THE MILITARY COMMANDER'S NECESSITY

The idea of military necessity lies at the centre of the law of armed conflict and yet it is less than fully understood. This book analyses which legal limits govern the commander's assessment of military necessity and it is argued that military necessity itself is not a limitation. Military necessity calls for a highly discretionary exercise: the assessment. Yet, there is little guidance as to how this discretionary process should be exercised, apart from the notions of 'a reasonable military commander'. A reasonable assessment of 'excessive' civilian losses are presumed to be almost intuitive. Objective standards for determining excessive civilian losses are difficult to identify, particularly when that 'excessiveness' will be understood in relative terms. The perpetual question arises: are civilian losses acceptable if the war can be won? The result is a heavy burden of assessment placed on the shoulders of the military commander.

Sigrid Redse Johansen is Judge Advocate General of Norway. In this capacity she is both the Director General of Military Prosecutions leading the military prosecutors and advisor to the Chief of Defence in cases and matters concerning criminal law, criminal procedure and summary punishment. She was previously an associate professor and lecturer in international and operational law at the Norwegian Defence Command and Staff College, where she was responsible for teaching programmes in the Law of Armed Conflict. She has also practised as an attorney at law, acting as defence counsel for the accused in criminal cases in the district courts, courts of appeal and before the Supreme Court of Norway.

The Military Commander's Necessity

THE LAW OF ARMED CONFLICT AND ITS LIMITS

SIGRID REDSE JOHANSEN
Norwegian Defence University College

Judge Advocate General for the Norwegian Armed Forces

CAMBRIDGE
UNIVERSITY PRESS

CAMBRIDGE
UNIVERSITY PRESS

University Printing House, Cambridge CB2 8BS, United Kingdom

One Liberty Plaza, 20th Floor, New York, NY 10006, USA

477 Williamstown Road, Port Melbourne, VIC 3207, Australia

314–321, 3rd Floor, Plot 3, Splendor Forum, Jasola District Centre, New Delhi – 110025, India

79 Anson Road, #06–04/06, Singapore 079906

Cambridge University Press is part of the University of Cambridge.

It furthers the University's mission by disseminating knowledge in the pursuit of education, learning, and research at the highest international levels of excellence.

www.cambridge.org
Information on this title: www.cambridge.org/9781108493925
DOI: 10.1017/9781108637060

First published 2019

Printed and bound in Great Britain by Clays Ltd, Elcograf S.p.A.

A catalogue record for this publication is available from the British Library.

Library of Congress Cataloging-in-Publication Data
NAMES: Johansen, Sigrid Redse, author.
TITLE: The military commander's necessity : the law of armed conflict and its limits / Sigrid Redse Johansen, Norwegian Defence University College.
DESCRIPTION: New York, NY : Cambridge University Press, 2019. | Includes bibliographical references and index.
IDENTIFIERS: LCCN 2019019731 | ISBN 9781108493925 (alk. paper)
SUBJECTS: LCSH: Necessity (International law) | Military necessity. | Armed Forces – Law and legislation. | Aggression (International law) | War (International law)
CLASSIFICATION: LCC KZ6415 .J65 2019 | DDC 341.6/3–dc23
LC record available at https://lccn.loc.gov/2019019731

ISBN 978-1-108-49392-5 Hardback
ISBN 978-1-108-71361-0 Paperback

For Axel

Contents

Preface

The picture on the cover page of this book shows the Norwegian Chief of Defence watching the hoisting of the flag at Akershus Fortress on the Norwegian liberation and veteran day. This book has been made possible thanks to my years in the Norwegian Armed Forces, at the University College located at Akershus Fortress. The topic of the military commander's necessity has matured while teaching staff officers for more than ten years. I have had the unique experience of the meeting between law and operational realities in these premises and I am sincerely grateful for the lessons taught to me by Norwegian officers. All armies probably have room for improvement, and mistakes occur, but my main sentiment after twelve years among tomorrow's commanding officers is genuine pride. To all of you in uniform out there on our behalf: you have impressed me by your ability to be pragmatic and fix things, to be brave and show concern – and to be true to our humane principles when that is required.

This book is based upon my PhD book *On military necessity: And the commander's assessment of military necessity under the international law of armed conflict during conduct of hostilities*, submitted at the University of Oslo in 2017. The road from undertaking this task, while I was working at the Norwegian Defence University College and up until today, has been a long journey.

I was at a stumbling, early stage, but with a clear interest for the topic chosen, when Professor Yoram Dinstein accepted my request to supervise the writing of my PhD. Writing a doctoral book under his supervision has been, to me, like attending an exclusive research academy. His tireless, precise, prompt and constructive comments for almost six years have been invaluable. Professor Dinstein's ability to see my desired aim and firmly, yet delicately, helping me to see the way forward in order to reach this aim the best I can, has been impressive. Yoram, I am truly grateful for having been able to participate in such a privileged, but also demanding, venture.

Professor Kjetil Mujezinovic Larsen was my supervisor at the Norwegian Centre for Human Rights. Kjetil, I am grateful for your gentle, reasonable, patient and constructive part in this process.

My research would not have been possible without my generous previous employer the Norwegian Defence University College – and with my protective and encouraging superiors, and previous superiors, in the military chain of command: Arne Røksund, John Andreas Olsen, Henning Frantzen, Gjert Lage Dyndal and Atle Stai. Thank you for your immense patience and encouragement! A very particular thank you goes to my long-standing colleague and superior: Tom Staib. Tom, your loyalty, encouragement, protection, creativity, humour and care for me throughout eleven years has been priceless.

To live every day with a research project hanging over you requires a sense of humour in order not to turn insane. For this – and for combining scholarly discussion with discussions on life itself – I am ridiculously grateful for the help from my previous colleagues at the Norwegian Defence University College: Camilla Guldahl Cooper, Bödvar Ingvarsson, Jo Sannem, Thomas Slensvik, Tor Arne Berntsen, Harald Høiback, Roar Wold – and my superior (after Tom) Andreas Wangberg.

Other colleagues have also shared their knowledge with me. I have been privileged with the advice and very constructive feedback with comments on parts of my work from William Boothby. Bill, thank you for your efficient, detailed and constructive comments! Rogier Bartels, thank you for your last minute valuable and friendly criminal advice. Jeroen van den Boogaard and Barbara Sonczyk, thank you for endless discussions and support.

In my present position at the Norwegian Military Prosecution Authority I am blessed with super colleagues and friends. A huge thank to each one of you for receiving me so well. Joachim Nordgreen, you persistently undermine your own priceless value. Thank you for coping with last minute good ideas and digressions from your superior. Reidar Bruusgaard, thank you for the friendly sharing of a proper prosecutor's thoughts on academic ideas.

To live around someone every day for many years who has an ongoing research project requires a portion of sane endurance. Olav, thank you for keeping up with my modes of passion – but most of all thank you for your endless guidance into the world of the military: whenever I throw my ideas at you at full speed, at any time of the day, you grab them and turn them, consistently, into the examples I want.

Needless to say, all errors in this book are mine alone.

Finally, my parents have been my invaluable back office for years. You have been babysitters, you have done homework, picked up from the kindergarten, driven to and from school, gone to numerous museums and cinemas and read endless goodnight stories. But most of all, you have raised me to believe that the most important thing when it comes to profession is to choose from one's desires and not pure reason. I have always felt that I could not have been provided with a better balance between sense and sensibility than what you have always offered me.

To you, my precious son, Axel: for laconically pointing out that 'she might have finished her book, but she will find something new to write'. I dedicate my book to you and hope you will be able to do everything you want in life.

Table of Cases

Table of Treaties

Declaration Respecting Maritime Law 16 April 1856, printed in Schindler, Dietrich and Toman, Jiri, eds., *The Laws of Armed Conflicts* (Martinus Nijhoff Publishers, 2004), at page 1055, 54

Instructions for the Government of Armies of the United States in the Field (Lieber Code) (1863), printed in Schindler, Dietrich and Toman, Jiri, eds., *The Laws of Armed Conflicts* (Martinus Nijhoff Publishers, 2004), at pages 3 ff, 54

Declaration Renouncing the Use, in Time of War, of Explosive Projectiles under 400 Grammes Weight (St Petersburg Declaration) (1868), printed in Schindler, Dietrich and Toman, Jiri, eds., *The Laws of Armed Conflicts* (Martinus Nijhoff Publishers, 2004), at pages 91 ff, 58

Brussels Conference of 1874, Project of an International Declaration Concerning the Laws and Customs of War (Brussels Declaration), printed in Schindler, Dietrich and Toman, Jiri, eds., *The Laws of Armed Conflicts* (Martinus Nijhoff Publishers, 2004), at pages 23 ff, 58

The Laws of War on Land: Manual published by the Institute of International Law (Oxford Manual) (1880), printed in Schindler, Dietrich and Toman, Jiri, eds., *The Laws of Armed Conflicts* (Martinus Nijhoff Publishers, 2004), at page 29, 171

Convention (II) with Respect to the Laws and Customs of War on Land (1899 Hague Convention) (1899), printed in Schindler, Dietrich and Toman, Jiri, eds., *The Laws of Armed Conflicts* (Martinus Nijhoff Publishers, 2004), at page 61, 14

Declaration (IV,3) Concerning Expanding Bullets (1899), printed in Schindler, Dietrich and Toman, Jiri, eds., *The Laws of Armed Conflicts* (Martinus Nijhoff Publishers, 2004), at pages 99–100, 175

Statute of the International Tribunal for the Prosecution of Persons Responsible for Serious Violations of International Humanitarian Law Committed in the Territory of the Former Yugoslavia since 1991 (1993), printed in Schindler, Dietrich and Toman, Jiri, eds., *The Laws of Armed Conflicts* (Martinus Nijhoff Publishers, 2004), at page 1288, 8

Convention on the Prohibition of the Development, Production, Stockpiling and Use of Chemical Weapons and on Their Destruction (CWC) (1993), *International Legal Materials* (ILM), vol. 32, page 800, 174

Protocol on Blinding Laser Weapons (Protocol IV of the CCW) (1995), printed in Schindler, Dietrich and Toman, Jiri, eds., *The Laws of Armed Conflicts* (Martinus Nijhoff Publishers, 2004), at page 212, 175

Convention on the Prohibition of the Use, Stockpiling, Production and Transfer of Anti-Personnel Mines and Other Destruction (Ottawa Convention) (1997), printed in Schindler, Dietrich and Toman, Jiri, eds., *The Laws of Armed Conflicts* (Martinus Nijhoff Publishers, 2004), at page 285, 5

Rome Statute of the International Criminal Court (1998), printed in Schindler, Dietrich and Toman, Jiri, eds., *The Laws of Armed Conflicts* (Martinus Nijhoff Publishers, 2004), at pages 1309 ff, 5

Second Protocol to the Hague Convention of 1954 for the Protection of Cultural Property in the Event of Armed Conflict (1999), printed in Schindler, Dietrich and Toman, Jiri, eds., *The Laws of Armed Conflicts* (Martinus Nijhoff Publishers, 2004), at page 1037, 5

1

Introduction

1.1 THE TOPIC

Considerations and conceptions of military necessity can be traced back as long as law has been governing aspects of war, and in close connection to the idea of restraint[1] in war due to humanitarian concerns.[2] Military necessity in the context of humanitarian concerns has also been said to illustrate a deeply rooted contradiction: 'Ambiguity and contradiction ... mark in general the whole of our Europe-based philosophy of war, which is found in the reconciliation of the principles of military necessity and humanitarian concern.'[3]

To choose a topic such as the legal concept of military necessity is therefore almost as ambitious as attempting to write a book 'on everything about law and war'. Nevertheless, unless it is sufficiently in-depth, it is not truly interesting. I have therefore chosen to pursue the following question in this book:

> What are the legal limits of the commander's assessment of military necessity under the International Law of Armed Conflict during the conduct of hostilities?

The term 'military necessity' calls for a discretionary judgment – the 'assessment' – by the military commander in the field during combat operations. The

1 On the conceptual idea of restraint in war in a historical perspective, see for example Best, 'Restraint in war', 3–26. See also Howard, 'Constraints on warfare', at page 2–3.

2 On the balance between military necessity and humanitarian concerns in general, see for example Draper, 'Military necessity and humanitarian imperatives', at page 130; Kelsen and Tucker, *Principles of International Law*; Pictet, *Development and Principles of International Humanitarian Law*; Schmitt, 'Military necessity and humanity in international humanitarian law'; Dinstein, 'Military necessity', at para. 1–7. See also Hayashi 'Military necessity as normative indifference', 675–782. On the question of whether military necessity and humanitarian concerns are always opposed, see Chapter 6.

3 Best, 'Restraint in war', at page 5.

'assessment' thus lies at the heart of this book, and the conceptual findings with regard to this discretionary judgment, referred to as the 'military margin of appreciation', is encapsulated in Chapter 4. In order to approach the core of the question however, I address different legal concepts under the international Law of Armed Conflict (LOAC) governing the conduct of hostilities and which in its own way strongly embodies the concept of military necessity. Among these concepts, civilian immunity from attacks (covering both persons and objects) and the proportionality rule protecting civilians and civilian objects from damage which will be excessive in relation to the concrete and direct military advantage anticipated, are prominent. Throughout this – also historical – survey I attempt to analyse, discuss and frame the limits of the assessment of military necessity via treaty law, state practice, case law and doctrinal debate.

In 1924 the legal scholar Spaight wrote: 'War, after all, is only a means to an end.'[4] The remark could also have been quoted elsewhere, from another time, and definitely not necessarily from a legal scholar. For the purpose of the present book however, the point is exactly that *even* from a legal point of view it appears impossible to escape the difficult relationship between *means* of warfare and *ends* of war. And in the midst of this difficulty is the legal concept of *military necessity* – simply because any notion of 'necessity' connotes a 'for what' – the means and methods considered necessary in order to achieve a military purpose.[5] It is no understatement to point out the vagueness of this point of departure: 'As with many abstract concepts, the answers to specific questions depend on the circumstances, appraised in the light of the humanitarian ends that justify the restraints. *Determining the proper relation between means and ends in situations of great complexity and uncertainty is never easy*.'[6]

With the privilege of hindsight US Secretary of Defence Robert McNamara (1961–8) has stated with regard to World War II (WWII) that:

> Why was it necessary to drop the nuclear bomb if Le May was burning up Japan? And he went on from Tokyo to firebomb other cities. 58% of Yokohama. Yokohama is roughly the size of Cleveland. 58% of Cleveland destroyed. Tokyo is roughly the size of New York. 51% of New York destroyed. 99% of the equivalent of Chattanooga, which was Toyama. 40% of the equivalent of Los Angeles, which was Nagoya. This was all done before the

4 Spaight, *Air Power and War Rights*, at page 2.
5 This question is further addressed in Chapter 2.
6 See Schachter's remarks in 'Implementing limitations on the use of force', at page 39, where the quotation is from his comments upon the questions of proportionality and necessity. Emphasis added.

> dropping of the nuclear bomb, which by the way was dropped by Le May's command. Proportionality should be a guideline in war. Killing 50% to 90% of the people of 67 Japanese cities and then bombing them with two nuclear bombs is not proportional, in the minds of some people, to the objectives we were trying to achieve.[7]

The concept of 'military necessity' is liable to abuse. And what is perhaps worse: abuse can be exercised with the best of intentions if based on flimsy or flawed intelligence or poor knowledge of the law. This book is devoted to the limits placed on military commanders in order to avoid such abuse.

1.2 DEFINING 'NECESSITY' AT THE OUTSET

'Necessity' is a generic term referring to a certain state of being required, an 'indispensable thing',[8] or, as stated in *Black's Law Dictionary*: 'something that must be done or accomplished for any one of various reasons ... context normally supplies a sense of the degree of urgency'.[9] Correspondingly, the adjective 'necessary' may be understood as a term referring to what is 'required to be done', or what is 'inevitably resulting from the nature of things'.[10] Under the LOAC it is considered *necessary* to disable as many enemy combatants as possible from continued fighting in order to weaken the enemy forces and gain military advantages for own forces.[11] Bearing in mind these ordinary meanings given to the terms, the meaning of 'necessity' and 'necessary' under international law must be understood as specifically related to the area of law in question. The present book is concerned exclusively with the concept of necessity under the LOAC, namely *military necessity*, and must thus be distinguished from the concept as it appears under areas of law adjacent, but not identical, to the LOAC, such as the *jus ad bellum*, the law on Responsibility of States for Internationally Wrongful Acts and the international human rights law.[12]

7 From the film *Fog of War* (2003), directed and produced by Errol Morris.

8 Soanes and Stevenson (eds.), *Concise Oxford English Dictionary*, page 956.

9 Garner (ed.), *Black's Law Dictionary*, at page 1193.

10 Soanes and Stevenson, *Concise Oxford English Dictionary*, page 956. In *Black's Law Dictionary*, the similar phrase is: 'needed for some purpose or reason; essential', at page 1192.

11 The notion of combatants is dealt with below, in Chapter 9, and the notion of military advantage – as well as the concept of 'weakening the enemy forces' – is dealt with in Chapter 14.

12 The relationship between the topic of this book and the *jus ad bellum*, the international law of state responsibility and the international human rights law (IHR), is dealt with below, in Sections 1.4 and 1.5.

1.3 MILITARY NECESSITY IN THE LAW OF INTERNATIONAL AND NON-INTERNATIONAL ARMED CONFLICT

In the present book military necessity is primarily dealt with in the framework for international armed conflicts (IACs). Acknowledging that a majority of armed conflicts in the world today are classified as non-international armed conflicts (NIACs), most of the legal framework (governing the conduct of hostilities) is still, at least as a matter of treaty law, drafted for IACs.[13] Having said this, core rules of the international Law of Armed Conflict also apply in their essence to NIACs.[14] Due to the selection of rules subject to analysis in this book, the findings will, in most cases, be applicable to NIACs as well. The concept of 'necessity' – albeit with different terminology – is referred to on a couple of occasions in the Protocol II Additional to the Geneva Conventions (AP II) concerning displacement of civilians if 'imperative reasons so demand'[15] and the duty to search for wounded, sick or shipwrecked persons 'whenever circumstances permit'.[16] Furthermore – and of more importance for the present book – the principles of distinction, unnecessary suffering, proportionality, precautions in attack and the prohibition of wanton destruction of property, which all contain in-built (or even explicit) considerations of military necessity, appear occasionally in treaty law applicable in NIAC,[17] and

[13] This is the case with the four Geneva Conventions (GC) as well as their Additional Protocol (AP). See Convention (I) for the Amelioration of the Condition of the Wounded and Sick in Armed Forces in the Field (GC I) (1949); Convention (II) for the Amelioration of the Condition of the Wounded, Sick and Shipwrecked Members of Armed Forces at Sea (GC II) (1949); Convention (III) Relative to the Treatment of Prisoners of War (GC III) (1949); Convention (IV) Relative to the Protection of Civilian Persons in Time of War (GC IV); Protocol Additional to the Geneva Conventions of 12 August 1949, and Relating to the Protection of Victims of International Armed Conflicts (Protocol I), (AP I) (1977). See common article 2 to the four GCs, and article 1 of the AP I.

[14] Dinstein, *Non-international Armed Conflicts in International Law*, at pages 213–19.

[15] Protocol Additional to the Geneva Conventions of 12 August 1949, and Relating to the Protection of Victims of Non-International Armed Conflicts (Protocol II), (AP II) (1977), article 17.

[16] AP II article 8.

[17] AP II article 13 and 13(3), as well as common article 3 to the four GCs, which embodies the rule on Direct Participation in Hostilities (DPH). A reference to military objectives is in AP II article 15 in the context of dangerous forces (the protection of works and installations containing dangerous forces is dealt with in Chapter 17 of this book). Protocol on Prohibitions or Restrictions on the Use of Mines, Booby-Traps and Other Devices, as Amended on 3 May 1996 (Protocol II of the CCW) replicates the definitions of military objectives and civilian objects in article 2(6) and (7), as well as the prohibition on unnecessary suffering in article 3(3), the prohibition on indiscriminate attacks 8(a) and (b), the proportionality rule in article 3(8)(c) and the duty to take precautionary measures in article 8(10). Convention on the Prohibition of the Use, Stockpiling,

is as well reflective of the customary law of NIAC.[18] Those parts of this book which are *not applicable* to NIACs are therefore, in essence, those sections dealing with lawful combatancy and the entitlement to prisoner of war status in Chapters 9 and 10.[19]

1.4 DISCIPLINES AND AREAS OF LAW WHICH ARE, AND ARE NOT, DEALT WITH

Let us return to the research question: what are the legal limits of the commander's assessment of military necessity under the LOAC during the conduct of hostilities? First of all, I deal with *legal* limits, not political restraint on military operations, nor ethical norms and moral obligations.[20] This must not be taken to diminish the practical importance of other limitations upon the commander's assessment, such as moral and political restraints. In fact, the commander's practical freedom of manoeuvre may be entirely dependent upon limitations other than international law, issued through the chain of

Production and Transfer of Anti-Personnel Mines and Other Destruction (Ottawa Convention) (1997) states in its preamble that the States parties are 'basing themselves' on the principle of limitation (on this principle, see further Chapter 7 of this book) and as well on the prohibition of unnecessary suffering and the principle of distinction. The Second Protocol to the Hague Convention of 1954 for the Protection of Cultural Property in the Event of Armed Conflict (1999) replicates the definition of military objectives in article 1(f), the proportionality rule and the duty to take precautionary measures with regard to cultural property in article 7, as well as including the notion of military necessity together with the target selection rule when protection is waived, in article 6. On the notion of military necessity in the target selection rule with regard to cultural property, see further Chapter 16 of this book. The Rome Statute of the International Criminal Court (Rome Statute) (1998) lists the war crimes that violate the principle of distinction and destruction of property not demanded by imperative military necessity in article 8(2)(e), (i) and (xii), at page 1320. Criminal law is dealt with in Chapter 5.

18 See Henckaerts and Doswald-Beck, *International Committee of the Red Cross Customary International Humanitarian Law* (CIHL), also accessible with updated commentaries at: ICRC, Customary IHL Database, https://ihl-databases.icrc.org/customary-ihl/eng/docs/v1 (2019) Rule 1 (distinction), Rule 11 (indiscriminate attacks), Rule 14 (proportionality), Rule 15 (precautions in attack), Rule 70 (unnecessary suffering) and Rule 50 (destruction of property). Dinstein, *Non-international Armed Conflicts in International Law*, also points out that the principles of distinction, unnecessary suffering, indiscriminate attacks, proportionality and precautions apply in NIACs, at pages 213–19.

19 These correspond to those parts of treaty law where the provisions in the AP I do not amount to customary law in international armed conflicts, see Section 1.6.1 below.

20 For discussions on military necessity with its roots in the legal discipline, but with a more interdisciplinary perspective, see for example O'Brien, *The Conduct of Just and Limited War*, at pages 79 ff.; Hayashi, 'Contextualizing military necessity', pages 195–220; Ohlin and May, *Necessity in International Law*.

command as rules of engagement (ROE) or standard operating procedures (SOP).[21] Some aspects of the relationship between limits under the LOAC and other limits are dealt with in Chapter 4, in order to illustrate the commander's margin of appreciation under the LOAC. Having said this, theoretical foundations and the structure of the LOAC as such *are*, to a certain extent, dealt with in this book. The very concept of military necessity may be perceived as a 'bridge' between facts and law and between facts and assessments of the facts and thus invite discussion of the relationship between the norm on the one hand and the person assessing the norm and its application on the other hand. This discussion is, in its general form, a part of Chapter 4. Another aspect of viewing military necessity as a 'bridge' between facts and law is as part of the discussion of *Kriegsraison* (in Chapter 6), where military necessity represents the outer limit of law as such. This study of military necessity as part of the LOAC is therefore bound to be an exercise of balance between dwelling into the theoretical underpinnings of the 'concept of law'[22] and the detailed analysis of how military necessity appears in concrete legal rules.

This book is about the concept of military necessity under the law governing the conduct of hostilities in international armed conflicts, the *jus in bello*, which applies 'to all cases of declared war or of any other armed conflict which may arise between two or more of the High Contracting Parties, even if the state of war is not recognized by one of them'.[23] The *jus in bello* has to be distinguished from the necessity of resort to use of force between States, the *jus ad bellum*. This distinction is dealt with specifically in Section 1.5 below. Furthermore, this book is *not* about necessity as a ground precluding wrongfulness under the International Law on State Responsibility, nor about international human rights law or criminal law as such.[24] The relationship to the law on State Responsibility and Human Rights law are commented upon briefly in the following.

Necessity as a ground precluding the wrongfulness of an act in general is governed by article 25 in the International Law Commission's Draft articles on Responsibility of States for Internationally Wrongful Acts

21 For an account of these limitations on the commander's room of manoeuvre, see Johansen, 'Mission command and command responsibility'.

22 The expression is taken from Hart, *The Concept of Law*.

23 Common article 2(1) to the four Geneva Conventions (in GC I).

24 A number of war crimes have in-built references to military necessity, such as destruction of property not justified by imperative military necessity. Where these provisions naturally occur, I address them in this book. Beyond this, I do not address conditions for criminal responsibility. See further my remarks in Section 1.6.4, below, on the practice of international courts and tribunals.

(2001).[25] Article 25(2)(a) excludes the possibility to invoke necessity if 'the international obligation in question excludes the possibility of invoking necessity'. In the commentary to this rule Crawford states that: 'the plea of necessity is not intended to cover conduct which is in principle regulated by the primary obligations. This has a particular importance in relation to the rules relating to the use of force in international relations and to the question of "military necessity".'[26]

The relationship between the general law on State responsibility and military necessity is also addressed in Section 2.6, with regard to the issue of military necessity as a permission or prohibition under the LOAC.[27]

International human rights law is a body of law distinct from the LOAC. This point of departure remains, although their areas of concurrent application may grow close on a number of occasions. Human rights obligations do not, in principle, cease to apply during situations of armed conflict. Yet, they are not drafted for the sole purpose of armed conflict. The LOAC, on the other hand, is drafted specifically for situations of armed conflict, which has consequently given rise to the LOAC being viewed as the *lex specialis* in the sense that it prevails in case of conflict of norms.

Finally, dealing with the law governing the conduct of hostilities, this book is not concerned with the law of belligerent occupation. Considerations of military necessity (or the similar considerations of 'security') by the occupant are numerous under the law of occupation. Yet, these considerations bear the distinctive mark of being made in situations of de facto control over a hostile territory.[28] During the conduct of hostilities, the situation is not the same. Although a comparison between assessments of military necessity done

25 Draft Articles on Responsibility of States for Internationally Wrongful Acts, with commentaries, in *Yearbook of the International Law Commission*, 2001, vol. II, Part Two, as corrected. On terminology in older literature, see also Schwarzenberger, *International Law as Applied by International Courts and Tribunals*, at pages 128–9. On the distinction between general and particular necessity under international law, see for example Agius, 'The invocation of necessity in international law', at pages 110 and 112, commenting on the relationship between Draft Articles on State Responsibility article 25 and the LOAC treaties. See also pages 121–2 commenting on the relationship between the concept of self-defence (or self-preservation) and military necessity, as well as referring to the doctrine of *Kriegsraison* as an expression of the conflation of these two concepts.

26 See Crawford, *The International Law Commission's Articles on State Responsibility*, at page 185.

27 That the two concepts are distinct was also emphasised in the Eighth Report on State Responsibility. See UN Doc. A/CN.4/318/Add.5–7, page 34, remarks by Roberto Ago, who points out that the concept of military necessity is not a 'subcategory' of those situations that may give rise to a state of necessity.

28 Convention (IV) Respecting the Laws and Customs of War on Land and its Annex: Regulations Respecting the Laws and Customs of War on Land (1907 Hague Regulations)

throughout belligerent occupation and assessments done during the conduct of hostilities would be interesting (not least with regard to the question of 'necessary for what?', as addressed in Chapter 2), the task of dealing with both is simply too comprehensive for the present study.[29]

1.5 THE SCOPE OF THE LOAC AND THE LIMITS OF CONTEXT: *JUS AD BELLUM* VS *JUS IN BELLO*

Lawyers distinguish between *jus ad bellum* and *jus in bello*. While *jus ad bellum* governs the initial right to resort to force between States, and lies outside the scope of this book, the *jus in bello* governs the use of force during armed conflict. In the distinction between these two sets of legal frameworks lies a presumption of independence: *jus in bello* applies equally to both parties to the armed conflict, regardless of which side is responsible for having started the war. An eventual violation of *jus ad bellum* rules does not impact on the application of *jus in bello* rules. This is the established legal point of departure.[30] Repeatedly, this sharp distinction has been challenged with reference to the moral inequality between the aggressor and the victim State.[31] Recently, the debate appears to have taken shape as a conflict between 'Separationists' and 'Conflationists', where the 'Conflationist' position is willing to merge the *jus ad bellum* and the *jus in bello*.[32] Although Conflationist views seem to be primarily *ethical*, there might be some 'spill over' to legal

(1907). Occupation is defined by article 42, to be when a territory 'is actually placed under the authority of the hostile army'.

29 A comparison is done for the purpose of addressing the scope of humanitarian assistance by Bashi, 'Justifying restrictions on reconstructing Gaza', at page 154. The difficulties of distinguishing between military and political objectives of warfare, during an occupation, appear to imply that the distinction is more easily upheld in targeting decisions. As discussed both in Chapter 2 and in Chapter 14 in this book, practice has shown that the distinction proves difficult everywhere – including during conduct of hostilities.

30 See AP I article 1(1), at page 715, which states that the duty to respect the rules exist in 'all circumstances', and Sandoz, Swinarski and Zimmermann (eds.), *Commentary on the Additional Protocols of 8 June 1977* (AP I Commentary), page 37, at para. 48. See also the Schmitt (general ed.), *Tallinn Manual 2.0 on the International Law Applicable to Cyber Operations*, in commentary 1 to rule 72, stating that: 'It is important to note that the conditions of necessity and proportionality in the *jus ad bellum* are distinct from the concept of military necessity and the rule of proportionality in the *jus in bello*.'

31 A brief account is given in the Final Report to the Prosecutor by the Committee Established to Review the NATO Bombing Campaign Against the Federal Republic of Yugoslavia (2000) (OTP Report) at the International Criminal Tribunal for the former Yugoslavia (ICTY), at para. 32.

32 See Weiler and Deshman, 'Far be it from thee to slay the righteous with the wicked', pages 25–61.

argumentation.[33] A regrettable source of confusion over the legal 'Separationist' point of departure can be found in the International Court of Justice (ICJ) Advisory Opinion on the Threat or Use of Nuclear Weapons from 1996. In this case the Court, among others, considered the use of nuclear weapons in light of the 'principles and rules of international humanitarian law (IHL) applicable in armed conflict and of the law of neutrality'[34] and stated (finally) that:

> Accordingly, in view of the present state of international law viewed as a whole, as examined above by the Court, and of the elements of fact at its disposal, the Court is led to observe that it cannot reach a definitive conclusion as to the legality or illegality of the use of nuclear weapons by a State in an extreme circumstance of self-defence, in which its very survival would be at stake.[35]

The Court seems to hold open the possibility that the legality of a particular means of warfare (nuclear weapons) can be considered differently in a situation of self-defence from other situations.[36] Unsurprisingly, considerations of military necessity are used as a driving force behind such positions,[37] although this use of the concept of military necessity is just as often rejected by scholars: 'Military necessity should be confined to the plight in which armed forces may find themselves under the stress of active warfare.'[38]

Among a number of scholars, the *jus ad bellum* is repeatedly held to impose restrictions on targeting during the conduct of hostilities, that is, as an additional (to the *jus in bello*) set of rules applicable in armed conflict.[39] Obviously, it cannot be denied that the *jus ad bellum* applies, sometimes concurrently, to

33 One such example is found in the article by Dunlap, 'The end of innocence', pages 9–17. Another recent example is found in Otieno, Wabuke and Otieno, 'The Fission and Fusion in International Use of Force', pages 303–28.

34 Legality of the Threat or Use of Nuclear Weapons, pages 226 ff., at para. 74.

35 Ibid., at para. 97.

36 In fact, the ICJ is not the first to lean on *jus ad bellum* considerations for a possible justification of the atomic bomb. On the same direction, see for example O'Brien, *The Conduct of Just and Limited War*, at page 76, where he refers to a proportionality assessment under necessity. The issue of proportionality as an alleged component of military necessity is dealt with in Chapter 13 in this book.

37 In this respect, see (again) O'Brien, ibid., at pages 84–5. An argument in favour of interpreting the laws of armed conflict differently, according to the different political purposes of war, is also given by Kelsen and Tucker, *Principles of International Law*, at pages 115–16

38 See Dunbar, 'Military necessity in war crimes trials', at page 443.

39 See for example Greenwood, *Essays on War in International Law*, at page 83, where he argues that *jus ad bellum* may have an effect upon what is to be considered a lawful target Green and Waters, 'Military targeting in the context of self-defence actions', who argue at page 23 that the *jus ad bellum* targeting rules does not absolutely prohibit the targeting of civilians. I disagree that *jus ad bellum* addresses targeting. Any measures taken as part of lawful self-defence must abide by the rules governing conduct of hostilities under *jus in bello* – and the targeting of civilians under these rules is prohibited, see Chapter 7.

the *jus in bello*. I do, however, contest that the *jus ad bellum* addresses the issue of targeting as such. Concrete activities comprising the conduct of hostilities, such as, for example, attacks and other military operations resulting in destruction or seizure of property or the capture of personnel, is governed particularly by the rules set out in *jus in bello*. In the case of conflict between norms, *jus in bello* prevails (*lex specialis*). In short, this book rests on the following view: military necessity neither transcends the scope of the *jus in bello* (it cannot be invoked to 'terminate the entire war'),[40] nor does it yield to requirements of the *jus ad bellum* as such (a lawful attack under *jus in bello* remains a lawful attack under *jus in bello*).[41] That said, a number of restrictions may be imposed on the actual conduct of hostilities, either by international law (such as the law of neutrality) or by States themselves, through mission specific regulations such as rules of engagement. These restrictions do not, however, alter the content of the *jus in bello* (by interpretation) nor the conception of military necessity per se.[42] To base the application of *jus in bello* upon the distinction in the *jus ad bellum* between the right-doer and the wrong-doer appears futile and dangerous.[43] Precisely because war is a political tool and an enterprise of means to achieve political ends, it is a continuous struggle to preserve a legal presumption of conduct that is 'purely military'.[44]

1.6 SPECIFIC ISSUES REGARDING SOURCES

As in any study or application of the law in the field of international law, this book is based on the two primary sources of international law: treaties and customary international law. The point of departure is stated in article 38 of

40 In support of this, see McDougal and Feliciano, *Law and Minimum World Order*, at page 527 who, in a critique of the Vietnam War in its aftermath, also illustrate the dangerous potential when writing into the principle of military necessity a conception of the legitimate 'purpose of war'. For a similar view in more recent literature, see for example Sassoli 'Ius ad bellum and Ius in bello', at page 249. In a slightly different direction, see Schmitt, 'Targeting and humanitarian law', at page 157 where he claims that the views of Sassoli are 'overly simplistic', although Schmitt himself also argues strongly in favour of upholding the separation between the *jus ad bellum* and the *jus in bello*.

41 An unclear phrase is found by O'Connell, 'Historical development and legal basis', at page 35.

42 On the application of the rules in different circumstances, see in particular Chapter 14, on the notion of military advantage.

43 See for example Schmitt, 'Targeting and humanitarian law', at page 160. This view is even more explicitly expressed in the OTP Report at para. 33. See also Boivin, 'The legal regime applicable to targeting military objectives', at page 28.

44 The expression is from Clausewitz, *On War*, at page 607.

the 1945 Statute of the International Court of Justice (ICJ Statute), and is recognised as an expression of general international law.[45]

A treaty is defined in the 1969 Vienna Convention of the Law of Treaties (VCLT) article 1(a) and can be applied in general and is not limited to the scope of the VCLT.[46] Apart from some older agreements (e.g. the Lieber Code as dealt with in Chapter 3), treaties of relevance for the application of the LOAC, and hence this book, are multilateral treaties falling within the scope of the VCLT.

Customary international law is referred to in the ICJ Statute article 38 as 'international custom, as evidence of a general practice accepted as law'. Customary law consists of two elements: 'general practice' and 'acceptance' as law. The latter element is usually referred to as a subjective element of *opinio juris* by States.[47] Both elements may prove – and do prove – challenging for the identification of customary LOAC. Some of these challenges are addressed in particular in Section 1.6.2. Before turning to these contentious issues I briefly introduce the presence of, and relationship between,[48] LOAC treaties and customary law of relevance for this book.

1.6.1 *Treaty and Customary Law in the LOAC*

The LOAC is rich in both customary and treaty law.[49] While treaty law governing the conduct of hostilities and victims of war (historically referred

45 The whole provision of the Statute of the International Court of Justice (ICJ Statute) article 38, states:

'1. The Court, whose function is to decide in accordance with international law such disputes as are submitted to it, shall apply:
   a. international conventions, whether general or particular, establishing rules expressly recognized by the contesting states;
   b. international custom, as evidence of a general practice accepted as law;
   c. the general principles of law recognized by civilized nations ;
   d. subject to the provisions of Article 59, judicial decisions and the teachings of the most highly qualified publicists of the various nations, as subsidiary means for the determination of rules of law.

2. This provision shall not prejudice the power of the Court to decide a case ex aequo et bond, if the parties agree thereto.'

46 Dinstein, 'The interaction between customary international law and treaties', page 325.

47 The expression 'subjective element' was used by the ICJ in the Judgment in the North Sea Continental Shelf cases, p. 44. See as well the Military and Paramilitary Activities in and against Nicaragua (*Nicaragua* v. *United States of America*). Merits, Judgment, p. 14 at para. 185.

48 For a thorough account on the relationship between treaty law and customary law in general, see Dinstein, 'The interaction between customary international law and treaties'.

49 See Dinstein, *Conduct of Hostilities*, at page 16; Kolb and Del Mar, 'Treaties for armed conflict', at page 51.

to as Hague and Geneva law) primarily developed from the middle of the nineteenth century, referred to in Chapter 3 as the Codification Era, customary LOAC is both of older as well as more recent origin. In the aftermath of WWII, customary LOAC was said to experience a 'revival' before turning dormant for years and then to enter the courtrooms of the international tribunals with all force.[50]

Some older instruments, of particular use for this book, are repeatedly being cited: the Lieber Code,[51] the St Petersburg Declaration[52] and the Brussels Declaration.[53] Among treaties are: the 1907 Hague Convention (IV) Laws and Customs of War on Land (1907 Hague Regulations), the 1949 four Geneva Conventions (GC I–IV), the 1954 Hague Convention on Cultural Property,[54] the 1977 Additional Protocols to the Geneva Conventions (AP I and II), the 1998 Rome Statute of the International Criminal Court (ICC) as well as a number of particular treaties governing restrictions or prohibitions on the use of weaponry.[55] With regard to customary LOAC, proof of custom and *opinio juris* can (first and foremost) be retrieved from the numerous military manuals published by States, as well as their actual behaviour and accompanying public statements throughout history (see Section 1.6.2). Other efforts to identify and collect customary rules are accounted for just below.

While treaties are binding only upon contracting States, customary LOAC is, in principle, binding upon all States.[56] Of particular importance with regard to the present topic is the customary status of the AP I. While the 1907 Hague Regulations and the GC I–IV generally also are acknowledged to express customary LOAC (obviously with some limitations upon the distinction between international and non-international armed conflicts, as well as towards belligerent occupation), some parts of the AP I remain a matter of controversy.[57] It is important to clarify which parts these are. A number of rules in the AP I governing conduct of hostilities are subject to controversy

50 Meron, 'Customary humanitarian law today', at pages 37–8.
51 Instructions for the Government of Armies of the United States in the Field (Lieber Code) (1863).
52 Declaration Renouncing the Use, in Time of War, of Explosive Projectiles under 400 Grammes Weight (St Petersburg Declaration) (1868).
53 Brussels Conference of 1874, Project of an International Declaration Concerning the Laws and Customs of War (Brussels Declaration).
54 Convention for the Protection of Cultural Property in the Event of Armed Conflict (1954 Hague Convention on Cultural Property) (1954).
55 For a selection, see Chapter 9 and the account given there of the prohibition of means and methods of warfare calculated to cause superfluous injury or unnecessary suffering.
56 With regard to LOAC, this general point is for example made by Kolb and Del Mar, 'Treaties for armed conflict', at page 53.
57 Ibid.

regarding details of interpretation. The discussion of the interpretation of the term 'effective contribution to military action', as an element of the definition of military objectives, is one such example of relevance for this book. This international legal debate is accounted for in Chapter 8. It is, however, with regard to the notion of lawful combatancy that the clash of opinions has been most significant, also being (parts of) a reason for the lack of accessions by some States.[58] What is more, the different conceptions among States in this regard lie, and have done so throughout history, deeply embedded in the controversy over the necessity for (or, conversely, the danger of) irregular warfare and thereby the justification for the status of (lawful) combatancy for irregulars. This feature of the debate is dealt into some detail in Chapter 9 and illustrates a more general point for this book, namely the particular function(s) of military necessity inherent, implicitly or explicitly, in the LOAC. The different functions of military necessity within the LOAC are addressed more comprehensively in Chapter 2.

In situations where a customary rule exists alongside treaty law, governing the same conduct, one must clarify to what extent these two complement each other.[59] As stated by the ICJ in the Nicaragua case: 'even if a treaty norm and a customary norm relevant to the present dispute were to have exactly the same content, this would not be a reason for the Court to take the view that the operation of the treaty process must necessarily deprive the customary norm of its separate applicability'.[60] Furthermore, that: 'More generally, there are no grounds for holding that when customary international law is comprised of rules identical to those of treaty law, the latter "supervenes" the former, so that the customary international law has no further existence of its own.'[61]

This point of departure must be applied specifically to the legal rules at hand. In this book, those are the rules of the LOAC referring to (or implementing considerations of) military necessity. The notion of 'military necessity' in the LOAC has a particular history in this regard. First, it is true that several rules of LOAC treaty law have taken military necessity into account, and that these rules also reflect customary law. In these situations, customary law and treaty law complement each other. This is the case for the definition of

58 The most profiled abstention in this regard is that of the United States. See further Chapters 9 and 10 below.

59 Dinstein, 'The interaction between customary international law and treaties', at page 385, 'The result is coexistence between custom and treaty in the sense that the two strata of international law do not clash but complement one another.'

60 Military and Paramilitary Activities in and against Nicaragua (*Nicaragua* v. *United States of America*), at para. 175.

61 Ibid., at para. 177. In this passage, the Court relied on the statement made in the North Sea Continental Shelf Cases, at para. 63.

military objectives and the proportionality rule, both expressed in the AP I and reflecting customary LOAC. Second, military necessity may only be invoked as an exceptive clause for conduct which is otherwise prohibited, where the exception is explicitly provided for in treaty law.[62] That is to say, military necessity cannot be invoked by reference to customary law in order to overrule a treaty prohibition (also of customary status). As noted by the British Military Tribunal in the von Manstein case 'military necessity has already been discounted in drawing up these rules'.[63] Thus, there are (at least) two possible ways of viewing the specific rejection of *Kriegsraison* (i.e. the rejection of the *blanco* invocation of military necessity) under the LOAC. It may (a) be viewed as a rebuttal of the point of departure made by the ICJ (above) that treaty law does not 'supervene' customary law, or it may (b) be viewed as complete identification of treaty and customary law, in other words that the possibility of invoking military necessity as an exception under customary law is not in any way broader than what is already accounted for in the treaty provisions. Either way, (a) or (b) arrives at the same result. This, in theory, simple point of departure when it comes to military necessity under the LOAC is revisited in a number of different contexts throughout this book.

Another specific feature of the companionship between treaty and customary LOAC is the role of the much cited, so-called, Martens Clause. The version of the Clause which appears in the preamble of the 1907 Hague Convention says:

> Until a more complete code of the laws of war has been issued, the High Contracting Parties deem it expedient to declare that, in cases not included in the Regulations adopted by them, the inhabitants and the belligerents remain under the protection and the rule of the principles of the law of nations, as they result from the usages established among civilized peoples, from the laws of humanity and the dictates of the public conscience.[64]

Despite the fact that present treaty law has left many fewer areas of warfare unregulated, the Clause is repeated in the AP I article 1(2) where it alludes to the application of customary law alongside treaty law, just as stated in the point

[62] See in particular the account given in Chapter 6 of the doctrine of *Kriegsraison*.

[63] In re von Lewinski (called von Manstein), at page 512.

[64] The Martens Clause appeared for the first time in the preamble to the Convention (II) with Respect to the Laws and Customs of War on Land (1899 Hague Convention) (1899) and was later recited in the preamble to the Convention (IX) Concerning Bombardment by Naval Forces in time of War (1907 Hague Convention IX) (1907) Hague Regulations, as well as in AP I article 1(2), and AP II, in the preamble (limited to the 'human person').

of departure above.[65] The side-by-side application must here be understood within the auspices laid down just above, with regard to the force of military necessity as a limited exception. The Clause has inspired both international tribunals and national courts, as well as legal scholars, to dwell upon its current status under international law. Those parts of the debate of further relevance for this book are dealt with partly in Chapter 2 as part of the relationship between permissions and prohibitions, partly in Chapter 6 with regard to the notion of the 'laws of humanity', and partly in Chapter 4 with regard to the application of flexible norms as part of the military commander's margin of appreciation.

As referred to above, considerable effort has been made in the international legal community to identify the content of customary LOAC. Among these initiatives is the International Committee of the Red Cross (ICRC) Customary Law Study (CIHL) which was first published in 2009, identifying 161 rules with allegedly customary status. Despite the fact that the CIHL has been subject to considerable critique, and must be used cautiously, its standing as a work of reference is indisputable. Also other non-binding productions identify customary LOAC to a considerable degree: the 1994 San Remo Manual,[66] the 2009 AMW Manual[67] and the 2013 Tallinn Manual (with a 2017 update), all of which have acquired solid legal standing, both among States as well as international tribunals and other practitioners and legal scholars. Parts of these works are used as valuable reference material in this book. I now turn to one of the contentious issues concerning formation of customary LOAC.

1.6.2 *Violation of Legal Norms vs Formation of Customary Law*

While it is generally accepted that the formation of customary international law rests on both general practice and *opinio juris*, the particularities of both elements are difficult to apply in practice. As has been stated by Meron: 'It is difficult to find positive, concrete state practice with regard to rules that are largely prohibitive – as the rules of humanitarian law generally are – because such rules are largely respected through abstention from violations, rather than affirmative practice.'[68]

65 See AP I Commentary to AP I article 1(2), at page 39, para. 56 and Dinstein, 'The interaction between customary international law and treaties', at pages 384–5.

66 Doswald-Beck (general ed.) and International Institute of Humanitarian Law, *San Remo Manual on International Law Applicable to Armed Conflicts at Sea*.

67 Program on Humanitarian Policy and Conflict Research Harvard University (HPCR), *Commentary on the HPCR Manual on International Law Applicable to Air and Missile Warfare* (AMW Manual) (2010).

68 Meron, 'Customary humanitarian law today', page 41.

One recurring issue is therefore the question whether a certain practice, of one or more States, is to be considered as formative for customary law or as an example of a violation of existing law. The ICJ has stated a point of departure in this regard, in the Nicaragua case, where the court noted that the 'corresponding practice' of a rule does not need to be 'in absolutely rigorous conformity with the rule'. The practice should 'in general, be consistent with such rules, and that instances of State conduct inconsistent with a given rule should generally have been treated as breaches of that rule, not as indications of the recognition of a new rule'.[69] The question thereby appears to be where the threshold for a practice that is 'in general' consistent with the rule is, and when 'contrary practice reaches such a critical mass that the norm in question cannot be said to be customary'.[70]

Some features of the actual practice of States during the conduct of hostilities, throughout history, are particularly troublesome to label: the practice of area bombardment (in particular during WWII), attacks on war sustaining capabilities and States' conception of military advantages as opposed to other advantages.[71] The significance of history in determining the content of customary LOAC is obvious. Parks points out that: 'The determination of customary international law is based in part on the "practice of nations", a synonym for history.'[72] A similar position is taken by Roberts: 'In short, the study of law needs to be integrated with the study of history: if not, it is inadequate.'[73] However, equating state practice with the study of history appears problematic if it turns into a pure 'apology' for State interests, lacking the normative element that turn that practice into *law*.[74] This problem is addressed with regard to the practice of area bombardment during WWII, by Blix, where he, on the basis that the practice of unrestricted bombing was stamped neither legal nor illegal by the Nuremberg tribunal after the war, points out that: 'Military necessity is not simply to be equated with every past

69 Military and Paramilitary Activities in and against Nicaragua (*Nicaragua* v. *United States of America*), at para. 186. The Court continues: 'If a State acts in a way prima facie incompatible with a recognized rule, but defends its conduct by appealing to exceptions or justifications contained within the rule itself, then whether or not the State's conduct is in fact justifiable on that basis, the significance of that attitude is to confirm rather than to weaken the rule.'

70 Meron, 'Customary humanitarian law today', page 40.

71 These legal questions are addressed with regard to military necessity in Chapters 8 and 14.

72 Parks, 'Perspectives and the importance of history', at page 377.

73 Roberts, 'Land warfare: from Hague to Nuremberg', at page 117.

74 I here rely on the description of 'apology' as presented by Koskenniemi, *From Apology to Utopia*, page 17.

military practice, however, but must be assessed as objectively as possible.'[75] The statement is agreeable, but not very informative.

In an opposite direction, where the importance of history is actually being downplayed in the formation of customary law, is the following view on the Martens Clause[76] as to where it, according to (for example) Meron, 'reinforces a trend, which is already strong in international institutions and tribunals, towards basing the existence of customary law primarily on *opinion juris* rather than actual battlefield practice'.[77] An illustration of this 'trend' can be seen in the International Criminal Tribunal for the Former Yugoslavia (ICTY) Trial Chamber judgment in the Kupreskic Case, over the issue of reprisals against civilians (dealt with in detail in Chapter 12). Contrary to state practice and the traditional view of customary LOAC, the Trial Chamber held, by referring – among others – to the Martens Clause, that:

> The aforementioned elements seem to support the contention that the demands of humanity and the dictates of public conscience, as manifested in *opinio necessitatis*, have by now brought about the formation of a customary rule also binding upon those few States that at some stage did not intend to exclude the abstract legal possibility of resorting to the reprisals under discussion.[78]

While this 'trend' bears a creative aspect in the formation of law, the truth should, ideally, lie somewhere in between or, rather, in the unification of practice and *opinio juris*, as the definition of customary international law itself ascertains. As applied in the domain of the LOAC, 'The point is obviously to find an interpretation which takes into account military and humanitarian needs in a balanced way.'[79] This balance is the topic of Chapter 6 in this book, where both the reality of practice and contrary practice is acknowledged, as well as a sincere search for States' expressions confirming their subjective conviction as to the adherence to practice *as law*. This ideal path has proven a continuous challenge throughout this book.

75 Blix, 'Area bombardment: rules and reasons', at page 40.

76 Quoted and dealt with into more detail below, in Chapters 2, 4 and 6, as well as in Section 1.6.3 just below.

77 Meron, *The Humanization of International Law*, at page 28. In the same vein, see Kolb and Del Mar, 'Treaties for armed conflict', at page 58.

78 International Criminal Tribunal for the former Yugoslavia (ICTY), Kupreskic Case, Trial Chamber Judgment, at para. 533. See further Chapter 12, for a discussion of reprisals and the position taken by the ICTY.

79 Kolb and Del Mar, 'Treaties for armed conflict', at page 80.

1.6.3 *Interpretation of Relevant Treaty Provisions*

As stated above, the VCLT applies to the LOAC treaties, leaving its 'general rule of interpretation' the point of departure for application of treaty rules to any given facts.[80] Article 31(1) states that 'A treaty shall be interpreted in good faith in accordance with the ordinary meaning to be given to the terms of the treaty in their context and in light of its object and purpose.' The provision refers to four elements: 'good faith', 'ordinary meaning', 'context' and 'object and purpose', of which all have some specific relevance for the interpretation of treaties applicable to the topic for the present book.

Among those terms which are of essential interest here are 'necessity' and 'advantage'. These are words that are not defined by treaty law and where interpretations are numerous – they are flexible terms subject to the commander's assessment (see Chapter 4). The ordinary meanings given to these terms have proven a valuable point of departure. This is particularly the case because references to these terms in court decisions as well as in legal literature appear to rely exactly upon a shared pre-understanding of the 'ordinary meaning' given to the terms. For example, such as the point made in Chapter 14, that the meaning given to 'military advantage' seems to have been presumed known during the treaty negotiations, yet never defined. Furthermore, the terms are so common, both in daily language and in military jargon, that they are given meaning almost intuitively. This intuitive distribution of meaning to the terms may in turn give rise to different interpretations that are not necessarily easy to discern at first glance. For example: 'necessity' refers to something that I *have to do*. Does this mean that, by the ordinary meaning given to term, the desired outcome cannot occur unless I act as described (i.e. that the act is *sine qua non* to the result, such as oxygen to fire)? These questions are addressed in a general manner in Chapter 2.

The notion of 'good faith' plays a particular role in the LOAC in that it constitutes one out of two elements required to be a 'reasonable commander', as dealt with in detail in Chapters 4 and 5. Under the LOAC, 'good faith' is an attribute of the commander which has originated from international criminal law, but which today is commonly referred to as almost integrated with the meaning of the treaty rule itself and not merely an issue of criminal responsibility.

The context as well as object and purpose of LOAC treaty rules are extensively referred to, either implicitly or explicitly, by legal scholars particularly, when arguments are made in favour of a specific legal position. LOAC

80 See for example, ibid., at page 79.

rules serve a twofold purpose, which is to strike a balance between two (mostly) competing interests: humanitarian considerations and military necessity. The result of treaty interpretation within the LOAC is thus often coloured by the relative weight distributed to each of these competing interests. The fundamental balance between humanitarian considerations and military necessity is dealt with in detail in Chapter 6. Reference to the Martens Clause is often also seen in this context (as well as regarding the formation of customary law as dealt with above), with the argument that the humanitarian considerations expressed in the Clause must serve as a guideline for the interpretation of the LOAC treaties. The validity of this argument is discussed in Chapter 4.

1.6.4 *The Practice of International Courts and Tribunals*

According to the ICJ Statute article 38(2), judicial decisions shall be applied as 'subsidiary means' for the determination of rules of law. The legal status of the different international tribunals within the field of the LOAC, throughout history, differs considerably. Yet, judgments from various international tribunals are quoted extensively, almost without reference to their formal status As referred to at the beginning of Section 1.6.1, customary law has 'entered the courtrooms of the international tribunals with all force'. Since WWII, the practice, in particular, of the International Military Tribunal at Nuremberg (IMT) (as well as the practice of the subsequent trials for the national military courts), the ICTY and the ICC have been cited and discussed in almost endless aspects. When suitable for the purpose of the present book, judgments are also being cited here. There is, however, (at least) one concern: the mentioned tribunals are erected for criminal prosecution of individuals, while the rules of the LOAC are not drafted as criminal provisions (see Chapter 5). Yet, the LOAC provisions are interpreted in the context of criminal prosecution on countless occasions and in insurmountable length. At least in the practice of the ICTY, interpretations of the LOAC are not always consistent and they do not necessarily serve the purpose of the LOAC. In this book, inconsistencies are pointed out, for example concerning wanton destruction of property, as well as regarding the scope of the notion 'concrete and direct military advantage' under the proportionality assessment. At the present stage, it therefore suffices to recall with caution the following statement by Meron: 'it is certainly true that, in practice, courts are giving greater weight to judicial decisions than what is suggested by the text of Article 38 of the ICJ Statute'.[81] Further remarks on the relationship between international criminal law and the LOAC is offered below, in Chapter 5.

[81] Meron, 'Customary humanitarian law today', page 40.

1.7 THE ROAD AHEAD

This book consists of seventeen chapters, and a conclusion. In acknowledging the core function of military necessity within the LOAC, core notions and core rules are addressed. Chapter 2 is a 'conceptual chapter' addressing the elements of military necessity which comprises its *function* in the law of armed conflict as well as its *content* ('nature').[82] The first refers *to where, when and how references to* military necessity are found and applied, and the second refers to *what* the factual circumstances constituting military necessity amount to. Then, having already pointed out the importance of history, Chapter 3 embarks on history all the way back to Grotius. Chapter 4 turns towards the military commander and their assessment, which is a core feature of the whole book. Chapter 5 addresses some aspects of the commander's criminal responsibility for violations of core rules governing conduct of hostilities. Chapter 6 addresses the fundamental balance to be struck between humanitarian considerations and military necessity and these need to be subject to continuous assessment by the commander, or have concrete limits placed on them. This may be addressed from numerous angles, out of which I have chosen to focus on the so-called doctrine of *Kriegsraison* and the rule of limitation. Then, Chapters 7, 8, 9, 10 and 11 deal with the rule of distinction, which is presented here as a limitation upon military necessity. However, Chapter 9 on combatants as lawful targets, addresses more than the rule of distinction between civilian objects and persons on the one hand and military objectives on the other – it also deals with limitations upon attacks on combatants – the rule prohibiting unnecessary suffering. Chapters 12 and 13 address the 'add on' to the rule of distinction – the prohibition of indiscriminate attacks and, hereunder, the prohibition of launching attacks which may be expected to cause excessive collateral damage (the proportionality principle). Chapter 14 is devoted in its entirety to the notion of military advantage, which appears as a constituting element of both the definition of lawful military objectives and the proportionality principle. Chapter 15 addresses core features of assessment of the foregoing basic rules, namely the assessment of excessiveness and the notion of feasibility. Chapter 16 deals with destruction of property and the distinction between destruction that is wanton and destruction that is

82 McCoubrey upholds a distinction between the 'nature' of necessity on the one hand and how it is applied by courts and tribunals, as well as appearing in treaty provisions, on the other hand. See McCoubrey, 'The nature of the modern doctrine of military necessity'. See also Hayashi, 'Requirements of military necessity in international humanitarian law and international criminal law'. Hayashi distinguishes between 'Material Reality', 'Norm Creation' and 'Positive Law'.

militarily necessary. Hereunder, I discuss the practical scope of the rule in the Hague Regulations alongside the rules in AP I dealing with attacks against military objectives (as dealt with in Chapters 8 and 9). The last chapter, Chapter 17 (before the concluding chapter), addresses rules on special protection and the role of military necessity in this regard.

PART I

CONCEPT, HISTORY AND BASICS

2

Elements of Military Necessity

2.1 INITIAL DEFINITION OF MILITARY NECESSITY

The notion of 'military necessity' is not defined by treaty law. Apart from the provisions in the Lieber Code governing the American Civil War more than a century ago (and which is not an international treaty), there are no general treaty definitions to retrieve.[1] Notwithstanding the various definitions found in States' military manuals, which are accounted for in Section 2.3, we need a basic working definition in order to address the point of departure for the legal concept of military necessity. In Chapter 1 'necessity' is defined, according to the ordinary meaning of the word, as a state of being required or as measures that are required (necessary). Recalling that the enterprise of war is 'only a means to an end',[2] a preliminary working definition of 'military necessity' is therefore: 'doing what is necessary to achieve a war aim'.[3] This rudimentary definition of military necessity reflects the actual practice of military operations.[4] It seems to be a widely shared opinion of States that: 'A winning military strategy hinges on the successful union of Ends (objectives), Ways (broad approaches) and Means (resources).'[5] When it comes to the legal conception of military necessity it therefore seems, at the outset, to be interwoven with this (fairly general) approach. In *The German War Book* from the

[1] Lieber Code article 14 is dealt with below, in Chapter 3. In the Lieber Code, the phrase 'ends of the war' is used to express what I here, initially, refer to as 'war aim'. Different expressions are dealt with further below, in Section 2.3 and in Chapter 3. Also the limitational rules in AP I article 35, and the 1907 Hague Regulations, article 22, are dealt with in Chapter 6. They do not contain definitions of military necessity as such.

[2] Spaight, *Air Power and War Rights*.

[3] Verri, *Dictionary of International Law of Armed Conflict*, at page 75. Recited by the ICTY in the Galic Case, Trial Chamber Judgment, in footnote 76 to para. 44.

[4] Military necessity understood as actual practice – and not the legal norm – is described as 'material military necessity' by Hayashi, 'Basic principles', at page 90.

[5] NATO, Allied Joint Publication (AJP) 01, at para. 3.7-3.10, page 3-2.

last half of the nineteenth century it was held that: 'What is permissible includes every means of war without which the object of the war cannot be obtained; what is reprehensible on the other hand includes every act of violence and destruction which is not demanded by the object of war.'[6]

Although the limitless reference ('every means') to what is demanded (by military necessity) is abandoned[7] in modern publications, the notion of 'means to ends' as a part of military necessity is still present: 'Military necessity includes two elements: (1) a military requirement to undertake a certain measure, (2) not forbidden by the laws of war. A commander must articulate a military requirement, select a measure to achieve it, and ensure neither violates the law of armed conflict.'[8]

From this outset, we can discern eight elements, or ingredients, of military necessity under the LOAC – which are being introduced in this chapter. Before these elements are presented one by one in the following sections, they are introduced here. First, *military* necessity must be distinguished from other necessities, such as political, economic or social – or even a 'state of necessity'. Second, military necessity relates to the war aim and therefore the war aim needs to be defined for the purposes of answering the question 'necessary for what?'. Third, the relational aspect of military necessity also hinges on a question of cause and effect – what is the legal requirement of proximity or suitability between the measures taken and the ends sought? Fourth, having established that military necessity relates to those measures necessary for a war aim, we can rule out as non-necessary (or unnecessary) those measures that *lack* a war aim. Those are, in practice, wanton acts of war. Fifth, those measures that are considered necessary to achieve a war aim address the whole fundament of the LOAC. As such, military necessity serves as a justification or permission for lawful acts of war. Sixth, having established that military necessity serves as a justification, we must address the different faces of military necessity throughout the legal framework of the LOAC. Seventh, and in the continuation of the sixth, what does the different aggravations of necessity (such as imperative and absolute) entail? Eight, 'doing what is necessary to achieve a war aim' requires a continuous assessment by the military commander. The legal notion of military necessity is thus inextricably linked to the assessment of it, and hereunder the inevitable use of discretion by the commander (his margin of appreciation).

6 Morgan, *The German War Book*, at page 64.

7 On the doctrine of *Kriegsraison* – and the critique against it – see below, Chapter 6.

8 See *US Law of Armed Conflict Deskbook* (US LOAC Deskbook), at page 134. Similar formulations are adopted in the US Department of Defence (DoD) *Law of War Manual* (US DoD Manual) para. 2.2, pages 52 ff. See further below, Section 2.3.

2.2 THE NATURE OF *MILITARY* NECESSITY AS OPPOSED TO OTHER NECESSITIES

The legal framework governing conduct of hostilities is only concerned with necessity which is *military in nature*. This leaves out considerations which are of a non-military nature such as political, economic, diplomatic or personal[9] considerations.[10] Situations of military necessity must also be distinguished from situations arising to a *state of necessity* precluding international State responsibility.[11] The point of departure appears clear, stemming from the wording of the concept itself, but two aspects have the potential for repeated confusion: first the fact that an armed conflict is a political tool for pursuing political ends[12] and second that the concept of 'military necessity' under the LOAC is law, not politics. Neither of the two can be viewed in isolation (as if the other does not exist), yet it is crucial not to merge them. Needless to say, if war aims are achieved, these achievements will ultimately turn into political benefits. On the other hand, when military aims and objectives are set out in military planning, they are done so with the background of political ends. Yet, military necessity as part of the law does not permit the application of military force solely based on political, diplomatic or economic aims.

On the other hand, military necessity should not be equated with military considerations of 'economy of force'. Force economy, as part of the military 'principles of war', means the concerted effort of force required in order to accomplish a certain task. It is in practice closely related, but not identical, to military necessity. First and foremost because economy of force is not a legal concept, but a part of military doctrine. Second, because economy of force contains limiting aspects[13] on the use of force which cannot automatically be read into military necessity.[14] The question remains: if not necessary for solely political, diplomatic or economic aim, then what is necessity considered for?

9 On wantonness as opposed to necessity, see Section 2.5 and Chapter 16.

10 Dinstein, 'Military necessity', paras. 20 and 25–6. Political considerations are specifically included in GC III article 76 and GC IV article 112, see further Section 2.9 below. The distinction is particularly important to draw with regard to the notion of the military nature of military *advantage*, which is dealt with in Chapter 14.

11 On the relationship between the international law on State responsibility and military necessity, see Section 1.6. This point is also emphasised by Geiss, 'Military necessity', at page 556.

12 See for example Geiss, ibid., at page 564: 'War itself ultimately remains a political act, and in the grey zones it may not be entirely clear when military considerations stop being military and become rather political.'

13 On the general rule of limitation, see Chapter 6.

14 In this respect economy of force is more easily comparable to proportionality (as distinct from necessity), and commented upon as such, in Chapter 14, with regard to the security of the attacking force. For an (*lex ferenda*) argument in favour of using military necessity as

2.3 MILITARY NECESSITY AND THE QUESTION OF 'NECESSARY FOR WHAT'?

If military necessity broadly speaking refers to those measures which are necessary to achieve a war aim, we need to define the war aim. Due to the nature of military necessity as 'a relational concept'[15] the question 'necessary for what?' quickly arises as the first question of means to ends in warfare.[16] To answer the question 'necessary for what?' we must formulate *ends* in warfare in a legal context, beyond simply referring to the 'war aim' as done hitherto. Based on this first question, there is a question of whether this 'end' encapsulates the whole war and points back at means necessary to 'terminate' the war.[17] The question of how certain means *relate* to certain *ends* is the second question of means to ends in warfare, and is discussed in the Section 2.4.

The only treaty text dealing with the war aim, as the coinage 'object of war', is the St Petersburg Declaration from 1868. The Declaration states that 'the only legitimate object which States should endeavour to accomplish during war is to weaken the military forces of the enemy'.[18] The status of the Declaration in general and the meaning of this phrase specifically is discussed into more detail in Chapter 3 where at least three different meanings of the phrase 'object of war' are presented.

The difficulties of subduing the 'object of war' to treaty regulation clearly became visible during the treaty negotiations prior to the adoption of the AP I. The drafting process of the basic rule of distinction in article 48 is accounted for in Chapter 7, but it is worthwhile to have an early look at draft article 43 which said: '. . . the Parties to the conflict shall confine their operations to the destruction or weakening of the military resources of the adversary . . .'[19] The passage was rejected and the only remaining means to discern the views among States is through their military manuals. Military necessity is addressed in a number of States' military manuals, and the wording used to describe the 'object of war' or the 'aim of warfare' varies.

a reducing factor, see Beer, 'Humanity considerations cannot reduce wars hazards alone', pages 803 and 807.

15 Solf, 'Protection of civilians against the effects of hostilities under customary international law and under Protocol I', at page 128.

16 McDougal and Feliciano, *Law and Minimum World Order*, at page 528. See also Geiss, 'Military necessity', at page 556 as well as below, Section 3.2.2.

17 This phrase is from Grotius, see Chapter 3.

18 St Petersburg Declaration. The Declaration is cited more extensively below, in Chapter 3.

19 Official Records of the Diplomatic Conference on the Reaffirmation and Development of International Humanitarian Law Applicable in Armed Conflicts (from Draft article 43 (final article 48)).

The most recited version is of US origin, also denoted as the 'Anglo-American doctrine of military necessity'.[20] The US definition (subsequent to the older Lieber Code) first appeared in the Hostage Case before the US Military Tribunal after WWII: 'Military necessity permits a belligerent, subject to the laws of war, to apply any amount and kind of force to compel the *complete submission* of the enemy with the least possible expenditure of time, life, and money.'[21]

And later in the US Field Manual, originally from 1957 and reiterated in the US Operational Law Handbook: '"military necessity" which has been defined as that principle which justifies those measures not forbidden by international law which are indispensable for securing the *complete submission* of the enemy as soon as possible'.[22]

Finally, the US DoD LOAC Manual states that: 'Military necessity may be defined as the principle that justifies the use of all measures needed to *defeat* the enemy as quickly and efficiently as possible that are not prohibited by the law of war.'[23]

The 'object of war' is here referred to as the 'complete submission' or the 'defeat' of the enemy. The same approach is chosen in the Canadian Manual[24] whereas in a US military dictionary, the 'object' is more broadly referred to as: 'the *successful conclusion* of a military operation'.[25] A similar wording is chosen in the German Manual, which in turn relies on the North Atlantic Treaty Organization (NATO) definition: 'According to the principle of military necessity, all military measures are permissible in armed conflict which are required for the *successful execution* of military operations in order to engage the enemy, provided that these measures are not forbidden by the LOAC.'[26]

20 See the remarks by Goldie, in Trooboff, *Law and Responsibility in Warfare*, at page 84.

21 *United States* v. *Wilhelm List and others* (Hostage Case), at page 66. Emphasis added.

22 FM 27-10, US Department of the Army Field Manual, *The Law of Land Warfare* (US Field Manual), Appendix A-1; International and Operational Law Department, *Operational Law Handbook*, at page 11. Emphasis added.

23 US DoD Manual, para. 2.2. Emphasis added.

24 Joint Doctrine Manual, *Law of Armed Conflict at the Tactical and Operational Levels* (Canadian Manual), at page 2-1: 'Military necessity is related to the primary aim of armed conflict – the complete submission of the enemy at the earliest possible moment with the least possible expenditure of personnel and resources.'

25 Joint Publication 1-02 (Dictionary of Military and Associated Terms). Emphasis added.

26 German Federal Ministry of Defence, Joint Service Regulation (ZDv) 15/2, *Law of Armed Conflict Manual* (German Manual), at page 25. The same definition appears in NATO, *Glossary of Terms and Definitions*, AAP-6 (NATO, AAP-6) (2013), at page 2-M-6.

This definition, resembling also the ones in the Norwegian Manual[27] and the Australian Air Force,[28] entails a change from the previous German Manual, then appearing in Fleck's handbook, where the expression 'defeat' was chosen,[29] accompanied with a confusing commentary relying upon the right to self-defence as recognised in the UN Charter.[30]

In the UK Manual, the 'object of war' is tied to the purpose of the entire conflict. The manual states:

> Military necessity permits a state engaged in an armed conflict to use only that degree and kind of force, not otherwise prohibited by the law of armed conflict, that is required in order to achieve the *legitimate purpose of the conflict*, namely the *complete or partial submission of the enemy* at the earliest possible moment with the minimum expenditure of life and resources.[31]

At the outset, it is not clear what the differences between 'complete submission', 'complete or partial submission', 'defeat' or the 'successful execution of military operations' amount to – if there are any differences in substance at all. Apparently, the expression 'complete *or partial* submission of the enemy' in the UK Manual has been chosen to reflect the modern development of the law

27 The Norwegian Manual states that military necessity 'grants military forces permission to use force necessary to achieve military objectives, typically to weaken the enemy forces militarily'. The (Norwegian) chosen solution leaves the possibility open for other examples of 'military objectives' than those explicitly exemplified. Norwegian Manual, Forsvaret, *Manual i krigens folkerett*, at page 13. The Norwegian text says: 'Prinsippet om militær nødvendighet gir militære styrker tillatelse til å bruke den makt som er nødvendig for å oppnå militære målsettinger, typisk å svekke motparten militært.'

28 Where military necessity is defined as: 'The principle that combatants may use the minimum amount of force necessary to achieve a legitimate military objective.' Recited from Henderson, *The Contemporary Law of Targeting*, at page 35.

29 See O'Connell, 'Historical development and legal basis', para. 132, at page 34. 'In war, a belligerent may apply only that amount and kind of force necessary to defeat the enemy. Acts of war are only permissible if they are directed against military objectives, if they are not likely to cause unnecessary suffering and if they are not perfidious.' The statement is problematic with regard to destruction of property beyond the scope of attacks, which are lawful acts of war not directed against military objectives. See further Chapter 16.

30 In ibid., at page 35 it is stated that: 'Prior to 1945, once a state was justified in going to war it was invariably entitled to seek the complete submission of its adversary and to employ all force, subject only to the constraints of humanitarian law, to achieve that goal. That is no longer permissible. Under the Charter of the United Nations (UN Charter), a state which is entitled to exercise the right of self-defence is justified only in seeking to achieve the goals of defending itself immediately and taking reasonable measures to provide for its future security in light of the nature of the violation of Article 2(4).' And then: 'In an extreme case the achievement of these defensive goals might be possible only by securing the complete submission of the adversary, but that will generally not be the case.'

31 UK Ministry of Defence, *The Manual of the Law of Armed* (UK Manual), at pages 21–2. Emphasis added.

in the aftermath of WWII, recognising that 'war can have a limited purpose'.[32] Similarly, the expression 'successful execution of military operations' seems to reflect the practice of States of conducting military operations not only in order to seek the defeat or submission of the enemy, but also – for example – to enhance security or establish freedom of movement in an area. In other words, the notion of the 'object of war', as a response to the question of 'necessary for what', appears to be understood broadly – and hence not specifically – by States.

Various references to the understanding of the 'object of war' can also be found among legal scholars, particularly in the aftermath of WWII. Dunbar relates military necessity to 'the stress of active warfare',[33] whereas Downey appears to borrow language from the St Petersburg Declaration stating that: 'Regulated violence is generally considered as that violence directed or authorized by superior authority for the purpose of disabling the greatest possible number of the enemy, but the military effect of which is not disproportionate to the suffering it entails.'[34]

The explicit notion of 'means to ends' has been pointed out in relation to military necessity as a: 'fundamental principle that the procedure of war is a means to an end and consequently all measures employed must have a direct or at least indirect relation to the submission of the enemy'.[35] These examples support the broad and non-specific approach taken by States, as referred to above.

It should be noted that the view of military necessity, or rather the scope of military necessity in relation to the 'object of war', easily appears to be coloured by the view of international law. A policy approach[36] was presented by McDougal in the 1960s, when he, in an answer to the question of 'necessary for what', argued in favour of a more limited approach to the 'object of war' and that military necessity: 'Permit[s] the exercise of that violence which is indispensably necessary (proportionate and relevant) for promptly repelling and terminating highly intense initiating coercion against "territorial integrity" or "political independence" – indispensably necessary, in a word, for successful defense or community enforcement actions.'[37] McDougal makes a direct link between military necessity and the 'territorial integrity' and 'political independence' of a State. Despite being made with the apparent

32 Rogers, *Law on the Battlefield*, at page 9.
33 See Dunbar, 'Military necessity in war crimes trials', page 443.
34 Downey, 'The law of war and military necessity', at pages 260–1. Emphasis added.
35 Rauch, 'The concept of military necessity in the context of the law of war', at page 4.
36 This expression is from Koskenniemi, *From Apology to Utopia*, at pages 201–9.
37 McDougal and Feliciano, *Law and Minimum World Order*, at page 528.

intention of limiting the use of force to certain specified purposes, his statement may very well be used in favour of an expansive and purpose-oriented use of force, rather than use of force limited to that which is related to the actual war-fighting, that is to say: within the context of the armed conflict.

It therefore suffices to state the point of departure that the 'object of war' must be understood broadly, yet within the context of the armed conflict – it must relate to actual war-fighting and not the resort to armed force as such.[38]

2.4 MILITARY NECESSITY AND CAUSE AND EFFECT

The second question of means to ends in warfare is introduced above as a question of cause and effect: What is the legal requirement of causality between the measures taken and the ends sought? Treaty LOAC referring to military necessity does not expound on the issue of the causal relationship between the means and the ends in warfare in general.[39] Causal[40] relationship is, however, addressed specifically in certain rules where military necessity are expressed implicitly,[41] such as the rule governing *direct* participation in hostilities and the proportionality rule prohibiting attacks which may be expected to cause collateral damage excessive to the concrete and *direct* military advantage anticipated.

In essence, the issue of the causal relationship between means and ends in warfare is a question of the suitability or 'relevance'[42] of the means adopted in order to reach the ends. For example, in order to reach the desired objective of weakening the opposing forces it is necessary to *cause* that effect by disabling as many enemy combatants as possible, by means of attacking them (or eventually capturing them).[43] Attacks against enemy combatants are *suited* to weaken enemy forces, just as destruction and seizure of enemy property may be.[44] Those measures that are *un*suited, that is not necessary according to the

38 See Chapter 1 for a distinction to the *jus ad bellum*.

39 As opposed to general international law, which in article 25 of the Draft Articles on State Responsibility qualifies an act of necessity to be 'the only way for the State to safeguard an essential interest against a grave and imminent peril'.

40 On causal terminology and law in general, see Hart and Honoré, *Causation in the Law*, at pages 27–9.

41 See Section 2.7.

42 McDougal and Feliciano, *Law and Minimum World Order*, at page 524. Later supported by Bothe, Partsch and Solf, *New Rules for Victims of Armed Conflicts*, at page 224; as well as Higgins, *Problems and Process: International Law and How We Use It*, page 232. The requirement of relevance is usually presented together with a requirement of proportionality, as a 'silent condition' of necessity. See Chapter 13.

43 On the alleged duty to capture rather than killing an enemy combatant, see Chapter 9.

44 See Chapter 16.

law, in order to reach the desired objective will, for practical purposes, amount to wanton acts of war, as dealt with in Section 2.5.

Two treaty provisions address the causal connection as part of the notion of military necessity in general: the Lieber Code[45] stating that the means must be '*indispensable*' for securing the ends of war and the St Petersburg Declaration stating that it is only allowed for those means which are '*sufficient* to disable the greatest possible number of men'.[46]

The phrase in the Lieber Code appears to have been the preferred American phrase,[47] up until the DoD *Law of War Manual* from 2015 where it is referred to 'all measures *needed* to defeat the enemy as quickly and efficiently as possible...'[48] It is, however, not easy to trace a consistent pattern with regard to the chosen formulations among States and in legal literature. Phrases such as 'essential condition'[49] and 'inevitably requires'[50] are found in the literature – pointing in the direction of being read as synonyms to 'indispensable'.[51] In the post-WWII Hostage Case, the causal requirement in military necessity is referred to with an add-on of reasonableness: 'Destruction as an end in itself is a violation of international law. There must be some *reasonable connection* between the destruction of property and the overcoming of the enemy forces.'[52]

The phrase 'reasonable connection' is recited in earlier manuals[53] and literature, but without further commenting specifically on the aspect of causality.[54] Instead of referring to the objective characteristics of the relation

45 On the Lieber Code as a legal source of international law, see Chapter 1. The Lieber Code is dealt with in more detail below, in Chapter 3.

46 Both provisions are cited in full and dealt with in more detail below, in Chapter 3.

47 See US Field Manual, Appendix A-1; US Operational Law Handbook, at page 11; and US LOAC Deskbook, at page 134. See also McDougal and Feliciano, *Law and Minimum World Order*, at pages 523–4, and O'Brien, 'The meaning of "military necessity" in international law', at pages 138 ff.

48 US DoD Manual, at page 52. With regard to destruction of property, however, the wording from the Hostage Case – reasonable connection – is used, see page 262.

49 AP I Commentary to AP I article 35, at page 396, para. 1396; and Meyrowitz, 'The principle of superfluous injury or unnecessary suffering', at page 100.

50 Oeter, 'Methods and means of combat', at page 122. A similar phrase is found in the US LOAC Deskbook, at page 134, cited above.

51 The AP I Commentary uses these phrases interchangeably, see paras. 1396, 1389 and 1406. The definition of military necessity in States' military manuals is also dealt with in Section 2.6 under the discussion of permissions vs prohibitions.

52 Hostage Case, page 66. Emphasis added.

53 US Field Manual, Appendix A-14.

54 See Dinstein, *Conduct of Hostilities*, at page 11; as well as Schmitt, 'Military necessity and humanity in international humanitarian law', at page 797; and Downey, 'The law of war and military necessity', at page 257.

between the means and the end – such as 'indispensable' – the notion of 'reasonable connection' refers to something other than strict (and objective) causality, namely the subjective element of reasonableness: the connection between means and ends must appear reasonable. This requirement hits at the core of the main topic of this book: the legal limits of the military commander's assessment of military necessity. The explicit requirement of reasonableness is dealt with in more detail below (in Chapter 4) and the inevitable use of discretion by the military commander is introduced at the end of this chapter.

The disruption or destruction of enemy supplies (such as fuel, food and military materiel) has a reasonable connection to the aim of hampering enemy advance, because supplies are essential to the ability to move forward. Conversely, destruction of food supplies for the civilian population does not have a reasonable connection to the aim of hampering enemy advance.[55] Although imposing hardship on the enemy civilian population ultimately may also be to the detriment of enemy military forces, the connection to the military aim is too remote to make it permissible. These examples reflect the law as it is today, where positive rules have in-built considerations of military necessity, as discussed later in this chapter. In fact, the causal requirement inherent in military necessity does not necessarily add or detract meaning to the rules of the LOAC in general, as each and every rule may have acquired its own requirement of causality, not only those where causality is mentioned explicitly. This observation stems from the fact that after the adoption of the AP I in 1977 practically all acts of warfare are subject to specific regulation, falling within the scope of either attacks or other acts amounting to destruction or seizure of property. However, due to the fact that States' military manuals (still) also contain general references to military necessity as a basic tenure of the LOAC – and hereunder the notion of causality in it – a few more remarks are offered in the following on the, often confusing, notion of causality.

Two aspects of causality are usually addressed when dealing with causality as a matter of natural science or – for example – as part of criminal law. With regard to the notion of military necessity under the LOAC, these are more sporadically addressed, but may nevertheless cause confusion. These aspects are: first, the question of whether necessity means that measures taken must be measures required in a strict logical sense, that is, whether they must be *sine*

[55] The special protection devoted to objects that are indispensable for the survival of the civilian population is dealt with in more detail in Chapter 17.

qua non[56] to the desired end or aim.[57] Second, the question of whether necessity means that the measure taken must be the only available course of action.

The different wording chosen by States in their manuals, as well as the two phrases from the Lieber Code and the St Petersburg Declaration, do not point in the same direction with regard to these questions. Naturally, treaty texts and States' manuals are not drafted for logical analysis and should not be read as such. They should, as stated in the VCLT, be read according to the ordinary meaning of the words.[58]

The word 'indispensable' seems to require that the measures taken are *sine qua non* to the desired military end. The same cannot be said about the wording in the St Petersburg Declaration, referring to *sufficiency* – meaning (logically) a measure that is suited to cause the desired end, but leaving the possibility open for achieving the result by other measures. Again, the wording in the St Petersburg Declaration is not a matter of logic and uses instead a prohibitive language: it is forbidden to do *more* than what is sufficient.[59] The inconsistent use of terminology among States also supports the assertion that measures taken during warfare need not be *sine qua non* to the result in order to be necessary, and lawful.

Second, there is the question of alternatives. As already pointed out at the outset of this section, treaty LOAC does not address this issue in general, although general international law does, requiring that there is 'no choice', but to act as chosen.[60] Although case law in the field of the LOAC in some instances has referred to situations where no other choice was possible, and the situation thus was one of necessity, this does not imply that situations of necessity require that no other choices are available in every case.[61] Even though 'no choice' implies necessity, there is no basis to assert that necessity *requires* a situation of 'no choice'.

56 When something is *sine qua non* for the desired effect, it is bound to be present when the effect is a fact. See for example Hart and Honoré, *Causation in the Law*, at page 113 which uses the presence of oxygen in order to produce a fire as an example of a condition *sine qua non*. Or, understood negatively, if the effect is there, the cause has also been present. Also known as a contrafactual. Contrafactual theory on causation was first discussed by Hume, *Philosophical Essays*. For more recent discussions see Lewis, *Counterfactuals*, and Menzies, *Counterfactual Theories of Causation*.

57 The concept of *sine qua non* is also addressed below, in Chapter 11 on the notion of direct participation in hostilities.

58 VCLT, article 31.

59 On the issue of proportionality as an alleged element of necessity, see Chapter 13.

60 See above, with the reference to Draft Articles on State Responsibility, article 25.

61 See *Luzon Sugar Refining Company Ltd. (Great Britain) v. United States* (the Luzon Case); and Chapter 16 on destruction of property.

Rather than focusing on the issue of '*no* choice', the practical difficulties more often concern situations where choices have to be made between alternative means in order to reach a desired effect. For example: the enemy may be denied access to an area by use of minefields as well as destruction of a bridge. Another example is whether a commander is required to use ground forces in a specific operation in order to avoid civilian casualties or whether he can choose to stick to air strikes in order to preserve his own forces.[62] The question will thus be whether the commander is free to decide between the alternatives or whether the law places an obligation to choose one alternative. One author has summed up the practice of national and international judicial decisions as follows:

> it would seem from the pattern of judicial and quasi-judicial decisions over the past 150 years or so that military necessity is effectively limited to actions dictated by circumstances precluding reasonable alternatives in pursuit of an objective legitimate in terms, at least of the jus in bello in itself. It seems doubtful whether an absolute absence of alternatives is demanded.[63]

Similar to the issue discussed just above, of reasonable connection between the measures taken and the ends sought, we may therefore argue that the alternative measure chosen is one that was reasonable in light of other alternatives, although not the only one existing. That said, some rules have specific requirements, such as the precautionary duty to select a target causing the least collateral damage if that target offers a similar military advantage to another target.[64]

Furthermore, the assessment must not be done *post facto*. If an earthquake has happened to destroy a bridge that was also under attack, attacking the bridge by military force may still have been 'necessary' in a legal context. Hence, the law does not require that the chosen alternative was the only way to accomplish the mission, neither does it permit conduct which is otherwise prohibited even if it was the only way to win the war.[65]

62 See further below, Chapter 14, on the notion of military advantage and issue of force protection.

63 McCoubrey, 'The nature of the modern doctrine of military necessity', at page 226. McCoubrey supports his view, among others, by relying on *United States* v. *Wilhelm von Leeb et al.* (the High Command Case), commenting on the legality of the scorched earth policy.

64 Military necessity and the duty to take precautionary measures are dealt with in more detail below, in Chapter 15.

65 See Blix, 'Area bombardment', page 291, referring to Spaight who argues that area bombardment was lawful if it was the only way to win the war. Blix argues that Spaight stretches the notion of imperative necessity too far. On area bombardment and military necessity in general, see below, Chapter 12. On military necessity used as *Kriegsraison*, see below Chapter 6.

2.5 ACTS WHICH ARE NOT MOTIVATED BY MILITARY NECESSITY

At the outset of this chapter I introduced, as the fourth element of military necessity, that we may rule out as non-necessary (or unnecessary) those measures that *lack* a war aim. Above all, these acts comprise cruelty (i.e. infliction of pain for the purpose of inflicting pain) and wanton acts (i.e. destruction as an end in itself) of war.[66] Such acts may be motivated by reasons other than those related to the success of the armed conflict and are prohibited by the LOAC.[67]

Apart from acts of cruelty and wantonness, which are clearly not motivated by military necessity, what other acts (if any?) are *unnecessary?* First, we may rule out harmless unmotivated acts, simply because of their irrelevance to the conduct of hostilities. Second, attacks that may be expected to cause excessive collateral damage (i.e. will violate the rule on proportionality, see Chapter 13) do not necessarily fit under the labels cruel or wanton within the ordinary meaning of those words. They are prohibited, but not on the basis of lack of necessity, rather due to the competing humanitarian concerns. Hence, cruel and wanton acts of war, here implying the very opposite of acts motivated by military necessity, must be distinguished from acts that may be considered necessary, but yet prohibited because necessity under the circumstances must yield to humanitarian considerations. This balance, between military necessity and humanitarian considerations, is dealt with in detail below, in Chapter 6. Although the distinction between acts which are clearly wanton on the one hand and acts which may be considered necessary, yet unlawful, on the other hand, in principle is possible to draw clearly – practice may prove otherwise – such as the prohibition against terror attacks against the civilian population (see Chapter 12). Throughout history, attacks on civilian morale have been justified by States by reference to military necessity, but nevertheless prohibited due to humanitarian considerations in the AP I in 1977.[68] Regardless of repeated State practice, some have persistently considered terror attacks as unnecessary (futile) for military purposes and used this as the basis for prohibition.[69]

66 Lieber Code article 16; Hostage Case, at page 66; US DoD Manual, at page 58. Wantonness is defined and dealt with in more detail in Chapter 16 on destruction of property and in Chapter 13 as distinct from military advantage. Cruelty, as opposed to 'humanity', is dealt with in Chapter 6 below within the scope of the balance between military necessity and humanitarian considerations. Cruelty as prohibited by the rule prohibiting unnecessary suffering to combatants is dealt with in Chapter 9.

67 See Chapter 16 for a discussion of the rule prohibiting acts not required by imperative reasons of military necessity.

68 AP I article 51(2).

69 See the discussion below in Section 12.1.3.

2.6 MILITARY NECESSITY AS PERMISSION OR PROHIBITION

At the beginning of this chapter I stated that those measures which are considered necessary in order to achieve a war aim address the whole fundament of the LOAC. As such, military necessity serves as a justification or permission for lawful acts of war. The question of whether the law is prohibitive or permissive is, in principle, common for both international law in general and the LOAC in particular.[70] A general point of departure regarding this question is found in the Lotus Case, where the free will of States is pointed out and that 'restrictions upon the independence of States cannot therefore be presumed'.[71]

In other words: unless States have committed themselves otherwise (through treaty or customary law), they are free to act. This position chimes well (at least at the outset) with the LOAC treaty framework which consists mainly of prohibitions.[72] Military necessity has been commented upon specifically in the context of State responsibility, where it has been said to serve as the reason – the *ratio* – for departure from peacetime law.[73] That is to say, as a point of departure, military necessity serves as a permission while specific treaty regulations mainly impose prohibitions.

Some argue in favour of a more restrictive position with reference to the much debated and celebrated Martens Clause.[74] The ICRC Commentary to AP I article 1(2) states that: 'the Martens clause prevents the assumption that anything which is not explicitly prohibited by the relevant treaties is therefore permitted'.[75] However, and as shown below in Sections 4.2 and 6.3 the legal force of the Clause is not at the level of a general prohibition, it is rather

70 For the question asked in this way, see Henderson, *The Contemporary Law of Targeting*, at page 38.

71 The Case of the S.S. 'Lotus' (the Lotus Case), at page 18.

72 In the Hostage Case, it was stated that: 'International law is prohibitive law', at page 66. With regard to literature, see: Dinstein, *Conduct of Hostilities*, at page 11; Henderson, *The Contemporary Law of Targeting*, at page 39; Kleffner, 'Section IX of the ICRC Interpretive Guidance on Direct Participation in Hostilities', at page 39.

73 See for example the Eighth Report on State Responsibility, at pages 34–5. The same approach is taken in the Commentary to the rules, by Crawford, *The International Law Commission's Articles on State Responsibility*, at page 186 (footnote omitted).

74 The Clause is cited above, in Section 1.6.1. See Draper, 'Military necessity and humanitarian imperatives', at page 132: 'It is not sufficient to claim that the law of war is a series of prohibitions. Neither is it a sound statement in juridical terms. The express prohibitions established in the Hague Convention No IV and its annexed Regulations stand as illustrative of the principles spelled out in the Preamble of de Martens. This negates the proposition that that which is not forbidden by the Law of War is implicitly illicit.'

75 AP I Commentary to article 1(2), at page 39, para. 55.

a confirmation that in cases *not covered* by the treaty persons remain under the protection already offered them by customary law.[76] Baxter describes the situation as follows:

> Animated by considerations of humanity and by the desire to prevent unnecessary suffering, states have nevertheless recognized limits on the unfettered power which they would otherwise actually enjoy in time of war. The law of war is, in the descriptive words of a war crimes tribunal, 'prohibitive law', in the sense that it forbids rather than authorizes certain manifestations of force.[77]

The prohibitive language of the treaty rules has been a feature since the first Hague Conventions. Solf explains why the Hague Conventions left out reasons for the rules (as had been kept in, in the Lieber Code) and instead simply stated prohibitions. This was apparently based on a belief by 'humanitarian scholars that a humanitarian instrument should provide what is to be spared, and should not explicitly authorize violence'. Solf, however, continues – with a key role devoted to military necessity:

> Frequently, this restraint sacrificed clarity; military men tended to consider permissible any measure not expressly prohibited. This was in error, for customary law remained in full force, except to the extent modified by conventional law. . . . The reluctance to express what is authorized under customary law made it necessary for military manuals to fill in the lacunae, including a statement as to the meaning and limitations of military necessity.[78]

If the Hague Rules featured a restrictive approach to formulate permissions on the conduct of hostilities – the Additional Protocols to the Geneva Conventions are nothing less – the unwillingness to 'draw up the rules for the conduct of war' in a humanitarian treaty was clearly present in the Diplomatic Conference.[79] It is, however, true, as stated by Solf, that States themselves have presupposed the permissions in their manuals. In a number of States' manuals, definitions of military necessity contain the terms 'permits'[80] or 'justifies'.[81] The difference in wording does not indicate any difference in substance. A permissive view is also

76 Meron, *The Humanization of International Law*, at page 27. See as well Chapters 4 and 6 on the impact of the Clause on the application of the LOAC in concrete situations.

77 Baxter, 'So-called unprivileged belligerency', at page 324.

78 Solf, 'Protection of civilians', at pages 121–2.

79 Official Records of the Diplomatic Conference CDDH/III/14, page 32, statement from the Syrian delegate. See also statements from the Canadian delegate at page 32, as well as Czechoslovakia and Ghana at pages 19 and 20.

80 See the UK Manual, the Norwegian Manual, at pages 13–14, as well as the Hostage Case, at page 66, also cited above in Section 2.3.

81 US Field Manual, US Operational Law Handbook and US DoD Manual, also cited above in Section 2.3.

upheld by scholars.[82] Schmitt points out that military necessity is not 'as sometimes asserted, [a] limitation on military operations. Instead the principle recognizes the appropriateness of considering military factors in setting the rules of warfare.'[83] That is to say, military necessity is referred to as a fundamental – and permissive – ingredient in the positive rules.[84] The consideration of military necessity, present in each and every rule, functions as the threshold towards arbitrariness. Dinstein expresses the room for manoeuvre for States as follows: 'This implies tangible operational latitude, but not lack of restraint. The dynamics of the law are such that whatever is required by military necessity, and is not excluded on the ground of humanitarianism, is permissible.'[85]

Military necessity thus serves as justification for acts not necessarily enumerated by the law.[86] As pointed out by Rauch: 'International law does not attempt to enumerate those particular acts of warfare which in consequence of military necessity may lawfully be committed.'[87] The same approach is chosen in the US DoD Manual which provide lists of actions that are justified by military necessity.[88]

The position taken by the Interpretive Guidance that the Martens Clause serves as a constant reminder and that it is: 'not necessarily lawful simply because it is not expressly prohibited or otherwise regulated in treaty law',[89] appears misleading, Both because the point of departure is – as argued just above – the opposite, and because the Martens Clause does not amount to an independent legal source.[90]

82 See Bill, 'The Rendulic "Rule"', at page 131: 'Military necessity is a meta-principle of the law of war, . . . in the sense that it justifies destruction in war.'

83 Schmitt, 'Military necessity and humanity in international humanitarian law', at pages 796 and 799. In the same direction, see also Kleffner, 'Section IX of the ICRC Interpretive Guidance on Direct Participation in Hostilities'; as well as Dunbar, 'Military necessity in war crimes trials', page 444.

84 See also Chapter 6.

85 Dinstein, *Conduct of Hostilities*, at page 10.

86 In practice, however, it is hard to see any practical room for such acts after the adoption of the AP I. On this issue, see Chapter 14.

87 Rauch, 'The concept of military necessity in the context of the law of war', at page 4.

88 US DoD Manual, para. 2.2.2.2, at pages 55–6.

89 Interpretive Guidance on the Notion of Direct Participation in Hostilities under International Humanitarian Law (Interpretive Guidance), at page 1042, footnote 219.

90 One version of this is also seen in Jean Pictet's 'use of force continuum', accounted for below in Chapter 9. See also Henderson, *The Contemporary Law of Targeting*, at pages 39–40 for the combination of a correct point of departure followed by an exaggerated weight devoted to the Martens Clause.

2.7 THE DIFFERENT FACES OF MILITARY NECESSITY

Related to the question discussed in the foregoing section is the question of how military necessity appears on the face[91] of law. Having already stated (above) that military necessity appears as an underlying permission within rules, it has the function of a *foundation* (justification for conduct) when it is *implicitly* expressed in the rule. Furthermore, it serves as an *exception* to other prohibitions when this is *explicitly* accounted for in the rule. These two functions relate, in that military necessity cannot be invoked to justify conduct which is otherwise prohibited and that it can *only* be invoked as an exception to otherwise prohibited conduct when the exception is explicit.[92] These two appearances are seen in the core rules of the LOAC. The rules defining military objectives, combatants and the proportionality rule are examples of where military necessity appear as a foundation.[93] That is to say, considerations of military necessity are built into the treaty (and customary) rule.[94] For example, lawful targets are considered necessary to attack per se.[95] Military necessity is a driving force[96] and justifies a departure from peacetime rules.[97] As stated in the ICRC Commentary to the AP I article 35: 'Finally, it is important to realize that this formula [the definition of military necessity] is normally applied purely and simply as a result of respect for the rules of the Protocol, since these rules encompass all considerations of military necessity.'[98]

91 A similar expression is used by Geiss, 'Military necessity', at page 557, where he refers to military necessity as a 'Janus-faced principle of International Humanitarian Law'.

92 See Chapter 6, where the *Kriegsraison* doctrine is accounted for.

93 The same approach is taken in the US DoD Manual, para. 2.1, at page 50, where it is stated that the principle of military necessity (together with humanity and honour) 'provide the foundation for other law of war principles, such as proportionality and distinction, and most of the treaty and customary rules of the law of war'. In a similar direction, see Geiss, 'Military necessity', at page 559, where he argues that: 'The fact that IHL has not made any provision for such decreased levels of military necessity indicates the presumption that the existence of an armed conflict automatically invokes a certain "basic level" of military necessity' Chapters 8, 9 and 12 of this book account for these rules.

94 This function appears to resemble what Hayashi calls military necessity as a 'reason-giving consideration in LOAC norm-creation', see Hayashi, 'Basic principles', at page 90. Bill argues in 'The Rendulic "Rule"', at page 131, that military necessity 'permeates all subsidiary rules'. See as well Section 14.3.6 with regard to the role of military necessity after the adoption of AP I vis-à-vis other principles of the LOAC.

95 The notion of lawful targets is dealt with in Chapters 8 and 9 in this book. With regard to the basic principle of distinction, see for example Sassoli, 'Targeting', at pages 183–4.

96 The expression 'driving force' is from Dinstein, *Conduct of Hostilities*, at page 8.

97 See above, the position taken in the Eighth Report on State Responsibility.

98 AP I Commentary, at page 396, para. 1397.

When military necessity appears as an exception, it serves as an exception to conduct otherwise prescribed or prohibited. The rule permitting destruction of enemy property contains the most general example of exceptive military necessity, and is addressed in detail in Chapter 16. Exceptional clauses are noteworthy in (at least) two dimensions: first, that they are exceptive as opposed to foundations of the rule and second, that they may be invoked *only when specifically* accounted for in the rule in question. Military necessity as an exception may differ from necessity where it appears in an in-built function, as a foundation, with regard to, among others, severity, relativity and objectivity. The distinction between military advantage and military necessity is the most illustrative example here, and is dealt with in Chapter 14. However, one of the distinctive features that distinguishes military necessity from military advantage – the severity[99] – is introduced in general in the following section.

2.8 AGGRAVATIONS OF MILITARY NECESSITY AND AN ELEMENT OF TIME

The term 'military necessity' is frequently accompanied by aggravating adjectives, such as 'imperative' or 'absolute'. Neither treaty law nor States' manuals are, however, consistent in their use of these aggravations. Where do aggravations appear and what do they entail? In the Hague Regulations the adjective 'imperative' appears.[100] Also the 1929 re-drafted Geneva Convention on Wounded and Sick and the new Convention on Prisoners of War use apparently synonyms for the term 'military necessity' – 'military exigencies'[101] and 'military considerations',[102] as well as the aggravated form of necessity: 'urgent necessity'.[103] In the Tokyo Draft on the Protection of Civilians from 1934,

99 In the same direction, see Hayashi, 'Basic principles', at page 93, where he argues that the difference between military necessity and advantage may be seen as one of degrees.

100 1899 and 1907 Hague Regulations, cited below, Chapter 16.

101 See GC I article 12 on the duty to provide wounded and sick, who have to be left behind, with medical personnel and equipment as far as military exigencies permit, and article 22 with regard to the visibility for the enemy forces of the distinctive emblem, as far as military exigencies permit. In GC III, see article 78, on the duty to facilitate the performance of relief personnel as far as military exigencies permit. A similar provision is also found in the Draft International Convention on the Condition and Protection of Civilians of Enemy Nationality who are on Territory belonging to or Occupied by a Belligerent, Recommended by the XVth International Red Cross Conference (1934 Tokyo Draft on the Protection of Civilians).

102 GC III article 12, on the duty to return medical personnel to the belligerent party they belong.

103 Ibid., articles 15 and 16, at page 518.

'necessity' caused by the situation of the enemy civilians and the 'security of the detaining Power', authorises internment of enemy civilians.[104]

In the four existing Geneva Conventions of 1949, 'military necessity' appears with numerous different wordings. GC I, II and IV contain provisions on the duty to search and collect killed and wounded persons 'as far as military considerations allow',[105] and those who are compelled to be left behind are 'as far as military considerations permit' to be left with medical assistance and equipment.[106] Protected materiel is to be respected, but both GC I (article 33) and GC II (article 28) include the use by military commanders of such fixed materiel and sick bays 'in case of *urgent* military necessity, provided they make previous arrangements for the welfare of the wounded and sick who are nursed in them'.[107] Other examples of occurrences from the Conventions illustrate that the sanctity of medical personnel, their materiel and those who are interned is far from absolute: the GC I contains provisions with regard to return of medical personnel and persons from neutral countries 'as soon as military requirements permit'.[108] In GC I article 42, and GC IV article 18, the duty to ensure visibility of the distinctive emblem reach as 'far as military conditions permit'.[109] A further duty to mark internment camps is found in GC IV article 83: 'whenever military considerations permit'. In GC III article 76 and GC IV article 112 military reasons are juxtaposed to political reasons with regard to the necessity of censuring the correspondence of prisoners of war. The provision is noticeable, as political considerations under other circumstances cannot influence military measures.[110] Prisoners of war's contact with the outside is also granted through visits from representatives from the Protecting Powers or ICRC, a right which is not absolutely sacred, as visits may be prohibited in cases of '*imperative* military necessity'.[111] The provision was inserted for the first time in the 1949 Convention after a proposal by the

104 1934 Tokyo Draft on the Protection of Civilians, article 15.

105 See GC I article 15; GC II article 18; and GC IV article 16. GC I and II use the phrase 'all possible measures'.

106 GC I article 12.

107 GC I article 33. Emphasis added. The equivalent provision is found in GC II article 28.

108 GC I articles 30 and 32. A similar provision is found in GC II article 37. See also reference to military necessity in article 8 in GC I, GC II and GC III, with regard to the work of the delegates of the Protecting Powers, and the similar provision in article 9 in GC IV.

109 GC I article 42. See also GC II article 43, which requires that the distinctive emblem on ships and crafts shall be made 'sufficiently apparent', and as well GC II article 45, with regard to the prevention of abuse of the distinctive emblem and article 50 with regard to measures necessary for the suppression of acts in violation of the preceding articles. An equivalent provision to the one in GC II article 50, is found in GC III article 129, and GC IV article 146.

110 See Section 2.2 and Chapter 14.

111 GC III article 126, and GC IV article 143.

ICRC.[112] The ICRC Commentary to the provision does not specify which reasons that may amount to exceptional prohibition but does instead link the determination of imperative military necessity to the exercise of sovereignty: 'If they are to justify the prohibition of visits, military necessities must be imperative. Whether they are or not is a matter for the Detaining Power alone to decide and the light of supervision of the Protecting Powers is restricted by this exercise of sovereignty.'[113]

It is, however, emphasised that exceptional prohibitions of access must be temporary.[114] With this clarification the exercise of sovereignty is thus limited after all.

Furthermore, in the GC IV – which to a considerable degree is concerned with the security of the occupying State – approximately thirty occurrences of military necessity may be found.[115] The law of belligerent occupation falls outside the scope of this book, but for the sake of illustration it is useful to mention here the occurrences such as '*absolute* military security' in GC IV article 5, '*imperative* necessities of security' in GC IV article 9, '*absolutely* necessary' in GC IV articles 42 and 53 with regard to internment and destruction of property, '*imperative* military reasons' in GC IV article 49 with regard to total or partial evacuation of protected persons, as well as detention, '*imperative* military requirements' in GC IV article 55 with regard to temporary restrictions on food and medical supplies in occupied territories, and '*urgent* necessity' in GC IV article 60 with regard to diversions of relief consignments.[116]

There is neither immediate consistency nor clarity with regard to the use of the aggravated terms such as 'imperatively', 'absolutely' and 'urgent' within the Conventions themselves. For example GC IV article 42 authorises internment when it is '*absolutely* necessary', article 49 authorises evacuation (as an exception to the prohibition on deportation and forcible transfer) when there are '*imperative* military reasons'[117] and article 78 authorises internment when there are '*imperative* reasons of security'.

112 Pictet, *The Geneva Conventions of 12 August 1949* (ICRC Commentary of 1952), at page 611.
113 Ibid.
114 ICRC Commentary of 1952, at page 611.
115 See at least articles: 5, 9, 16, 18, 25, 27, 30, 35, 39, 40, 42, 49, 53, 55, 60, 62, 63, 64, 75, 78, 83, 108 and 112.
116 For the last, see ICRC Commentary of 1952, at page 324.
117 The right to evacuate is an exception to the prohibition to forcibly transfer or deport the civilian population, as stated in article 49(1) of the same Convention. The distinction between the prohibition of deportation and the right to evacuate is touched upon in the von Manstein Case, where the Judgment by the Tribunal seems to have been even more strict than GC IV

Common in these occurrences of military necessity in the Geneva Conventions is that they explicitly allow for departure from conduct which is otherwise prohibited; they have the face of exceptions, as accounted for above.[118] Military necessity may in certain (urgent) situations trump the humanitarian considerations for the wounded and sick.[119] What 'necessity' actually amounts to is, however, unclear. The ICRC Commentary to the Conventions states for example that: 'If tactical considerations demand that a medical establishment be used for another purpose, they will be imperative.'[120] It is difficult to read from this what amounts to '*urgent* military necessity' as opposed to 'simple' military necessity. It is even difficult to read from 'tactical considerations' what amounts to military necessity as an exception and thus what may lead to deprive the medical facilities of their specially protected status. Furthermore, the ICRC Commentary does not include in the matter of urgency either specific or other comments than that of 'imperative necessity'.[121]

In the Hague Regulations, the adjective 'imperative' accompanies military necessity as the qualifying permission to destroy enemy property. The addition of 'imperative' to the Hague Rule is discussed into more detail below, in Chapter 16. As pointed out there, the difference in wording between the Geneva Conventions and the Hague Rule does not necessarily represent a different threshold, *and* confusion over the word imperative may stem from the linguistic meaning of the word itself as 'imperative' also may be interpreted as a component of 'necessity'.[122] This approach appears to be one reflected in case law from the international tribunals as well as the ICRC Commentary and some scholars.

In the aftermath of WWII, an expression by the US Military Tribunal in the Hostage Case has led commentators[123] to include a requirement of urgency in the definition of military necessity. The tribunal stated with regard to the

article 49, where the first seemingly denies any other reason for evacuating the population than their own security (and not leaving military necessity an alternative). This point is among others expressed by the ICTY, Krstiæ Case, Trial Chamber Judgment, at page 526. See also Hayashi, 'Requirements of military necessity', at page 92.

118 Draper, 'Military necessity and humanitarian imperatives', at page 138.

119 Ibid., at page 139.

120 See ICRC Commentary of 1952, at page 275.

121 Ibid. In particular, the matter of 'urgency' is not dealt with in ICRC, *Commentary on the First Geneva Convention* (ICRC Commentary on the First Geneva Convention 2016).

122 See Section 1.6 with regard to interpretation of treaties and the specific issue of the 'ordinary meaning'.

123 See Downey, 'The law of war and military necessity', at page 254; McCoubrey, 'The nature of the modern doctrine of military necessity', page 226. Also the AP I Commentary to article 35 seems to rely upon a requirement of urgency, see page 396, para. 1396.

Hague Regulations that: 'The prohibitions therein contained, control, and are superior to military necessities of the most *urgent nature* except where the Regulations themselves specifically provide the contrary.' And furthermore with regard to the case of Rendulic: 'We are not called upon to determine whether *urgent* military necessity for the devastation and destruction in the province of Finmark actually existed.'[124] Also in the von Manstein trial, it was remarked by the British Military Court that 'the requirement is "necessity" and not "advantage"' and that 'necessity must be an imperative one'.[125] Furthermore that 'it was really the carrying out of a policy planned a considerable time before, a policy which the accused had in fact been prepared to carry out on two previous occasions and now is carrying out in its entirety and carrying out irrespective of any question of military necessity'.[126] A similar approach was taken in the High Command Case, upon which McCoubrey argues that '"Necessity" is a judgment made upon particular circumstances in the detailed conduct of armed conflict and not something determined *a priori* by reference to grand political or strategic objectives.'[127]

The practical distinction between 'military necessity' in simple terms and the aggravated version, 'imperative military necessity' (or absolute, or urgent), is far from clear, as pointed out in the literature.[128] One suggestion to overcome the lack of clarity is to read the aggravated form as an emphasis on the 'severity of the "necessities"',[129] provided that it is possible to detect any material difference between the terms at all. At least it must be clear that even the aggravated form of military necessity does not mean 'impossibility', but rather 'impractical'; however, not simply 'tactical and strategic convenience'.[130]

To conclude on this issue, the point of departure for this book is that it is impossible to discern difference in substance between different aggravations accompanying the phrase 'military necessity' (or its equivalent) that will have

124 The Hostage Case, in the case against Lothar Rendulic, at page 69. Emphasis added. The case concerning Rendulic is dealt with further below, in Chapter 4 on the military margin of appreciation.

125 Von Manstein case, at page 522. The distinction between necessity and advantage is dealt with into detail below, in Chapter 14.

126 Ibid., at pages 522–3.

127 McCoubrey, 'The nature of the modern doctrine of military necessity', at page 227.

128 Ibid., at pages 224 and 234; Dinstein, *Conduct of Hostilities*, at page 12.

129 McCoubrey, 'The nature of the modern doctrine of military necessity', page 234. In the same direction, see Geiss, 'Military necessity', at page 559.

130 McCoubrey, 'The nature of the modern doctrine of military necessity', at page 237. See also Detter, *The Law of War*, at page 396: 'any derogation from the Conventions must be substantiated as a compelling military necessity as no one can be held to do the impossible'.

any practical bearing upon military operations. However, the notion of military necessity appears to contain an *element of time* as reflected in the different references to 'urgency' by the practice of international tribunals. The exact scope of this element of time remains to be settled by practice.

2.9 MILITARY NECESSITY AND THE INEVITABLE USE OF DISCRETION BY THE MILITARY COMMANDER

'Military necessity' is a vague term and, as already stated at the very beginning of this book, the term calls for a discretionary judgment (the assessment) by the commander in the field during combat operations. The question of what amounts to military necessity is both one of objective (ontological) fact and a matter of law. 'Military necessity is not simply to be equated with every past military practice, however, but must be assessed as objectively as possible ... What then are the "military necessities" which cannot be disregarded, and what rules of restraint will they allow?'[131]

Ultimately, military necessity under the law could be what the commander assesses it to be. In this case, military necessity may turn into a purely subjective assessment. Yet, in practice the decision must balance between objective facts and how these are assessed by the commander. Therein lies their margin of appreciation, which is discussed in detail in Chapter 4. For the present purpose, the point of departure shall be stated: a margin of appreciation is an inevitable ingredient of the legal concept of military necessity.[132] At any given time during the conduct of hostilities *someone* has to determine what measures are reasonably required to attain certain ends. The limits to this decision is the overall topic throughout this book.

Like 'proportionality' and 'necessity', 'margin of appreciation' is a generic term which has a wider area of application under public international law in general, than under the LOAC. It is not possible to derive any meaningful guidance simply from referring to international law as such (unless the aim is a comparative analysis, which is not the aim of this book). This book is thus *not* concerned with the general features of the concept under public international law, nor the specific features of the margin of appreciation under the international human rights law regime (where the jurisprudence of the European Court and literature is overwhelming in total) nor the *jus ad bellum*, but with a military margin of appreciation in the LOAC.

131 Blix, 'Area bombardment', at page 40.

132 In the same direction see Bill, 'The Rendulic "Rule"', at pages 130–1: 'military necessity invests the commander with a certain amount of discretion'.

3

Military Necessity and Its History

3.1 EARLY WRITINGS

Even though we may trace the predecessors of the regulation of armed conflict all the way back to ancient and early Christian times,[1] it is first and foremost along with the emergence of the nation state in the seventeenth century that 'modern international law' – and the legal regulation of armed conflict – appeared as the legal concept which is recognisable today.[2]

Throughout history, arguments for or against the restraint of war have been a conglomerate of political philosophy, military theory and religious thought.[3] The views which throughout the past have been referred to as particularly influential when it comes to the early development of international law of armed conflict in a more modern sense are those of Alberico Gentili, Hugo Grotius and Emmerich de Vattel. References to 'military necessity' (or simply to 'necessity') appear in the works of all three authors, as part of their discussions on lawful conduct in war.

3.1.1 *Gentili, Grotius and Vattel*

In 1612 the Italian law professor Alberico Gentili discussed means and methods of warfare extensively in *The Three Books on the Law of War*.[4] When arguing in favour of a prohibition against poison as means of warfare he discusses

[1] For early examples, see, Howard, 'Constraints on warfare'. See further Neff, *War and the Law of Nations*, at pages 13–39. See also Reichberg et al., *The Ethics of War*.

[2] See Neff, *War and the Law of Nations*, at page 85.

[3] For a compact presentation of this subject, see Detter, *The Law of War*, at pages 151 ff. On the law of war in the Middle Ages in general, see Keen, *The Laws of War in the Late Middle Ages*. For a general overview of the factors shaping the law of war in the seventeenth and eighteenth centuries, see Neff, *War and the Law of Nations*, at pages 85 ff.

[4] Gentili, *De Iure Belli Libri Tres*.

necessity as a possibility for deviation from what is otherwise prohibited. He states:

> You will perhaps inquire if it is allowed in case of great necessity. For what the law does not permit, necessity makes allowable. ... But we reply that our necessity does not oblige us to violate the rights of our adversaries, or even the rights of anyone. For although it is believed that it is lawful to steal in case of necessity, the defence is made that it is not theft, since in time of necessity all edibles are common property. It is also a rule of war to throw the enemy into insuperable difficulties. And if it is lawful for him to escape from these in any and every way, it will surely be allowed him to be perjured and treacherous; and why not? And thus all intercourse between enemies and every law of war will be done away with. 'I cannot easily be induced', says Saint Bernard, 'to admit that what gives rise to so much that is unlawful is itself lawful'.[5]

This line of argument implies that what is necessary is not unlawful, but to apply necessity *in toto* would imply that the law of war could be set aside in its entirety – and this implication does not seem to be endorsed by Gentili.

The thoughts of Gentili were in many aspects drawn upon by the more well-known works of the Dutch lawyer Hugo Grotius, *De jure belli ac pacis*, from 1625,[6] who has often been assigned a prominent place in history.[7] The concept of military necessity is enshrined in the following general *passus*:

> ... the means employed in the pursuit of any object must, in a great degree, derive the complexion of their moral character from the nature of the end to which they lead. It is evident therefore that we may justly avail ourselves of those means, provided they be lawful, which are necessary to the attainment of any right.[8]

With regard to the understanding of what is the 'right' to attain, he then proceeds: 'Right in this place means what is strictly so called, signifying the moral power of action, which any one as a member of society possesses.'[9]

5 See Gentili, *De Iure Belli Libri Tres*, at page 159.

6 Grotius, *The Rights of War and Peace*.

7 For a comprehensive analysis, see Tuck, *The Rights of War and Peace: Political Thought and the International Order from Grotius to Kant*. Tuck also points out that Grotius was drawing on Gentili without acknowledgement, see page 105. See also Frits Kalshoven, *Reflections on the Law of War: Collected Essays*, in Chapter 12: 'Grotius' Jus in Bello, with Special Reference to Ruses of War and Perfidy'. With regard to the general conception of the influence of Grotius, see also for example Rogers, *Law on the Battlefield*, at page 1. In other publications Grotius is, however, completely absent from the historical outline of the law applicable in armed conflicts, see for example Detter, *The Law of War*, at pages 151 ff.

8 Grotius, *The Rights of War and Peace*, at pages 290–1.

9 Ibid.

When it comes to 'necessary means' in the quotations above, Jean Barbeyrac as editor of the 1738 edition of Grotius' work, has interestingly noted:

> Our Author does not mean Things essentially bad, and which, as such, cannot be lawful in any Case, or to any End whatsoever; but only those, which a Man could not do otherwise, without the necessary Connection they have with a lawful End. . . . Things bad in their Nature are indeed generally not necessary, with Regard to the Necessity in Question.[10]

When it then comes to which means the editor labels 'essentially bad', he mentions, among others, blasphemy and adultery. It is worth noticing the emphasis on the strength of the connection between means and ends – as only those means which 'cannot be done without' in order to achieve a certain end. This is in other words a reference to necessity in a strict logical sense, which cannot be read from Grotius . It is also a *qualified* conception of Grotius' necessity, qualified in the sense that not everything which can be perceived as necessary is to be understood as lawful necessity.

Grotius then deduces the lawful conduct in war, from the 'end'. The function of (military) necessity consequently appears in a number of places, such as: 'So too when punishment is lawful and just, all the means absolutely necessary to enforce its execution are also lawful and just . . .'[11] It is worth noticing the use of the word 'absolutely' in connection with necessity, an adverb which does not add clarity to the concept, but which indicates a certain strength and which reappears in modern treaty texts.[12] This view was criticised by Grotius' contemporary, Pufendorf, when it comes to the lawful character of 'punishing' other people or nations without having political authority over them.[13] The disagreement is related to what necessity is deduced from: if it is not lawful to punish, then the means for achieving punishment are not lawful.[14] When it comes to the seizure of property owned by enemy individuals, Grotius further states that: 'Yet this is a practice, which nothing but necessity could justify; for, on any other ground it would be opening a door to innumerable acts of wanton aggression and injustice against individuals.'[15] This quotation is illustrative as it points out the contrast between acts which are necessary and acts which are wanton: a core of the understanding of

10 Ibid.

11 Ibid., at page 291.

12 See above, Chapter 2 on the different aggravations of military necessity.

13 See Tuck, *The Rights of War and Peace*, at pages 142–5 where Tuck argues that an often held conception of similarities between Hugo Grotius and Samuel Pufendorf is mistaken.

14 On the notion of the 'object of war', see Chapter 2 above, as well as Section 3.2.2 below, on the St Petersburg Declaration.

15 Grotius, *The Rights of War and Peace*, at page 308.

necessity concerning property destruction which has survived up until present time.[16]

Grotius sets a balance between the prosecution of 'rights' during wartime and the protection of human life, which implies limitations upon reprisals against 'innocent subjects':

> Indeed a person may ACCIDENTALLY though not INTENTIONALLY be killed by us in attempting to prevent him from violently obstructing us in the prosecution of a lawful right. Yet if such an accidental calamity could be foreseen, the law of charity, setting so pre-eminent a value upon the life of man, would in such a case prescribe the forbearance of our right.[17]

As the past has shown as well, reprisals and considerations of necessity often go hand in hand, whereby considerations of necessity may motivate certain reprisals.[18] Reprisals (or retaliation) are also held by Pufendorf to be the only lawful resort towards a breach of the law – in contrast to punishment, which is included by Grotius.[19]

It is, however, when it comes to conduct which may be permissible (done with impunity), but at the same time morally wrong,[20] that his prescribed restraints are most visibly linked to a balance between 'necessity' and 'humanity'. Restraint in war is prescribed through 'Moderation' and 'Humanity': 'Though there may be circumstances, in which absolute justice will not condemn the sacrifice of lives in war, yet humanity will require that the greatest precaution should be used against involving the innocent in danger, except in cases of extreme urgency and utility.'[21]

He then exempts children, women and men 'whose modes of life are entirely remote from the use of arms', from the calamities of war. He furthermore rejects the necessity of retaliation, or 'striking terror', and, 'all actions no way conducive to obtain a contested right, or to bring the war to a termination, but calculated merely to display the strength of either side are totally repugnant to the duties of a Christian and the principles of humanity. So that it behooves Christian princes to prohibit all unnecessary effusion of blood ...'[22]

16 On the distinction between wantonness and necessity, see above, Chapter 2 as well as Chapter 14 on the difference between military advantage and military necessity, and Chapter 16 on destruction of property.

17 Grotius, *The Rights of War and Peace*, at page 312.

18 Kalshoven, *Belligerent Reprisals*, at page 365.

19 Tuck, *The Rights of War and Peace*, at pages 158–9.

20 On this point of distinction between *lex lata* and *lex ferenda*, see Kalshoven, *Reflections on the Law of War*, at page 328.

21 Grotius, *The Rights of War and Peace*, pages 361–2.

22 Ibid., at pages 363–4.

Grotius's distinction between those acts which are necessary and those which are wanton, are also subject to further 'moderations': 'It may be possible, under some circumstances, to detain what belongs to an enemy, so as to prevent his deriving advantage from it, in which case it would be an unnecessary and wanton act to destroy it.'[23] He refers to moderations which even today seem far-reaching, when he holds that fruit trees, agriculture and everything *supportive* of man ought (therefore) to be spared. The same is the case for works of art and things devoted to the purpose of religion. Destruction which does not in the least tend to impair an enemy's strength, nor to increase that of the destroyer, is labelled madness.[24] Closely related to considerations of necessity – and despite the lack of specific guidance as to any conceptual differences between references to necessity and utility – we may read his remarks on 'utility': 'Rules and practices derive much of their merit from the utility, with which they are attended.'[25]

Many features of the law as expressed by Grotius also appear in the works of de Vattel in the middle of the eighteenth century. At first glance, de Vattel presents the concept of necessity in war in a seemingly unrestricted way:

> The whole is to be deduced from one single principle, – from the object of a just war: for, when the end is lawful, he who has the right to pursue that end, has of course, a right to employ all the means which are necessary for its attainment. . . . As soon, therefore, as we have declared war, we have a right to do against the enemy whatever we find necessary for the attainment of that end, – for the purpose of bringing him to reason, and obtaining justice and security from him.[26]

This wide open point of departure is, however, followed by quite sophisticated regulations on the actual conduct of warfare and by placing emphasis on the requirement of connection between means and ends: 'The lawfulness of the end does not give us a real right to do anything further than barely the means necessary for the attainment of that end.'[27] Also de Vattel, along with Grotius, prescribes further restrictions on warfare than those required by 'general lawfulness', in order to remain 'innocent before God' and his 'gentler methods'.[28] Towards the enemy who were taking part in the war, every

23 Ibid., at page 366.

24 Ibid., at page 367. Today protection of objects indispensable to the survival of the civilian population are protected by AP I article 54, which is dealt with in Chapter 17.

25 Grotius, *The Rights of War and Peace*, page 367.

26 See de Vattel, *The Law of Nations or the Principles of Natural Law*, book 3, Chapter 8, § 136.

27 Ibid., § 137.

28 Ibid. Certain of the rules prescribed by de Vattel were to be codified about a hundred years later, see further below Section 3.2, on the era of codification from the last half of the nineteenth century.

measure necessary in order to *weaken him* was lawful – provided that the measure was not of an odious kind, unjustifiable in themselves and prohibited by the law of nature.[29] Like his predecessors, de Vattel gave reprisals an important role: the duty to give quarter to surrendering enemy personnel was subject to an exception in cases where the prisoners were guilty of serious crimes, as well as in cases of reprisals and in cases of 'impossibility' due to the 'greatest necessity'.[30] As was the case with Grotius, it is worth noticing the reference to necessity in the aggravated sense, by use of the word 'greatest', and again with no guidance as to the distinction between 'simple necessity' and the 'greatest necessity'.[31]

3.1.2 *General Features*

Some general features of the legal concept of military necessity may be drawn from the works of Gentili, Grotius and de Vattel: considerations of 'humanity' give rise to restrictions upon warfare which do not entail strict legal obligations but are motivated by the desire to remain innocent towards metaphysical powers (God and one's own conscience). However, even strict law admits limitations. Those means which are necessary in order to attain a lawful end are lawful (permissible), but they do not cover all means. Certain means are considered 'odious' and therefore not permissible. Emphasis is placed on the relationship between the lawful 'end' and the 'means' applied in order to reach that end. Yet, the lawfulness of certain ends is disputed. 'Necessity' seems to be characterised as the very opposite of 'wantonness' when it comes to destruction of property. In fact, the backbone of these early features already illustrates the elements of military necessity as outlined above, in Chapter 2. In particular, the two questions of means to ends as well as the fact that those measures that *lack* a war aim are juxtaposed to wantonness or cruelty. Finally, reprisals are given an important role when it comes to counter breaches of the law by the enemy. Considerations of necessity can motivate quite harsh measures as reprisals, even denial of quarter.

29 See ibid., §§ 138 and 145. Women, children, aged and sick were regarded as enemies, but when showing no resistance by taking part in the war, there was no right to use violence against them.

30 See ibid., §§ 140–2 dealing with quarter, punishment and reprisals. See ibid., § 151 dealing with circumstances of 'impossibility'. De Vattel refers to the battle of Agincourt in 1415 where French prisoners were slayed at the battlefield due to King Henry V's fear of the prisoners being freed and able to rejoin their army.

31 See Section 2.8 above, on the different aggravations of military necessity.

Leaving aside the works of early modern thinkers, one may also find early and sporadic examples of treaty provisions mitigating the effects of war on the war victims, from the period of the formation of nation states as we know them.[32] In Scandinavia, one such example is found in the war articles for Denmark–Norway of 1564 and 1611. These articles contained provisions protecting evangelic preachers, the elderly, women and children.[33] The importance of treaty law for the formation of the legal concept of military necessity as seen today, however, may first and foremost be traced back to the last half of the nineteenth century.

3.2 THE CODIFICATION ERA: LIEBER CODE AND THE DEPARTURE OF MODERN TREATY LAW

This period, labelled by some the second period of codification,[34] (the first being the seventeenth century as discussed above and the third being the late twentieth and the twenty-first centuries as discussed in subsequent chapters) is marked by a profound disagreement (in the Western world) between Imperial Germany and other Western States over the definition of military necessity,[35] a disagreement which was to colour legal debate and publications way into the twentieth century, and which is dealt with subsequently in this book. Disagreements aside, the period in the last half of the nineteenth century is also referred to as 'an era of belief in progress in controlling war' and that this 'passion for codification'[36] started with the 1856 Paris Declaration on Maritime Law.[37] It was, however, with the Lieber Code and the St Petersburg Declaration that the legal regulations of interest for the present topic first saw light.

3.2.1 *Lieber Code: Justifications and Limitations*

From the last half of the nineteenth century, the LOAC gained its modern shape through the first attempts of codifying customary law into treaty law.[38]

32 See examples in Detter, *The Law of War*, pages 151–2.

33 Boye, *Haandbok i Folkeret*, at page 126.

34 For a much narrower (narrow in time) approach to a codification period within the same time frame, but limited to 1864–99, see Kolb, 'The main epochs of international humanitarian law since 1864', at pages 25–40.

35 Hull, 'Military necessity and the laws of war in Imperial Germany', at page 352.

36 Ibid. The 'passion' is also described in a different tone by Kolb, 'The main epochs of international humanitarian law since 1864', at page 28.

37 Declaration Respecting Maritime Law, 16 April 1856.

38 See Rogers, *Law on the Battlefield*, at page 1. See also Detter, *The Law of War*, at page 153, as well as Green, *The Contemporary Law of Armed Conflict*, at page 36.

Out of these acts of codification, the Lieber Code,[39] prepared by Professor Francis Lieber and promulgated by President Abraham Lincoln for the armed forces in the field during the American Civil War (1861–5), contains an early, and later well known, definition of military necessity in its article 14: 'Military necessity, as understood by modern civilized nations, consists in the necessity of those measures which are indispensable for securing the ends of the war, and which are lawful according to the modern law and usages of war.'[40]

Even though the Lieber Code has been widely referred to as codification of the law[41] – not least by Lieber himself – its area of application was limited. The instructions were not an international treaty; they were only binding upon US forces, despite being of influence on international law.[42] Furthermore, the instructions were based upon a premise of reciprocity between civilised parties, and they did therefore not apply in the Indian wars which took place during the same period – in the same country.[43] Thus, the instructions were even more limited than what has been preached by some authors.[44]

Military necessity, as it appears in the Lieber Code, has been viewed as a justification for 'all measures of regulated violence indispensable for bringing about the submission of the enemy.'[45] It has also been described as the 'American concept of military necessity',[46] and as a general legal principle to limit violence, in the absence of any other rule.[47]

In the same way as being termed a limitation, it has also been referred to as an 'enlightened advance', away from the wanton destruction of property; however, it also has the potential of being used as a licence for

39 Lieber Code at page 6.

40 Ibid.

41 With regard to literature, the references are vast. See for example O'Brien, 'The meaning of "military necessity" in international law', at page 128 who states that the Lieber Code 'now commands universal adherence'. See further, Kalshoven, *Belligerent Reprisals*, at page 45. See also Meron, 'Francis Lieber's Code and principles of humanity', at pages 271 and 278, with further references. See O'Connell, 'Historical development and legal basis', at page 21, as well as Solf, 'Protection of civilians', at page 121.

42 For an emphasis on the domestic aspect, see Kolb, 'The main epochs of international humanitarian law since 1864', at pages 25–6.

43 Lieber Code article 24. Maguire, *Law and War*, at page 37.

44 O'Brien, 'The meaning of "military necessity" in international law', at page 129 argues that 'Under the Lieber doctrine there is no question of reversion to an earlier type of warfare simply because of necessity.' It may prove difficult to make this statement harmonise with the denunciation clause with regard to *civilised* nations.

45 Dunbar, 'Military necessity in war crimes trials', at page 444.

46 See Downey, 'The law of war and military necessity', at page 252. See also Chapter 2, Section 2.3.

47 See Carnahan, 'Lincoln, Lieber and the laws of war', at page 216. For my position regarding military necessity and the notion of 'limitation', see Chapter 6.

mischief.[48] This characterisation is, however, not precise. Wanton destruction was already held by Gentili (as shown above) to be the very opposite of permissible, necessary, conduct.

An interesting remark concerning limitation and 'advance' is made by O'Brien, when commenting upon the Lieber Code. He argues that military necessity turned into a legal principle and not purely a 'factual statement of military utility which is often in opposition to the law'.[49] This statement implies both a limitation and an advance – away from 'pure military utility' – but it also indicates a difference between two categories of measures which are both useful in order to reach a purpose: utility and necessity. Out of these, the first has nothing to do with legality and the second is a legal concept.[50] This distinction is difficult to grasp properly and, as we shall see further below, other authors[51] take a different stand, making the picture even more untidy.

Even though repetitively cited, the content of the term 'indispensable' does not seem to have raised much attention. While the Lieber Code provides exemplification of permissible and impermissible conduct on the basis of military necessity, the connection between *means* and *ends* was not addressed in greater detail.[52] With regard to specific conduct which is permitted, article 15 states:

> Military necessity admits of all direct destruction of life or limb of 'armed' enemies, and of other persons whose destruction is incidentally 'unavoidable' in the armed contests of the war; it allows of the capturing of every armed enemy, and every enemy of importance to the hostile government, or of peculiar danger to the captor; it allows of all destruction of property, and obstruction of the ways and channels of traffic, travel, or communication, and of all withholding of sustenance or means of life from the enemy; of the appropriation of whatever an enemy's country affords necessary for the subsistence and safety of the army, and of such deception as does not involve the breaking of good faith either positively pledged, regarding agreements

48 Ibid., at page 217.

49 O'Brien, 'The meaning of "military necessity" in international law', at pages 129–30.

50 For a similar distinction, however not with the presumption that the factual necessity always challenges the legal, see Hayashi, 'Military necessity as normative indifference', at pages 681–5, where he distinguishes between 'material' military necessity, 'normative' military necessity and 'juridical' military necessity. As I read it, the comparison to O'Brien's distinction between 'utility' and 'necessity' goes between 'material' military necessity on the one hand and 'normative' and 'juridical' military necessity on the other hand, where O'Brien makes no attempt to single out the general 'normative' from the legal-specific norm: 'juridical' military necessity.

51 See the view of Kelsen and Tucker, *Principles of International Law*, below.

52 The causal connection between means and ends, hereunder the notion of 'indispensable', is discussed in general above, in Chapter 2.

> entered into during the war, or supposed by the modern law of war to exist. Men who take up arms against one another in public war do not cease on this account to be moral beings, responsible to one another and to God.[53]

Whereas the limits of military necessity – hereunder its contrast to wanton destruction – are spelled out in Lieber Code article 16:

> Military necessity does not admit of cruelty – that is, the infliction of suffering for the sake of suffering or for revenge, nor of maiming or wounding except in fight, nor of torture to extort confessions. It does not admit of the use of poison in any way, nor of the wanton devastation of a district. It admits of deception, but disclaims acts of perfidy; and, in general, military necessity does not include any act of hostility which makes the return to peace unnecessarily difficult.[54]

Whether it is correct to regard a reference to necessity as one of 'limitation' is, however, questionable. In Chapter 6, I argue why I consider that the right to invoke military necessity is limited, but that military necessity as such is not *a* limitation. Others take a different position, describing the concept of necessity as encompassing 'both a positive, expansive, violence-permitting role, and a negative, restrictive, violence-limiting role'.[55] Others again place just as much emphasis on the permissive part, arguing that the principle of necessity recognises the appropriateness of 'considering military factors in setting the rules of warfare'.[56] Whether or not viewed upon as a limitation, the Lieber Code did not simply refer to 'limited warfare'[57] and the balance between humanitarian concerns and military necessity 'did not always further the dictates of humanity . . .', as has been correctly pointed out.[58] One way to read these three articles is as a 'mini-encapsulation' of what has later been named the LOAC,[59] which truly embodies the balance between

53 Lieber Code article 15, at page 6.
54 Lieber Code article 16.
55 Kolb, 'The main epochs of international humanitarian law since 1864'.
56 In this regard, see Schmitt, 'Military necessity and humanity in international humanitarian law', at page 799.
57 On the phrase 'limited warfare', see also further below, in Chapter 6, where it is argued that a 'principle of limited warfare' is a misconception in legal terms.
58 For example: Lieber Code articles 17 and 18 allowed for starvation as a method of warfare that also included the non-combatant population. Taking of hostages was allowed, though considered a rare practice, see articles 54–5. Furthermore, see articles 60–6, which open up the possibility for denial of quarter 'in great straits'. See also Meron, 'Francis Lieber's Code and principles of humanity', at pages 271–3.
59 Article 16 contains prohibitions which are upheld today in the different later treaty texts, among which the prohibition on wanton destruction of property is found in the 1907 Hague Convention article 23(g) (see also Chapter 16).

humanitarian concerns and military necessity. Instead of separate and detailed prohibitions governing means and methods of warfare (as has been more frequent in recent time) the quoted articles from the Lieber Code contain prohibitions specifically derived from considerations of necessity. The limited right to invoke military necessity therefore functioned as a limitation upon the destruction and seizure of civilian property, 'at each stage of strategy';[60] however, not to 'unduly' limit 'the military's discretion' or to curtail its ability to 'win a victory'.[61] It has also been pointed out that Lieber's work made it clear that the difficulties related to interpreting 'military necessity' involved the impact of war on non-combatants.[62]

3.2.2 *St Petersburg Declaration and the 'Object of War': Military Necessity and the Question of 'Necessary for What?'*

The Lieber Code gained attention and terrain internationally, and were of influence when the St Petersburg Declaration of 1868 was drafted, as well as the text adopted at the Brussels Conference in 1874.[63] The St Petersburg Declaration was drafted with the purpose of banning a newly invented projectile, but it (should be safe to say that it) has been frequently cited way beyond the intended purpose.

In the adopted text of the Declaration, a connection between *means and ends* is spelled out:

> That the only legitimate object which States should endeavour to accomplish during war is to weaken the military forces of the enemy;
>
> That for this purpose it is sufficient to disable the greatest possible number of men;
>
> That this object would be exceeded by the employment of arms which uselessly aggravate the sufferings of disabled men, or render their death inevitable; ...[64]

The Declaration gained widespread support,[65] although it was also said to be an 'answer' to the earlier ideas of the German military thinker Carl von

60 See for example Carnahan, 'Lincoln, Lieber and the laws of war', at page 228 in 'At each stage of strategy, military necessity dictated the imposition of different limits on the destruction and seizure of civilian property.'

61 Meron, 'Francis Lieber's Code and principles of humanity', at page 272. With regard to the military's discretion, see further below, Chapter 4.

62 Hull, 'Military necessity and the laws of war in Imperial Germany', at page 356.

63 With regard to its influence, see for example Best, *Humanity in Warfare*, at pages 160 ff. and 180, and Kalshoven, *Belligerent Reprisals*, at page 45. See also Meron, 'Francis Lieber's Code and principles of humanity', at page 279.

64 St Petersburg Declaration, preamble.

65 The Declaration is ratified by twenty States, which includes all of Europe except Spain and also includes Brazil and Persia as non-European States. Some do, however, contest the customary status of the Declaration; see Baxter at page 65 in Trooboff, *Law and*

Clausewitz, who denied the application of 'a principle of moderation' in war.[66] As noted already in Chapter 2, the Declaration limits the *object of war* to that of *weakening the military forces of the enemy*.

The wording in the phrase is far from clear. As has been correctly pointed out, the wording is vague and possibly broad[67] – by some even denoted 'terribly problematical' in the twentieth century[68] – as well as referring to 'the extreme conceptual and terminological confusion surrounding this notion'.[69] Indeed, States have not agreed on later treaty provisions of the same – or alternative – wording. It is thus difficult to discern any 'original' meaning of the wording dealing with the 'object of war' in the Declaration, even though some seem to refer to a given, common conception by the Declaration's drafters.[70]

Despite the lack of clarity from the concept itself, the issue must be addressed in order to grasp the concept of necessity. Let's first address the phrase 'object of war', before turning to the expression 'weakening the military forces of the enemy' – even though the two are to be read together. The notion of the 'object of war' alludes to the first question of means to ends in warfare, as introduced in general in Chapter 2, namely: 'necessary for what'?[71] For obvious linguistic reasons, it is difficult to grasp any concept of 'necessity' without having an idea of the latter question. 'Necessary' means or methods must relate to *something* to achieve – a goal or an aim – or an objective. 'The object of war' is therefore one such 'something'. Military advantage can be another. At the outset, the expression 'object of war' can be interpreted in (at least) three different ways.

Responsibility in Warfare: the Vietnam experience, calling the Declaration 'an interesting historical landmark – a primitive attempt at weapons control. To argue that the "spirit" of this century-old instrument proscribes certain conduct as part of customary international law is really to argue by analogy.' On the actual scope of the provision, see further below.

66 McCoubrey, 'The nature of the modern doctrine of military necessity', at page 221.

67 Parks, 'Asymmetries and the identification of legitimate military objectives', at page 68. On the other hand, but also recognising the wide wording, see Meyrowitz, 'The principle of superfluous injury or unnecessary suffering', at pages 106–7. See also Geiss, 'Military necessity', who states on page 563 that 'IHL has been haunted by the vagueness of its legitimate aims throughout history'.

68 Roberts, 'Land warfare', at page 119.

69 Meyrowitz, 'Reflections on the centenary of the Declaration of St. Petersburg', at page 613.

70 See for example Hayashi, 'Requirements of military necessity', at page 47 claiming that the Declaration: 'has acquired a meaning and dimension not present in the minds of those gathered at St. Petersburg in 1868'. The statement is, however, not accompanied by any further explanation of what this 'meaning and dimension' more concretely implies.

71 McDougal and Feliciano, *Law and Minimum World Order*. The question is recited by 'Protection of Civilians', at page 128. See also Hayashi, 'Requirements of military necessity', at page 60.

First, 'the object of war' can be understood as a reference to the desired political outcome of the war as such. A number of expressions appear to be synonyms describing the same concept. Clausewitz refers both to the 'political purpose of war' as well as the 'political object – the original motive for the war'[72] while others prefer 'aim'[73] or 'end'[74] of war. NATO documents use the term 'End State', to describe the situation to be attained at the end of an operation.[75] In this book I prefer the expression 'aim of war/war aim', but other expressions may occur, depending on the specific context. A political war aim can vary from the conquest of land in earlier times to vaguer expectations of a 'safe and secure environment' in the present. Another example stated by the USA at the commencement of the first Gulf War in August 1990 is: 'Immediate, complete, and unconditional withdrawal of all Iraqi forces from Kuwait; restoration of Kuwait's legitimate government; security and stability of Saudi Arabia and the Persian Gulf; and safety and protection of the lives of American citizens abroad.'[76] An older example of a wide interpretation, is in Schwarzenberger, who equates necessities of war with 'sovereignty at large'.[77]

Second, the 'object of war' can mean what Clausewitz refers to as the 'aim of warfare is to disarm the enemy'.[78] Also here, different terms are used, with the risk of confusion. Oppenheim prefers the expression 'purpose of war',[79] to describe what appears to be the same as Clausewitz's 'aim of warfare'. Oppenheim argues that the purpose of war is the 'overpowering and utter defeat of the enemy',[80] and thus is the same in every war. As stated by Greenspan: 'To compel the submission of an enemy, it is necessary to weaken and destroy his powers of resistance.'[81] The 'purpose of war' (in this context

72 Clausewitz, *On War*, at pages 90 and 81 respectively.

73 This term is used by Meyrowitz in 'Reflections on the centenary of the Declaration of St. Petersburg', at page 614. The phrase 'war aim' is, however, also used beyond the specific scope of the political. See ICRC Dictionary of the LOAC, cited in the Galic Case, at footnote 76.

74 This term is used by Oppenheim in Oppenheim and Lauterpacht, *Disputes, War and Neutrality*, at page 225.

75 In NATO, the 'End State' is referred to as 'The political and/or military situation to be attained at the end of an operation, which indicates that the objective has been achieved.' See NATO, AAP-6.

76 Conduct of the Persian Gulf Conflict: An Interim Report to Congress, at page 1-1 and Final Report to Congress: Conduct of the Persian Gulf War, at page 74.

77 Schwarzenberger, *International Law*, at page 135.

78 Clausewitz, *On War*, at page 77.

79 Oppenheim and Lauterpacht, *Disputes, War and Neutrality*, uses 'purpose of war', and holds that this must not be confused with the 'object of war'.

80 Ibid., at page 225.

81 Greenspan, *The Modern Law of Land Warfare*, at page 316.

and not in the context above) can therefore be read as a reference to one of the elements of the nature of war; parallel to how one would describe the purpose of a hammer to be to hit nails. As opposed to the first interpretation above, this second understanding of the 'object of war' chimes well with the wording in the St Petersburg Declaration.

Third, the 'object'[82] can be understood as a reference to the *objectives* pursued during war-fighting,[83] *objectives* which may be identified at the different levels of military command, but nevertheless *military*, as opposed to *political*. This distinction, between the military and the political aim of the operation,[84] was to prove difficult in the century to come after the adoption of the St Petersburg Declaration. At the same time, the distinction may appear crucial for the answer to the question presented as 'necessary for what?' Brief, sweeping statements in legal theory are sometimes seemingly in conflict on the question of what military necessity points at: overpowering the enemy or only military objectives (understood as aims, not objects). Whereas Oppenheim's point of departure is: 'the principle that a belligerent is justified in applying any amount and any kind of force which is necessary for the realisation of the purpose of war – namely the overpowering of the opponent'.[85]

Others seem to disagree completely on this point, arguing that 'However, at the root of the difficulty is probably the uncertainty as to what exactly military necessity implies: it cannot be the global aim of "overpowering the enemy", which is a definition so wide as to be useless.'[86] The critique appears, however, to be based on a (mis)reading of Oppenheim where he apparently does 'equate military necessity with the purpose of

82 Meyrowitz refers to this as the 'object in war', as opposed to the 'object of war' which is reserved for a higher level in the 'hierarchy'. See Meyrowitz, 'Reflections on the centenary of the Declaration of St. Petersburg', at page 614.

83 In NATO, an objective is generically defined as: 'A clearly defined and attainable goal for a military operation, for example seizing a terrain feature, neutralizing an adversary's force or capability or achieving some other desired outcome that is essential to a commander's plan and towards which the operation is directed.' See NATO, AAP-6.

84 See also above, Chapter 2, Section 2.2 as well as below, in Chapter 14 on the military nature of the military advantage.

85 Oppenheim and Lauterpacht, *Disputes, War and Neutrality*, at pages 208 and 227. Oppenheim's position may be based on the von Manstein case where it was held that: 'The purpose of war is the overpowering of the enemy', see transcript 3139, cited from Dunbar 'Military necessity in war crimes trials', at page 445. The point of view seems to be shared by Meyrowitz in 'Reflections on the centenary of the Declaration of St. Petersburg', at page 614, although Meyrowitz points out that the concept of the purpose of war 'assumes an abstract character which goes beyond the scope of law'.

86 Detter, *The Law of War*, at page 396. See also Chapter 1 on the distinction between the *jus ad bellum* and the *jus in bello*.

war'.[87] Apart from being a misreading, the statement is imprecise; the critique should be confined to the question of what necessity is *deduced from*, for as pointed out: 'a certain amount of violence, can be appraised necessary or unnecessary only in relation to attainment of a specified objective'.[88] This statement seems to lie at the heart of the discussion. While literature seems to differ, and state practice certainly challenges the question of 'necessary for what?', the two latter meanings of the 'object of war' seem uncontested: it is undoubtedly here we find the primary area of application for the St Petersburg Declaration,[89] and hence the LOAC.

Interpretative demands do not rest there however, for the second phrase in the St Petersburg Declaration has complemented the debate on the object of war. According to one view, 'weakening the military forces' has been juxtaposed to that of 'the enemy nation's ability to resist', stating that: 'Military objectives that support or sustain an enemy nation's ability to resist are integral to weakening its military forces.'[90] In the same context, the expression from the Declaration is described as a 'historic anomaly' and thus that a 'restrictive interpretation would not be consistent with State Practice in the Twentieth Century or recent conflicts'.[91] In other words, and according to this view, the Declaration is not to be taken on its word, and at least not to be read restrictively. On the other hand, the phrase has been held to be so wide that 'the notion of "object" is therefore irrelevant to the law of armed conflicts'.[92]

Both views agree on the possible wide interpretation of the Declaration. However, while the first position acknowledges the fact that States have applied exactly such a wide interpretation, the second position seems to refuse to accept that such state practice may have created law[93] or – provided a more favourable reading of the second position – one may argue that such a wide interpretation certainly no longer is an expression of *lex lata*.

87 The critique is presented by Detter, ibid., at page 396 in footnote 41 which refers to Oppenheim and Lauterpacht's 1952 edition, at page 232. This edition can, however, not possibly be read as Detter does. Page 232 explains the *Kriegsraison* argument.

88 McDougal and Feliciano, *Law and Minimum World Order*, at page 525.

89 This is explicitly argued at least by Meyrowitz, 'Reflections on the centenary of the Declaration of St. Petersburg', at page 614.

90 Parks, 'Asymmetries and the identification of legitimate military objectives', at page 68.

91 Ibid., this is a methodological argument which places clear emphasis on the practice of states when it comes to interpretation of treaty provisions, and can be viewed as stating the following: 'it cannot have been a restrictive clause, because it was not applied restrictively'. Footnotes omitted.

92 Meyrowitz, 'The principle of superfluous injury or unnecessary suffering', at page 107.

93 On the general issue of formation of customary law and the role of state practice during conduct of hostilities, see Chapter 1.

Later attempts to define – or to refer to – the 'object of war' in treaty law have failed.[94] Furthermore, States' military manuals have adapted similar, but not identical language as references to the notion of 'object of war'. The reading of the manuals supports (see Chapter 2) a broad interpretation of the notion of 'object of war', yet limited to actual war-fighting and not the resort to armed force as such.

Although measures of war have political implications, the political decision of *resort to war* as a tool for conflict settlement has been kept outside the discussions of military necessity.[95] We may say that war is a political instrument, but military necessity is *apolitical.* In the 1950s Greenspan stated that: 'War is a political weapon, used to gain by force what cannot be settled by negotiation. Gratuitous suffering or cruelty as such is irrelevant to its purpose.'[96] The view is upheld in recent literature as well.[97] Despite this, repeated examples throughout history have shown that the distinction is difficult to uphold in practice. For example, the bombardment of Paris in 1871 during the Franco-Prussian War had apparently 'no military reason', and its only objective was to attack the morale of the 'stubborn Parisians'.[98] Unfortunately, the firm belief in the secondary, non-military, effects of military power in a specifically advantageous direction for own forces, has survived war after war. These 'beliefs' are addressed within different contexts later in this book, such as in Chapter 12 concerning the prohibition of terror attacks and in Chapter 14 with regard to the definition of military advantage. I then leave history, and turn to one part of the core of the research question: the military commander's assessment.

94 See Chapter 2, Section 2.3.

95 Oppenheim and Lauterpacht, *Disputes, War and Neutrality*. McDougal and Feliciano, *Law and Minimum World Order*, at page 223.

96 Greenspan, *The Modern Law of Land Warfare*, at page 315.

97 Dinstein, *Conduct of Hostilities*, at page 103. Hampson, 'Necessity and proportionality in the Gulf conflict', at page 47. Oeter, 'Methods and means of combat', at pages 169–70. By some the question appears more open, although as part of the difficult decisions. See for example McCoubrey, 'The nature of the modern doctrine of military necessity', at page 232, and the discussions following below.

98 Cited below, Chapter 12.

4

Assessing Military Necessity through a Military Margin of Appreciation

4.1 MARGIN OF APPRECIATION: GENERAL REMARKS

A margin of appreciation – in general legal terms – can mean at least two things: a subsidiarity of a Court's review (judicial deference) and a discretionary competence for the legal subject to assess the content of specific legal norms.[1] The first meaning relates to procedure, the latter to material content. In this book I am concerned with a margin of appreciation in the latter sense which, arguably, is not a true 'margin of appreciation' in the sense of judicial deference, but a margin granted commanders, among others, due to the 'fog of war' and the fact of being close to the battlefield.

All legal norms with a flexible wording calls for a discretionary assessment, as opposed to an almost mechanical application of the law such as for example the enforcement of speed limits. Flexible norms do not only grant the legal subject a certain freedom or latitude, they also imply a *duty* to assess. In the case of the LOAC, the military commander has no choice but to use his/her discretion. The question remains as to whether the commander uses his/her discretion *reasonably* or not.

Although it appears obviously sensible that any application of the law requires some sort of 'human touch' in the sense that the application is distinct from a completely mechanical exercise, treaty negotiations prior to the AP I were remarkably burdened with views trying to avoid 'subjectivity'.[2]

Military necessity lies at the very heart of the commander's military margin of appreciation.[3] The task of issuing limits to the commander's assessment has accompanied the development of treaty law. As pointed out in Chapter 2,

1 Christoffersen, *Fair Balance*, at page 236.

2 See Section 4.3.2.

3 Melzer: 'Targeted killing or less harmful means?', argues at page 106 that: 'the role of military necessity appear[s] when IHL leave a margin of judgment'.

a 'margin of appreciation' is a generic term. What are the distinctive characteristics of a margin of appreciation under the LOAC?

4.2 MILITARY MARGIN OF APPRECIATION: AS A CONSTRUCT OF MILITARY NECESSITY

4.2.1 *Early Conceptions, Limiting Arbitrariness*

The scope of a military margin of appreciation may be approached from two extremes which may be traced back to the turn of the last century.[4] On the one hand, the 1899 and 1907 Preambles to the Hague II and Hague IV Conventions states that: 'the High Contracting Parties clearly do not intend that unforeseen cases should, in the absence of a written undertaking, be left to the arbitrary judgment of military commanders'.[5] On the other hand, the German General Staff argued during the same epoch that the military commanders enjoy full discretion in the field and that their (the commanders) 'subjective freedom and arbitrary judgment' only is guided by the 'precepts of civilization, freedom and honour, the traditions prevalent in the army and the general usages of war'.[6]

These two positions are extremes in the sense that the first acknowledges the limits of positive law, whereas the latter dismisses legal limitations beyond military necessity *as the force of law*.[7] In other words: the assessment of military necessity becomes military necessity. In another sense, however, it is – at least at first glance – difficult to discern the differences of the positions, apart from the fact that the German War Book uses the word 'arbitrary'. The *guidelines* attached to the prescribed judgment do, however, point away from arbitrariness, and resemble the guidelines of the *reasonable commander* (see below). The notion of the military margin of appreciation lies here: between the black letter of the law and the *reasoning of the commander*. Furthermore, the notion of the military margin of appreciation is illustrated by the concept of necessity which, as shown by the discussions of *Kriegsraison* (in Chapter 6) bears the potential to justify (rightly or wrongly) conduct either within or outside positive law – and thus for the critics, label conduct as arbitrary.

4 See Section 6.5.1 on the Franco-Prussian War and the German General Staff below.

5 1907 Hague Regulations, preamble.

6 Cited from Morgan, *The German War Book*, at page 64; also cited in Section 6.5.1.

7 See Section 6.5.1. This is the essence of the notion of *Kriegsraison*. Such position also resembles early appearances of the doctrine of military necessity, as seen in Chapter 3, for example by de Vattel, *The Law of Nations or the Principles of Natural Law*, book 3, Chapter 8, at para. 137, where he argues that 'each nation decides for himself'.

The limitless discretion inherent in the doctrine of *Kriegsraison* has been repeatedly condemned by scholars. In the speech made by Elihu Root (then President of the American Society of International Law) in 1921, at the annual meeting of the Society, he argued that: 'As the belligerent is to be the sole judge of the necessity, the doctrine [of *Kriegsraison*] really is that a belligerent may violate the law or repudiate it or ignore it whenever that is deemed to be for its military advantage ...'[8] This last point, on arbitrariness, lies at the heart of any legal discussion of 'margins' because arbitrariness encapsulates the very opposite of *justice* – which is to be promoted by the law. Perhaps we may go even further, and say that arbitrariness is the opposite of *law* – and therefore the *legal* fundament of a 'margin of appreciation' becomes crucial. Appreciation beyond the limits of law becomes the incarnation of arbitrariness. Yet, words calling for assessment or discretion, without fixed limits, are common, necessary ingredients of a functional legal system – in particular in the highly 'context-dependent' field of law, the LOAC. Then what, more concrete, is the military margin of appreciation in the context of military necessity?

4.2.2 *Two Faces: Assessment of Necessity Where It Is Implicitly and Explicitly Provided For*

As with the different faces of military necessity under the LOAC, the commander's assessment of military necessity also appears to reflect these faces. The military margin of appreciation is exercised both where military necessity is *implicitly* expressed in the rule and where military necessity is *explicitly* referred to as an exception from conduct which is otherwise prohibited.[9] Examples of the first category are norms calling for a concrete discretionary assessment where considerations of military necessity are in-built in the rule, such as the notion of 'excessiveness' under the proportionality rule, the notion of 'military advantage' and the notion of 'feasibility' with regard to precautions in attack. Assessments under these norms are dealt with into more detail in Chapters 14 and 15. Examples of the latter category are the prohibition of destruction of enemy property unless required by military necessity and specific protection of persons and objects unless military necessity (according to specific rules and procedures) justifies waiver of protection. These assessments are dealt with into more detail in Chapters 16 and 17.

8 Quoted in Downey, 'The law of war and military necessity', at page 253.

9 On the different faces of military necessity and military necessity as a justification, see Chapter 2, Section 2.7.

4.2.3 *Two Dimensions: the Norm and the Person*

A military margin of appreciation does appear with two different faces, but it also has two dimensions when it comes to the actual assessment: the flexible rule and the person who assesses it. For example: the margin of appreciation encapsulates both the zone of flexibility inherent in the notion of 'excessiveness' (the rule itself) and the expectations of the commander's assessment – the yardstick of assessment (the assessment of the rule). Both these aspects are dealt with successively in the following. Sometimes the rule and the assessment of the rule are so closely linked that we may say that the rule becomes what the commander assesses it to be.

The ICRC Commentary points out with regard to the drafting of AP I article 57 that: 'The differences of opinion were mainly related to the very heavy burden of responsibility imposed by this article on military commanders, particularly as the various provisions are relatively imprecise and are open to a fairly broad margin of judgment.'[10] The passage illustrates the relationship between the two dimensions of a margin of appreciation: that a vague norm implies not only a corresponding degree of margin, but also the responsibility to assess, as pointed out above. Furthermore, that the aim of succeeding in war-fighting often will be a buffer against turning the 'margin' into arbitrariness. The ICRC Commentary states that: 'In fact it is clear that no responsible military commander would wish to attack objectives which were of no military interest. In this respect humanitarian interests and military interests coincide.'[11] The distinction between subjective assessment and arbitrariness is dealt with into more detail below.[12]

4.3 CHARACTERISTICS OF A FLEXIBLE NORM: 'SUBJECTIVITY VS OBJECTIVITY'

4.3.1 *Three Categories of Limitations to the Commander's Assessment*

Two dimensions of the margin of appreciation were introduced above: the norm and the person assessing the norm. The core of this book is the legal limits to the assessment of the norm and hence exactly the relationship

[10] See AP I Commentary, at para. 2187.
[11] AP I Commentary, at para. 2195.
[12] On the rejection of arbitrariness, see for example the Hostage Case, at page 64 where it was held that: 'It is a fundamental rule of justice that the lives of persons may not be arbitrarily taken. A fair trial before a judicial body affords the surest protection against arbitrary, vindictive or whimsical application of the right to shoot human beings in reprisal.'

between the norm and the person. The legal norm is an objective standard.[13] Yet, flexible norms call for a subjective assessment. The subjective assessment must be within the objective threshold established in the legal norm. Obviously, different rules allow for a different 'margin' of subjectivity. As shown later in this book, the notion of military advantage is primarily a matter of subjectivity, while the notion of military necessity primarily is a matter of objective fact.[14] The pending issue for the LOAC appears to be to strike a balance between subjective assessments of rapidly changing circumstances and objective expectations of the human behaviour on the battlefield. While too much allowance left for subjective assessments can lead to arbitrariness, too narrow an opening for subjectivity can leave the rules inflexible and inapplicable to real life scenarios. This subtle balance is also reflected in the stated aim of the 1899 and 1907 Hague II and Hague IV Conventions of not to leave unforeseen cases to the 'arbitrary judgment of the military commanders'.[15] And it has accompanied treaty law until the drafting of the AP I, where the aim was to also 'at least reduce grey areas of legal uncertainty emanating from the complex pattern of modern armed conflicts or discretionary power of the commander in action'.[16]

Naturally, the key to strike a proper balance is to combine realistic room for subjective manoeuvre with objective limits to the commander's concrete assessment. In this book, I deal with limits to the commander's assessment in three categories: first, the limits inherent in the established interpretation of the legal rules. Second, eventual limits shaped as guidelines for interpretation of the LOAC rules and, third, the limits to the subjective appraisal shaped as the standard of the 'reasonable commander'. At the outset, the two first categories are references to objective requirements, while the third category addresses the subjective ingredients in the military commander's decision making. It must, however, be clear that these distinctions between subjectivity and objectivity are only at the outset. The first category dominates the legal discussions in Chapters 7–13 on the rules on humanitarian considerations, distinction and proportionality. The second and third categories are given a generic presentation in the present chapter, and then revisited again in Chapter 16 on destruction of property. Chapters 14 and 15 touch upon the interplay between the objective content of the norm and the level of subjective expectations of the commander. The interplay between objective standards

13 In the same direction, specifically with regard to the 'Rendulic Rule', see Bill, 'The Rendulic "Rule"', at page 136.

14 See Chapter 14.

15 Quoted below, Section 6.5.1. See as well Chapter 3, for a historical account.

16 Rauch, 'The concept of military necessity in the context of the law of war', page 27.

and subjective assessment is a particular feature for the proportionality rule. Some aspects are addressed in the following.

4.3.2 *Proportionality: the Ultimate Subjective–Objective Concept*

The proportionality rule met harsh opposition and was subject to heavy debate during its drafting process. This process is accounted for below, in Chapter 13. One point is, however, of interest here, and that is the deeply rooted scepticism towards – and the attention devoted to – the *subjectivity* inherent in the concept of proportionality.

Among others, it was remarked during the Diplomatic Conference that: '... the rule of proportionality, which called for a comparison between things that were not comparable, and thus precluded objective judgment'.[17] A rather nuanced allowance of subjectivity is expressed in the US DoD Manual: 'The decisions and judgments required by the principle of proportionality in conducting attacks have subjective aspects.'[18] Furthermore, references to the 'subjective assessment' in the proportionality rule occur frequently among legal scholars. Oeter refers to the 'considerable margin of appreciation' and that 'objective standards for the appraisal of expected collateral damage and intended military advantage are virtually non-existent'.[19] In the same direction Schmitt argues that 'it is the subjective perspective of the party carrying out the proportionality assessment that matters'.[20] Other scholars maintain similar views[21] pointing out, among others, that the rule is 'easily subject to abuse, because its application presupposes subjective reasoning'.[22] Furthermore that 'It could be argued that this rule leaves far too much to the discretion of the military commander'[23] and that 'the best that can be expected of the decision maker is that he act honestly and competently. This action must be judged on the basis of information of facts and circumstances available to him at the time, not on the basis of hindsight.'[24]

17 Official Records of the Diplomatic Conference CDDH/III/SR.6 at pages 48–9, the comments of the Hungarian delegate.
18 US DoD Manual, at para. 5.10.2.3, at page 244.
19 Oeter, 'Methods and means of combat', at page 197.
20 Schmitt, 'Asymmetrical warfare and international humanitarian law', at page 28.
21 See Dinstein, *Conduct of Hostilities*, at page 158. Bothe, Partsch and Solf, *New Rules*, argue at page 351 that: 'As both sides of the equation are variables, and as they involve a balancing of different values which are difficult to compare the judgment must be subjective.'
22 Rauch, 'The concept of military necessity in the context of the law of war', page 25. See also Gardam, 'Proportionality and force in international law', at page 407.
23 Rauch, 'The concept of military necessity in the context of the law of war', page 25.
24 Bothe, Partsch and Solf, *New Rules*, at pages 351–2.

Despite having argued that there is a lack of objective means or benchmarks, the *test* is in fact objective. As stated in the Canadian military manual: 'The test for determining whether the required standard of care has been met is an objective one: Did the commander, planner or staff officer do what a reasonable person would have done in the circumstances?'[25] Despite gloomy predictions and opposition towards the 'subjective' proportionality rule – the rule in AP I article 51(5)(b) is considered one of the keystone instruments to provide protection for civilians during combat.[26] The key issue (which is not limited to the notion of proportionality) thus remains: how to limit and 'streamline' the commander's assessment while maintaining the very essence of flexibility?

There are, roughly said, two ways to limit the commander's assessment: through guidelines for the interpretation of the treaty text and through the level of 'reasonableness'. First a few remarks on interpretative issues.

4.4 APPLICATION OF FLEXIBLE RULES IN THE LOAC: NECESSITY VS HUMANITY?

Above, I have pointed out two dimensions of a margin of appreciation: the flexible rule and the assessment of the rule (the actual application of the rule). In this section I shall discuss more closely the first dimension: the scope of the (flexible) rule itself. As stated in Chapter 1, flexible rules also giving a wider room for interpretation must be interpreted 'in accordance with the ordinary meaning to be given to the terms of the treaty and in their context and in light of its object and purpose'.[27] The challenge pointed out at the outset, that some words are so common that their meanings appear to rely on a shared pre-understanding and that this pre-understanding of meaning is distributed almost intuitively, applies in particular with regard to 'humanity' and 'necessity'. For example: it may be an intuitive conception that the killing of a combatant is inhumane when it is possible to capture him. While capture may be ethically sound, killing is not unlawful (see Chapter 9). We may therefore ask whether the two fundamental and opposing considerations of humanity and necessity, underlying the very essence of the LOAC, give additional guidance when it comes to interpretation of vague terms and expressions. It is, for example, *not* a given fact that 'The lack of precision

25 Canadian Manual, at para. 418(3), pages 4–5.
26 Dinstein, *Conduct of Hostilities*, at pages 152–3.
27 VCLT, article 31(1). See Section 1.6.

operates in the interest of the military rather than that of civilians.'[28] Considerations of humanity in relation to treaty interpretation are addressed in the following.

4.4.1 *General Guidelines of Interpretation: the Scope of the Martens Clause*

This section addresses the possible impact of humanitarian considerations on the interpretation of the LOAC treaties. More specifically, the role of the Martens Clause. While the Martens Clause itself is not synonymous with a margin of appreciation,[29] it addresses a highly discretionary exercise: the application of 'principles of humanity'. The version of the Martens Clause appearing in the preamble to the 1907 Hague Convention V is cited above, in Chapter 1. The point made there was the link to customary LOAC, made by the phrase 'usages established among civilized peoples' (the equivalent of 'established custom' in the passage below). AP I article 1(2) contains a renewed version of the Clause: 'In cases not covered by this Protocol or by other international agreements, civilians and combatants remain under the protection and authority of the principles of international law derived from established custom, from the principles of humanity and from the dictates of public conscience.'

The legal status of the Martens Clause has been commented upon by national and international courts[30] and tribunals, as well as being subject to scholarly discussion.[31] Despite some divergence with regard to practice from national courts after WWII,[32] the view presented by the ICTY in the Kupreskic case may serve as a point of departure:

> ... this Clause may not be taken to mean that the 'principles of humanity' and the 'dictates of public conscience' have been elevated to the rank of

28 Gardam, 'Proportionality and force in international law', at page 407.

29 See Dolzer, 'Commentary', at page 391.

30 Legality of the Threat or Use of Nuclear Weapons, Advisory Opinion, at para. 78, which speaks of the Martens Clause as 'an effective means of addressing the rapid evolution of military technology'.

31 See for example Cassese, 'The Martens Clause', pages 193–202. See also Meron, 'The Martens Clause', pages 78–89.

32 From Norwegian case law see RAM-15–23 'Klingedommen', as well as Rt. 1948 page 1088 and Rt. 1947 page 468. The last case is particularly illustrative as the Court argues, with the Martens Clause as a point of departure, that: '... International law recognises certain fundamental principles as invariable. These rules, if they are to have any meaning, must be binding notwithstanding whether national law violates them.' My translation from Norwegian. The case is also commented in Johansen, 'The occupied and the occupier', at pages 212–13.

independent sources of international law, for this conclusion is belied by international practice. However, this Clause enjoins, as a minimum, reference to those principles and dictates any time a rule of international humanitarian law is not sufficiently rigorous or precise: in those instances the scope and purport of the rule must be defined with reference to those principles and dictates.[33]

In other words, the tribunal states that the Martens Clause may serve as interpretive guidance. The tribunal's exact use of the Clause in the same case was, however, rather 'progressive',[34] than merely a reference to 'guidance'. With reference to the Clause the tribunal stated that the 'cumulative effect of attacks on military objectives' may be 'contrary to the demands of humanity', although they 'do not appear on their face to fall foul per se'.[35] Such 'cumulative effects' (as described by the tribunal) of attacks on military objectives are rejected below (see Chapter 14), as they fall outside the scope of the 'attack as a whole' in the proportionality rule. Moreover, an interpretation of the rules in question, as done by the tribunal in this case, contravenes not only the wording in the specific rule (the proportionality rule referring to the notion of 'excessiveness'), but also the wording of the Martens Clause itself. There is no indication in the Clause that it should circumscribe the content of other positive rules – the scope of the Clause is the opposite: to give guidance in cases *not covered by the protocol*. Positive rules of the protocol leaving a wide margin of appreciation to the belligerents are not beyond the scope of the protocol[36] – the margin is a part of the protocol. It is sometimes a matter for the belligerent party 'alone to decide' that military necessities are imperative.[37]

It therefore appears as a circumscription of the law when the ICTY states that in order to limit this margin 'elementary considerations of humanity . . . should be fully used when interpreting and applying loose international rules, on the basis that they are illustrative of a general principle of international

33 Kupreskic Case, at para. 525. See also Chapter 12 with regard to reprisals.

34 The label 'progressive' is from the ICTY body itself, in the OTP Report, at para. 52. See also Chapter 14.

35 Kupreskic Case, at para. 526.

36 It seems to be implied by the ICTY when arguing in the Kupreskic Case that there is a 'wide margin of discretion to belligerents by using language that might be regarded as leaving the last word to the attacking party', see Kupreskic Case, paras. 524–6.

37 See for example GC III article 126, on prohibition of visits of POWs by representatives from the Protecting Powers and ICRC. The ICRC Commentary of 1952, states at page 611 that: 'If they are to justify the prohibition of visits, military necessities must be imperative. Whether they are or not is a matter for the Detaining Power alone to decide and the light of supervision of the Protecting Powers is restricted by this exercise of sovereignty.'

law'.[38] Furthermore, that the provisions governing precautions in attack should be 'interpreted so as to construe as narrowly as possible the discretionary power to attack belligerents and, by the same token, so as to expand the protection accorded to civilians'.[39] It appears reasonable, however, to argue that the rules, in case of doubt, should be interpreted 'consistently with the principles of humanity and the dictates of public conscience'.[40] It must be stressed that a 'consistent interpretation' in this case cannot mean that humanity will tip any consideration to the detriment of military necessity. On the contrary, the interpretation must reflect *the balance* between humanitarian considerations and the necessities of war already inherent in the rules. This appears to be in concordance with the view expressed by the ICRC as well, arguing in the Commentary to AP I that the interpretation is a matter of 'common sense and good faith'[41] and that 'The entire law of armed conflict is, of course, the result of an equitable balance between the necessities of war and humanitarian requirements. There is no implicit clause in the Conventions which would give priority to military requirements. The principles of the Conventions are precisely aimed at determining where the limits lie; the principle of proportionality contributes to this.'[42]

Turning back to the point of departure above, the impact of the Martens Clause as 'interpretive guidance' appears modest. A general rule favouring humanitarian considerations contravenes not only each positive rule of the LOAC – which is already drafted upon a balance between humanity and necessity – it also contravenes the essence of the Clause itself, which is to give guidance in cases *beyond* the scope of positive rules. That said, in (rare) cases where an ordinary interpretation of the rule at hand indicates that a situation appears to fall outside the scope of positive law, the Clause does have an interpretative function.

4.4.2 *Other Guidelines Limiting the Commander's Assessment?*

Few, if any, of the numerous flexible terms and expressions in the rules of the LOAC are accompanied by concrete guidelines for application. The notion of military necessity is a good example in this regard.[43] This (absence) has led scholars and organizations to provide suggested interpretive guidelines, such

38 Kupreskic Case, at para. 524. The case is also quoted and commented in Chapters 7, 11 and 12.
39 Kupreskic Case, at para. 525.
40 Meron, *The Humanization of International Law*, at page 27.
41 See AP I Commentary to article 57, at pages 681–2, para. 2198.
42 AP I Commentary to article 57, at page 683, para. 2206.
43 See for example Geiss, 'Military necessity', at page 558.

as the ICRC Interpretive Guidance on Direct Participation in Hostilities, from 2009, where it is argued that: 'The aim cannot be to replace the judgment of the military commander by inflexible or unrealistic standards; rather it is to avoid error arbitrariness, and abuse by providing guiding principles for the choice of means and methods of warfare based on his or her assessment of the situation.'[44]

A range of different 'guidelines' can be retrieved in States' military manuals and in manuals drafted by scholars. As for States' military manuals, they are (obviously) not binding upon other States, but may be viewed as examples of State practice formative for customary international law. One example is the discussion over the definition of military objectives.[45] Treaty law does not provide lists of objects qualifying as military objectives, while military manuals often do. The same is the case with regard to activities which usually amount to direct participation in hostilities for persons.[46] Interpretive guidance is, however, rare to find when it comes to the proportionality balance. The lack of guidance (such as numerous, publicly accessible examples of attacks that do and do not violate the threshold of excessive collateral damage) may induce the commander to blindly stumble while performing his or her assessment. Furthermore, case law may stumble blindly as well, when assessing the commander's assessment in the absence of suitable and exemplifying standards. One such illustration is found in the ICTY case law, discussed below.

Naturally, the aim should not be to create 'inflexible or unrealistic standards'. On the other hand, if guiding principles are to have any effect, there is no point in simply replacing one vague standard with another.[47] In the Gotovina case the ICTY Trial Chamber attempted to replace the commander's assessment with an inflexible and unrealistic standard of a 200-metre 'margin of error' around military objectives. The tribunal considered that all artillery projectiles falling beyond the range of 200 metres outside the lawful target were considered to be deliberate attacks on civilians or civilian property and thus unlawful.[48] The 200-metre standard was rejected in the Appeals Chamber decision on the basis that the Trial Chamber had not based the standard on the evidence before it, and that it had offered no explanation for

44 Interpretive Guidance, at page 1042. The study is dealt with in more detail in Chapter 11.

45 See Chapter 8, where discussion of whether the definition in AP I should be formulated as a generic and abstract formula or a list of objectives – or both.

46 UK Manual, at pages 56–7; the AMW Manual with Commentary, in rules 26 and 27, at pages 111–16 with regard to direct participation in hostilities and in rule 29, at pages 121–3 with regard to aircrafts. For a further discussion, see Chapter 11.

47 See also Chapter 15, where this point is made with regard to the assessment of excessiveness.

48 ICTY, Gotovina Case, Trial Chamber Judgment, at para. 1898.

arriving at 200 metres, instead of 400 metres.[49] Furthermore, the Trial Chamber did not take the changes in circumstances (such as wind, speed and distance) into account.[50] The unfounded 200-metre standard was therefore applied mechanically to the facts before it.[51] Therefore, the Gotovina Trial Chamber judgment is an illustrative example of unjustified replacement of the margin of *appreciation*, which includes by its very nature, room for considering each case based on the circumstances ruling at the time, by a margin of *error*.

Another, and more specific, way of limiting the commander's discretion is to issue mission specific rules for the military operation through, among others, ROEs or SOPs.[52] However, the challenge with ROEs, if these are to function as guidelines for the assessment, is that they usually are classified and therefore of little guidance for customising the commander's discretion in a general manner. Obviously, ROEs can be of invaluable importance in order to control the use of force for mission accomplishment, but ROEs do not develop or determine the scope of the LOAC. An example of the exercise of control for accomplishing the mission, can be found in the Norwegian implementation of UN Security Council Resolution 1973 (2011) for Libya,[53] where the Ministry of Defence explicitly stated in a letter to the Defence Staff that:

> The conditions for use of force laid down in the Resolution is that force is used to protect civilians or civilian populated areas in Libya threatened by attack. Other offensive use of force is not authorised in order to protect civilians . . . Existing ROE for the operation, in the form these are authorised with amendments by the Norwegian Ministry of Defence, do not authorise operations or the use of force beyond what is permitted under LOAC or Security Council resolution 1973.[54]

The letter furthermore stated that particular care was to be shown towards the principles of proportionality and distinction under the LOAC. According to

49 ICTY, Gotovina Case, Appeals Chamber Judgment, at para. 58.

50 Ibid., at para. 60.

51 Ibid., at para. 54.

52 This is the model presumed by Bothe, Partsch and Solf, *New Rules*, at page 352.

53 The UN mandate was implemented by the Norwegian Government in a Royal Decree dated 23 March 2011: Det Kongelige Forsvarsdepartement, Kongelig Resolusjon, 23.03.2011, 'Fullmakt til deltakelse med norske militære bidrag i operasjoner til gjennomføring av FNs sikkerhetsrådsresolusjon 1973 (2011).' The decree gives the Norwegian Armed Forces authorisation to participate with six F-16 fighter planes in order to implement Security Council resolution 1973 on Norway's behalf. All translations from Norwegian are mine.

54 Letter from the Norwegian Ministry of Defence to the Defence Staff, dated 24 March 2011. On hand with author. All translations from Norwegian are mine.

this view, it appears clear that the LOAC and the obligations from the Security Council resolution apply simultaneously and autonomously.[55] The guidelines applied for the exercise of the military commander's margin of appreciation under the LOAC were thus limited to show 'particular care' towards the rules on distinction and proportionality, as well as to abide by eventual classified procedures within the scope of the ROEs. Any superior, from the troop commander to the Minister of Defence, is entitled (within the limits of their command) to cancel or suspend attacks on objects that are otherwise lawful according to the LOAC. Such control is frequently exercised through the use of ROEs and this practice must not be confused with issuing interpretive guidelines for the application of the LOAC. Furthermore, this practice does not change the content of the LOAC.

The actual assessment done by the commander is subject to the yardstick of the reasonable commander, dealt with in the following.

4.5 THE YARDSTICK OF ASSESSMENT: THE REASONABLE COMMANDER

4.5.1 *The 'Rendulic Rule': a Comparison with a Reasonable Commander*

In the case against Lothar Rendulic before the US Military Tribunal at Nuremberg (the Hostage Case) after WWII, the indictment covered, among others, destruction of property not justified by military necessity. Rendulic had applied the scorched earth policy in Finnmark, in the north-east of Norway, in order to hamper Russian advance from the east.[56] The Tribunal found that no military necessity had actually existed, but nevertheless held that: 'But we are obliged to judge the situation as it appeared to the defendant at the time. If the facts were such as would justify the action by the exercise of judgment, after giving consideration to all the factors and existing possibilities, even though the conclusion reached may have been faulty, it cannot be said to be criminal.'[57] The content of this passage has later been labelled the 'Rendulic

55 Having this view, I do not see a conflict of norms between the LOAC and the UN Charter article 103. Article 103 says: 'In the event of a conflict between the obligations of the Members of the United Nations under the present Charter and their obligations under any other international agreement, their obligations under the present Charter shall prevail.' On the interpretation of the Security Council resolution 1973 among other States, see Chapter 14 on military advantage.

56 On the scorched earth tactics and destruction of property in general, see Chapter 16.

57 Hostage Case, at pages 68–9.

Rule' and given widespread acceptance, such as the reference in the US Operational Law Handbook:

'The Rendulic case also stands for a broader standard regarding liability for battlefield acts: commanders and personnel should be evaluated based on information reasonably available at the time of decision.'[58] A number of States have quoted similar passages in ratification statements to the AP I.[59] Also the ICTY has embraced the Rendulic Rule in its adjudication, such as in the Galic case. As parts of the remarks upon proportionality, the Tribunal argued that: 'In determining whether an attack was proportionate it is necessary to examine whether a reasonably well-informed person in the circumstances of the actual perpetrator, making reasonable use of the information available to him or her, could have expected excessive civilian casualties to result from the attack.'[60] The comparison to what a 'reasonably well-informed person' under the same circumstances would have assessed, is also referred to as a standard of 'the reasonable military commander'.[61]

4.5.2 *Two Elements: 'Good Faith' and 'Information Reasonably Available at the Time'*

A 'reasonable commander' must live up to two requirements: acting in good faith and relying upon information reasonably available at the time. The duty to apply the law in good faith is an explicit treaty obligation stated in the VCLT, article 31(1).[62] The notion of good faith is also embraced in a number

[58] US Operational Law Handbook, at page 12. Footnote omitted. The same position is upheld in the US DoD Manual, at pages 195–7, referring to the quoted passage from the Hostage Case.

[59] See for statements by Australia, Roberts and Guelff, *Documents on the Laws of War*, at page 500; Austria, ibid., at page 500; Belgium, ibid., at page 501; Canada, ibid., at page 502; Federal Republic of Germany, ibid., at page 505; Ireland, ibid., at page 506; Italy, ibid., at page 507; The Netherlands and New Zealand, ibid., at page 508; Spain, ibid., at page 509; and the United Kingdom, ibid., at page 510.

[60] Galic Case, at para. 58. The same perspective is taken in the Strugar Case, with regard to military objectives. See ICTY, Strugar Case, Trial Chamber Judgment, at para. 295: 'Whether a military advantage can be achieved must be decided, as the Trial Chamber in the Galic case held, from the perspective of the "person contemplating the attack, including the information available to the latter, that the object is being used to make an effective contribution to military action".'

[61] In the OTP Report at para. 49 it is stated with regard to the proportionality rule that: 'It is suggested that the determination of relative values must be that of the "reasonable military commander". Although there will be room for argument in close cases, there will be many cases where reasonable military commanders will agree that the injury to noncombatants or the damage to civilian objects was clearly disproportionate to the military advantage gained.'

[62] On the interpretation of flexible rules in the LOAC, see Section 4.4.

of military manuals[63] and by the ICRC.[64] What the notion of 'good faith' entails in practice may appear unclear. In the Blaskic case, the ICTY stated with regard to the border between acts lacking 'sound military judgment' and criminal acts that:

> the nature of the attack of 18 July 1993 cannot be categorically defined as that of a criminal act, in that there was still the presence of a considerable number of ABiH [Armija Bosne i Hercegovine] soldiers in Stari Vitez at that time. The operation itself may have been a wilful one lacking sound military judgement, but that wilful aspect of the attack does not make it a crime in terms of the Statute.[65]

Good faith is the opposite of ignorance of fact or 'turning the blind eye' to apparent circumstances. However, the distinction between excusable and culpable lack of information may be a fine line in practice.[66] The requirements of good faith and information reasonably available are thus connected and partly overlapping.

The emphasis placed on what information that is reasonably available 'at the time', rules out considerations of hindsight. This point is often specified to be: '... not on the basis of hindsight'.[67] Assessment based on 'information reasonably available at the time' relates to all decisions during conduct of hostilities.[68] Furthermore, assessment relates in practice to the commander's decision cycle,[69] which as a minimum consists of three phases: assessment, decision and action. Applying the rule of distinction is often referred to by scholars as a two-step task: first gathering of information and then decision making based on the gathered information (leaving out the obvious third step; 'action').[70] But what information, under the circumstances, is reasonably *available* at the time? The answer to the question obviously relies (among other things) upon what available assets for Information Surveillance and Reconnaissance (ISR) the commander possesses. In the notion of 'reasonably

63 US DoD Manual, at page 56; Canadian Manual, at pages 2-2 and 4-4, cited below.

64 See the AP I Commentary to articles 51(4) and (5), at para. 1978, page 625.

65 ICTY, Blaskic Case, Appeals Chamber Judgment, at para. 463.

66 For examples, see Chapter 7 on the discussion of the rule of distinction and the presumption of civilian status.

67 Quoted from Bothe, Partsch and Solf, *New Rules*, at pages 351–2. The same point is emphasised in the US DoD Manual, at page 193.

68 See for example the US DoD Manual, at page 192 and Bill, 'The Rendulic "Rule"', at pages 137 and 138.

69 In military literature often referred to as the OODA loop; 'Observe, Orient, Decide and Act'. A concept developed by the American military strategist John Boyd.

70 Merriam, 'Affirmative target identification', page 90 and Henderson, *The Contemporary Law of Targeting*, page 237.

available', it is not possible to deduce a duty to exploit all potential assets his or her State possesses. On the other hand, the State is obliged to have assets which are capable of abiding by the law.[71] Furthermore, it appears reasonable to require that the commander actually *knows* what ISR collection assets he or she can benefit from, and how they are used. In this direction, see for example the Canadian Manual, stating with regard to the rule of distinction that 'Commanders must make reasonable, good faith efforts to gather intelligence and to review the intelligence available to them.'[72] In many cases the threshold of what information is 'reasonably available at the time' coincides with the duty to do everything 'feasible' to verify that the target is a military objective.[73] The commander ought to possess basic knowledge about his or her own forces' capacities and capabilities, as well as that of the enemy, in order to assess potential military advantages and/or necessities.[74] The commander should have an initial understanding of the enemy's basic strength and vulnerabilities. For example, if intelligence shows that the enemy's most critical asset is his northern fleet, this information must be presumed known to the rest of the command group. Accordingly, the commander must possess an initial knowledge of where an attack may be presumed to produce the greatest advantage. Having said this, the expected level of available information must allow for the confusion stemming from the 'fog of war' (see Section 4.6). Naturally, intelligence may prove wrong and liable to the enemy's deception. Finally, the expected level of available information does not rule out that decisions during combat necessarily will be made under a certain level of doubt.

One example with terrible consequences that subsequently questioned the good faith of the commanders in charge, was the US bombing of the Al-Firdus shelter/bunker[75] the night between 13 and 14 February in 1991, during the first Gulf War. The shelter/bunker was built as a civil defence air shelter during the Iran–Iraq war, but US intelligence had assessed that it was being used as a C2 and C3 bunker for Saddam's forces.[76] The intelligence was based on electronic signals apparently coming from the bunker and images from satellites of

71 AP I Commentary, at para. 1871; Henderson, *The Contemporary Law of Targeting*, at page 162.

72 Canadian Manual, at page 2-2.

73 AP I article 57(2)(a)(i). The specific notion of feasibility is dealt with in Chapter 15.

74 The Canadian Manual may also be read in support of this view. See para. 415, at page 4-4.

75 Terminology depends on whether the object is identified as a military objective or as a civilian object. The White House has for example used the phrase 'Bunker-Shelter' when dealing with the case in retrospect. See The White House, Crafting Tragedy. The bunker/shelter is also referred to as the al-Amariyya shelter, for example by Human Rights Watch in its report, Needless Deaths in the Gulf War, at pages 126 ff.

76 Final Report to Congress, at page 141. Human Rights Watch, Needless Deaths in the Gulf War, at pages 126–31.

persons and vehicles moving in and out of the shelter.[77] The USA argued that it was also covered with camouflage and surrounded by barbed wire – although the camouflage was contested by other witnesses.[78] The USA claimed not to know that the bunker was also being used – at the time of the attack – as a regular bomb shelter for the civilian population. At the time of the attack there were between 200 and 300 persons inside, incarcerated by the heat following the attack. The US position following the attack was clear: they did not know that civilians were allowed into the bunker and Saddam conducted a deliberate use of the Iraqi civilian population in order to shield military activities and gain sympathy in international media.[79] While the USA in the aftermath also argued that the attack was lawful on the basis of military necessity,[80] critique and questions were raised – in particular from Human Rights Watch, who questioned the core elements of the commanders' assessment: good faith and the information reasonably available at the time. At the heart of the critique lies the question: how could the USA reasonably not know that there were civilians present in the bunker, when they had images of military use?[81] The preliminary answer lies in the facts accounted for above, that the reuse as a bomb shelter had commenced recently and as part of a greater intermingling of military activity among the civilian population. More detailed questions raised by the attack, such as whether the circumstances should have created a substantial doubt and whether the USA had done everything feasible to minimise collateral damage, are addressed elsewhere in this book.[82] The following section deals with the acceptable level of doubt and the interaction between doubt and the margin of appreciation.

4.5.3 *A Military Margin of Appreciation and the Issue of Doubt*

The commander's assessment of military necessity is not a matter of exact science. Some doubt is unavoidable[83] under the stress of warfare – and the

77 Human Rights Watch, Needless Deaths in the Gulf War, at page 133.
78 Ibid., at page 132, in interview with a journalist.
79 Final Report to Congress, at page 617. See also the passages cited from public statements in Human Rights Watch, Needless Deaths in the Gulf War, at pages 131–3.
80 Final Report to Congress, at page 617.
81 Human Rights Watch, Needless Deaths in the Gulf War, at page 137.
82 See Chapter 7 on civilians; Chapter 15 on precautions in attack; and Chapter 5 on criminal responsibility.
83 See for example the Tallinn Manual in commentary 12 to rule 113, at page 475, commenting on the proportionality rule, emphasising that 'Expectation and anticipation do not require absolute certainty of occurrence.'

'someone' who doubts is the military commander.[84] This is a common feature for all decisions taken by commanders in wartime. During the Diplomatic Conference prior to the AP I the British delegate presented a rather pragmatic approach: 'In cases of doubt such as were envisaged by the paragraph some element of subjectivity was unavoidable. The sponsors of the proposal had tried to make the criteria as strict as possible to put a heavy burden of proof on the soldier.'[85]

Strings of doubt accompany assessments of military objectives, military advantage, collateral damage as well as all predictions regarding enemy behaviour and the indeterminate size 'fog of war'.[86] The commander's margin of appreciation is not the same as leeway for doubt, but doubt is also subject to the commander's judgment.[87] As such, the two issues may appear inextricably linked. For example: the assessment of whether destruction of a compound will offer a definite military advantage under the circumstances ruling at the time, is a decision within the commander's margin of appreciation. This assessment may rely upon the assumption that the compound is actually used to house C2 facilities. This latter decision may be a matter of doubt – is it reasonable to rely on the information available in order to verify that the object is in fact used to make an effective contribution to military action?[88] Finally, the issue whether the commander has done everything feasible to verify (hereunder to gather information) that the compound is a C2 facility, is a concrete issue of precautionary duties regulated in AP I article 57. The threshold of feasibility relies upon the commander's assessment of the need and possibility to call for additional information when he or she is in doubt about the object's status. Ultimately, the notion of feasibility takes the necessities of war into account, as assessed by the commander under the umbrella of practical possibilities under the circumstances (for example whether it was possible under the circumstances to verify the object by human intelligence

84 See Bill, 'The Rendulic "Rule"', at page 139, where he states that: '*Someone* has to "doubt", and *someone* has the [*sic*] resolve the doubt: the commander is the person to do so.'

85 Official Records of the Diplomatic Conference CDDH/III/SR.6, at page 47. The statement was made with regard to the presumption of civilian status in matters of doubt (now encompassed in article 50(1)) and discussed in relation to draft article 45(4). The burden of proof is commented upon further below.

86 On the 'fog of war', see further Section 4.6.

87 The AP I Commentary to article 53(3) on the presumption of civilian status for objects which are normally so used, states at page 638: 'However, it remains the case that the text adopted by the Diplomatic Conference largely relies on the judgment of soldiers who will have to apply these provisions.'

88 In the Gotovina Case, Appeals Chamber Judgment, the ICTY argued at para. 13 that: 'Regarding errors of fact, the Appeals Chamber will apply a standard of reasonableness.'

sources or only images). The notion of 'practical possibilities' is an interwoven part of the commander's margin of appreciation. As such, the issue of doubt, feasibility and margin of appreciation appear circular.

Doubt is explicitly regulated with regard to the principle of distinction and the definition of civilians and military objectives in AP I articles 50(1) and 52(3). These provisions are dealt with successively in Chapter 7, whereas the notion of feasibility is addressed in Chapter 15.

4.5.4 *The Burden of Proof*

At the outset, the 'burden of proof' is placed differently during conduct of hostilities and with regard to criminal defences. While it is a fundamental notion in criminal law that the prosecution bears the burden of proof for establishing criminal guilt, the situation is slightly different as a point of departure when it comes to the question whether an act of warfare was lawful or not.[89] I first deal with the question of 'proof' outside the scope of criminal responsibility. With regard to 'proof' of military necessity, Draper states that: 'The defence of military necessity being exceptive, the onus of establishing that imperative military necessity will lie upon those invoking it once they are confronted with a violation of the norm to which military necessity is exceptive.'[90] In a similar direction Downey asks: 'how is the person making such a decision to know whether some court at a later date may not overrule him?' He then answers his own question by referring to the U.S. Supreme Court in the Mitchell case: 'He must show by proof the nature and character of the emergency, such as he had reasonable ground to believe it to be.'[91]

With regard to exceptive military necessity, the situation appears easy: the commander must justify (provide proof), either explicitly or implicitly, the amount of force he/she uses. Sometimes this 'justification' is evident and implicit, such as with attacks on enemy combatants or tanks. In other cases, such as assessments made under the proportionality rule, the justification requires more from the commander. Although the function of military necessity is different when the commander assesses military objectives and the proportionality rule from military necessity in an exceptional provision, the burden of proof appears to rely on the commander in both cases. This does not mean that a commander in an eventual criminal case will have to prove his/

89 On the presumption of innocence in criminal law, Chapter 5.
90 Draper, 'Military necessity and humanitarian imperatives', at page 133.
91 Downey, 'The law of war and military necessity', at page 256.

her own innocence.[92] A delicate balance between providing proof for the commander's assessment of the necessity of an attack and the presumption of innocence in criminal matters can be seen in the following passages from the practice of the ICTY. In the Strugar case, the Tribunal stated: 'As regards the Defence submission concerning alleged military activities of the Crisis Staff, the headquarters of which was located in the Old Town, the Chamber notes that no persuasive evidence has been supplied to the effect that the Crisis Staff was conducting military operations from the Old Town.'[93] Then, in the Gotovina Appeals Chamber case, it was stated that:

> the Trial Chamber erred in excluding the possibility of mobile targets of opportunity such as military trucks and tanks. The possibility of shelling such mobile targets, combined with the lack of any dependable range of error estimation, raises reasonable doubt about whether even artillery impact sites particularly distant from fixed artillery targets considered legitimate by the Trial Chamber demonstrate that unlawful shelling took place.[94]

The relationship between the LOAC and international criminal law with regard to military necessity is dealt with in Chapter 5.

4.5.5 *Who Is the Commander?*

Having established the notion of reasonableness as a general point of departure, another issue is to determine the context of reasonableness. Who is the ideal reasonable commander? Is it the four-star general or the second lieutenant? Is it someone particularly skilful or particularly brave under the stress of combat? The overall question of who is the reasonable commander thus has at least two sub-questions: the question of level of command (or military rank) and the question of subjective skills or qualities.

The point of departure appears clear. The standard of reasonableness applies to the entire military chain of command.[95] This point is envisaged for example in the AP I article 57, which require feasible precautions to be taken by 'those who plan or decide upon an attack'.[96] As the wording indicates, some obligations are by their nature addressing those who plan an attack,

92 See Chapter 5.

93 Strugar Case, Trial Chamber Judgment, at para. 284.

94 Gotovina Case, Appeals Chamber judgment, at para. 66. See as well para. 63.

95 See for example, Bill, 'The Rendulic "Rule"', at page 144.

96 The wording is slightly different in the San Remo Manual and the AMW Manual with regard to sea and air war respectively The San Remo Manual article 46 juxtaposes those who plan and decide upon an attack with those who execute the attack, while the AMW Manual article 32 (a)–(c) has a more generic language and simply refers to the duty to take constant care.

while others, such as the duty to cancel or suspend an attack,[97] also point at lower echelons of command.[98]

In each case there is a question of which level of command bears the responsibility for the different parts of the planning and execution of an attack.[99] During the Diplomatic Conference prior to the AP I, some States argued that the duty to take precautions in attack primarily fell upon battalion commanders and above, due to the limited access to information further down the chain of command.[100] Legitimate concern was raised over whether the phrase 'those who plan or decide upon an attack': '. . . could lay a heavy burden of responsibility on subordinate officers who are not always capable of taking such decisions, which should really fall upon higher ranking officers'.[101] Other States tie the obligations to the information and discretion available at any given time, at each level of command – in principle from soldier to force commander.[102] The two views do not need to depart significantly in practice. The practical approach appears to be that the obligations apply to every level of command,[103] but that expectations with regard to reasonableness when it comes to verification of targets and assessment of proportionality,[104] in particular the assessment of the relative importance of the military objective under attack, often fall at higher levels of command.[105] The duty to cancel or suspend an attack may, in principle, apply all the way down to the individual soldier,[106] although it is unlikely that an infantry soldier will be in a position to cancel an attack in which he takes part. In broad terms, it suffices to state that the

There are, however, no indications to state that the differences in terminology relate to differences in substance with regard to land, air and sea warfare.

97 AP I article 57(2)(b) and (c).

98 See for example the remarks by Sweden in the Official Records of the Diplomatic Conference in O.R. VI, CDDH/SR.42, Annex, at page 237. See as well the AP I Commentary, at paras. 2220 and 2222.

99 This is also pointed out in the Commentary to rule 15 in the ICRC CIHL (using the phrase 'constant care').

100 Afghanistan and Switzerland are mentioned in particular, Official Records of the Diplomatic Conference O.R. VI, CDDH/SR.42, Annex, pages 219 and 236.

101 AP I Commentary, at para. 2197, page 681. In the same direction, see Rauch, 'The concept of military necessity in the context of the law of war', at page 24.

102 UK manual, page 85, para. 5.32.9

103 Norwegian Manual, page 36. Henderson, *The Contemporary Law of Targeting*, at page 159 and Boivin, 'The legal regime applicable to targeting military objectives in the context of contemporary warfare', at page 35.

104 See for example Fenrick, 'The rule of proportionality and Protocol I in conventional warfare', at page 98.

105 See Bothe, Partsch and Solf, *New Rules*, at page 409.

106 In this direction, see Norwegian Manual, at pages 35–6 and Dinstein, *Conduct of Hostilities*, page 167.

expectations of a reasonable commander, when it comes to precautions in attack, adjust and increase in accordance with the level of command.[107] The duty incumbent upon higher levels of command comprises the duty to 'instruct personnel adequately so that the latter, even if of low rank, can act correctly in the situations envisaged'.[108]

One example of how responsibility and expectations adjust to level of command and access to information is the case where a pilot, having eyes on target, observes something else than what has been passed to him through the chain of command. There might be civilians approaching an area previously presumed to be of solely military use, forcing the pilot to suspend the attack in order to not to violate the proportionality rule. Considering the information and situational awareness possibly available at higher levels of command, the question for the pilot appears as 'whether the commander's determination is *evidently* faulty in view of what is visible on site'.[109] In other words: supervening reasons are required if a decision from higher command is reasonably expected to be altered. Normally, it is neither expected nor permitted that a soldier (which in many cases is not comparable to a fighter pilot) overrules considerations made by higher command.[110] For practical purposes, the 'reasonable commander' will usually be a person vested with command authority according to national laws or regulations.

Having stated that the reasonable commander in practice may be a four-star general or a junior officer, the next issue at hand is the different subjective background that each commander naturally possesses. The OTP Report addresses the issue, stating with regard to the proportionality assessment that:

> the answers may differ depending on the background and values of the decision maker. It is unlikely that a human rights lawyer and an experienced combat commander would assign the same relative values to military advantage and to injury to noncombatants. Further, it is unlikely that military commanders with different doctrinal backgrounds and differing degrees of combat experience or national military histories would always agree in close cases.[111]

The latter is probably true For example, in a case where an older pilot would decline to drop a bomb over an assigned target, a younger pilot may very well not hesitate. Obviously, they may both be 'reasonable commanders'. Reasonableness

107 ICRC CIHL, at page 359 and Henderson, *The Contemporary Law of Targeting*, page 160.
108 AP I Commentary, at para. 2197, page 681.
109 AMW Manual, commentary 4 to rule 32(a). Emphasis added.
110 Boothby, *The Law of Targeting*, at page 120.
111 OTP Report, at para. 50. On the proportionality assessment in general, see Chapter 13.

cannot be the same as only one reasonable alternative – although that *might* also be the case, depending on the circumstances. The demanding task is therefore to establish the zone of reasonableness, including room for the more experienced and the less experienced commanders, but excluding the irresponsible and untrained ones when the standard is set. Finally, the comparison is to be done with a *commander*, not a 'human rights lawyer', as mentioned in the OPT Report above.[112]

4.5.6 *Transfer of Authority*

In principle, the same point of departure applies also in cases where command is transferred to, for example, an international force, either an international organisation, such as the UN or the EU, or a coalition (such as will be the case in a NATO operation). The standard of reasonableness applies to each level of command. When States transfer authority over their forces to an international organisation or a multinational coalition, the practice is to transfer operational command or operational control, but not full command, leaving 'operational matters' under the command of the international force commander, but not 'administrative or logistic control'.[113] The military chain of command may thus consist of troops with different doctrinal and cultural backgrounds, all being compared to the standard of a reasonable commander while performing the same or similar tasks. Furthermore, the possibilities of control may arguably get weaker when command is shared or transferred to an international organisation.[114] This weakness may eventually affect the possibility to instruct personnel as required to secure reasonableness at all levels of command throughout the mission.

4.6 THE MILITARY COMMANDER'S ASSESSMENT AND THE 'FOG OF WAR'

4.6.1 *The Inevitable 'Fog of War'*

Behind the legal 'margin' devoted to military commanders during conduct of hostilities lies the need for adapting the law to rapidly changing factual

112 Bothe, 'The protection of the civilian population and NATO bombing on Yugoslavia', at page 535, can be read as to include civilians in the comparison. I do not share this position.

113 NATO AAP-6, page 2-0-3.

114 European Commission for Democracy through Law (Venice Commission), Report on the Democratic Control of the Armed Forces, at page 35.

circumstances, the so-called 'fog of war'.[115] Military necessity grants this margin and may be 'perceived as the placeholder of realism in war'.[116]

Apart from the never-ending challenge of striking the right balance between concrete flexibility on the one hand and normative predictability on the other, there are differences in practice when it comes to the actual margin left to commanders on behalf of their respective governments. To a certain extent, these two issues are related. Broadly, governments usually find that commanders are those best suited to assess military matters, to make military plans and to perform the 'operational art'. Depending on the nature of the conflict however, some matters will be kept for the political level to decide, while others are more easily left to the military. In short, the intensity of civilian control with the armed forces – and hereunder with their actual margin of appreciation – varies. Consequently, the political involvement in matters which by law are presumed to be military, occurs to a varying degree. The varying intensity of civilian control is not, as such, an issue of the LOAC. The actual practice of the commander's discretion (as a representative of the State) may, however, be illustrative in order to show how States view the commander's margin in light of the 'fog of war' and therefore how wide a margin the States grant themselves as a point of departure.

4.6.2 *Civilian Control: the Point of Departure*

Civilian control is not part of the legal limits to the commander's assessment of military necessity according to the LOAC. Concerning the LOAC, the argument in favour of democratic (civilian) control[117] is more indirect: as a prerequisite to avoid state responsibility for acts not wanted by the (civilian) authorities of the state, and to be able to prosecute violations of the LOAC amounting to crimes.[118] Although civilian control is presumed to be strong in democracies, the special features of military decisions are recognised, such as by the Venice Commission of democracy, pointing out the special features of speed, urgency, secrecy and discretion.[119] Furthermore, that operational issues

115 See McClintock, 'The Law of War', at pages 644–5, where he argues that the acquittal of Rendulic in the Hostage Case, 'reflects the deference given to decisions made while the commander is enshrouded in the "fog of war"'.

116 Geiss, 'Military necessity', at page 557.

117 Venice Commission, *Report on the Democratic Control of the Armed Forces*, at pages 14 and 16, states that civilian control is a *sine qua non* for democracy.

118 Ibid., at page 19.

119 Ibid., at page 92.

'should benefit from a greater margin of appreciation left to the military', than policy issues.[120]

Leaving this as a point of departure for the concrete assessment of facts by the reasonable commander, I shall move to the examples from history. Such examples may be illustrative in two aspects: first, as expressions of the distinction between law and politics and second, as expressions of the practice of States with regard to the actual margin offered by the law.

4.6.3 What Has Been Left to the Military in Past Wars?

During the Franco-Prussian War in the 1870s the Prussian General Staff under General von Moltke enjoyed almost maximum freedom in making the overall war strategy[121] that led to victory. While abstaining from active participation in political affairs, Moltke was granted the possibility of direct appeal to 'one level above', to King Wilhelm I of Prussia.[122] The Prussian discretionary freedom is commented upon below (in Section 6.5.1) as one of two extremes (the Preamble to the 1907 Hague Convention being the other) with regard to the commander's margin of appreciation. The commander himself determined the content of military necessity entirely. In other words, the norm of military necessity was indistinguishable from the commander's subjective assessment of the facts.[123] While limits on the commander's discretion appeared to hardly exist as a public policy under Prussian tradition, the Allied powers attacked the Prussian doctrine harshly during the (much later) aftermath of WWII. While attacking the Prussian tradition of an apparently unfettered approach to the assessment of military necessity, the actual practice of the allied commanders could hardly be recognised as being more 'fettered'. In WWII the allied strategy of weakening the resistance of the civilian population[124] left 'a good deal of latitude for interpretation for the field commanders'.[125] The latitude given would thus include the determination of means considered militarily necessary in order to attain the objective.

After WWII the actual leeway granted military commanders varies according to the political climate during the armed conflict. While being exceptionally

120 Ibid.

121 For an interpretation of Napoleon's art of war, who Prussia had previously lost against, see Holborn, 'The Prusso-German school', at page 283.

122 Ibid., at page 285.

123 See as well Section 6.2 below, on the humanity–necessity balance, where necessity in the German War Book was given the force of law.

124 On the 'morale attacks' conducted during WWII, see below, Chapter 12.

125 Biddle, *Rhetoric and Reality in Air Warfare*, at page 215.

narrow during parts of the Vietnam War (in particular Operation Rolling Thunder) and the Kosovo War (Operation Allied Force), the pendulum has swung in a more flexible direction between and after these wars.[126] Both the Gulf War of 1991 (Operation Desert Storm) and the Libya War of 2011 (Operation Unified Protector) were featured by a lesser degree of civilian control over operational matters, while the non-international armed conflict in Afghanistan has been reigned by an increasing pattern of procedural checklists.[127] The development from Operation Rolling Thunder in the Vietnam War to Operation Desert Storm in the Gulf War is particularly illustrative. While political control over Operation Rolling Thunder has been labelled by critics in the aftermath as being not only outstandingly tight, but also unreasonably so, not exploiting either the law nor military doctrine to the benefit of the campaign, Operation Desert Storm was the opposite on all points. An unprecedented latitude was permitted to General Horner on his way to compel Saddam out of Kuwait.[128] Consequently, the margin inherent in the LOAC appears to be grasped by States and handed over to military commanders whenever considered politically suitable. For the State, the margin is truly flexible and the commander is dependent upon his or her government.

[126] An account of the margin devoted to the military commanders during these wars is given in my article, Johansen, 'Mission command and command responsibility'.

[127] For examples of this, see Chapter 15 on the practice of taking feasible precautions under attack in Afghanistan.

[128] See my article, Johansen, 'Mission command and command responsibility' with further references.

5

Assessing Necessity and Criminal Responsibility

5.1 SANCTIONS AS LIMITS ON THE COMMANDER'S ASSESSMENT

This book is about the *legal limits to the military commander's assessment of military necessity during conduct of hostilities*. Ultimately, these limits are illustrated by enforcing sanctions upon violations of the LOAC. The present chapter is about the military commander's criminal responsibility for wrongful assessments of military necessity under the LOAC.

International and national law offer a catalogue of sanction regimes. In this chapter I leave out sanctions in the broader picture, such as fact-finding commissions, reparations and countermeasures (however, reprisals are dealt with in a specific context in Section 12.4), and concentrate on the individual role of the military commander. The purpose here is to address the ultimate outer limits to the commander's assessment of military necessity during conduct of hostilities, through comparisons between a LOAC rule and its corresponding war crime – but first a presentation of the context: three pillars of liability.

5.2 THE COMMANDER'S THREE PILLARS OF LIABILITY

The commander is placed under different regimes of liability, which sometimes make the assessments truly demanding. First, commanders have an individual duty under national law to obey superiors' orders and are, obviously, criminally responsible for conduct ordered by themselves, or performed by themselves. An 'order' must be understood widely, and includes a wide array from 'missions' to specific, concrete orders – both written and unwritten. State armed forces being under a command responsible for their conduct, shall also be subject to an internal disciplinary system which shall enforce compliance with the LOAC.[1] All violations of the LOAC, as well as orders limiting the conduct of commanders beyond the LOAC, for example in the form of ROEs, may be subject to disciplinary sanctions by the State.[2]

Second, the commander is a representative for the State and all acts conducted within line of duty (and not ultra vires) are 'acts of State', which attributes State responsibility for unlawful acts of war.[3] As opposed to the duty to obey orders and command responsibility, State responsibility for internationally wrongful acts does not entail individual criminal responsibility – but, as the wording indicates, a responsibility for the State to provide reparation for the injury.[4]

Third, the commander may be criminally responsible for crimes committed by subordinates within his/her 'effective command and control' – 'command responsibility'.[5] This rather far-reaching criminal responsibility aims at framing military commanders in higher echelons of command. Command responsibility holds a military commander responsible for conduct by subordinates, if the commander failed to take all necessary and reasonable measures within his or her power to 'prevent or repress' the commission of the crime or to submit the matter to the competent authorities for investigation or prosecution.[5] Command responsibility is construed to force military commanders (as well as civilian leaders) to never 'turn a blind eye' and actively pursue rumours of misconduct.

This chapter is limited to liability in the first sense: the military commander's individual criminal responsibility for war crimes ordered or performed by themselves.

5.3 BASIC FEATURES OF WAR CRIMES

5.3.1 *The Definition*

The international notion of war crimes comprises, in short, grave (or 'serious') breaches of the LOAC, hereunder both violations of the four Geneva Conventions and other treaties and customs of war.[7] The fact that war crimes

1 AP I article 43(1).
2 On the relationship between ROEs and the LOAC, see Section 4.4.2.
3 AP I article 91 and Hague Regulations article 3, ICRC CIHL rule 149, as well as Draft articles on Responsibility of States for Internationally Wrongful Acts, articles 2 and 5.
4 Ibid., article 34.
5 Rome Statute article 28, ICTY article 7(3) and ICTR article 6(3).
6 Rome Statute articles 28 (1)(b) and (2)(c).
7 ICTY, Tadic Case, Appeals Chamber decision, at para. 94; Rome Statute article 8; ICTY articles 2 and 3; and the London Agreement for the International Military Tribunal, article 6(b).

entail violations of both treaty law and *customs* of war is, in particular, seen from a civil national law perspective and the basic principle of legality.[8] While the standing of custom has been upheld throughout the aftermath of WWII and the ad hoc tribunals, there has been a shift in this regard with the establishment of the ICC and the Rome Statute.

As with international law governing conduct of hostilities, there is also a basic distinction in international criminal law between international armed conflicts and non-international armed conflicts. Under the Rome Statute, neither the crime of launching an attack in violation of the proportionality rule, nor the law of weaponry is reflected in the Statute – with the deficits this entails for enforcement.[9]

It is a basic premise of modern criminal law – both international law and the various national legal systems – that individual criminal responsibility requires both a specific conduct (*actus reus*) *and* a mental requirement (subjective guilt or *mens rea*).[10] Despite being a basic premise, the Rome Statute article 30 is the first and only instrument under international criminal law which explicitly states the content of the mental element of the crime. The mental requirement established in the Rome Statute has, however, been subject to criticism because it, at least allegedly, departs from the customary law requirement of 'wilfulness' (see below). As with any criminal case, the question of guilt is not necessarily straightforward to establish. The inherent challenges in prosecuting crimes which may have taken place long ago, without immediate access to evidence, is particularly prominent as far as war crimes are concerned. Furthermore, it is difficult to prosecute military commanders, particularly those belonging to state armed forces, if they argue that they were doing their best, acting as reasonable commanders under the fog of war (see Section 5.3.4).

5.3.2 *Few Cases but Large Impact*

Compared to national courts, international courts deal with few cases. Compared to the number of armed conflicts going on, the number of victims of war and the number of persons participating in an armed conflict at any given time, there are few war crime cases, and most likely many more crimes. In light of their relatively low numbers, each case achieves tremendous

8 For an outline of the principle and its different conceptions, see Cassese, *International Criminal Law*, pages 36–41.

9 See for example criticism posed by Cryer, *Prosecuting International Crimes*, at page 283.

10 See for example, Cassese, *International Criminal Law*, page 53; ICTY Trial Chamber judgment, *Prosecutor* v. *Mucic et al.*, paras. 424–5; and the ICC Elements of Crimes.

international attention (at least among those who care about international criminal law or the specific armed conflict). Many perpetrators of crimes go free, but the prosecution of one specific war criminal can have a large signal-effect. Furthermore, those cases that have been brought to court have made international criminal an engine in the development of the LOAC (see Section 1.6.4).[11] For this reason, numerous references to judgments by international courts and tribunals (in particular the ICTY) are made throughout this book. As shown on various places, jurisprudence is not always perfectly consistent. The impression of war crimes trials today leaves a partly fragmented and partly overwhelming picture (at least when it comes to the length of the judgments).

5.3.3 *Different Purposes*

The purposes of the International Criminal Law (ICL) and the LOAC are different. Where the purpose of the first is to avoid impunity, the purpose of the second is to achieve a minimum of protection for victims – and to alleviate the sufferings of war. In order to enforce the rule of distinction, the LOAC has established a presumption of civilian status in case of doubt of whether a person is a civilian or not.[12] Under criminal law the accused benefits from the presumption of innocence.[13] To a certain extent the presumption of civilian status under the LOAC may 'work against' the criminal law presumption of innocence.[14] By this is meant that the benefit of doubt may *not* be accredited the accused when it comes to the question of civilian status.

Having said this, enforcement through prosecution is a part of securing proper conduct in war – to the benefit of the victims of war. ICL is particularly shaped to this purpose as far as war crimes are concerned. In this respect the two areas of law have a common purpose to serve and ICL can be described as an 'accessory to IHL'.[15]

5.3.4 *Application of Flexible Rules*

As accounted for in Chapter 4, the LOAC is scattered with flexible terms and expressions, where some of them are so common that their meanings appear to

[11] See for example Bartels, 'Dealing with the principle of proportionality in armed conflict in retrospect', at page 277.

[12] See Section 7.9.

[13] See for example Rome Statute article 66.

[14] Bartels, 'Armed conflict proportionality in international criminal trials', at page 279.

[15] Bartels, 'Discrepancies between international humanitarian law on the battlefield and in the courtroom', at page 341.

rely on a shared pre-understanding and that this pre-understanding is distributed almost intuitively (Section 4.4). The challenges attached to the application of such terms are no less under criminal law. To a certain extent we may even state that all the difficulties of applying the LOAC on the battlefield are accentuated when enforcing violations in the courtroom. The core premise of applying the LOAC, with the military commander in focus, that the *post facto* assessment has to be done based on foresight and not hindsight. This means, necessarily, that foresight needs to be construed in retrospect. This is not an easy task, taking into account that the inevitable 'fog of war' described in Section 4.6 also clouds criminal trials.[16] This fog may certainly obscure the possibilities for obtaining timely and reliable evidence and as such seriously hamper the trial.

The very essence of flexible rules is that they aim to encapsulate changes in circumstances and call for the commander's discretion or value judgment (see Chapter 4).[17] The subjective elements, which are bound to accompany a value judgment, are sometimes difficult to distinguish from the objective (conduct) element. Some material elements contain an adjectival phrase that *sounds like a mental state*.[18] This is particularly the case when it comes to military necessity and the military margin of appreciation, which consists of two dimensions: the norm and the person assessing the norm. These two dimensions are sometimes so closely linked that we may say that the rule becomes what the commander assesses it to be.[19] The notions of 'excessiveness', 'feasibility' and 'military advantage' are examples of such terms, which contain a large portion of subjective ingredients – and eventually pose challenges when it comes to prosecution. I shall return to these challenges below, when dealing with the proportionality rule.

5.4 THE NOTION OF SEVERITY AND THE FUNCTION OF MILITARY NECESSITY

5.4.1 *'Grave' Breaches*

As pointed out elsewhere in this book, it is difficult to discern a meaningful difference between aggravations and simple forms of conduct, such as

[16] For this point in the ICL perspective, see Bartels, 'Armed conflict proportionality in international criminal trials', at page 279.
[17] For this point in the ICL perspective, see ibid., at page 277.
[18] Pigaroff and Robinson, 'Article 30: mental element', page 1116.
[19] See Section 4.2.3 above.

between 'imperative military necessity' and simple 'military necessity'.[20] The same point of departure is valid for the distinction between breaches and grave breaches of the LOAC, which practically speaking concern matters of life and death. With one important remark: violations of rules of war amounting to attacks on civilians or attacks on military objectives with incidental effects on civilians causing death or injury *are* serious. These crimes are therefore addressed below. Before turning to the war crimes of attacking civilians and causing excessive collateral damage, I shall present some reflections on the function of military necessity as an element of the crime.

5.4.2 *Military Necessity As an Element of the Crime*

Military necessity is undoubtedly an element – either implicit or explicit – of core war crimes and breaches of the LOAC not amounting to grave breaches (and thus punishable solely by national law). The absence of military necessity has been described as a 'negative' element,[21] indicating that conduct which is *not* justified by military necessity amounts to a crime. For some crimes this description is surely correct, but not for all. When it comes to the crime of intentionally directing attacks against the civilian population or civilians not taking direct part in hostilities,[22] the conduct (the attack) may very well be motivated by considerations of military necessity, yet it is unlawful. As argued in Chapters 7 and 12, the prohibition under the LOAC (and thus the criminalisation) is a *limitation* upon military necessity. Furthermore, the prohibition is more fruitfully applied *without* references to military necessity, recognising that perceptions of military necessity will vary considerably as the armed conflict proceeds. It ought to be pointed out that this position is a pedagogical one: military necessity should not be understood as either justifying conduct which is otherwise prohibited (such as directing attacks against civilians), or prohibiting conduct which is otherwise permitted (such as attacks against a military weapon system – this is *ipso facto* militarily necessary).[23] Military necessity may therefore be seen as an element of crimes (but not necessarily a *negative* one), or more closely as a reflection of how military necessity appears in the LOAC framework constituting the basis for the crime. The commander's assessment of military necessity ought not to be

20 See Sections 2.8 and 15.7.

21 Hayashi, *Military Necessity*, pages 219–20.

22 Rome Statute, article 8(2)(b)(i), see further below.

23 See for example Section 16.5, where this point is made with regard to destruction of property which qualifies as a military objective.

viewed as a separate dimension of the crime.[24] As in the underlying LOAC framework, military necessity is in-built in the description of the criminal conduct – or where the material element sounds like a mental element.

5.4.3 *Categories of Conduct*

For the present purposes there are, roughly speaking, five relevant *categories of conduct* which may give rise to criminal responsibility: attacks violating the rule of distinction,[25] employing means and methods of warfare violating the prohibition of unnecessary suffering on combatants,[26] destruction of property not required by military necessity,[27] violations of other specific methods of warfare (perfidy and starvation)[28] and violations of the duty to take feasible precautions in attack.[29] Out of these categories, it is only the first four which amount to war crimes. Violations of the duty to take feasible precautions in attack is not a war crime *as such*. In this chapter I limit the presentation to deal with violations of the rule of distinction and its add-on: the proportionality rule.

The categories of conduct mentioned do not have a uniform expression under treaty law. They are partly derived from the list of grave breaches in the AP I[30] and partly from the 'laws and customs' of war.[31] The latter category is rather rudimentarily spelled out in the ICTY Statute and more detailed in the Rome Statute which more closely reflects the underlying LOAC rules, and on occasion verbatim repeats the wording of, inter alia, the Hague Regulations,[32] thereby leading to the Rome Statute being partially made up of rather archaic language. For most practical purposes, the material elements of the crimes reflect the underlying LOAC rules, and are as such dealt with throughout this book. It is only *when and how the crime differs in its material aspects* from the LOAC rule that some material elements are given specific attention here. This leaves the mental

24 A misleading remark in this regard is the Blaskic Case Trial Chamber Judgment, at para. 180, page 60, quoted below, Section 11.2.
25 Rome Statute articles 8(2)(b)(i)–(iii), as well as (iv), where the latter is a violation of the proportionality rule.
26 Rome Statute article 8(2)(b)(xx) and the ICTY Statute article 3(a) (the use of weapons).
27 Rome Statute articles 8(2)(a)(iv) and (b)(xiii).
28 Rome Statute article 8(2)(xxv).
29 AP I article 57 and no corresponding war crime.
30 AP I article 85(3).
31 Rome Statute article 8(2)(b) and ICTY Statute article 3. The chapeau and heading respectively.
32 See for example Rome Statute article 8(2)(xi) and Hague Regulations article 23(b).

(subjective) element of the respective crime the pending issue in the present context.

5.4.4 *Violations of Distinction and Proportionality As War Crimes*

The crime as formulated in the Rome Statute articles 8(2)(i–iii) of intentionally directing attacks against civilians, the civilian population or civilian objects is based upon AP I article 51(2).[33] The notions of 'directing attacks', 'civilians' and 'taking direct part in hostilities' are understood similarly as under the LOAC and dealt with in Chapter 11 of this book. As pointed out above, there is no requirement to assess military necessity specifically as an element of this crime. Regardless of whether it was perceived as a necessity, directing an attack against a civilian (who is not taking direct part in hostilities) is prohibited and a crime.[34] Obviously, it is often not easy to determine whether a person at the time was taking direct part in hostilities. These issues are dealt with in Chapter 11 and may pose particular challenges for determination of guilt (see Section 5.5).

The only *treaty* formulation of the crime of violating the proportionality rule is found in the Rome Statute. Article 8(2)(b)(iv) criminalises: 'Intentionally launching an attack in the knowledge that such attack will cause incidental loss of life or injury to civilians or damage to civilian objects or widespread, long-term and severe damage to the natural environment which would be clearly excessive in relation to the concrete and direct overall military advantage anticipated.' The wording of this crime differs from the rule in AP I article 51(5)(b) (dealt with in Chapters 13 and 14) in three aspects as far as the material elements are concerned: the causal requirement of the collateral damage is referred to as 'will cause' instead of 'expected' to cause, and this collateral damage must be 'clearly' excessive in relation to the 'overall' military advantage anticipated. As explained in Chapter 14, the latter difference in wording is in reality obsolete. The insertion of 'clearly', however, was allegedly made in order to permit the commanders to enjoy a wider margin of appreciation and, hence, a higher threshold for criminal responsibility.[35] The totality of changes in wording implies a raised threshold which has been subject to criticism for making it unduly difficult to prosecute.[36]

33 Dörmann, 'Article 8: mental element', page 255.
34 See further Section 11.2.
35 See Arnold and Wehrenberg, 'Article 8: mental element', at page 377.
36 See for example Cryer, *Prosecuting International Crimes*, at page 277.

5.5 THE LIMITS OF REASONABLENESS

5.5.1 *General Remarks*

The construct of the *reasonable commander* is, as accounted for in Section 4.5, an import from international criminal law to the LOAC. The test for both lawfulness and criminality would, according to customary law, depend upon whether a reasonable commander under the circumstances ruling at the time would have acted similarly. As pointed out numerous times in this book, the comparison to a reasonable commander's assessment of the flexible norms – such as 'excessiveness', 'advantage' and 'necessity' in the LOAC – is the backbone of the legality test. It is obvious that the prosecution of these value-judged decisions is burdened with challenge, but the fact that it is difficult does not preclude prosecution. The vexed question after the adoption of the mental (subjective) element in the Rome Statute is, however, whether the standard of reasonableness has ceased to be of help with prosecuting, in particular, violations of the principle of proportionality. In order to address this question I shall therefore compare the subjective requirements under customary law and the Rome Statute respectively.

5.5.2 *Wilfulness*

Customary law and the ICTY article 2 requires that grave breaches of the Geneva Conventions are committed 'wilful/wilfully'. The wording reappears in the Rome Statute article 8(2)(a) as far as violations of the Geneva Conventions are concerned (but not violations of the 'Hague law' in article 8(2)(b)).

The phrase 'wilful' is based on the wording in the Geneva Conventions I-IV[37] and the AP I article 85 governing repression of breaches, and has been interpreted to encompass intent and recklessness. Intent and recklessness is described as follows in the Commentary to AP I article 85:

> the accused must have acted consciously and with intent, i.e., with his mind on the act and its consequences, and willing the ('criminal intent' or 'malice aforethought'); this encompasses the concepts of 'wrongful intent' or 'recklessness', viz., the attitude of an agent who, without being certain of a particular result, accepts the possibility of it happening; on the other hand, ordinary negligence or lack of foresight is not covered, i.e., when a man acts without having his mind on the act or its consequences.[38]

37 GC I article 50; GC II article 51; GC III article 130; GC IV article 147.
38 Commentary to AP I article 85, para. 3474.

It follows from the abovementioned that recklessness is here understood as *dolus eventualis*, which in some states is understood as a subcategory of intent.[39] As we shall see, among the pending questions after the establishment of the International Criminal Court is whether the notion of 'intent and knowledge' encompasses *dolus eventualis*. For certain crimes, where the crime of violating the principle of proportionality is the primary example, the answer to this question is of practical importance for the possibility to actually prosecute.

5.5.3 *Intent and Knowledge*

The mental element in the Rome Statute article 30 says:

1. Unless otherwise provided, a person shall be criminally responsible and liable for punishment for a crime within the jurisdiction of the Court only if the material elements are committed with intent and knowledge.
2. For the purposes of this article, a person has intent where:
   (a) In relation to conduct, that person means to engage in the conduct;
   (b) In relation to a consequence, that person means to cause that consequence or is aware that it will occur in the ordinary course of events.
3. For the purposes of this article, 'knowledge' means awareness that a circumstance exists or a consequence will occur in the ordinary course of events. 'Know' and 'knowingly' shall be construed accordingly.

Unless otherwise provided in other, specific provisions, the conduct, consequences or circumstances described (material elements) must be committed with 'intent and knowledge'. The notion of 'intent' (*dolus directus*) encapsulates situations where, for example, a commander is aware that by engaging in a specific shooting he/she will cause the death of certain persons *and* has the will to cause their death.[40]

[39] See for example the Norwegian Criminal Code § 22 which says:
'Intent exists when a person commits an act that fits the description of the offence in a penal provision

a) deliberately,
b) with the awareness that the act with certainty or most likely fits the description of the offence, or
c) considers it possible that the act fits the description of the offence, and chooses to act even if that should be the case.

Intent exists even if the offender is unaware that the act is unlawful, see Section 26' (translation by the Norwegian Ministry of Justice).

[40] See for example, Cassese, *International Criminal Law*, at page 60.

The term 'intentionally' thus relates to both directing the attack *and* to the object of attack.[41] With regard to 'knowledge', the wording of article 30(3) is clear enough. It is, however, not entirely clear how this requirement is to be applied with regard to the consequences described in each of the crimes.

The General Introduction to the Elements of Crimes, paragraphs 3 and 4, state that: 'Existence of intent and knowledge can be inferred from relevant facts and circumstances', and 'With respect to mental elements associated with elements involving value judgment, such as those using terms "inhumane" or "severe", it is not necessary that the perpetrator personally completed a particular value judgment, unless otherwise indicated.' Based on these general paragraphs, it would not be necessary to prove that the commander in fact assessed the foreseen collateral damage as 'clearly excessive'. Furthermore, 'knowledge' is, as the point of departure, first and foremost crucial to establish as regards the underlying *facts*. However, a particular footnote to the elements of crime of violating the proportionality rule dictates otherwise (just below).

On some occasions throughout the Rome Statute there are double (superfluous) references to 'intent'. Apparently, this is a result of the negotiating process where the crime has been imported from the LOAC rules.[42] This is the case with regard to violations of the rules of distinction and proportionality in articles 8(2)(b)(i–iv). Sometimes there are also (somewhat confusingly) references to 'wilful' – apparently for the same reason.[43] The lack of clarity with regard to the mental element is particularly pertinent when it comes to the proportionality rule.

5.5.4 *Applied to the Proportionality Rule*

The war crime in the Rome Statute of violating the proportionality rule requires that the attack must be launched intentionally, which means that the person must mean to engage in the conduct of the attack. For most practical purposes this part of the mental element does not appear too troublesome to apply. The pending issue appears to be to establish intent in relation to the consequence of *clearly excessive collateral damage*. The wording of Rome Statute article 8(2)(b)(iv) uses the phrase: 'knowledge that such attack will cause', while article 30(3) defines knowledge in this regard, namely: awareness that a consequence will occur in the ordinary course of events. In footnote 37

41 Dörmann, 'Article 8: mental element', page 359.
42 See Pigaroff and Robinson, 'Article 30: mental element', page 1117.
43 Pigaroff and Robinson, 'Article 30: mental element', page 1120.

to Element 3 of the crime (stating the 'perpetrator knew that the attack would cause incidental death or injury to civilians or damage to civilian objects . . . and that . . . would be of such an extent as to be clearly excessive in relation to the concrete and direct overall military advantage anticipated') it is, however, said that: 'As opposed to the general rule set forth in paragraph 4 of the General Introduction, this knowledge element requires that the perpetrator make the value judgment as described therein. An evaluation of that value judgment must be based on the requisite information available to the perpetrator at the time.' In other words, it is not enough to establish knowledge about the underlying facts; the actual (very subjective exercise of the) value judgment must be proven. This footnote has gained criticism for making prosecution unnecessarily difficult and for departing too much from the customary rule (of including recklessness as mental element) without good enough reason for it.[44] The result is undoubtedly at odds with an ordinary reading of the wording of the crime. The proportionality rule is by its very essence a rule relying on the reasonable commander. By the drafting of the rule in the Rome Statute, this standard has been departed from as the basis for the crime. Its application undoubtedly causes peculiar results, and the outcome has, quite precisely, been described as a 'flawed interpretation of the notions of mistake of law and intent'.[45] With this outcome, the tendency described above, and particularly in Chapter 4, that the norm and the persons melts together, becomes acute.

The use of explosive weapons in populated areas may serve as example. If a military commander uses some kinds of 122 mm rocket artillery at maximum range, the weapon is expected to function in an elliptic area which is 168 metres in length and 80 metres in azimuth.[46] Collateral damage within this area is a consequence in the ordinary course of events and we may say that the mental element for that part of the crime is fulfilled. (Some may even argue that the attack was actually *directed* at civilian persons or personnel within this area.[47]) So far, the physics of weaponry determine the ordinary course of events. Furthermore, the military commanders are presumed to know the basic accuracy of their weapon systems. The existence of their knowledge about these facts can, in other words, be inferred from the circumstances.[48]

44 See for example Cryer, *Prosecuting International Crimes*, at pages 278–9.

45 Bothe, 'War crimes', at page 400.

46 These numbers are collected from Cross, Dullum and Jensen-Jonez, Explosive weapons in populated areas, page 32.

47 As required by the crime of violating the rule of distinction in the Rome Statute articles 8(2)(b)(ii) and (iii).

48 See also ICC General Introduction to the Elements of Crimes, para. 3, which states that: 'Existence of intent and knowledge can be inferred from relevant facts and circumstances.'

Depending on the circumstances, other random errors related to launch direction and wind[49] may even make the area considerably bigger.

While physics can determine the ordinary course of events with regard to *where* damage will occur and *how* large the damage will be that occurs to the affected persons or objects, it is a separate assessment to determine how *many* civilians will be in the area. This assessment is bound to be concrete and – also here – knowledge may be inferred from the circumstances. Such circumstances may be obvious and there may be publicly available information about the population in the area, but also concrete information obtained by own intelligence sources. For many practical purposes it will be a thin line between assessing the eventual lack of feasible precautions taken prior to the attack[50] (which is not a war crime in itself) and the circumstances giving rise to stating a commander's knowledge about a certain fact. In more concrete words: it may be a thin line between, on the one hand, stating that a commander did not do everything feasible to verify that there were not more than, let us say, two civilians near a highway bridge used by the armed force, and, on the other hand, to infer his knowledge about the other twenty-five persons present on and by the bridge, from the fact that the bridge under normal circumstances is traversed by a minimum of twelve cars at any given time of the day. The latter is an example of turning a blind eye to obvious circumstances and may arguably fall within the ambit of the coinage 'intent and knowledge'.[51] Obviously, one can imagine numerous incidents where the facts of the commander's knowledge are not possible to infer so easily. Having stated the commander's knowledge about the facts, one could, by the main rule in article 30 and the General Introduction to the Elements of Crimes, hold the commander responsible for the crime if an assessment of the facts, according to a comparison with a reasonable commander's assessment of the facts, would amount to *clearly excessive collateral damage* in legal terms. With the additional 'footnote 37', however, the prosecution would have to prove that the commander in question him- or herself made this judgment. It is not a very likely procedure. It remains to be seen how the ICC will interpret the rule.

49 These numbers are from Cross, Dullum & Jensen-Jonez, 'Explosive weapons in populated areas', at pages 32–3.

50 See AP I article 57, dealt with in Chapter 15.

51 On 'wilful blindness' and its uncertain application under the Rome Statute, see Pigaroff and Robinson, 'Article 30: mental element', at page 1124.

6

Military Necessity and Humanitarian Considerations

6.1 THE POINT OF DEPARTURE: TO CONCILIATE MILITARY NECESSITY WITH HUMANITY

Humanitarian considerations pose a major limitation upon the commander's assessment of military necessity. These limiting considerations are the topic of this chapter.

Where the Lieber Code had been a comprehensive code of permissible and non-permissible conduct, the St Petersburg Declaration was originally drafted to establish an international ban on the use of a newly invented projectile.[1] The preamble, however, boldly states that the Declaration aspires to fix: '... the technical limits at which the necessities of war ought to yield to the requirements of humanity ...' These aspirations are repeated towards the end of the Declaration where the States have reserved the option to achieve further improvements adjusted to the technological developments of armaments, in order to: '... maintain the principles which they have established, and to conciliate the necessities of war with the laws of humanity'.[2]

These phrases are far more expansive than to ban a single type of ammunition. The quotation enshrines the underlying driving forces,[3] as mentioned above, of military necessity and humanitarian considerations which – throughout the modern history of the LOAC – has permeated the entire legal framework.[4]

[1] Best, *Humanity in Warfare*, at page 159.

[2] St Petersburg Declaration, the preamble.

[3] Dinstein, *Conduct of Hostilities*, at page 8.

[4] Hans Blix thus refers to military necessity and humanity, as described in the quotation from the St Petersburg Declaration, as 'The two pillars upon which the law of armed conflict rests.' See Blix, 'Area bombardment', at page 32.

6.2 HUMANITY AND NECESSITY: REMARKS ON A BALANCE

Two words found in the quotes are of guidance for performing the balance: *yield* and *conciliate*. When does military necessity have to *yield* to humanity and what lies in a *conciliation* of the two?[5] One answer to this question is found in the proportionality balance established in treaty law more than hundred years after the St Petersburg Declaration, and discussed in Chapter 13. At the present stage, however, we are concerned with the point of departure, the conceptual balance between two considerations.[6] Additional questions immediately arise. First of all, the substantive questions of the content of both military necessity and humanity, of which the first is the actual topic of this book. With regard to the content of humanity, however, this conceptual question is left for another forum. We are, however, going to address the questions of whether the balance is one of diametrically opposed concerns, what the legal status of humanity is with regard to necessity and the relative weight of the two concepts.

One conceptual point of departure can be found in the 1966 edition (by Tucker) of Kelsen's *Principles*, where it is asserted that:

> Mention must be made of the widely held belief that the principles of military necessity and humanity largely contradict one another, that they serve opposing purposes, and that it is the task of the law of war to attempt to balance considerations of military necessity against the requirements of humanity. This belief must be questioned. Rather than 'contradict' the principle of humanity, the principle of military necessity implies the former principle. The principle of necessity does not allow the employment of force unnecessary or superfluous to the purposes of war. Nor does the principle of humanity oppose human suffering or physical destruction as such. It is the unnecessary infliction of human suffering and the wanton destruction of property that is opposed, both by the principle of military necessity and by the principle of humanity.[7]

According to this conception (which seems, more or less, to be shared by other contemporaries), there is a *principle of humanity*, which is already *implied* in

5 See McCoubrey, 'The nature of the modern doctrine of military necessity' at page 221, which refers to this quotation as 'the essence of the enterprise'.

6 Schmitt argues that the 'balance between military necessity and necessity pervades IHL in both a general and a specific sense' and that the balance also appears as a 'foundational principle'. See Schmitt, 'Military necessity and humanity in international humanitarian law', at pages 799–800.

7 Kelsen and Tucker, *Principles of International Law*, at page 115, in footnote 112.

the principle of necessity.[8] This statement, however, presupposes a *relative* conception of humanity where human suffering is not considered to violate humanity unless the suffering is not unnecessary for the purpose of war. The argument seems tautological[9] because it presupposes that the balance between military necessity and humanity is already performed when the question of balance is presented. Having said this, tautology might to a certain extent not be avoided.[10] It seems more important to clarify at what level *humanity* is referred to: to a 'meta-juridical level'[11] or to rules expressed in positive law? An expression of the first is presented by Dinstein:

> In the final analysis, the law of international armed conflict is a product of reconciliation between demands of military necessity and humanitarian considerations. If military necessity were to prevail completely, belligerent parties would have full freedom of action, with a view to winning a war. If humanitarian considerations were the only guide to the conduct of hostilities, the waging of war would become impossible by dint of the death, injury, and suffering that unavoidably accompany it. The law of international armed conflict therefore takes a middle road, rendering unto military necessity what is due to it, while protecting and respecting at least a minimal level of humanitarianism even in the midst of hostilities.[12]

This passage reveals what humanity could entail if understood absolutely (and not relative to military necessity as shown in the quote by Kelsen and Tucker above), namely the absence of war. Similar positions (and more than fifty years earlier) are taken by Downey, arguing that 'This definition [of regulated violence] is a compromise between the conflicting *military* and *humanitarian* concepts of the purpose of war',[13] and by Schwarzenberger pointing out the tension between the 'standard of civilization' and the 'necessities of war',[14] as well as more recent literature. Pictet refers to 'The fundamental opposition between humanity and necessity . . .',[15] and Schmitt to 'often contradictory interests'.[16] Other scholars also present more or less

8 See also Greenspan, *The Modern Law of Land Warfare*, page 315, which states the following and attaches the statement to the St Petersburg Declaration: 'The second principle is that of humanity, which forbids the employment of all such kinds and degrees of violence as are not necessary for the purpose of war.'

9 McDougal and Feliciano, *Law and Minimum World Order*, at page 522.

10 Ibid., at pages 522–3.

11 Dinstein, 'The Principle of Proportionality', at page 73.

12 Dinstein, 'Military necessity', at para. 2.

13 Downey, 'The law of war and military necessity', at page 261.

14 Schwarzenberger, *International Law*, at page 135.

15 Pictet, *Development and Principles of International Humanitarian Law*, at pages 61–2.

16 Schmitt, 'Military necessity and humanity in international humanitarian law', at page 799.

loose references to a foundational balance, not necessarily emphasising whether the interests would always be at conflict.[17]

A further discussion of whether humanity is truly – and always – opposed to military necessity is primarily interesting for theoretical purposes.[18] There may certainly be cases where the best military solution, all things considered, is the one which also is best suited to save lives.[19] In this case one may say that military necessity coincides with humanity, but it is in reality only *better* for the purpose of humanity than another military alternative.[20] It is not the solution which considerations of humanity alone would prescribe, from the top of the shelf. The fact that some inhumane acts would not be militarily necessary (for example torture) does not alter the point of departure that military necessity and humanitarian considerations are opposing interests.[21]

6.3 THE STATUS OF 'HUMANITY': WHAT IS NECESSITY TO BE WEIGHED AGAINST?

To perform a balance between military necessity and humanity requires a certain conception of humanity. The obvious difficulty of defining humanity

17 See for example Draper, 'Military necessity and humanitarian imperatives', at page 129 arguing that the laws of war have 'sought to achieve some modest balance between military needs and the imperatives of humanitarianism'. In the same direction see McCoubrey, 'The nature of the modern doctrine of military necessity', at page 220, which aspires to 'examine the nature of military necessity and to derive therefrom a coherent theoretical base for the doctrine'; and Meron, 'Francis Lieber's Code and principles of humanity', at page 271.

18 Such critique is raised by Hayashi in 'Military necessity as normative indifference' where he denies a so-called 'inevitable conflict' that he attributes to Dinstein and Schmitt. See pages 688 ff. As part of this critique, on page 695 it is argued that 'The inevitable conflict book needs more than mere non-coincidence between material military necessity and descriptive humanity.' This argument is correct, provided that the book is actually one of *inevitable conflict* in strictly logical terms, and provided that strict logic is a requirement for the description of the values underpinning the LOAC. Both these presumptions, however, are incorrect, and thus so is the argument.

19 In this direction see Beer, 'Humanity considerations cannot reduce war's hazards alone', at pages 802–3 where he refers to economy of force and 'professional restraints' by the armed forces themselves. Beer further argues in favour of 'revitalizing' military necessity as a constraining principle, see for example page 807. I have sympathy for his views, but I do not share his arguments.

20 Such an example with the use of incendiary weapons is provided by Schmitt, 'Military necessity and humanity in international humanitarian law', at page 816. Hayashi comments that there is a 'limited possibility that military necessity and humanity may coincide', see Hayashi, 'Military necessity as normative indifference', at page 691.

21 See Hayashi, 'Military necessity as normative indifference', at pages 705–6 where he argues that military necessity and humanity align. The argument, however, does not show that warfare in any cases is truly *humane*, it simply shows that lawful warfare is less brutal than torture, due to considerations of humanity.

is pointed out by a number of authors,[22] and the concept of humanity appears in a different guise in the parts of international law touching upon armed conflict, from being referred to as a somewhat vague principle – applicable just as much in peacetime as in armed conflict – in the jurisprudence of the ICJ,[23] to a source of legal development in the Martens Clause (cited above, in its different versions, in Sections 1.6.1 and 4.4.1) and as a 'crime against humanity' in the statutes of international criminal tribunals.[24] It is, however, the Martens Clause which primarily has been linked to the question of the scope of 'humanity' under the LOAC. When it comes to the content (for remarks with regard to *status*, see Chapter 4) and status of 'humanity', the Martens Clause thus deserves some additional attention. Although being termed a 'principle' in legal literature,[25] the more correct reference to 'humanity' therefore seems to be to give 'considerations of humanity' a role to 'pave the road to the creation of legal norms and thus explain the evolution of IHL'.[26] Furthermore, the Clause is a reminder of the protection offered persons by

[22] For an overview, see Coupland, 'Humanity', pages 969–90. See also Hayashi, 'Military necessity as normative indifference', at page 688; and Larsen, Cooper and Nystuen, 'Introduction by the editors: is there a "principle of humanity" in international humanitarian law?', at page 1.

[23] Corfu Channel Case, *ICJ Reports* 1949, at page 4. At page 22 the Court affirms the duty for Albanian authorities to warn approaching vessels of the danger of mines in the water of the Corfu Channel and states that: 'Such obligations are based, not on the Hague Convention of 1907, No. VIII, which is applicable in time of war, but on certain general and well-recognized principles, namely: elementary considerations of humanity, even more exacting in peace than in war.' This phrase was recited by the Court both in the Legality of the Threat or Use of Nuclear Weapons, Advisory Opinion, as well as in the Jurisdictional Immunities of the State (*Germany* v. *Italy*: Greece intervening), Judgment, ICJ Reports 2012, at page 99, para. 52.

[24] See Rome Statute article 7, which defines 'crimes against humanity'.

[25] See Kelsen and Tucker, *Principles of International Law*. See also Greenspan, *The Modern Law of Land Warfare*, at page 315, which draws upon the St Petersburg Declaration and uses the principle of humanity as a circumvention of necessity; 'The second principle is that of humanity, which forbids the employment of all such kinds and degrees of violence as are not necessary for the purpose of war.' In the same direction, see Pictet, *Development and Principles of International Humanitarian Law*, at page 61, who states that: 'We might formulate the Principle of Human Law as follows: Military necessity and the maintenance of public order must always be compatible with respect for the human person.' Both statements are to be noted also with regard to the question of whether necessity is to be understood as an 'additional layer' upon otherwise lawful acts. This position is rejected also elsewhere in this book, see for example Chapters 9 and 13.

[26] Dinstein, 'The principle of proportionality', at page 73, where it is also stated: 'Humanity is not an obligation (or set of obligations) incorporated per se in positive IHL. There is no overarching, binding, norm of humanity that tells us what we must do (or not do) in wartime.' In the same direction see Schmitt's comments on the Martens Clause in Schmitt, 'Military necessity and humanity in international humanitarian law', at pages 800–1.

customary international law and not included in the codifying treaty text.[27] Having said this, more conceptual discussions of 'humanity' and the 'principle of humanity' may be valuable,[28] but nevertheless beyond the scope of this book, which aims to analyse military necessity rather than humanity.

6.4 PERFORMING THE BALANCE: A POINT OF DEPARTURE

Of more interest for the application of the law – and surely for this book – is the actual balancing of military necessities against humanitarian interests. We thus return to the question posted above, based on the wording from the St Petersburg Declaration: 'at what point ought the former to yield to the latter?'[29] Having stated that humanitarian considerations as such (when not expressed as positive law) serve as modest interpretative guidance, it is of interest to analyse the relative weight given these considerations. At the present stage, we are concerned with the general level, and only with the aim of establishing a point of departure. Chapters 14 and 15 are particularly concerned with the actual balance under the principle of proportionality, and the latitude given to the military while performing this balance.

A number of authors argue that a gradual shift has taken place in the period from the end of the nineteenth century and up until today: 'Historically, of course, the line of compromise has, more frequently than not, tended to be located closer to the polar terminus of military necessity than to that of humanity.'[30] And, in an even more unveiled manner with regard to the period until WWII: 'Throughout this period, military necessity reigned supreme, while humanity served primarily to protect the armed forces.'[31] Then, with regard to the shift: 'Since the nineteenth century, it has moved steadily in the direction of humanity and away from that of military necessity.'[32] Some even regard this shift as deeply problematic.[33] Others again point out the more pragmatic point of departure, that both considerations were: 'entirely

27 Meron, *The Humanization of International Law*, at page 27.

28 Two valuable contributions in this direction are Coupland, 'Humanity', and Larsen, Guldahl Cooper and Nystuen, 'Introduction by the editors: is there a "principle of humanity" in international humanitarian law?'

29 Kalshoven, *Reflections on the Law of War*, at page 370.

30 McDougal and Feliciano, *Law and Minimum World Order*, at page 523. In the same direction see Kolb, 'The main epochs of international humanitarian law since 1864', at pages 23–4.

31 Schmitt, 'Military necessity and humanity in international humanitarian law', at page 807. See as well Kalshoven, *Reflections on the Law of War*, at page 377.

32 Schmitt, 'Military necessity and humanity in international humanitarian law', at page 805. See as well Kolb, 'The main epochs of international humanitarian law since 1864', at page 33.

33 Reeves and Thurnher, 'Are we reaching a tipping point?', at page 12.

legitimate considerations in the eyes of the members of the International Military Commission, and they have remained so to the present day'.[34] Yet others point out that humanitarian considerations have not in fact contributed to mitigate the evils of war and hence that the constraining force of law should not lie on the 'thin shoulders' of humanitarian considerations alone.[35] I do not share this latter view. Although the law is not abided by, it does not necessarily mean that its meta-legal foundation is weak.

The relative weight devoted to military necessity in the actual practice of States was perhaps most visible through the doctrine of *Kriegsraison* which stemmed from German General Staff in the late half of the nineteenth century and granted the military huge discretion and 'absolute dependence' on military necessity.[36] Although most visible, and certainly most condemned, in the German *Kriegsraison* doctrine, the dependence on military necessity at the expense of humanity was by no means absent from the application of armed force by other States (among others those facing the German war machinery) during the same time span. With regard to the 'steady movement' in the direction of humanity throughout the twentieth century, this is without doubt true when it comes to arguments presented in the aftermath of WWII, such as: 'Not everything necessary for the purposes of war is allowed by the law of war'[37] – and also true with regard to the magnitude of treaty obligations – but whether the actual practice of States truly has moved in the humanity direction remains an open question.

6.5 'HEAVY-WEIGHT' NECESSITY: THE DOCTRINE OF *KRIEGSRAISON*

The doctrine of *Kriegsraison* appeared primarily in the German literature around the turn of the nineteenth century and aroused harsh critics both then and later. The birth of the doctrine must be seen in light of the views and publications of the German General Staff as well as the actual practice of the Prussian army.

6.5.1 *The Franco-Prussian War and the German General Staff*

The Franco-Prussian War of 1870–1 was one of the most decisive conflicts in the modern history of Europe and has given rise to considerable scholarly

34 Kalshoven, *Reflections on the Law of War*, at page 370.
35 Beer, 'Humanity considerations cannot reduce war's hazards alone', at page 802.
36 *Kriegsraison* and the German General Staff is dealt with into more detail in Section 6.5.
37 Kelsen and Tucker, *Principles of International Law*, at page 100.

analysis.[38] The Prussian Army was at the height of its strength,[39] led by the German General Staff and General von Moltke, and was directly subordinate to the Prussian king.[40]

The views presented in the German War Book and by Von Hartmann illustrate an era and an environment where the reference and importance devoted to 'military necessity' perhaps was at its all-time-high: 'The unmitigated conduct of war is to the good of humanity. Violently fought wars run a brief course.'[41]

And its parallel expression in the German War Book: '. . . all means which modern inventions afford, including the fullest, most massive, and most dangerous, means of destruction, may be utilized; these last, just because they attain the object of war as quickly as possible, are on that account to be regarded as indispensable and, when closely considered, the most human.'[42] This view, that short, sharp and brutal wars are the most humane, turned into a trade-mark for the German militarism in the same epoch.[43] Such way of promoting 'humanism' is evident all through the views of Von Hartmann, and has later acquired negative connotations, with only a few exceptions[44] – although State practice during WWII were prone to the same thinking when dropping the atomic bomb.[45] Von Hartmann argues that 'civilized warfare' is meaningless, if by civilization one understands the 'equilibrium of rights and duties',[46] and furthermore that 'civilized warfare' contains an 'inevitable contradiction': that wars can be fought humanely, but that they cannot be fought in a 'civilized manner'.[47] Hartmann does not, however, regard 'the concepts of war and humanity' as 'mutually exclusive',[48] it is only the idea of 'civilized warfare' which to Hartmann appears as absurd – and the weight openly attributed to military necessity is clear: 'Military necessity and humanity must be weighed against the other; now one will prevail, now the other', and in times of conflict: 'the necessity of attaining a military end must always be the

38 For an account of the most important works in this regard, see Howard, *The Franco-Prussian War*.
39 Holborn, 'The Prusso-German School', at pages 286–7.
40 Ibid., at page 284.
41 From the translation in Andler, *'Frightfulness' in Theory and Practice*, at pages 75–6.
42 German War Book, page 65.
43 See as well Adler, 'Targets in war', at pages 13–14.
44 A fairly recent (and thus rare) view in the same direction – but with no further comparative points – can be found in Luttwak, 'Give war a chance'.
45 Adler, 'Targets in war', at page 14.
46 From Andler, *'Frightfulness' in Theory and Practice*, page 77.
47 Ibid.
48 Ibid., at page 85.

deciding motive'.[49] This clear weighting in favour of military necessity did not, however, seem to allow absolutely everything: 'acts of brutality committed upon unarmed persons, pillage, and the gathering of booty were regarded as crimes'.[50] Then, the role of military necessity is given the most prominent place; 'once war is declared only the demands of military necessity have the force of law'.[51]

The exclusive reference to military necessity as the sole legal principle applicable must also be seen in its military-political context: Prussia (and later Germany) found itself in an existential war with France – and the existential character of that war seemed to have been perceived as a permanent feature of war as such.[52] Both the German War Book and Von Hartmann acknowledge full discretion for the military commander in the field. The German War Book refers to the commanders' 'subjective freedom and arbitrary judgment', only *guided* by 'the precepts of civilization, freedom and honour, the traditions prevalent in the army and the general usages of war'.[53] Von Hartmann has been said to recognise only two limitations upon warfare: the ethical and legal convictions *of the warrior* himself and considerations of reciprocity.[54] Thus, the warrior himself was expected to show the most disciplined chivalry and to determine upon the content of military necessity.[55] The view of Von Hartmann has, by critics, not been regarded as representative for the realities which took place during the Franco-Prussian War.[56] Whether the Prussian soldiers actually were in possession of the chivalrous temper is one question, whether the decision is to be left to them alone is another, yet related, question. That the views of Von Hartmann and Germany were at odds with the contemporary, international *conception* of law seems undoubted, but whether the actual practice of *other* States also differed clearly from the German views is another matter to be examined below. The dissonant *perceived conception* of law was for example visible in the preamble of the 1899 Hague Convention which states the following as a prelude to the Martens Clause:[57] 'On the other hand, it

49 Ibid., at page 87.

50 Ibid.

51 Ibid., at page 81.

52 Hull, 'Military necessity and the laws of war in Imperial Germany', at pages 356–60.

53 German War Book page 64. On subjectivity and discretion in general, see Chapter 4.

54 See also O'Brien, 'The meaning of "military necessity" in international law', at page 125, where he also cites the German War Book and emphasises the German dismissal of the binding force of the law.

55 Hull, 'Military necessity and the laws of war in Imperial Germany', at pages 356–60. See Chapter 4 for a more thorough discussion of the military margin of appreciation.

56 Andler *'Frightfulness' in Theory and Practice*, at page 48, criticises that the soldiers are to be sole judges of military necessity.

57 On the Martens Clause, see Section 6.3 and Chapter 4.

could not be intended by the High Contracting Parties that the cases not provided for should, for want of a written provision, be left to the *arbitrary judgment of the military commanders.*'[58] This judgment of the military commander was therefore a pivotal point of disagreement, where one view regarded it as potentially 'arbitrary' and where another (the Prussian) saw it as the only sensible way to conduct warfare.

During the 1870s, Prussia had been working against the Codification attempts at the Brussels Conference in 1874[59] (but had accepted the Geneva Convention of 1864), because it was held that rules had to accrue out of practice, and that the suggested legal framework did not.[60] Von Hartmann explored his views on the legal framework as follows:

> States may proclaim a code of war which prescribes, to the military powers, certain fixed rules of humanity. But the same states must not be guided in such matters by the general principles of law; they must eliminate from their stipulations all that might in any way hamper or compromise the liberty and conformity of military action; so that here again they *are absolutely dependant on the particular concrete circumstances which are entailed by war; that is to say, on military necessity.*[61]

His dependence on reality, here shown by the phrase 'particular concrete circumstances' (regarded as realism[62]) was further substantiated by his meta-perspective on legal regulations of warfare: 'The Utopian idea of war construed a priori must be abandoned.'[63] Hence, war had to be seen as 'variable kind' and therefore the circumstances of war were 'object of a subjective appreciation which, when a decision must be taken, can recognize no other law than that of military necessity'.[64] In simple words: military necessity was the only legal rule suitable to adjust to the realities of war.

6.5.2 *The Doctrine As Presented by Scholars*

It has been said that *Kriegsraison* 'means military necessity and is linked with the basic right of self-preservation of States'.[65] An early version of the doctrine

58 Convention (II) with respect to the Laws and Customs of War on Land (1899 Hague Convention). Emphasis added.
59 On the Brussels Conference, see further above, Chapter 3.
60 Hull, 'Military necessity and the laws of war in Imperial Germany', at pages 356–60.
61 From Andler, *'Frightfulness' in Theory and Practice*, at page 81. Emphasis added.
62 See Hull, 'Military necessity and the laws of war in Imperial Germany', at pages 356–60.
63 From Andler, *'Frightfulness' in Theory and Practice*, at page 81.
64 Ibid., at page 82.
65 O'Brien, 'The meaning of "military necessity" in international law', at pages 119–20.

was represented (among others) by the German lawyer Lueder,[66] who later became to be regarded as a proponent of the famous doctrine.[67] The views of Lueder have also somewhat imprecisely been described as 'Lieber without limitations'.[68] The core of the doctrine of *Kriegsraison*, which later was subjected to massive condemnation,[69] was a twofold exemption from the laws of war: in cases of extreme necessity, where the object of war could not be achieved without non-observance of the rules, and in cases of retaliation where the enemy has performed unlawful non-observance of the laws of war.[70] It is in its first form that the *Kriegsraison* has been considered most controversial. The proponents of the *Kriegsraison* doctrine argued strongly for deviation from the laws of war in order achieve the 'supreme object of war: breaking the enemy will and winning the war'.[71]

When the argument of *Kriegsraison* received such harsh criticism it was not because necessity gave reason for exemptions from the law – which it did, also according to treaty law. It was said to be due to the 'limitless fashion in which it was advocated'.[72] The reference to 'limitless' is a truth subject to modifications, but it may serve as a point of departure.

Kriegsraison in its most crude form implies that *any conduct* in principle may be justified by reference to extreme necessity. In other words, the doctrine implies that no prohibitions are truly absolute. Such a view seems to be in contrast to that advocated in the early modern times, and as shown above, by Gentili, Grotius and de Vattel, as well as in the St Petersburg Declaration.[73] Perhaps the most prominent critique against the doctrine by Lueder's

66 von Holtzendorff, *Handbuch des Völkerrechts*, at page 255 ff. See also von Liszt, *Das Völkerrecht*. Liszt confines his presentation to merely a reference to the *Kriegsraison* as necessity, and then exemplifies some cases with regard to the withholding of neutral merchant ships and the sale of enemy property. Lueder's other contemporary, von Ullmann, 'Völkerrecht', is commented upon below.

67 Westlake, *International Law*; O'Brien, 'The meaning of "military necessity" in international law'; Best, *Humanity in Warfare*, at page 172.

68 Best, *Humanity in Warfare*, at page 172.

69 See further Section 6.6.

70 See von Holtzendorff, *Handbuch des Völkerrechts*, at page 255. See also Best *Humanity in Warfare*, at page 173. See as well O'Brien 'The meaning of "military necessity" in international law'. This twofold approach was also upheld outside Germany, see for example Kleen, *Kodificerad Handbok i Krigets Lagar*, pages 88–9. On Kleen, see further Section 6.5.3.

71 Lueder, 'Krieg und Kriegsrecht', pages 255–6, and Best, *Humanity in Warfare*, page 174. On general observations of the 'object of war', see Chapter 2.

72 Best, *Humanity in Warfare*, page 173.

73 Lueder himself referred to the writings of Grotius and Pufendorf: see 'Krieg und Kriegsrecht', at page 256. The limitations entailed therein are, however, not cited.

contemporaries was raised, among others, by Westlake,[74] who argued that the real question raised under the term *Kriegsraison* was whether the success of war was to break down the legal code – 'a code in which humanity to the enemy on the one side, and the essential needs of war on the other, have been considered'.[75] Westlake's critique of Lueder has to be set in perspective. First, Lueder published his works in 1889, before the binding and comprehensive regulations in the 1899 Hague Conventions (but, truly, after the adoption of the St Petersburg Declaration in 1868 and the Brussels Declarations in 1874). Westlake, on his side, published his critique *after* the adoption of the Hague Conventions. The impact on the doctrine of *Kriegsraison* of the adoption of the Hague Conventions is discussed in a quite thorough analysis done by Max Huber in 1913. I shall return to the views of Max Huber just below. Second, Lueder advocated that the invocation of *Kriegsraison* was entirely exceptional.[76] This view was endorsed by his contemporary, Ullmann, stating that the *Kriegsraison* were to be invoked only if it was a question of (for example) surrendering the existence of the state, and – even more – Ullmann held that *Kriegsraison* was not to be applied without limits: some rules were of an absolute binding character 'unbedingt bindende Kraft', such as for example the use of poisonous weapons and the resort to perfidy.[77] Westlake *could* therefore (if he was offering the German authors the benefit of the doubt) view the German arguments as an illustration of the difference between State practice[78] and treaty law. Third, it is doubtful whether the critique was truly of a purely humanitarian character, but rather primarily reasoned by considerations of reciprocity.[79] After all, Westlake also acknowledged the institute of reprisals as a matter of law, even though their status and content were left unclear after the diplomatic conferences at Brussels and at The Hague.[80] Unconditional humanitarian considerations were excluded, because of the general participation clause also in the Hague Conventions.[81]

74 Westlake, *International Law: Part II: War*. See in particular page 115. Westlake here concurs with later conceptions of how the balance between military necessity and humanity is expressed in treaty law.

75 Westlake, *International Law*, at pages 244–6.

76 Lueder, 'Krieg und Kriegsrecht', at page 255.

77 See von Ullmann, 'Völkerrecht'. O'Brien, 'The meaning of "military necessity" in international law', comments von Ullmann's views at page 123, but for some reason leaves out this important point.

78 On State practice in the same period, see above.

79 On reciprocal arguments during the Franco-Prussian War and the South African War, see above.

80 See Westlake, *International Law*, at pages 112–15.

81 See article 2 in the 1899 and 1907 Hague Conventions. The treaty only applies directly (notwithstanding the question of application of the content as customary law) in cases where all the belligerents are parties to the Convention.

Fourth, the scholarly discussions of the doctrine of *Kriegsraison* must also be viewed in their broader historical context – as presented above – where British writers in a response to the threat from a (militaristically) strong, united Germany 'showed themselves less inclined than their Teutonic cousins to glorify war as the supreme act of the State, and adopted a more pragmatic and defensive approach to the military problems which confronted them'.[82]

The doctrine of *Kriegsraison* has been attributed primarily to German writers, but there were also proponents in other countries highly influenced by German thoughts. One such example is found by the Swede, Richard Kleen, who belonged to the Swedish Ministry of Defence and embraced the doctrine in 1909. With regard to the two aspects of reprisals and necessity, Kleen holds the latter to be the one of controversy.[83] With regard to *Kriegsraison* as necessity he claims that: 'one cannot expect *Kriegsmanier* from a small people being assaulted by a greater, in the defence of their homeland against barbaric lust for personal gain'.[84] He then uses the Boer against the Englishmen, and the Spanish guerrillas against the French invasion as examples. He further holds that another controversial aspect is that whether the war against 'uncivilized opponents' and 'wild peoples' can set aside all *Kriegsmanier*.[85] Kleen does not dismiss the argument completely; he argues the rules cannot be set aside in their entirety, but keeps the possibility open for a 'middle road' where *Kriegsraison* can be used as ground for reprisals if the uncivilised opponent does not abide by the rules – and he reminds that the 'laws of war' apply between 'civilized nations'.[86] This last point resembles a mixture of a reference to reprisals and to necessity. The views of Kleen is not visible in the works of later Swedish authors or governmental reports, or in any other Scandinavian representative literature for that matter. The particular development in Sweden is dealt with separately in Section 6.5.3.

The pre-WWI doctrine of *Kriegsraison* was subject to thorough a discussion in an article by Max Huber, published in 1913. Some emphasis is to be placed on the article here. Huber addresses the question which is left out by Westlake: the relationship between the earlier unwritten *Kriegsmanier* and the later treaty law in the Hague Conventions from 1899 and 1907. Huber addresses

82 Howard, 'Empire, Race and War in pre-1914 Britain', at page 10.

83 Kleen, *Kodificerad Handbok i Krigets Lagar*, pages 88–9.

84 Ibid., at page 89. My translation from Swedish. The Swedish text says: 'man kan ikke forvente krigsmaner av et lite folk som blir overfalt av en stor til forsvar av sitt fosterland mot barbarisk vinningslyst'.

85 Ibid., at page 90. The terms are translated by me from Swedish to English. The Swedish terms are 'vilda folkslag' and 'uciviliserade motstandere'.

86 Ibid., at page 91.

four different situations of necessity: *Staatsnotwendigkeit* (in order to preserve vital interests of the State), *Kriegsnotwendigkeit* (in order to achieve the purpose[87] of war (in order for example to place a capital under siege)), *militärische Notwendigkeit* (in order to accomplish a single military operation) and *eigentlicher Notstand* (in order to save the life of a single person).[88] He then distinguishes between 'Recht' and 'Sitte'/'Manier', where the first is understood as unconditionally binding, while the latter is to be understood as what is usually adhered to ('was regelmäßig beobachtet wird').[89] *Kriegsmanier* was not to be adhered to in the case of *Kriegsraison*.[90] According to Huber, the real question arises after the codification of major parts of the Law of War (*Kriegsrechts*) through treaties in 1899 and 1907: whether the binding force of treaty norms, through *Kriegsraison*, through military necessity, could also be set aside.[91] This question he answers separately for each of the four different situations of necessity just mentioned.

With regard to 'Staatsnotwendigkeit', he argues that the answer is affirmative because: 'wenn die Erfüllung Eier Plicht mit der Existenz, Unabhängigkeit, wesentlichen Lebensbedingungen und der moralischen Integrität eines Staates unvereinbar ist, dann diese Pflicht dahinfällt, . . .'[92] Huber adds that such situations, were the existing conventions to be set aside, are hardly thinkable.[93]

When it comes to 'Kriegsnotwendigkeit', limitations are imposed first and foremost with regard to the enemy population in land warfare.[94] The question therefore arises whether *Kriegsraison* can justify terrorising the enemy population and to weaken the economy of the enemy State.[95] Huber points out that even before the Hague Conferences, freedom of people and property was recognised in international law, and the St Petersburg Declaration had established that the fight was to take place (only) against the enemy troops.[96] He then contrasts the picture by referring to State practice subsequent to the

87 I have translated the term 'Zweck' as 'purpose'. Huber also use the term 'Ziel' in a different place in the article, when apparently addressing the same concept. See Huber, 'Die kriegsrechtlichen Verträge und die Kriegsraison', at pages 354 and 365 respectively.

88 Ibid., pages 354–5.

89 Ibid., at page 361.

90 Ibid., at page 362.

91 Ibid., at page 363.

92 Ibid., at page 364.

93 Ibid.

94 Ibid., at page 356.

95 Ibid., at page 366. Questions which bear a connection to the question of the relationship between means and ends and how the ends are formulated, see further Chapter 2.

96 Ibid.

St Petersburg Declaration, but prior to the Hague Conventions, in order to show examples of either explicit or implicit reference to measures against the peaceful, enemy population. He argues that the measures taken against the Franc-tireurs in the Franco-Prussian War[97] came pretty close to terrorising the population and, furthermore, that the British use of concentration camps in the English–Boer war[98] deprived the civilians of their rights which were later codified in the Hague Convention of 1907 article 46.[99] He concludes that the law (he then refers to the binding Hague Convention) could only be disregarded on the basis of 'Kriegsnotwendigkeit' when the situation resembled that of 'Staatsnotwendigkeit'.[100] Huber furthermore recognises the existence of a 'militarische Notwendigkeit', which concerns the actual conduct of hostilities, and thus perhaps is what is most commonly referred to as the core of the *Kriegsraison.*[101] In this connection he appears to attempt to enlighten as well as justify its area of application and explain why the criticism against the doctrine has been so harsh (without referring to the exact critique, for example by Westlake). He emphasises the binding force of the law[102] and the exceptional character of the *Kriegsraison.* Furthermore, he dismisses the idea that their adherence is solely up to the discretion of each party, and thus seems to be at odds with what had been preached by Von Hartmann and the German General Staff earlier.[103] Then he turns to the circumstances at the Diplomatic Conferences, reminding that every treaty is a compromise and that each situation (in war) is not the same for the contracting parties.[104] He argues that during the discussions at the Brussels in 1874 and at The Hague in 1899, reservations towards the *Kriegsraison* were growing as a reflection of the growing uncertainties with regard to the discussions of the content of treaty law.[105]

Huber seems to imply that these reservations were merely a state of confusion and thus did not express a diminished role for *Kriegsraison* as a matter of

97 On the Franco-Prussian War and the methods taken against the Franc-tireurs, see further Section 6.5.1.

98 On the Boer War as an example, see also above, where Kleen uses this war as an example where the Boer could possibly have relied on the *Kriegsraison* for their defence in their fight against the English.

99 See Huber, 'Die kriegsrechtlichen Verträge und die Kriegsraison', page 367. The wording of article 46 says: 'Family honour and rights, the lives of persons, and private property, as well as religious convictions and practice, must be respected. Private property cannot be confiscated.'

100 Ibid., at page 367.

101 Ibid., at page 368.

102 Ibid., at page 369.

103 Ibid., at page 370.

104 Ibid., at page 372.

105 Ibid.

law. A point of view which might not prove entirely wrong; after all the discussions of *reprisals* surely did not succeed at the Brussels Conference, which in turn left an unsolved question in international debate up until the adoption of the Additional Protocols in 1977.[106]

Despite Huber's wholehearted attempt – and influential views – of revitalising the doctrine in a nuanced version, the term has remained understood in a highly disparaging way throughout the aftermath of these early discussions.[107] It should also be pointed out that the *Kriegsraison* was not understood as 'the German doctrine' even at the turn of the last century.[108] Its much detested aura must be seen in relation to the attempts by the German accused war criminals during the Nuremberg trials after WWII of relying on the doctrine as a valid criminal defence. The modern rejection of *Kriegsraison* is accounted for in Section 6.6.2.

6.5.3 *A Note on the Swedish Development: from* Kriegsraison *to Non-existence*

The view of the role of military necessity has undergone a remarkable development in Sweden and is therefore worth some specific remarks. The Swedish development shows a noticeable path away from reliance on military necessity: from the great importance devoted to military necessity in the writings of Kleen[109] at the turn of the last century and up until today – where military necessity does not seem to flourish in Swedish thinking almost at all. In Sweden, the LOAC[110] has been subject to two public reports during the last thirty years, where the concept of military necessity has moved from being marginal to apparently non-existent. Under the discussions that led to the 1984 report,[111] the International Law Committee (*Folkrättskomitten*) did not find

[106] See Best, *Humanity in Warfare*, at page 171.

[107] Examples from early post-WWII literature include, but are not limited to, Oppenheim and Lauterpacht, *Disputes, War and Neutrality*, at pages 231–3, where Oppenheim supports Westlake; O'Brien, 'The meaning of "military necessity" in international law', at page 128; Dunbar, 'Military necessity in war crimes trials', at pages 444–5; Downey, 'The law of war and military necessity', at pages 253–4. Kelsen and Tucker, *Principles of International Law*, at page 100, who do not refer to the term *Kriegsraison*, but treat the concept as a wide version of necessity; Schwarzenberger, *International Law*, at page 136. See also Best, *War and Law since 1945*, at page 188.

[108] O'Brien, 'The meaning of "military necessity" in international law', at page 128.

[109] See Section 6.5.2, Kleen, *Kodificerad Handbok i Krigets Lagar*. Kleen's view was comparable to the German writers advocating the reviled *Kriegsraison* doctrine.

[110] The Swedish documents use the term 'international humanitarian law' (IHL), but for reasons of consistency on this book, I use the term LOAC.

[111] Folkrätten i krig, Statens Offentliga Utredningar (SOU) 1984:56.

anything in the development of international law which indicated that military necessity was to exist as a 'general and overarching principle'.[112] Whereas in the 2010 report – which entailed a proposition for a Swedish manual on international humanitarian law – the step is taken even further, where no definition of military necessity can be found. The phrase 'military necessity' is mentioned, but then, inter alia, with regard to the principle of proportionality, because the latter establishes a 'link between military necessity and the requirement of humanity'.[113] Sweden has, in a short time, gone from one extreme to the other. From heavy reliance upon military necessity to virtually none.

6.6 THE GENERAL RULE OF LIMITATION: DENIAL OF *KRIEGSRAISON*

6.6.1 *A Rule Placing Limitations upon Military Necessity*

Although being referred to as 'unsuccessful' in one matter and as 'scarcely ever applicable due to the general participation clause',[114] the 1899 and the 1907 Hague Conventions concerning the Laws and Customs of War on Land were the first steps towards comprehensive treaty regulations governing the conduct of hostilities.[115] Parts of the treaty texts are, as in other diplomatic products, unmistakably vague, possibly wide and also abstract, due to States' unwillingness to 'give away anything that could be of use'[116] to them. Therefore, 'the best we have' should not be a shameful argument – bearing in mind that diplomatic success is a novelty – at least in this area of the law.

As indicated in their preambles, military necessity permeates the whole framework. This basic premise has found the following expression in the text of the 1907 Hague Convention: 'According to the views of the High Contracting Parties, these provisions, the wording of which has been inspired by the desire to diminish the evils of war, as far as military requirements permit, are intended to serve as a general rule of conduct for the belligerents in their mutual relations and in their relations with the inhabitants.' The

112 Bring and Körlof-Askholt, *Folkrätt i krig, kris och fredsoperationer*, at page 76. The translation is mine.

113 *Folkrätt i væpnad konflikt: svensk tolkning och tillempning*, SOU 2010:72 Attachment 7, see page 47. The Swedish text says: 'Proportionalitetsprincipen etablerar en lank mellan militär nödvendighet och kravet på humanitet.'

114 Oeter, 'Methods and means of combat', at page 116.

115 Best, 'Restraint in war', at page 19.

116 Ibid., at page 20.

quoted passage from the 1907 text is the same as the 1899 text, with the exception of the replacement of the phrase 'military necessities', which appeared in the 1899 text, with the phrase from the St Petersburg Declaration: 'military requirements'. These two different phrases, however, appear to be synonyms.[117] Actually, the preamble has been taken to express three principles, out of which military necessity is the most dominant.[118]

The general, 'basic' rule imposing limitations on the use of weapons is, however, found in article 22: 'The right of belligerents to adopt means of injuring the enemy is not unlimited.'[119] The rule is often mentioned in close connection with the concept of military necessity,[120] such as by Adler: 'Although military necessity was a primary consideration in The Hague Conventions, it was implicitly limited to the use of only that degree of force which is required to attain a given objective.'[121] The rule of limitation codified, in an abstract manner, parameters for the balance set out above, between military necessity and humanitarian considerations.[122] Just as much as this rule has been viewed to encapsulate the balancing of necessities of war with the requirements of humanity, it has been seen as a reference to the prohibitions in the existing legal framework:[123] 'Consequently, many writers considered that military necessity was discounted when the rules of warfare were drawn up, and that their strict observance is only to be relaxed when reprisals are warranted.'[124]

Even though gaining almost unanimous support in its aftermath, this point was contested by some, in particular German, authors at its time of adoption.

117 See below. In article 15 the replacement has taken place the 'other way around', which can indicate that the swopping of words is merely random. See for example also Dunbar, 'Military necessity in war crimes trials', at page 444, treating the reference to military requirements as a reference to military necessity. See also Schwarzenberger, *International Law*, at page 128 which explicitly regards the two terms (and other terms) as synonyms.

118 Greenspan, *The Modern Law of Land Warfare*. The two other principles referred to are those of humanity (taken from the St Petersburg Declaration) and chivalry.

119 For the reference to 'basic', see Oeter, 'Methods and means of combat', at page 122.

120 Greenspan, *The Modern Law of Land Warfare*, at page 314. AP I Commentary, at page 390, uses this provision as the point of departure for the whole discussion of military necessity. Oeter, 'Methods and means of combat', at page 122: 'The formula puts in a nutshell the customary principle that any act of warfare should be guided by the requirements of military necessity.'

121 Adler, 'Targets in war: legal considerations', at page 15. In seemingly the same direction, see also Beer, 'Humanity considerations cannot reduce war's hazards alone', at page 807.

122 Bothe, Partsch and Solf, *New Rules*, at page 224.

123 Ibid., at pages 224–5 and Best, 'Restraint in war', at page 17.

124 Dunbar, 'Military necessity in war crimes trials', at page 444. For a similar position, see Oppenheim and Lauterpacht, *Disputes, War and Neutrality*, at page 231.

This dissent was seen in the much contested doctrine of *Kriegsraison*,[125] which warrants military necessity an *in principle* unlimited exceptional role, also with regard to treaty provisions.

The rule of limitation has thus been standing solid until the present day and has been reaffirmed in the AP I article 35(1): 'In any armed conflict, the right of the Parties to the conflict to choose methods or means of warfare is not unlimited.' In the AP I provision the scope of the article is broadened to encompass both *methods* as well as means of warfare, nevertheless maintaining a solid status as an expression of customary law.[126] In AP I article 35 the reference to 'not unlimited' is by the ICRC held both as an opposition to the old doctrine of *Kriegsraison*, and as a statement that there are no situations which can preclude the wrongfulness of a State by reference to a 'State of Necessity'.[127]

The wording of the AP I provision is reiterated in the military manuals of today[128] and also linked directly to the view presented above 'that military necessity does not justify any exception ... unless such an exception is expressly stated in the Rule'.[129]

As the heading of this sub-section indicates, the rule of limitation *limits* considerations of military necessity to what is otherwise permitted by the LOAC. For this reason, I find it misleading to label military necessity as such as a limitation.[130] Other scholars argue the opposite, that military necessity is a 'restraining principle'.[131] However, reflections of military necessity do work as limitations – such as the prohibitions on unnecessary suffering (see Chapter 9) and wanton destruction of property (see Chapter 16). Nevertheless, it is a conceptual difference between stating that military necessity is limiting conduct and that the resort to military necessity is limited. The latter is certainly true (e.g. military necessity cannot be invoked to justify terror attacks, to pursue purely political aims or to set aside other prohibitions: *Kriegsraison*), while the former is confusing at best. The different appearances of limitations

125 See Section 6.5.

126 Bothe, Partsch and Solf, *New Rules*, at page 223, AP I Commentary, at page 390, Dinstein, *Conduct of Hostilities*, at page 4.

127 See AP I Commentary, at paras. 1386 and 1387.

128 The provision in the German manual is found in rule 142, at page 25. In the UK Manual, it is simply stated that 'The means to achieve military victory are not unlimited', see page 23.

129 AMW Manual rule 4, at page 62.

130 In the same direction, see Schmitt, cited in Section 2.6, where I also argue that military necessity should be viewed (in essence) as permissive, subject to prohibitions.

131 See for example Venturini, 'Necessity in the law of armed conflict and in international criminal law', at page 48; Beer, 'Humanity considerations cannot reduce war's hazards alone', at page 807; and Blum, 'The fog of victory', at page 415.

upon military necessity, and the commander's assessment of it, is a core element of this book. In the present chapter, the focus is on humanitarian considerations as basic limitations upon military necessity.

6.6.2 *Military Necessity As a Limited Exception*

In the ICRC Commentary, military necessity is referred to as the 'necessity for measures which are essential to attain the goals of war, and which are lawful in accordance with the laws and customs of war. Consequently a rule of the law of armed conflict cannot be derogated from by invoking military necessity unless this possibility is explicitly provided for by the rule in question.'[132] The passage contains two (main) aspects, which both are introduced in Chapter 2: first, the question of the relationship between means and ends, expressed by '*essential* to attain *the goals of war*' and, second, the denial of a possibility to use military necessity as an exception beyond what is provided for in the rule in question – in practice a denial of *Kriegsraison*. The second aspect is the point of primary concern here and has been firmly established since the aftermath of WWII both during the Nuremberg trials and by States' military manuals.[133] As a response to the German plea of *Kriegsraison* during the war crimes trials, the US Tribunal stated in the Hostage Case that: 'Military necessity or expediency do not justify a violation of positive rules. International law is prohibitive law. ... The rights of the innocent population therein set forth must be respected even if military necessity or expediency decree otherwise.'[134] And later, in the High Command Case:

> ... the doctrine of military necessity has been widely urged. In the various treatises on International Law there has been much discussion on this question. It has been the viewpoint of many German writers and to a certain extent has been contended in this case that military necessity includes the right to do anything that contributes to the winning of a war.[135]

Also in the Krupp case, the US Military Tribunal emphasised that: 'War is by definition a risky and hazardous business' and that the rules are designed

132 AP I Commentary, at para. 1389.

133 See for example: US DoD Manual, para. 2.2.2.1 at pages 53–4, German Manual, at para. 142, page 25, Norwegian Manual, para. 1.25, page 14, *Militærmanual om folkeret for danske væbnede styrker in internationale militære operationer* (Danish Manual), page 110, Canadian Manual, para. 202 at page 2-1, and UK Manual, at para. 2.3, page 23. See as well the NATO AAP-6, cited in Section 2.3 above.

134 Hostage Case, at pages 66–7.

135 *United States* v. *Wilhelm von Leeb et al.* (High Command Case), at page 93.

specifically for all phases of the war.[136] By the same token, post-WWII case law is clear on the relationship between treaty and customary law (as introduced in Section 1.6): the rejection of invoking *Kriegsraison* covers both customary and treaty law – there was no exceptional military necessity which had survived the treaty process at the Hague.[137] This point is unaltered – and even reaffirmed (see the ICRC Commentary above) – after the adoption of the GC I–IV and the AP I.

The position taken at Nuremberg and in States' manuals also appears uncontroversial among legal scholars.[138] The clear point of departure, despite confusion, seems to arise when some scholars and practitioners are confronted with specific cases. By way of illustration, Henderson poses the following question: 'At the individual level, the question might arise whether a soldier could use a weapon otherwise prohibited under IHL in defence against a lawful attack where the attack would without use of the prohibited weapon be likely to cause serious death or injury to the soldier'.[139] The answer to the question is clear. A prohibited weapon cannot be used to avoid death or injury. This lies at the core of the statement made in the Krupp case cited above – that war is a risky business by definition.

Military necessity can be invoked as an exception in a number of situations as accounted for in treaty law. Traditionally, the rule permitting destruction of enemy property when imperatively required by military necessity has been among those provisions of most practical relevance for the conduct of hostilities. Apart from this rule, the 1907 Hague Regulations provided for exceptional military necessity in two contexts worth mentioning today. First, with regard to prisoners of war (POWs): their internment[140] and their eventual acts of insubordination[141] and, second, with regard to facilities for the performance

[136] *In re Krupp and others* v. *US Military Tribunal at Nuremberg*, page 628.

[137] High Command Case, at page 89 ff. where it is stated that the Hague Conventions binding as declaratory law, even if the state was not a party to the Convention.

[138] See for example Dunbar, 'Military necessity in war crimes trials', at page 451. Oppenheim and Lauterpacht, *Disputes, War and Neutrality*, at page 233. Downey, 'The law of war and military necessity', at pages 253–4. Dinstein, *Conduct of Hostilities*, at page 10. See also Solis, *The Law of Armed Conflict*, at page 261, citing the High Command Case.

[139] Henderson, *The Contemporary Law of Targeting*, at page 35, footnote 73. Henderson himself dismisses the argument at page 38, with reference to the Krupp case.

[140] Conditions of internment of POWs 'cannot be confined except as in indispensable measure of safety *and only while the circumstances which necessitate the measure continue to exist*'. Emphasis added on the text amended from the 1899 to the 1907 Hague Convention.

[141] In the 1907 Hague Convention, article 8 it is stated: 'Any act of insubordination justifies the adoption towards them of such measures of severity as may be considered necessary.'

of the humane tasks of relief personnel.[142] Today, military necessity appears as an exceptive clause in numerous provisions in GC I–IV and in the AP I (in addition to the appearances under Hague law). A brief account of the different appearances of military necessity (and its corresponding different aggravations) under Geneva law is given in Section 2.8. As pointed out there, the differences in wording (both with regard to necessity as such and with regard to the adjectival aggravation, such as 'absolute' and 'imperative') hardly reflect differences in substance. For the purpose of the present sub-section, this means that the invocation by a military commander of a limited exception from conduct which is otherwise prohibited, more often than not, will have the same (in gravity) scope of application. Regrettably, the differences in wording may not provide additional clarity for commanders in the field. A number of the core specific rules providing special protection, and the loss of such due to military necessity, are the topic of Chapter 17.

6.6.3 *Limitation but Not Necessarily a 'Limited War'*

The reference to limitations should not be confused with a duty to conduct a 'limited war'. In the ICRC Commentary to AP I the following is stated:

> Thus the first Section of Part III '(Methods and means of warfare)' is concerned with the reaffirmation of these principles. This implies *accepting the principle of limited warfare,* as opposed to total warfare which discards all rules. It has a key function in relation to the other provisions of the Protocol, since non-respect for the rules of combat entails non-respect for all other rules. It should be considered as a constructive reaffirmation of the law of The Hague.[143]

This view should not be a source of confusion over a *practice* of limited warfare with the notion of military necessity or – even worse – as a prohibition of engaging in an existential war mobilising the entire nation. Some authors argue that this rule (of limitation) relies on a 'final rejection of the idea of "total war"' and that the 'principle of limited warfare' is 'intimately connected to' the condition of 'military necessity' in this regard.[144] While the rule prohibits

[142] Ibid., article 15 it is stated that their performance is subject to 'the bounds imposed by military necessities and administrative regulations'. In this provision 'military necessities' has replaced the phrase 'military requirements', which was used in the 1899 text, the opposite change to what had been done in the text in the preamble which strengthens the view that the two phrases are to be seen as synonyms.

[143] AP I Commentary, at para. 1367. Emphasis added.

[144] Oeter, 'Methods and means of combat', at page 122 (footnotes omitted). The view appears to be supported by Kolb and Hyde, *An Introduction to the International Law of Armed Conflicts*, at page 125.

a limitless resort to military means and methods, the rule does not prohibit a certain *kind of war.*[145]

The ICRC Commentary states in this regard:

> The principle contained in this paragraph reaffirms the law in force. Whether the armed conflict concerned is considered by the protagonists to be lawful or unlawful, general or local, a war of liberation or a war of conquest, a war of aggression or of self-defence, limited or 'total' war, using conventional weapons or not, the Parties to the conflict are not free to use any methods or any means of warfare whatsoever.[146]

The definition of a 'total war', or a massive national mobilisation to engage in one, lies outside the scope of law. That said, a State engaged in a 'total war' may encounter numerous legal challenges, for example the inevitable challenge to enforce the principle of distinction. The rule of limitation (as well as other core rules in the AP I) are certainly better suited to a 'limited war' than to a 'total war'.

145 The difference between certain kinds of war and the rules of warfare is also discussed in Chapter 14 with regard to the scope of the military advantage.

146 AP I Commentary, at page 390, para. 1382.

PART II

DISTINCTION AS LIMITATION UPON MILITARY NECESSITY IN THE LAW OF ARMED CONFLICT

7

The Principle of Distinction: Also a Limitation upon Military Necessity

7.1 A BASIC RULE WITH TWO ELEMENTS

The principle of distinction is one of two (the other being the prohibition of unnecessary suffering[1]) 'cardinal principles' constituting the 'fabric of international humanitarian law', to use the words of the ICJ in the Advisory Opinion of the Nuclear Weapons Case.[2] Being a 'cardinal principle' its position as part of customary international law is uncontested today.[3] The formulation of the customary rule of distinction appears in different guises. The version of the AMW Manual is being presented here: 'In accordance with the basic principle of distinction, attacks must be confined to lawful targets.'[4]

The core of the rule of distinction has been a part of customary law from long before the treaty definition in the AP I[5] – with traces all the way back to

[1] See Chapter 9.

[2] Legality of the Threat or Use of Nuclear Weapons, Advisory Opinion (see Chapter 3), at page 257, para. 78.

[3] AP I Commentary, para. 1863, page 598. ICRC CIHL rule 1, at page 3. Tallinn Manual, rule 93, at page 420. For use by the ICTY in practice, see for example the Kupreskic Case, at para. 521; the Galic Case, at para. 45, with a historical account in footnote 78. See also Blaskic Case, Appeals Chamber Judgment, at para. 109. In legal literature, see for example: Solf, 'Protection of civilians', page 129; Boothby, *The Law of Targeting*, at pages 60–2; Rogers, *Law on the Battlefield*, pages 11–21; Dinstein, *Conduct of Hostilities*, at page 12; Pictet, *Development and Principles of International Humanitarian Law*, at page 72; Kalshoven and Zegveld, *Constraints on the Waging of War*, at page 40; Corn et.al., *The Law of Armed Conflict: An Operational Approach*, at page 120.

[4] AMW Manual, rule 10(a), at page 83. See also page 106. The formulation of the rule in the ICRC CIHL (rule 1) has been criticised for being misleading in the sense that it appears as more demanding than the AP I rule. See Boothby, *The Law of Targeting*, at pages 61–2.

[5] Hague Rules on Aerial Warfare (1923) article 24. The definition of *military objectives* in the Hague Rules was contested at the time, but not the core of distinction – see Oeter, 'Methods and means of combat', at page 123. See further below, Chapter 8. On the basic rule of distinction prior to AP I, see further: ICRC Draft Rules for the Limitation of the Dangers Incurred by the Civilian Population in time of War, 1956, articles 6 and 7. UN GA res 2444

the St Petersburg Declaration which limited the objectives of States to be to 'weaken the military forces of the enemy'.[6] The protection of the civilian population was, however, rudimentarily and unsatisfyingly established in treaty law through the prohibition of attacks and bombardment against 'undefended towns, villages, dwellings, or buildings' in the Hague Regulations of 1907.[7]

It was not until the adoption of the AP I in 1977 that the principle of distinction was expressed in a treaty. The *basic* rule in AP I article 48 now states: 'In order to ensure respect for and protection of the civilian population and civilian objects, the Parties to the conflict shall at all times distinguish between the civilian population and combatants and between civilian objects and military objectives and accordingly shall direct their operations only against military objectives.'[8]

The overarching aim and purpose of the principle of distinction is to protect civilians and the civilian population from the effects of hostilities.[9] The principle is thus founded on humanitarian considerations and expresses one of the core limitations upon warfare and military necessity – it does not, however, contain a general duty to conduct a 'limited war' (see Chapter 6).[10]

The balance which is struck in the rule of distinction can be explained from two alternative (theoretical) approaches: by arguing that it is not necessary to direct attacks against those persons who are falling outside the scope of the definition of combatants[11] or to say that necessity is easily outweighed by humanitarian considerations and yields completely to these. I argue that the most suitable approach with regard to the rule of distinction is something in between: that if military necessity easily can be argued to yield to humanity, then the weight devoted to necessity will easily diminish as well.

(1968). See also Kalshoven and Zegveld *Constraints on the Waging of War*, at page 40. Greenspan, *The Modern Law of Land Warfare*, at page 334.

6 The St Petersburg Declaration is quoted, in Chapter 3. On the link between the Declaration and the rule of distinction, see for example Boothby, *The Law of Targeting*, at page 62; ICRC CIHL rule 1, and Kalshoven and Zegveld, *Constraints on the Waging of War*, page 38.

7 1907 Hague Regulations, article 25. Oeter 'Methods and means of combat', at page 123.

8 AP I article 48. Draft article 43 (now 48) is also commented upon below, in Chapter 14 on military advantage.

9 AP I Commentary at para. 1863, page 598.

10 See for example, Kolb and Hyde, *An Introduction to the International Law of Armed Conflicts*, page 125.

11 This approach seems to be taken by Sassoli, 'Targeting', at pages 183–4 where he argues with regard to the basic principle of distinction that: 'If a military action is not even militarily necessary, it is therefore always prohibited because with regard to it, no compromise between military necessity and humanity is needed; humanity may entirely prevail and any violence is prohibited.' See as well Chapter 2.

7.2 TWO ELEMENTS: PROHIBITIVE AND PERMISSIVE

The rule of distinction consists of two elements. It is shaped as a prohibition against directing attacks against civilians, the civilian population and civilian objects,[12] and it also rests on one of the basic premises of the LOAC: the permission to direct attacks against lawful targets.[13] The prohibitive aspect is expressed explicitly in the related treaty provisions in the AP I. With regard to persons, article 51(1) states: 'The civilian population as such, as well as individual civilians, shall not be the object of attack.' And, with regard to objects, article 52 (1) states: 'Civilian objects shall not be the object of attack or of reprisals.' The elements of protection and the scope of the prohibition is accounted for into more detail later in the following chapters. The permissive aspect can be viewed in close connection to military necessity: 'Focusing on the target, the question is whether the selected object may actually figure as an object of attack. There can only be argument for a positive answer, and this must be found in the military necessity of the attack.'[14]

7.3 *ABSOLUTE* PROHIBITION

The prohibition to make civilians and civilian objects the object of attack[15] is often referred to as an 'absolute prohibition'. It has been emphasised by the ICTY on a number of occasions, such as in the Blaskic Case: 'The Appeals Chamber underscores that there is an absolute prohibition on the targeting of civilians in customary international law.'[16] By 'absolute' is meant 'from which there is no exception'. This is first and foremost a rejection of exceptional military necessity, such as expressed in the Galic case: 'Under no circumstance are civilians to be considered legitimate military targets. Consequently, attacking civilians or the civilian population as such cannot be justified by invoking military necessity.'[17]

[12] See the Kupreskic Case, at para. 521 where it is held that: 'It is now a universally recognised principle, recently restated by the International Court of Justice, that deliberate attacks on civilians or civilian objects are absolutely prohibited by International humanitarian law.' The prohibition is as well restated in the Galic Case, at para. 44 as well as the Blaskic Case, Appeals Chamber Judgment, at para. 109.

[13] Dinstein, *Conduct of Hostilities*, at page 102. On the character of the LOAC as being permissive and prohibitive and the notion of military necessity in general, see Chapter 2.

[14] Kalshoven, 'Remarks', page 41.

[15] 'the object of attack' is the formulation used in AP I articles 51(2) and 52(2).

[16] Blaskic Case, Appeals Chamber Judgment, at para. 109.

[17] Galic Case, at footnote 76 to para. 44. The same point is emphasised in the Tallinn Manual, Commentary 6 to rule 93, at page 422.

Although there is no exception, the prohibition is contingent upon civilians abstaining from participation in hostilities, i.e. they are protected against direct attacks 'unless and for such time as they take a direct part in hostilities'.[18]

The absolute feature of the basic rule has been continuously challenged throughout history. In fact, the invocation of military necessity has been a repeated pledge from States – in particular when it comes to the alleged necessity of affecting enemy (civilian) morale in order to 'end the war' (terror attacks), as well as the alleged necessity of reprisal attacks against civilians (both dealt with separately and in detail in Chapter 12). Both with regard to terror attacks as well as reprisal attacks against civilians, the law has developed in favour of humanitarian considerations and towards the absolute feature the rule of distinction possesses today. However, a discrepancy between treaty law and customary law when it comes to the lawfulness of reprisal attacks against civilians is present. In reality, this discrepancy challenges the true notion of an 'absolute prohibition'. The details regarding invocation of military necessity as justification for both terror attacks as well as reprisal attacks are accounted for in Chapter 12.

7.4 ABSOLUTE PROHIBITION BUT NOT ABSOLUTE PROTECTION

The rule of distinction may be characterised as an 'absolute prohibition', but this characterisation must not be confused with an *absolute protection* against the effects of hostilities. The wording in AP I article 51(1) refers to the civilian population and civilian individuals 'as such', indicating that the rule offers no guarantee against the effects from attacks directed at otherwise lawful targets.[19] As spelled out in the abovementioned Galic case: 'The principle of military necessity acknowledges the potential for unavoidable civilian death and injury ancillary to the conduct of legitimate military operations.'[20]

The drafting history of the AP I illustrates this as well: in an early ICRC draft proposal the protection of persons belonging to the civilian population was formulated as to being 'spared as much as possible'.[21] The threshold of 'as much as possible' clearly reflects the 'necessities of war'.[22]

In result, the protection of civilians in the AP I is designed with a twofold immunity: 'by a complete ban on military attacks or operations against civilian

18 Among others expressed in AP I article 51(3). See Chapter 11.

19 Bothe, Partsch and Solf, *New Rules*, at page 341.

20 Galic Case, at footnote 76 to para. 44.

21 Quoted in AP I Commentary at para. 1868, page 599.

22 Ibid. See further below, Section 11.1 on the definition of civilians.

populations and civilian objects as such and, second, by limiting the effects of military operations which, although directed against military objectives, might incidentally or accidentally endanger the civilian population and civilian objects in the vicinity'.[23] While the first aspect of this twofold immunity reflects the principle of distinction as introduced here, the second aspect is a reflection of the prohibition of indiscriminate attacks, as well as the proportionality rule in the LOAC. The prohibition of indiscriminate attacks is accounted for in Chapter 12 whereas the specifics related to the proportionality rule is dealt with in Chapters 13 and 14.

7.5 FORMATION AND VIOLATION OF THE RULE OF DISTINCTION

Although it has an undisputed status as customary law, repeated violations of the rule of distinction has raised the question whether the practice of States in the past represented violations of the law or creation of new law:

> However, it was above all the development of weaponry after this conflict [WWI] and its use during the Second World War which radically changed the situation. As a result the customary rule was affected to such an extent that *one might have wondered whether it still existed.* By the repeated use of reprisals the point was reached where attacks were systematically directed at towns and their inhabitants.[24]

The question is, however, presented in such a rhetorical manner in the Commentary, that the ICRC answer seems to emanate from the undertone; there was – and certainly is – a rule, but repeated violations challenged the rule at a certain point of time. A similar approach – with an emphasis on the role of military necessity – can be found in legal literature in the aftermath of WWII, such as: 'The distinction between combatants and the civilian population has been characterized not only as one of the fundamental principles of international law, but as its greatest triumph. . . . both in point of fact and in theory the distinction has been so whittled down by the demands of military necessity that it has become more apparent than real.'[25] This tendency of 'whittling down' the distinction had been illustrated by attempts to extend the definition

[23] Official Records of the Diplomatic Conference CDDH/III/SR.2 at page 13, the comments made by the ICRC representative.

[24] AP I Commentary, page 598, paras. 1866–7, footnote omitted. Emphasis added. For a discussion of attacks by way of reprisals, see further Section 12.3.

[25] Nurick, 'The distinction between combatant and noncombatant in the law of war', at page 680.

of combatants to include almost all elements of the enemy civilian population. The latter seems to be the key challenge to the application of the principle of distinction – also today. Although the basic rule is firmly established and uncontested, its different elements are nevertheless subject to controversy. During the Disarmament Conference in Geneva in 1923–4 the participants were already 'obsessed with civilians' and their protection from the dangers from the air – but: 'What was wrong was that no one stopped to ask who the "civilians" were about whom so much concern was shown.'[26] And with regard to military objectives – perhaps even more illustratively from WWII strategic air war campaigns: 'The devil, as ever, lurked in the details of the phrase "legitimate military objectives".'[27]

In the following, the two parts of the rule of distinction – those of lawful targets and protected persons and objects – will be addressed. Particular aspects of destruction of property are dealt with below in Chapter 16 and persons and objects with *special protection* are dealt with in Chapter 17.

7.6 LAWFUL TARGETS: COMBATANTS, CIVILIANS DIRECTLY PARTICIPATING IN HOSTILITIES AND MILITARY OBJECTIVES

The enumeration of lawful targets as combatants, civilians directly participating in hostilities and military objects is not explicitly stated in a treaty provision, but stems from an overall reading of AP I articles 48, 51(3) and 52(2) which on this point clearly express customary law. While article 52(2) (below) does not mention combatants explicitly, article 48 does, and article 52(2) first sentence contains no limitation to objects (as does the second sentence).[28]

The focus on persons (as well as objects) can of course also (again) be traced all the way back to the St Petersburg Declaration's reference to 'weaken the military forces of the enemy'.[29] The details on the enumeration of lawful targets are accounted for in the following chapters.

26 Spaight, *Air Power and War Rights*, at page 43.
27 Biddle, *Rhetoric and Reality in Air Warfare*, at page 181.
28 UK Manual, at page 54; Norwegian Manual, at page 28; Dinstein, *Conduct of Hostilities*, at page 105.
29 On the St Petersburg Declaration, see Chapter 3. For an approach to lawful targets via the language of the Declaration in this specific regard, see for example Rogers, *Law on the Battlefield*, at page 11; and Kalshoven and Zegveld, *Constraints on the Waging of War*, at page 38.

7.7 THE TREATY DEFINITION OF MILITARY OBJECTIVES: LEAVING TOO MUCH FOR THE COMMANDER'S ASSESSMENT?

The adoption of the treaty definition of 'military objectives' in AP I article 52(2) in 1977 was the result of a long and controversial process,[30] but nevertheless represents a 'cornerstone' in the modern law of armed conflict.[31] The present treaty definition reads: 'In so far as objects are concerned, military objectives are limited to those objects which by their nature, location, purpose, or use make an effective contribution to military action and whose total or partial destruction, capture or neutralization, in the circumstances ruling at the time, offers a definite military advantage.'[32]

The contemporary treaty text defining military objectives can be viewed as confining the role of military necessity: 'only for the purpose of combat against such objectives does the regulation of customary international law recognize military necessity'.[33] And in a more basic manner: 'The notion of military necessity is also part of the concept of military objective . . .'[34] Or, as stated in the US DoD Manual, 'Thus, *military necessity* underlies law of war concepts that explain when persons and property may be the object of attack, *e.g.*, the concepts of "taking a direct part in hostilities" and "military objective".'[35] And finally as expressed by Kalshoven: 'Focusing on the target, the question is whether the selected object may actually figure as an object. There can be only one argument for a positive answer, and this must be found in the military necessity of the attack. Targets that may be so attacked are referred to as "military objectives".'[36]

30 AP I Commentary, at page 630, para. 1994; Bothe, Partsch and Solf, *New Rules*, at page 363; Oeter, 'Methods and means of combat', at pages 169–70. For an overview of the history of the identification of legitimate military objectives, see for example Parks, 'Asymmetries and the identification of legitimate military objectives'; and Boivin, 'The legal regime applicable to targeting military objectives', at pages 8–13.

31 Rauch, 'The concept of military necessity in the context of the law of war', at page 18.

32 The wording is repeated as well in Protocol II to the CCW and Protocol on Prohibitions or Restrictions on the Use of Incendiary Weapons (Protocol III to the CCW), and in the Second Protocol to the Hague Convention on Cultural Property.

33 Oeter, 'Methods and means of combat', page 166. In a similar direction see Boivin, 'The legal regime applicable to targeting military objectives', at page 17 where it is argued: 'the principle of restricting destruction to what is militarily necessary is part and parcel of the two-pronged test'. The two-pronged test is discussed below in Chapter 8.

34 Rauch, 'The concept of military necessity in the context of the law of war', at page 8. See as well the reference to Kalshoven, 'Remarks'.

35 US DoD Manual, para. 2.2.1, at pages 52–3. Emphasis in original. Footnotes in original omitted.

36 Kalshoven, 'Remarks' at page 41.

With regard to the legal expression 'military objectives' it has been said that: 'The term has developed around carefully negotiated criteria that leave room for interpretation according to the circumstances ruling at the time, while seeking to coin an acceptable balance between humanitarian and military considerations.'[37] This balance which is struck in the definition does not, however, imply that the application of the rule requires a balance to be struck each time the rule is applied to a concrete case – as opposed to the proportionality assessment (see below).[38]

The treaty definition is reiterated in Protocol II and III to the CCW[39] as well as the Second Protocol on Cultural Property.[40] The AP I definition is widely cited by States[41] and generally considered reflective of customary law although there are interpretative challenges to be settled.[42] Among the critics to the adopted definition is Parks who, 'not necessarily accept[s] the conclusion of the International Committee of the Red Cross in its *Customary International Humanitarian Law Study* that the definition has attained customary law status'.[43] His critique is based on the alleged lack of treaty implementation and actual practice of States.[44]

As was the case with regard to the negotiations of the principle of proportionality,[45] the Diplomatic Conference aroused discussions with regard to the fact that a humanitarian treaty should define which objects that were lawful to attack.[46] An argument which was presented was thus that article 52(2) solely prohibits direct attacks on civilian objects and not incidental damage as the result of an (otherwise lawful) attack on a military objective.[47]

37 Boivin, 'The legal regime applicable to targeting military objectives', at page 8.

38 See Hampson, 'Necessity and proportionality in the Gulf conflict', at page 49, where she argues that: 'The definition of a military objective does require a balance to be struck, which is the nature of a proportionality requirement; it does require a standard to be met.'

39 Protocol II of the CCW, article 2(4) and article 2(6).

40 Second Protocol to the Hague Convention of 1954 for the Protection of Cultural Property, article 1(f).

41 UK Manual, at page 54; US DoD Manual, para. 5.6.3, page 210; German Manual, para. 407, page 54; Norwegian Manual, at page 32; Canadian Manual; Swedish proposed manual, Folkrätt i væpnad konflikt: svensk tolkning och tillempning, SOU 2010:72, rule 8, at page 345.

42 Dörmann, 'The definition of military objectives', at pages 78–9; Dinstein, 'Legitimate military objectives under the current jus in bello', at page 141; Boothby, *The Law of Targeting*, at pages 63 and 101; Boivin, 'The legal regime applicable to targeting military objectives', at page 15; AMW Manual, rule 1(y), with Commentary 1, at page 49; ICRC CIHL, rule 8, at page 29, which is partly based on the OTP Report.

43 Parks, 'Asymmetries and the identification of legitimate military objectives', at page 91.

44 Ibid., at pages 91–2.

45 See Chapter 13.

46 AP I Commentary, at para. 2015, page 635. On these arguments with regard to the proportionality rule, Chapters 13 and 14.

47 See for example the UK position in UK Manual, at page 54. See as well Bothe, Partsch and Solf, *New Rules*, at page 364.

Pending questions have been whether the treaty definition in AP I should be formulated as a generic and abstract formula or through a list of specific objectives (casuistic) – or both – and whether the definition should be negative (denoting objects which are protected and prohibited to attack) or positive (denoting objects which are lawful objects of attack, namely military objectives).[48] The solution in AP I landed on a generic and abstract definition which is both positive (with regard to military objectives) and negative (what are not military objectives are civilian objects). The lack of a specific list – despite attempts in treaty drafts and examples of older treaties[49] – has by some been pointed out as a regrettable fact and certainly makes the application of the law to practical cases more difficult for commanders in the field. For this reason, non-exhaustive lists of military objectives have been provided in legal literature, such as in the AMW Manual, rules 22 and 23[50] and by Dinstein and Rogers.[51] The same approach is taken in the US DoD Manual and the UK Manual which provide non-exhaustive lists of possible military objectives, the latter emphasising that the list does not mean that the object 'is necessarily a military objective'.[52] Those who are not in favour of a list of military objectives argue that a general definition is the only 'realistically available solution to a vexed problem'[53] or even that a list would be 'liable to cause confusion or to result in apparent arbitrariness'.[54] That a non-exhaustive list of exemplification would result in 'arbitrariness' is difficult to grasp; after all, non-exhaustive lists are common tools in ordinary legislation – obviously without inducing arbitrariness.

During negotiations over the Draft Hague Rules on Aerial Warfare (1922), the term 'military objective' instigated opposing views with regard

48 AP I Commentary, at para. 2004, page 633.

49 Convention (IX) Concerning Bombardment by Naval Forces in time of War (1907 Hague Convention IX), article 1; Hague Rules of Aerial Warfare, article 24; 1954 Hague Convention on Cultural Property, article 8; and ICRC 1956 Draft Rules, article 7, with the list in appendix.

50 AMW Manual, rules 22(a)–(d) with commentaries and rule 23 with commentaries, at pages 107–9.

51 Rogers, *Law on the Battlefield*, pages 122–4. Dinstein, 'Legitimate military objectives under the current jus in bello', at pages 141–2 and *Conduct of Hostilities* at pages 110–11. Dinstein's position is supported by for example Sassoli, 'Targeting', at page 185, and on a general basis by Parks, 'Asymmetries and the identification of legitimate military objectives', at pages 92–3, although Parks considers Green and Dinstein's list as 'more restrictive than State practice', see in particular pages 94–5. See also Green, *The Contemporary Law of Armed Conflict*, at page 191. Rogers' list is also cited in the OTP Report, at para. 38.

52 UK Manual, at pages 56–7. US DoD Manual, para. 5.6.4, at pages 211 ff.

53 Kalshoven and Zegveld, *Constraints on the Waging of War*, at page 106. In the same direction, see Dörmann, 'The definition of military objectives', at page 84 where he concludes that 'the definition is fine, but there may be potential for interpretive clarification'.

54 Boothby, *The Law of Targeting*, at page 102.

to discretion. Parks notes: 'The British delegation set great store in "military objective" as having a limitative effect, while the U.S. delegation argued the phrase left too much to the discretion of the individual commander.'[55]

Due to the inherent flexibility in the notion of 'military objective', the perceptions of its suitability were diametrically opposed. Furthermore, without being somewhere near arbitrary decisions, a 'margin of appreciation' should in any case be granted for the commander when determining military objectives.[56]

7.8 A HISTORY OF MILITARY OBJECTIVES UNDER THE UMBRELLA OF MILITARY NECESSITIES

The concept of 'military objectives' was first sought to be codified in the Hague Rules on Aerial Warfare, and then introducing as well the concept of an 'obvious military advantage'.[57] The 1923 Hague Rules of Air Warfare refer to 'necessity' on a couple of occasions in the articles governing wireless telegraphy in time of war (articles 4 and 7). It is, however, with regard to aerial bombardment in articles 22–6 that the attempted regulations with regard to the purpose of the present book can be traced. These provisions aspire to regulate both the limits of the lawful *purpose*[58] of bombardment, and the objects of attack, the military objectives:

> Art. 24. 1. An air bombardment is legitimate only when is directed against a military objective, i.e. an objective whereof the total or partial destruction would constitute an obvious military advantage for the belligerent;
>
> 2. Such bombardment is legitimate only when directed exclusively against the following objectives: military forces, military works, military establishments or depots, manufacturing plants constituting important and well-known centres for the production of arms, ammunition or characterized military supplies, lines of communication or of transport which are used for military purposes. . . .[59]

55 Parks, 'Asymmetries and the identification of legitimate military objectives', at page 72.

56 Oeter, 'Methods and means of combat', page 171. Boothby, *The Law of Targeting*, at page 99, relying on Dinstein, *Conduct of Hostilities*, at pages 103–4. On the margin of appreciation in general, see Chapter 4.

57 Hague Rules of Aerial Warfare, page 315.

58 The purpose was also restrained in article 23 with regard to enforced requisitions and payments.

59 Hague Rules of Aerial Warfare, at page 319. Article 24(3) is discussed below in Chapter 12 with regard to the prohibition of indiscriminate attacks. Articles 24(4) and (5) govern a predecessor to the regulation of collateral damage, and are discussed below, in Chapter 13.

The Hague Rules remained a draft – albeit an 'authoritative attempt'[60] – and their status as customary law at the time remained a matter of controversy. States allegedly found the rules on bombardment too strict, and the definition of military objectives proved too difficult to reach.[61] With respect to this last point, it could be seen as a symptomatic start of a feature of the twentieth century warfare which would more than forty years later be described as a: 'constant expansion of the military objective'.[62] However, its importance as a 'starting point' is notable.[63] Therefore, some remarks on the draft and its contemporary critics can be fruitful. The appearance of the concept of 'military objectives' was in the 1930s described as 'too vague to be of practical importance'[64] and in the present time as a 'very imprecise' concept.[65] The vagueness and imprecision is unquestionable, but the definition found in article 24 appears as both modern and practical compared to the text in AP I article 52(2), which misses a list with examples of military objectives.

After the failure of achieving ratification of the Hague Rules, it is State practice which dominate the period until 1974–7 when it comes to the definition of military objectives.[66]

At the outset of WWII the Allies agreed to confine their attacks strictly to military objectives and to exclude objectives with no strictly defined military purpose. However, military necessity played a vital role in the transition away from this restrictive and impeccable point of departure towards the abyss of unlimited area bombardment.[67]

The lack of a definition of military objectives inevitably led to wide open discretionary powers for the State: '. . . in fact, during the Second World War and during several armed conflicts which have taken place since then, each

60 See Robertson, 'The principle of the military objective in the law of armed conflict', at page 37 with further references. See also Boivin, 'The legal regime applicable to targeting military objectives', at page 9.

61 See for example Spaight, *Air Power and War Rights*, at pages 244–5. Kalshoven, *Reflections on the Law of War*, at page 438. See as well Hancke, 'The 1923 Hague Rules of Air Warfare', particularly pages 19–20 and 28. Parks, 'Asymmetries and the identification of legitimate military objectives', at page 75.

62 Kelsen and Tucker, *Principles of International Law*, at page 122.

63 Parks, 'Asymmetries and the identification of legitimate military objectives', at page 74.

64 See Biddle, *Rhetoric and Reality in Air Warfare*, at page 153, quoting an essay by Jonathan Mitchell for the New Republic in 1937.

65 Hancke, 'The 1923 Hague Rules of Air Warfare', at page 14.

66 Parks, 'Asymmetries and the identification of legitimate military objectives', at page 76, commenting that the Hague Rules were the 'first, last, and only formal effort at defining military objective until the 1974–1977 Diplomatic Conference that promulgated Additional Protocol I'.

67 See below, Chapter 12.

belligerent determined what should be understood by such objectives as it pleased.'[68] Accordingly, the place devoted to military necessity was a sovereign matter for each belligerent and actual limitations were few, but practice seemed to be fairly homogenous (at least with regard to air force): 'All bombed the same categories of targets ...'[69] The widespread practice of bombing without discrimination was also documented by the belligerents themselves, as pointed out in the US Bombing Survey: 'the proper target ... was the basic economic and social fabric of the country'.[70] With the lack of precise parameters, aggressive tactics in determining the military objective during WWII period has been identified in the aftermath: 'An object became a military objective if it was determined to contribute effectively towards the destruction of the enemy nation's means to resistance, and lowering of its determination to fight.'[71] And furthermore that: '*Military objective* was viewed in a strategic as well as tactical sense.' As an example of the strategic sense Parks uses the 'Doolittle Raid' in 1942, where 'medium bombers with very small bomb loads of military objectives in Tokyo made no "effective contribution to the *military* action" in the sense of a tactical gain, but had a "major strategic effect in the Pacific War".'[72]

The feature of WWII as a total war has even induced writers to argue that what may constitute a legitimate military objective 'may vary from conflict to conflict'.[73] The rationale behind such an argument seems to be that the desired *contribution* of the military objective in order to reach a desired aim varies accordingly with the nature of the armed conflict. The reasoning is unsettling – and criticised elsewhere[74] – if it is presented as an expression of existing law; for the purpose of describing State practice during WWII, however, it can pass. In the post-AP I era, the military objective must make an 'effective contribution to military action' and its destruction must 'offer

68 AP I Commentary, at para. 2000, page 631. In the same direction, see Boivin, 'The legal regime applicable to targeting military objectives', at pages 9–10. On discretion in general, see Chapter 4.

69 Parks, 'Asymmetries and the identification of legitimate military objectives', at page 82. On State practice during WWII bombing campaigns, see also Chapter 12.

70 See US Strategic Bombing Surveys, European War/Pacific War, at page 83.

71 Parks, 'Asymmetries and the identification of legitimate military objectives', at page 83.

72 Ibid.

73 See the discussion (with further references) in Robertson, 'The principle of the military objective in the law of armed conflict', at page 48. That the definition is flexible according to the conflict also seems to be the position in Fenrick, 'Targeting and proportionality during the NATO bombing campaign against Yugoslavia', page 494. See also Chapter 14 with regard to the 'circumstances ruling at the time'.

74 Robertson, 'The principle of the military objective in the law of armed conflict'; Sassoli, 'Targeting', at pages 199–200.

a definite military advantage'. These cumulative criteria are dealt with in detail, in Chapters 8 and 14.

The practice experienced throughout the World Wars necessitated, in the views of the ICRC, a 'restrictive definition' of military objectives in treaty law.[75] What, however, amounts to a definition which truly is 'restrictive', is unclear. At least two codification attempts were made before the final adoption in the AP I: the 1956 ICRC Draft and the 1969 text prepared by the Institute of International Law. In the 1956 Draft the connection to military necessity is obvious, as the definition of military objectives is tied to objects of 'military importance' – together with a list of objects.[76] The Draft furthermore contained a reference to 'military interest' which was left out in the final text.[77] Seen in relation to the treaty text which was finally adopted, however, the requirement of 'military interest' appears superfluous. The 1969 text is even closer to the present treaty text, and includes an alternative criterion of 'generally recognized military significance', in addition to the requirement of offering a 'substantial, specific and immediate military advantage to those who are in a position to destroy them'.[78]

7.9 THE DOUBT RULES: PRESUMING CIVILIAN STATUS

The AP I contains two rules with a presumption of civilian status, for persons and objects. The AP I article 50(1) states 'that in case of doubt whether a person is a civilian, that person shall be considered to be a civilian'. Whereas article 52(3) states that: 'In case of doubt whether an object which is normally dedicated to civilian purposes, such as a place of worship, a house or other dwelling or a school, is being used to make an effective contribution to military action, it shall be presumed not to be so used.'

The two rules are similar – but not identical – and difficult in many aspects. While the rule in article 50(1) by wording applies to all persons, presumption of civilian use in article 52(3) applies – as the wording indicates by the phrase *normally dedicated to civilian purposes* – to objects which do not normally have a significant military use or purpose.[79] For example, if there is doubt whether a school is used as ammunition storage, the school shall be presumed

75 Ibid.

76 1956 ICRC Draft Rules, article 7.

77 AP I Commentary, at para. 2019.

78 The Distinction between Military Objectives in General and Particularly the Problems Associated with Weapons of Mass Destruction, Resolution adopted by the Institute of International Law at its session in Edinburgh, 9 September 1969.

79 Bothe, Partsch and Solf, *New Rules*, at page 368; Boothby, *The Law of Targeting*, at page 71.

to maintain its civilian status. Objects that are military by nature, however, do not fall within the ambit of the rule.

The customary status of both rules is contested[80] (primarily by the USA) with the argument that: 'A legal presumption of civilian status in cases of doubt may demand a certain degree of certainty that would not account for the realities of war.'[81] Upon ratification, the UK made the reservation with regard to article 50(1) that it 'applies only in cases of substantial doubt still remaining after the assessment referred to at paragraph (c) above has been made ...'[82] The UK view seems to have gained widespread support. In fact, it is a bit difficult to grasp the difference (if any) between the accepted customary rule and the treaty rules as understood with interpretive reservations. The treaty rules do not require certainty (as the wording could indicate),[83] but a reasonable belief (as does customary law) that the object or person is actually a military objective.[84] Certainty would, for all practical matters rule out doubt all together. Hence, not every theoretical doubt will release the civilian presumption, but a reasonable doubt.[85] As always, the notion of reasonableness hinges on the specific circumstances included in the commander's assessment. Furthermore, the devil lies in the practical application of the rule in detail. The recurring question for practical purposes appears to be: when is the belief 'reasonable'? I return to this issue just below, but first a couple of exemplifications.

80 With regard to objects, see the account given in Bothe, Partsch and Solf, *New Rules*, at page 368 with regard to the disagreement over 'objects in the contact zone'. On the same matter, see as well the ICRC CIHL, Commentary to rule 10; Dinstein, *Conduct of Hostilities*, at page 113; Rogers, *Law on the Battlefield*, at page 105; Boothby, *The Law of Targeting*, at page 71.

81 US DoD Manual, para. 5.4.3.2, at page 201. The same position has previously also been upheld by the US. See for example Final Report to Congress, page 616, where a similar statement is made: 'This imbalance ignores the realities of war in demanding a degree of certainty of an attacker that seldom exists in combat.' On the USA position with regard to assessment of information in general during conduct of hostilities, see Chapter 4.

82 UK reservation to AP I.

83 The AP I Commentary, page 638, at para. 2034 uses the word 'certain' with regard to buildings normally used for civilian purposes, even if they are in the contact zone.

84 AMW Manual, at page 87 in Commentary. Boothby, *The Law of Targeting*, at page 107. De Cock, 'Operation Unified Protector and the protection of civilians in Libya', at page 231, argues that 'PID [positive identification] is the reasonable certainty that a given object is a valid military objective.' In the Galic Case, the ICTY stated that: 'The Trial Chamber understands that such an object shall not be attacked when it is not reasonable to believe, in the circumstances of the person contemplating the attack, including the information available to the latter, that the object is being used to make an effective contribution to military action', at para. 51. 'Reasonableness' is dealt with in more detail in general in Chapter 4.

85 Tallinn Manual, Commentary 3 to rule 95, at page 424; Dinstein, *Conduct of Hostilities*, at page 113; Schmitt, 'Targeting and international humanitarian law in Afghanistan', at page 320, refers to 'substantial doubt'.

With regard to persons, applying the rule may depend upon the adversary's compliance with the duty to distinguish themselves (see Chapter 10). Repeated perfidious behaviour may degrade the presumption.[86] A particular issue arises when the enemy largely consists of civilians taking part in hostilities and thus lose their civilian protection. Whether or not a person behaves in a way that would qualify as direct participation in hostilities may rely on the cultural-contextual facts. For example, a male individual holding a gun outside his house may indicate participation in hostilities or it may indicate that he is protecting his home according to local customs.[87] Whether the doubt is reasonable relies on the expected knowledge of the commander. Carrying weapons has for example been a common feature among Afghan men and this fact should be presumed to be known to military commanders. Hence, if spotting a man carrying a weapon, this fact alone should raise substantial doubt as to whether there is sufficient nexus to the armed conflict (see below).

With regard to objects, the tragic bombing of the Al-Firdus bunker, which was still being (re)used as an air-raid shelter, can also provide an example here.[88] As indicated in Chapter 4, parts of the questioning from Human Rights Watch concerned the rule on presumption of doubt.[89] The questions with regard to doubt appear as Should there have been substantial doubt as to whether the bunker was, at the time, still being used as a military bunker for C2 purposes? Or, was it reasonable to rely on the intelligence already provided? Being built as an air-raid shelter, the rule on presumption of civilian status applies by treaty law. However, as pointed out above, the customary status of the treaty rule is contested by the USA, so the general point of departure regarding good faith in the assessment of information reasonably available at the time applies. Exactly which feasible measures that could be expected in order to verify that the object was (still) a military objective is dealt with in Chapter 15. When it comes to doubt, it suffices to state that with regard to the regrettable practice by Saddam Hussein to exploit the presence of the Iraqi civilian population for propaganda purposes,[90] it appears to have been within

86 Bothe, Partsch and Solf, *New Rules*, at page 336. For examples related to perfidy, see Section 17.3 on loss of special protection by resort to perfidy.

87 See the Norwegian Manual, at page 32; and Schmitt, 'Targeting and international humanitarian law in Afghanistan', at page 319, for similar points.

88 See Chapter 4 for a presentation of the facts.

89 Human Rights Watch, Needless Deaths in the Gulf War, at page 137.

90 For a USA view on this practice, see Final Report to Congress, at page 615. See also, for example, The White House, Crafting Tragedy.

the ambit of good faith on behalf of the USA to rely on the information available at the time.[91]

Now, turning back to the general issue of when the belief appears reasonable, the LOAC appears carefully drafted in not dealing with probabilities, but rather with reasonableness. In order to come closer to a concrete example, we may turn the issue of doubt upside down: how certain must the commander be that the person or object is a military objective? Or, what probability is in most cases considered 'reasonable'? First it is important to emphasise that reasonable belief must not be confused with 'beyond reasonable doubt' – as is the common expression in criminal law. In most cases it is impractical to foresee attacks being launched unless it is more likely than not that the target is a military objective.[92] After all, there is no military sense in wasting ammunition.[93] For all practical purposes the pending question thus seems to lie on a scale between considering that it is 'highly likely' that the target is a military objective and 'likely' that it is so. Whether to launch an attack on the basis of intelligence concluding that it is likely that the person is actually administering a weapons cache, or that the house is actually being a weapons cache, is finally a matter for the commander's margin of appreciation to decide. The key to resolve the question in practice seems to lie on the threshold for what is required of the 'reasonable commander' when taking precautions in attack.[94] Whether he or she had done everything feasible in order to reach the established knowledge is dealt with in Chapter 15.

91 The USA position is presented in Final Report to Congress, at pages 141 and 615–17. See also Barber, 'Scuds, shelters and retreating soldiers', at page 689.

92 In the Norwegian Manual the level of knowledge is explicitly stated at page 29: 'An attack can only be launched if it is highly probable that the person or the object is a lawful target, regardless of the importance of the target.'

93 For a remark on 'Economy of force', see Chapter 2.

94 In this direction see also the ICRC CIHL, Commentary to rule 10.

8

Military Objects

8.1 THE 'TWO-PRONGED TEST'

The AP I definition of military objectives in article 52(2) refers to 'objects', which are military objectives in the legal sense, and must be distinguished from military objectives in the military operational usage.[1] The treaty definition clearly encapsulates *objects* and not aims or purposes (but *humans* are not excluded).[2] The provision thus addresses material and tangible things, not 'victory' or 'public will'.[3]

The definition of military objectives (in article 52(2)) succeeds the foregoing negative definition of civilian objects (in article 52(1)). Although all objects which are not military objectives are civilian objects and immune from direct attacks,[4] this does not *exclude any civilian object* from changing status into a military objective.

The requirement for acquiring status as a military objective comprises two cumulative criteria – a 'two-pronged test':[5] that the nature, location, purpose or use 'make an effective contribution to military action', and that the destruction, capture or neutralisation of the object, in the circumstances at the time,

1 See Tallinn Manual, page 436, where it is stated the term military objective is 'a term of art in the law of armed conflict. This legal term is not to be confused with the meaning of the military objective in operational usage, that is, the goal of a military operation.' On the 'object of war', see Chapter 2.

2 AP I Commentary, at para. 2010, page 634. See as well Dinstein, 'Legitimate military objectives under the current jus in bello', at page 142, emphasising that combatants are not exempted from the category.

3 Dörmann, 'The definition of military objectives', at page 79. On 'enemy (civilian) morale', see Chapter 12.

4 See Bothe, Partsch and Solf, *New Rules*, at page 361.

5 For the use of this phrase, see for example Robertson, 'The principle of the military objective in the law of armed conflict', at page 48; Bothe, Partsch and Solf, *New Rules*, at page 365. Boivin, 'The legal regime applicable to targeting military objectives', at pages 15–16.

offers a 'definite military advantage'. This 'two-pronged' test has been said to consist of an 'objective' and a 'subjective' element: the 'objective' element – the 'effective contribution to military action' – refers to the nexus between the object in question and the military action on the side of the attacked party to the conflict; whereas the 'subjective' element – the definite military advantage – refers to the expected outcome of the attack (as a whole) to the benefit of the attacker.[6] Some argue that the first element, of being 'objectively' an effective contribution to military action, reflects the 'requirement of military necessity'.[7] The relationship between the (subjective) notion of military advantage and (objective) military necessity is addressed in more detail in Chapter 14.

The two elements of the definition of military objectives do not need to be related.[8] Bothe, Partsch and Solf use the example of the Allied deceptive attacks against targets in Pas de Calais in 1944, where the effective contribution these objects on German military action did not relate to the Allied advantage of creating the impression of a forthcoming amphibious assault against Pas de Calais rather than Normandy.[9] Having said this, it is certainly not the case that there need not be a relationship at all; it is exactly the relationship between the destruction on the one hand and the advantage on the other which actually makes the object a lawful target, but the advantage for own forces does not need to be an exact reflection of the effective contribution to the opposing forces military action. The function of the legal definition of military objectives is, however, to establish a more fixed (although still flexible) standard for the 'necessity of the attack', and to structure and limit the assessment which will have to be done by military commanders.[10]

It has furthermore been discussed whether the cumulative requirement of the two tests implies that they need to be fulfilled *simultaneously*, which is the word used in the ICRC Commentary.[11] This position appears too rigid and connotes poorly with the concept of one of the two 'prongs': the military advantage.[12] As argued in Chapter 14, military advantages may materialise sometime in the future (but not include 'the entire war'[13]), subject to the limitations of being 'definite' or 'concrete and direct'.[14]

6 Oeter, 'Methods and means of combat', at pages 170–1. The distinction is also upheld by Henderson, *The Contemporary Law of Targeting*, at page 52.

7 Henderson, *The Contemporary Law of Targeting*.

8 Bothe, Partsch and Solf, *New Rules*, at page 366.

9 Ibid. On military advantage vs military necessity, see Chapter 14.

10 See Chapter 4.

11 See AP I Commentary, at para. 2018, page 635. See the discussion as well in Henderson, *The Contemporary Law of Targeting*, at page 52.

12 In the same direction see the US DoD Manual, para. 5.6.5, at page 212.

13 Dörmann, 'The definition of military objectives', page 80.

14 See Section 14.5 for a thorough discussion of these aspects.

More often than not, the two tests will probably be related and to a certain degree the assessment of the two criteria will naturally overlap in practice. When an object makes an 'effective contribution to military action', its destruction will often also offer a 'definite military advantage'.[15] The degree of overlap is criticised by some, arguing that 'The logic of this approach, however, endangers collapsing the two-prong test into one.' And, furthermore, that: 'This logic reduces the two-prong test to one that strongly favours the attacking Party.'[16] This critique does not, however, appear convincing: a degree of overlap does not imply that the tests are collapsing into one; the definition of military objectives still consists of two distinct tests which must both be satisfied.[17] The assessment of the tests with regard to the different alternatives of 'nature, location, purpose or use', is dealt with throughout the following sub-sections.

8.2 'EFFECTIVE CONTRIBUTION' TO 'MILITARY ACTION' AND THE CONTROVERSY OVER 'WAR-SUSTAINING CAPABILITIES'

During the decade after the adoption of the definition of military objectives in the Additional Protocol of 1977, the theoretical debate was relatively silent in that writers more or less referred to the definition of military objectives found in the treaty provision, without discussing it.[18] There has, however, been a continuous source of controversy over the requirement of 'effective contribution to military action'.

The phrase encompasses two sub-elements: that of 'effective contribution' as well as 'military action'. The requirement of 'effective' means that there must in fact be a contribution to the military action, but this contribution does not need to be significant.[19] Furthermore, the expression 'effective contribution' does not require a 'direct connection with combat operations' – as opposed to the rule on DPH with regard to persons.[20] The Norwegian Manual states on the other hand that the contribution must be direct, but

[15] Sassoli, Bouvier and Quintin, *How Does Law Protect in War*, at page 252, footnote 196.

[16] Boivin, 'The legal regime applicable to targeting military objectives', at pages 15–16.

[17] AMW Manual, Commentary 3 to rule 1(y), at page 49. See as well Hampson, 'Necessity and proportionality in the Gulf conflict', at page 49. In the same direction, see Boothby, *The Law of Targeting*, at page 100, footnote 106.

[18] See Fenrick, 'Targeting and proportionality during the NATO bombing campaign against Yugoslavia', at page 495.

[19] AMW Manual, Commentary 4 to rule 1(y), at page 49.

[20] AMW Manual, rule 24, Commentary, at page 110; Bothe, Partsch and Solf, *New Rules*, at page 365; Dinstein, 'Legitimate military objectives under the current jus in bello', at page 145. On loss of civilian protection due to DPH, see further below.

not to a particular combat operation; it can be a direct contribution to the 'end state' of the operation.[21] The 'end state' must be understood here as the military and not the political end state and has a direct reference to the understanding of the notion of 'military action', which: 'means military action generally, not a limited or specific military operation',[22] and more than 'hostilities proper'.[23] Thus, whether one argues that the connection between the military action and the military objective need to be direct or indirect is to a certain extent coloured by the view of the scope of 'military action'. After all, the treaty text does not deal with directness vs indirectness but with effectiveness and military action. The example used in the AMW Manual of storage depots far from the battlefield[24] may serve to illustrate: the AMW Manual deals with this as an indirect contribution to military action or as an indirect connection to ongoing operations. This is true, but if military action is viewed as broader than ongoing operations, the connection may also be viewed as direct – this appears for example to be the position taken in the Norwegian Manual.[25]

The scope of 'military action' has been subject to controversy. Primarily due to the US position juxtaposing 'military action' with 'war-fighting' or 'war-sustaining capability', such as stated in the US DoD Manual:

> Military action has a broad meaning and is understood to mean the general prosecution of the war. It is not necessary that the object provide immediate tactical or operational gains or that the object make an effective contribution to a specific military operation. Rather, the object's effective contribution to the war-fighting or war-sustaining capability of an opposing force is sufficient. Although terms such as 'war-fighting,' 'war-supporting,' and 'war- sustaining' are not explicitly reflected in the treaty definitions of military objective, the United States has interpreted the military objective definition to include these concepts.[26]

This position is supported by some – primarily American – writers who argue that this includes 'objects that contribute to an opposing state's ability to wage war'[27] and as well 'economic targets that indirectly but effectively support enemy operations'.[28] The US position is, furthermore, that 'economic objects associated with military operations or with war-supporting or war-sustaining

21 Norwegian Manual, at page 140. In the same direction, placing emphasis on the 'direct' contribution, see Sassoli, 'Targeting', at pages 186 and 196.
22 UK Manual, at page 56. See as well the US DoD Manual, para. 5.6.6.2, at page 214.
23 Kalshoven and Zegveld, *Constraints on the Waging of War*, at page 106.
24 AMW Manual, rule 24, Commentary 1, at page 110.
25 Norwegian Manual, at page 140.
26 US DoD Manual, para. 5.6.6.2, at page 214.
27 Parks, 'Asymmetries and the identification of legitimate military objectives', at page 87.
28 Green, *The Contemporary Law of Armed Conflict*, at pages 218–19.

industries' are regarded as military objectives.[29] In a White House Report from 2016 it is stated that 'Under certain conditions, attacks on money and revenue-generating objects are consistent with the law of armed conflict.'[30] The question has raised increased attention after the war in, and around, Syria. The armed coalition, engaging in a non-international armed conflict against Islamic State of Iraq and the Levant (ISIL), has targeted ISIL oil exports (tanker trucks), as well as storage sites that were used to store the money under ISIL control.[31] The impact on the law of this practice must not, however, be exaggerated, as it relates to a NIAC and not an IAC, where the primary measure applicable between belligerent States in order to block economic income supporting the war is blockade.

The question of 'economic targets' and the notion of war-sustaining capabilities is raised and rejected elsewhere (outside the USA) in both military manuals[32] and literature as 'going too far'[33] and that the 'causal linkage between damage to or destruction of financial or commercial facilities not otherwise linked to the military war effort and military advantage is insufficiently direct'.[34] This position is exemplified in the Norwegian Manual by objects which make an indirect contribution to military action, such as a factory which by its production contributes financially to the national income and thus to the war effort.[35] Other examples are presented in the AMW Manual, referring to export oil production intended for neutral States[36] – but all sorts of export objects vital for the national economy can fulfil the same role, from fish or bananas to cotton or coffee.[37] Hence, the contribution must be effective to the *military phase*[38] of the war effort and not only to 'war-sustaining' activities.[39]

29 US DoD Manual, para. 5.6.8.5, at page 219.

30 See The White House, Report on the Legal and Policy Frameworks Guiding the United States' Use of Military Force.

31 The White House, Report on the Legal and Policy Frameworks Guiding the United States' Use of Military Force, at page 24.

32 Norwegian Manual, at page 140.

33 Dinstein, 'Legitimate military objectives under the current jus in bello', at page 145.

34 Boothby, *The Law of Targeting*, page 106. See also Rogers, *Law on the Battlefield*, pages 109–10.

35 Boothby, *The Law of Targeting*.

36 AMW Manual, Commentary 2 to rule 24, at page 110. The Group of Experts drafting the AMW Manual were divided on the matter of war-sustaining economic targets. The majority took the view that such objects did not constitute military objectives.

37 Rogers, *Law on the Battlefield*, at pages 109–10 makes the example of bananas or coffee. From a Norwegian perspective salmon or oil could serve the same purpose. The example of cotton production stems from the Confederate production during the American Civil War and is part of the US conception – criticised by Dinstein, *Conduct of Hostilities*, at pages 109–10.

38 Bothe, Partsch and Solf, *New Rules*, at page 366. See also Boivin, 'The legal regime applicable to targeting', at page 18.

39 Dinstein, *Conduct of Hostilities*, at pages 109–10.

The inherent challenge of determining when an object makes an effective contribution to military action is illustrated by the post-WWII urge to reject total-war arguments, as seen in Chapter 6.[40] Oeter points out that the approach chosen in the AP I article 52(2) 'considerably limits the military opportunities for a belligerent and is therefore not without problems, since successful modern warfare requires great strategic and tactical flexibility'. However, he continues, that 'if the intention directly to influence the enemy population's determination to fight were recognized as a legitimate objective for military force, then no limit to warfare would remain'.[41] The core of this argument makes sense: that legal standards ought to be realistic to achieve, in every armed conflict, taking a reasonable account of both States' perception of necessity as well as the imperative to protect the civilian population from the effects of hostilities. The needs of States are addressed by some authors, arguing that the scope of 'military action' is: '. . . broad enough to encompass certain economic activities without opening the door to attacks against "the main export industries, the stock market or the taxation authorities"'.[42] The issue can therefore be seen as another expression of the balance to be struck between military necessity and humanitarian considerations.

A related issue to that of war-sustaining capabilities and the scope of 'military action' is the scope of the 'military advantage' (the second 'prong' of the test to determine whether an object is a military objective) as opposed to other advantages. The scope of 'military advantage', as well as States' practice in pursuing such advantages, is dealt with in detail in Chapter 14.

Beyond the scope of those objects which are military by nature, the categories of 'purpose', 'location' or 'use' must meet the cumulative test set out in article 52(2). These alternative forms of qualification are accounted for in the following.

8.3 MILITARY OBJECTIVES BY 'NATURE'

'Nature' relates to objects which are intrinsically military,[43] such as – but not limited to – weapons, weapons platforms, ammunitions depots, military transports, command and control centres, military ports, docks and airfields as well

40 See in particular Section 6.6.3 on the rule of limitation which is not a general reference to 'a limited war'.
41 Oeter, 'Methods and means of combat', at pages 169–70.
42 Sassoli, 'Targeting', at page 196.
43 The AMW Manual use the phrase 'inherent characteristic or attribute which contributes to military action', see Commentary 1 to rule 22(a), at page 107.

as communications stations for military use.[44] These objects are military objectives even when they are not in use (during armed conflict).[45] This distinguishes military objectives by nature from military objectives by use – where the latter category clearly contains a temporal aspect.[46] There is, however, disagreement with regard to whether an object which is military by nature is also subject to the two-pronged test of effective contribution to military action and direct military advantage. While the position taken by the majority of Experts in the AMW Manual is that an object which is military by nature is a military objective in all circumstances (see, however, the 'compromise-solution' for objects of infrastructure and industry),[47] Boothby disagrees and argues that the two tests must always be applied in every case.[48] In the Norwegian Manual a pragmatic approach is chosen, stating that for 'objects which are military by nature it is normally not necessary to make a concrete assessment of whether these objects offer an effective contribution to military action, since it is presumed that they actually do'.[49] Dinstein is more explicit than this and argues that in order to be a military objective by nature the object 'must be endowed with some inherent attribute which *eo ipso* makes an effective contribution to military action'.[50] It appears that the disagreement to a large extent will depend on the scope of 'military objectives by nature'. Given a narrow approach, the application of the two tests will become moot. Given a wider approach, however, the two tests must obviously be applied in order not to water down the whole definition.

44 UK Manual, at page 55; Norwegian Manual, at pages 139–40. In legal literature, helpful lists are provided by Dinstein, *Conduct of Hostilities*, at pages 110–11 and 'Legitimate military objectives under the current jus in bello', at pages 146–7 and Rogers, *Law on the Battlefield*, at pages 83–4. See also Parks, 'Asymmetries and the identification of legitimate military objectives', at page 93, who agrees on the abovementioned list proposed by Dinstein, but emphasises the illustrative character of the list and regards it as 'more restrictive' than State practice.

45 AMW Manual, Commentary 1 to rule 22(a), at page 107. Robertson, 'The principle of the military objective in the law of armed conflict', at page 49.

46 On the criteria of use, see below. The temporal aspect is, however, challenged to a certain degree if one considers that not even objectives which are military by nature are lawful to attack at all times. See further below on the discussion of the scope of military objectives by nature and the diverging views expressed in the AMW Manual.

47 AMW Manual, Commentary 1 to rules 22(a) and 23, at page 109. Certain industrial objects, such as energy production, are dealt with below in the section on 'dual-use' objects, while certain infrastructure objects are dealt with in the section on bridges below.

48 Boothby, *The Law of Targeting*, at page 103.

49 Norwegian Manual, at page 140. My translation from Norwegian. The Norwegian text says: 'For objekter som etter sin art er militære, vil det normalt ikke være nødvendig å foreta en konkret vurdering av hvorvidt disse objektene gir et effektivt bidrag til militære operasjoner, da det forutsettes at de faktisk gjør det.'

50 Dinstein, *Conduct of Hostilities*, at page 110.

In fact, the distinction made in the AMW Manual rule 22(a) and rule 23 (supported by the majority of the Group of Experts and referred to as the 'compromise-solution' above) is based on a wide vs narrow approach to the group of objects, where the former will be military objectives only in light of the circumstances ruling at the time.[51] Having said this, the disagreement by Boothby presented above seems to touch upon even the narrow group of objects which are military by nature. He uses as example 'a military aircraft remote from servicing' and argues that this will have to be subject to the two tests.[52] It is hard to see that the attack on a military aircraft in an armed conflict will have to pass the two-pronged test.[53] This issue appears rather to be about military priorities than a matter of law, and hence up to the discretion of the military commander. Attacking military aircrafts even remote from military operations do not endanger the principle of distinction as such. When it comes to objects which are military by nature – but remote from servicing – they would normally appear to be either too remote for being a military priority or they are close enough to be of actual military value and hence obviously a military objective by nature – and lawful to attack at any time.[54] That 'the principle of necessity' should prohibit the attack on a military aircraft on its way to surrender[55] appears detached from the issue of whether objects which are military by nature automatically are military objectives, and could preferably be dealt with according to the rules of surrender (for the persons, as the object cannot be *hors de combat*), which in turn require that intent to surrender must be communicated in a clear way to the enemy.[56] A clear communication from an aircraft must preferably take the form of radio communication to the enemy.[57] Hence, it is true that military necessity – or the lack of such – is the basis for the protection devoted persons surrendering in an aircraft, but the object does not cease to be a military objective by nature, it simply gains temporary protection from attack because the personnel are surrendering.[58]

51 AMW Manual, at pages 107 and 109.

52 Boothby, *The Law of Targeting*, page 103, footnote 124, mentions the example of a military aircraft remote from servicing, fuelling arrangements and runway.

53 In support of this, see the illustration provided by Henderson, *The Contemporary Law of Targeting*, at pages 55–6, referring to the remote positioning of fighter aircrafts and abandoned military vehicles during the first and second Gulf Wars.

54 In this direction, see Henderson, *The Contemporary Law of Targeting*.

55 This example and argument is used by Kolb and Hyde, *An Introduction to the International Law of Armed Conflicts*, at page 131.

56 AP I article 41(2)(b). AMW Manual, rule 127(a), at page 266. Surrender is dealt with in Chapter 17.

57 AMW Manual, rule 128, Commentary 3, at page 267.

58 On the notion of special protection enemy combatants *hors de combat*, see further Chapter 17.

8.4 MILITARY OBJECTIVES BY 'USE'

Any civilian object can be 'used' in a way to make an effective contribution to military action; also objects entitled to special protection may lose their protection through military use, if military necessity requires it.[59] To enlarge the category even further: *any (military) use* may qualify as use – for as long as the use continues.[60] Examples are numerous: civilian houses may be used as shelter for troops[61] or for ammunition depots, and radio and television broadcasting facilities may be used for command and control purposes.[62] Civilian vehicles, airfields, airplanes and ships may become military objectives if used to launch military aircrafts or transport troops, ammunition and military materiel.[63] The criteria of use has a temporal aspect; military use of an object turns that object into a military objective – but only for so long as the use lasts.[64] This temporal aspect aside, it cannot be understood so rigidly that the object regains its original protection the moment a group of soldiers disembarks from a vehicle – for example for a rest – if the vehicle has been used for military purposes for a number of days.[65] If the issue concerns continued use of an object in the future, the consideration belongs under the criteria of purpose (dealt with below) and reliable evidence has to support the assumption of future use.[66] The temporal aspect is also envisaged in the additional criteria of 'circumstances ruling at the time' (see Chapter 14). Although the point of departure with regard to the criteria of 'use' is easy to grasp, or almost self-explanatory, this category has given rise to considerable debate regarding the so-called 'dual-use' objects.[67]

8.5 THE ISSUE OF 'DUAL-USE OBJECTS'

If the military use takes place alongside civilian use, such as may be the case for instance with an airfield which was originally civilian but in the event of an

59 AMW Manual, rule 22(d), Commentary 4, at page 108; 1954 Hague Convention on Cultural Property article 4; see further Chapter 17.

60 AMW Manual, Commentary to rule 22.

61 Robertson, 'The principle of the military objective in the law of armed conflict', at page 49; Henderson, *The Contemporary Law of Targeting*, at page 58.

62 AMW Manual, rule 22(d), Commentary 2, at page 108.

63 AP I Commentary at para. 2022, page 636; AMW Manual, rule 22(d), Commentary 2, at page 108.

64 Boothby, *The Law of Targeting*, at page 104. Dörmann, 'The definition of military objectives', at page 80.

65 Henderson, *The Contemporary Law of Targeting*, at page 58.

66 AMW Manual, rule 22(d), Commentary 4, at page 108.

67 AP I Commentary, para. 2023, at page 636.

armed conflict is also used by the armed forces, or with computer networks and other cyber infrastructure, the object (or the use of the object) is often denoted 'dual-use'.[68] The term may, however, appear misleading[69] as the object is either a military objective according to the definition or it is not – and 'dual-use' objects are military objectives.[70] Nevertheless, quite a few objects fall within the category and these so-called 'dual-use' objects have been the centre of attraction for legal controversy. Among the objects which raise discussion are airfields/airports/maritime ports, bridges (see also Section 8.8), industrial facilities, power generation plants, TV and radio stations, oil/coal and other mineral resources as well as trains and trucks.[71] Taking into account the simultaneous civilian use, the question of whether the object may be attacked depends upon the application of the proportionality rule, by the military commander.[72]

The first Gulf War in 1991[73] led to disagreement (among others) with regard to the lawfulness of attacks on electricity production facilities which served both the armed forces as well as the Iraqi civilian population (bridges are dealt with below). Electricity, oil refining and refined oil products were among the strategic targets identified by the USA during the war.[74] Critics reported 'near-apocalyptic results upon the economic infrastructure'[75] as a result of the attacks on Iraqi power supplies – but the pending issue with regard to the legality of the attacks was not whether the object was a lawful target but

68 AMW Manual, rule 22(d), Commentary 7, at page 109; Tallinn Manual, Commentary 1 to rule 101, at page 445. The terminology is of US origin, dating back to the first Gulf War in 1991. For a brief account of the inception of the term, see Parks, 'Asymmetries and the identification of legitimate military objectives', at pages 103–7.

69 Boivin, 'The legal regime applicable to targeting military objectives', at page 23.

70 Tallinn Manual, rule 101, at page 445; Boothby, *The Law of Targeting*, at pages 104–5; Hampson, 'Necessity and proportionality in the Gulf conflict', at page 50.

71 See Dinstein, 'Legitimate military objectives under the current jus in bello', at pages 153–8. Parks, 'Asymmetries and the identification of legitimate military objectives', at pages 103–7; Rogers, *Law on the Battlefield*, at pages 69–85; Oeter, 'Methods and means of combat', at pages 173–4.

72 AMW Manual, rule 22(d), Commentary 7, at page 109. On the principle of proportionality, see Chapter 13.

73 The first Gulf War (also referred to as the Persian Gulf War and Operation Desert Storm) started with the Iraqi invasion of Kuwait on 2 August 1990 and was followed by the USA led attack on Iraq from 17 January 1991 to 28 February 1991. As the Iraqi invasion in Kuwait aroused immediate international condemnation and agreement on UN Security Council Resolutions 660 and 661, the USA led Operation Desert Storm attacked Iraqi forces on 17 January, subsequent to the passing of UN Security Council resolution 678, authorising States to use 'all necessary means' in order to force Iraq out of Kuwait after 15 January.

74 Final Report to Congress, at page 122.

75 Human Rights Watch, Needless Deaths in the Gulf War. The report is based on the report of a UN Mission visiting Iraq in 1991.

whether the attacks violated the proportionality rule.[76] With regard to the status as lawful military objectives the conclusion seems to be clear: 'Power supplies provided significant military support', and thus an effective contribution to military action.[77] In the view of the majority of the Group of Experts drafting the AMW Manual, even energy production facilities are military objectives by nature, in light of the circumstances ruling at the time.[78] In Iraq, in the Gulf War, the classification of the objects was, however, that they were military objectives by *use*.

While electricity and power supplies were categorised as strategic targets[79] during Operation Desert Storm in the Gulf War, those targets were not hit at all during Operation Unified Protector (OUP) over Libya in 2011.[80] Due to reasons which were also non-legal,[81] air strikes were directed almost exclusively at military objectives by nature (the attack on Tripoli TV station is discussed below).[82] The two wars show how the different circumstances will dictate the different importance of the military objectives individually, for each conflict. During the first Gulf War, Saddam Hussein's regime was strongly centralised and it was therefore of paramount importance to paralyse the command and control (C2) functions[83] in order to hamper the movement of massive forces. It was also important for the air campaign to prepare for the

76 Rogers, *Law on the Battlefield*, at pages 75–6. See further Chapter 13.

77 Final Report to Congress, at page 148; Parks, 'Asymmetries and the identification of legitimate military objectives', at pages 103–4; Dinstein, 'Legitimate military objectives under the current jus in bello', at page 155; Dinstein, *Conduct of Hostilities*, at page 121; Rogers, *Law on the Battlefield*, at page 75; Hampson, 'Necessity and proportionality in the Gulf conflict', at page 50; Boivin, 'The legal regime applicable to targeting military objectives', at page 50, footnotes 191 and 193.

78 AMW Manual, rule 23, at page 109 in Commentary. The 'third view' in the AMW Manual is dealt with below as well, when discussing particular questions related to bridges.

79 On the definition and weight devoted to strategic targets in the proportionality assessment, see Chapter 15.

80 Operation Unified Protector was mandated in UN Security Council Resolution 1973 from 17 March 2011 which authorised the use of 'all necessary means' to 'protect civilians and civilian populated areas under threat of attack in the Libyan Arab Jamahiriya, including Benghazi, while excluding a foreign occupation force of any form on any part of Libyan territory, and requests the Member States concerned to inform the Secretary-General immediately of the measures they take pursuant to the authorization conferred by this paragraph which shall be immediately reported to the Security Council'.

81 On the political impact of the assessment of the military advantage, see Chapter 14.

82 For a chronological account on a daily basis of the key targets and engagements from 1 April to 25 October 2011, see Operational Media Update, NATO and Libya. On target selection during OUP see also below on the discussion of 'circumstances ruling at the time' as well as Chapter 4 on the commander's assessment.

83 See for example, Final Report to Congress, at pages 148–9; Parks, 'Asymmetries and the identification of legitimate military objectives', at page 103.

ground campaign and therefore a potential great risk for loss of own troops. The Libya War was, on the other hand, not a ground operation from NATO's side and the hampering of mass movement of troops was not an issue compared to the Gulf War.[84] These circumstances, seen together with the strong political impact of the mandate which stressed the protection of civilians, can easily explain the actual limitation to direct attacks primarily at those objects which belong to the core of objects and are military by nature. This practice of NATO States does therefore not diminish the status of power supplies as military objectives either by use or even (according to the circumstances) by nature.

Among the controversial 'dual-use' objects which have been subject to discussion since 1990, are those of radio and TV stations – which have been attacked several times during the last decades. The USA bombed TV and radio facilities in Baghdad during the first Gulf War and argued subsequently that: 'Civil TV and radio facilities *could be used* easily for C3 backup for military purposes. The Saddam Hussein regime also controlled TV and radio and used them as the principal media for Iraqi propaganda. Thus, these installations also were struck.'[85] The notion of 'could be used' has been criticised, and rightly so, as insufficient for the military objective test in AP I[86] – not only because 'could be' does not amount to actual use, but also according to the 'purpose' criteria, which addresses the intended future use of an object and is commented upon below.

Since 1990, NATO forces have bombed such objects both in April 1999, in Belgrade, and in July 2011 in Tripoli. The aim of the attack on the Serbian TV and radio had a twofold guise, which resembles the US argument from the Gulf War above: (a) that it was a part of Milosevic's command, control and communication (C3)[87] and/or (b) that it was a part of the war propaganda.[88] The latter alternative was clearly dubious and has been rejected as 'use' which makes an 'effective contribution to military action'.[89] As a part of C3, however, TV and radio stations have also been considered lawful targets in its aftermath, although subject to criticism.[90] On

84 I thank LTC Geir Ødegaard for helpful discussions on this matter.
85 Final Report to Congress, at page 149. Emphasis added.
86 Henderson, *The Contemporary Law of Targeting*, at page 60.
87 OTP Report, at para. 72.
88 Ibid., at para. 74.
89 Ibid., at para. 76; Dörmann, 'The definition of military objectives', at page 82.
90 Dinstein, 'Legitimate military objectives under the current jus in bello', at page 157; Rogers, *Law on the Battlefield*, at pages 82–3. For a critical perspective, see Laursen, 'NATO, The war over Kosovo, and the ICTY investigation', at pages 789–90.

29 July 2011 NATO again bombed a TV station, this time in Tripoli, Libya, during Operation Unified Protector.[91]

There is no doubt that broadcasting facilities may easily be used for military purposes. In the 1954 Hague Convention it is even exemplified as a military objective in article 8(1)(a). But it is difficult to take it further and conclude whether media is a 'legitimate target group' or not.[92] As long as broadcasting facilities, in particular those that are state owned, are mostly used for civilian purposes but have easy access for (State) military forces to make use of them, the point of departure remains accordingly: they are civilian objects which easily may turn into military objectives. Further attempts of 'grouping' such objectives may make the actual application of the law unnecessarily difficult. Each case must eventually be decided, by the commander, after a careful assessment of the facts reasonably available at the time.

8.6 MILITARY OBJECTIVES BY 'PURPOSE'

When it comes to 'purpose', this relates to the 'intended future use' of an object,[93] as opposed to the notion of 'use', which refers to the present use of an object.

To fulfil the criteria of military objective by purpose, the future use must be *intended*, and not only hypothetical or speculative. This means that there must be concrete, intelligence based evidence that the opposing forces actually intend to use the object as a military objective. It is not enough that the object in theory could be suited to military purposes, such as a church spire which could offer a good sniper position or observation post, or that civilian broadcasting facilities easily could be used for military command and control purposes.[94] A historical example which has been subject to differing opinions in this regard is the Allied destruction of the Monte Cassino Abbey in 1944.

91 On Operation Unified Protector, see above. On the report of the hit of the TV satellite dishes, see Operational Media Update 29 July 2011. See also *The Guardian*, 30 July 2011. A NATO spokesperson said on the following day that: 'Our intervention was necessary as TV was being used as an integral component of the regime apparatus designed to systematically oppress and threaten civilians and to incite attacks against them.' See, 'NATO strikes Libyan TV satellite facility'. On the relationship to serious crimes, see OTP Report, at paras. 47 and 76; and Section 14.9 below.

92 See Laursen, 'NATO, the War over Kosovo, and the ICTY investigation', at page 777. Henderson tries to 'go beyond' mere general statements in *The Contemporary Law of Targeting*, at pages 130–9.

93 AP I Commentary, at para. 2022, page 636; Norwegian Manual, at page 140; UK Manual, at page 56; AMW Manual, rule 22(c), at page 107 in Commentary; Dinstein, 'Legitimate military objectives under the current jus in bello', at page 148.

94 On this point, see above, on 'dual-use' objects.

The Abbey was situated on top of a hill, a perfect spot for observation and reconnaissance by the Germans. The Germans, however, did not intend to use the Abbey, due to its protected status as cultural heritage.

The bombings have been used as an example by critics of being based on insufficient intelligence, and hence unlawful.[95] Others argue completely the opposite, that the Abbey was a lawful military objective and that the attack was lawful (taking sufficient precautions in attack as well).[96] The differing in opinion seems to stem from how they judge the commander's assessment of the available intelligence under the given circumstances.[97]

The practical importance of the criteria of purpose is being downplayed by some, arguing that: 'It is hard to think of an example of a case where "purpose" will be the deciding factor, especially given the limitation of "in the circumstances ruling at the time".'[98] The practical importance, however, can be found exactly in the 'circumstances at the time'; when the criteria of 'purpose' allows a party to the conflict to direct an attack against an objective based on intelligence revealing the intent of the other party. Examples where the intentions are rather easily accessible are civilian houses which are being re-built or renovated for military accommodation. In such cases there is no need to await an attack until the actual use commences.[99] The enemy's intentions may also be based on '... specified preconditions prior to actual implementation of any existing plans'[100] such as an overt contingency plan to use civilian transports in case of need for military purposes. It is not enough to be aware of the plan; the civilian object assumes status as a military objective first when steps are taken to activate the plan – although the actual use is still civilian.[101] Examples of such contingency plans were numerous in the Norwegian 'mobilisation defence'. Passenger ferries were for example equipped with facilities in order to be able to be quickly re-built for mine laying, but used in civilian transport until being eventually summoned for military service in the case of an armed attack.[102] During the eventual 're-build' phase, the ferries would have been lawful targets, despite not yet being in military use.

95 Dinstein, *Conduct of Hostilities*, at page 114 and 'Legitimate military objectives under the current jus in bello', at page 148.

96 Rogers, *Law on the Battlefield*, at page 94.

97 The level of expectancy of the commander's judgment is dealt with in general in Chapters 4 and 5.

98 Rogers, *Law on the Battlefield*, at page 66–67.

99 AMW Manual, Commentary 2 to rule 22(c), at page 107.

100 Ibid., Commentary 4 to rule 22(c), at page 108.

101 Ibid.

102 For an account of civilian ships subject to military requisition throughout the 1970s and 1980s, see Gjelsten, 'Marinens beredskap 1960-90; Kampklar i Nordflåtens skygge', at pages 40–1. 602 ships were subject to pre-requisition.

8.7 MILITARY OBJECTIVES BY 'LOCATION'

The alternative that a civilian object may become a military objective by location encapsulates situations where a specific area of land, such as a specific hillside, a bridgehead and other spots of operational value become military objectives because the area makes an effective contribution to military action.[103] The piece of land in question becomes a military objective irrespective of the actual use or intended use (purpose) by the enemy; the crucial aspect lies in *denying* the options of the enemy forces.[104] Examples are to deny the possibility of retreat or advance over a bridge or through a mountain pass or to take territorial control over a certain hillside. Obviously, the area cannot be of indefinite size, but must have a distinct feature which turns it into a military objective.[105]

Some also point out that objects which otherwise are considered civilian become military objectives by location in cases where, for example, a supermarket is located within a military base or a merchant vessel is anchored in a military port.[106] Beyond this, however, the question of co-location of civilian objects together with military objectives is an issue of proportionality.

8.8 PARTICULAR QUESTIONS RELATED TO BRIDGES

The categorisation of bridges has been subject to controversy. While some argue that bridges are military objectives *by nature*,[107] others disagree and argue that they are only military objectives in so far as they can be so according to their actual use, intended future purpose or location.[108] In the view of the majority of Experts drafting the AMW Manual, bridges are categorised alongside, inter alia: roads, tunnels, airfields, energy production facilities and oil storage depots as the compromise solution of the two foregoing views. According to this compromise-solution (see Section 8.3), those objects are military objectives by nature, but only in light of the circumstances at the time.[109]

103 AMW Manual, rule 22(b) with commentary at page 107. AP I Commentary at page 636, para. 2021. Bothe, Partsch and Solf, *New Rules*, at page 367.

104 AMW Manual; Bothe, Partsch and Solf, *New Rules*; Boothby, *The Law of Targeting*, at page 103; Rogers, *Law on the Battlefield*, at page 69.

105 AP I Commentary, at page 2026. Dinstein, 'Legitimate military objectives under the current jus in bello', at page 150.

106 Dinstein, 'Legitimate military objectives under the current jus in bello', at page 150.

107 Dinstein, *Conduct of Hostilities*, at page 115. For the opposite view, see Hampson, 'Necessity and proportionality in the Gulf conflict', at page 49.

108 See for example Hampson, 'Necessity and proportionality in the Gulf conflict'.

109 AMW Manual, Commentary 1 to rule 23, at page 109.

Hence, there is no question that a bridge easily may acquire the status of a military objective[110] – such as bridges during the first Gulf War,[111] where the US position was that: 'Baghdad bridges crossing the Euphrates River contained the multiple fiber-optic links that provided Saddam Hussein with secure communications to his southern group of forces. Attack of these bridges severed those secure communication links, while restricting movement of Iraqi military forces and deployment of CW [chemical weapons] and BW [biological weapons] warfare capabilities.'[112]

Disagreement persists with regard to whether bridges (and railways) can be categorised by reference to an 'abstract target categorization' – as always being military objectives by nature – or whether an individual assessment is required with regard to the circumstances at the time (either by nature, location, purpose or use).[113]

The underlying question for where opinions differ can be formulated as done by Sassoli: 'Are all bridges and railway lines of a country military objectives from the very first day of a war, independently of where fighting erupts and where troops have to move to and fro?'[114]

Those answering this question in the negative base their arguments on whether the moving of 'military supplies from one place to another' has (in their opinion) any significance for the conflict.[115] When destruction of bridges during the first Gulf War obviously would offer a military advantage,[116] their destruction during the Kosovo Campaign in 1999 has been criticised.[117]

110 See for example the enumeration of objectives in the 1956 ICRC Draft Rules from where the categories listed in the annex contain: 'Those of the lines and means of communications (railway lines, roads, bridges, tunnels and canals) which are of fundamental military importance.' See as well Norwegian Manual, at page 140, places bridges as an example of an object which easily acquire the status of a military objective by purpose.

111 Hampson, 'Necessity and proportionality in the Gulf conflict', at page 51. Dinstein, 'Legitimate military objectives under the current jus in bello', at page 151. Rogers, *Law on the Battlefield*, at pages 71–2.

112 Final Report to Congress, at page 613. See also Parks, 'Asymmetries and the identification of legitimate military objectives', at pages 104–5.

113 See above on the discussion of military objectives by nature, and the three views presented in the AMW Manual with regard to rules 22(a) and 23. Human Rights Watch criticise even the attack on bridges during the Gulf War, in the report: Needless Deaths in the Gulf War, Chapter 3. The position of the Human Rights Watch Report is shared by Henderson, *The Contemporary Law of Targeting*, at pages 76–7.

114 Sassoli, 'Targeting', at page 197.

115 This is the positions of Bothe, 'The protection of the civilian population and NATO bombing on Yugoslavia', at page 534.

116 See also, however, the criticism by Human Rights Watch with regard to the attacks on bridges during the Gulf War, dealt with above.

117 During the bombing campaign a passenger train was hit (unintentionally) as a result of an (intentional) attack on the bridge at Grdelica Gorge. During the assessment of the hit on the

8.9 RETURNING TO THE COMMANDER'S ASSESSMENT

The decision as to whether an object qualifies as a military objective rests with the military commander. In Section 7.7 I dealt with questions raised during, and after, the adoption of the AP I: would the treaty definition leave too much room for the commander's assessment and would exemplifying lists of military objectives contribute to guidance for the commander's assessment or, rather, to arbitrary decisions? As argued there: it is hard to see that exemplifying lists (belonging to the second category of limitations to the commander's assessment of military necessity, introduced in Section 4.3) contributes to arbitrariness – on the contrary. Having said that, the interpretive controversy existing over the scope of the notion of 'effective contribution to military action' as well as concerning the alternative criterion 'by nature', is a regrettable fact as far as clarity for commanders is concerned. Clarity in this regard could have provided military commanders with better guidance, and limitation (in the shape of the first category introduced in Section 4.3), in their decision making.

In the two mentioned issues of controversy, the former (whether the notion of 'effective contribution to military action' includes 'war-sustaining capabilities') appears to bear most practical impact upon the commander's assessment. The assessment of 'effective contribution to military action' – alongside the assessment of 'military advantage', as dealt with in Chapter 14 – amounts to an implicit assessment of military necessity (see Section 4.2) and is a demanding assessment for any reasonable commander. At the core of the challenge lies the fact that different views upon the scope of the notion of effective contribution to military action often entail different perceptions of whether it is a necessity to destroy economic targets. Needless to say, these differences in perception may lead to significant differences in practice. Furthermore, differences in perceptions of necessity should also be seen in a broader perspective, and are dealt with in Chapter 12 (protection of the civilian population and perceptions of military necessity) and in Chapter 14 (military necessity and the scope of military advantage).

The second issue of controversy (the scope of the alternative 'by nature') may arguably have a lesser practical impact, although different perceptions of necessity may also be hidden in the controversies here: is it presumably a necessity to destroy bridges in armed conflict, like there is a presumable necessity to disable enemy combatants and military materiel, or is the

train, the OTP Report simply stated that the bridge was considered a military objective (the bridge was used on a Serbian supply route). See the OTP Report, at para. 62. The position taken in the OTP Report is criticised by Bothe, 'The protection of the civilian population and NATO bombing on Yugoslavia'.

destruction of bridges (and railway lines) dependent upon the circumstances of the time?[118]

However, the alternative categories of 'nature', 'location', 'purpose' or 'use' encapsulate a broad range of possible situations in which an object may turn into a military objective. For a commander it is, arguably, of less importance which one of the categories an object falls into, as long as the mission can be accomplished. The decisive element appears to the degree of information required in order to determine that an object actually fulfils the requirement of the definition. For objects qualifying as military objectives by nature, it is usually not necessary to make a concrete assessment of whether these objects make an effective contribution to military action, since it is presumed that they do so (see Section 8.3).

118 'Circumstances ruling at the time' is dealt with in Chapter 14.

9

Combatants As Lawful Targets

9.1 GENERAL REMARKS

This chapter addresses which persons are classed as combatants, the military necessity considerations that underpin the right to direct attacks against combatants and the principle that limits this right, i.e. the prohibition of means and methods of warfare of a nature to cause superfluous injury or unnecessary suffering. The protection of combatants *hors de combat* is dealt with in Chapter 17.

As stated in Chapter 7, the principle of distinction places limitations upon (the commander's assessment of) military necessity. In order to implement the principle of distinction it must be practically possible for combatants to *actually distinguish* those who are lawful targets from those who enjoy protection from attack. As we shall see, the notion of *lawful combatancy* is therefore inextricably linked to *how* combatants distinguish themselves from civilians and the civilian population – this issue is dealt with separately in Chapter 10.

9.2 WHO ARE COMBATANTS?

The notion of 'combatants' under the international LOAC is found today in the 1907 Hague Regulations articles 1 and 3 and is reflected in GC III article 4A and AP I article 43.[1] Neither the Hague Regulations nor the GC III actually defines combatants. The 1907 Hague Regulations refers to the 'qualification of belligerents' (in the heading) as well as to armies, militia and volunteer corps, while the GC III article 4 governs the right to POW status for armed forces,

[1] 1907 Hague Regulations, article 1; GC III article 4; AP I article 43.

militia, volunteer corps, organised resistance movements as well as inhabitants of a non-occupied territory who spontaneously take up arms (*levee en masse*).[2]

The only explicit reference to combatants is found in article 3 in the 1907 Hague Regulations where it is stated that: 'The armed forces of the belligerent parties may consist of combatants and non-combatants. In the case of capture by the enemy, both have a right to be treated as prisoners of war.'

Customary law[3] and AP I article 43(2)[4] define combatants as being all members of the armed forces of a belligerent party to the conflict, except those who enjoy protection as medical or religious personnel. The definition in AP I article 43(2) explicitly links the term 'combatants' to the right to participate in hostilities – although this right also has been part of the law prior to the AP I.[5] The AP I also dissolves the distinction made in the 1907 Hague Regulations article 3, since *all* members of the armed forces are now considered combatants.[6]

When dealing with the notion of combatants it is important to distinguish between the primary and secondary status as combatants. By primary status I refer here to the status as a lawful target and by secondary status I refer to the status as prisoner of war upon capture. While the GC III explicitly governs the secondary status as POW,[7] the AP I and customary law are concerned with combatancy both in the primary and secondary sense. In the AP I this follows from the relationship between articles 48 and 50. Article 48 limits the right to direct operations only to military objectives and confirms the duty to distinguish between combatants and the civilian population. With regard to the latter (the distinction between combatants and the civilian population), article 50 entails a negative definition of civilians as all those who do not fall into any of the categories as combatants. The categories of civilians and combatants are thus said to be mutually exclusive; a person is either a combatant or a civilian (on the definition and scope of protection on civilians, see Chapter 11).[8]

2 1907 Hague Regulations, article 1; GC III article 4A. The provisions are cited in full and accounted for in more detail below, Section 10.1. Those categories mentioned in GC III articles 4A (4) and (5) are not combatants according to the AP I article 50 (the definition of civilians) although they are entitled to POW status.

3 ICRC CIHL, rule 3; AMW Manual, rule 10(b)(i), Commentary at page 84; and commentaries 1 and 4 to rule 87 of the Tallinn Manual, at pages 402–3.

4 AP I article 43(2).

5 AP I Commentary to AP I article 43, page 515, para. 1677; Dörmann, 'The legal situation of "unlawful/unprivileged combatants"', at page 45; Boothby, *The Law of Targeting*, at page 65.

6 AP I Commentary to AP I article 43, at page 515, para. 1677. The explicit exclusion follows from AP I article 44(2).

7 AP I Commentary to AP I article 43, at page 515, para. 1677.

8 Boothby, *The Law of Targeting*, at page 69.

The expression 'combatant' has been used with two meanings: in the first sense as a reference to a person who actually engages in hostilities – regardless of whether that person is entitled to such participation; and in the second sense as a reference to only those who have the combatant's privilege, i.e. the right to participate in hostilities.[9] If one takes the first position, a subsequent distinction between lawful and unlawful combatants makes more sense than if one confines the group of combatants to members of the armed forces as defined in AP I article 43.[10] The question of how to label those who do not fulfil the criteria as (lawful) combatants remains however. As a solution to this some States' military manuals distinguish between combatants as those who are entitled to take a direct part in hostilities on the one hand and unlawful combatants as those who are not entitled to, but who do take part in hostilities.[11] Others again distinguish between lawful combatants on the one hand and 'other combatants' on the other hand.[12] The latter terminology is aimed at describing the physical phenomenon that a heterogeneous group of people actually fighting in hostilities are lawful objects of attack and do not enjoy the privileges of POW. The further consequences of unlawful combatancy are dealt with in Chapter 10.

Because participation in hostilities is not unlawful as such under international law,[13] the phrase 'unlawful combatant' may appear misleading. An unlawful or unprivileged combatant is simply a person who takes a direct part in hostilities without being entitled to do so and therefore does not enjoy the privilege of POW status upon capture by the opposing forces.[14] However, whether one chooses to label those who fight as 'unlawful combatants', 'unprivileged combatants' or as 'civilians' is not per se decisive, but becomes so if one attaches substantive consequences to the terminology.

9 UK Manual, at page 38. The discussion is also referred to in the AMW Manual, rule 10(b)(i), Commentary 4, at page 84. The first position is held by Dinstein, *Conduct of Hostilities*, at pages 41–2, where he argues that 'civilians are assimilated to combatants for such time as they engage in the hostilities'. The latter position is taken by the ICRC. See for example AP I Commentary to article 43, at page 515, para. 1677

10 This point is made by Garraway, '"Combatants" – substance or semantics?', at page 327. Boothby argues in *The Law of Targeting*, at page 66, that: '. . .for States that are Party to API there is no such thing as an "unlawful combatant". That would be an oxymoron.'

11 Canadian Manual, at page 3-1, Section 302.

12 Norwegian Manual, at page 46.

13 Tallinn Manual, commentaries 1 and 2 to rule 86, at page 401; Dinstein, 'Unlawful combatancy', at page 251; Pejic, 'Unlawful/enemy combatants', at page 338.

14 Dörmann, 'The Legal situation of "unlawful/unprivileged combatants"', at page 46; Pejic, 'Unlawful/enemy combatants', at page 338.

The categories of lawful and unlawful combatants are dealt with in more detail in Chapter 10, but a list of subcategories is presented here. Lawful combatants are: members of the armed forces of a party to the conflict (except for chaplains and medical personnel who are non-combatants), members of militia, volunteer corps and organised resistance movements belonging to a party to the conflict, and participants in a *levee en masse* against an invading force. Other persons sometimes described combatants/unlawful combatants include: members of the groups listed above which do not fulfil the criteria for lawful combatancy (see below), members of organised armed groups not belonging to a State, spies, mercenaries and civilians directly participating in hostilities.

The first (uncontested) category of combatants, the armed forces of a party to the conflict, consists of all organised armed forces, both regular and irregular as well as paramilitary forces, under a responsible command.[15] The task each individual member of the armed forces actually fulfils is irrelevant (beyond medical and religious personnel); they are considered combatants.[16] This will include a range of functions, such as cooks, administrative personnel and legal advisors.[17] Instead, the solution in AP I is based on status alone.[18]

The notion of a 'party to the conflict' is primarily understood as referring to States which are parties to an international armed conflict (including governments of an occupied country which are in exile[19]), while the AP I extends the notion of a party also to entities which are not States under a provision that never seems to have been applied in practice.[20] This latter extension is highly contested and not a part of customary international law.[21] Hence, the status as combatant only exists in international armed conflicts and in conflicts treated as such.[22]

15 GC III articles 4(A)(1), (2) and(3). AP I articles 43(1) and (3).

16 AP I Commentary to article 43, at page 515, para. 1677.

17 AP I Commentary to article 43, at page 515, para. 1677; Bothe, Partsch and Solf, *New Rules*, at pages 273–4; Dinstein, *Conduct of Hostilities*, at page 41; Henderson, *The Contemporary Law of Targeting*, at page 81

18 Garraway, '"Combatants" – substance or semantics?', at page 325.

19 Bothe, Partsch and Solf, *New Rules*, at page 269. One such example is the Norwegian 'Homefront' during WWII, which was under the command of the Norwegian Government in exile in London (when not under the actual command of the British Government).

20 AP I article 1(4); and the AP I Commentary to article 43, at para. 1661, page 507.

21 This point is most notable when it comes to the recognition of POW status for irregular forces according to the criteria of AP I article 44(3). This discussion is dealt with in more detail below.

22 ICRC CIHL, Commentary to rule 3; Pejic, 'Unlawful/enemy combatants', at page 335; Dörmann, 'The legal situation of "unlawful/unprivileged combatants"', at page 47.

9.3 MILITARY NECESSITY AND COMBATANTS AS LAWFUL TARGETS

In the Lieber Code article 15 it is stated that: 'Military necessity admits of all direct destruction of life or limb or *armed* enemies . . .'[23] Later formulations of military necessity in States' military manuals refer to the amount of force necessary in order to compel the submission (partial or complete) of the enemy.[24]

Injury to enemy forces is also referred to in the Preamble to the St Petersburg Declaration which states:

> That the only legitimate object which States should endeavour to accomplish during war is to weaken the military forces of the enemy;
>
> That for this purpose it is sufficient to disable the greatest possible number of men . . .

Attacks against enemy armed forces are thus at the core of what is considered necessary and lawful under the LOAC. Military necessity permits[25] attacks against the enemy armed forces.

Furthermore, the LOAC contains a presumption for the necessity of attacks against individuals who come within the understanding of the word 'combatants'. While an armed conflict between States is taking place, combatants can be attacked at any time and at any place within the limitations mentioned later in this chapter and in Chapter 17.[26] The status of combatants as lawful targets is not bound by the functional criteria for objects (see Chapter 8) and civilians directly participating in hostilities (see Chapter 11). The military commander does not need to prove in each case that combatants are making an effective contribution to military action – they are already presumed to do so.[27] However, combatants are only lawful targets for as long they are not *hors de combat* and thus gain protection either as incapacitated wounded or sick, if they are clearly surrendering, or as POWs.[28] Again, considerations of military necessity underpin the distinction: any combatant who has surrendered or is *hors de combat* (due to wounds or sickness, and therefore is incapable of defending himself, provided that he abstains from any hostile act and does not attempt to escape), is already deprived the possibility to harm the

23 Lieber Code article 15. Emphasis in original. Bill argues in 'The Rendulic "Rule"', at page 134, in this regard that 'In other words, targeting a combatant is always militarily necessary.'

24 See Sections 2.3 and 2.4, citing the US, UK, German and Norwegian manuals.

25 On military necessity as permission, see Section 2.7.

26 Dinstein, *Conduct of Hostilities*, at page 42.

27 See the discussion below of the alleged duty to 'capture rather than kill' in Section 9.4.

28 AP I article 41(2). Rules on special protection are dealt with in Chapter 17.

opponent and there is no reason to direct an attack towards him.[29] For the same purpose – of solely pursuing the necessities of war – the rule prohibiting means and methods inflicting unnecessary suffering (see below) to combatants places limitations on kinds of attack against otherwise lawful targets. Beyond these limitations – as well as specific weapons regulations derived from the unnecessary suffering principle – belligerents are left with a range of possibilities in choosing means and methods of warfare. The possibilities include the freedom to choose whether a combatant is to be captured or subject to lethal attack – although this freedom has been questioned (see below).

Finally, a remark with regard to the link between combatant and POW status: although the principle of distinction is reflected in the list of those entitled to POW status, the secondary status as POW must not be confused with combatant status and the liability to be attacked. The categories of combatants and POWs are distinct – although partly (with regard to combatants) derived from the same provision. Only combatants in AP I terms and lawful combatants in the US lexicon acquire POW status, while *all those participating in combat* are lawful targets.[30]

9.4 MILITARY NECESSITY AND THE ALLEGED DUTY TO 'CAPTURE RATHER THAN KILL' A COMBATANT

The question of whether there is a duty to capture rather than kill has been inextricably linked to the conception of military necessity and discussed with variable intensity at least since Jean Pictet published *The Principles of International Humanitarian Law* in 1966. The book was republished in 1985 after the adoption of the Additional Protocols of 1977. In the 1985 edition Pictet writes:

> To diminish the enemy's human potential – consisting of the persons who contribute directly to the war effort – a belligerent may kill, wound or capture them. These three means are equivalent so far as military effectiveness is concerned, for they all eliminate the enemy's active forces. The reasoning in humanitarian terms is quite different, and the three means are not at all equivalent, for humanity insists that capture is preferable to wounding an enemy, and wounding him better than killing him; that non-combatants shall be spared as far as possible; that wounds inflicted be as light as possible, so that

[29] Bothe, Partsch and Solf, *New Rules*, at page 252. See also Chapter 17.

[30] This follows explicitly from a reading of AP I article 50, together with AP I articles 43–4 and GC III article 4.

> the injured can be treated and cured; that the wounds cause the least possible pain; that captivity be made as endurable as possible.[31]

The views of Pictet, referred to by critics as 'Pictet's use of force continuum',[32] were raised at the Diplomatic Conference prior to the drafting of the Certain Conventional Weapons (CCW) Convention,[33] but his views apparently gained little serious support from government delegations[34] and were contested by other expert participants.[35] Nevertheless, the position of 'capture rather than kill' as a legal duty was put forward by the ICRC in the 'Interpretive Guidance on Direct Participation in Hostilities'.[36] Based on rather general references to military necessity and humanity as well as the mentioned 'Pictet's use of force continuum' (the Interpretive Guidance actually – and without sufficient reason – argues that 'implicit in the principle of military necessity is the principle of humanity'[37]) the Interpretive Guidance concludes:

> In sum, while operating forces can hardly be required to take additional risks for themselves or the civilian population in order to capture an armed adversary alive, it would defy basic notions of humanity to kill an adversary or to refrain from giving him or her an opportunity to surrender where there manifestly is no necessity for the use of lethal force.[38]

This notion of additional legal restraint on the basis of military necessity of the use of force against otherwise lawful targets has been so seriously contested in the aftermath of the publication of the Interpretive Guidance that a general consensus *rejecting* the view seems to have emerged: a choir of critics have firmly upheld that the LOAC does not contain a duty to 'capture a combatant

31 Pictet, *Development and Principles of International Humanitarian Law*, at page 62.
32 Parks, 'Part IX of the ICRC DPH Study', at page 785.
33 Convention on Prohibitions or Restrictions on the Use of Certain Conventional Weapons Which May be Deemed to be Excessively Injurious or to Have Indiscriminate Effects (1980).
34 Parks, 'Part IX of the ICRC DPH Study', at page 787.
35 Kalshoven, *Reflections on the Law of War*, at pages 369–71.
36 Interpretive Guidance, at page 1040. For a discussion of the notion of direct participation in hostilities, see Chapter 11.
37 Ibid., at page 1042. On the balance and relationship between military necessity and humanitarian considerations in general, see Chapter 6.
38 Ibid., at pages 1044–5. A position resembling that of the ICRC was also published by Melzer, 'Targeted killing or less harmful means?', at page 108, referring to the 'restrictive function of military necessity'. Support for the proponents of the view has also been retrieved in the so called 'Targeted Killings Judgment' in *The Public Committee Against Torture et al.* v. *The Government of Israel et al.* This decision does, however, concern Israeli administrative law and cannot be applied directly to questions pertaining to the LOAC.

rather than killing him'.[39] Some also explicitly point out that the assumption of necessity vis-à-vis combatants does not 'amount to an extension of the principle of proportionality towards combatants'.[40] The same (rejecting) position has been upheld in States' military manuals,[41] and strengthens the impression that for the purpose of attack on lawful targets: 'specific customary and treaty rules set forth in IHL have already taken military necessity into account' and that the notions of military necessity and humanity are 'principles underlying the positive rules'.[42]

Examples from State practice also support the position that lawful objects of attack are subject to no further legal restrictions than the definition of a military objective. The US attacks on retreating Iraqi armed forces during the first Gulf War (see Section 9.5.4) can be viewed in this regard. Although the 'Highways of Death' gained considerable attention and criticism, there appears to be widespread support for the legality of the attacks.[43] The US position in the DoD Manual is also explicit in this regard, stating that 'overwhelming force' may be used against enemy military objectives.[44]

9.5 THE PROHIBITION OF UNNECESSARY SUFFERING ON COMBATANTS

9.5.1 *The Rule as Expressed in Treaties*

In the St Petersburg Declaration, subsequent to the phrases quoted earlier,[45] the following is stated:

39 Parks, 'Part IX of the ICRC DPH Study'; Watkin, 'Opportunity lost'; Boothby, 'And for such time as'; Schmitt, 'Deconstructing direct participation in hostilities'.

40 See Geiss, 'Military necessity', at page 562. On proportionality as an alleged 'silent condition' of military necessity, see Chapter 13.

41 Norwegian Manual, at page 45, which states that 'it is not a requirement according to international law to capture someone instead of shooting them, unless the person clearly intends to surrender' (my translation). The Norwegian text says: 'Det innebærer blant annet at det ikke er et folkerettslig krav om å ta noen til fange i stedet for å skyte med mindre personen gir tegn til å ville overgi seg.'

42 Schmitt, 'The Interpretive Guidance on the Notion of Direct Participation in Hostilities', at pages 40–1. See also for example Gardam, *Necessity, Proportionality and the Use of Force by States*, at page 7.

43 Dinstein, *Conduct of Hostilities*, at page 117; and De Cock, 'Operation Unified Protector and the protection of civilians in Libya', at page 230.

44 US DoD Manual, para. 2.2.3.1, at page 57. The passage is also commented upon in Section 13.2.1 below.

45 See Chapter 3. See also Chapter 2 with regard to the term 'object of war'.

> That this object would be exceeded by the employment of arms which uselessly aggravate the sufferings of disabled men, or render their death inevitable;
>
> That the employment of such arms would, therefore, be contrary to the laws of humanity . . .

This prohibition is thus a specific prohibition, protecting combatants, rooted in considerations of necessity[46] as well as humanity. In fact, the core of the rule is to prohibit injury which 'lacks military utility'.[47] The wording from the St Petersburg Declaration was repeated with slight alterations – and subsequent discussions – in the Brussels Declaration of 1874[48] as well as in the Oxford Manual.[49] The Hague Regulations of 1899, article 23(e) stated in English that it was prohibited: 'To employ arms, projectiles, or material of a nature to cause superfluous injury . . .'

This text was directly translated from the binding French version.[50] In the Hague Regulations of 1907 however, the English (not authentic) text changed, although the French had not. The English translation of article 23(e) reads: 'To employ arms, projectiles, or material calculated to cause unnecessary suffering . . .' The debate concerning the differences between 'superfluous injury' and 'unnecessary suffering' and between 'of a nature to cause' and 'calculated to cause' are now obsolete, subsequent to the adoption of the provision in AP I article 35(2): 'It is prohibited to employ weapons, projectiles and material and methods of warfare of a nature to cause superfluous injury or unnecessary suffering.'

Today the prohibition also enjoys the status of customary international law,[51] and has even been considered by the ICJ to be one of two 'cardinal

46 See for example the US DoD Manual, where it is stated in para. 6.6.2, at page 359, that 'the superfluous injury rule prohibits weapons that are designed to increase the injury or suffering of the persons attacked beyond that justified by military necessity'.

47 Boothby, *The Law of Targeting*, at page 258.

48 Brussels Declaration article 12 says: 'The employment of arms, projectiles or material calculated to cause unnecessary suffering, as well as the use of projectiles prohibited by the Declaration of St. Petersburg of 1868'.

49 The Laws of War on Land, manual published by the Institute of International Law (Oxford Manual) (1880) article 9 says: 'It is forbidden:

(a) To employ arms, projectiles, or materials of any kind calculated to cause superfluous suffering, or to aggravate wounds – notably projectiles of less weight than four hundred grams which are explosive or are charged with fulminating or inflammable substances (Declaration of St. Petersburg).'

50 The French text says: 'd'employer des armes, des projectiles ou des matières propres à causer des maux superflus'.

51 ICRC CIHL, rule 70; Tallinn Manual, rule 104.

principles'[52] of the LOAC, governing specifically the law of weaponry. Nevertheless, the core of the concept of superfluous injury and unnecessary suffering remains unclear and controversial.[53] As of today, the prohibition encapsulates both 'means' (weapons, weapon systems and platforms) as well as 'methods' of warfare; it applies to *all* means and methods of warfare,[54] and it is criminalised in the Statutes of the ICTY[55] as well as in the Rome Statute of the ICC.[56]

The ICRC Commentary to AP I article 35 refers to the aim of the ICRC at the time of preparations prior to the Diplomatic Conference: 'It was not only concerned with saving those who did not participate in the hostilities, but also with avoiding any injury or suffering of the combatants in excess of that necessary to put the enemy "hors de combat".'[57]

9.5.2 *The 'Yardsticks': When Is Suffering Unavoidable?*

Leaving aside, for the time being, the discussions of the constituent elements of a weapon in order to be embraced by the prohibition and the medical conditions which actually amount to 'suffering' or 'injury',[58] some general features are to be pointed out.

A simple way of renaming the prohibition has been demonstrated by the ICJ by referring to: 'a harm greater than that unavoidable to achieve legitimate military objectives'.[59] The reference to a measurement of 'greater than that unavoidable' seems to encounter different conceptions. Many regard this as a matter of 'proportionality'. In the US DoD Manual it is said that: 'The test for whether a weapon is prohibited by the superfluous injury rule is whether the suffering caused by the weapon provides no military advantage or is otherwise clearly disproportionate to the military advantage reasonably expected from

52 Legality of the Threat or Use of Nuclear Weapons, Advisory Opinion, at para. 78. The other principle being the one of distinction.
53 Gardam, *Necessity, Proportionality and the Use of Force by States*, at page 67. For a critical point of view to the whole prohibition, see Kelsen and Tucker, *Principles of International Law*, at page 113, where it is argued that the provision is 'without substantial effect'.
54 See Legality of the Threat or Use of Nuclear Weapons, Advisory Opinion, at paras. 74–8.
55 Statute of the International Tribunal for the Prosecution of Persons Responsible for Serious Violations of International Humanitarian Law committed in the Territory of the former Yugoslavia since 1991 (1993) (ICTY Statutes), article 3(a).
56 Rome Statute, article 8(2)(b)(xx).
57 AP I Commentary to article 35, para. 1410, at page 400.
58 Gardam, *Necessity, Proportionality and the Use of Force by States*, at page 68. With regard to medical criteria, see the ICRC's work which has resulted in Coupland, *The SIrUS Project: Towards a determination of which weapons cause 'superfluous injury or unnecessary suffering'*.
59 Legality of the Threat or Use of Nuclear Weapons, Advisory Opinion, at para. 78.

the use of the weapon. Thus, the suffering must be assessed in relation to the military utility of the weapon.'[60]

A 'proportionality' test has also been upheld by others, relying among others on the preparatory works of the CCW, stating that 'the concept entailed a "balancing" or "equation" rather than a prohibition against a significant degree or even a vast amount of suffering'.[61] A proportionality test has its parallels in the 'proportionality' requirement argued by some to also be inherent in the concept of military necessity. An alleged proportionality requirement is, however, also duly criticised in both contexts.[62] According to the critics, no 'equation' is to be performed, and instead of the proportionality consideration, the proper test involves a true reference to 'avoidable', and consists of two main yardsticks: whether there is an alternative weapon available causing less suffering or injury, and whether the effects produced by the alternative weapon are sufficiently effective in neutralising enemy personnel.[63] It is even argued that in order to breach the rule, the injury must be 'significantly greater than that to be expected of alternative weapons that yield the same generic military advantage or utility'.[64] The ICRC Commentary to article 35 is somewhat unclear on the yardsticks or 'proportionality'[65] but sums up the conceptual character of the prohibition in a rather pragmatic way:

> The concept of superfluous injury or unnecessary suffering, its objective effect on the victim (severity of the injury, intensity of suffering), and its relation to military necessity (rendering the enemy 'hors de combat') are not

60 US DoD Manual, para. 6.6.3, at page 359.

61 Quoted from the dissenting opinion of Judge Higgins in Legality of the Threat or Use of Nuclear Weapons, Advisory Opinion, at para. 15, page 586. In the same direction see Bothe, Partsch and Solf, *New Rules*, at pages 225–6. See also Gardam, *Necessity, Proportionality and the Use of Force by States*, at page 68, who argues: 'But whether a weapon falls within the prohibition is clearly a question of balance or proportionality: "unnecessary" "involved some sort of equation between, on the one hand, the degree of injury or suffering inflicted (the humanitarian aspect) and, on the other, the degree of necessity underlying the choice of a particular weapon (the military aspect)".'

62 For a criticism with regard to unnecessary suffering, see Meyrowitz, 'The principle of superfluous injury or unnecessary suffering', at page 109. Meyrowitz is supported by Dinstein, *Conduct of Hostilities*, at page 75. With regard to the concept of necessity, see further Chapter 13.

63 See Meyrowitz, 'The principle of superfluous injury or unnecessary suffering', at pages 110–12. The same position is taken by Dinstein in *Conduct of Hostilities*, at pages 75–6.

64 Boothby, *The Law of Targeting*, at page 259.

65 The Commentary concurs with a phrase from the Rapporteur during the preparatory works: 'several representatives wished to have it recorded that they understood the injuries covered by that phrase to be limited to those which were more severe than would be necessary to render an adversary hors de combat', AP I Commentary, at page 403.

> interpreted in a consistent and generally accepted manner. This concept continues to be the basis on which judgment is formed, but debates have shown its relative and imprecise character.[66]

The assessment must consider the weapon/weapons system under its normal circumstances – leaving aside the possibilities of misuse[67] or malfunction which is not to be blamed upon the operators. Whether one uses the phrase 'proportionality' or not, it seems clear that the assessment involves a consideration of the utility of the weapon and that vast suffering as such is not prohibited. Some practical examples follow in the next section.

9.5.3 *Means of Warfare*

The principle prohibiting unnecessary suffering is primarily a rule governing the use of weapons (as opposed to methods of warfare, commented upon below) – as was the case with its treaty origin in the St Petersburg Declaration and the 1907 Hague Regulations article 23(e) (see above). States' military manuals as well as legal scholars primarily comment on the principle as part of the general regulation of weapons.[68] Its practical scope (see further below) primarily links to specific rules restricting or prohibiting the use of certain weapons. The preamble to the CCW Convention states that the treaty is based on the two principles of limitation of means and methods of warfare and of prohibition of means and methods of a nature to cause superfluous injury or unnecessary suffering.[69] Despite this reference to considerations underpinning the protection of combatants, a large portion (arguably the majority) of existing law of weaponry is drafted in order to protect civilians against indiscriminate effects.[70]

Among those rules construed in order to protect combatants against unnecessary suffering are the prohibition on chemical[71] and biological[72] weapons,

66 AP I Commentary, at pages 409–10. See also Melzer, 'Targeted killing or less harmful means?', at page 97.

67 Boothby, *The Law of Targeting*, page 259.

68 UK Manual, at page 101; Norwegian Manual, at page 154; Swedish SOU, 2010:72, at page 92; US DoD Manual, para. 6.6, at page 357; Canadian Manual, at page 5-1, Section 502; Boothby, *The Law of Targeting*, page 258; Dinstein, *Conduct of Hostilities*, page 73.

69 Preamble to the CCW, in Roberts and Guelff, *Documents on the Laws of War*, at page 520.

70 See for example the remark made by Kalshoven and Zegveld in *Constraints on the Waging of War*, at page 174.

71 Convention on the Prohibition of the Development, Production, Stockpiling and Use of Chemical Weapons and on their Destruction (CWC) (1993).

72 Convention on the Prohibition of the Development, Production and Stockpiling of Bacteriological (Biological) and Toxin Weapons and on their Destruction (1972).

poison[73] (these three may naturally also have indiscriminate effects), certain booby-traps[74] (the rest are aimed at avoiding indiscriminate effects), blinding laser weapons,[75] fragments which are not detectable on X-ray,[76] expanding or flattening ammunition ('dum-dum'),[77] asphyxiating gases,[78] explosive ammunition[79] and modifications of bullets and bayonets, such as dipping bullets in poison, serrated edges on bayonets and lances with barbed heads.[80]

Some comments will now be made on some of the different regulations, starting with the last – modification of existing weapons or bullets. The Canadian Manual provides an illustrative example of the infliction of unnecessary suffering in this regard: '... soldiers may use their bayonets against an adversary. However, they may not "notch" their bayonets to cause a jagged wound that results in suffering out of proportion to the aim of using the bayonets in the first place.'[81] The advantage of using the bayonet is to render the enemy soldier *hors de combat*; it is not to torment him when this advantage is achieved. As such, the rule is closely linked to the protection given enemy combatants once they are rendered *hors de combat*, as accounted for in Chapter 17.

Another conventional weapon, not subject to specific regulation, is the regular hand-grenade that fragments and may create multiple wounds upon detonation/fragmentation. States do not, however, consider hand-grenades to inflict unnecessary suffering, although unconventional fragmentation weapons filled with other projectiles such as glass, nails or similar are considered to do so.[82] Some argue that glass fragments will fall under the prohibition of fragments 'which in the human body escape the detection by X-rays', and thus are prohibited by the CCW Protocol I.[83] Modern radiology technology (a

73 1907 Hague Regulations, article 23(a).
74 Protocol II of the CCW, article 6(2), with amendments as of 1996, article 3(3).
75 Protocol on Blinding Laser Weapons (Protocol IV of the CCW) (1995).
76 Protocol on Non-Detectable Fragments (Protocol I of the CCW) (1980).
77 Declaration (IV,3) Concerning Expanding Bullets (1899).
78 Protocol for the Prohibition of the Use in War of Asphyxiating, Poisonous or other Gases, and Bacteriological Methods of Warfare (Geneva Gas Protocol) (1925).
79 St Petersburg Declaration, cited in Chapter 3.
80 Customary International law as expressed for example in Canadian Manual, at page 5-1, Section 503. See also page 5-2, para. 510. The same position is taken in the UK Manual, at page 105, where modifications such as barbed heads, serrated edges or spreading of substances designed to inflame wounds are mentioned with regard to bayonets and swords. The US DoD Manual refers to poison or other substances in order to make the wound more painful, at page 340. See also AP I Commentary to article 35, at para. 1419, pages 404–5.
81 Canadian Manual, page 5-1.
82 UK Manual, at page 110.
83 Protocol I of the CCW. The Protocol consists of only one provision: 'It is prohibited to use any weapon the primary effect of which is to injure by fragments which in the human body escape

combination of conventional X-ray, computed tomography (CT) scan and ultrasonography) seems, however, to discover glass, stone and metal fragments quite easily. More difficult substances seem to be wood and different sorts of plastic material, such as Bakelite, and as well acryl.[84]

The issue of fragmentation is – together with the prohibition of explosive and expanding ammunition – noteworthy in the broader context of how soldiers and commanders perceive the LOAC. While some fragmentation weapons do not have the primary effect of injuring by non-detectable fragments and therefore escape the prohibition, others may fall within the prohibition yet cause less suffering. Likewise, for exploding and expanding projectiles, while expanding ('dum-dum', see above) projectiles are permissible during policing operations, they are prohibited as means of warfare. The effect on the human body is the same, but the legal assessment is different. In law enforcement situations use of the projectile is not considered to cause unnecessary suffering because of the care shown towards the civilian surroundings, such as in a hostage situation.[85] Exploding projectiles are prohibited when designed to explode upon contact with or intrusion in the human body, but not when designed to break through armoured surfaces. In the latter case, the impact on a human person (instead of an armoured tank) will be fatal, yet lawful. For soldiers and junior officers whom I have taught, these facts of law appear blatantly inconsistent. One lieutenant asked me: 'Why prohibit a projectile that flattens or expands in the human body but permit a hand grenade? Or worse, why permit a weapon that causes a hole in the human body the size of a football [and as such be fatal], but prohibit smaller projectiles exploding upon contact?' Obviously, he could not see consistency in that one type of use was considered necessary suffering and the other not. On the one hand, it seems fair to argue that there is not (sufficient) coherence between considerations of necessity and established treaty law governing means of warfare. On the other hand, however, the treaty patchwork on weapons and ammunition is precisely an expression of the necessities of war as perceived by the negotiating States, yet these do not appear consistent in all aspects – or they only appear consistent when viewed in a bigger perspective. Rauch points out that 'military necessity in this context carries a wider meaning and has an undeniable connection with the military balance between the

detection by X-rays.' Glass fragments are mentioned by Dinstein, *Conduct of Hostilities*, at page 80; and in the Norwegian Manual, at page 164.

84 See for example Aras et al., 'Comparison of the sensitivity for detecting foreign bodies among conventional plain radiography, computed tomography and ultrasonography', at pages 72–8.

85 Boothby, *The Law of Targeting*, at page 258.

parties concerned'.[86] Judge Higgins states in her dissenting opinion in the Nuclear Weapons case that: 'States have been able to move to a specific prohibition of dum-dum bullets, whereas certain weapons that cause vastly greater suffering have neither been the subject of specific prohibitions, nor, in the general State practice, been regarded as clearly prohibited by application of the "unnecessary suffering" principle.'[87]

Furthermore, and as pointed out in the US DoD Manual, there is a range of utilities of a weapon that justifies its use beyond rendering an enemy combatant *hors de combat*.[88] Among these are area-denial weapons, whose effects easily may become indiscriminate. Anti-personnel mines, most booby-traps,[89] incendiary weapons[90] and cluster munitions are prohibited by treaty law, or their use is restricted, in order to avoid their indiscriminate effects and not because they are considered of a nature to cause unnecessary suffering or superfluous injury, although some booby-traps may be of a nature to cause unnecessary suffering.[91] The booby-traps that are of a nature to cause unnecessary suffering which the drafters had in mind consist of hidden holes dug in the ground, like traps, and filled with spears erected from the bottom. The suffering entailed from the spears is unnecessary to the aim of trapping and disabling the combatant; it gains no military advantage.[92]

As with other core rules of the LOAC, nuclear weapons represent a particular challenge. Based on the negotiations that led to the adoption of AP I it was the opinion of a number of States that the Protocol solely applies to conventional weapons.[93] Nuclear weapons are, however, subject to the customary international law principle prohibiting means of warfare of a nature to cause unnecessary suffering or superfluous injury. Regrettably, there seems to be no willingness in the international community of States to consider nuclear weapons as prohibited as such. Their devastating effects, however, are to an even greater extent challenging the rule prohibiting indiscriminate attacks.[94]

86 Rauch, 'The concept of military necessity in the context of the law of war', at page 7.

87 Judge Higgins, dissenting opinion in the Nuclear Weapons Case, at para. 16, page 586.

88 US DoD Manual, para. 6.6.3.1, at pages 360–1 where a list of areas of use is provided, with reference to military necessity.

89 Kalshoven and Zegveld, *Constraints on the Waging of War*, at page 174.

90 Protocol III to the CCW, article 2, which confines the Protocol to the protection of civilians. This point is emphasised by Kalshoven and Zegveld, *Constraints on the Waging of War*, at page 179.

91 Protocol II of the CCW, article 6(2).

92 Kalshoven and Zegveld, *Constraints on the Waging of War*, at page 177; Dinstein, *Conduct of Hostilities*, at pages 81–2.

93 Canadian Manual, para. 526, pages 5-8 and 5-9; UK Manual, at page 117; US DoD Manual, para. 6.18.3, at pages 418–17.

94 Indiscriminate attacks are dealt with in Chapter 12.

The ICJ stated in its Advisory Opinion from 1996 that: 'Nor can the Court make a determination on the validity of the view that the recourse to nuclear weapons would be illegal in any circumstance owing to their inherent and total incompatibility with the law applicable in armed conflict.'[95] The Court's abdication was to a certain extent rebutted by Judge Higgins in her dissenting opinion, where she argued with regard to the matter of unnecessary suffering that:

> There remains unanswered the crucial question: what military necessity is so great that the sort of suffering that would be inflicted on military personnel by the use of nuclear weapons would even be justified? ... If the suffering is of the sort traditionally associated with the use of nuclear weapons – blast, radiation, shock, together with risk of escalation, risk of spread through space and time – then only the most extreme circumstances (defence against untold suffering or the obliteration of a State or peoples) could conceivably 'balance' the equation between necessity and humanity.[96]

The legal question remains, however and regrettably, open and subject to considerations of military necessity in an undesirable manner.

9.5.4 *Methods of Warfare*

As indicated above, it is difficult to see the rule's area of application regarding methods of warfare. Beyond those methods already regulated by the AP I, those States who actually include methods of warfare in their manuals[97] give no further exemplification of methods of warfare that may violate the prohibition.[98] The scope of the rule with regard to methods must therefore be seen in relation to the rules prohibiting denial of quarter and the protection of enemy combatants *hors de combat* (on these rules, see further Chapter 17).[99] One example has, however, been discussed under the auspices of unnecessary suffering – the US attacks on Iraqi armed forces retreating from Kuwait on Highways 80 and 8 (subsequently often named 'Highways of Death') during the first Gulf War in 1991 (see also Section 9.4).

The attacks took place on 26 and 27 February (Highway 80) and on 2 March (Highway 8) in 1991, following the retreat of Iraqi forces from Kuwait, leaving

95 Legality of the Threat or Use of Nuclear Weapons, Advisory Opinion, at para. 95, page 262.

96 Legality of the Threat or Use of Nuclear Weapons, Advisory Opinion, dissenting opinion of Judge Higgins, at page 587, para. 18.

97 For examples of States who do not mention 'methods', see the US DoD Manual, Chapter VI and the Canadian Manual, at page 5-1, para. 502.

98 ICRC CIHL, Commentary to rule 70 and Norwegian Manual page 168.

99 Barber, 'Scuds, shelters and retreating soldiers', at page 678.

tens of kilometres with destroyed vehicles and corpses.[100] Both the facts and the subsequent legal assessment of the attacks have been subject to controversies,[101] in particular as to whether there was any potential military gain to be expected from the attacks or whether the purpose was simply to 'rub in the defeat' of the Iraqi forces, and not truly a weakening effect which would enhance the US operations.[102] Controversies aside, there does not appear to be widespread support for the position that the incident was a violation of the prohibition of unnecessary suffering.

9.5.5 *The Practical Scope of the Rule and the Assessment of the Commander*

The rule addresses States, rather than individual combatants.[103] In the UK Manual the rule is referred to as a 'guiding principle upon which specific prohibitions or restrictions can be built'.[104] In the same vein, one scholar argues, 'The principle is still too abstract, however, to warrant immediate result'.[105] This appears to be the customary status of the scope of the rule, even acknowledged by the ICRC in the Customary Law Study.[106] Thus, the rule is hardly for each commander to assess during the conduct of hostilities. The US DoD Manual refers to the 'test' as to whether the suffering entails no military advantage or is clearly disproportionate to the advantage reasonably expected from the use of the weapon, but it does not appear to be a test to be performed by each military commander in the field.[107] Although the duty primarily rests on the States as such, this does not preclude commanders from being obliged to assess a particular method or the use of a particular weapon under unusual or new circumstances not assessed by the State in accordance with AP I article 36.

100 The numbers vary, in particular regarding the number of dead soldiers. Some figures are approximately 1,400 vehicles on Highway 80, over a distance of about 60 km. The number of dead soldiers range from 300 to several thousands. A number of soldiers were reported to be fleeing into the desert.

101 See for example the in-depth and post-war assessment done by Hersh, 'Overwhelming force'. The case may also be seen in light of AP 1 article 40, prohibiting the denial of quarter, and its predecessor in the 1907 Hague Regulations article 23(d).

102 The incident is also commented upon below, in Chapter 17 on the distinction between surrendering combatants and retreating combatants.

103 Boothby, *The Law of Targeting*, at pages 259–60.

104 UK Manual, at page 103.

105 Kalshoven and Zegveld, *Constraints on the Waging of War*, at page 35.

106 See ICRC CIHL, Commentary to rule 70.

107 US DoD Manual, at pages 338–9.

10

Military Necessity and the Notion of 'Lawful Combatancy'

10.1 LAWFUL COMBATANCY AND THE POW PRIVILEGE

The definition of lawful combatants is tied to the rule of distinction, in that it distinguishes those who are entitled to participate in hostilities from the civilian population who enjoy protection from attack. As with the rule of distinction in general, the notion of lawful combatancy consists of prohibitive and permissive elements, reflecting the balance between military necessity and humanitarian considerations.[1]

Combatants – when fulfilling the legal requirements – 'have the right to participate directly in hostilities',[2] which for practical purposes implies a permission, a right to direct attacks against other lawful targets – a 'license to kill'.[3] The aim is to confine the war-fighting to a contest between those who are lawful combatants and distinguish themselves from the civilian population. By doing this, the civilian population may be spared to the extent which is possible, taking the necessities of war into account. This distinction may, however, be jeopardised when combatants do not distinguish themselves. The necessity to direct attacks against them remains, but then at the expense of the civilian protection. The reflection of the permission to participate in hostilities is immunity from criminal liability for performing lawful acts of war – a core essence of the POW privilege. The further consequences of unlawful combatancy are dealt with separately below.

1 On prohibitive and permissive elements in the rule of distinction, see Section 7.1. On permissive and prohibitive elements in general, see Chapter 2.

2 AP I article 43(2); see Section 9.3.

3 Dörmann, 'The legal situation of "unlawful/unprivileged combatants"', at page 45. Dinstein, *Conduct of Hostilities*, at page 42.

The question of status as lawful combatant has been subject to discussion and controversy[4] since the early 1900s. In the ICRC Commentary to AP I article 43, the following is stated with regard to the Hague Conferences of 1899 and 1907:

> Some wished to impose strict conditions on the definition of the status of members of the armed forces, bearing in mind the necessities of war; others would not allow any restriction to the right and duty of taking up arms, apart from the organization required to maintain the basic rules of good faith pertaining to warfare and to prevent banditry.[5]

There were in other words two views on the right to participate in hostilities with the accompanying status as lawful combatants: one narrow – arguing that the status as a lawful combatant was to be confined to those fulfilling specific criteria. And one wider – arguing in favour of an almost unrestricted scope for the group entitled to take part in hostilities. The reference to 'the necessities of war', as a basis for strict conditions for lawful combatancy, appears unclear. As we shall see, the 'necessities of war' was more frequently referred to during the treaty history as an argument in favour of a liberal right to participate in hostilities, than against it. Furthermore, the principle of distinction – the limitation upon military necessity – has been referred to as an argument in favour of strict conditions.[6] Today, these different approaches have in fact led to two standards[7] for lawful combatancy and POW status under international law: one under the Hague and Geneva Conventions which reflect customary law and one under the AP I, where the AP I standard contains a more lenient and controversial requirement of distinction. The Hague conditions for lawful combatancy are stated in articles 1 and 2:

> Article 1. The laws, rights, and duties of war apply not only to armies, but also to militia and volunteer corps fulfilling the following conditions:
>
> 1. To be commanded by a person responsible for his subordinates;
> 2. To have a fixed distinctive emblem recognizable at a distance;
> 3. To carry arms openly; and
> 4. To conduct their operations in accordance with the laws and customs of war.

4 On the historical discussion between the 'patriot school' and the 'military school', see further Section 10.5 See as well Section 10.6 for a separate discussion of the requirement of distinction.

5 AP I Commentary to article 43, at pages 509–10, para. 1670.

6 See further, Section 10.6.

7 Dinstein, *Conduct of Hostilities*, at pages 61–4.

> In countries where militia or volunteer corps constitute the army, or form part of it, they are included under the denomination 'army'.
>
> Art. 2. The inhabitants of a territory which has not been occupied, who, on the approach of the enemy, spontaneously take up arms to resist the invading troops without having had time to organize themselves in accordance with Article 1, shall be regarded as belligerents if they carry arms openly and if they respect the laws and customs of war.[8]

And in the GC III article 4, the requirements for achieving POW status are as follows:

> A. Prisoners of war, in the sense of the present Convention, are persons belonging to one of the following categories, who have fallen into the power of the enemy:
>
> (1) Members of the armed forces of a Party to the conflict as well as members of militias or volunteer corps forming part of such armed forces.
>
> (2) Members of other militias and members of other volunteer corps, including those of organized resistance movements, belonging to a Party to the conflict and operating in or outside their own territory, even if this territory is occupied, provided that such militias or volunteer corps, including such organized resistance movements, fulfil the following conditions:
>
> (a) that of being commanded by a person responsible for his subordinates;
>
> (b) that of having a fixed distinctive sign recognizable at a distance;
>
> (c) that of carrying arms openly;
>
> (d) that of conducting their operations in accordance with the laws and customs of war.
>
> (3) Members of regular armed forces who profess allegiance to a government or an authority not recognized by the Detaining Power.
>
> (4) Persons who accompany the armed forces without actually being members thereof, such as civilian members of military aircraft crews, war correspondents, supply contractors, members of labour units or of services responsible for the welfare of the armed forces, provided that they have received authorization from the armed forces which they accompany, who shall provide them for that purpose with an identity card similar to the annexed model.

8 1907 Hague Regulations, articles 1 and 2.

(5) Members of crews, including masters, pilots and apprentices, of the merchant marine and the crews of civil aircraft of the Parties to the conflict, who do not benefit by more favourable treatment under any other provisions of international law.
(6) Inhabitants of a non-occupied territory, who on the approach of the enemy spontaneously take up arms to resist the invading forces, without having had time to form themselves into regular armed units, provided they carry arms openly and respect the laws and customs of war.

The requirements deserve some further comments. While the requirements of the 1907 Hague Regulations articles 1(2) and (3) and GC III articles 4(2)(b) and (c) are dealt with separately below, the remaining requirements are commented upon in the following.[9]

The requirement that combatants must belong to a party to the conflict is explicitly stated in the GC III and the AP I, and is undoubtedly customary international law, although not stated in the 1907 Hague Regulations.[10] The treaties do not define a 'party to the conflict' and the ICRC Commentary to the AP I states that the notion of a 'Party to the conflict' is implied to be a 'known concept'.[11] The link between the party to the conflict and the armed force must be a 'de facto' relationship, which includes for example governments in exile.[12]

The requirement of being under a command responsible for its subordinates is established in the 1907 Hague Regulations, the Geneva Convention, as well as in the AP I.[13] This requirement must be seen in relation to the initial requirement of belonging to a party to the conflict, as the command, in order to be responsible, must answer in a chain of command to the party to the conflict and not wage a private war.[14]

The requirement of 'organization' does not appear in the 1907 Hague Regulations nor in the GC III, but is a part of customary international law and is expressed explicitly in AP I article 43(1).[15] The notion of

9 See, however, Section 10.5.2 on *levee en masse*.

10 AP I article 43(1), and GC III article 4 A(1); Bothe, Partsch and Solf, *New Rules*, at page 268; and AMW Manual, Commentary to rule 10(b)(i), Commentary 2, at page 84.

11 AP I Commentary to article 43, at page 506, para. 1659.

12 ICRC Commentary of 1952 to GC III articles 4A(1 and 2), at page 57; Tallinn Manual, Commentary 8 to rule 87, at page 404; and Bothe, Partsch and Solf, *New Rules*, at page 270, which states that the requirement was not to be understood differently in the AP I from the GC III.

13 1907 Hague Regulations, article 1(1), at page 66; GC III article 4A(2)(a); and AP I article 43(1).

14 AP I Commentary at page 512, para. 1672. Bothe, Partsch and Solf, *New Rules*, at page 271. Dinstein, 'Unlawful combatancy', at page 256.

15 AP I article 43(1). See Bothe, Partsch and Solf, *New Rules*, at page 268; and AMW Manual, Commentary to rule 10(b)(i), Commentary 2, at page 84.

'organization'[16] is understood to be rather flexible and aims at distinguishing war-fighting from fighting which does not have a collective character.[17]

The duty to uphold an internal disciplinary system and enforce violations of the LOAC is established in the Hague Regulations, the GC III as well as the AP I[18] and must be seen together with the duty and responsibility of commanders under the AP I articles 86 and 87. The requirement of compliance with the rules of the LOAC does, however, apply somewhat differently in the Hague and Geneva rules from the AP I. The 1907 Hague Regulations as well as the GC III distinguishes between regular armed forces and militia groups regarding the right to retain their status as POWs after having committed a violation of the LOAC. While regular armed forces retain their status, irregular forces have to 'prove that they acted in accordance with the laws and customs of war in their operations'.[19] In the AP I article 44(2) this distinction is abandoned, stating that 'violations of these rules shall not deprive a combatant of his right to be a combatant, or, if he falls into the power of an adverse Party, of his right to be a prisoner of war, except as provided for in paragraphs 3 and 4.' On this point the AP I probably goes further than existing customary law.[20] The requirement of compliance with the laws of armed conflict for armed groups under the Hague and Geneva provisions is understood as a group requirement[21] and although it may imply the loss of POW status, it does not imply that each and every violation of the law will result in the loss of status as lawful combatants (and POWs). This understanding is supported by the formulation of the customary rule in the AMW Manual, where it is expressed as a requirement to 'generally conduct their operations in accordance with the laws and customs of warfare'.[22] With regard to the loss of POW status for armed groups, Dinstein points at four different scenarios where the relationship between the group and the individual is emphasised.[23] First, the case when a group

16 In the Tallinn Manual, the requirement of being under responsible command is seen as a feature of the requirement of 'organization', see Commentary 10 to rule 87, at page 404.

17 AP I Commentary at page 512, para. 1672.

18 1907 Hague Regulations, article 1(4); GC III article 4A(2)(d); and AP I article 43(1).

19 AP I Commentary to article 44(2), at page 526, para. 1689.

20 AP I Commentary to article 44(2), at pages 525–6, para. 1689.

21 Tallinn Manual, Commentary 15 to rule 87, at page 406. Dinstein, *Conduct of Hostilities*, at page 54. With regard to the position of the AP I, see Bothe, Partsch and Solf, *New Rules*, at page 272, who point out that any violations of the LOAC will not imply that the force is being disqualified from being a lawful force.

22 AMW Manual, Commentary 2 to rule 10(b)(i), at page 84.

23 Dinstein, *Conduct of Hostilities*, at pages 59–60.

largely conducts its operations in accordance with the LOAC – a single perpetrator will not be considered an 'unlawful combatant' (and not even if he commits a war crime, which makes him a war criminal and without POW status). Second, if the group largely does *not* conduct its operations in accordance with the LOAC, the unlawfulness will also taint individuals – they may be considered unlawful combatants. The 9/11 attack on World Trade Center has been used as an example of so flagrant and extensive violations of the LOAC that it precluded the possibility of POW status for the Al Qaida group.[24] The disqualification of individual members of an armed group which largely does not conduct its operations in accordance with the LOAC can, however (and third), be rebutted: if it can be shown that the individual has a record of compliance with the LOAC, then the behaviour of the group should not be used against him. Finally, if the pattern of the group is unclear, the benefit of the doubt should be given the soldier.

Violations of the LOAC which amounts to war crimes are in a separate category, however. During the drafting of GC III article 85 (which grants continued POW status to those who are prosecuted or convicted of offences committed prior to capture) considerable resistance was raised, and a number of States have made reservations to the provision – arguing that war criminals should lose their POW status.[25] Notwithstanding the controversy – the application of article 85 does not imply more than the offering of due process requirements – the perpetrator may still be convicted for war crimes in accordance with the gravity of the offence.[26] It should also be pointed out that there is no necessary connection between those who are war criminals and those who will eventually be 'unlawful combatants'.

The requirement of distinction from the civilian population is explicitly stated in the 1907 Hague Regulations articles 1(2) and (3), the GC III articles 4(2)(b) and (c) and AP I article 44(3), as well as customary law.[27] The traditional requirements for distinction encompasses carrying arms openly as well as having a fixed distinctive sign recognisable at a distance, while the AP I requirements only uphold the requirement of carrying arms openly *within a limited time frame*.[28] The requirement of distinction is discussed in more detail in Section 10.6.

24 Dinstein, 'Unlawful combatancy', at page 268.
25 ICRC Commentary of 1952, to GC III article 85, at pages 414–15.
26 Dinstein, *Conduct of Hostilities*, at page 303.
27 AMW Manual, rule 10(b)(i), Commentary 2, at page 84. ICRC CIHL, rule 106
28 ICRC CIHL, rule 106.

An additional requirement of not having a duty of allegiance to the detaining power is upheld by some,[29] and contested by others with reference to the lack of a nationality clause in the conventions.[30]

Although there are semantic differences with regard to the application of requirements for regular and irregular armed forces, all the requirements listed in the foregoing applies in order to achieve, and maintain, the status as lawful combatants.

10.2 'UNLAWFUL COMBATANCY': LEGAL STATUS AND CONSEQUENCES

Having drawn up the criteria for lawful combatancy, it remains to examine the legal framework for those who do not fulfil the requirements but nevertheless participate in hostilities (on the explicit notion of direct participation in hostilities as a rule for loss of protection against direct attacks, see further Chapter 11).

First, those who fail to comply with the requirements of lawful combatancy lose their entitlement to combatant immunity and POW status.[31] The further categorisation of those who do not fulfil the criteria for being lawful combatants is controversial. Shall they be considered as civilians (who have lost their protection against attack) or as 'unlawful combatants'/'unprivileged combatants'?[32]

Questions related to terminology and legal consequences are deeply tied to the question of what to do with 'unlawful combatants' upon capture[33] – can they be denied quarter due to considerations of necessity? As referred to above, the question of combatants' status has been a revolving matter of controversy, and a number of questions are not explicitly dealt with in the treaty texts – partly due to States' urge to deal with saboteurs and terrorists according to their

[29] Dinstein argues in *Conduct of Hostilities*, at pages 51–6, that there are in total seven requirements. These seven requirements are: to be commanded by a person responsible for his subordinates, to have a fixed distinctive sign and to carry arms openly during military engagement and deployment to such (on this controversy, see below), to conduct military operations in accordance with the law, to belong to a party to the conflict, to be in a certain degree of organisation and to have no duty of allegiance to the detaining power. In this direction see also Rogers, 'Combatant status', at page 107. See as well Bothe, Partsch and Solf, *New Rules* at page 268.

[30] Rogers, *Law on the Battlefield*, at pages 31–2.

[31] Tallinn Manual, rule 87 with accompanying commentary at page 402.

[32] AMW Manual, Commentary 4 to rule 10(b)(i), at page 84.

[33] Kalshoven, *Reflections on the Law of War*, at pages 475–6.

national regulations.[34] In the ICRC Commentary to the AP I article 43 it is noted that:

> Finally the question was resolved at The Hague along the lines indicated above, which means that for combatants who do not fulfil the conditions imposed, nothing is provided in the Regulations, either in their favour or against them. These are rules of unwritten law, in accordance with the principles of the law of nations referred to in the Preamble (Martens clause). Therefore it is clear that nothing in the Regulations should be considered as tending to lessen 'or suppress the right that belongs to the population of an invaded country, to carry out its duty of opposing to the invaders by any lawful means the most energetic patriotic resistance'.[35]

In fact, the range of activities, which may amount to 'unlawful combatancy' is wide and encompasses all activities in which those persons do not fulfil the criteria for lawful combatancy. Often, unlawful combatancy may amount to methods that are termed sabotage, guerrilla or even terrorism.[36]

10.3 CONSEQUENCES OF 'UNLAWFUL COMBATANCY': HUMANE PROVISIONS VS THE NECESSITY OF HARSH MEANS

Having stated that an 'unlawful combatant' loses his or her POW privileges, the question remains how much else he or she will lose upon capture. Is an unlawful combatant, who fails to meet the criteria of GC III, also deprived of the protection offered by the GC IV?

The underlying view which was visible during the preparatory works for the AP I was that 'unlawful combatants' were not entitled to the same protection as prisoners of war, nor to all the protection accorded to 'peaceful civilians' – but to humane treatment.[37] Being outside the scope of POW privilege they may also be punished by national law for the mere participation in hostilities.[38] Beyond this, controversy exists when it comes to the legal consequences of taking a direct part in hostilities without being a lawful combatant (unlawful combatancy). Can 'those found guilty of acts of "unprivileged belligerency", whether consisting in actual fighting, espionage, sabotage, or terrorism' be

34 See Section 10.5 on the different conceptions of necessity and different sorts of irregular combatants.

35 AP I Commentary to article 43, at, pages 509–10, para. 1670.

36 For an account of the concept and definition of 'guerrilla', see Kalshoven, *Reflections on the Law of War*, at pages 467–9.

37 Dörmann, 'The legal situation of "unlawful/unprivileged combatants"', at pages 52–3.

38 Dinstein, 'Unlawful combatancy', at pages 250–1.

executed after trial according to the 'law of combat',[39] or to what extent are they protected by the GC IV on protection of the civilian population? The views differ. First, there are those who argue that the scope of GC IV article 4 encompasses all persons fulfilling the nationality criteria, notwithstanding whether they are captured during active combat, on their own territory, by enemy forces, prior to occupation or during occupation or on enemy territory.[40] Second, there are those who argue that persons who choose to participate in hostilities without being entitled to, lose their protection under GC IV (some also include the Additional Protocol here[41]) as well as that of GC III. With regard to the latter view, the solution is based on the scope of GC IV article 4 as well as the scope of GC IV article 5 – where the latter grants the right to derogations from article 4. Article 5 authorises two levels of derogations: first, the loss of rights and privileges under the Convention for persons engaged in activities hostile to the security of the State, and second, a less extensive right to derogate in cases of occupation – where the detained person may lose his or her right to communication 'where absolute military security so requires'.[42] The GC IV article 4 (as well as the corresponding right to derogate in article 5) does, however, fail to regulate situations of combat where an 'unlawful combatant' is caught on his or her home territory by enemy armed forces (outside actual occupation).[43] This 'failure' has led Baxter to argue that:

39 Kalshoven, *Reflections on the Law of War*, argues at page 480 that: 'the law of combat applies, and the view has been widely defended that this law permits the execution after trial of those found guilty of acts of "unprivileged belligerency", whether consisting in actual fighting, espionage, sabotage, or terrorism, and no matter how one might regard these acts from a viewpoint less biased than that of the enemy.' If these persons were to fall under the protective regime of GC IV article 68 places limits on the access to inflict the death penalty. That customary law permits the death penalty is also referred to by Bothe, Partsch and Solf, *New Rules*, at page 278.

40 ICRC Commentary of 1952, to GC IV article 4, at pages 50–1; Dörmann, 'The legal situation of "unlawful/unprivileged combatants"', at page 46; Pejic, 'Unlawful/enemy combatants', at pages 339–41. The same position as the ICRC is also taken by the ICTY in the Delalic Case, at paras. 271–2.

41 Garraway, '"Combatants" – substance or semantics', at page 332.

42 GC IV article 5.

43 Baxter, 'So-called unprivileged belligerency', at page 328. Kalshoven, *Reflections on the Law of War*, at page 478. Dinstein, *Conduct of Hostilities*, at page 44. Draper, 'The status of combatants and the question of guerilla warfare', at pages 173–218, only addresses the nationality criteria of articles 4 and 5 in GC IV and does not specifically address the situations of combat in a non-occupied territory where guerrilla forces approach an invading force, see page 193. Dörmann criticises this view and argues that it's not truly based on an interpretation of article 4, but on earlier (national) case law.

> A category of persons who are not entitled to treatment either as peaceful civilians or as prisoners of war by reason of the fact that they have engaged in hostile conduct without meeting the qualifications established by Article 4 of the Geneva Prisoners of War Convention of 1949 thus continues to exist and to be subject to the maximum penalty which the detaining belligerent desires to impose.[44]

This view represents the latter group referred to just above and has later been extensively referenced. Although a number of scholars support this notion of a 'third category' of persons,[45] the position remains contested.[46]

For the case that GC IV does not apply, there seems to be general agreement that AP I article 75 and common article 3 applies as a minimum framework for protection, but the actual scope of this protection when it comes to the contested group of persons also remains unclear.[47] While those arguing in favour of a more *narrow* scope of GC IV article 4 (and 5) also argue in favour of a right for the captor-state to impose the death penalty after trial for the mere participation in conflict – those arguing in favour of a *wider* scope of GC IV also seem to marginalise the difference when it comes to actual protection. Dörmann argues for example that the effect of AP I article 75 'virtually neutralizes the derogations permitted under Art. 5 of the Fourth Convention, except for persons held as spies'.[48] The underpinnings of necessity for harsh means against irregulars on the one hand and the necessity of resorting to irregular methods on the other hand are dealt with separately in the section just below.

To sum up a rather extensive debate quite shortly: while controversy exists regarding scope of consequences for unlawful combatancy after capture, three basic consequences are, however, uncontested: the persons are lawful objects of attack, they are not entitled to POW status and can be prosecuted nationally

44 Baxter, 'So-called unprivileged belligerency', at page 328.

45 See above and also Garraway, '"Combatants" – substance or semantics', at page 332. He does not link his position to Baxter's, but they appear at the outset to be the same – the exception is that Garraway does not differentiate the scope of article 4 according to its literal meaning; he appears to solely exclude protection, which in reality goes much wider than the views of Baxter, Draper, Kalshoven and Dinstein.

46 Dörmann, 'The legal situation of "unlawful/unprivileged combatants"', at pages 59–61. He also finds support for his views in the ICTY Delalic Case which bases its view on the ICRC Commentary, that a person is either a prisoner of war or a protected person according to GC IV.

47 See AP I article 45(3); and Dörmann, 'The legal situation of "unlawful/unprivileged combatants"', at page 64; Dinstein, *Conduct of Hostilities*, at pages 47–8; and Garraway, '"Combatants" – substance or semantics', at page 333.

48 Dörmann, 'The legal situation of "unlawful/unprivileged combatants"', at pages 68–9.

for the mere participation in hostilities, and they are (at least) entitled to humane treatment according to CA 3 and AP I article 75.

10.4 PARTICULAR GROUPS: SPIES AND MERCENARIES

10.4.1 *Spies*

While the status of saboteurs was considered adequately dealt with in the general rules on combatancy in AP I, spies were considered to raise special issues.[49] As stated above with unlawful combatancy in general, espionage is not a prohibited method of warfare under international law.[50] The act of espionage is nonetheless – as with sabotage and guerrilla methods – considered to be particularly dangerous for the opposing forces and have necessitated harsh measures in response.[51] When qualifying as a spy, the person does not fulfil the requirements as lawful combatants (and POW status), and is consequently liable for domestic punishment.[52]

When it comes to the definition of spies, the 1907 Hague Regulations article 29(1) states that: 'A person can only be considered a spy when, acting clandestinely or on false pretences, he obtains or endeavours to obtain information in the zone of operations of a belligerent, with the intention of communicating it to the hostile party.' Neither the Geneva Conventions nor the AP I contain a more precise definition of spies, the latter giving a description of those who shall *not* be considered a spy in article 46.[53] However, by this negative definition the AP I provision does shed light on the definition of spies. The AP I provision is based on the definition in the Hague Regulation, but goes one step further with regard to the zone of operations of spies and extends this – in accordance with established interpretation of customary law – to: 'territory controlled by an adverse party'.[54] The AP I rule also clarifies the ambiguous terms in the 1907 Hague Regulations of 'clandestinely or on false pretences', by substituting them with a reference to 'uniform'.[55] The requirement of 'uniform' must not be read as to change the content of the 1907 Hague Regulations

49 Bothe, Partsch and Solf, *New Rules*, at page 299.
50 Ibid.
51 On the necessity of irregular methods of warfare, see Section 10.5.
52 UK Manual, at page 46. Dinstein, *Conduct of Hostilities*, at pages 278–9.
53 AP I Commentary to article 46, at page 565, para. 1774.
54 AP I Commentary to article 46, at page 566, para. 1775. Dinstein, *Conduct of Hostilities*, at page 280. Ipsen, 'Combatants and non-combatants', at page 108.
55 Norwegian Manual, at page 60. Ipsen 'Combatants and non-combatants', at page 107. Dinstein, *Conduct of Hostilities*, at page 281.

article 29(2) which refers to 'soldiers not wearing a disguise'.[56] In article 46(3) however, which governs occupied territory, is the formulation of the Hague Regulations upheld when it states that persons who are resident in the territory are only to be considered spies when gathering or attempting to gather information of military value 'under false pretences or deliberately in a clandestine manner'.[57] According to the ICRC, this requirement reflects the exceptional minimum criteria in AP I article 44(3), arguing that

> ... the absence of uniform or what takes the place of uniform, is not automatically equivalent to an activity undertaken 'through an act of false pretences or deliberately in a clandestine manner', since in certain situations which arise particularly or exclusively in occupied territory, guerrilla combatants are expressly exempt from the obligation to distinguish themselves from the civilian population (Article 44 'Combatants and prisoners of war,' paragraph 3).[58]

In other words: gathering of information by resident combatants (resistance movements who are members of the armed forces) in an occupied territory does not qualify as espionage simply by being conducted in civilian clothing[59] – they will retain their combatant and POW status according to the threshold of article 44(3) – provided that the capturing state is bound by the AP I provisions.

10.4.2 *Mercenaries*

Mercenaries are not lawful combatants and do not have the right to POW status.[60] The AP I contains a rather extensive definition of mercenaries in

56 Bothe, Partsch and Solf, *New Rules*, at page 300. AP I Commentary to article 46, at pages 566–7, para. 1776: 'The problem of uniform is possibly an even more vexed question. One delegate at a plenary meeting asked what significance it should be given "in the case of combatants who were not required to wear uniform, and who, in any case, had no chance of wearing one". The question was by no means irrelevant, although it is understood that the word "uniform" applied not only to a uniform in the conventional sense, but to any distinguishing sign which warranted that the activity in question had nothing clandestine about it. In addition, the Rapporteur declared that this means that: "any customary uniform which clearly distinguished the member wearing it from a non-member [of the armed forces], should suffice". All the same, that does not alter the fact that certain categories of combatants can, as we have seen, be exempt from all distinguishing signs with the exception of the open carrying of arms.' On the requirement of distinction as a condition for POW status, see further below.

57 AP I article 46(3).

58 AP I Commentary to article 46(3), at page 568, para. 1779.

59 Bothe, Partsch and Solf, *New Rules*, at page 301.

60 AP I article 47(1).

article 47.[61] The provision does not, however, reflect customary law – which has not even established the concept of mercenaries as unlawful combatants.[62] The AP I rule is therefore an attempt to define this group of persons for the first time.[63] Mercenaries depart from the other groups of unlawful combatants since their status is not linked to the lack of fulfilment of the principle of distinction, but to the motivation of profit for private gain.[64]

10.5 THE NECESSITY OF IRREGULAR WARFARE: UNDERPINNINGS OF THE DEBATE OVER THE REQUIREMENT OF DISTINCTION

10.5.1 *Remarks on the Military Necessity–Humanity Equilibrium with Regard to Lawful Combatancy*

When it comes to the notion of combatancy, the legal rule does not simply reflect a military necessity–humanity equilibrium. Some scholars include loose references to considerations of chivalry, honour and 'fair play' as well.[65] The difficulty, however, has first and foremost been to strike a proper balance between military necessity and humanitarian considerations.[66] More precisely, between the necessity of guerrilla warfare and guerrilla methods on

61 AP I article 47(2) says:
'A mercenary is any person who:
(a) is specially recruited locally or abroad in order to fight in an armed conflict;
(b) does, in fact, take a direct part in the hostilities;
(c) is motivated to take part in the hostilities essentially by the desire for private gain and, in fact, is promised, by or on behalf of a Party to the conflict, material compensation substantially in excess of that promised or paid to combatants of similar ranks and functions in the armed forces of that Party;
(d) is neither a national of a Party to the conflict nor a resident of territory controlled by a Party to the conflict;
(e) is not a member of the armed forces of a Party to the conflict; and
(f) has not been sent by a State which is not a Party to the conflict on official duty as a member of its armed forces.'

62 Dinstein, *Conduct of Hostilities*, at page 67.

63 AP I Commentary to article 47, at page 574, para. 1793.

64 Bothe, Partsch and Solf, *New Rules*, at page 304. Dinstein, *Conduct of Hostilities*, at page 67.

65 For a historical approach to these considerations with regard to combatancy, see Draper, 'The status of combatants and the question of guerilla warfare', at pages 173–5. See also Keen, *The Laws of War in the Late Middle Ages*, at pages 69 ff.

66 This historical difficulty (of striking an equilibrium with regard to combatancy) was also pointed out by the ICRC delegate to the Diplomatic Conference, see Official Records of the Diplomatic Conference CDDH/III/SR. 33–6, Annex. Other state representatives uphold the provision in AP I article 44 as a success in this regard, see ibid., CDDH/SR/40, para. 75 (Hungary), and that it 'struck a delicate balance'.

the one hand and the protection of civilians from being blended in with the combatants on the other. During the treaty negotiations prior to the AP I, the necessity of guerrilla warfare was, by some delegates, linked to an emphasis on legalising the 'struggle of oppressed peoples'.[67]

This latter argument, the legalisation of irregular combatants, has a deeper, highly political backdrop: the protection of small States' limited resources for resistance. We must turn back more than a century in order to grasp the picture sufficiently.

The participation in 'public war' (as distinguished from cowardly assassinations) has throughout history been seen as a 'privilege of a privileged class of men',[68] while the 'unorthodox methods', such as guerrilla warfare, take advantage of being clandestine and thus pose danger to the opposing forces.[69] Although being on the border (or below) of being conceived as 'fair play', these unorthodox methods have more often than not been the small States' (sometimes only) advantage or necessity.[70] The emphasis on this necessity has therefore trumped the concern of civilian protection. This necessity of the agent is thus reflected in the danger for the State exposed.[71] As the foregoing introduction indicates, the different perceptions of military necessity over the issue of lawful combatancy has played out – and plays out – primarily at the level of treaty formulation. In turn, the room for the military commander's assessment of military necessity is, in cases concerning lawful combatancy, substantially limited.

10.5.2 *The Clash of Opinions from 1874 to Post-1949: 'Military School' vs the 'Patriot School'*

The clash of opinions (or needs) became apparent at the Brussels Conference in 1874 as well as at the 1899 and 1907 Hague Conferences, in discussions

67 See the remarks by the Yugoslavian delegate during the Diplomatic Conference prior to the adoption of AP I article 44(3). See CDDH/SR/40, para. 76: 'It was not merely that the article widened the area of humanitarian protection, but also that it laid the foundation for future relations between aggressor and victim: the old rules which had expressly tied the status of combatant to formal and rigid legal conditions, making matters easier for an aggressor and occupying Power, by the same token restricted the opportunities for combating aggression; while the article which had just been adopted unequivocally legalized the struggle of oppressed peoples against occupation and aggression of every kind. It granted the status of combatant to members of the civilian population who in exceptional circumstances might take up arms to defend their country.'

68 Draper, 'The status of combatants and the question of guerilla warfare', at page 174.

69 Ibid., at pages 177–8. Hostage Case, at page 58.

70 Draper, 'The status of combatants and the question of guerilla warfare', at page 184.

71 The danger is pointed out by Baxter, 'So-called unprivileged belligerency', at page 343; and Draper, 'The status of combatants and the question of guerilla warfare', at page 183.

between supporters of the 'military school' (such as the militarily powerful Prussia) on the one side and the 'patriot school' on the other side (such as Belgium or France when opposing the Prussian invasion in the 1870s).[72]

The Brussels Conference sought to establish a balance between humanitarian considerations and military requirements and in this token 'confirmed the idea of the popular resistance in the form of a *levee en masse*'.[73] The initiative was primarily driven through by the small powers: the 'patriot school'.[74] The *levee en masse* institute is expressed in the GC III article 4(6) and the 1907 Hague Regulations article 2 (cited Section 10.1), and refers to a spontaneous 'mass uprising' by citizens who are not members of the armed forces. The concept illustrates a deeply rooted necessity of resort to arms by *the nation*, to resist an advancing enemy. Its historic origin in the French Revolution illustrates as well that of a total war, in the sense that the total resources of the nation mobilises for war.[75]

Although it is not a requirement that the inhabitants are taken by surprise, the right is limited to a very short period during the actual invasion; the inhabitants must not have had time to organise themselves.[76] Situations falling within the scope of the provision are the only ones where the cumulative criteria otherwise applicable for lawful combatancy are relieved. Only the requirements of carrying arms openly and respecting the LOAC apply. In other words: situations of spontaneous and limited uprisings against an invading force are the only situations where the necessity of resort to irregular methods (lack of organisation and discipline and lack of distinction) is properly acknowledged. Due to the limited scope of application, the *levee en masse* institute does not solve the issue of partisans' fight against an already established occupant. Partisans and *levee en masse* must, however, be viewed as 'components of the same problem'[77] and where the right to spontaneous mass risings against an invading force ends, the vexed question of partisan war/guerrilla war and combatant status continues.

The necessity of the 'patriot' to resort to 'unorthodox methods' was adhered to by the patriot school, while the military school wanted an exclusive

72 See Bothe, Partsch and Solf, *New Rules*, at pages 278–9; Draper, 'The status of combatants and the question of guerilla warfare', at pages 180–1; and Rogers, 'Combatant status', at pages 104–5.

73 Rabus, 'A new definition of the levee en masse', at page 234. On the balance between humanitarian considerations and military requirements in general, see Chapter 4.

74 Rabus, 'A new definition of the levee en masse', at page 234.

75 On the origins of the concept, see Rabus, 'A new definition of the levee en masse', at pages 232–4. On total war and the military necessity–humanity balance, see also Chapter 6.

76 ICRC Commentary of 1952, at page 68. Dinstein, *The International Law of Belligerent Occupation*, at page 97.

77 Rabus, 'A new definition of the levee en masse', at page 239.

definition of combatants and severe penalties for those who dared take a part in hostilities. The Norwegian author Andenæs writes from a small State perspective in the aftermath of WWII that:

> Small States wanted the recognition of an unconditional right to resistance for the population in an occupied territory, while the powerful States emphasised the soldier's right to protection from being attacked by an apparently peaceful population and the dangers of brutalisation of warfare when the civilian population took part in hostilities. After an in many ways unclear debate were those proposals which aimed at a recognition of the right to resistance beyond the scope of articles 1 and 2 [of the Hague regulations] withdrawn. By this, it was not the intention of those fronting the proposal to abandon their claims; the tacit agreement was that the question was to remain unsolved. The way the regulations were shaped, however, does not leave much room for expanding the protection of the resistance fight beyond what follows from articles 1 and 2.[78]

The status after the 1907 Hague Conference was thus a compromise between the opposing schools.[79] The clash of opinions emerged again during the preparatory work for the Diplomatic Conferences prior to the Geneva Conventions III of 1949:

> . . . two schools of thought were observed. Some delegates considered that partisans should have to fulfil conditions even stricter than those laid down by the Hague Regulations in order to benefit by the provisions of the Convention. On the other hand, other experts or delegates held the view that resistance movements should be given more latitude. The problem was finally solved by the assimilation of resistance movements to militias and corps of volunteers 'not forming part of the armed forces' of a Party to the conflict. However, contrary to the interpretation generally given to the corresponding provision in the Hague Regulations, it was recognized that such units might operate in occupied territory. That was an important innovation which grew out of the experience of the Second World War.[80]

78 Andenæs, 'Okkupasjonstidens likvidasjoner i et rettslig lys', at pages 4–5. My translation from Norwegian. The Norwegian text says: 'Småstatene ønsket å få anerkjent en ubetinget motstandsrett for befolkningen på det besatte område, mens stormaktene fremhevet soldatens krav på vern mot angrep fra den tilsynelatende fredelige befolkning og faren for en brutalisering av krigføringen ved deltagelse fra sivilbefolkningen. Etter en på mange måter uklar debatt ble de forslag som tok sikte på en anerkjennelse for motstandsretten ut over området for art. 1 og 2, trukket tilbake. Det var ikke med dette forslagsstillernes mening å oppgi sitt standpunkt, forutsetningen var at spørsmålet skulle stå uløst. Slik som reglementet ble formet, lar det seg imidlertid ikke godt gjøre å utvide området for den rettsbeskyttede motstand ut over det som følger av art. 1 og 2.'

79 Rogers, 'Combatant status', at page 105.

80 ICRC Commentary of 1952, at pages 49–50.

This 'compromise' solution is also criticised, and rarely fulfilled in practice.[81] Draper argues that the solution in the Hague Regulations and the GC III (which is an expression of the customary law today, see further below): 'seeks to preserve the military needs of the occupant and the humanitarian treatment of the partisan'[82] but that it is doubtful whether this purpose has been achieved and that there is a: 'considerable need for revision of the law on this matter in order to reassert the balance between military and humanitarian needs in the contest of modern weaponry and techniques for fast moving land fighting.'[83] The weight devoted to necessities of the irregulars must yield, he argues: 'The military advantage of the irregular against his regular adversary must not mask the humanitarian risk to the ordinary civilian.'[84] The solution in the AP I went in another direction, however.

10.5.3 The Necessity of Irregular Warfare: a Victory for the Patriot at the Expense of the Civilian Population in 1977

In the treaty text finally adopted in 1977 it is stated in article 44(3) (cited and discussed into detail below) that the drafters were 'recognizing however ... that there are situations ... where ... an armed combatant cannot so distinguish himself'. Hence, the patriot's argument finally made it through and lowered the threshold for acquiring status as a lawful combatant. During the treaty negotiations, the views were split (as they had been before and were to be after) over the issue whether these 'situations' in reality permitted the arbitrary application of the principle of distinction or whether a suitable balance between humanitarian considerations and military necessity was found. The Swiss delegate expressed the Swiss abstention from voting on the final draft of the AP I at the Diplomatic Conference, by arguing that:

> Situations of armed conflict in which, because of the hostilities the combatants were unable to distinguish themselves from the civilian population were not defined, but left to each party to appraise as it pleased and arbitrarily. The conditions added in sub-paragraphs (a) and (b) were without value. The Swiss delegation was therefore afraid that the article would only have the effect of doing away with the distinctions between combatants and civilians. The consequence would be that the adverse party could take draconian measures against civilians suspected of being combatants. Lastly, the explanations of

81 Bothe, Partsch and Solf, *New Rules*, at page 279. For an account of State practice in this regard, see Parks, '"Special Forces" wear of non-standard uniforms', at pages 526–39.

82 Draper, 'The status of combatants and the question of guerilla warfare', at page 202.

83 Ibid., at page 203, see also page 178.

84 Draper, 'Military necessity and humanitarian imperatives', at page 143.

vote by the delegations which had spoken on that article made it clearly apparent that no unity of view existed concerning it.[85]

The Norwegian delegate represented the opposite, small State, patriot's view and argued that:

If international humanitarian law applicable in armed conflicts was not to become a dead letter, it was essential, first that the rules of that law should place the parties on an equal footing – in other words that the rules should be equally binding on all the parties to the conflict; secondly, that those rules should constitute a well-balanced compromise between humanitarian considerations and military necessity; lastly, that they should be drafted in such a way as to ensure that all the parties to the conflict would have an equal interest in their application. His delegation did not consider that the ICRC draft articles 35, 40, 41 and 42 took those principles sufficiently into account. In particular with regard to article 35, military necessity, in guerrilla operations, was disregarded.[86]

Based on this, the Norwegian delegation proposed an addition to article 35 (which governed perfidy[87] in the Draft Articles) which surely took the necessity of acting clandestinely for guerrilla forces into account, stating that: 'Attacks from ambush, even if carried out in civilian clothing, are not prohibited.'[88] The proposal met opposition[89] and was never adopted, but truly illustrates the patriot's view on the necessity of guerrilla forces – a view shared by the Egyptian delegation, which commented with regard to article 42, that: 'The article established a fair balance between the humanitarian protection of the civilian population and the military necessities of guerrillas.'[90] The remarks made by the delegate of Vietnam also favoured draft article 42, but placed emphasis on the humanitarian arguments of protecting liberation movements: 'The notion of humanity based on justice for national and social liberation movements and the notion of the protection of the civilian population was acquired and formed in the ever evolving

85 Official Records of the Diplomatic Conference CDDH/SR.40, at pages 130–1, paras. 68–9. The Swiss view was shared by for example Uruguay, see CDDH/SR.40, para. 18.

86 Official Records of the Diplomatic Conference CDDH/III/SR 28, paras. 8–9.

87 The link to perfidy – that acts which comply with the requirements of distinction are not perfidious – is today expressed in AP I article 44(3)(b), *in fine*.

88 Norwegian proposal to article 35(2), in Official Records of the Diplomatic Conference CDDH/III/81.

89 See for example the comment by the US delegate that such a rule would create confusion and the comment by the Spanish delegate that such ambush would be against the law, see CDDH/III/SR.28, paras. 24 and 29 respectively.

90 CDDH/SR.41, para. 20, page 145 (Egypt).

humanitarian conscience only in proportion as the liberation movements of the weak and oppressed peoples expanded.'[91]As indicated above, the views upon the military necessity–humanity equilibrium were – and are – diverse: while some States and commentators place emphasis on the humanitarian protection of the civilian population[92] as well as the necessity of conventional forces to counter guerrilla forces in an open manner, others (as seen in the Norwegian proposal quoted above) place emphasis on the necessity of resort to guerrilla warfare[93] (in particular when seen as liberation movements) against an overwhelming military force.[94] The two-poled positions remain (at least at the outset, see just below), and the opposition against the AP I provision has been upheld after its entry into force: 'The United States rejected AP I in part due to this provision, has long vehemently opposed it, and does not accept it as customary law. Encouraging enemy forces to blur the distinction between combatants and civilians undermines a core principle and obligation of the LOAC.'[95] The criticism is emphasised in legal literature as well,[96] and even States who have ratified the contested provision, have acknowledged the danger posed to civilians as a consequence of the AP I rule.[97]

Regardless of the US view referred to above, the necessity of using sub-standard uniforms on certain occasions, also for US forces, is emphasised by Parks: 'The decision to wear something other than a standard uniform first

[91] CDDH/SR.41, para. 56, page 153 (Vietnam).

[92] See for example New Zealand in CDDH/SR.40, para. 71; Canada, CDDH/III/SR.27, para. 51; and Israel in CDDH/SR.40, paras. 18–19.

[93] For an example of this focus see the remarks made by the Yugoslavian delegate in CDDH/SR.40, at page 76, arguing that the provision actually widened the scope of humanitarian protection and that the older rules had made matters easier for an occupant or an aggressor. See also the remarks by the Dutch delegate in CDDH/SR.41, para. 4.

[94] See for example the comment made by the Philippine delegate that guerrillas blending in with civilians is the only way to counter the superior military strength of the aggressor, in CDDH/III/SR.28, para. 25. See as well the comment by the Vietnamese delegate that the necessity of guerrilla tactics was triggered by the super-power opponents, as well as imperialism, see Official Records of the Diplomatic Conference CDDH/III/SR.33, para. 37. In the same direction see as well the comments of Kenya, Uganda and Romania in CDDH/SR.40, paras. 54, 57 and 61 respectively. And even further the remarks of the Sudanese delegate in CDDH/SR.40, para. 138 and the remarks of the Afghan delegate in CDDH/SR.41, para. 2.

[95] From Operational Law Handbook, at page 17. The position is upheld in the US DoD Manual, para. 4.6.1.2, at page 119. See as well the account given by Parks in '"Special Forces" wear of non-standard uniforms', at pages 519–20.

[96] Dinstein, *Conduct of Hostilities*, at pages 61–4.

[97] See for example the remarks made by Austria in Official Records of the Diplomatic Conference CDDH/SR.40, para. 38; and Germany, para. 78. See also Norwegian Manual, page 113, where it is warned against a liberal application of the exceptional rule in AP I article 44(3).

requires military necessity.'[98] He points out the fact (which is discussed in Section 10.6.1) that wearing a partial uniform, or even civilian clothing, is not a crime as such and is illegal under international law only if it involves perfidy.[99] The different modes of military necessity therefore become apparent if one views both sides of clandestine warfare. As argued by Baxter: '... the power of a belligerent to punish espionage directed against him arose not from the fact that the law prohibited activity, but from the danger which clandestine acts created and the resulting necessity that they be dealt with severely'.[100] Although the act of espionage is not equivalent to guerrilla fighting as such, the need to operate clandestinely is usually present in both modes of warfare, as well as reflected in the necessity for the affected party to counter such methods severely. The AP I solution favoured the necessity for the former one step further by granting POW status to a group of irregulars who earlier could have been dealt with as spies.

10.6 THE REQUIREMENT OF DISTINCTION

10.6.1 What Is the Obligation to Distinguish Oneself?

Two questions arise: what is the content of the obligation to distinguish oneself, and what are the consequences of breaching the obligation? While the first question is dealt with subsequently below, the second question shall be briefly addressed initially.

In the 1907 Hague Regulations and GC III (as reflecting customary law[101]) the obligation to distinguish oneself is inextricably linked to the loss of POW status upon breach – and only this. The AP I article 44(3) first sentence, however, arguably establishes a new rule of international law.[102] It states that: 'In order to promote the protection of the civilian population from the effects of hostilities, combatants are obliged to distinguish themselves from the civilian population while they are engaged in an attack or in a military operation preparatory to an attack.' Although placed in a provision which deals with POW status, the sentence is not, by wording, limited to the

98 Parks, '"Special Forces" wear of non-standard uniforms', at page 513. See also pages 521, 523, 529 and 542.

99 Ibid., at pages 512–13 and 521.

100 Baxter, 'So-called unprivileged belligerency', at page 329.

101 ICRC CIHL, rule 106. AMW Manual, rule 10(b)(i), at page 84. See as well for example UK Manual, at page 145; Norwegian Manual, at page 111; AP I Commentary to article 44, at page 527, para. 1691; Ipsen, 'Combatants and non-combatants', at pages 89–90. Henderson, *The Contemporary Law of Targeting*, page 82.

102 Bothe, Partsch and Solf, *New Rules*, at page 285.

achievement of POW status, and a breach of the rule may, arguably, be considered a separate violation of the LOAC, but not a war crime as such. Failure to distinguish oneself may amount to an international crime only in cases where the act in question amount to treacherous killing or perfidy.[103] This rule in AP I article 44(3) is, however, limited to the scope of the AP I and binding only upon States' parties to this.

The duty to distinguish oneself has been described as a reciprocal duty: as a 'quid pro quo' relationship where civilians are protected and combatants are obliged to distinguish themselves in order to enforce civilian protection and that each party to the conflict can expect this from the opposing forces.[104] Lack of distinction – and danger posed to civilians – is sanctioned by loss of POW privilege.[105] Military necessity cannot be invoked as a general exception to the requirements for POW status.[106] The exceptional (minimum) criteria for obtaining POW status are dealt with separately below – according to the different standards in the 1907 Hague Regulations and the GC III on the one hand and the AP I on the other.

Although the treaty texts of the 1907 Hague Regulations and the GC III do not contain an explicit duty for regular armed forces to distinguish themselves (as part of the POW requirements), it is understood as an inherent presumption that States' regular armed forces wear uniforms and thus that the minimum requirements are not necessary to express explicitly.[107] The crucial element is that they are distinguishable from the civilian population.[108] The practical difficulties related to a 'fixed distinctive emblem' (see further below) and the lack of definition of a uniform remain, however.[109]

The wearing of a standard uniform is not a requirement, although it is normally being used.[110] Some seem to argue though, that regular armed forces are obliged to wear a uniform, while militia and organised resistance movements ('irregular forces') as mentioned in GC III article 4A(2) is the only

103 Ibid. On perfidy, see Chapter 17.
104 See Ferrell, 'No shirt, no shoes, no status', at page 105.
105 Dinstein, *Conduct of Hostilities*, at page 44.
106 Dinstein, 'Unlawful combatancy', at page 267.
107 AP I Commentary to AP I article 44, at page 527, para. 1692. Tallinn Manual, Commentary 11 to rule 87, at page 405. See also Ferrell, 'No shirt, no shoes, no status', at page 106.
108 See for example the comments by the US delegate during the Diplomatic Conference stating that there is no duty to wear a uniform under international law, nor on the definition of a uniform, but that there is a duty to distinguish oneself, see Official Records of the Diplomatic Conference CDDH/III/SR.27, para. 23. Ferrell, 'No shirt, no shoes, no status', page 106.
109 Parks, '"Special Forces" wear of non-standard uniforms', at page 516.
110 Dinstein, *Conduct of Hostilities*, at pages 52–3. Parks, '"Special Forces" wear of non-standard uniforms', at page 508. Norwegian Manual, at page 111.

category exempted from the duty to wear a uniform.[111] This view is rebutted by the interpretation of the provision in AP I article 44(7) which refers to the 'generally accepted practice of States with respect to the wearing of the uniform . . .' Apparently, it was meant here to uphold the practice of wearing of uniform as the principal rule for regular combatants, and at the same time to also acknowledge the need for regular members to adopt to guerrilla means (and the requirements of article 44(3)) when assigned to such tasks.[112]

10.6.2 *The Hague and Geneva Requirements of Distinction for Irregular Forces*

According to the 1907 Hague Regulations, the GC III, as well as customary law,[113] the requirement linked to distinction for irregular forces – the 'partisans'[114] – is twofold: the Hague Regulation article 1(2) and GC III article 4 A(2)(b) require the wearing of a 'fixed distinctive sign recognizable at a distance' and the same articles 1(3) and 4 A(2)(c) require 'carrying arms openly'. Both requirements deserve some further comments.

A 'fixed distinctive sign' is meant to identify and characterise the armed force[115] and must therefore be distinct for that armed force and be worn by all members of the force, constantly in all circumstances (hence 'fixed').[116] The requirement can be fulfilled by wearing the most distinctive sign of all, the regular uniform, but may just as well be another piece of clothing such as a cap, a coat, a shirt, an armband or an emblem worn on the chest.[117] The option of a cap has been criticised for not being sufficiently 'fixed',[118] but if 'fixed' is to be understood as 'irremovable', the same argument would apply to a shirt or a coat.[119] In fact, nothing is actually 'irremovable'. The point is that

111 Ipsen 'Combatants and non-combatants', at pages 89–90. A very clear statement in this direction was made by the Egyptian delegate during the Diplomatic Conference as well. See Official Records of the Diplomatic Conference CDDH/SR.41, para. 19, stating that regular combatants were not released from their obligation to wear uniform and that failure to do so would amount to perfidy. This position is clearly too rigid.

112 Bothe, Partsch and Solf, *New Rules*, at page 291.

113 AMW Manual, rule 10(b)(i), Commentary 2, at page 84.

114 ICRC Commentary of 1952, to GC III article 4, page 49. Although the provision is made to cover conduct by partisans, it also applies to regular forces doing irregular warfare.

115 Dinstein, *Conduct of Hostilities*, at page 52.

116 ICRC Commentary of 1952, to GC III article 4, at page 59.

117 ICRC Commentary of 1952, at page 60; AMW Manual, rule 10(b)(i), Commentary 2, at page 84.

118 Ferrell, 'No shirt, no shoes, no status', page 107.

119 In this direction, see also Parks, '"Special Forces" wear of non-standard uniforms', at page 517, where he argues that despite the clear wording 'fixed', the device need not be permanent or fixed.

the emblem should not be taken on and off. Actually, it has also been suggested that a distinctive headgear is the most distinctive sign.[120] With regard to irregular forces it is the element of permanency (which lies in the requirement of 'fixed'), which can prove to be a major difficulty, since it has practical implications for the possibility to operate clandestinely.[121]

What then lies in the requirement of being recognisable at a distance? When it comes to the understanding of 'distance', it is the view of the ICRC that 'the distinctive sign should be recognizable by a person at a distance not too great to permit a uniform to be recognized'.[122] 'Distance' is still a relative notion and must be understood in relation to what physical circumstances reasonably permit. For example, it is not required that the combatant illuminates himself during dark[123] or otherwise draws attention to himself at the cost of staying alive: 'Combatants seeking to stay alive do not attempt to draw attention to themselves.'[124] Furthermore, camouflage is a common way of operating as long as the camouflage seeks to blend in with topography (landscape) rather than demography (people). The aim of the provision is to frame the false impression, not to make them visible at all times.[125]

The requirement of carrying arms openly is aimed at identifying the combatants, as a 'real distinctive mark of combatants'.[126] The duty to carry arms openly according to the GC III does not mean that all sorts of weaponry have to be visible at every time. The view of the ICRC is that:

> although the difference may seem slight, there must be no confusion between carrying arms 'openly' and carrying them 'visibly' or 'ostensibly'. Surprise is a factor in any war operation, whether or not involving regular troops. This provision is intended to guarantee the loyalty of the fighting, it is not an attempt to prescribe that a hand-grenade or a revolver must be carried at belt or shoulder rather than in a pocket or under a coat.
>
> The enemy must be able to recognize partisans as combatants in the same way as members of regular armed forces, whatever their weapons. Thus, a civilian could not enter a military post on a false pretext and then open fire, having taken unfair advantage of his adversaries.[127]

120 Draper, 'The status of combatants and the question of guerilla warfare', at page 202.
121 Ibid. On the necessities of the guerrilla-warfare methods, see further Section 10.5.
122 ICRC Commentary of 1952, to the GC III article 4, at page 60.
123 Parks, '"Special Forces" wear of non-standard uniforms', at page 517.
124 Dinstein, 'Unlawful combatancy', at page 257.
125 Ibid.
126 Draper, 'The status of combatants and the question of guerilla warfare', at page 203.
127 ICRC Commentary of 1952, to the GC III article 4, at page 61.

The core of the provision thus seems to be weapons which are normally worn openly, such as a rifle, should not be hidden with the purpose of concealing arms.[128] Beyond this it is not clear from the quoted passage what 'loyalty of the fighting' means in more practical terms. The duty to carry arms openly is an alternative to the presumed, regular mode of distinction: the uniform. The rule does not impose any requirement for regular combatants in uniform to carry arms openly.[129]

The requirement of carrying arms openly is repeated in the exceptional provision in AP I article 44(3), but then with and additional time-factor which is discussed separately below.

10.6.3 *When Combatants 'Cannot So Distinguish Themselves' According to the AP I*

One of the most controversial and time-consuming issues during the drafting process of AP I was the question of combatant and POW status for national liberation movements.[130] Among the pending issues which had to be solved with regard to status was the question of distinction between the civilian population and combatants. After stating the general duty of combatants to distinguish themselves (on this issue, see above), article 44(3) says:

> Recognizing, however, that there are situations in armed conflicts where, owing to the nature of the hostilities an armed combatant cannot so distinguish himself, he shall retain his status as a combatant, provided that, in such situations he carries his arms openly:
>
> a) During each military engagement, and
> b) During such time as he is visible to the adversary while he is engaged in a military deployment preceding the launching of an attack in which he is to participate. Acts which comply with the requirements of this paragraph shall not be considered as perfidious within the meaning of Article 37, paragraph 1(c).

Several interpretative questions arise from the reading of this passage. Among these, the interpretation of the exceptional phrase 'nature of the hostilities'. The phrase is an obvious recognition of the military necessity of guerrilla warfare (as accounted for above), but which situations are actually referred to? The question was discussed during the treaty negotiations and the views were

128 Dinstein, *Conduct of Hostilities*, at page 54.
129 Norwegian Manual, at page 111.
130 Bothe, Partsch and Solf, *New Rules*, at page 282.

divided: can the exceptional minimum criteria be invoked only during occupation or wars of liberation as mentioned in article 1(4) or is the rule of a general nature? A majority of States and commentators seem to favour the first interpretation,[131] while others point out that the wording is general and that this in reality left the consideration 'to each party to appraise as it pleased and arbitrarily'.[132] The latter view reflects the controversy over the whole article as such. It furthermore raises a question with regard to the practice of States' regular armed forces and their use of/non-use of uniform.

While it is clear, on the one hand, that the exceptional rule in AP I article 44(3) does not represent customary law with regard to POW status for irregular forces it is, on the other hand, also clear (from the wording of article 44(7)) that the rule does not change customary law with regard to States' armed forces use of uniform.[133] This (State) practice reflects at least three aspects: first, that 'uniform' includes different types of non-standard uniform (see Section 10.6.2), second that States practice assignment of members of the armed forces to certain (non-fighting) positions where they wear civilian clothing,[134] and third that the practice of States also includes the use of the 'militia requirements' for distinguishing regular armed forces – when military necessity requires exception from a more standard uniform.[135] However, as pointed out above with regard to the general requirement of distinction: military necessity cannot be invoked as an exception beyond the criteria especially accounted for – either in the AP I or GC III expressing customary law. This applies notwithstanding possible violations from the opposing forces: 'These criteria admit of no exception, not even in the unusual circumstances of Afghanistan',[136] not for Taliban, not for Al Qaida and not for US forces.[137] A seemingly opposite position is taken

131 In favour of a limited application, see for example the views of Canada in Official Records of the Diplomatic Conference CDDH/SR.41, para. 24; and UK in CDDH/SR.40, para. 74. In this direction, see as well Bothe, Partsch and Solf, *New Rules*, at page 289. German Manual, para. 316, at page 41. The AP I Commentary to article 44 seems mostly to acknowledge that the issue is disputed and gives an account of the differences, see pages 529–30, para. 1698.

132 See the view presented by the Swiss delegate, pointing out that the rule is of a general nature in Official Records of the Diplomatic Conference CDDH/SR.40, para. 66. For the critical view of Switzerland in general, see above.

133 Bothe, Partsch and Solf, *New Rules*, at page 291.

134 Ibid. and Parks, '"Special Forces" wear of non-standard uniforms', at page 520. See also the related discussion in the Tallinn Manual, regarding persons engaged in cyber operations at a distance from the area of operations or clearly separated from the civilian population, in commentaries 11–13 to rule 87, at pages 405–6.

135 See in particular the view presented by Parks in '"Special Forces" wear of non-standard Uniforms', at page 543.

136 Dinstein, 'Unlawful combatancy', at page 267.

137 Ibid., at page 269.

by a minority of the Experts in the Tallinn Manual, arguing that 'the sole condition for combatant status for members of the armed forces is their status as members'.[138]

The AP I rule has reduced the duty to distinguish oneself from 'all times' to 'during military engagement' and the time he is 'visible to the adversary while engaged in a military deployment preceding the launching of an attack'. The understanding of the notion of 'military deployment' becomes crucial. During the drafting process controversy existed over whether the phrase encapsulates 'any movement of the military formation towards the place from which the attack was to be launched''[139] or 'the last step when the combatants were taking their firing positions, just before the commencement of hostilities'.[140] The majority of States seem to favour the first interpretation.[141]

The limitation to 'military engagement' and 'military deployment' preceding an attack, must not only be understood in a temporal aspect. This limitation also leaves out other modes of warfare-related activities, such as training, administration and law enforcement.[142] One particular example (of warfare-related activity) is the so-called 'resident combatants' who are not considered spies even if they are wearing civilian clothing during information gathering (see Section 10.4.1). The duty to carry arms openly exists for the time the combatant is 'visible to the adversary'. This phrase raises additional interpretative questions: does it imply that the obligation does not arise if the combatant does not know nor should have known that he was visible?[143] Does visibility refer to what can be spotted by the naked eye, or does it include binoculars and/or infrared equipment?[144] Commentators seem to favour the latter solution.[145]

Having discussed all the interpretative difficulties and controversies which may arise during the application of AP I article 44(3), the result in practice may simply prove to be that the combatant will nevertheless benefit from the POW treatment, due to the rule in article 44(4), which says:

> A combatant which falls into the power of an adverse Party while failing to meet the requirements set forth in the second sentence of paragraph 3 shall forfeit his right to be a prisoner of war, but he shall, nevertheless, be given

138 Tallinn Manual, Commentary 6 to rule 87, at page 402.
139 Official Records of the Diplomatic Conference CDDH/SR.40, para. 23 (Italy), para. 74 (UK); CDDH/SR.41, para. 6 (The Netherlands); CDDH/SR.41, para. 24 (Canada).
140 CDDH/SR.41, para. 21 (Egypt) and para. 28 (PLO).
141 Bothe, Partsch and Solf, *New Rules*, at page 288.
142 Ibid., at page 286.
143 Dinstein, 'Unlawful combatancy', at page 265.
144 Ibid.
145 Bothe, Partsch and Solf, *New Rules*, at page 289.

> protections equivalent to those accorded to prisoners of war by the Third Convention and by this Protocol. The protection includes protections equivalent to those accorded to prisoners of war by the Third Convention in the case where such a person is tried and punished for any offences he has committed.

The effect of this rule has been firmly criticised for in reality allowing the question of distinction to become moot.[146]

10.7 RETURNING TO THE COMMANDER'S ASSESSMENT

The question of 'lawful combatancy' is not frequently a matter within the commander's margin of appreciation. As seen, this vexed issue has been consumed by the historical discourse concerning the necessity for irregular warfare. Finally, the notion of lawful combatancy has been resolved at the level of treaty formulation – in two different standards. Having said that, commanders will have to assess how their subordinates shall distinguish themselves from the civilian population when participating in hostilities, i.e. by the wearing of uniforms or other distinctive signs.

In cases governed by the AP I standard for lawful combatancy, commanders may admittedly be left small, yet significant, room for discretion: the assessment of situations when combatants 'cannot so distinguish themselves' in the AP I article 44(3). This assessment – if and when left to commanders – has to be performed on the basis of each State's different perception of necessity vis-à-vis humanity, which in turn may prove to also be a deeply rooted matter of State policy. The assessment may prove quite a challenge for a military commander to perform, if not equipped with proper guidance from his or her government.

146 Dinstein, 'Unlawful combatancy', at pages 265–6.

11

Who Are Civilians and When Do They Lose Their Protection?

11.1 DEFINITION OF CIVILIANS

Civilians are defined – for the first time in a treaty[1] – negatively in AP I article 50, as all those *who do not* enjoy status as combatants:

1. A civilian is any person who does not belong to one of the categories of persons referred to in article 4 A (1), (2), (3) and (6) of the Third Convention and in article 43 of this Protocol. In case of doubt whether a person is a civilian, that person shall be considered to be a civilian.
2. The civilian population comprises all persons who are civilians.
3. The presence within the civilian population of individuals who do not come within the definition of civilians does not deprive the population of its civilian character.

The definition of combatants is accounted for in Chapters 8 and 9. Civilians comprise all those who fall outside the scope of the definition of combatants. This negative definition was chosen to the benefit of the civilian population,[2] in the favour of humanitarian concerns and (possibly) to the detriment of military necessities. The negative definition is as well considered an expression of customary law in the following formula: 'Civilians are persons who are not members of the armed forces. The civilian population comprises all persons who are civilians.'[3] Or as put by the ICTY, adding a time element to the membership in the armed forces: 'Civilians within the meaning of

[1] Conference of Governmental Experts (1971), vol. III, at page 17. Bothe, Partsch and Solf, *New Rules*, at page 334.

[2] Conference of Governmental Experts (1971), vol. III, at pages 19–20.

[3] ICRC CIHL, rule 5. For support of the ICRC Customary rule, see for example Boothby, *The Law of Targeting*, at page 69.

Article 3 are persons who are not, or no longer, members of the armed forces.'[4]

Although the GC IV in its title refers to the protection of civilian persons in time of war, the Convention does not define the civilian population as such, only those who are granted the protection according to the Convention: enemy nationals in a belligerent State, and inhabitants in an occupied territory.[5] Nor does the Convention contain a provision establishing the protection from attacks or the effects of hostilities. The need to actually define the civilian population seems to have emerged together with the concept of a total war, but also of the industrial war as well as the development of air power and its ability to strike at the war industry in the 'hinterland'.[6] Hence, both a greater necessity to actually strike at the war machinery (to destroy the industry) as well as a possibility to do it (by air power), have accompanied the debate of who actually *deserved* the status as a protected civilian.[7]

The category of civilians also comprises certain individuals who are granted the secondary status as prisoners of war upon capture. These are those mentioned in GC III articles 4 A(4) and (5) and encompass persons who accompany the armed forces without being members thereof and crews of the merchant marine and civil aircraft who do not enjoy more favourable treatment.

During the drafting process it was discussed – as touched upon above with regard to the definition of the category of combatants in Section 9.2 – whether the definition of civilians should exclude those who were directly participating in 'military operations' – as opposed to those who were participating in the 'war effort'.[8] The role of civilians in a nation's war effort has been a revolving issue at least throughout the modern history of war. As pointed out by Baxter: 'The view that war makes individuals in belligerent nations enemies one to the other persisted throughout the eighteenth and nineteenth centuries and still perhaps serves as a fundamental assumption of the law.'[9] During the American Civil War the Lieber Code stated that persons (men) who committed hostilities without being part of the armed forces were to lose their POW status and

4 ICTY Blaskic Case, Trial Chamber Judgment, at para. 180, page 60.
5 GC IV article 4.
6 See for example, Nurick, 'The distinction between combatant and noncombatant in the law of war', at pages 689–91.
7 See for example Spaight, *Air Power and War Rights*, at pages 43–4; Solf, 'Protection of civilians', at pages 120, 127.
8 Conference of Governmental Experts (1971), vol. III, at pages 27–8. See as well Bothe, Partsch and Solf, *New Rules*, at page 335.
9 Baxter, 'So-called unprivileged belligerency', at page 325.

to be dealt with as robbers or pirates.[10] When speaking of civilians, the notion of 'innocence' has been close at hand; civilians have been considered to deserve protection only when they are innocent.[11] And furthermore: '. . . the civilian has often voluntarily become a participant in warfare, as a guerrilla or as a member of the underground or as a secret agent, requiring, *inter alia*, stringent control of his activities or even internment if he is present on the domestic territory of a belligerent'.[12]

The distinction between participation in military operations and participation in the war effort reflects the later adopted rule on direct participation in hostilities in article 51(3), which is accounted for in Section 11.3. The distinction also reflects the question of whether civilians who lose their protection also lose their *status* as civilians. The ICRC claim that status as civilian is not lost, while others disagree.[13] Earlier texts, which have gained widespread support,[14] such as the General Assembly Resolution 2675 (XXV), supports the notion that the status is also lost: 'In the conduct of military operations in armed conflicts, a distinction must be made at all times between persons actively taking part in the hostilities and civilian populations.'[15]

Notwithstanding the position chosen on the question of status, civilians remain civilians even though *individual* combatants are present among them. This is stated in article 50(3) and also emphasised in the jurisprudence of the ICTY.[16] In the Strugar Case it was held that: 'It is possible that there may have been individuals in the Old Town on 6 December 1991 who were connected with the Croatian defending forces, however, any such persons did not fire on JNA forces or undertake any overt military activity. Their

10 Lieber Code article 82. See also Boothby, *The Law of Targeting*, at page 144.

11 See for example the historical account given by Solf, 'Protection of civilians', at page 119.

12 Baxter, 'So-called unprivileged belligerency', at page 326.

13 Bothe, Partsch and Solf, *New Rules*, at page 335. Dinstein, *Conduct of Hostilities*, at pages 105 and 174, where he argues that civilians taking direct part in hostilities assimilate themselves to combatants.

14 The resolution is held in the Conference of Governmental Experts (1971), vol. III, at page 14 to reflect *opinio juris*.

15 UN General Assembly Resolution 2675 (XXV) (1970), at para. 2.

16 Galic Case, at para. 50. See also AP I Commentary, at para. 1922. The Appeals Chamber, however, reverted the Trial Chamber judgment's conclusion of unlawfulness, based on the finding that there was still a considerable number of soldiers in the town at the time of the attack. On the question of a number of combatants or military objects within a civilian population or town, see also jurisprudence from the Blaskic, Strugar and Gotovina cases.

presence could not change the character of the population.'[17] Having said this, civilians who are serving the armed forces *within* a military objective run a specific risk which arguably attributes to them less weight than other civilians under the proportionality assessment, as dealt with in Chapters 13 and 15 below.[18]

11.2 THE ELEMENTS OF PROTECTION: AND THEIR LIMITATIONS

AP I article 51(1) states the general rule that 'the civilian population and individual civilians shall enjoy general protection against dangers arising from military operations'.[19] This protection is to be effectuated through the rules to follow in article 51. The fundamental – and absolute[20] – prohibition against direct attacks is thus spelled out in 51(2), first sentence: 'The civilian population as such, as well as individual civilians, shall not be the object of attack.'[21] Article 51 furthermore enumerates those rules which together form the protection of the civilian population, and which in part are to be accounted for in this and the next chapter. Roughly considered, the rules contained in article 51 comprise: first, the prohibition of direct attacks against civilians where the civilian person/civilian object is the intended object of attack, unless and for such time as civilians directly participate in hostilities and notwithstanding the alleged justification of reprisals or affecting civilian 'morale'. Second, the prohibition of indiscriminate attacks – which are of a nature to strike without distinction, either due to the intrinsic character of the weapon or how the weapon or the weapon system is used (the method). Third, the prohibition of disproportionate attacks, which are directed against a lawful target, but where the incidental damage on civilians/civilian objects is excessive compared to the expected military advantage. This latter category is dealt with separately in Chapter 13. The following part of the present chapter is devoted to the loss of civilian protection due to direct participation in hostilities whereas the remaining categories are dealt with in Chapter 12. These categories of protection may, however, also be viewed at the outset from their limitations. As formulated by the ICTY in the Kupreskic Case:

17 Strugar Case, Trial Chamber Judgment, at para. 284.
18 Bothe, Partsch and Solf, *New Rules*, at page 336. On the weight devoted to different relata under the proportionality assessment, see Chapters 13 and 14.
19 AP I article 51(1), first sentence.
20 On the notion of absolute protection, see Section 7.3.
21 Also cited in Section 7.2.

> The protection of civilians and civilian objects provided by modern international law may cease entirely or be reduced or suspended in three exceptional circumstances: (i) when civilians abuse their rights; (ii) when, although the object of a military attack is comprised of military objectives, belligerents cannot avoid causing so-called collateral damage to civilians; and (iii) at least according to some authorities, when civilians may legitimately be the object of reprisals.[22]

A misleading and unfortunate reference to the (not absolute) protection of civilians according to the rule of distinction and military necessity is found in the Blaskic Case from the ICTY: 'Targeting civilians or civilian property is an offence when not justified by military necessity. . . . Such an attack must have been conducted intentionally in the knowledge, or when it was impossible not to know, that civilians or civilian property were being targeted not through military necessity.'[23] The reference to military necessity in this latter passage is superfluous at best. Military necessity cannot render the attack on civilians lawful. Although the aim of the remark is obviously to state the contrary. The aim of the general protection is to reduce to a minimum the dangers arising from the armed conflict – acknowledging that dangers for the civilian population is an inevitable consequence of hostilities.[24] The fundamental protection against direct attacks is to be distinguished from the special protection devoted to certain categories of personnel, dealt with in Chapter 17.[25]

The presence of the balance between military necessity and humanitarian concerns has been conspicuous throughout the drafting history: 'The expression "to the effect that the latter be spared", indicates the chief object and concern of humanitarian international law. On the other hand, the words "as much as possible", are a concession to the principle of military necessity, a concession which seemed to the experts to be both realistic and inevitable.'[26] The duty to spare the civilian population 'as much as possible' connotes not only to the basic rule of distinction which prohibits directing attacks against civilians, but just as much to the rules which are to set the principle into effect: the prohibition against indiscriminate attacks. The standard of 'as much as possible' may also be seen as reflecting time; the development of the prohibition of terror attacks (see Chapter 12) is one such example.

22 Kupreskic Case, at para. 522, page 204.
23 Blaskic Case Trial Chamber Judgment at para. 180, page 60. See also Chapter 5.
24 AP I Commentary to article 51(1), at para. 1935, page 617.
25 Bothe, Partsch and Solf, *New Rules*, at page 341.
26 Conference of Governmental Experts (1971), vol. III, at page 25.

11.3 LOSS OF CIVILIAN PROTECTION DUE TO DIRECT PARTICIPATION IN HOSTILITIES

AP I article 51 is a key article[27] to understand the relationship between the protection devoted to civilians, as introduced above in Section 11.2, and the loss of such protection. The first major exception from protection is the rule on 'direct participation in hostilities' (DPH), which is, among others, expressed in article 51(3): 'Civilians shall enjoy the protection afforded by this Section, unless and for such time as they take a direct part in hostilities.'

An identical provision is found in the AP II article 13(3) and similar, but not identical,[28] provisions are also found elsewhere in the Additional Protocols and the four Geneva Conventions,[29] as well as in rules formulated to express customary LOAC.[30] The semantic difference to the rule in article 3 Common to the four GCs, which makes use of the term 'active part', is generally understood not to imply material differences.[31] The reason behind the rule is clear: when civilians take part in hostilities, the military necessity of directing attacks towards them reappears and the rationale for protection becomes moot.

The ambiguities left open by the DPH rule have been pointed out as a regrettable fact[32] and, evidently, this short and important provision has given rise to considerable debate. The debate has been actualised more than ever since the ICRC Interpretive Guidance on the Notion of Direct Participation in Hostilities under International Humanitarian Law in 2008, illustrating to the fullest the potential for ambiguities in the rule.

27 AP I Commentary, at para. 1923, page 615.

28 For an attempt to distinguish between these different expressions, see Bothe, Partsch and Solf, *New Rules*, at pages 344–5 with further references.

29 In AP I similar provisions are found in articles 8(a) and (b) with regard to the loss of protection for wounded, sick and shipwrecked when performing 'any act of hostility', and in article 41(2) which prohibits making personnel 'hors de combat' the object of attack, provided that he 'abstains from any hostile act', as well as article 42(2) granting descending airmen immunity from attack in order to be able to surrender unless 'it is apparent that he is engaging in a hostile act'. Then, last in the AP I (but not least practical) are the rules in articles 13(1) and 65(1) which prescribe the loss of protection from being the object of attack for medical units and civil defence organisations when they are performing 'outside their humanitarian function' 'acts harmful to the enemy'. The preceding provisions are also found in the GC I article 22 with regard to medical personnel (although not explicitly in this provision); GC II article 34 with regard to hospital ships and sick bays; and GC IV article 19 with regard to hospitals.

30 Rome Statute article 8(2)(b)(i); AMW Manual, rule 28, page 118; and ICRC CIHL, rule 6. The positions also seems to be undisputed in legal literature. See for example Schmitt, 'The interpretive guidance on the notion of direct participation in hostilities', at page 13.

31 Boothby, *The Law of Targeting*, at page 145; Interpretive Guidance, at pages 1013–14; Dinstein, *Conduct of Hostilities*, at page 174.

32 Bothe, Partsch and Solf, *New Rules*, at page 344.

Both considerations of military necessity and humanity may align in favour of a broad interpretation of the notion of DPH. While considerations of necessity certainly may favour a wide interpretation of DPH, the protection of the civilian population as such may also benefit from a clear and reasonably wide understanding of the concept of DPH, in order to make the distinction to the peaceful population as clear as possible.[33]

11.3.1 *The Notion of Organised Armed Groups and the Scope of the DPH Rule*

Among the controversial issues discussed during, and after, the Interpretive Guidance was the question (introduced above) whether a person who takes a direct part in hostilities loses his/her status as civilian and becomes an unlawful combatant, or whether the person remains a civilian.[34] This question is closely related to the time dimension of the DPH rule (addressed separately below) which adds a time limitation to the loss of civilian protection due to direct participation in hostilities.

In the Interpretive Guidance the concept of 'civilian' encompasses all persons who do not belong to a State party to a conflict and all those who do not fulfil a 'continuous combat function' in an organised armed group (OAG) in a non-international armed conflict.[35] This position is highly contested and criticised for being 'fatally flawed'.[36] At the heart of the diverging views are the differing opinions over the threshold for comparing – or mirroring – the notion of armed forces (who are lawful targets at all times) to that of organised armed groups.[37] The result of the approach taken in the Interpretive Guidance is that members of non-State organised armed groups in an international armed conflict are considered as civilians, and do not lose their civilian protection on a continuous basis.[38] Considerations of military necessity may reasonably advocate different positions from that of the Interpretive Guidance. The ICRC view may arguably provide the non-State armed groups with an unfair advantage to the benefit of States' regular armed forces.[39] The US view is, for example, that persons belonging to a hostile, non-State armed group are

33 Schmitt, 'Humanitarian law', at page 17.

34 Dinstein, 'Distinction and loss of civilian protection', at pages 188–9.

35 Interpretive Guidance, at pages 997 and 1002.

36 Schmitt, 'Deconstructing direct participation in hostilities', at page 738.

37 The division of opinion is illustrated among the Experts in the Tallinn Manual, see Commentary 4 to rule 96, at page 426.

38 A critique of this view is for example presented by Watkin, 'Opportunity lost', at page 651.

39 Boothby, *The Law of Targeting*, at page 150. See also below, this argument is also valid against the Interpretive Guidance view on the scope of the time dimension to DPH.

not civilians, and are liable to attack unless they are rendered *hors de combat.*[40] However, and as pointed out by the US DoD LOAC Manual, one may argue that these persons are still civilians, but nevertheless liable to attack on a continuous basis, due to their membership in an armed group which 'is engaged in hostilities as a form of taking a direct part in hostilities'.[41] This latter view is rather widely shared,[42] and the position may be less limited than the Interpretive Guidance in two aspects: first, that the notion of armed groups may also encompass international armed conflicts, and second, a rejection (or a watering down) of the ICRC requirement of 'continuous combat function'. The solution in the Norwegian Manual is, for example, to apply the same criteria for members of organised armed groups (not acting on behalf of a State) to both international and non-international armed conflicts, and not to define their status as either combatants or civilians. Furthermore, the ICRC requirement of continuous combat function is upheld in the Norwegian Manual, but interpreted so widely that it resembles an actual reflection of the armed forces.[43]

Although the overall picture is not clear, it seems correct to state that the customary law definition of civilians concerning the DPH rule is not reflected in the Interpretive Guidance.

Beyond the time dimension of the DPH rule, the question of a person's status is only of interest with regard to the question of treatment after capture – not with regard to the status as a lawful target. In other words: notwithstanding whether the person is to be considered to have turned into a combatant or to remain a civilian – he or she has lost the protection against direct attacks.[44] If a person is considered a civilian, and captured, he or she enjoys the protection according to the GC IV, while the protection of unlawful combatants after capture may be less extensive.[45]

11.3.2 *The Elements of the Direct Participation Rule: 'Hostilities' and 'Direct Participation'*

The notion of direct participation in hostilities comprises two elements: that of the collective 'hostilities' and that of individual 'direct participation'.[46]

40 US DoD Manual, para. 5.7.3, at pages 222 ff.

41 US DoD Manual, para. 5.8.2.1, at page 228.

42 AMW Manual, Commentary 4 to rule 28, at page 119. Boothby, *The Law of Targeting*, at pages 150–1.

43 See the Norwegian Manual, at pages 58–9. The example used to illustrate 'combat function' in an armed group is that of a chef who is accompanying the group on tactical manoeuvres, hiding in the mountains and otherwise acting as if they are an integrated part of the group.

44 Boothby, *The Law of Targeting*, at page 148.

45 On the consequences of unlawful combatancy, see Section 10.3.

46 AMW Manual, at page 117; and Interpretive Guidance, at page 1013.

The notion of 'hostilities' is not defined in the treaty text, and also terminology switches between 'hostilities', 'warfare' and 'military operations' (or simply 'operations').[47] It is, however, clear that the notion of 'hostilities' refers to situations occurring within armed conflict (either international or non-international) – although certainly not *all* situations within the scope of armed conflict.[48] This includes – but is not limited to – acts of violence, and must be distinguished from the 'general war effort'.[49] Within the spectrum of 'hostilities' we thus find the use of traditional means and methods of warfare, on behalf of a party to the conflict and against an adversary, as well as logistics, communication and military planning. Outside the scope of 'hostilities' is for example the use of violence as part of law enforcement.[50]

The Interpretive Guidance furthermore identifies three cumulative, constitutive elements of DPH: the threshold of harm, direct causal link and belligerent nexus.[51] The three elements also gain support, in principle, in certain military manuals,[52] while the views among critics vary, and it is doubtful whether the criteria can be said to reflect customary law.[53] Having said this, among the different aspects of the DPH rule, the three elements are less controversial than the time dimension and the concept of civilians.[54]

The element of the 'threshold of harm' can be linked directly to the balance between military necessity and humanitarian considerations,[55] as done by Schmitt:

> The direct participation rule represents a paradigmatic example of this dynamic in that attack is permitted against civilians only in the face of clear military necessity – where those civilians are so harming the enemy (or benefitting its opponents, a point missed by the Guidance) that withdrawal of their protection from attack is merited. The quandary lies in determining the nature and degree of 'harm' justifying such a dramatic step. Does any

47 AMW Manual; and references in AP I, part III, Section I, in the title and in article 35; 1907 Hague Regulations, Section II, title, and the GCs.

48 Interpretive Guidance, at page 1012; Gasser and Dörmann 'Protection of the civilian population', at page 256.

49 Norwegian Manual, at pages 12 and 54.

50 Ibid.

51 Interpretive Guidance, at page 1016.

52 In the Norwegian Manual, at page 52, the criteria are enumerated as threshold of harm, direct cause and intent to cause harm to the adversary for the benefit of own forces.

53 Schmitt, 'The interpretive guidance on the notion of direct participation in hostilities', at page 27, seems to support the general notion of the criteria. See, however, the statement made in the AMW Manual, at page 121, Commentary 5 to rule 29, where it is pointed out that there was no agreement among the experts that the criteria reflect customary law.

54 Schmitt, 'Deconstructing direct participation in hostilities', at page 738.

55 See Chapter 6 for a general discussion of this issue.

action disadvantaging a side to the conflict suffice or do situations exist where the harm lacks the severity necessary to outweigh humanitarian considerations?[56]

Does military necessity require loss of civilian protection against attack in all instances where harm is inflicted upon an adversary or is it meaningful to establish a 'threshold of harm'? If one does not limit the 'threshold' criterion only to a quantitative consideration, but rather to an assessment of the nature of the harm, the requirement can make sense.[57]

'Harm' clearly encompasses effects of a military nature:[58] even if it does not result in physical damage, the effect may for example be to deny the adversary access to an area or to disrupt command, control and communications facilities through the use of computer network attack (CNA) or electronic countermeasures (ECM).[59] A limitation to harm which is of a military nature may be supported by the definition of military objectives in AP I article 52(2) (see Chapter 8 above), which requires that the objects make an effective contribution to military action and that their capture or destruction offers a definite military advantage.[60] *Military* necessity supports the notion that the expected harm be of a *military* nature. Discussions go further however, and one may reasonably ask whether the scope of 'harm' must be understood not only as harm inflicted directly upon the adversary's enemy forces, but also as acts which create an advantage for the own party's forces.[61] Considerations of military necessity support this notion, bearing in mind that the basic tenet of military necessity is a reference to those measures which weakens enemy forces at the benefit of one's own (see Chapter 2).

Beyond harm of a military nature, the ICRC argues that an act may constitute DPH even if it is not likely that it will harm the adversary militarily. In such cases, the ICRC argues, the act must be likely to result in death, injury or destruction on protected persons or objects.[62] The military necessity of directing attacks against persons who inflict death, injury or destruction on protected objects or persons is likely to be less apparent than where harm of

56 Schmitt, 'Deconstructing direct participation in hostilities', at page 713.

57 In this direction, see ibid., at page 716.

58 The general support of the notion, that harm is that of a military nature, is also found in the AP I Commentary to article 51(3), at pages 618–19, para. 1942; and as well in the US DoD Manual, para. 5.8.3, at page 228.

59 Interpretive Guidance, at pages 1017–18.

60 Schmitt, 'Deconstructing direct participation in hostilities', at page 717.

61 Schmitt, ibid., argues at page 720 that harm and beneficiary should be seen as the same. Schmitt is supported by Boothby in *The Law of Targeting*, at page 153.

62 Interpretive Guidance, at page 1019.

a military nature is inflicted on enemy forces. Although there are obviously good reasons to protect those under attack, the reasons for doing so are not apparently military at the outset. One may, however, argue that there is an indirect advantage of securing protected persons/objects and, depending on the concrete mission of the operation, there may be a clear necessity in order to achieve the aim of the operation.[63] Furthermore, considerations of military necessity may give reason to direct attack against civilians (the necessity certainly does not make such attacks lawful, since humanitarian considerations have trumped necessity in this regard under international law, but attacks may still be perceived as necessary to the attacker), and consequently, there is a necessity to also attack those directing attacks against the civilians. Among those acts which an attacker may perceive as necessary – and that are linked to the ongoing hostilities – are deportation of civilians, hostage-taking and attacks directed against the civilian population in order to shatter their morale.[64] Out of these, neither deportation nor hostage-taking necessarily amount to the infliction of death or injury and the ICRC approach is criticised for being under-inclusive in this regard.[65] The criticism seems valid, especially considering what appears to be the most pertinent challenge with regard to civilians attacking civilians: the establishment of sufficient nexus to the armed conflict.

The obvious challenge, with acts where civilians attack civilians, is to establish a sufficient nexus to the armed conflict, and to distinguish the violence from mere criminality. Examples of situations that have aroused controversy are discussed further in Section 11.3.5.

The requirement of belligerent nexus relates to the link between the act and the ongoing armed conflict. A harmful act must not be made out of let's say economic motives, for example the robbery of a combatant for cash, whereas an attack on the same combatant may very well constitute DPH.[66] Since the attacker's mind cannot be read from the outside, his or her subjective intent must be construed based on objective facts.[67] The act in question must be *shaped* to cause the required threshold of harm, in support of one party to the conflict, to the detriment of the other.[68] This requirement

63 See for example the mandate of Operation Unified Protector (Libya) in 2011, in UN Security Council resolution 1973, where the protection of civilians was a specific military task.

64 On 'morale attacks', see Section 12.1. For a fairly recent such example see the ICTY Strugar Case, Trail Chamber Judgment, at para. 286.

65 Schmitt, 'Deconstructing direct participation in hostilities', at page 724.

66 Schmitt, 'Humanitarian law', page 18.

67 Ibid.

68 Interpretive Guidance, page 1030.

cannot be read as a reference to the subjective mind of the person, but to the design of the act.[69]

11.3.3 *What Is 'Direct' Participation? A Question of Causation and a Question of Participation in the 'War Effort'*

What is the actual meaning of *direct* participation, as distinguished from participation which is merely indirect?[70] When does the causal connection between the act and the ongoing hostilities make it a military necessity to attack the individual? Schmitt says that: 'In other words, sometimes causation is so direct that the shield of humanitarian considerations must yield in the face of military necessity, while in other situations the causal connection is too weak to overcome humanitarian factors.'[71] The element of the legal rule – direct participation – is, arguably, based on two factors: the causal strength and the corresponding weight of military necessity. Disagreement exists, however, over when the causal strength is 'sufficiently close'.[72] As a point of departure, there seem to be general agreement that direct participation must be distinguished from situations where civilians are only taking part in the war effort – which may be seen as mere indirect participation.[73] This distinction is emphasised by the ICRC Commentary, stating the following:

> There should be a clear distinction between direct participation in hostilities and participation in the war effort. The latter is often required from the population as a whole to various degrees. Without such a distinction the efforts made to reaffirm and develop international humanitarian law could become meaningless. In fact, in modern conflicts, many activities of the nation contribute to the conduct of hostilities, directly or indirectly; even the morale of the population plays a role in this context.[74]

This point of departure does not, however, solve the issue of causal strength – how close to hostilities should the act be, for the person conducting it to be liable for attack? One approach is to list examples of activities which rise above the threshold. This approach is presented below (Section 11.3.5). In the present section follows a brief conceptual approach.

69 AMW Manual, Commentary, at page 121. In another direction (referring to the subjective mindset of the person), see the Norwegian Manual, at page 53. Also Schmitt argues that the *mens rea* of the civilian is decisive, in 'Humanitarian law', at page 19.

70 See Bothe, Partsch and Solf, *New Rules*, at page 344.

71 Schmitt, 'Deconstructing direct participation in hostilities', at page 726.

72 Expression taken from the Interpretive Guidance, at page 1021.

73 US DoD Manual, para. 5.8.3, at page 229.

74 AP I Commentary, at para. 1945, page 619. On attacks on civilian morale, see further Chapter 12.

During the working group meetings, between 2004 and the adoption of the Interpretive Guidance in 2008, the question of causality was – as were the majority of questions – subject to controversy. Controversy emerged over at least two causal aspects: the question of necessary vs sufficient causes for an effect and the question of causal proximity. These two aspects are easily confused with each other. Furthermore, although the question of causality seems to arise primarily with regard to the requirement of *direct* participation, it is also arguably intertwined with the notion of *hostilities*.[75] If *hostilities* are understood widely, the threshold for *sufficiently direct* participation in these hostilities would in practice appear lower.

First, to the question of necessary vs sufficient causes: during the 2004 meeting it was proposed by Schmitt, who was one of the experts, that the causal requirement was one of 'but-for':[76] if the harm would not have occurred without the act performed by the civilian, then the causal requirement was not fulfilled. This position was contested, arguably because it would imply lowering the threshold for participation from the alternative requirement of 'direct causation'.[77] Since it is possible to think of acts which would constitute conditions *sine qua non* ('but-for'), and still have a longer causal chain to the effect, the argument that it would imply lowering a threshold *can* be correct – but not necessarily. The requirement of *sine qua non*[78] is usually a strict requirement. It is furthermore so, that the question of whether an act is *sine qua non* with regard to a certain effect is *a different question* from the one of causal proximity. Therefore, it is not necessary to reject the argument of *sine qua non*, by referring to causal proximity. An act which is *sine qua non*, can be both direct and indirect to the effect, and an eventual requirement of direct causation can be upheld or disregarded regardless of the question of *sine qua non*. I therefore argue that *both the requirements of sine qua non and direct causation are too strict*. The Interpretive Guidance seems to be arguing correctly when including for example contributory causes[79] and when excluding participation in the general war effort, as well as when rejecting the requirement of

75 Third Expert Meeting on the Notion of Direct Participation in Hostilities (2005), at page 30.

76 Second Expert Meeting on the Notion of Direct Participation in Hostilities (2004), page 11. See also Schmitt, 'The interpretive guidance on the notion of direct participation in hostilities', at page 29.

77 Second Expert Meeting on the Notion of Direct Participation in Hostilities, at page 25, where it is argued that: 'Instead, this expert required "but for causation", that is to say that, without the act in question, the damage would not have occurred. This would be a standard slightly lower than direct causation and would include, for instance, an analysis of the tactical intelligence that was to be immediately transmitted to a shooter.'

78 On causality and military necessity in general, see Chapter 2.

79 Interpretive Guidance, at page 1022: 'The standard of direct causation must therefore be interpreted to include conduct that causes harm only in conjunction with other acts.'

sine qua non. It appears to be a better solution to leave aside the references to logical causal connection and instead rely on the reference to acts that are an 'integral part of combat operations' – which is the chosen solution in both the US DoD Manual[80] as well as the AMW Manual and with other scholars.[81] The AMW Manual says that the act need not be a sufficient cause in order to create an effect, but may be integrated with other acts in order to result in the desired outcome.[82]

Then, second, to the question of causal proximity: the Interpretive Guidance does not seem to give a correct reflection of customary law by requiring that 'the harm in question must be brought about in one causal step'.[83] The requirement of 'one causal step' seems unfounded, and the finding actually supports a conception that it appears as 'merely a poorly drafted explanation of the agreed upon need for a clear link between the act and the ensuing harm ...'[84] A requirement of 'one causal step' is not found in States' military manuals either. The Norwegian Manual states explicitly that it is: 'not only the last, decisive act in a chain of facts that can be viewed as direct participation, such as for example firing a rocket, but also those acts which made the attack possible, for example planning the attack or transport of personnel and weapons to a suitable place'.[85]

Neither the UK Manual[86] nor the US or Canadian manuals address the matter.[87] The AMW Manual refers to the criteria of the Interpretive Guidance, but also states that the criteria were not adopted unanimously.[88]

Finally, having discussed the theoretical threshold for direct causation, the question of foreseeability remains. The AP I Commentary has stated that: 'acts of war which by their nature or purpose are *likely to cause* actual harm to the

80 US DoD Manual, para. 5.8.3, at page 228.

81 Schmitt, 'Deconstructing direct participation in hostilities', at page 729; Boothby, *The Law of Targeting*, at page 154.

82 AMW Manual, Commentary 3 to rule 29, at page 120.

83 Interpretive Guidance, at page 1021.

84 Schmitt, 'The interpretive guidance on the notion of direct participation in hostilities', at page 30. The argument continues: '... or whether it reflects an actual, and if so, flawed, requirement'. I support the first supposition.

85 Norwegian Manual, at pages 52–3 (my translation). The Norwegian text says: 'Det er med andre ord ikke kun den siste avgjørende handling i en handlingsrekke som kan oppfattes som direkte deltakelse, slik som for eksempel det å avfyre en rakett, men også de handlinger som gjorde angrepet mulig, for eksempel planlegging av angrepet eller transport av personell og våpen til egnet sted.'

86 The UK Manual only contains a short passage on the DPH rule which refers to practical examples, and no statement on the constituent elements argued in the Interpretive Guidance, see page 54.

87 The Canadian Manual also only refers to the DPH rule and labels civilians who fulfil the criteria as 'unlawful combatants', see pages 3–5. The US DoD Manual mentions that the act must be 'intended to cause', and that the act may be a 'but for' cause of death, injury or damage, and as well to the 'degree to which the act is connected to the hostilities', para. 5.8.3, at page 230.

88 AMW Manual, at page 121.

personnel and equipment of the enemy armed forces'.[89] After negotiations this position is upheld in the Interpretive Guidance stating that the requirement of direct causation is satisfied if the act 'may reasonably be expected to directly' cause the harm.[90] The same position is held in the AMW Manual, referring to 'harm which may reasonably be expected to result from an act in the prevailing circumstances'.[91]

Again, here the assessment is subject to the standard of the reasonable commander, as accounted for above, in Chapter 4. The challenges facing military commanders due to the open-endedness of the terms in the DPH rule can be illustrated all the way back to examples of confusing remarks during the Diplomatic Conference: the provision in 51(3) is identical to the one presented by the ICRC in the draft article 46(2) during the Diplomatic Conference.[92] Alternative, and more extensive, formulations which could *not* be read as offering civilians *lesser* protection,[93] were, however, presented during the Conference, but rejected. Interesting to note though, are examples from the comments made by delegates to the alternative (and rejected) proposal, which could not be supported 'because it gave the erroneous impression that all the civilian population *taking part in the war effort* could be the subject to attack'.[94] This erroneous remark is noteworthy because it illustrates the ambiguity inherent in probably *any* formulation of the DPH concept. The differences between the rejected draft article and the final provision did not – in the present author's view – invite the condemnation of the one for the benefit of the other; the possible interpretative width can be read out of *both provisions*, if interpreting the words in accordance with their ordinary meaning.[95]

11.3.4 The Time Dimension: 'for Such Time'

The notion of 'for such time' is a part of customary law, but controversies have emerged over the understanding of the time-factor.[96] The first and obvious

89 AP I Commentary to article 51(3), at para. 1944. Emphasis added. See also the Third Expert Meeting on the Notion of Direct Participation in Hostilities, at page 28, where the quotation is recited with regard to the question of causal proximity.
90 Interpretive Guidance, at page 1025.
91 AMW Manual, Commentary to rule 29, at page 120.
92 Official Records of the Diplomatic Conference CDDH/I at page 16.
93 See CDDH/III/10 Romanian proposal: 'the civilian population in general, and individual civilians not taking a direct and immediate part in hostilities shall never under circumstances be made the object of any form of attack'. At page 200.
94 CDDH/III/SR.7, at page 52, remarks by the delegate of Ghana. Emphasis added.
95 VCLT, article 31.
96 AMW Manual, Commentary 2 to rule 28, at page 118.

pending issue is that of when the participation starts and ends. A second contested issue is the scope of continued loss of protection. This second issue covers two separate questions: one being the question of which groups of persons qualify for the continued loss of protection (this question is dealt with above together with the notion of organised armed groups) and another being the so-called issue of the 'revolving door'.[97]

First a few remarks on the beginning and end of participation. In the Interpretive Guidance it is argued that the essence of preparatory measures, which are also considered as DPH, are 'military operations preparatory to an attack' – a wording found in AP I article 44(3).[98] These acts can, however, only be seen as the core of preparatory acts since DPH surely also covers acts which do not amount to an attack.[99] Furthermore, geographical proximity is neither a necessary nor a sufficient criterion for a preparatory act.[100] Particular issues in this regard may arise in the cyber context. The majority of Experts in the Tallinn Manual hold that 'logic bombs', designed to activate at some future point, accrue the direct participation of the individual(s) for the same period as the delayed effect of the bomb.[101]

Whether the preparations themselves need to be proximate to the act has also been contested. While Boothby argues that concealing a weapon or assembling an IED with a view to use it is continued DPH, the Interpretive Guidance argues otherwise, specifically noting that the act of DPH typically may end when the individual is hiding a weapon and retreating from combat.[102] The differing in opinion may lie in the understanding of 'hiding a weapon'. If the purpose of 'hiding' is only with the purpose of reuse the next day, considerations of military necessity argue strongly against limiting the notion of DPH in this regard. If, on the other hand, the weapon is hidden with the purpose of actual retreat from combat – and not only to go to sleep – the hiding of a weapon may indicate the end of DPH. This view is also compatible with military necessity; if a person in fact ceases his/her participation in combat, it is not necessary to direct an attack against that person. This latter view is emphasised by the USA in the DoD Manual, where it is argued that civilians 'must not be made the object of attack after they have *permanently* ceased their participation because there would be no military

97 Boothby, 'And for such time as', at page 743.
98 Interpretive Guidance, at page 1031.
99 Boothby, 'And for such time as', at page 746.
100 Interpretive Guidance, page 1032; Boothby, 'And for such time as', at page 747.
101 Tallinn Manual, Commentary 9 to rule 97, at page 431.
102 Boothby, 'And for such time as', at page 749; Interpretive Guidance, page 1033.

necessity for attacking them'.[103] In other words it is the US view that the necessity of attacking civilians only ceases after the *permanent* withdrawal from hostilities.

The question of permanent vs temporary withdrawal from participation in hostilities is the essence of the issue whether the law may offer a 'revolving door' of protection. By this, it is referring to the situation where, for instance, a civilian is taking a direct part in active combat during the night, and returning to his fields during daytime. If he is granted immunity from attack while doing farming in the daytime, the law grants him a 'revolving door' of protection. The question is whether this is the position of the law. The USA has explicitly argued that this is not an option – that the law does not really provide a revolving door of protection – civilians will lose their protection permanently unless they permanently cease their participation.[104] Other States and commentators are less clear, and argue that civilians will lose their protection permanently if they participate in hostilities on a regular basis.[105] The opposite view is that the wording of AP I clearly will offer a revolving door of protection in some situations.[106] This latter position entails that the scope of loss of protection is twofold: protection is lost on a permanent basis for members of an organised armed group in a non-international armed conflict, whereas for all others, protection is lost only for the duration of each 'specific act'.[107]

Considerations of military necessity underpin a large portion of the critique against the view presented in the Interpretive Guidance. Michael Schmitt refers in his critique of the Interpretive Guidance to the 'very delicate balance between two principles: military necessity and humanity' and argues that: 'It is in this regard that the Interpretive Guidance falters. Although it represents an important and valuable contribution to understanding the complex notion of

103 US DoD Manual, para. 5.8.4.1, at page 234. Emphasis added.

104 US DoD Manual, para. 5.8.4.2, at page 235.

105 In the Norwegian Manual, at page 57, this is presented as the exceptional rule when civilians take part in hostilities on a regular basis (and are not members of organised armed groups). Boothby, *The Law of Targeting*, also seems to advocate a similar position, although not presenting it as 'exceptional'. Schmitt, 'Direct participation in hostilities', at page 510, and Dinstein, *Conduct of Hostilities*, at pages 176–7, both argue that protection is lost permanently when a person takes part in hostilities on a regular basis and that protection only is regained when the person unambiguously disentangles themself from the activity.

106 Interpretive Guidance, page 1035. AP I Commentary to article 51(3) states in para. 1944, at page 619 that the person regains their protection 'once he ceases to participate' in hostilities. See also Henderson, *The Contemporary Law of Targeting*, at page 96, who seems to argue in this direction.

107 Interpretive Guidance, page 1037.

direct participation in hostilities, on repeated occasions its interpretations skew the balance towards humanity.'[108]

The obvious imbalance, between States' armed forces on the one hand and civilians taking a direct part in hostilities on the other, complements this picture.[109] While State armed forces are lawful targets at all times, the notion of DPH does not reflect this. As suggested by Boothby,[110] this is in particular problematic if one follows the ICRC view that an individual may change from having a continuous combat function in an organised armed group to fulfil a non-combat role in the same group – but continues to take a direct part in hostilities on a sporadic basis. If that individual then regains his protection between the sporadic acts, it gives him a legally constructed advantage to the opposing regular armed forces. If this 'specific act' approach is upheld, and a civilian is allowed to regain his protection under such circumstances, it does not only sacrifice the military necessity of the regular armed forces, but may also be counter-productive from a humanitarian perspective. If the opposing forces consist of civilians opting in and out of protection, planning procedures for own forces may become seriously hampered. If a person may be the object of attack only while caught in a 'specific act', the long-term perspective disappears and so does the ability to take proper precautions in attack. The risk of collateral damage may actually increase, since the planning of military operations may turn into 'split-second' decisions. In turn, such a rule (as advocated in the Interpretive Guidance) appears to try to circumvent war into something which it is not.

11.3.5 Which Acts Do We Talk About?

An alternative (or in addition to the three constituent elements discussed above) approach to define the scope of the DPH rule is simply to provide examples of activities which may amount to DPH, according to the circumstances.[111] The increased practice of using civilian contractors in support of military operations has been devoted considerable attention – not least due to the extensive use of civilian contractors in the 2003 Iraq War.[112] The following examples include those where civilian contractors are used.

108 Schmitt, 'The interpretive guidance on the notion of direct participation in hostilities', at page 6. On the balance in general, see Chapter 6.

109 See Section 11.3.1, where this argument is made with regard to the notion of organised armed groups.

110 Boothby, *The Law of Targeting*, at page 162.

111 For this approach in military manuals, see US DoD Manual, para. 5.8.3.1, at page 231; UK Manual, at page 54. In literature, see Dinstein, *Conduct of Hostilities*, at page 178.

112 Schmitt, 'Humanitarian law'; Boothby, *The Law of Targeting*, at page 147.

(a) Every use of weapons and weapons system in combat amount to DPH, regardless of the distance to the actual combat zone. Also, the operating of a long-distance weapon system amounts to DPH,[113] as will a computer network attack launched from a far distance.[114] The same goes for the killing and capturing of enemy personnel without the use of weapons, as well as infliction of injury and destruction of enemy materiel – or *trying to* produce any of the mentioned effects.[115] The use of weapons and infliction of death, injury or destruction include the preparation and return from combat.[116]
(b) It is not only the preparation of combat that amounts to DPH, the planning, authorisation or implementation of a combat operation also amounts to DPH.[117]
(c) The supply of weapons to the combat zone amounts to DPH, while weapons production in a rear-area factory does not.[118] In the first case, the supply is direct enough, but in the latter the proximity to the war-fighting is too remote. The same goes for supply of fuel or other needs to the armed forces. While the rear-area production is too remote and generally is considered a civilian contribution to the entire war effort alongside the production of food, clothing and housing, serving the front line with military logistics is proximate both in time and geography and amounts to DPH.[119] Transport of ammunition is commented upon in particular below, due to the international attention given to this particular example.
(d) To provide tactical intelligence on the ground amounts to DPH, whereas the transmission of strategic intelligence will not necessarily amount to DPH.[120] Along the same lines as provision of tactical intelligence is the functioning as a forward air controller (FAC) or artillery spotter or otherwise directing fire against a target.[121]

113 Dinstein, *Conduct of Hostilities*, at pages 178–80. Schmitt, 'Humanitarian law', page 18; Boothby, *The Law of Targeting*, at page 157. Rogers, *Law on the Battlefield*, at page 11.
114 Schmitt, 'Humanitarian law', at pages 19 and 22.
115 US DoD Manual, para. 5.8.3.1, at pages 231–3
116 US DoD Manual, para. 5.8.3.1; Boothby, *The Law of Targeting*, at pages 158–60; Rogers, *Law on the Battlefield*, at page 11. On the time dimension, see further above.
117 US DoD Manual, para. 5.8.3.1, at page 231; Norwegian Manual, at page 55; Schmitt, 'Humanitarian law', at page 22.
118 US DoD Manual, para. 5.8.3.1, at page 231; Norwegian Manual, at page 55.
119 Schmitt, 'Humanitarian law', at page 23; Norwegian Manual, at page 56. Boothby argues in *The Law of Targeting*, at page 157, that the transportation of military supplies may or may not be DPH, depending on the circumstances.
120 AMW Manual, rule 29(iv); Schmitt, 'Humanitarian law', at page 23; Dinstein. *Conduct of Hostilities*, at page 179.
121 US DoD Manual, para. 5.8.3.1, at page 231; Norwegian Manual, at page 55; Boothby, *The Law of Targeting*, at page 157.

(e) The notion of 'human shields' raises a number of pending questions with regard to the protection of civilians, among these the question of what categories of 'human shielding' amount to DPH.[122] There is a clear duty upon the attacker not to use civilians in order to render certain objects immune from attack.[123] In situations where civilians are compelled to shield military objectives in order to render the latter immune from attack – either by placing them in front of, or on, military materiel, or by placing military materiel in the midst of densely inhabited civilian areas – the civilians will not be considered to take a direct part in hostilities.[124] When it comes to the act of voluntarily defending a military objective, opinions are divided: the AMW Manual clearly contends that the conduct of hostilities comprises not only offensive but also defensive acts and hence that the defence of military objectives is direct participation in hostilities.[125] This view is supported elsewhere,[126] while the Interpretive Guidance distinguishes between voluntary human shields who provide a cover for military objectives in ground operations and human shields who try to cover military objectives against artillery or air attacks. It is the ICRC view that, in the latter case, the shielding does not have any impact on the adversary and that the act therefore does not – under such circumstances – reach the required 'threshold of harm', and hence does not amount to DPH.[127] The latter view illustrates the difficulties of breaking the DPH rule down into criteria which might turn out to be too technical for its own good. When the element of harm is too narrowly understood (see above on the contested ICRC view that harm only entails harm to the *adversary*, and not also to *the benefit of own* force), it rules out cases in an unreasonable way. After all, the effect of shielding an object in front of ground forces or air forces appears the same. This is due to the purpose of shielding in the first place, which is to bar an attack on an otherwise lawful object by rendering it immune by the presence of protected persons. The reasons for depriving these persons of their protection remains the same in both scenarios: it is not the physical

122 On human shields and the proportionality rule, see Chapter 15.

123 GC IV article 28; and AP I article 57(7). The act is also criminalised as a war crime in the Rome Statute article 8(2)(b)(xxiii).

124 On the proportionality assessment in these situations, see further Chapters 13 and 15.

125 Commentary to the AMW Manual, at page 121, rule 29(i).

126 Norwegian Manual, at page 55; Schmitt, 'Deconstructing direct participation in hostilities', at page 732.

127 Interpretive Guidance, at page 1024.

hampering of advancement of opposing forces which is desired effect, but the infliction of a duty to deter from attack.

(f) The training of personnel with a specific military operation in sight may amount to DPH.[128] This may include in-camp training of local military forces on foreign soil. The decisive criteria must be the proximity to the actual combat operations in time and geography: in other words that the training is combat specific. General education of military personnel does not, however, amount to DPH since the relation to the battlefield is too remote, and hence not 'direct participation'.[129]

(g) The example where a civilian is driving an ammunition truck has been used frequently to illustrate the different situational modes of DPH.[130] The driver of an ammunition truck, on his or her way to the front line, takes a direct part in hostilities.[131] That is to say, if he or she detaches himself or herself from the vehicle during the transport, he or she is also a lawful target for the time he or she is out of the truck. The driver of an ammunition transport in the rear-areas, however, for example driving to a port for further shipping, does not participate directly in hostilities.[132] The truck remains a lawful target for the whole time and the driver will count as collateral damage when not being considered to take a direct part in hostilities.

128 Norwegian Manual, at page 55; Schmitt, 'Humanitarian law', at page 24; AMW Manual, rule 29 (xii).

129 Schmitt, 'Humanitarian law', page 24.

130 The example first arose at a conference of Experts in The Hague in 2003, convened by the TMC Asser Institute. See for example Rogers, *Law on the Battlefield*, at page 10.

131 Interpretive Guidance, at pages 1023–4; Norwegian Manual, at page 55; US DoD Manual, para. 5.8.3.1, at pages 231–2.

132 Interpretive Guidance, at pages 1023–4.

PART III

EFFECTUATING DISTINCTION: ENFORCING AN ULTIMATE BALANCE BETWEEN NECESSITIES OF WAR AND CONSIDERATIONS OF HUMANITY

12

Protection of the Civilian Population and Perceptions of Military Necessity

12.1 INTRODUCTORY REMARKS: PROHIBITIONS AND PERCEPTIONS OF MILITARY NECESSITY

The present chapter deals with the protection of the civilian population against specific means and methods of warfare with a common feature: they are often – rightly or wrongly – perceived (and assessed) by belligerents as necessary, yet they have become prohibited.

The first part of this chapter is devoted to the past practice of 'morale attacks' as well as the present prohibition of terror attacks, now outlawing attacks directed against civilian morale even though such attacks may be perceived by belligerents as effective game-changers in the war. Section 12.4 of this chapter is also devoted to a past practice now subject to a far-reaching – but not absolute – ban: attacks by way of reprisals against civilians. Precisely because both morale attacks and reprisal attacks have gained much attention due to their perceived necessity, they are devoted particular space in this chapter. With regard to both morale attacks and reprisal attacks (as well as reprisal prisoners, which is subject to an absolute prohibition), treaty law now balances military necessity and humanitarian concerns in a compromised way, where some perceptions of military necessity have yielded to humanitarian concerns.

12.2 PROHIBITION OF 'TERROR ATTACKS' AGAINST CIVILIANS

The necessity of shattering civilian morale has been an argument frequently resorted to throughout history. The line between attacks against lawful targets with incidental effects on civilian morale, and attacks with the sole purpose of terrorising the civilian population, has been a hard one to draw – and during history reached its breaking point[1] (see further below). Terror attacks are now explicitly prohibited in the AP I. Regardless of whether it may be perceived as a necessity to direct attacks against civilians for the purpose of undermining their morale and thus shorten the war, the following is now the law: humanitarian considerations have trumped military necessity by the AP I prohibition of terror attacks, which is also reflective of customary law.[2] AP I article 51(2), second sentence, prohibits attacks or threats of attacks with the *specific purpose* of terrorising the civilian population: 'Acts or threats of violence the primary purpose of which is to spread terror among the civilian population are prohibited.' Almost all attacks may have a frightening effect on the civilian population. It is therefore a practical difficulty to distinguish those attacks which have a primary purpose to terrorise, from those which 'only' have a secondary effect of terror.[3] The following sections offer first a historical account of the thin line between terror attacks on civilians and attacks with secondary effects on civilians and, second, an analysis of the present prohibition of terror attacks in AP I article 51(2).

12.2.1 *Morale Attacks and Military Necessity: a Historical Backdrop*

Attacks on enemy 'morale' go back in time, even before the use of air power, although 'morale attacks' first and foremost are inextricably linked to an unfettered belief in the psychological effects of air power. As early as 1905 the British 'Manual of Military Ballooning' argued that the use of balloons as a means of warfare might have a 'moral effect on the enemy that should not be lost sight of',[4] and this faith remained a mantra all through the post-WWI period.[5] Attacks on civilian 'morale', however, had already been conducted in the Franco-Prussian War (for example by the bombardment of Paris in 1871)[6]

1 See for example Parks, 'Military objectives', at page 75.

2 ICRC CIHL, rule 2.

3 Bothe, Partsch and Solf, *New Rules*, at page 342.

4 Biddle, *Rhetoric and Reality in Air Warfare*, at pages 13–14.

5 See Parks, 'Asymmetries and the identification of legitimate military objectives', at page 77, where he holds that: '"Attacks on morale" became a shibboleth, a mantra, exhorted as a matter of blind faith by airpower advocates in behalf of aviation service survival and development in the post-World War I budget battles with land and naval forces.'

6 On the Franco-Prussian War see also above, Chapter 6, within the context of the doctrine of *Kriegsraison*. On the bombardment of Paris, Howard writes: 'For this attack on the civilian population, as for that at Strasbourg, there was no military reason. Its only excuse, and it was to be one increasingly used by belligerents of all lands with equally little justification, *was that by directly attacking their morale it would incline the stubborn Parisians the earlier to peace.*' Howard, *The Franco-Prussian War*, at page 361. Emphasis added. Footnotes omitted. In the same direction of Howard, see also Andler, *'Frightfulness' in Theory and Practice*, at pages 52–3.

and the South African (Boer) War. These early examples of the concept also show how the perceived necessity of 'morale attacks' rests on a 'total war' argument. The Prussian general Von Hartmann said that 'the necessity of imposing this burden results from the conception of national war',[7] while a British defence of burning of farms was formulated as: 'when a nation adopts guerrilla tactics it deliberately courts those sufferings to the whole country which such tactics invariably entail'.[8] In other words: when civilian and military resources are impossible to distinguish from each other in a guerrilla posture, even attacks against the civilian population are perceived as 'necessary'. The total war argument was also used – and in a more familiar way, related to a big, industrial war where the whole nation was taking part in the war effort – in the two World Wars. In the directive to the UK Bomber Command issued on 14 February 1942 attacks were ordered with the aim of 'undermining the morale of the enemy civil population and in particular, of the industrial workers'.[9] Then, one year later, in January 1943, an allied objective for the strategic air force in Europe was reached in Casablanca, stating: 'Destruction and dislocation of the German Military, industrial, and economic system and the undermining of the morale of the German people to the point where their capacity for armed resistance is fatally weakened.'[10] The accomplishment of this strategy (by both the British and the Allied forces) was, among others, performed in an iconic manner by Air Chief Marshal Sir Arthur Harris ('Bomber Harris') with a reported 'shock-effect' on Hamburg in August 1943,[11] and as well a number of other terrible attacks on German cities, including the firebombing of Dresden in 1945.[12] Towards the end of the war the fire-bombing in order to break enemy morale was eventually reconsidered – but not with regard to their inhuman impact, rather with regard to their utility (necessity) for the Allied forces (in this case the UK). In a memo from 1 April 1945 Churchill stated:

> It seems to me that the moment has come when the question of the so called 'area-bombing' of German cities should be reviewed from the point of view of

[7] Andler, *'Frightfulness' in Theory and Practice*, at page 83.

[8] Conan Doyle, *The War in South Africa*, at page 84.

[9] Biddle, *Rhetoric and Reality in Air Warfare*, at page 197.

[10] US Strategic Bombing Survey, at page 197.

[11] US Strategic Bombing Survey, at pages 10 and 13. Apparently, only 20 per cent of the US 'precision bombs' hit their targets. The reported shock-effect was apparently also to a great extent upheld by Harris himself, see Biddle, *Rhetoric and Reality in Air Warfare*, pages 177 and 214.

[12] See the account given by Harris himself in AIR 16/487: Despatch on War Operations, February 1942–May 1945.

> our own interests. If we come into control of an entirely ruined land, there will be a great shortage of accommodation for ourselves and our allies . . . We must see to it that our attacks do no more harm to ourselves in the long run than they do to the enemy's war effort.[13]

The instigation of attacks on enemy civilian morale must also be seen in relation to arguments of retaliation, or rather a spiral of retaliation, which are accounted for below in Section 12.4.[14]

12.2.2 *The AP I Prohibition of Attacks 'with a Primary Purpose' to Spread Terror*

A treaty prohibition of terror attacks had already been proposed in the Hague Regulations on Air Warfare article 22: 'Any air bombardment for the purpose of terrorizing the civil population or destroying or damaging private property without military character or injuring non-combatants, is forbidden.' The provision which was finally adopted in the AP I article 51(2) does not prohibit terror effects, but the *purpose of achieving* such effects.[15] This element makes the provision obviously difficult to apply in real life, as evidence for *primary purpose* would be almost impossible to retrieve from belligerent parties – unless the parties openly admit such a policy.[16] The prohibition of terror attacks is also held to be customary international law.[17] The rule is as well reaffirmed by the ICTY, in the Galic Case[18] where it was found that: 'a campaign of sniping and shelling was conducted against the civilian population of ABiH-held areas of Sarajevo with the primary purpose of spreading terror'.[19] The ruling in the Galic Case has also been supported in literature.[20]

13 Taylor, *Dresden: Tuesday 13 February 1945*, at page 434.

14 See also Chapter 13 with regard to the question of proportionality as a 'silent condition' of military necessity.

15 Bothe, Partsch and Solf, *New Rules*, at page 342.

16 Kalshoven, *Reflections on the Law of War*, states at page 445 that 'This conclusion may only be drawn on the basis of reliable evidence – in times of armed conflict, a rare commodity.'

17 In military manuals, see for example the US DoD Manual, para. 5.2.2, at page 189; the UK Manual, at page 67; the Norwegian manual, at page 187; and the Canadian Manual, at pages 4–6, rule 423. Beyond States' military manuals, see other manuals: AMW Manual, rule 18: 'Acts or threats of violence in the course of air or missile operations cannot be pursued for the sole or primary purpose of spreading terror among the civilian population', see Commentary, at page 102; ICRC CIHL, rule 2. The latter rule repeats the wording of the AP I provision. Tallinn Manual, rule 98, at page 433.

18 Galic Case, at paras. 87–90.

19 Galic Case, at para. 597. See also paras. 745–7 with regard to the findings of criminal responsibility for Galic.

20 Schmitt, 'Military necessity and humanity in international humanitarian law', at page 818.

The prohibition encompasses attacks where the *primary purpose* is to spread terror, which leaves lawful those situations where attacks on otherwise lawful targets *also* create fear and a perception of terror among the civilian population as a side effect.[21] In the ICRC Commentary it is stated in this regard that:

> In the second sentence the Conference wished to indicate that the prohibition covers acts intended to spread terror; there is no doubt that acts of violence related to a state of war almost always give rise to some degree of terror among the population and sometimes also among the armed forces. It also happens that attacks on armed forces are purposely conducted brutally in order to intimidate the enemy soldiers and persuade them to surrender. This is not the sort of terror envisaged here.[22]

Fenrick even seems to take the argument one step further: 'It would appear, however, that it is lawful to attempt to undermine enemy civilian support for the war effort by other means, including attacks on military objectives.'[23] This has, however, been subject to some controversy. The wording of article 51(2) gives no specific guidance on the question of whether the prohibition only serves a strengthened protection of civilians, or whether attacks directed at military objectives fall within the protection if they are committed with the primary purpose of spreading terror.[24]

According to the commentary by Bothe, Partsch and Solf, the provision is confined to prohibit specific kinds of attack or threats of attacks *on civilians*.[25] This view is, however, contested by Kalshoven, arguing that neither the textual reading nor the drafting history provide convincing answers and that there are good reasons, based on the actual practice of belligerents, to also include attacks on military objectives with the primary purpose of spreading terror.[26] Kalshoven argues: 'The point that comes into mind here is the guerrilla technique of attacking relatively minor targets with the expectation and, indeed, primary purpose of thereby achieving much wider results, for instance, through the spreading of terror among the civilian population.'[27] Although the situation referred to here – of attacking 'minor targets' – might be less suited to illustrate the point ('minor targets' may very well be attacked with

21 Norwegian Manual, at page 187; AMW Manual, at page 102, Commentary 5 to rule 18; UK Manual, at page 67.
22 AP I Commentary, at page 618.
23 Fenrick, 'Targeting and proportionality during the NATO bombing campaign against Yugoslavia', at page 497. Footnotes omitted.
24 Kalshoven, *Reflections on the Law of War*, at page 446.
25 Bothe, Partsch and Solf, *New Rules*, at page 342.
26 Kalshoven, *Reflections on the Law of War*, at pages 446–7.
27 Ibid., at page 447.

the purpose of achieving greater effects as a part of a plan to hit the enemy's 'centre of gravity'), the point made has also found support in the commentary to the AMW Manual: 'if the presence of lawful targets in the area is used merely as an excuse to conduct the operation, and in fact the "primary" purpose of the act of violence (or the threat thereof) is to terrorize the civilian population, the operation is prohibited under rule 18'.[28]

The key to answer the question may thus lie in the requirement of 'primary' purpose.[29] If the primary purpose of an attack is the creation of fear within the civilian population it would be hard to reconcile it with achieving a definite military advantage from destroying or neutralising the object in the first place (see Chapters 8 and 14). The following passage from the ICRC Commentary might also support such a view. The Commentary states with regard to the notion of 'primary purpose' that: 'This provision is intended to prohibit acts of violence the primary purpose of which is to spread terror among the civilian population without offering substantial military advantage.'[30]

Notwithstanding possible disagreement regarding the use of the adjective 'substantial' here – if attacks on objects in the area are used merely as excuse for terrorising the civilian population they may be considered unlawful terror attacks. However, they may also be unlawful attacks per se, since the objects themselves may not even reach the definition of being military objectives (unless they are military objectives by nature).[31] From this perspective it is difficult to see the independent scope of article 51(2) with regard to actual attacks (it obviously has an independent scope with regard to *threats*) beyond the prohibition of indiscriminate attacks in AP I article 51(5)(a): 'which treats as a single military objective a number of clearly separated and distinct military objectives'.[32] Moreover, questions of evidence with regard to establishing a true 'primary purpose' will most likely render the practical application of the provision quite difficult. In some cases it is for example possible to *lawfully* attack military objectives as an excuse for achieving something else,

[28] AMW Manual, at page 102, Commentary 5 to rule 18.

[29] The Norwegian Manual may be read in the same direction when stating at page 187: 'I en væpnet konflikt vil militære aksjoner kunne oppleves som terror av sivilbefolkningen fordi de medfører frykt og andre ulemper. Slike militære aksjoner vil imidlertid kun være forbudt dersom det er opplevelsen av terror hos sivilbefolkningen som er hovedhensikten med aksjonene.' Which in English could be (my translation): 'In an armed conflict military actions may be felt as terror by the civilian population because of the fear and other inconveniences they entail. Such military action will, however, only be prohibited if it is the perception of terror by the civilian population which is the primary purpose of the action.'

[30] AP I Commentary, at page 618.

[31] Wording from the AP I article 52(2).

[32] Ibid.

for example if military necessity requires a deceptive manoeuvre – and hence an example of ruses of war.

12.2.3 *The Alleged Necessity of Terror Attacks*

Leaving aside the unsettled issue of the scope (with regard to military objectives) of article 51(2) and moving to another pending and unsettled issue – which might even be central to the prohibition of terror attacks: the question of their potential utility. Strictly speaking, there is less need for a prohibition of terror attacks unless military commanders as well as civilian leadership are convinced of their potential necessity. As shown by the history of (primarily) air-war strategy, belief in morale attacks (which would fall within the scope of terror attacks in AP I article 51(2)) has been significant. The controversy has been live up to present day. In the commentary to the AMW Manual it is stated that: 'some commentators contend that attacks designed to destroy civilian morale may be permissible should it lead to an early termination of hostilities. The majority of the Group of Experts believed that the prohibition of terrorizing the civilian population is unacceptable even if it can be explained along so-called utilitarian lines.'[33]

The issue can be distilled into separate questions: the necessity of depriving the population of their resistance and will to fight and the means considered (a) necessary to reach that aim and (b) lawful according to the humanity–necessity balance struck in the legal framework. The true controversy does not arise over the first question; it is – broadly speaking – considered desirable to deprive the population of their resistance and will to fight against own forces. As expressed by Fenrick:

> Neither the civilian population nor civilian morale constitute legitimate military objectives. This generally accepted legal norm is, at least in part, the result of a defensible legal fiction. In most states, the will to wage military operations is dependent upon popular support. If the civilian population does not support the war effort, the national will to wage war and, usually, the national ability to wage war will be degraded. The United States lost the Vietnam conflict because the American people eventually indicated they did not support the war.[34]

The question of controversy arises first and foremost with regard to the next questions (the means considered necessary and lawful in order to reach the

33 AMW Manual, at page 102, Commentary 7 to rule 18.

34 Fenrick, 'Targeting and proportionality during the NATO bombing campaign against Yugoslavia', at page 497. Footnotes omitted.

desired aim). A strong proponent of the view *against* the actual necessity of terror attacks is Hans Blix (who was a diplomatic representative to the treaty negotiations and expressed a related view with regard to reprisals there[35]) who argues that:

> Even in large-scale international conflicts, bombardment affecting the civilian population has taken place with the purpose of destroying its morale and its allegiance to the opponent. Such 'terror' bombardment does not appear to be defended on legal grounds by anyone and where it has taken place it has been presented as having another alleged justification. *Thus, although the morale and allegiance of the civilian population may have some relevance to the armed contest, no one seems ready to argue that it is legally justifiable to bombard the population for this reason.* There are, moreover, serious doubts as to whether morale and allegiance can be pulverized by bombs. If these doubts should be well-founded, there would be no rational reason for such bombardment and, hence, in any case no justification under the basic principle.[36]

According to Blix, bombs are neither suited to reach the ends militarily, nor lawful. The first aspect of the quoted passage – of means to ends – touches upon the question of what constitutes a military advantage – both in terms of facts and law (see Chapter 14). The latter aspect of the quotation addresses the balance between humanitarian considerations and military necessity enshrined in the treaty prohibition of terror attacks. As expressed by Fenrick: 'Quite clearly, taking action, which will adversely affect enemy civilian support for the war, can result in substantial military benefit. That being said, attacking civilians or civilian objects is unacceptable because it is unlawful and morally abhorrent.'[37] While the view that attacks against civilians for the purpose of affecting their morale is 'morally abhorrent', as well as unlawful, seems to be prevailing today – others have suggested otherwise. In the aftermath of the Kosovo air campaign Dunlap argued that: 'A new paradigm for non-combatancy may be in order in the post-Kosovo era.'[38] Dunlap's argument is normative; he recognises that the legal order today does not accept attacks against the civilian population, but argues that humanitarian considerations are credited too much weight at the expense of military necessity. Apart from agreeing that civilians '"contribute" to the country's armed

35 See Section 12.4, on reprisal attacks against civilians.

36 Blix, 'Area bombardment', at pages 32–3. Emphasis added.

37 Fenrick, 'Targeting and proportionality during the NATO bombing campaign against Yugoslavia', at page 497. Footnotes omitted.

38 Dunlap, 'The end of innocence', at page 9.

strength', Dunlap makes use of non-legal moral-sociological literature and takes the argument further to argue that the notion of 'innocent civilians' is not true; civilians are morally responsible.[39] He furthermore revitalises the belief in air power on enemy civilian morale which had been upheld during WWII (see above) by arguing that its potential simply has not been utilised enough.[40] This position is accompanied with a fetish for expanding the existing categories of lawful targets by arguing:

> Specifically, when facing a society whose moral compass is wildly askew, it may well behoove democracies to consider a similarly sweeping campaign against property – despite its terrible destructiveness … We need a new paradigm when using force against societies with malevolent propensities. We must hold at risk the very way of life that sustains their depredations, and we must threaten to destroy the world as they know it if they persist. This means that the air weapon should be unleashed against entirely new categories of property that current conceptions of LOAC put off-limits.[41]

Michael Schmitt criticises Dunlap for moving on to a 'slippery slope', risking the spiral that may lead into unlawful reprisals (see further Section 12.4). Furthermore, that introducing 'moral imbalance' as a criterion for depriving someone of their protection against attacks may result in the situation where a malevolent leader can effectively deprive his own population of protection. Schmitt argues: 'There is nothing inherently immoral or illegal about targeting the will of the people or their leader. That said, humanitarian law does, and should, dictate how that may be accomplished.'[42] Schmitt thus aligns with the prevailing view: that the will of the people may constitute a military advantage, but that humanitarian concerns prevail in the legal balance against military necessity. Not even the necessity of 'shortening the war' interferes with the balance struck in the prohibition of terror attacks.

Prohibited terror attacks must be distinguished from operations 'designed to affect civilian morale without spreading terror'.[43] Such operations do not amount to 'attacks' according to AP I article 49[44] and are therefore not prohibited by article 51(2). Operations designed to affect the civilian population can include for example psychological operations which aim to influence the civilian population in order to gain support for own operations at the

39 Ibid., at page 10.
40 Ibid., at pages 11–12.
41 Ibid., at page 14.
42 Schmitt, 'Targeting and humanitarian law', at page 160.
43 AMW Manual, Commentary 6 to rule 18, at page 102.
44 'Attacks means acts of violence against the adversary, whether in offence or in defence.'

expense of the adversary (operations commonly placed under the umbrella of 'effects based approach to operations').

12.3 PROHIBITION OF INDISCRIMINATE ATTACKS

The present prohibition of indiscriminate attacks can be traced back to the formulation in the Draft Hague Rules on Aerial Warfare article 24(3):

> Any bombardment of cities, towns, villages, habitations and buildings which are not situated in the immediate vicinity of the operations of the land forces, is forbidden. Should the objectives specified in paragraph 2 be so situated that they could not be bombed but that an undiscriminating bombardment of the civil population would result therefrom, the aircraft must abstain from bombing; . . .[45]

The Hague Rules distinguish between objects and places which are and are not in the 'immediate vicinity' of the operations of the land forces. Military necessity played a crucial part in this distinction: 'it followed that military necessity had to be recognized at least to the extent that less strict limits were placed on attacks near the front than those carried out far behind the lines where the civilian population would be taken by surprise'.[46] The rule in article 24(3) thus represented the stricter version, leaving less leeway for military necessity.

The Hague Rules remained a draft, but the core of these provisions hits at the centre of the prohibition of indiscriminate attacks: that the attack is launched recklessly or carelessly towards its aim. The widespread practice of area bombardment that took place during WWII (as well as later) is an example of what the prohibition is seeking to address.[47] Because of its nonchalance,[48] or recklessness,[49] the attack is compared to that of a direct attack against civilians or civilian objects.

The present treaty rule contains an emphasis on the intent of the attacker, rather than the actual result of the attack.[50] Furthermore, the question of

45 Articles 24(1) and (2) are quoted and discussed above, in Chapter 7, with regard to the definition of military objectives.

46 Hancke, 'The 1923 Hague Rules of Air Warfare', at page 23. On the provision which places less limits on the belligerents, see further Chapter 13 on proportionality.

47 AP I Commentary, at para. 1946, page 619.

48 See Dinstein, *Conduct of Hostilities*, at page 147.

49 See Chapter 5.

50 Hancke, 'The 1923 Hague Rules of Air Warfare', at pages 25–6. On the subjective notion of intent, see further Chapter 4 on the military margin of appreciation. See further UK manual, at page 69, commenting on the AP I article 51(4) rule.

military necessity has remained in contention. 'Probably the most controversial question of the whole Protocol I has become, whether and if so to what extent the prohibition of indiscriminate attacks in Art.51 par.4 contains an indirect reference to military necessity.'[51] Whether it is the most controversial question of the whole Protocol remains an open question, but the definition and scope of the adopted definition is certainly controversial.

12.3.1 *Attacks Which Are of a 'Nature to Strike without Distinction'*

Today the treaty prohibition against indiscriminate attacks is – among others – found in the AP I article 51(4), which states that:

> Indiscriminate attacks are prohibited. Indiscriminate attacks are:
> (a) Those which are not directed at a specific military objective;
> (b) Those which employ a method or means of combat which cannot be directed at a specific military objective; or
> (c) Those which employ a method or means of combat the effects of which cannot be limited as required by this Protocol; and consequently, in each such case, are of a nature to strike military objectives and civilians or civilian objects without distinction.

The elements of *litera* (a) and (b) of this definition are repeated in Protocol II to the CCW article 3(b) with regard to the use of mines, booby-traps and other devices,[52] but *litera* (c) is left out. In the Rome Statute, only the act of 'intentionally directing attacks' against civilians/civilian objects is criminalised as a war crime, as well as 'intentionally *launching*' an attack in violation of the proportionality rule.[53] It is noticeable that the launching of attacks which 'cannot be directed', or where the 'effects cannot be limited', are not made separate war crimes. For the purpose of criminal responsibility it is thus not an issue to merge the proportionality rule and the assessment of collateral damage with the notion of indiscriminate attacks.[54] Despite the fact that both the ICRC Customary Law Study and certain military manuals[55] define indiscriminate attacks equally as in AP I article 51(4) (a) to (c), in rule 12, and that

51 Rauch, 'The concept of military necessity in the context of the law of war', at page 26.

52 Protocol II of the CCW, at page 198. See as well Chapter 9.

53 Rome Statute articles 8(2)(b)(i), (ii) and (iv).

54 Ibid. See as well ICC Elements of crimes, at page 18, where it is a requirement that the perpetrator intended that the civilian person/object should be the object of attack. On specific issues regarding the mental element and the proportionality rule, see Chapter 5.

55 UK manual, at pages 68–9, recites the AP I article 51(4) provision; Canadian Manual, at page 4-4. The Norwegian Manual refers to AP I articles 51(4)(a)–(c) without reciting the whole provision or integrating it into examples, at pages 32–3.

the AMW Manual recites the passage of prohibiting attacks where the 'effects cannot be limited' as required by the LOAC,[56] the customary scope of 51(4)(c) remains dubious and controversial. It is for example not found in the US DoD Manual. In fact, it is difficult enough to establish the treaty scope of the provision in *litera* (c).[57] I shall come back to the unclear content of *litera* (c) below, but first I address the key core content of the definition in *literas* (a) and (b), common also to the CCW Protocol II and customary law.

The essence of indiscriminate attacks is that they 'are of a nature to strike . . . without distinction'.[58] This 'nature' points back at either the inherent character of the weapon, the weapons system or how either of these are being used. In the case where the attack is 'not directed at a specific military objective' (*litera* (a)), the assessment is therefore first and foremost linked to the question of whether everything feasible was done in order to verify the status as a military objective according to AP I article 57 (2)(a)(i).[59] In this context, the requirement of 'feasibility' illustrates the balancing of military necessity against the protection of civilians from the effects of hostilities.[60] One example is to fire blindly with an automatic weapon in an area without taking feasible precautions in order to verify that there are no civilians present.[61] Firing blindly must, however, not be confused with harassing fires or interdiction fires in order to disturb resting enemy combatants or to deny the adversary access to a certain area.[62] In both cases the same requirement of taking feasible precautions applies. Harassing fires appear random, on purpose, but are directed at the enemy forces. Interdiction fires may be fired at random intervals, but must likewise be directed at an area which qualifies as a military objective by nature or purpose (understood as possible future use, since the 'use' is what is sought to be prevented).

Second (in *litera* (b)), attacks which cannot be directed at a military objective cover the use of 'blind' weapons and weapons systems, as well as the use of weapons and weapons system under circumstances where it is impossible to

56 AMW Manual, rule 13(b), at page 89 in Commentaries. ICRC CIHL, rule 12.

57 Bothe, Partsch and Solf, *New Rules*, at pages 346–7. Oeter, 'Methods and means of combat', at page 194, refers to the provision as 'the most controversial part of the definition of indiscriminate attacks'.

58 AP I article 51(4).

59 See AP I Commentary, at para. 1952, page 620. The duty to take precautions in attack – and the content of the notion of 'feasible' – are further dealt with below in Chapter 15. See as well Oeter 'Methods and means of combat', at page 192; Blix, 'Area bombardment', at pages 48–9.

60 The notion of feasibility is dealt with in more detail in Chapter 15.

61 This example is used in the Norwegian Manual, at pages 32–3.

62 Bothe, Partsch and Solf, *New Rules*, at pages 348–9; Dinstein, *Conduct of Hostilities*, at page 148. For an example of NATO definitions used as background here, see AAP-6.

distinguish between civilians/civilian objects and combatants/military objectives.[63] Examples of 'blind' weapons are the V2 rockets used during WWII and the Scud missiles used by Iraq during the first Gulf War (1991).[64] Examples of weapons systems which can arguably, or under the circumstances (depending on the ammunition and use), be seen as incapable of being directed at a military target are cluster munitions as well as artillery and different versions of the truck loaded multiple rocket launcher systems.[65] In the Martic Case the ICTY considered the use of a cluster weapon (M-87 Orkan) over Zagreb city and held that:

> the Trial Chamber notes the characteristics of the weapon, it being a non-guided high dispersion weapon. The Trial Chamber therefore concludes that the M-87 Orkan, by virtue of its characteristics and the firing range in this specific instance, was incapable of hitting specific targets. For these reasons, the Trial Chamber also finds that the M-87 Orkan is an indiscriminate weapon, the use of which in densely populated civilian areas, such as Zagreb, will result in the infliction of severe casualties.[66]

Another example is the multiple rocket launcher systems that have been used in a variety of ways since WWII, today appearing in both guided as well as unguided artillery-like systems. The use of one version, Grads (used in Ukraine in 2014), was subject to criticism by Human Rights Watch, who argued that the weapons were indiscriminate and violating the LOAC.[67]

Regular artillery is an area weapon as well, but has not been considered inherently indiscriminate simply because of its character as an area weapon. The use of fixed 'error-zones' in order to determine whether an attack was indiscriminate has been rejected by the ICTY Appeals Chamber in the Gotovina Case.[68] The use of artillery can certainly be viewed under article 51(5)(a) as well (see Chapters 5 and 13).[69]

It has been argued that these two types of indiscriminate attacks mentioned so far (AP I articles 51(4)(a) and (b) and the Protocol II to the CCW article 3

63 Bothe, Partsch and Solf, *New Rules*, at page 346. Oeter 'Methods and means of combat', at pages 193–4; Blix, 'Area bombardment', at page 50.

64 Oeter, 'Methods and means of combat', at page 193. UK Manual, at page 68.

65 Multiple rocket launcher systems come in a variety of forms, from those that are precision guided to those which are cheap to build and by nature an area weapon. Some examples of the latter kind are frequently used by insurgents, such as the Russian modified 'Katuysha' rockets.

66 ICTY Martic Case, Trial Chamber Judgment, at para. 463.

67 See Human Rights Watch, 'Ukraine: unguided missiles killing civilians'.

68 Gotovina Case, Appeals Chamber Judgment, at para. 67. On the standardisation of the commander's assessment and the Gotovina Case, see Chapter 4.

69 Oeter 'Methods and means of combat', at pages 194–5; UK Manual, footnote 96, at page 68.

(b)) 'leave no room whatsoever for considerations of military necessity'.[70] This statement seems to align with the point of departure in the Hague Regulations (see Chapter 6), as an example of where military necessity clearly has yielded to considerations of humanity in order to protect civilians against the effects of attack. Apart from the link (in *litera* (a)) to the duty to take feasible precautions in attack regarding the verification of lawful targets, the military commander's margin of appreciation is therefore of limited (close to non-existent) scope as far as the application of the rules in AP I articles 51(4)(a) and (b) (and corresponding customary law) is concerned.

When it comes to the scope of 51(4)(c) and the wording of the prohibition of attacks 'the effects of which cannot be limited as required by this Protocol', some[71] refer to the surrounding articles in the AP I which govern attacks against dams and dykes (article 56, see Chapter 17), the natural environment (articles 35(3) and 55, see Chapter 17) and as well as the proportionality rule (articles 51(5)(b) and 57, see Chapters 13 and 15). Others argue that the scope of article 51(4)(c) is not simply consumed by other provisions, and that the provision does not deal with collateral damage.[72] In the rejection of the notion of collateral damage in article 51(4)(c) also lies the rejection of military necessity – since the weight of collateral damage clearly bears upon the balance between military necessity and humanitarian considerations. Seen as such, the rule in article 51(5)(b) extends rather than restricts the scope of article 51(4).[73] Without, or before, taking a position on the question whether *litera* (c) deals with collateral damage it is of interest to examine the practical impact of the scope of this provision seen in relation to the rest of article 51(4) and article 51(5). Attacks of which the effects cannot be limited can for example be attacks by the use of weapons which are also prohibited by other instruments – as well as by *litera* (b) and 51(5) – such as gas, biological and chemical weapons.[74] The same goes for the use of cluster munitions and other anti-personnel mines – depending on the circumstances and the treaty obligations of the respective State.[75] An attack would, for example, fall within the scope of article 51(4)(c) when used in a way such that the effects are not possible to limit. This could be the case with gas in the air or poison in the

70 Rauch, 'The concept of military necessity in the context of the law of war', at page 26.

71 Bothe, Partsch and Solf, *New Rules*, at pages 346–7; Oeter 'Methods and means of Combat', at page 194. This also seems to be the position in the UK Manual which refers to 'incidental effect', at page 68.

72 Rauch, 'The concept of military necessity in the context of the law of war', at page 32.

73 Ibid.

74 AP I Commentary, at paras. 1962–3, pages 622–3.

75 See AP I Commentary, at paras. 1962–3, pages 622–3. On the specific prohibition of poisonous gases and biological and chemical weapons, see Chapter 9.

water.[76] Taking into account that the scope of the provision, beyond what is already accounted for (in *literas* (a) and (b)), is unclear as well as not being a part of the CCW, nor being made a specific war crime, its practical application appears less significant, despite being 'controversial'.

12.3.2 A *Remark on Nuclear Weapons and Indiscriminate Attacks*

The particular issue of nuclear weapons and the prohibition of indiscriminate attacks as defined in AP I article 51(4) requires some specific remarks. There is no specific prohibition on the use of nuclear weapons which can be inferred from treaty law.[77] We are left with the task of examining the use of nuclear weapons as any other weapon, according to the general rules of the LOAC. As asked by the ICJ, whether: 'such weapons would kill and destroy in a necessarily indiscriminate manner, on account of the blast, heat and radiation occasioned by the nuclear explosion and the effects induced ...'[78] The Court itself answers this question in the negative, arguing that it: 'does not have sufficient elements to enable it to conclude with certainty that the use of nuclear weapons would be at variance with the principles and rules of law applicable in armed conflict in any circumstance'.[79] Although the use of nuclear weapons would be 'scarcely reconcilable' with the requirements of the LOAC.[80] The position of the Court has been criticised in the Dissenting Opinion of Judge Higgins – who argues that the Court does not enter into a systematic analysis of the law before reaching the conclusions mentioned, but nevertheless concurs with the result that 'there may be very limited prospects of a State being able to comply with the requirements of humanitarian law'[81] – and the Dissenting Opinion of Judge Koroma – who argues that the use of nuclear weapons 'in any circumstance would be unlawful'.[82] It is possible to view these differing, dissenting opinions as also representative of the differences in opinion in literature elsewhere. Some authors argue that the use of some guided nuclear warheads can remain permissible, while the use in

76 Ibid., at para. 1965, page 623.
77 Legality of the Threat or Use of Nuclear Weapons, Advisory Opinion, at page 253, para. 63.
78 Ibid., at page 262, para. 92.
79 Ibid., at page 263, para. 95.
80 Ibid., at page 263, para. 95.
81 Dissenting Opinion of Judge Higgins, ibid., at page 584. See also at page 593 where she argues that: 'It is not clear to me that either a pronouncement of illegality in all circumstances of the use of nuclear weapons or the answers formulated by the Court in paragraph 2E best serve to protect mankind against that unimaginable suffering that we all fear.'
82 Dissenting Opinion of Judge Koroma, ibid., at page 556.

densely populated areas remains unlawful.[83] Others argue firmly that the use of nuclear weapons, due to the extreme danger of escalation, renders their use unlawful in every case.[84] I consider the use of nuclear weapons as almost impossible to reconcile with maintaining a legal order – due to their inherently devastating, widespread effects. It is perhaps with regard to the latter point that the use of nuclear weapons raises the most delicate legal issue: that of using nuclear weapons as area bombardment by way of reprisals in reply to a first attack – as a measure of 'extreme military necessity'. This issue addresses in particular (beside the issue of reprisals) the notion of area bombardment which is governed as a particular type of indiscriminate attack in AP I article 51(5)(a).

12.3.3 *Area Bombardment*

Article 51(5)(a) states:

> Among others, the following types of attacks are to be considered as indiscriminate:
>
> (a) an attack by bombardment by any methods or means which treats as a single military objective a number of clearly separated and distinct military objectives located in a city, town, village or other area containing a similar concentration of civilians or civilian objects; . . .

An attack which violates article 51(5)(a) is commonly viewed as also violating the general rules in 51(4) (or already covered by 51(4)(a)[85]). The particular need for a separate provision dealing with area bombardment has its historic origin in the widespread practice of area bombardment during WWII (and also later) which was aimed at leaving an area completely devastated and useless.[86] The general view today is that the treaty rule expresses customary international law.[87] Legal reasoning in the aftermath of WWII was, however, more dubious[88] and clung to imperative[89] military

83 Oeter 'Methods and means of combat', at page 195.

84 Ragone, 'The applicability of military necessity in the nuclear age', at pages 710–11.

85 AP I Commentary, at para. 1973, pages 624–5.

86 AP I Commentary, at paras. 1967–8, pages 623–4; AMW Manual, Commentaries 2 and 3 to rule 13(c); Bothe, Partsch and Solf, *New Rules*, at page 347.

87 AMW Manual, rule 13(c); ICRC CIHL, rule 13; UK Manual, para. 5.23; Norwegian Manual, page 33; Canadian Manual, page 4-4; German Manual, para. 403, at page 53.

88 See the account given by Blix in 'Area bombardment', at pages 288–91. On the difference between military necessity which must yield to other considerations and militarily necessary vs unnecessary, see Chapter 2.

89 On the different versions of military necessity in general, see Chapter 2.

necessity as justification,[90] arguing in favour of legality if the area bombardment was the only possible solution to achieve the desired military result. As argued by Spaight:

> Military effectiveness has been the test, and by that test the target-area bombing passes muster. It could be condemned only if it involved acts repugnant to humanity. It was approved, however, by public opinion, generally, in Britain and America. There was no such widespread doubt about it as there was about the subsequent resort to atomic bombing, which did gravely disturb the public conscience.[91]

This line of reasoning has been criticised for being dangerous and prone to advance different rules for the just and the unjust.[92] The post-WWII reasoning by Spaight certainly shows the willingness to infer considerable weight upon military necessity – at the expense of humanitarian concerns. This weight has, however, been reduced to a vanishing point under the present rule – or even claimed to be viewed as a waste of force.[93] Viewed in light of the technological development in weaponry since the aftermath of WWII, it does not seem far-fetched to argue that, more often than not, area bombardment would prove to be unnecessary.[94] As with regard to 51(4)(a) there is no room for considering the military necessity of the attack; if the attack is of a nature to strike indiscriminately because the military objectives are 'clearly separated and distinct', the attack is unlawful when directed at all of these objects at once. Despite this absolute feature, the meaning of the phrase 'clearly separated and distinct' has been subject to discussion,[95] and clearly leaves some interpretative latitude to the attacker.[96] This interpretative latitude must not, however, be confused with the latitude to determine the weight of military necessity. The subjective notion in the provision is left to the determination of 'clearly separated and distinct'. The interpretation of this passage will as well inevitably reflect, to a certain extent, the weapons used: the more precise the weapons, the more distinct the objectives may appear.[97] This does not,

90 As pointed out by Blix, 'Area bombardment', at page 291.
91 Spaight, *Air Power and War Rights*, at pages 271 and 276.
92 Blix, 'Area bombardment', at page 291.
93 Ibid., page 294.
94 In this direction, see Boohtby, *The Law of Targeting*, page 94, where he states that: 'Arguably, therefore, article 51(5)(a) is another example of where humanitarian law rules and military interests converge.'
95 See AP I Commentary which refers to the drafting process, at para. 1969, page 624.
96 AP I Commentary, at para. 1973, pages 624–5. On the 'latitude' devoted to military commanders in general when determining military necessity, see Chapter 4 above.
97 Blix, 'Area bombardment', at page 302.

however, imply that there is a general duty to apply precision weapons.[98] The assessment of indiscriminateness is a concrete one.

The prohibition of area bombardment, which treats several separated military objectives as one, must also be seen in relation to the prohibition of terror attacks. The alleged necessity to affect civilian morale has frequently been used as basis for the practice of area bombardment. Furthermore, terror attacks have usually been conducted as area bombardment,[99] and also reprisal attacks against civilians have been practiced as area bombardment. In fact, States' necessity for reprisals have made the UK formulate a reservation (see below) to the AP I article 51(5)(a) prohibition of area bombardment.

12.4 ATTACKS BY WAY OF REPRISALS AGAINST CIVILIANS

12.4.1 *The Definition*

Belligerent reprisals are 'extreme measures'[100] applied by a belligerent party in order to enforce compliance with the LOAC by the adverse party. In the ICRC Customary Law Study belligerent reprisals are defined as: 'A belligerent reprisal consists of an action that would otherwise be unlawful but that in exceptional cases is considered lawful under international law when used as an enforcement measure in reaction to unlawful acts of an adversary.'[101] Belligerent reprisals are thus measures of 'self-help' for States in order to enforce abidance of the law and are recognised as a part of customary international law, albeit subject to strict conditions: that resort to reprisals is the ultimate solution, after the wrongdoing state has been called upon to stop and been given a warning; that the reprisal is proportionate to the foregoing wrongful act and authorised by the highest level of command (since the act entails State responsibility[102]); and finally that the reprisal is terminated as soon as the initial wrongful activity ceases.[103]

98 Boothby, *The Law of Targeting*, at page 93.
99 See Section 12.2 and Blix, 'Area bombardment', at pages 45 and 52.
100 UK Manual, at page 418.
101 ICRC CIHL, rule 145, Commentary.
102 See Draft articles on Responsibility of States article 30 which lays down the duty to cease the commission of any wrongful act and article 50 which refers to the duty not to violate obligations of a humanitarian character prohibiting reprisals during countermeasures. On the general distinction to the law on State responsibility, see Chapter 1.
103 UK Manual, at page 419; German Manual, at para. 1528; Canadian Manual, page 15-2.

12.4.2 *Specific Prohibitions of Reprisals*

The position of reprisals *as such* under the LOAC is firmly established. Its *scope with regard to objects of attack* is, however, contested. Treaty law today prohibits reprisals against protected personnel and property.[104] Certain parts of the treaty prohibition are, however, contested[105] because they are not covered by the customary law prohibition on specific reprisals. It is first and foremost with regard to area bombardment that the issue of reprisals is at stake. For the purpose of the present chapter, emphasis is placed on the status of civilians and civilian objects (in the combat zone and not in the hands of the adversary, such as occupation) with regard to reprisals under customary international law. According to the AP I article 51(6) civilians enjoy absolute protection against reprisals: 'Attacks against the civilian population or civilians by way of reprisals are prohibited.' The absolute character of this prohibition rules out the possibility of invoking military necessity as an exception, whereas customary law until the adoption of the AP I has allowed reprisals against enemy civilians (provided that the reprisal fulfils the criteria mentioned above). I return to the present customary status of reprisals below, but first some remarks on the historic connection between military necessity and reprisals against civilians.

12.4.3 *Military Necessity and Reprisal Attacks in History*

History has clearly shown the link between military necessity and the invocation of certain belligerent reprisals, where military necessity often has motivated the 'selection of specific reprisals'.[106] Military necessity was hotly debated with regard to reprisals at the Brussels Conference in 1874, but the participants did not manage to reach an agreement.[107] The disagreement over reprisals disclosed – inter alia – different points of view between Germany – which held military necessity to be the sole legal principle applicable in war – and other European States. These differences in opinion must, to a great extent, be seen in relation to the (then) recent Franco-Prussian War

104 See for example GC I article 46; GC II article 47; GC III article 13; and GC IV article 33; as well as AP I article 20.

105 See the UK Manual, at page 420, listing the prohibitions in AP I articles 51–5: civilians and civilian population, historic and cultural monuments, objects indispensable for the survival of the civilian population, the natural environment, and works and installations containing dangerous forces.

106 Kalshoven, *Belligerent Reprisals*, at page 365.

107 Hull, 'Military necessity and the laws of war in Imperial Germany', at page 357; Best, *Humanity in Warfare*, at pages 171–2.

(1870–1).[108] After the Brussels Conference the topic of reprisals left the arena of diplomatic conferences for a decade, and returned first during the negotiations of the AP I. Meanwhile, however, military necessity was frequently used as an exception during WWII,[109] and led to 'confusion about legitimate targets'.[110] The development into a spiral of reprisals quickly followed on from the noble point of departure given by President Roosevelt at the beginning of WWII that: 'every Government … shall in no event and under no circumstances undertake bombardment from the air of civilian populations or unfortified cities, upon the understanding that the same rules of warfare shall be scrupulously observed by their opponents'.[111]

In the UK a legal report to the Foreign Office had preached a similarly restrictive policy, but accompanied by a cover letter which proclaimed that the rules – which were stricter than the Draft Hague Rules on Aerial Warfare – would 'be subject to modification if the enemy commenced indiscriminate bombing'.[112] Then, in May 1940, the British Foreign Office publicly proclaimed that they 'reserve to themselves the right to take any action which they consider appropriate in the event of bombing by the enemy of civil populations, whether in the United Kingdom, France or in countries assisted by the United Kingdom'.[113] Retaliation immediately developed after this,[114] with strategic air offensives over Germany and the German reply by the bombing of London on 7 September,[115] until the removal of all restrictions by the Air Ministry's statement in 1942: 'Consequent upon the enemy's adoption of unrestricted warfare, the Cabinet have authorized a bombing policy which includes the attack on enemy morale.'[116] The cat was out of the bag and

108 Best, *Humanity in Warfare*, at page 171; Kalshoven, *Belligerent Reprisals*, at page 48. The difference in opinion can be seen as closely related to the controversies over the doctrine of *Kriegsraison*. See Chapter 6 on this doctrine and the Franco-Prussian War.

109 AP I Commentary, at page 626, para. 1984.

110 Rogers, *Law on the Battlefield*, at page 14.

111 Roosevelt's appeal to the governments of the UK, France, Germany and Poland, and embraced by the UK and France. Quoted from Spaight, *Air Power and War Rights*, at page 259.

112 Biddle, *Rhetoric and Reality in Air Warfare*, at page 182.

113 Quotation from Spaight, *Air Power and War Rights*, at page 266. Kalshoven argues that this British 'feeling' of no longer being bound by their legal obligations did not in fact release them from the same obligations. See *Belligerent Reprisals*, at page 169, where he also contends that the proclamation was not a real invocation of reprisals as justification for their acts.

114 For an account of this period with regard to belligerent reprisals, see Kalshoven, *Belligerent Reprisals*, at pages 163–7.

115 Spaight, *Air Power and War Rights*, at page 269. Kalshoven argues, after some hesitation, that the bombings in London also lack justification as reprisal, see pages 177–8.

116 From Biddle, *Rhetoric and Reality in Air Warfare*, at page 197. Attacks on enemy morale are dealt with separately in Section 12.2.

civilian Germany was in flames due to the alleged *necessity* of retaliatory bombardment. A perception of necessity aside, it was arguably not sufficient to justify the bombing as reprisals: 'both parties in the war had by then resorted to indiscriminate bombing on too many occasions for an attempt to justify a particular instance as a reprisal to be taken seriously any longer . . .'[117] Or as put by one scholar with regard to the aim of avoiding civilian casualties: 'As the conflict developed, however, the perceived demands of military necessity eroded these standards.'[118]

12.4.4 *The Customary Status of Reprisal Attacks against Civilians*

Prior to the adoption of the AP I prohibition, views on the utility and need for reprisals against enemy civilians were divided.[119] Among the views *against* a total ban on reprisals against civilians and the civilian population was the view that governments could not sit idly by and watch repeated violations of the Protocol against their own population when the only way of stopping the wrongful act was to do the same against the civilian population of the perpetrating State. To sit passively was viewed as both unrealistic and possibly weakening for the whole Protocol.[120] By others it was argued that 'terror raids' and area bombardment had proven to be of limited military value and hence that the protection of the civilian population should be strengthened accordingly.[121] In other words, the opinions regarding the actual *military necessity* of reprisal attacks differed.

It is doubtful whether States which are *not* parties to the AP I are bound by a customary prohibition to direct reprisals against civilians – customary law as prior to the AP I is arguably (and regrettably) still in force with regard to reprisals against civilians.[122]

The treaty reservation to the AP I articles 51–5 by the United Kingdom illustrates the States' persistence in upholding the customary law position prior to the AP I prohibitions on reprisals which may amount to different versions of area bombardment:

117 Kalshoven, *Belligerent Reprisals*, at page 178.
118 Gardam, *Necessity, Proportionality and the Use of Force by States*, at page 56.
119 Kalshoven and Zegveld, *Constraints on the Waging of War*, at pages 144–5.
120 See the views of Canada, the USA and France in Official Records of the Diplomatic Conference CDDH/III/SR 7, para. 33 and CDDH/III/SR/8, paras. 50 and 56.
121 Swedish representative, Hans Blix, in CDDH/III/SR/8, para. 8.
122 UK Manual, at pages 420–1; Kalshoven and Zegveld *Constraints on the Waging of War*, at page 146; Dinstein, *Conduct of Hostilities*, at page 295; Rogers, *Law on the Battlefield*, page 14.

> The obligations of Articles 51 and 55 are accepted on the basis that any adverse party against which the United Kingdom might be engaged will itself scrupulously observe those obligations. If an adverse party makes serious and deliberate attacks, in violation of Article 51 or Article 52 against the civilian population or civilians or against civilian objects, or, in violation of Articles 53, 54 and 55, on objects or items protected by those Articles, the United Kingdom will regard itself as entitled to take measures otherwise prohibited by the Articles in question to the extent that it considers such measures necessary for the sole purpose of compelling the adverse party to cease committing violations under those Articles, but only after formal warning to the adverse party requiring cessation of the violations has been disregarded and then only after a decision taken at the highest level of government. Any measures thus taken by the United Kingdom will not be disproportionate to the violations giving rise there to and will not involve any action prohibited by the Geneva Conventions of 1949 nor will such measures be continued after the violations have ceased. The United Kingdom will notify the Protecting Powers of any such formal warning given to an adverse party, and if that warning has been disregarded, of any measures taken as a result.[123]

The UK position has been referred to as one reflecting the position in customary international law.[124] The practice of the ICTY has been inconsistent on the matter. In the Kupreskic Case, the tribunal relied upon the Martens Clause and argued that:

> The aforementioned elements seem to support the contention that the demands of humanity and the dictates of the public conscience, as manifested in *opinio necessitatis*, have by now brought about the formation of customary rule also binding upon those few States that at some stage did not intend to exclude the abstract legal possibility of resorting to the reprisals under discussion.[125]

Although the tribunal in this case was willing to disregard or diminish the weight of the practice of States in order to reach a customary prohibition of reprisal attacks against civilians, the tribunal apparently changed the course in the Martic Case (yet referring to the Kupreskic Case), arguing that 'reprisals, in order to be considered lawful, are subject to strict conditions' and that 'acts of reprisal must respect the "laws of humanity and dictates of public conscience"'. The latter phrase meant, according to the tribunal, that the reprisal must be exercised: 'to the extent possible, in keeping with the principle of the

[123] Cited from Schindler and Toman, *The Laws of Armed Conflicts*, at page 817.
[124] Kalshoven and Zegveld *Constraints on the Waging of War*, at page 146.
[125] Kupreskic Case, at para. 533, page 211.

protection of the civilian population in armed conflict and the general prohibition of targeting civilians'.[126] By including the phrase 'the extent possible', it appears that even the ICTY is on the same page as the view presented on the customary status of reprisals above.

The realm of (some) States' nuclear strategies lie at the heart of the reluctance by (the same) States to accept a total ban on reprisals against the civilian population. In order to be able to keep the possibility to maintain a contingency plan (within the scope of the law) of the use of nuclear weapons as a 'second-strike' option, subsequent to a first-hit nuclear strike by an adversary, the position as expressed by the UK appears rational. The underlying problem of such a position is, however, disturbing. Apart from the obvious similarities to the rhetorical justification of the terror attacks and area bombardment conducted during WWII, the position – of accepting reprisals against the civilian population by the use of area bombardment – represents a litmus test for the overall legal framework in armed conflict. A nuclear strike ought not to be seen as anything other than sweeping away the whole fundament for the *legal restraint* in war and blowing the road wide open for exceptional military necessity in its widest sense. Nevertheless, this regrettable situation seems to be the law. Certainly, there are other legal aspects related to the use of nuclear weapons, which are dealt with elsewhere in this book.[127]

The majority of States parties to the AP I however – those who do not possess nuclear weapons – seem to have interpreted the wording of the prohibition in accordance with its ordinary meaning, and hence encompassing a total ban on directing attacks on civilians – even as reprisals subject to strict conditions.[128]

12.4.5 *The Particular Issue of 'Reprisal Prisoners' (Hostages)*

It is unequivocally prohibited to take hostages during conduct of hostilities. The prohibition is firmly established as part of both treaty and customary law.[129] The prohibition includes the taking of hostages even if it is not accompanied by the threat of killing them.[130] The sweeping prohibition is,

[126] Martic Case, at paras. 465–7, pages 167–8.
[127] See Chapter 13 on proportionality and Chapter 9 on unnecessary suffering.
[128] Norwegian Manual, at pages 287–8; German Manual, at paras. 490 and 1528; Canadian Manual, at page 15-2.
[129] GC IV article 34; GC I-IV common article 3; Rome Statute article 8(2)(a)(viii); CIHL, rule 96.
[130] See the ICTY Blaskic Case, Appeals Chamber Judgment, at para. 639.

however, of fairly recent origin. In the immediate aftermath of WWII the situation was different.

The issue of hostages was first and foremost dealt with in the Hostage Case, where the tribunal held that 'The question of hostages is closely integrated with that of reprisals'[131] and that:

> An examination of the available evidence on the subject convinces us that hostages may be taken in order to guarantee the peaceful conduct of the populations of occupied territories and, when certain conditions exist and the necessary preliminaries have been taken, they may, as a last resort, be shot. The taking of hostages is based fundamentally on a theory of collective responsibility.[132]

The reasoning behind the position of the Tribunal is 'provided it can be shown that the *population* is a party to the offense, either actively *or passively*'.[133] Thus, those liable to be killed were somehow being collectively held responsible for the 'peaceful conduct' in an area. To establish the facts it required a judicial inquiry, but not without exception: 'The only exception to this rule is where it appears that the *necessity for the reprisal* requires immediate action to accomplish the desired purpose and which would be otherwise defeated by the invocation of judicial inquiry.'[134]

This position of the Tribunal illustrates at least two aspects: first, that the conception of which measures that are *necessary* during warfare (and occupation) have changed, and second, that the overall idea of a 'total war' (in the sense that a society's total resources, civilian and military, are thrown into the war effort) permeated the thinking on lawful conduct of hostilities at the time of WWII and its aftermath (there is no other way that 'the population' can be a party to the offence). It must be emphasised that the Tribunal viewed the practice as accepted by States, but nevertheless a 'complete failure on the part of the nations of the world to limit or mitigate the practice by conventional rule', and therefore argued that 'This requires us to apply customary law',[135] a statement from the Tribunal which actually illustrates the strong position of military necessity in customary international law at the time. Today, this position is weakened. Necessity has yielded to humanitarian concerns (also) concerning reprisal prisoners.

[131] Hostage Case, at page 61.

[132] Ibid.

[133] Ibid., at page 62. Emphasis added.

[134] Ibid., at page 64. Emphasis added. With regard to the question of killing helpless survivors at sea, for the sake of preserving one's own life, see as well *British Military Court for the Trial of War Criminals* v. *Kapteinleutnant Hans Eck and four others* (The Peleus Trial I).

[135] Hostage Case, at page 63.

13

Military Necessity and Proportionality

13.1 'PROPORTIONALITY' IN GENERAL AND THE SPECIFIC 'PRINCIPLE OF PROPORTIONALITY' IN THE LOAC

The term 'proportionality' simply refers to a commensurable relationship between two relata. The notion of proportionality in general is understood as a general and almost intuitive guide to the distribution of equal weight to different interests. Literally, the word is put together from two words: *pro portio*, in equal shares.[1] As a legal principle (a norm) a more specific approach is, however, required, and the purpose of this chapter is to distinguish different facets of the meaning of 'proportionality' and to address more closely those meanings of proportionality which are inextricably linked to the concept of military necessity under conduct of hostilities.

A concept of 'proportionality' is devoted considerable attention in public international law, beyond the LOAC. The views of the status of 'proportionality' vary, from those arguing that it is a general doctrine – or principle – of public international law,[2] to those who strongly contest the tenet of 'proportionality' being a general principle of international law.[3] While a concept of proportionality certainly have many normative faces in international law, it seems fair to argue – with the words of Rosalyn Higgins – that proportionality is

[1] Soanes and Stevenson, *Concise Oxford English Dictionary*, at page 1151, also referred to as 'corresponding in size or amount to something else'. For a general approach to the linguistic background, see Christoffersen, *Fair Balance*, at page 35.

[2] See for example Engle, 'The history of the general principle of proportionality', at page 3, who argues that: 'Today the general principle of proportionality is a worldwide principle of law.' See as well the *Beit Sourik Village Council* v. *The Government of Israel and the Commander of the IDF Forces in the West Bank* (HCJ 2056/04), (Israeli High Court) (Beit Sourik Case) at paras. 36–7.

[3] Dinstein, 'The principle of proportionality', at page 74, also criticising the abovementioned Beit Sourik Case.

not a 'substantive norm' in international law such as, for example the use of force, but a concept which eases the appropriate application of norms in particular cases.[4]

In this book the concept of proportionality is apparent – and discussed – in two normative structures: that of military necessity (where some argue that it is *implied*) and that of the rule prohibiting attacks which may be expected to cause excessive collateral damage (generally referred to as the principle of proportionality under the LOAC). The latter rule is a 'genuine military principle' as opposed to a 'general principle of proportionality'.[5]

The concept of proportionality does, however, also appear in two normative structures which often are confused – to a certain extent – with the concept as it appears under the LOAC: the principle of proportionality as an element of the right to self-defence under the *jus ad bellum*,[6] and the principle of proportionality in the jurisprudence of the European Court of Human Rights (ECtHR) (see below).

As stated already at the outset of this book, the proportionality requirement under the *jus ad bellum* must not be confused with proportionality during armed conflict. Some authors seem to argue that the proportionality requirement under the *jus ad bellum* continues to apply throughout the course of war – as an extra layer of assessment[7] – and not only governs the initial use of force in order to repel an armed attack.[8] However, the consideration of proportionality under the *jus ad bellum* and the *jus in bello* (LOAC) ought to be kept apart. When the *jus ad bellum* proportionality 'concerns the relationship between that action and its purpose, namely ... that of halting and repelling the attack'[9] (symmetry in modes of attack and response is not

4 Higgins, *Problems and Process*, at page 219.

5 Heintschel von Heinegg and Dreist, 'The 2009 Kunduz Air Attack', at page 848. The cited position is that of the German Public-Prosecutor.

6 UN Charter article 51. The element of proportionality is interpreted by the ICJ to constitute an integrated requirement of the resort to force in self-defence, see *Nicaragua* v. *United States of America*, at paras. 176–94 and Legality of the Threat or Use of Nuclear Weapons, Advisory Opinion, at paras. 40–1. See also Gardam, *Necessity, Proportionality and the Use of Force by States*, at page 11.

7 This position is taken among others by Gardam, *Necessity, Proportionality and the Use of Force by States*, at page 156.

8 This diametrically opposite position is fronted among others by Dinstein, *War, Aggression and Self-Defence*, at pages 237–8, who argues that: 'There is no support in the practice of States for the notion that proportionality remains relevant – and has to be constantly assessed – throughout the hostilities in the course of war.' See also page 240 with further reference to Oppenheim and Lauterpacht, *Disputes, War and Neutrality*, at page 225.

9 Eighth Report on State Responsibility, at page 69, para. 121. See also Gray, *International Law and the Use of Force*, at page 121.

required),[10] the *jus in bello* proportionality (in the proper sense) amounts to an equation between military advantage and expected collateral damage. Many references can, however, also be found to a second version of proportionality under the *jus in bello*, resembling that of the *jus ad bellum*, namely as 'one of two elements comprising necessity, the other being relevance'.[11] This version of proportionality under the *jus in bello* is named a 'silent condition of necessity' and dealt with in Section 13.3.

A concept of proportionality is inherent as well – and to a major extent – in the European Convention of Human Rights and its application is well developed in the case law of the Court.[12] The human rights law regime is distinct from the LOAC and aimed at striking a 'fair balance between the protection of the interests of the community and respects for the rights and freedoms safeguarded by the Convention'.[13] Although areas of life in reality sometimes overlap (for the purpose of the present book this is particularly so with regard to situations falling under ECHR article 2[14] which protects the right to life), the legal norms of proportionality are not the same under the two sets of rules, and a comparative study requires a separate analysis which goes beyond the scope of this book.

13.2 THE LOAC RULE: PROPORTIONALITY AS A PROHIBITION OF EXCESSIVE COLLATERAL DAMAGE

Alongside the principle of distinction, the principle of proportionality under the LOAC is a limitation on military necessity[15] and for the purpose of this book, a limitation upon the military commander's assessment of military necessity. As envisaged in the ICRC Commentary to the AP I: 'The entire law of armed conflict is, of course, the result of an equitable balance

10 See Legality of the Threat or Use of Nuclear Weapons, Advisory Opinion, dissenting opinion of Judge Higgins, at para. 3 (judgment page 583), who relies upon the Eighth Report on State Responsibility written by Professor Ago.

11 Higgins, *Problems and Process*, at page 232. The same position is taken by Bothe, Partsch and Solf, *New Rules*, at page 224.

12 Proportionality is also visible in the jurisprudence of other human rights organs. For an overview of this status, see Christoffersen, *Fair Balance*, at pages 40–3.

13 European Court of Human Rights, Case *'Relating to certain aspects of the laws on the use of languages in education in Belgium'* v. *Belgium* (Merits), 23 July 1968, Series A, no 6, at page 40, para. 7. Emphasis added. See as well the position taken in European Court of Human Rights, *Sporrong and Lönnroth* v. *Sweden* (Merits), 23 September 1982, at para. 69.

14 Convention for the Protection of Human Rights and Fundamental Freedoms, article 2.

15 On military necessity in general and the aspect of limitation, see Chapter 7. In the same direction of treating proportionality as a limitation, see for example Cannizzaro, 'Proportionality in the Law of Armed Conflict', at page 333.

between the necessities of war and humanitarian requirements. There is no implicit clause in the Conventions which would give priority to military requirements. The principles of the Conventions are precisely aimed at determining where the limits lie; the principle of proportionality contributes to this.'[16]

The principle of proportionality is also explained as being 'a link between the principles of military necessity and humanity'.[17] If military necessity was to rule without this limitation one would not need to take into account the incidental damages of a necessary attack. Necessity would be sufficient for lawfulness. The proportionality rule is expressed in the AP I article 51(5)(b) as: 'an attack which may be expected to cause incidental loss of civilian life, injury to civilians, damage to civilian objects, or a combination thereof, which would be excessive in relation to the concrete and direct military advantage anticipated'. The provision in AP I article 51(5)(b) 'represents the first concrete codification of the principle of proportionality as it applies to collateral civilian casualties'.[18] The rule is of rather recent origin, and by some even characterised as 'innovative'.[19] The wording is reiterated in article 57(2)(a)(iii) with regard to precautions in attack, as well as in other – and more recent – treaty provisions,[20] such as in the Rome Statute[21] which confirms the rule with the addition of 'clearly' in front of the requirement of 'excessive' as well as 'overall' in front of the military advantage anticipated. The impact of these additions is dealt with in Chapters 5 and 14.

Despite its recent treaty origin, the proportionality rule has an unequivocal status as customary international law. The wording of the AP I provision is reiterated in both the ICRC Customary Law Study and the AMW Manual[22] as well as referred to in States' military manuals[23] and legal literature.[24]

16 AP I Commentary, at page 683, para. 2206.
17 UK Manual, at page 25.
18 Bothe, Partsch and Solf, *New Rules*, at page 350.
19 Cohen, 'The Lebanon War and the application of the proportionality principle', at page 9.
20 Protocol II of the CCW article 3(3)(c), and Protocol II (1996 amendment) article 3(8)(c).
21 Rome Statute article 8(2)(b)(iv).
22 See CIHL, rule 14 and AMW Manual, rule 14, at page 91 in Commentary.
23 UK Manual, at pages 25 and 86; US DoD Manual, at page 241; German Manual, para. 404, at pages 53–4; Norwegian Manual, at pages 14 and 33; Canadian Manual, at page 4-3; Swedish proposed manual, in SOU 2010:72, at page 47.
24 See for example: Dinstein, 'The principle of proportionality', at page 74; Boothby, *The Law of Targeting*, at page 71; Rogers, *Law on the Battlefield*, at page 17; Henderson, *The Contemporary Law of Targeting*, at page 181; Schmitt, 'Military necessity and humanity in international humanitarian law', at page 804.

Case law and actual State practice on the application of the proportionality rule have been scarce,[25] although examples in different shapes can be found in the case law of the ICTY[26] as well as in State practice from the Vietnam War, the first Gulf War, the Kosovo War, the armed conflict in Afghanistan during the 2000s[27] and, more recently, the war in Libya in 2011 and in Syria from 2011 until present date (2017). Almost certainly, the scattered case law before 1977 stems from the fact that the rule was not yet formulated, but also from an apparent unwillingness among the Allied in the aftermath of WWII to bring to court cases which obviously could be perceived as a mirror of their own conduct.[28]

Obviously, the principle of proportionality is 'much easier to formulate' than to apply in concrete cases.[29] The AP I introduces the principle in two different contexts: as a particular type of prohibited indiscriminate attack in article 51(5)(b) and – under the duty to take precautions in attack in article 57(2)(a)(iii) – a duty to cancel, suspend or re-plan the attack if it may be expected that the attack will violate the proportionality principle. The essence of the proportionality rule is the assessment of 'excessive collateral damage'. Both the notion of collateral damage as well as excessiveness will be accounted for in more detail, but first a historical outline on the relationship between military necessity and the proportionality rule.

13.2.1 *Necessity and Proportionality: Historical Underpinnings*

The proportionality rule found its place in a treaty for the first time in AP I in 1977, but traces of similar considerations can be found also in older instruments. The Lieber Code article 15 states that: 'Military necessity admits of all direct destruction of life of *armed* enemies, and of other persons whose destruction is incidentally *unavoidable* in the armed contests of war . . .'[30] The reference to destruction which is 'incidentally unavoidable' resembles

25 For an account of this up until 1982, see Fenrick, 'The rule of proportionality and Protocol I in conventional warfare', at pages 112–17.

26 For an account, see Bartels, 'Dealing with the principle of proportionality in armed conflict in retrospect'.

27 See for example the 'Kunduz Air Attack' incident, dealt with in Section 14.10 with regard to the security of the attacking forces, as well as in Chapter 15 with regard to feasible precautions in attack.

28 See for example, Olasolo, *Unlawful Attacks in Combat Situations*, at page 156.

29 See for example Fenrick, 'The rule of proportionality and Protocol I in conventional warfare', at page 94.

30 The point is made by Bothe, Partsch and Solf, *New Rules*, at page 350. Lieber Code. Emphasis in original.

today's rule which tolerates damage or injury which is not excessive. The threshold for tolerated damage or destruction is thus inextricably linked to considerations of military necessity.

Also the 1907 Hague Regulations and the 1907 Hague Convention IX on naval bombardment contain provisions which may be seen as predecessors to a proportionality rule. Articles 25 and 1, respectively, prohibit bombardment of undefended towns,[31] while articles 27 and 6 establish a duty to spare 'as far as possible, buildings dedicated to religion, art, science, or charitable purposes, historic monuments, hospitals, and places where the sick and wounded are collected'. Again, the duty to spare protected buildings does not go further than what can be tolerated due to military necessity, as seen in the phrase 'as far as possible'. The Hague Convention on Bombardment by Naval Forces contains in addition an exceptional clause in article 2 (which is not also found in the 1907 Hague Regulations on Land Warfare) referring to a situation: 'If for military reasons immediate action is necessary', the commander 'shall take all due measures in order that the town may suffer as little harm as possible'. Although this is certainly not the proportionality rule of today, the rule prescribes a balance to be struck between the harms of a civilian town and the military necessities of the attack (the bombardment).

Furthermore, another step in the direction of a proportionality rule – which never reached the status of a ratified treaty – is article 24(4) of the Hague Rules on Aerial Warfare, which states:[32] 'In the immediate vicinity of the operations of the land forces, the bombardment of cities, towns, villages, habitations and buildings is legitimate, provided there is a reasonable presumption that the military concentration is important enough to justify the bombardment, taking into account the danger to which the civil population will thus be exposed.' This proposed rule contains a more explicit reference to the balancing of harms: the importance of the military concentration (military necessity) must outweigh (justify) the danger to the civil population.

However, as the Hague Rules got no longer than the negotiating table, the legal situation prior to and during WWII was that no proportionality rule existed in treaty or customary law. As opposed to the rule of distinction (which evidently also was under severe pressure), hardly any signs can be

[31] The link between the proportionality rule and the Hague Convention IX on naval bombardment is for example made in the Swedish proposed manual SOU 2010:72, at page 47.

[32] The Hague Rules followed the first attempts of regulation of aerial warfare in 1899 and 1907, which recalled the 'sentiments' from the St Petersburg Declaration. The Declaration forbade the launching of projectiles and explosives from balloons and was of limited duration.

found in the practice of States throughout the inter-war period and WWII to support a rule of proportionality.[33] It is therefore misleading to evaluate WWII bombings in light of the principle of proportionality as envisaged in the AP I.[34]

After WWII, a new attempt was made in the ICRC Draft Rules of 1956, which stated in article 8(b) that: 'He is required to refrain from the attack if, after due consideration, it is apparent that the loss and destruction would be disproportionate to the military advantage anticipated.' The expression 'disproportionate' survived all the way up to the draft article 46(3)(b) to the AP I, which suggested that it was prohibited to: 'launch attacks which may be expected to entail incidental losses among the civilian population and cause the destruction of civilian objects to an extent disproportionate to the direct and substantial military advantage anticipated'.[35]

Fenrick later identified three conflicting views that emerged during the negotiating process. First, a view which recognised proportionality as an essential element of the law of armed conflict, second, a view which denied the existence of such a rule as a part of the law of armed conflict, and third, a view which partially recognised proportionality as part of the law.[36] A number of States stood behind three alternative formulations to a rule where the expression 'disproportionate' was upheld.[37] The opposition towards explicitly introducing a relative protection of civilians was, however, substantial.[38] Four alternative formulations without the expression 'disproportionate' were presented, and a majority of the States supported this latter solution, where the formulation 'excessive' came in as a substitute.[39]

33 See for example the account given by Blix, 'Area bombardment', at pages 35–7.

34 For an example of this, see Jaworski, 'Military necessity and civilian immunity', at page 182, who seems to apply the proportionality rule on the Hiroshima and Nagasaki nuclear attacks.

35 Official Records of the Diplomatic Conference CDDH/I at page 16.

36 Fenrick, 'The rule of proportionality and Protocol I in conventional warfare', at page 102.

37 See proposition of Australia in Official Records of the Diplomatic Conference CDDH/III/43/Rev.1; the proposition of Sweden in CDDH/III/44; the proposition of Brazil, Canada, Federal Republic of Germany and Nicaragua in ibid., CDDH/III/27.

38 See the account given by Fenrick in 'The rule of proportionality and Protocol I in conventional warfare', at pages 102–6, and by Blix, 'Area bombardment', at page 51.

39 See the propositions of Czechoslovakia, German Democratic Republic, Hungary and Poland in Official Records of the Diplomatic Conference CDDH/III/8; Romania in CDDH/111/10; Algeria, Arab Republic of Egypt, Democratic Yemen, Iraq, Kuwait, Libyan Arab Republic, Morocco, Sudan, Syrian Arab Republic and United Arab Emirates in CGGH/III/48; and Philippines in CDDH/III/51. The scepticism against 'subjectivity' which lay behind the opposition towards the expression 'disproportionate' is dealt with in more detail in Chapter 4.

13.2.2 *Proportionality As the Ultimate Balancing of Military Necessity and Humanitarian Considerations*

In Chapter 4 proportionality was introduced as the 'ultimate subjective-objective concept' and, in this context, the deeply rooted scepticism towards 'subjectivity' in the rule. The margin left to the commander's discretion lies at the very heart of the controversy over 'subjectivity'. The object of this (partly) 'subjective assessment'[40] is, precisely, the necessity–humanity balance, in the heading of this section referred to as the 'ultimate' balancing to be performed by the commander. In Chapter 4, I posed the question: how to streamline this assessment? I proposed two approaches to this streamlining: through guidelines of interpretation and through the prescribed level of reasonableness. The latter point is emphasised with regard to the proportionality rule in the US DoD Manual, where it is stated that: 'For example, the commander must be able to explain the expected military importance of the target and why the anticipated civilian collateral injury or damage is not expected to be excessive.'[41] The commander's task of assessing excessiveness and advantage is subject to separate scrutiny below. The present section is devoted to the point of departure: the characteristics of the 'balance' and the commander's performance of this.

In the aftermath of the first Gulf War, Frits Kalshoven presented a scheme of limitations on military action, which implies a two-step approach in which military necessity is identified as a crucial ingredient. The first step is to determine that the object of attack is a military objective and the second step: 'Taking into consideration any values outside the chosen military objective that do not themselves constitute military objectives, the next step is to determine whether "collateral damage" to such values should be accepted as an unavoidable side effect of the attack. Once again, the sole argument for an affirmative answer is the military necessity of attacking the target.'[42]

The proportionality rule has been viewed as the 'most conspicuous balancing'[43] between military necessity and humanitarian considerations, where: 'there is a requirement for a subordinate rule to perform the balancing function between military and humanitarian requirements. This rule is the rule of proportionality.'[44] Even though one may view the principle of distinction as the 'most outstanding illustration of the balance',[45] and probably rightly

40 US DoD Manual, at para. 5.10.2.3, page 244.
41 US DoD Manual, at para. 5.10.2.2, page 244 (footnotes omitted).
42 Kalshoven, 'Remarks', at page 41.
43 Schmitt, 'Military necessity and humanity in international humanitarian law', at page 804.
44 Fenrick, 'The rule of proportionality and Protocol I in conventional warfare', at page 94.
45 Dinstein, 'The principle of proportionality', at page 73.

so, taking into account that the principle of proportionality presupposes the principle of distinction, the proportionality assessment is not diminished in practical importance compared to the rule of distinction.

As already pointed out, the humanity–military necessity balance struck in the proportionality rule requires in practice the balancing of incomparable things collateral damage and military advantage.[46] To perform this balance amounts to an obvious difficulty which also has been referred to as the 'moral roots of the dilemma'.[47] But what sort of balance is actually sought here? The answer lies in the notion of 'excessiveness', which is dealt with in Chapter 15. A few overall remarks shall, however, be made here.

Is it true, for the principle of proportionality, that 'various external pressures have fuelled a gradual shift in emphasis toward humanitarian considerations'?[48] While the negative definition of civilians, which underpins the rule of distinction, by some was said to be too wide in order to favour humanitarian concerns, the proportionality rule was actually said to do the opposite, to grant more room for military necessity: '. . . it has been necessary, to counterbalance this broad definition [of civilians] favourable to the civilian population, to make a restriction in favour of the principle of military necessity by indicating the high risks run by these persons who do not, in practice, enjoy the same degree of protection as other civilians, within the strict limits of their functions'.[49] For, as pointed out even by the ICRC, 'only peace could guarantee effective protection for the civilian population within or near military objectives'.[50]

These were, however, views presented at the inception of the proportionality rule as a treaty rule in the AP I. The question of whether there has been a later shift towards humanitarian considerations can be addressed in at least two different layers: as a question of whether the content of military necessity[51] actually changes or can be changed, and second, as a question of whether the relative weight attached to military necessity is subject to change. Strictly speaking, it is only the second layer which deals with a shift in the balancing of values, while the first layer refers to the actual values which are subject to weighing. For example: in military theory, it is often argued that 'air

46 In the context of military necessity, this is among others pointed out by Rauch in 'The concept of military necessity in the context of the law of war', at page 25.

47 Watkin, 'Assessing Proportionality', at page 5.

48 Schmitt, 'Military necessity and humanity in international humanitarian law', at page 796. The question also is raised in Chapter 6.

49 Conference of Governmental Experts, (1971) Vol. III, at page 28.

50 Official Records of the Diplomatic Conference CDDH/III/SR.5 at page 37.

51 The question of content is pointed out by the OTP Report, at para. 49.

superiority is a necessity'.[52] If we argue that this, due to the changing character of war, is not the truth anymore, it is an argument of the actual content of military necessity – the first layer referred too. If, on the other hand, we still argue that air superiority is a necessity for military success, but that humanitarian considerations place restrictions on the measures which can be taken in order to achieve air superiority, it is an argument of the relative weight devoted to necessity – the second layer referred to.

The two layers do, however, often merge together in legal argumentation. Gardam argues that: 'The gulf conflict graphically illustrated that, if the requirements of Article 51(5)(b) are to be complied with, military necessity will require considerable reappraisal.'[53] It is not clear whether she argues that the content of military necessity ought to be changed (reappraised) or whether the relative weight attached to necessity ought to be subject to reappraisal. Watkin replies by referring to both layers subsequently, first the issue of the content of military necessity: 'it is unlikely that the nature of warfare, and with it the application of military necessity, can be easily altered'.[54]

He then continues by referring to a 'strategic approach' to the attachment of relative weight to military necessity: 'Ultimately, the answer to this dilemma may be found in identifying the limits that a broader cumulative strategic approach would require if it is to support an acceptable weighing of humanitarian goals and military necessity.'[55]

As seen and as will be shown, there are different views both on the actual performance of the balance between military necessity and humanitarian considerations as well as on the material content of necessity – and whether this content is subject to change. When weighing military necessity on a scale against humanitarian considerations, it is not only the obvious problem of comparing the incomparable, it is also the inherent problem of relativity.[56] The problem of relativity points at the scope of military necessity: the question of 'necessary for what' reappears (see Chapter 2). In the proportionality assessment, the 'necessary for what' question links to the notion of military advantage – which may be approached by the following quote: 'The meaning to be given to this term introduces fundamental questions regarding the goals of armed conflict, how campaigns are waged and the impact of the levels of warfare on "proportionality".'[57]

52 Warden, *The Air Campaign*, at page 10.
53 Gardam, 'Proportionality and force in international law', at page 409.
54 Watkin, 'Assessing proportionality', at page 121.
55 Ibid.
56 This problem is for example pointed out in the OTP Report, at para. 49.
57 Watkin, 'Assessing proportionality', at page 17.

Before turning to another conception of proportionality under the LOAC, and eventually the notion of the military advantage, we shall move to the other, incomparable, side of the scale and address the content of incidental damage to civilian persons or objects – the collateral damage.

13.2.3 *The 'Humanitarian Side' of the Scale: Collateral Damage*

The expression 'collateral damage' does not appear in the treaty text itself, but it is often understood as encapsulating incidental 'loss of civilian life, injury to civilians and damage to civilian objects', as specified in the treaty rule on proportionality.[58] Although the two (loss of life or injury to persons on the one hand and damage to objects on the other) are merged into one in the coinage 'collateral damage', this does not necessarily mean that they count equally under the proportionality assessment,[59] which is subject to separate discussion in Chapter 15.[60] 'Collateral damage' refers to damage or loss of life or injury which is *incidental*. This incidental damage may be caused both during transit and because of the attack itself. Damage caused during transit may happen for example in the conduct of cyber attacks launched via satellites or civilian communication cables,[61] or in the conduct of missile attacks while the missile is in its midcourse phase on its way to its target. This means that damage which is inflected intentionally upon civilians/civilian objects is unlawful per se (as a violation of the principle of distinction) and not considered collateral damage. Moreover, intentional damage inflected directly upon civilians will never meet a proportionality assessment. Incidental damage is the unintentional side effect of an attack directed against an otherwise lawful target. Civilians directly participating in hostilities are lawful targets (see Chapter 11), and will therefore never constitute collateral damage.[62] By treaty wording, collateral damage comprises only civilians and civilian objects and not military medical personnel or combatants even when the latter are protected against direct attack as *hors de combat*.[63] The ICRC (and others) have, however, argued that this distinction is now obsolete, and that medical personnel,

58 AP I article 51(5)(b). I here use the notion of collateral damage as laid down in the AMW Manual, rule 1(l), at page 33 in the Commentary.

59 See Arai-Takahashi, 'Excessive collateral civilian casualties and military necessity', at page 327.

60 See as well the US DoD Manual, at paras. 5.12.1.1 and 5.12.3.3, at page 261.

61 Tallinn Manual, Commentary 3 to rule 113.

62 AMW Manual, rule 1(l), page 33 in the Commentary.

63 See Henderson, *The Contemporary Law of Targeting*, at page 206. See also the US DoD Manual, at paras, 5.10.1 and 5.10.1.2, pages 241–2, where it is stated that although the protection does not extend to military personnel and objects, feasible precautions should be taken.

wounded and sick combatants and POWs also enjoy protection as collateral damage.[64] The issue remains unresolved. Most States do, however, take these categories into account in the collateral damage estimates.

The expression 'may be expected to cause', which accompanies the notion of collateral damage, clearly establishes that the proportionality rule is an obligation which relates to foresight and not hindsight.[65] The position of the AMW Manual in this regard is that 'harm to civilians and civilian objects that the attacker did not expect is not collateral damage included in proportionality calculations'.[66] Collateral damage may be seen as 'caused' by the attack if the outcome was expected to occur in the attack in the ordinary course of events.[67] Even collateral damage which is expected – and included in the proportionality calculations – can be lawful;[68] it is only when the collateral damage is *excessive* in relation to the concrete and direct military advantage anticipated that the attack becomes unlawful. Civilians being incorporated into a military objective, such as in a munitions factory, remain civilians and thus count as collateral damage – but whether the relative weight of collateral damage in these situations are to count less than civilians who are 'completely innocent', has been raised as a question and is dealt with in Chapter 15.[69]

Collateral damage amounts to physical injury or loss of life, not inconveniences for the civilian population as a result of the hostilities, such as loss of economic income[70] or reduced access to different sorts of food.[71] *Lack* of food can arguably be considered an 'injury',[72] and starvation as a method of warfare is specifically prohibited. Stress or fear from ongoing hostilities do not amount to collateral damage, but attacks whose primary purpose is to spread fear are prohibited as terror attacks (see Chapter 12).

It can be difficult to assess whether damage or injury that is remote or indirect from the actual attack should count as collateral damage. Two considerations lie at hand in this regard: whether the damage could reasonably have been expected (see below, on foresight) and/or whether the damage was

64 See GC I Commentary, at para. 1357.
65 UK Manual, at page 86; AMW Manual, Commentary 5 to rule 14, at page 91.
66 AMW Manual, Commentary 4 to rule 1(l), at page 33.
67 The same point of departure is taken in criminal law, see Chapter 5. See also Gillard, 'Proportionality in the conduct of hostilities', at page 14.
68 Dinstein, 'The principle of proportionality', at page 77.
69 Oeter 'Methods and means of combat', at para. 446, page 176; and Parks, 'Air war and the law of war', at page 164. See as well the US DoD Manual, at para. 5.10.2.1.
70 US DoD Manual, para. 5.12.1.2, at page 261.
71 Ibid.
72 Norwegian Manual, at page 34.

too remote to actually be considered as *caused* by the attack. In practice the two questions would probably merge into one consideration of which damage that could be reasonable to expect.[73] The issue of remote or indirect damage appears to be unsettled by the law,[74] although some States take a rather clear position. The US position is that: 'Remote harms that could result from the attack do not need to be considered in applying this prohibition.'[75]

This position is problematic. If one leaves out 'remote harms' from the equation, the real balancing between military necessity and humanitarian concerns under the proportionality rule easily becomes moot. The massive attacks on the Iraqi electrical power systems during the first Gulf War (1991) may serve as an example. The effects of Allied bombing on Iraqi electricity power supplies were substantial,[76] but so were the side effects. Human Rights Watch argues in its report that: 'Predictably, the effects of this massive destruction on Iraq's water supply, sewage-treatment system, agricultural production and food distribution systems, and public-health system were severe and continue to be felt.'[77] Among the side effects, from shortage of clean water supply to lack of energy to the hospitals, the reports were devastating.[78]

The question remains: are (any of) these reported harmful effects too remote to be considered collateral damage? Some argue, although regrettably, that there appears to be a gap to be filled.[79] Others again argue that the Gulf experience calls for refining the definition of collateral damage to 'require a more detailed examination of the potential reverberating effects of aerial attacks'.[80]

Obviously, the task of predicting harms is a difficult one, and it is not truly a *military* task. The assessment may depend on technical calculations etc. Yet,

73 Both considerations are mentioned in the Report from the Expert meeting on Targeting Military Objectives, at page 15. See also below, in the more recent position taken by the ICRC.

74 AMW Manual, Commentary 4 to rule 14, at page 91. See also the discussion reflected in the report from the Report from the Expert meeting on Targeting Military Objectives, at page 15 as well as Gillard, 'Proportionality in the conduct of hostilities', at page 18.

75 US DoD Manual, para. 5.12.1.3, at page 261.

76 Human Rights Watch, Needless Deaths in the Gulf War, reports that the energy production was down to 3–4% of its original level immediately after the war, and still at only 23% of its original level at the time of the Report (1991), see pages 171–2.

77 Ibid., at page 177.

78 Ibid., at page 183.

79 Hampson, 'Necessity and proportionality in the Gulf conflict', at page 51; and Kalshoven, 'Remarks', at page 45.

80 Crawford, 'The law of noncombatant immunity and the targeting of national electrical power systems', at page 111.

it is a task for the reasonable military commander. The ICRC has taken the position that reverberating effects which are foreseeable by the reasonable commander should count in the proportionality assessment.[81] A similar position is taken in recent reports and the Tallinn Manual, where it is argued that collateral damage includes 'any indirect effects that should be expected by those individuals planning, approving or executing a cyber attack'.[82] Beyond cyber attacks, this position is of particular relevance with regard to the use of explosive weapons in densely populated areas, nuclear weapons and the natural environment.[83] In fact, the task of including foreseeable (expectable) reverberating effects in the proportionality assessment may prove to be among the current significant challenges for commanders today. While collateral damage estimates are usually performed by armed forces, these estimates are, apparently, rarely incorporated a standard for evaluating reverberating effects.[84]

13.3 PROPORTIONALITY AS A 'SILENT CONDITION' OF NECESSITY

13.3.1 *What Is a 'Silent' Condition of Necessity?*

As introduced above, the concept of proportionality is discussed in two normative structures in the present book. In the present section, I discuss proportionality as a 'silent' or 'implied' condition of necessity.[85]

As a commentary to the basic rule of limitation in AP I article 35(1), Bothe, Solf and Partsch comment that:

> The second layer of limitation are those inherent in the complementary principles of necessity and humanity which underlie the law governing the conduct of hostilities. The principle of necessity justifies those measures of military violence, and only those measures, not *forbidden by international law* which are relevant and proportionate to securing the prompt submission of the enemy with the least possible expenditure of economic or human resources.[86]

81 International humanitarian law and the challenges of contemporary armed conflicts, Report by the International Committee of the Red Cross (Geneva, October 2015, 32IC/15/11), (ICRC 2015 Report) at page 52.

82 Tallinn Manual, Commentary 6 to rule 113. Gillard 'Proportionality in the conduct of hostilities', at pages 18–20.

83 ICRC 2015 Report, at pages 41, 52, 53 and 58.

84 See ibid., at page 53, where 'significant doubt' is raised with regard to practice.

85 The terminology of 'silent' is collected from Higgins, *Problems and Process*, at pages 252–3.

86 Bothe, Partsch and Solf, *New Rules*, page 224. Emphasis in original.

The conception of necessary measures as comprising those that are 'relevant and proportionate' is repeated by the same authors also with regard to articles 51 and 52,[87] and as well by other authors.[88]

In this view, proportionality is added to the (strictly) causal relationship which necessity inevitably entails. As accounted for in Chapter 2, the notion of necessity entails a question of 'necessary for what', which again is a circumscription of the military question of (necessary) 'means to ends'. This question addresses the relativity of 'necessary'. Necessary means are understood *relative* to the ends sought. For example: in order to weaken the enemy forces it may be considered necessary to direct attacks against enemy soldiers and enemy military materiel. Bombs are often considered necessary, in the meaning 'relevant' or 'suited', to destroy military materiel. So far I agree that necessity entails a requirement of 'relevance'. The question is whether 'necessary' also implies a requirement that bombs shall be suited to destroy, *but not more*. This is what would be the implication of implying that necessary also means proportionate. For example: by arguing that necessary also means proportionate, one could argue that a 200 pound bomb is suitable to destroy a military tank, but since a military tank would be destroyed also by a 100 pound bomb, a 200 pound bomb is unnecessary and unlawful. In simple terms: does the conception of necessity under the LOAC imply a duty 'not to shoot a bird with a cannon'? This seems to be the position in the Commentary of the ICRC:

> In order to comply with the conditions, the attack must be directed against a military objective with means which are not disproportionate in relation to the objective, but are suited to destroying only that objective, and the effects of the attacks must be limited in the way required by the Protocol; 'moreover', even after those conditions are fulfilled, the incidental civilian losses and damages must not be excessive.[89]

87 See ibid., at page 350 commenting on article 51(5)(b). See as well page 362 where the authors comments on article 52 where this provision is linked back to the rule in 1907 Hague Convention, article 23(g), characterised to be 'an application of the principle that destruction which is not necessary (relevant and proportionate) to the attainment of a military advantage is prohibited'.

88 See Higgins, *Problems and Process*, at pages 232–3, where she argues that military necessity justifies those measures that are 'relevant and proportionate to securing the prompt submission of the enemy with the least expenditure of economic or human resources'. See also Gardam, 'Proportionality and force in international law', at page 406. Another, recent, example – of proportionality as an element of necessity – is suggested by Bashi, in 'Military necessity and humanitarian assistance', with regard to security measures under the law of occupation, at page 155.

89 AP I Commentary, at para. 1979, pages 625–6.

There are certainly good reasons not to shoot birds with a cannon and, more often than not, military tactics would favour such solutions. However, this does not appear to be a legal duty, and has been specifically contested for example in the US DoD Manual, where it is stated in the context of military necessity that 'the law of war may justify the use of overwhelming force against enemy military objectives'.[90] Yet, the notion of 'proportionality' re-emerges in States' military manuals (also elsewhere in the US DoD Manual), among scholars and in judgments by international tribunals. The following sub-sections give an account of the views.

13.3.2 *From 'Indispensable' to 'Relevant and Proportionate'*

In Chapter 1 (see Section 1.6.3), I introduced the possible challenge attached to the general rule of interpretation under international law: that terms are to be interpreted in accordance with their 'ordinary meaning'. The attribution of a silent requirement of proportionality into the concept of necessity appears to be an interpretative result that might be intuitive rather than illustrative of the law today.

The phrase 'relevant and proportionate', as used by Bothe and Solf, stems from an interpretation of the earlier American definition of military necessity.[91] In a footnote in the Commentary it is stated that: '"Relevant and proportionate" is used in this Commentary in preference to "indispensable" which is frequently used in definitions of the principle of military necessity',[92] and stems from the formulations in the Lieber Code where military necessity is defined as '. . . those measures which are indispensable for securing the ends of the war . . .'[93]

In the US Field Manual from 1956 it is stated that:

> Particularly in the circumstances referred to in the preceding paragraph, loss of life and damage to property must not be out of proportion to the military advantage to be gained. Once a fort or defended locality has surrendered,

[90] US DoD Manual, para. 2.2.3.1, at page 57.

[91] The 'American view' has in particular been fronted by O'Brien, in 'The meaning of "military necessity" in international law', and *The Conduct of Just and Limited War*, at page 40. He finalises his views in a definition of 'legitimate military necessity' in *The Conduct of Just and Limited War*, at page 66, where he presents the following, rather extensive, definition of military necessity: 'Legitimate military necessity consists in all measures immediately indispensable and proportionate to a legitimate military end, provided that they are not prohibited by the laws of war or the natural law, when taken on the decision of a responsible commander, subject to review.'

[92] Bothe, Partsch and Solf, *New Rules*, page 224, footnote 7.

[93] Lieber Code, article 15.

> only such further damage is permitted as is demanded by the exigencies of war, such as the removal of fortifications, demolition of military buildings, and destruction of stores (*GC, art.147*; par. 502 herein).[94]

Then, in the DoD Law of War Manual from 2015 (as amended in 2016), a similar requirement of proportionality appears with regard to the notion of military advantage: 'There must be a good faith expectation that the attack will make a *relevant and proportional* contribution to the goal of the military attack involved.'[95] In the UK Manual the reference is to force necessary to achieve the 'complete or partial submission of the enemy',[96] but it is also added that 'It is generally accepted that the use of force must be *proportionate to its overall objective*.'[97] The Canadian Manual upholds a limitation between ends and means which may resemble that of a proportionality requirement: that the concept of military necessity presupposes 'that the amount of force used is *limited to* what is needed to achieve prompt submission'.[98] The Norwegian Manual does not recite a requirement of proportionality as an element of military necessity, but states that the 'principle of military necessity gives the armed forces permission to use that amount of force necessary to achieve military goals'.[99] In another context, however, the Norwegian MoD has stated that: 'The proportionality requirement means that more force than necessary cannot be used in order to achieve the military aim of the operation.'[100] A similar approach appears to have been chosen in the Danish Manual where it is stated that military necessity implies a 'requirement' that a party to the conflict is 'only permitted to use that amount of force which is necessary to achieve the legitimate goal of the of the conflict' and that this means to enforce the complete or partial submission of the enemy with 'the least possible loss of human life and resources'.[101] None of the Manuals provide accompanying examples of the actual scope of this silent condition of proportionality. In fact, some appear contradictory to statements elsewhere, such as in the US DoD Manual, where 'overwhelming force' is explicitly included as permissible, while the generic reference to proportionality is included elsewhere (see above). The overall impression is that the coinage 'relevant and

94 FM 27-10, appendix A-12, rule 41.

95 US DoD Manual, para. 5.12.2, at page 262. Emphasis added.

96 UK Manual, at page 22.

97 Ibid., at page 26. Emphasis added.

98 Canadian Manual, at page 2-1. Emphasis added.

99 Norwegian Manual, at page 13. My translation from Norwegian.

100 Letter to the Chief of Defence regarding the use of Cyber Warfare in the armed forces (Norwegian Ministry of Defence, 3 September 2012). My translation.

101 Danish Manual, at pages 109–10. My translation from Danish.

proportionate' appears to have been borne within the fold of the American definition of military necessity, and simply restated since. *If* proportionality is included into the concept of necessity as a silent condition, this implies that necessity contains also a restraint, a limitation upon the use of force (contrary to what I have argued in Chapter 6). However, in the following I argue that this is not the case and that the correct reflection of the law is that resort to necessity is limited, but not *a* limitation. First, I present some consequences of a position where proportionality is a silent condition of military necessity.

13.3.3 *A Silent Condition As an Additional Restraint?*

What does it imply when the manuals – and literature – state that military necessity permits the use of force which is 'a proportional contribution' (US DoD Manual) or 'proportional to its overall objective' (UK Manual)? One part of this question addresses the topic of means to ends and must be seen as a question of causal strength, which is dealt with in general in Chapter 2, but the other part (relevant for the present section) can be formulated as follows: does the approach of permissive necessity and prohibitive rules imply an independent consideration of necessity in each and every attack? In other words, can attacks which are directed at otherwise lawful targets be unlawful if considered *unnecessary*? If this is the case, will military necessity not only provide a fundamental permission, but also impose an additional restraint? The view presented in the manuals above can be interpreted in that direction. The practice of the ICTY may also be of some guidance on the issue.

In the Blaskic Case the ICTY Trial Chamber concluded that: 'Generally speaking, the three attacks described above targeted the Muslim civilian population and were not designed as a response to a military aggression. At the very least, even if there had been such aggression, the assets and the method used could not be deemed proportionate to it.'[102] And then the tribunal continues:

> Consequently, it was impossible to ascertain any strategic or military reasons for the 16 April 1993 attack on Vitez and Stari Vitez. In the event that there had been, the devastation visited upon the town was out of all proportion with military necessity. On the contrary, the attack was designed to implement an expulsion plan, if necessary by killing Muslim civilians and destroying their possessions.[103]

102 Blaskic Case, Trial Chamber Judgment, at para. 507.
103 Blaskic Case, para. 510.

In the Appeals Chamber however, this view was rebutted:

> As has been found in relation to the attack of 16 April 1993 on the town of Vitez, the nature of the attack of 18 July 1993 cannot be categorically defined as that of a criminal act, *in that there was still the presence of a considerable number of ABiH soldiers in Stari Vitez at that time*. The operation itself may have been a wilful one lacking sound military judgement, but that wilful aspect of the attack does not make it a crime in terms of the Statute.[104]

Although the decision was altered by the Appeals Chamber, the reference to proportionality as a requirement under military necessity does not appear to be a part of the Appeals Chamber's rebuttal. The rebuttal seems rather to be directed at the concrete judgment of military necessity – which, according to the Appeals Chamber, *was* present. In a less clear-cut way, but yet possible to misread, is the statement made by the Trial Chamber in the Kordic Case that: 'In short, prohibited attacks are those launched deliberately against civilians or civilian objects in the course of an armed conflict and are not justified by military necessity.'[105] The possible source of confusion is the word 'and' – as if the attack must both be directed at a lawful target *and* be militarily necessary. Instead, military necessity is already included in the definition of lawful targets.

For this reason (of possible confusion) the UK manual has been criticised.[106] The criticism is based on the dismissal of the *Kriegsraison* doctrine (see Chapter 6) and construed as follows: when States (and scholars) argue that military necessity only may be invoked as an exception when explicitly provided for in the treaty, they must also (for the sake of consistency) argue that military necessity never is an additional restraint apart from when specifically mentioned by treaty (or customary) rule.[107] Surely, it can be perceived as disharmonious if necessity in one circumstance is applied only when explicitly accounted for, and in another is dealt with as an omnipresent restraint.

States' military manuals' insertion of military necessity as an (seemingly) additional restraint appears to rest on pragmatic reasons. States' manuals seem

104 Blaskic Case, Appeals Chamber Judgment, para. 463. Emphasis added. With regard to the last passage of the quotation, the judgment is also commented upon in Chapter 4 on the military margin of appreciation.

105 ICTY, Kordic Case, Trial Chamber Judgment, at para. 328.

106 Hayashi, 'Requirements of military necessity in international humanitarian law and international criminal law', at page 49. He uses the phrase 'quite mysterious'. His position is upheld in Hayashi, 'Basic principles', at page 92.

107 Hayashi, 'Requirements of military necessity in international humanitarian law and international criminal law', at page 49.

to address the definition of necessity in a meta-legal approach, rather than as a concrete rule. These introductory statements on military necessity should rather be perceived as a description of the function of military necessity *in other rules* than as a basic rule to be applied independently in every case. The manuals should, in other words, be read cautiously – and as such not necessarily inducing an additional restraint. Furthermore, the prohibition of wanton acts of war should not be confused with proportionality, as sometimes done in earlier literature. O'Brien offers an example of 'obvious' disproportionate behaviour, where: 'troops run through streets of a town, shooting, looting and burning, simply because a small bomb has derailed their train and injured one man slightly, there is clearly a lack of proportionality between the legitimate military objective of punishing those responsible for the act and discouraging repetitions, and the means employed to accomplish this.'[108]

O'Brien also offers the negative version of the alleged requirement of proportionality: 'All acts which are not immediately indispensable for and proportionate to a legitimate military end are forbidden.'[109] The primary problem with this statement is the effect it may provide when taken out of context. O'Brien's book (which is much cited[110]) was written before the adoption of the AP I and the treaty (and corresponding customary) definitions of lawful targets as well as the proportionality rule. His statement cannot be applied 'on top of' modern treaty (and customary) definitions of lawful attacks. The room for invoking military necessity *as such* is narrowed down in the post-AP I era (see Section 14.3.6 below). The answer to the question posed in the heading of this sub-section is therefore that if the requirement of a silent condition of military necessity is taken literally after the adoption of the AP I, it implies a 'double (additional) requirement' for lawfulness, which in turn is not consonant with the LOAC.

13.3.4 *As a Critique of the 'Morale Bombings'*

In fact, it seems that one of the main reasons for some scholars introducing a requirement of proportionality under the concept of necessity is that of being able (in the absence of the 'true' principle of proportionality protecting against

108 O'Brien, 'The meaning of "military necessity" in international law', at pages 148–9, where he also argues that: 'Proportionality of acts of war must, therefore, be determined upon the relation to the means employed and a legitimate military end.'

109 Ibid., at page 149.

110 See as well Ragone, 'The applicability of military necessity in the nuclear age', at page 707, supporting the position of O'Brien, and McDougal and Feliciano, *Law and Minimum World Order*, at page 525.

excessive collateral damage which is an element of law today) to duly criticise the strategic bombings during WWII (as well as Korea and Vietnam).[111] As seen above (Chapter 12), the Allied objectives during WWII included a desire to 'destroy the morale of the civilian population so that the will to continue the war would be eroded'.[112] O'Brien argues: 'Finally, it is clear that fire-storm bombing of German and Japanese cities was counter-value warfare, tending to be *disproportionate* per se in terms of normal military necessity.'[113] On the other hand, he argues that the atomic bombings of Hiroshima and Nagasaki were arguably lawful, as they 'did foreseeably and in fact end the war quickly'.[114]

The weight of such arguments ought to be toned down today for two reasons: first because they seem to lack foundation in *lex lata*, both then and now, and second because the *moral argument* which obviously lies behind the arguments in the post-WWII discourse is now protected in the AP I and the principle of proportionality (as well as the prohibition of indiscriminate attacks) as enshrined there. Adding a separate proportionality requirement under the concept of necessity is a disadvantage for clarity.

111 O'Brien, *The Conduct of Just and Limited War*, at page 79.
112 This quotation is taken from O'Brien ibid., at page 80.
113 Ibid., at page 83. Emphasis added.
114 Ibid., at page 86.

14

Military Necessity and the Scope and Nature of Military Advantage

14.1 PRELIMINARY REMARKS: THE ELEMENTS AND SCOPE OF MILITARY ADVANTAGE

The current and the next chapter (in parts) are devoted to the concept and assessment of military advantage, which by wording is a wide concept.[1] As we shall see, 'military advantage' allows for large subjective considerations,[2] but the adjectives 'concrete and direct' as well as the relation to the 'attack as a whole' under the circumstances ruling at the time, embody limitations upon the military commander's assessment of the advantage.

The expression 'military advantage' today appears in AP I articles 51(5)(b), 52(2), 57(2)(a) and(b) and 57(3). The notion of military advantage 'captures military necessity'[3] and constitutes a defining element in the definition of military objectives and one of two comparative elements in the proportionality balance, as well as being mirrored in the duty to take precautions in attack. The expression is also explicitly integrated in the war crimes definition of launching a disproportionate attack.[4] Treaty law contains no definition of the term, and it is certainly not easier to apply than 'military necessity'.[5] Beyond the adjectives 'definite' and 'concrete and direct',[6] treaty law does not contain any guidance as to what military advantages comprise.

A definition is offered by the *Air and Missile Warfare Manual*: '"Military advantage" means those benefits of a military nature that result from an attack ...'[7] Questions immediately arise. What are those benefits, or

[1] Dinstein, *Conduct of Hostilities*, at page 106.
[2] US DoD Manual, para. 12.3.2, at page 244.
[3] See Bill, 'The Rendulic "Rule"', at page 132.
[4] See Rome Statute, article 8(2)(b)(iv), also dealt with in Chapter 5.
[5] See Bill, 'The Rendulic "Rule"', at page 132.
[6] In AP I articles 52(2) and 51(5)(b). See as well the use of the adjective 'overall' in these provisions.
[7] AMW Manual, rule (1)(w), first sentence at page 44 in Commentary.

advantages, which are military, as opposed to another nature? Does advantage include the opponent's disadvantage? Is an advantage the same as necessity, and if not, where does the distinction go? How much value does one advantage carry as opposed to another advantage and, finally, as opposed to collateral damage?[8] Throughout this chapter, as well as in the next, I seek to address these questions. In the next sections I first address the relationship between military advantage and military necessity, before turning to the relative scope of military advantage. Thereafter I deal with the question of the nature of military advantage as opposed to other advantages as well as the security of the attacking force. Questions of doubt and uncertainty (when is the advantage 'anticipated'?) are dealt with partly in Chapter 4 and partly in Chapter 15.

Before turning to the historic backdrop, I shall introduce one feature of military advantage: its relative nature. Relativity connects to the questions asked above and easily touches upon the very essence of military advantage. I see at least two relative dimensions: first, what does military advantage relate to in light of the overall purpose of war, and second, how much weight does any military advantage carry related to collateral damage? The first relative dimension contains a range of sub-questions, among these the scope of the notion of 'concrete and direct' and the reference to the 'circumstances ruling at the time'. The second dimension is dealt with in Chapter 15, as a part of the assessment of military advantage.

14.2 THE RECENT TREATY ORIGIN OF MILITARY ADVANTAGE

The expression 'military advantage' appears for the first time in a treaty draft definition of military objectives, in article 24 of the Hague Rules of 1924 on air warfare, together with the adjective 'obvious'. As an element of a proposed rule on proportionality, 'military advantage' appears in article 8(b) in the ICRC Draft Rules of 1956. The term is subsequently referred to, without being defined, throughout the documentation of the treaty negotiations leading up to the ratification of the AP I. The ICRC Report from 1969 refers for example to the great suffering caused by the indiscriminate bombing during WWII – 'without even producing decisive military advantages', and recognises the need to regulate more closely the distinction between the civilian population and military objectives and as well the effects of indirect attacks against the

8 One may also raise the question of 'whose advantage?' in the context of coalition warfare, as done by Roscini in 'Targeting and contemporary aerial bombardment', at page 423.

civilian population.[9] The ICRC draft article 46(3) then referred to the 'substantial military advantage anticipated'.

Two impressions are worth pointing out from the negotiating documentation: first, that the meaning of the term 'military advantage' seems to have been presumed to be known, although vague,[10] and second, that there seems to have been no expressed identification of necessity and advantage. On the contrary, the potential wide and vague scope of the proportionality rule seemed to be a repeated source for opposition: "The rule of proportionality as expressed in the ICRC text would give military commanders the practically unlimited right to decide to launch an attack if they considered that there would be a military advantage."[11] It was suggested either to be deleted,[12] or to be amended in 'an improved form which would give even more protection' from area bombardment.[13] One reference to military necessity can be found in the remarks by the Norwegian delegate, and then as a reason for a more narrowly formulated rule:

> . . . the concept of military necessity had lost much of its meaning in many modern conflicts, where one side was often technologically superior to the other and where at least one of the sides was often fighting not for survival but for some other reason. It would therefore be neither unrealistic nor impossible to lay down very strict criteria providing the greatest possible protection for the civilian protection.[14]

And in this regard that the principle of proportionality 'needed more substantial amendment' and should be 'more restrictive'.[15] In support of the restrictive view, some even emphasised that 'the aim should be to put an end to the attacks which brought suffering to the civilian population, except perhaps when a party had *no other alternative* in the prevailing circumstance'.[16] The

9 XXI International Conference of the Red Cross, 'Reaffirmation and Development of the Laws and Customs Applicable in Armed Conflict', Report submitted by the ICRC, Geneva (1969) (ICRC Istanbul Report), at page 65.

10 Official Records of the Diplomatic Conference Volume XIV, CDDH/III/SR.8, page 69, remarks by the Hungarian delegate.

11 Ibid., Volume XIV, CDDH/III/SR.8, page 61, remarks by the Polish delegate.

12 Ibid., page 61, remarks by Uganda and page 62, remarks by Mauritania. The latter suggesting that 'the principle of proportionality should be replaced by more objective terms'. The same view was taken by Czechoslovakia and Indonesia, referred to at page 69, and by Albania, referred to at page 70.

13 Ibid., at page 60, remarks by the Swedish delegate. Supported by Iran, see page 64.

14 Ibid., at page 59, remarks by the Norwegian delegate.

15 Ibid., at page 59, remarks by the Norwegian delegate.

16 Ibid., at page 68, remarks by the Indian delegate. Emphasis added.

suggestion seems to refer to situations of necessity, where there is no other practical alternative.

Other State representatives saw the wide and flexible scope as the only way to cope with the realities of war, such as the UK statement: 'The Committee must not put forward formulations which could not in practice be followed. To do away with the rule of proportionality would remove a valuable humanitarian protection from the civilian population and a rule of law which could be followed by combatants.'[17]By the Finnish delegate it was argued that the rule 'struck a reasonable balance between the protection of the civilian population and military interests'.[18]

Both the critical views, as well as those in favour of the proportionality rule, thus shared the conception of a wide and flexible rule, which certainly left a range of alternatives open for the military commanders. Opinions collided, however, on the need for such flexibility – over whether considerations of necessity could justify such a potentially wide rule. From the outset then, military necessity appeared in a 'foundational' function and not in its exceptive form. References to the two concepts (of necessity and advantage) in a more symbiotic relationship are, however, also found: the term 'military advantage' has been described as an 'indirect definition'[19] of military necessity, the first since the definition in the Lieber Code. As the relationship between the distinct form of exceptional military necessity and the foundational function of military necessity remains unclear, I shall proceed with examining the relationship between the two.

14.3 THE DISTINCTION BETWEEN MILITARY ADVANTAGE AND MILITARY NECESSITY

In Chapter 2, I introduced two faces (or functions) of military necessity: as a foundational principle and as a specific exception. I also argued that the proportionality rule illustrates the foundational function of military necessity. The proportionality rule contains no specific reference to the expression 'military necessity', but has been viewed as the ultimate test for balancing military necessities against humanitarian considerations. So, what is the relation between the 'foundational' face of military necessity expressed as military

[17] Ibid., at page 64, remarks by the UK delegate. See as well page 62, remarks by the Australian delegate: 'Since area bombardment was unlikely to be abandoned, there should be a distinct code related to it.' See also the French remarks in favour of the rule, at page 65 and the US remark at page 67, arguing that the 'rule of proportionality was as far as the law could go'.

[18] Ibid., at page 66, remarks by the Finnish delegate.

[19] Best, 'Restraint in war', at page 15.

advantage and the explicit incorporations of (exceptional) military necessity in treaty law? First, there are linguistic differences. Second, there is a different matter of subjectivity. Third, there is a conception of military advantage as 'less severe'. Fourth, there are differences regarding the relation between means and ends. I shall address the relationship divided into these four aspects in the following.

14.3.1 *The Linguistic Differences between 'Necessity' and 'Advantage'*

An advantage, by the very meaning of the word,[20] indicates a 'condition or circumstance that puts one in a favourable position'.[21] Whereas necessity refers to 'the state or fact of being required or unavoidable' or 'a situation enforcing a certain course of action', and furthermore, necessary measures are those which 'need to be done'.[22]

The linguistic conception of the differences between necessity and advantage can be retrieved for example in the Manstein trial,[23] after WWII, where the Judge Advocate pointed out that: 'Now first and obvious comment on the wording of this article is that the requirement is "necessity" and not "advantage".'[24] In the same vein, the US Military Tribunal at Nuremberg stated in the Hostage Case that military necessity must not be confused with 'convenience and strategical interests'.[25] These views support that 'military advantage' is somewhat less severe than 'military necessity'. The question is how much less severe? And eventually, to whom? Both these two questions are revisited in the following sub-sections.

Furthermore, the military advantage is substantive, the end or goal to achieve. Military necessity, however, is often spoke of as those measures required *in order to* achieve military success. This ordinary meaning of the different terms seems to have come to an expression for example by the ICTY in the Galic Case: 'However, this principle [of military necessity] requires that destroying a particular military objective will provide some type of advantage in weakening the enemy military forces.'[26]

[20] Vienna Convention on the Law of Treaties, article 31(1).
[21] Soanes and Stevenson, *Concise Oxford English Dictionary*, page 18.
[22] See Chapter 1.
[23] Von Manstein case, at page 509 ff. The Manstein trial is also commented upon in Chapter 2, as an example of case law denying the application of the doctrine of *Kriegsraison*.
[24] Ibid., at page 522.
[25] Hostage Case, at page 63.
[26] Galic Case, at footnote 76 to para. 44. The Galic Case is also dealt with in Chapter 7 on the principle of distinction.

In Chapter 2, I discussed two questions of means to ends: the question of what the ends actually are (necessary for what) and the question of cause and effect. The linguistic distinction between military necessity and military advantage touches upon both questions. A military advantage represents an end, an object to achieve, but is not identical to the 'object of war', which encompasses more than military advantages. From this, the further distinction is difficult to grasp clearly. I start, however, by addressing the subjective notion of military advantage.

14.3.2 *The Subjective Notion of Advantage*

The question introduced above – to whom the military advantage relates – addresses the subjective notion[27] of advantage. Being a circumstance that puts one in a favourable position, the position is a subjective issue of assessment.[28] On the other hand, the question of whether a measure was necessary or not in order to reach a certain end is a matter of (ontological) objective fact. Let us consider the following example: for Commander X it was advantageous to position his reconnaissance and Special Forces teams in the south end of valley A and await reinforcement before advancing north. If his military objective (eventually) was to hold the territory of hillside B above valley A, it may be necessary, in order to acquire the advantage of terrain, to destroy a bridge located in the mountain pass at the south end of the valley. An attack against a passing, single enemy vehicle may, on the other hand, prove advantageous, but not necessary in order to reach the desired objective. Yet, the attack on the vehicle is clearly lawful. Furthermore, an attack on the vehicle may certainly amount to a necessity, if circumstances change and the enemy is about to spot the Special Forces team and call for air support.

The advantage of acquired territory is a subjective, yet undisputable, decision. Considering topography, it is objectively necessary to control access through a mountain pass, in order to reach the desired advantage. Whether it will produce an advantage or not to attack the enemy forces passing through the valley appears to be a circumstantial question depending, among others, on the subjective perception of risk.

27 As already presented at the outset, under Section 14.1, see the US DoD Manual, at page 244.

28 Schmitt, 'Asymmetrical warfare and international humanitarian law', at page 28: 'Ultimately, no objective means of valuing either incidental injury/collateral damage or military advantage exists. Instead, it is the subjective perspective of the party carrying out the proportionality assessment that matters.' Part of the passage is also quoted above, in Section 4.3.2.

The subjective notion does not, however, only encompass the 'to whom' aspect, it also relates to the *discretion* inherent in the concept of advantage. Just as military *advantage* appeared presumptively known (but undefined, as accounted for above) and distinct from necessity, the *subjectivity* of advantage appeared to be a common perception, both prior to[29] and during the Diplomatic Conference resulting in the AP I. This subjective aspect nurtured opposing views and scepticism on the proportionality rule.[30] While some State representatives seemed to juxtapose the subjective assessment of military advantage with arbitrariness,[31] others argued that flexibility was the only practical solution.[32] A subjective assessment might be liable for abuse or it might be the only realistic solution – or it might be both. Exactly how flexible and subjective the notion of advantage is in comparison to necessity remains to be clarified. At the outset though, it is clear that subjective discretion does not apply beyond the threshold of that of a 'reasonable commander'. This issue is dealt with in more detail in Chapters 4 and 15.

14.3.3 *The Notion of 'Less Severe'*

The answer to the question raised above, how much less severe military advantage is than military necessity, is far from a matter of exact science. The notion of 'less severe' is particularly vague because military advantage expresses foundational considerations of military necessity.

Treaty law is of little or no further guidance in respect of the severity distinction. Although some refer to 'urgency' as a general requirement of

29 ICRC Istanbul Report, at page 74: 'Moreover, the principle of proportionality is characteristic of a developed law. This idea, like that of "reasonable", proposed by an expert, cannot be dependent on the purely subjective and arbitrary appreciation of an assailant. Whatever difficulties are involved by this idea, which is again to be found in the rule placing limitations on reprisals, it conforms to the development of the law it is desired to introduce in this field. It also implies the existence of closer supervision of the humanitarian rules devolving from it.'

30 From the discussions, see for example as a point of departure: Official Records of the Diplomatic Conference CDDH/III/SR.5, at page 37, the comments of the ICRC delegate with regard to the expressions 'proportionate' and 'disproportionate'.

31 Ibid., CDDH/III/SR.7, at page 56, the opinion of the representative of the German Democratic Republic: 'To permit attacks against the civilian population and civilian objects if such attacks had military advantages was tantamount to making civilian protection dependent on subjective decisions taken by a single person, namely the military commander concerned.' On draft article 46 in general, see further Chapter 13.

32 Ibid., CDDH/777/SR.7, at page 55, the opinion of the representative of Canada: 'An absolute prohibition would result in a very difficult situation, for instance when there was a single civilian near a major military objective whose presence might deter an attack.'

military necessity,[33] this criterion[34] has not been specifically attached to the different appearances of 'military necessity' in the four Geneva Conventions nor the Hague convention on cultural property. On the contrary, 'urgency' appears alongside other forms of aggravation, such as 'imperative' or 'absolute'. The differences between, on the one hand, these different aggravated forms and, on the other hand, between 'simple' and 'aggravated' necessity, are inconclusive.[35]

A couple of examples may illustrate. One (fictive) example is a situation where one party to an armed conflict is severely weakened, estimated as having about 5 per cent of its offensive capacities left. An attack on the remaining 5 per cent of the military materiel may still offer the opposing party an advantage, yet the attack does not appear (severe enough) to be necessary.[36] Nevertheless, this lack of necessity does not make the attack unlawful. Having said this, economy of force or other non-legal considerations may certainly be a reason for not attacking anyhow – but this is a matter left to the appreciation of the military commander.

Another recent example is the NATO practice of bombing Gadhafi's (non-prioritised) massive weapons caches in the desert.[37] The practice took place while returning from sorties over Libya in 2011, during Operation Unified Protector. This practice may illustrate two aspects: first, that Gadhafi's old weapons caches were considered (without doubt), by the participating States, military objectives despite not being in active use, and second – in the prolongation from the first and what is important for the present context – that despite not being devoted the highest priority the attacks were considered a military advantage, not an objective necessity. In this context, the bombing of Gadhafi's stockpiled, massive weapons caches illustrates the presumptive necessity which is in-built in the definition of military objectives.

It is difficult and hardly fruitful to quantify 'severity', beyond examples as the foregoing, and consequently, considering the rather vague relation to the 'broader imperatives of winning the war'.[38]

33 In this direction see for example Downey, 'The law of war and military necessity'; and the AP I Commentary to article 35, both quoted in Chapter 6. The notion of urgency is introduced in Chapter 2.

34 The criteria appear to have been based on case law from the US Military tribunal, particularly in the Hostage Case, at page 69, as well as the British trial against von Manstein.

35 See Chapter 2 for an account of the different guises of military necessity in the Geneva Conventions.

36 On the issue of 'overwhelming force', see the US DoD Manual, cited in Section 13.3 above.

37 With regard to the historical stockpile of ammunition in the Libyan desert and its potential use, see for example Feinstein, 'Where is Gaddafis vast arms stockpile?'

38 US DoD Manual, para. 2.2.3.1, at page 56.

14.3.4 How the Means Relate to the Ends

As stated at the very beginning of this book, the entire enterprise of war is 'only a means to an end'[39] – or, put differently, the exercise of operational art.[40] It is the military commander's role to consider options and different courses of action[41] in order to achieve the desired aims and objectives of the operational plan (OPLAN), to select and determine military advantages.[42] The military advantage is thus always relative to the plan, as well as other circumstances at the time – in addition to always relate to 'for whom' the advantage is a benefit.

Occasionally, the question of how necessary means relate to the military advantages are addressed explicitly in treaty law. In the case of cultural property for example, the Second Protocol from 1999 determines that 'imperative military necessity' can be invoked after a cumulative test where the object is both a military objective and there is no other feasible alternative to obtain a similar military advantage.[43] This rule connects (imperative) military necessity to military advantages as means connects to ends, and requires a specific causal strength by reference to military necessity. This rule is, however, also an example of the fact that a necessity always will amount to a military advantage (although not all advantages amount to necessities). A similar consideration is required regarding dams, dykes and nuclear electrical generating stations. The special protection of these objects ceases only 'if it is used for other than its normal function and in regular, significant and direct support of military operations and if such attack is the only feasible way to terminate such support'.[44] The underlying question for the commander is this: is the attack necessary in order to achieve the advantage, which is to halt the advancement of the enemy forces? As pointed out above, the law does not require the commander to ask this question when attacking, for example, a tank. In addition to illustrate the role of military necessity as link between means and

39 Spaight, *Air Power and War Rights*, at page 2. Also quoted above, in Section 1.1. For a general introduction to 'ends, ways and means', see Chapter 2.

40 Defined for example in NATO, AAP-6, as: 'The employment of forces to attain strategic and/or operational objectives through the design, organization, integration and conduct of strategies, campaigns, major operations and battles.'

41 For a NATO description of the development of different courses of action, see Supreme Headquarters Allied Powers Europe, 'Allied Command Operations Comprehensive Operations Planning Directive (COPD V2.0)', (2013), at pages 4-63–4-77.

42 See for example COPD V2.0, at page 4-67.

43 Second Protocol on Cultural Property, article 6 (a), at page 1040.

44 1954 Hague Convention on Cultural Property, article 11(2); Second Protocol on Cultural Property, articles 6(a) and (b), at page 1040; and AP I article 56(2)a–c. Both issues are dealt with further in Chapter 17.

ends in certain contexts, the two foregoing examples illustrate military necessity where it is particularly severe.

In most other cases, treaty law does not spell out the relation between necessary measures and military advantages. Furthermore, there is no general requirement that the chosen alternative is the only feasible way to achieve the advantage.[45] The AP I article 57(3) clearly shows this in a 'target selection rule': 'When a choice is possible between several military objectives for obtaining a similar military advantage, the objective to be selected shall be that the attack on which may be expected to cause the least danger to civilian lives and to civilian objects.' The scope of the rule as customary LOAC is subject to careful assessment with regard to the interpretation of the notion of 'similar military advantage'.[46] The notion of 'possible choices' incorporates military necessity in a foundational function, and does not require militarily unreasonable choices.[47] For example in the case of denying the enemy access to fuel or power supplies, a similar advantage can (perhaps) be achieved by attacking pump stations as oil refineries.[48] In another case, it may prove to be a necessity to attack the refinery in order to hamper the access of fuel. We may express the relationship between necessity and advantage in this regard as follows: not all measures resulting in military advantages amount to military necessities, but all militarily necessary measures produce military advantages.

Then a final remark with regard to the 'overlap' between military necessity and military advantage – i.e. when necessary measures produce military advantages. This co-existence does not mean that necessity amounts to an additional legal norm, or an extra exception.[49] Although sometimes referred to

45 In an opposite direction, see Hancke, 'The 1923 Hague Rules of Air Warfare', at page 23, where he interprets the concept of military advantage offered in article 24(1) in the1923 Hague Rules: 'This advantage must be clearly apparent, i.e. it must not simply consist of a few minor advantages. Moreover, the destruction of the object in question must represent a conditio sine qua non for military success (advantage), although actual ultimate success is not required. But there must at least be a real possibility of success.'

46 See US DoD Manual, para. 5.11.7, at pages 259–60. The US view is that the customary status of the rule depends on the interpretation, that is, that a customary norm of target selection applies only 'when all other factors are equal'.

47 AMW Manual, Commentary 6 to rule 33, at page 129.

48 This solution was chosen in the 2011 Libya War. See also the AP I Commentary, at page 687, para. 2227, where the examples of railway lines vs railway station is used.

49 This point is also made with regard to the doctrine of *Kriegsraison* in Chapter 6. For a particular discussion of this issue with regard to the sometimes alleged duty to 'capture rather than kill', see Chapter 9. The same point is made, among others, by the ICTY in the Strugar Case, where it is held that: 'the absolute prohibition against attacking civilians "may not be derogated from because of military necessity"'. See: ICTY, Strugar Case, Appeals Chamber Judgment, at para. 275. The Strugar Case is also dealt with in Chapter 4 as well in Chapters 16 and 17.

as a 'two-step approach'[50] where considerations of military necessity occurs in the definitions of military objectives and proportionality, these 'two steps' do not imply a second legal requirement (see Section 13.3), it is simply a reference to the foundational function of military necessity in the two rules.

14.3.5 *Advantage and Necessity As Opposed to Wanton Acts of War*

Not every military advantage amounts to a necessity. Despite this, military advantage is an expression of military necessity in a foundational function and is as such the very opposite of 'wanton acts of war' as prohibited in article 23(g) of the 1907 Hague Regulations.[51]

Furthermore, when it comes to destruction of property when military necessity requires it, this rule has a broader scope than attacks, but a higher threshold to permitting destruction of civilian property. It therefore appears as a shortcut when the ICTY treats the definition of military objectives as an *equation* of military necessity, as defined in the crime of destruction of property. In the Strugar Case, the Court stated: 'The Chamber is of the view that military necessity may be usefully defined for present purposes with reference to the widely acknowledged definition of military objectives in Article 52 of Additional Protocol I.'[52] The statement entails a merging of the rules on the definition of military objectives and destruction of property – two rules where the function of military necessity is different. This issue is dealt with in more detail in Chapter 16.

14.3.6 *(A View on) The Foundational Face of Military Necessity to a Vanishing Point*

Some argue that after the adoption of the treaty rule in AP I, military necessity is left with 'no substantive content'.[53] This statement invites the questions: has

50 Kalshoven, 'Remarks', at page 41, cited above, Chapter 13.

51 Dinstein, 'Military necessity', at paras. 21–4.

52 ICTY, Strugar Case, Trial Chamber Judgment, at para. 295. The Trial Chamber findings were not altered by the Appeals Chamber. The Trial Chamber also refer to the Trial Chamber judgment in the Galic Case, at para. 51, but at this place (in the Galic Case) it is simply referred to the definition of military objectives without connecting this to the concept of military necessity. The ICTY's decision is also applauded for not treating 'military necessity as a constraint that was additional to the extant law' and that the Court in such cases (on the conduct of hostilities) 'has shown impressive sensitivity to maintaining the military necessity – humanity balance'. Schmitt, 'military necessity and humanity in international humanitarian law', at page 818. The credit devoted to the ICTY for preserving the balance is also visible in the Tribunal's dealing with waiving of protection for cultural property.

53 Gardam, *Necessity, Proportionality and the Use of Force by States*, at page 8.

military necessity in reality become completely absorbed by other positive rules? And – if so – what are the legal consequences of this?

In Section 13.3.3 above I argued that the room for invoking military necessity *as such* was narrowed down after the adoption of AP I and that an additional (double) requirement for lawfulness is not consonant with the LOAC. The content of the present section is related to the position taken above, but not identical to it. While the position taken above implied that military necessity cannot be understood to impose an additional restraint upon conduct which is otherwise in conformity with the LOAC, the issue here is whether military necessity in reality has evaporated where it is not explicitly accounted for.

The 1977 Additional Protocol represents a benchmark. Until 1977 the absence of written and agreed definitions of military objectives and lawful attacks (beyond the scope of the 1907 Hague Regulations) demanded a more active use of 'military necessity' in order to justify conduct of hostilities. The older definition of military necessity, found in the Lieber Code, the Hostage Case and the US FM 27–10 regulations of land warfare, was suited to distinguish lawful conduct from unlawful conduct – absent other and more precise rules. Some conduct might appear more necessary than other conduct, and it may therefore be appropriate to talk of a 'scale of necessities', or certain degrees of necessity. Since 1977, this 'scale' has to a large extent been replaced by 'advantage' at the one end and explicit 'necessity' at the other, where a necessity always will be an advantage, but an advantage will not necessarily amount to a necessity. The AP I rules on distinction and proportionality seem to have closed a gap. The rules regulate an area that was usually governed by more vague considerations of military necessity. Military necessity thus seems to have transformed from being *one* legal principle, into being *two* different concepts: a consideration and an exceptional rule. The 'foundational' necessity (the consideration) does not in itself constitute a legal norm that can be violated or upheld, but rather a 'driving force' behind the positive rules.[54] The exceptional rule is a legal norm like any other rule, and is either upheld or violated.

Confusion remains, however, because closing gaps with regard to military necessity does not appear to have been a specific intention of the AP I drafters. References to military necessity in its original and singular shape remain, as they were before 1977. International law is fragmented law in this regard, as

54 On the role of military necessity today, Bill argues in 'The Rendulic "Rule"', at page 131, that military necessity 'has little utility in practical terms when compared to the other primary principles of the law of war, namely distinction, proportionality, and unnecessary suffering'.

there is no legal body to secure internal logic and legal coherence.[55] The practice of 'double-references', such as seen frequently in military manuals, therefore invites confusion as follows: is military necessity completely absorbed and 'gone' or is it an 'additional restraint'? My answer to the question is that it is neither. Military necessity has developed from being one, to being two, where the two forms have arisen primarily out of the ratification of AP I.

14.4 'CONCRETE AND DIRECT' VS 'DEFINITE MILITARY ADVANTAGE'

As noted, the term military advantage appears both in AP I article 51(5) and 52(2), as well as in articles 57(2)(a)(i and iii) and (b) with regard to precautions in attack. The term is accompanied by different adjectives in the two provisions: 'concrete and direct' (which also appear in articles 57(2)(a)(iii) and (b)) when assessing the rule of proportionality, and 'definite' for the purpose of defining a military objective – a lawful object of attack. The ICRC originally suggested using same adjective in both provisions: the word 'substantial'.[56] From the preparatory work of Committee III it is stated with regard to the definition of military objectives that: 'Extensive discussion took place before agreement was reached on the word 'definite' in the phrase 'definite military advantage'. Among the words considered and rejected were 'distinct', 'direct', 'clear', 'immediate', 'obvious', 'specific' and 'substantial'.[57] It was then noted by the Rapporteur that: 'The Rapporteur is unable to draw any clear significance from this choice.'[58] The position of the Rapporteur is also supported by Kalshoven.[59]

The treaty texts are thus left for interpretation. Considering drafting history, the differences in wording should not be overemphasised. From the ordinary reading of the words in context, it might be inferred that 'concrete and direct' can give some additional guidance to the relative scope of the advantage under the proportionality assessment. After all, articles 51(5) and 57 do not have the addition 'under the circumstances ruling at the time', which is present in article 52(2) (see further below on this notion in a contextual perspective). 'Concrete and direct' might give equivalent guidance as 'the circumstances ruling at the time'. Both the commentaries of Bothe, Partsch and Solf and the

55 See Chapter 2 as well.

56 AP I Commentary, at page 2027.

57 Official Records of the Diplomatic Conference Vol. XV, CDDH/215/Rev.1, para. 64, at page 277.

58 Ibid., Vol. VX, CDDH/777/224, page 332.

59 Kalshoven, *Reflections on the Law of War*, at page 213.

ICRC seem at the outset to be willing to juxtapose the different expressions, when it comes to substantive content.[60] In the ICRC commentary to article 57, however, it is stated: 'it should be noted that the words "concrete and direct" impose stricter conditions on the attacker than those implied by the criteria defining military objectives in Article 52'.[61] The view presented by Rauch points in a similar direction: 'The definition of "military objective" in Art.52 speaks of a "definite military advantage". The language in Art.51 is apparently an attempt to reduce the weight to be attached to uncertain military advantages and to view them in the light of the actual military situation.'[62] As indicated above, an ordinary reading of the text might imply that 'concrete and direct' brings article 51(5) closer to a requirement similar to 'circumstances ruling at the time', which is found in article 52(2). I cannot see, however, that the scope of advantages should be understood as more narrow in article 51(5) than in article 52(2) – if this is what is indicated by Rauch. The reference to *weight* is not clear either, as the word 'definite' may correspond to the word 'concrete'. The difference rather relates to the causal strength, hence the word 'direct', which only appears in article 51(5).[63] Having said this, the requirement in article 52(2) that the objective shall 'make an effective contribution to military action' seems to tighten up the possibility for also relying on indirect advantages here. The requirement of 'effective contribution' has been said to express that there must be 'a proximate nexus to "war-fighting"'.[64] In sum, the differences do not seem to be apparent. One remark with regard to the conception of military advantage in context shall, however, be made: as far as objects are concerned, the military advantage must be assessed for each and every object. The assessment can be quick if many objects are similar or identical, but the requirement is linked to every object.[65] This is different when it comes to the proportionality assessment. Proportionality is assessed in light of the attack as a whole, which can include a number of objects under attack. In this context, it adds guidance to refer to the concrete and direct advantage of the attack as a whole. In the coming section, I shall concentrate on the requirement of the concrete and direct advantage from the attack as a whole.

[60] Bothe, Partsch and Solf, *New Rules*, at page 365. AP I Commentary, at para. 2027.

[61] AP I Commentary, at para. 2218.

[62] See Rauch, 'The concept of military necessity in the context of the law of war', at page 24.

[63] In this direction, see also Boivin, 'The legal regime applicable to targeting military objectives in the context of contemporary warfare', at page 43.

[64] Dinstein, *Conduct of Hostilities*, at page 109.

[65] AP I Commentary, at para. 2028.

14.5 THE REQUIREMENT OF 'CONCRETE AND DIRECT' ADVANTAGE FROM THE ATTACK AS A WHOLE

The requirements of 'concrete and direct' are evaluative limits to the commander's assessment of military advantage. The proportionality rule is referred to above as the ultimate balance of humanitarian considerations and military necessity – to be performed by the military commander at (in principle) any level of the military chain of command.[66] The combination of the requirement of 'concrete and direct' and the coinage 'attack as a whole' provide the commander with some guidance in his or her 'ultimate task'. The topic of the present section is to analyse the scope of this guidance.

14.5.1 *Specificity and a Qualified Causal Chain*

A *concrete* advantage means the opposite of a hypothetical, speculative or general advantage.[67] A concrete military advantage is for example to deny the adversary access to a naval port or an airfield – or the manifestation of denied access, namely control and use of the naval port and airfield for own forces.

The adjective *direct* connotes a causal chain, arguably 'without intervening condition of agency'.[68] As a point of departure it suffices to say that the coinage of 'concrete and direct' requires a certain degree of connection in time and space between the attack and the military advantage.[69] The ICRC Commentary to the AP I argues that the intention behind the chosen wording was that the military advantage should be '... substantial and relatively close, and that advantages which are hardly perceptible and those which would only appear in the long-term should be disregarded'.[70]

Although 'concrete and direct' relates to limits in time and space, there are no clear limits for the appraisal of 'advantage', neither in time nor geographically. It may include advantages that will materialise sometime in the future,[71] but not – as argued below – the future end of the war. The geographical aspect implies for example that a military operation can consist of a number of smaller attacks,[72] out of which one or more may have been instigated as

66 With regard to the level of command, see Chapter 4 and the US DoD Manual, at page 243.
67 Bothe, Partsch and Solf, *New* Rules, at page 365.
68 Ibid.
69 Gardam, *Necessity, Proportionality and the Use of Force by States*. See as well Hampson, 'Necessity and proportionality in the Gulf conflict', at page 47.
70 AP I Commentary, at para. 2209.
71 See US DoD Manual, para. 5.12.2, at page 263, where it is stated that the advantage need not be immediate. See also, for example, Henderson, *The Contemporary Law of Targeting*, at page 200.
72 Which is a different position from the one exposed in the Galic Case.

ruses of war, in order to draw attention away from the main effort.[73] The uncertainties with regard to scope have led to the numerous references to the 'attack as a whole'. I shall deal with this in the following as a part of the relative concept of military advantage, and a response to the question what does the advantage relate to?

14.5.2 *The Relative Concept of Advantage: Plans, Aims and Other Circumstances*

At the beginning of this chapter the relative aspects of military advantage were divided in two, out of which the first, the relation to the planning objectives, also embraces the evolving circumstances ruling at the time. The context-specific determination of military advantage thus relates to the attack as a whole – but not the war as a whole – and to the 'circumstances ruling at the time'. These two relative aspects partly overlap. The phrase 'circumstances ruling at the time' does not encapsulate the entire war.

Despite this, it is sometimes asserted that 'military necessity becomes most acute if there is a question of shortening the war as a whole'.[74] In between shortening the war as a whole and the attack as a whole, two questions arise: first, what does advantage encompass when it comes to tactical gains, operational gains, strategic gains – the entire war? Second, what are the 'circumstances at the time'? Two relative aspects appear inextricably linked: the military plans, aims and objectives on the one hand and other circumstances on the other hand.

Beyond the phrase referring to the 'circumstances at the time' in article 52(2), the wording of both articles 51(5)(b) and 52(2) – as well as 57(2)(a)(iii) and (b) – is silent on the relativity of 'advantage'. During the treaty negotiations it was for example remarked by the Hungarian delegate that: 'Military advantages were based on unpredictable strategical considerations which evolved more quickly than humanitarian law.'[75]

It has been clear from both subsequent treaty law, as well as the conception among ratifying States, that military advantage must be related to the 'attack as a whole'. The Rome Statute states in article 8 that: 'Intentionally launching an attack in the knowledge that such attack will cause incidental loss of life or injury to civilians or damage to civilian objects or widespread, long-term and severe

[73] AMW Manual, Commentary, at page 45.
[74] Detter, *The Law of War*, at page 394.
[75] Official Records of the Diplomatic Conference Volume XIV, CDDH/III/SR.8, at page 69.

damage to the natural environment which would be clearly excessive in relation to the concrete and direct *overall* military advantage anticipated.'[76]

Several States have filed a similar reservation text to AP I articles 51 and 57. A much cited version is the one filed by the UK: 'In the view of the United Kingdom, the military advantage anticipated from an attack is intended to refer to the advantage anticipated from the attack considered as a whole and not only from isolated or particular parts of the attack.'[77]

The same view is re-cited in States' military manuals,[78] in the Tallinn Manual[79] and in the AMW Manual. In the AMW Manual it is stated that the military advantage: '... relate[s] to the attack considered as whole and not merely to isolated or particular parts of the attack'.[80]

The notion of the 'attack as a whole' therefore appears as an established legal point of departure, despite the fact that the ICRC has expressed the view that the word 'overall' was redundant in the text.[81] It is not, however, utterly clear what the 'attack as a whole' embodies, but it is clearly meant to go beyond 'the level of each sniping and shelling incident' as argued by the ICTY in the Galic Case,[82] as well as by some critical commentators.[83] This very narrow approach to the military advantage does not even seem to be consistently upheld by the ICTY itself,

76 The Rome Statute, article 8(2)(b)(iv). Emphasis added.

77 UK Declaration of 28 January 1998. Similar declarations are posited by Australia on 24 June 1991, Canada on 20 November 1990, Belgium on 20 May 1986, Germany on 14 February 1991, Italy on 27 February 1986, The Netherlands on 26 June 1987, New Zealand on 8 February 1988 and Spain on 21 April 1989.

78 Norwegian Manual, at page 35: 'Den militære fordel som forventes oppnådd, kan være både den umiddelbare fordelen ved angrepet og den samlede fordelen for den overordnede taktiske operasjonen som angrepet utgjør en del av'; UK Manual, at page 67; Canadian Manual, at page 2-2 and para. 415 at page 4-4; German manual, para. 404, at pages 53–4.

79 Tallinn Manual, Commentary 10 to rule 113, at page 474.

80 AMW Manual, rule 1(w), second sentence, at page 44 in Commentary.

81 The view is cited in Dörmann, *Elements of War Crimes under the Rome Statute of the International Criminal Court*, at pages 169–70.

82 Galic Case, at para. 37 (the argument of the prosecutor). The position was upheld in the Judgment as well as by the Appeal Chamber, at para. 235. See also Fenrick, 'The rule of proportionality and Protocol I in conventional warfare', at page 107, who argues that it is unlikely that the concrete and direct military advantage from an attack is the military benefit derived from an attack on a single military objective; Olasolo, *Unlawful Attacks in Combat Situations*, at page 172, where he also rejects the position taken in the Galic Case.

83 In a critique of the US attacks on the power grids in Iraq in the first Gulf War, Gardam argued that military advantage should be assessed on a case by case basis and furthermore that: 'The Gulf Conflict graphically illustrated that, if the requirements of Article 51(5)(b) are to be complied with, military necessity will require considerable reappraisal.' See Gardam, 'Proportionality and force in international law', at page 409.

neither in the judgments,[84] nor by the Office of the Prosecutor. I shall return to the views of the Office of the Prosecutor just below.

The ratification statements on the 'attack as a whole' have been interpreted both to 'suggest that the notion of military advantage should include elements of more strategic importance to the opposing party to the conflict'[85] and that they 'extend the scope for the weighing of pros and cons beyond what is offered by the wording of the paragraph ...'[86] Where does this take us – what is a military advantage beyond tactical and operational gains?

At the outer end of 'strategic importance' we find the view taken by the Ethiopia-Eritrea Claims Commission. The Commission held that 'military advantage' had to be understood in the context of the military operations between the parties taken *as a whole*, and not only the advantage of the specific attack.[87] This position has been strongly criticised by Dinstein as a 'gross exaggeration', stating that the proper consideration concerns the 'attack as a whole' and not the 'armed conflict as a whole'.[88] Hampson presents a similar view, arguing that: 'Furthermore, it must be a *military* advantage. The ultimate advantage – the end of the war – appears to have too remote a connection with the attack. The alternative would be to deprive proportionality of all meaning, as it would appear to sanction a strategic nuclear strike, provided that the strike was thought likely to bring the conflict to an end.'[89]

The position taken in the US DoD Manual is a bit more difficult to grasp, when it is stated that the military advantage: 'is not restricted to immediate tactical gains, but may be assessed in the full context of the war strategy'.[90] The US view was also previously expressed, for example, in the Final Report after Operation Desert Storm in 1991, where it was held: '"Military advantage" is not restricted to tactical gains, but is linked to the full context of a war strategy, in this instance, the execution of the Coalition war plan for liberation of Kuwait.'[91] The ICRC Commentary to AP I article 57 takes a narrower approach: 'This article, like Article 51' (Protection of the civilian population), 'is not concerned with

84 In the Blaskic Case, Trial Chamber Judgment, the Court did not consider each mosque or school as an attack, but instead the entire village. See para. 543. In the Strugar Case, Trial Chamber decision, the Court took a similar approach with regard to an eventual proportionality assessment of the attack on the Old Town in Dubrovnik. See paras. 194–5.

85 Boothby, *The Law of Targeting*, at page 501.

86 Rauch, 'The concept of military necessity in the context of the law of war', at page 24.

87 Permanent Court of Arbitration, case no. 2001-02, Eritrea's Claims 1, 3, 5, 13, 14, 21, 25 and 26, at para. 113.

88 Dinstein, *Conduct of Hostilities*, at page 109.

89 Hampson, 'Necessity and proportionality in the Gulf conflict', at page 47.

90 US DoD Manual, para. 5.12.2.1, at page 264.

91 Final Report to Congress, at page 699.

strategic objectives but with the means to be used in a specific tactical operation.'[92] The commentary of Bothe, Partsch and Solf refers to the 'specific military operation of which the attack is a part taken as a whole . . .',[93] while other examples from military manuals add to the diversity of the picture: the Norwegian Manual refers to the military advantage of the 'overarching tactical operation'[94] and the Canadian Manual refers to the 'success of the overall operation'.[95] The ICTY states in a criticised passage that: 'The committee understands the above formulation, instead, to refer to an overall assessment of the totality of civilian victims as against the goals of the military campaign.'[96] In the critique of this statement, it has been argued that the number of civilian casualties could not be compared against the entire Operation Allied Force over Kosovo.[97] I agree with this last point, but I do not think that the critique actually frames the Report. When assessing the attack on the Serbian Radio and TV station, the Office of the Prosecutor does not compare the number of civilian casualties against 'the entire Operation Allied Force'. Instead, it is a concrete assessment of the coordinated pre-planned attack against C3 assets, more closely determined as radio relays, buildings and towers and electric power transformer stations.[98] The targets were considered to be 'strategic', but I do not agree, as some argue, that the Report by this use of the notion of 'attack' is synonymous with the entire military campaign.[99] The statement in the Report cited above is unfortunate as a generic expression, but it does not (in my view) reflect the actual considerations done by the Office of the Prosecutor, and the significance of the error should be toned down. In order not to be misread, it could have been inserted '*each* goal of the military campaign', and the statement would have been more representative for the discussions to come later in the Report.

Much of the apparent ambiguity seems to be buried in the lack of clarity over what 'tactical', 'operational' or 'strategic' entail or do not entail, and this is exactly what makes the question of 'strategic objectives' or 'tactical operation' difficult.[100] While there seems to be widespread acceptance of the inclusion of

92 AP I Commentary, at page 683, para. 2207.

93 Bothe, Partsch and Solf, *New Rules*, at page 352.

94 Norwegian Manual, at page 35.

95 Canadian Manual, at para. 415, page 4-4. Emphasis added.

96 See OTP Report, at para. 52, in a comment to the Kupreskic Trial Chamber Judgment on the role of the Martens Clause in interpreting the proportionality rule, arguing there that civilian casualties could cumulatively add up to a crime.

97 Laursen, 'NATO, the war over Kosovo, and the ICTY investigation', at page 792.

98 OTP Report, at para. 78.

99 Olasolo, *Unlawful Attacks in Combat Situations*, at pages 183–4.

100 For example, the ICTY Trial Chamber judgments in the Blaskic and Strugar cases are considered by Olasolo, in *Unlawful Attacks in Combat Situations*, at page 176, to illustrate proportionality assessments at the operational level. While I agree that the two judgments

'tactical operation', the pending issue seems to remain with advantages identified at the operational or strategic level of command – as illustrated with the controversy over the OTP Report. However, differences between 'tactical' or 'strategic/strategy' do not necessarily determine the scope of 'concrete and direct' military advantage. A tactical advantage may be the immediate advantage of neutralising an object, such as a pick-up truck loaded with artillery or the destruction of a number of bridges in order to prevent the advance of enemy forces through an area. A military advantage defined at the operational level (beyond the tactical operation) is for example to achieve air superiority. In order to establish air superiority it may be necessary to attack radar stations, airfields, military headquarters and air-defence systems.[101] In this case the advantage of attacking one radar station or one part of a nation's air-defence system cannot be considered in isolation, but as part of the coordinated attack in order to gain air superiority. The advantage of air superiority can prove vital for the success of the whole military operation, but is nonetheless a military advantage which, when set in a military plan, is concrete and direct to the attack. This is consonant with the view taken in the OTP Report with regard to attacks on C2 or C3 assets. The aim of paralysing C2 or C3 can be identified at each level of military planning, even at the political level. While keeping the 'whole war' and the 'entire war strategy' outside the scope of a concrete and direct military advantage, it is possible to come up with examples of strategic attacks, of which the advantage is still 'concrete and direct'. A strategic attack can be understood as one which is directed at a target 'specifically selected to achieve military strategic objectives'.[102] This model of military planning has sprung out of an idea that it is possible to detect the enemy's 'centre of gravity',[103] and that an attack on this centre produces a strategic effect which is directly linked to the adversary's will or capacity to sustain the war. A strategic attack may therefore be expected to produce a significant military (strategic) advantage – but it is not consonant with the 'entire war strategy', although naturally being linked to it. A strategic attack can for example be an attack on the supreme leader of the military operation, if this leader is expected to have the power to end the war (without simply being replaced by another leader). A strategic attack can also be an attack on industry which is, in addition to qualifying as a military objective, expected to be of decisive importance for sustaining the war machinery.

illustrate a practice that is wider than the one in the Galic Case, I cannot read an 'operational level' into them.

101 For an example in a similar direction, see Tallinn Manual, Commentary 10 to rule 113, at page 474.

102 This definition is taken from NATO, Standard, AJP-3.3(B), para. 1.5.2, page 1-10 (April 2016).

103 The centre of gravity is discussed in Section 14.7.

The reference to 'strategy' and 'strategic objectives', as done in the ICRC Commentary above, is therefore (in my view) partly misleading. A military advantage can be identified at each level of the military chain of command: from technical to tactical and to military strategic level. The military advantage will often be identified at a relatively high level of command, for example at the level of the joint operational headquarters, where joint operations are planned and synchronised. Finally, whether an advantage anticipated from an attack is (assessed by the military commander to be) of strategic value depends on the circumstances at the time.

The requirement of 'circumstances ruling at the time' consists of two elements: the factual, which comprises the actual 'circumstances', and the time dimension. I start with the 'circumstances' – what are these?

To begin with, 'circumstances' naturally include weather conditions, natural or demographic topography, the positioning of both parties' forces, the resources left, the stage of the war and the modus operandi of the belligerent parties, the available time, and certainly the status on available intelligence as well as other situation-specific facts.[104]

Some examples where the concrete context can lead to varying assessments of the military advantage are: one or more bridges[105] can offer a definite military advantage if they are destroyed in a conflict with defined fronts and large troops on the move. Such as was the situation in the first Gulf War, but perhaps not on the same scale in the Kosovo War, or the Libya War in 2011. C2 installations and facilities may offer a definite military (strategic or operational) advantage if the opposing forces are subject to a strong and centralised C2 structure. Again, the advantage of destroying C2 was probably expected to be higher in the first Gulf War than for example in Libya. In Syria, the C2 structure has occasionally been completely broken down among various armed groups and in such situations it may prove difficult to measure the definite military advantage expected from an attack. It is thus the war as it appears, that determines whether the destruction of an object is expected to result in a military advantage and what the relative weight attached to this advantage is. It is not, as sometimes asserted, whether the war is 'limited' or 'total' which is decisive (on the 'changing character of war', see further below).[106]

104 Dinstein, *Conduct of Hostilities*, at pages 104–105. Jachec-Neale, *The Concept of Military Objectives in International Law and Targeting Practice*, at page 136, refers to 'time and situation-specific factors'.

105 The example made here is not meant to undermine the point made in Chapter 8 that main lines of communication, including its bridges, most often will qualify as military objectives.

106 On this part I therefore disagree with the statement made by Fenrick in 'Targeting and proportionality during the NATO bombing campaign against Yugoslavia', at page 494, where

Then to the time dimension. During warfare, circumstances often change rapidly, and the requirement of 'at the time' is meant to cope with this fluent reality.[107] The reference to 'circumstances ruling at the time' was apparently a recognition of the 'dynamic nature of military operations'.[108] Dynamic realities imply rapid changes both ways: an object can be used for military purposes for two days, and not the third, and vice versa.[109] The requirement of 'at the time' therefore also precludes hypothetical changes in the wartime scenario.[110]

Different views upon the relative scope of military advantage seem to reappear in the aftermath of every armed conflict. On numerous occasions, the argumentation is tied to the 'nature of war', the 'character of war'[111] and the 'purpose of war' – and eventually to military necessity. Although the rules of AP I were 'expected to be applicable to all these different types of warfare',[112] the character of the war as limited, total, irregular, hybrid or conventional does not as such determine the military advantage of destroying a particular object. Having said this, we can certainly sum up different circumstances and, based on this, characterise a certain war as this or that. The content of law is not to be determined by a political purpose, but the rules are made flexible in order to suit all changing circumstances. The AP I contains 'abstract rules designed to cover all contingencies',[113] but the flexible notion of 'circumstances ruling at the time' is meant precisely *not* to induce commanders to rely on 'abstract categorizations in the determination of whether specific objects constitute military objectives'.[114]

Despite a rather concrete core of the notion of 'circumstances ruling at the time', where the military advantage is linked to the 'concrete military context',[115]

he argues that: 'A core of objects will be military objectives in virtually any conflict. Other objects may become military objectives in certain conflicts depending upon various factors, including the strategic objectives of the parties to the conflict and the degree to which the conflict approaches a total war.'

107 Dinstein, *Conduct of Hostilities*, at page 104; Jachec-Neale, *The Concept of Military Objectives in International Law and Targeting Practice*, at page 142.

108 Jachec-Neale, *The Concept of Military Objectives in International Law and Targeting Practice*, at page 136, where she also refers to the *travaux preparatoire*.

109 The link to the enemy's use of objects is for example done in the UK Manual, at page 56.

110 Boothby, *The Law of Targeting*, at page 100. Bothe, Partsch and Solf, *New Rules*, at page 365; Heintschel von Heinegg, 'The law of armed conflict at sea', at page 481.

111 For an example of the latter (and in my opinion not correct today) opinion, see Kelsen and Tucker, *Principles of International Law*, at page 114, where it is argued that 'But the concept of a military objective will necessarily vary as the character of war varies.'

112 Kalshoven, *Reflections on the Law of War*, at page 211.

113 Ibid.

114 Ibid., at page 213. 'Flexible rules' as such are discussed in Chapter 4.

115 Bothe, 'The protection of the civilian population and NATO bombing on Yugoslavia', at page 534.

confusion easily arises regarding the scope of this concrete context. In the OTP Report it is argued with regard to the definition of military objectives that: 'The application of the definition to particular objects may also differ depending on the scope and objectives of the conflict. Further, the scope and objectives of the conflict may change during the conflict.'[116] The passage does not appear to be a precise reflection of the law, when it juxtaposes the 'scope and objectives' of the conflict. The reference to military 'objectives' (understood as aims) is unproblematic. Military (planning) objectives inextricably link to the circumstances ruling at the time, although – as pointed out above – *objectives* are not identical to *circumstances*. A military objective is for example to 'secure sea lines of communication (SLOC) into port X'. In order to secure the SLOC, the capture of, or attack on, enemy merchant vessels carrying arms to the extent that they have both capacity (and possibly intention to) inflict damage on a warship[117] can produce a military advantage under the circumstances. The reference to the 'scope' of the conflict is more confusing. The term, which is ambiguous in this context, resembles a reference to the 'political purpose of war', which is beyond the scope of the LOAC. The political purpose of a military campaign may, for example, be to 'compel the compliance of government A to abide by the peace treaty B'. The ordinary meaning given to the term 'circumstances ruling at the time' does not include the purpose of political coercion. When the political purposes of war change from conflict to conflict, approaches like the one cited in the OTP Report seem to reappear, probably because it is impossible to keep politics out of war-fighting. Politics is, however, not a part of law and challenges arise. Allowing political purposes determine the scope of military advantages may, however, let politically motivated violence replace the constraints of the LOAC, to the detriment of humanitarian protection. Ironically, critics argue that the Kosovo War widened rather than tightened the scope of military objectives, despite often being referred to as a 'humanitarian intervention'.[118]

14.6 MILITARY ADVANTAGE AS DISTINCT FROM OTHER ADVANTAGES: THE POINT OF DEPARTURE

At the beginning of the this chapter, I presented the relativity of military advantage in two dimensions. One dimension is the question of what military advantage derives from, in order to be a *military* advantage by nature. What

116 OTP Report, at para. 37.

117 Heintschel von Heinegg, 'The law of armed conflict at sea', at page 488.

118 Bothe, 'The protection of the civilian population and NATO bombing on Yugoslavia', at page 534; and Fenrick, 'Targeting and proportionality during the NATO bombing campaign against Yugoslavia', at page 495.

distinguishes a *military* advantage from other advantages? This question is common to the conception of military advantage both in the definition of military objectives and the proportionality assessment.

The AMW Manual elaborates on the notion of 'military nature' in the commentaries, where it is stated: 'Military advantage does not refer to advantage which is solely political, psychological, economic, financial, social, or moral in nature. Thus forcing a change in the negotiating position of the enemy only by affecting civilian morale does not qualify as military advantage.'[119]

The ICRC goes quite far in narrowing the concept down and seems to juxtapose a military advantage with the object of 'weakening the enemy forces', stating that: 'A military advantage can only consist in ground gained and in annihilating or weakening the enemy armed forces.'[120] Clearly, 'weakening the enemy forces' can amount to a 'military advantage'. 'Military advantages' are, however, not only found within the ambit of 'weakening the enemy forces' (as argued by the ICRC). In the AMW Manual it is stated that: 'A better approach is to understand military advantage as any consequence of an attack which directly enhances friendly military operations or hinders those of the enemy.'[121] Sometimes States identify military objectives (aims) rather widely, such as the US military objectives for Operation Desert Storm[122] in Iraq, which among others, were to 'attack Iraqi political-military leadership and C2', as well as destroying the Republican Guard forces and liberating Kuwait City.[123] According to US reports, 'Military objectives were clear, attainable, and achieved.'[124] However, the liberation of Kuwait City and attacking political (military) leadership represent more than simply weakening the enemy forces.

Destruction of economic objects, such as the export of fish products, or oil export, is not usually considered to offer a *military* advantage.[125] Furthermore, it can hardly be considered a *direct* advantage. This latter point introduces the

119 Commentary to rule (1)(w), number 4.

120 AP I Commentary to article 57, para. 2218.

121 AMW Manual, Commentary 3 to rule 1(w), at page 45.

122 I do not deal with the objectives of Operation Desert Shield here, which were primarily to defend Saudi Arabia. See Final Report to Congress, at page 75.

123 Objectives were also more traditional military objectives, such as to 'gain and maintain air superiority', destroying weapons facilities and severing supply lines. See Conduct of the Persian Gulf Conflict: Interim Report to Congress at page 1-1; Final Report to Congress, at page 120, with further references to CENTCOM OPORD 91–001.

124 Conduct of the Persian Gulf Conflict: Interim Report to Congress at page 1-2. The positive development from the experiences from the Vietnam War in this regard (clarity and achievement) was emphasised. See Final Report to Congress, at page 25.

125 See for example Roscini, 'Targeting and contemporary aerial bombardment', at page 426. Note, however, that this point of departure has been challenged by the recent State practice

issue of particular interest in this regard: a political, diplomatic or economic advantage can indirectly be a military advantage, but only indirectly, due to its economic or political – and not military – nature. An opposite point of view is seen in the case from the Ethiopia-Eritrea Claims Commission, where it was held that a power plant had 'economic importance' to Eritrea and under the circumstances accrued to a 'definite military advantage' since it would 'influence the political will' of the opponent.[126] The fact that the operation is subject to a so-called 'effects based approach' (often labelled EBAO or EBO) does not alter this clear point of departure. The 'effects' should be military in nature.[127] Two non-military effects appear to create repeated disturbance with regard to the wording '*military* advantage': the effects of 'persuasion' and 'protection'.

14.7 ASSESSING THE MILITARY ADVANTAGE: NOT TO FORCE A CHANGE IN THE 'NEGOTIATING ATTITUDE' OF THE OTHER PARTY

The fact that military advantages must be kept distinct from advantages which are solely of a non-military nature, places limitations upon the military commander's assessment during the military planning process. While 'military advantage' calls for a subjective assessment, there are objective limits to the nature of the advantage. The military planning process is construed in order to transform political aims into military objectives, and finally to identify military advantages. Two points are worth repeating in this regard. First, that LOAC treaty law rests on a premise that military objectives (aims) can and shall be distinguished from political aims, and second, that this distinction is difficult to make in practice.

As stated in the AMW Commentary above, the military advantage must not be *solely* political, psychological, economic, financial, social or moral. In many instances, though, the military advantage will *also* be of another nature than solely military. The military advantage of gaining sea control in an area by taking control over enemy submarine assets may easily amount to a political, economic and psychological advantage *as well* as military. The

(2015/2016) in the non-international armed conflict against ISIL, where oil exports headed for Turkey have been targeted. This practice is also commented upon above, in Chapter 8.

126 Permanent Court of Arbitration, Case, no. 2001-02, Eritrea's Claims, at paras. 117–21.

127 Boothby, *The Law of Targeting*, at page 500: 'For the intended "effect" to count in that calculation, therefore, it would be necessary to show that the effect was military in nature, that it was concrete not speculative, and that it could properly be described as anticipated as a direct result of the attack.'

key is to assess when an advantage is solely, or purely,[128] political and not military. That a military campaign is labelled as 'political' – such as for example operation Rolling Thunder during the Vietnam War and operation Allied Force during the Kosovo War – does not automatically render the advantages political as well.[129]

The devil obviously lies in the details of perception in this regard. The military planning process supports (by its design) the LOAC premise that military objectives can and shall be distinguished from political aims. An example of a military planning procedure where strategic aims are transformed into military objectives can be as follows:

> The politically desired end state for the operation is that 'peace and security in the X region is restored and the sovereignty and territorial integrity of State Y is preserved'. The following political strategic objectives are that 'security in the X region is restored' and that 'Government of Y is supported in maintaining security and stability in Y'. Then, the military strategic objectives are 'Y internal security restored' and 'Z aggression deterred'. Finally, the corresponding military operational objectives are to 'neutralise NN insurgency' and to 'deter and counter Z intervention in Y'. It is first at this final level, which is still not describing the tactical tasks and manoeuvres, that it is possible to distinguish properly the military from the political. It is also at this level that it is possible to limit the objects of attack in order to sustain the military plan, not the political objectives. For example: in order to achieve the latter military operational objective, military action can be to 'establish air superiority' and 'conduct show of force by the Maritime Component Command' and, if required in order to establish air superiority: to 'destroy Z C2 facilities and air fields'.

Nevertheless, it appears – from the observation of history – to be particularly difficult to uphold this distinction in military operations referred to as 'coercive' or where the purpose is to 'target political will'.[130] Clausewitz states in

128 Dinstein, 'Legitimate military objectives under the current jus in bello', at page 144, where he explicitly points out that: 'The advantage gained must be military and not, say, purely political (hence, "forcing a change in the negotiating attitudes" of the adverse party cannot be deemed a proper military advantage).' See as well Sassoli, 'Targeting'; and Henderson, *The Contemporary Law of Targeting*, at page 128 ff., where he also criticises Michael Schmitt for implying (wrongly) that 'IHL should permit the use of force to achieve political or diplomatic ends'.

129 Parks, 'Rolling thunder and the law of war', describes the Operation Rolling Thunder, from March 1965–November 1968, as extremely 'political', resulting in an 'almost apologetic … graduated application of military power', at pages 3 and 9.

130 This expression is for example used by Boivin, 'The legal regime applicable to targeting military objectives in the context of contemporary warfare', at page 27.

a repeatedly cited phrase, 'War is thus an act of force to compel our enemy to do our will.'[131] The basic element of compulsion in war can be understood in a number of ways. Sometimes it is even used as a separate label on a particular type of armed conflicts, so-called 'coercive campaigns'. By coercion is here simply meant that force is used or threatened to be used in order to 'induce an adversary to behave differently than it otherwise would'.[132] The act of 'compelling compliance', or 'forcing to negotiate', obviously has a political dimension. In this regard, it is sometimes asked whether it is a military or a political goal to persuade the enemy to surrender.[133] As indicated above, the problem lies in the question itself: it is often both, not either-or.

The practice of 'strategic bombing' (long-range bombing) has been devoted particular attention due to its (assumed) 'psychological' aspect on the enemy. 'Strategic bombing' means different things to different authors,[134] but one generic description, which includes a 'psychological' aspect of effect on the enemy, is as follows: 'The concept implies that aircraft carrying bombs to an enemy's "vital centers" can undermine its ability and will to fight.'[135] The concept is, however, also referred to without the psychological aspect of effect, as 'bombing of targets in the interior, beyond the contact zone'.[136] Strategic bombing has been applied in order to achieve advantages that are not solely military. Such examples have been identified, in particular, in the aftermath of the Vietnam War and the Kosovo War.

In Linebacker II (sometimes referred to as the 'Christmas bombings') in the Vietnam War, the desired outcome was apparently twofold: 'planners sought two advantages: the interdiction, by hitting military targets, of military supplies ultimately destined for enemy forces in South Vietnam, and forcing a change in the negotiating attitudes of the North Vietnamese leadership'.[137] The first advantage is military in nature and the second is political. Judging the legality thus relies on which out of the two was decisive for the attack. Apparently, all military targets were already destroyed, and the desired political outcome of the operations therefore induced the US's planners to expand the target categories to include cities.[138] This led critics to argue that: 'the principle is

131 Clausewitz, *On War*, at page 75.
132 Byman, Waxman and Shapiro, 'The future of U.S. coercive airpower', at page 52.
133 Hampson, 'Military necessity, crimes of war'.
134 MacIsaac, 'Voices from the central blue', at page 625. A NATO definition of 'strategic attack' is offered above, in Section 14.5.
135 Biddle, *Rhetoric and Reality in Air Warfare*, at page 3. In the same direction, see Van Creveld, *The Age of Air Power*, at page 57.
136 Dinstein, *Conduct of Hostilities*, at page 135.
137 Carnahan, '"Linebacker II" and Protocol I', at page 867.
138 de Saussure and Glasser, 'Air warfare Christmas 1972', at pages 126–8.

well settled that military power is to be applied to gain military advantages, not to serve immediate and short-range political ends. The use of military power for immediate political gains only obscures the laws of war."[139]

With regard to Operation Allied Force during the Kosovo War, one military scholar has argued that: 'The general consensus was that quick, efficient, *diplomatic utilization of air power* was acceptable, but ongoing bombing was not.'[140] Furthermore, the NATO mindset was apparently the hope that 'the simple threat of air power might press Milosevic toward a negotiated solution'.[141] Neither the 'diplomatic utilization of air power', nor 'pressing Milosevic toward a negotiated solution', represents military advantages according to the AP I. Having said this, overall political justification for bombing campaigns are neither justified nor prohibited attacks under the LOAC. The legality for attacks must be determined by a concrete assessment of whether force in that particular case was used in order achieve political ends such as negotiating attitude, or in order to achieve a military advantage, such as cutting off military supplies. There is an apparent danger of confusion, since cutting off military supplies in turn may force a change in the negotiating attitudes of the opposing forces. The latter is, however, not a matter for the military plan. It does not belong to the commander's margin of appreciation to assess the political negotiating attitude – a position which seems to be supported by examples of State practice.[142] Yet, each military commander at a certain level of military command is presumed to pay attention to the political climate surrounding the military operation. This may leave a commander in a demanding situation. Political restraints and other precautionary measures in order to minimise unintended effects of the use of force are dealt with in Chapter 15.

139 In Trooboff, *Law and Responsibility in Warfare*, at pages 130–1, commenting on the so-called 'Christmas bombings' of Hanoi towards the end of the Vietnam War. It is also possible to find legal defence so strong for the chosen strategy that it resembles propaganda. See Walne, 'AFP 110-31', at pages 2 and 3.

140 Grant, 'Michael C. Short', at page 379. My emphasis.

141 Ibid., at page 378.

142 See the Beit Sourik Case. The Court discussed the legality of the erection of a separation fence in the West Bank, and argued – in response the arguments of the applicant – that: 'We accept that the military commander cannot order the construction of the separation fence if his reasons are political. The separation fence cannot be motivated by a desire to annex territories to the state of Israel. The purpose of the separation fence cannot be to draw a political border.' And furthermore, even more explicitly limiting: 'The military commander is not permitted to take the national, economic, or social interests of his own country into account . . . even the needs of the army are the army's military needs and not the national security interest in the broad meaning of the term.'

Additional examples of the difficulties attached to the commander's assessments of military advantages are attacks on strategic targets or (so-called) high value targets. In Operation Desert Storm in the first Gulf War,[143] General Horner wanted to develop a 'list of strategic targets' to deter Saddam Hussein from resort to chemical and biological weapons.[144] Rather than playing the supporting role to ground operations, the air campaign went offensively out, targeting the Iraqi leadership and regime itself.[145] Obviously, the impact of deterring Hussein from resorting to chemical and biological weapons was both military and social/political. The difficulties attached to the commander's assessment of military advantages do not only stem from the fact that the targets are 'strategic' or 'high value' and thus quickly become a political concern, they also emanate from the chosen approach to military planning more broadly, such as the practice of military planning where target categories are deducted from centres of gravity (CoG).[146] In a number of cases, CoGs are not military in nature. In Operation Desert Storm the Five Rings as extensions of the CoG covered Iraq as *a system*. This system also included the population and key power production. Hence, 'the system' had a much wider range than what Warden, who was the military officer behind the target plan, himself referred to as a 'military war'.[147] The objective of the military plan was to cut Iraq down to an 'acceptable postwar size' and to make it impossible for Iraq to do anything about it.[148] The plan set out in effect included parallel and paralysing attacks on the electrical power generating system, with the effects on the population as described in Chapter 13. Destruction of electrical power required for military C2 certainly offers a military advantage. Yet, the military advantage is not identical to the aim of cutting the Iraqi nation down to a post-war size. Furthermore, this raises the issue (dealt with in Chapter 15) of the

143 In Desert Storm, the military strategic approach was built upon a 'Five Rings Model', created by Colonel John A. Warden. The 'Rings' circle around a Centre of Gravity where the purpose of the strategy was 'to attack Iraq so as to change Iraq the system such that it would be compatible with the envisioned post war peace'. See, Warden, *The Air Campaign*, at page 145.

144 Hallion, 'Charles A. Horner', at pages 307–8.

145 Olsen, *Strategic Air Power in Desert Storm*, at page 64. Scholars argue that the air campaign took a deliberate, different path from the legacy from the Vietnam War. See Olsen, ibid., at pages 67–72, as well as Hallion, 'Charles A. Horner', at pages 303–4.

146 A theory behind the plan of Desert Storm was to pursue the CoG and hit the enemy where he is most vulnerable. The point is furthermore that the attack should have the best chance of being decisive for the entire campaign. See, Warden, *The Air Campaign*, at page 7. CoG is in NATO AAP-6 and is defined as: 'Characteristics, capabilities or localities from which a nation, an alliance, a military force or other grouping derives its freedom of action, physical strength or will to fight.'

147 Warden, *The Air Campaign*, at pages 144–6.

148 Ibid., at page 150.

relative weight of the military advantage when the advantage is of strategic importance.

With regard to the latter category mentioned further up, attacks on civilian morale, these are explicitly prohibited in the AP I article 51(2) as terror attacks (see Chapter 12) when applied for this purpose alone – regardless of whether the attacks may produce military advantages as well.[149] Prior to WWII, advantages of long-distance bombing were claimed to be twofold: to weaken the enemy directly, by damage to industrial, railway and military centres, and to weaken the enemy indirectly, 'by producing discontent and alarm amongst the industrial population'.[150] The British survey team upheld the same beliefs after the war,[151] that the 'moral effects' could outnumber the physical effects of bombing industrial towns.[152] These beliefs aside, humanitarian considerations[153] have trumped the military necessities (if the prospect of military advantages prove to be correct) and prohibited attacks where the purpose is to achieve fear.

14.8 MILITARY ADVANTAGE AS OPPOSED TO 'WINNING HEARTS AND MINDS'

Finally, a military advantage according to the LOAC is a military advantage despite being determined in the context of a so-called 'humanitarian war',

149 The 'civilian morale' has repeatedly been referred to as reason for launching an attack. See Blix, 'Area bombardment', at page 32; Dinstein, *Conduct of Hostilities*, at page 125.

150 See in particular the views proclaimed by the British Commander Hugh Trenchard, who was commanding the Independent Force (IF) and showed great influence on developing the strategies of strategic bombing from WWI to WWII. Trenchard later got the position as Chief of Air Staff under Winston Churchill in 1919, and therefore took part in forming the strategies of the British Royal Air Force (RAF). See Biddle, *Rhetoric and Reality in Air Warfare*, at pages 37 and 62.

151 The survey team concluded that the material damage done to the German war economy had been small and that the moral effect of bombing had been 'considerable', due to work stops caused by air raid alarms and so on. See Biddle, *Rhetoric and Reality in Air Warfare*, at page 58.

152 Ibid. See also MacIsaac, 'Voices from the central blue', at page 633. As seen in Chapter 12, State practice in the two World Wars did nothing to limit the wide conception of the 'object of war'. See also Parks, 'Asymmetries and the identification of legitimate military objectives', at pages 70–1.

153 On the fundamental balance between military necessities and humanitarian considerations, see Chapter 6 above. Parks argues, in 'Asymmetries and the identification of legitimate military objectives', at page 84, that: '"Attacks on morale" was at best a euphemism for relieving an attacker of any obligations with respect to collateral damage to civilian objects and incidental injury to the enemy civilian population.'

such as the air war over Libya in 2011.[154] A military advantage must thus be clearly distinguished from the objective of winning 'hearts and minds'[155] and exists, for example, where a territorial stronghold of opposing forces is reduced and advancement of own forces into the area is secured.

This is valid even though some are questioning the suitability of the notion of military necessity as a measurement of military success[156] and others ask whether 'more severe restraints would be imposed on the choice of military targets and of the balancing test applied for the purposes of the proportionality principle than in a "normal" armed conflict'.[157] Even if the ultimate aim of the entire conflict is to protect the civilian population from violence, the objectives destroyed must offer a definite *military* advantage – and when they offer a military advantage, they are lawful targets according to the LOAC[158] regardless of the overall purpose (and mandate) of the conflict.[159] If attacks on enemy C2 structures are likely to hamper the advancement of enemy forces (therefore hampering their advancement in attacking the civilian population), the attacks provide a military advantage. This view is supported by State practice and publicly announced statements during and in the aftermath of the

[154] By 'humanitarian wars', I refer to armed conflicts where the political aim of the war is explicitly humanitarian. The mandate for Operation Unified Protector was given in UN Security Council Resolution 1973 (2011), where the Council authorised the 'use of all necessary measures . . . to protect civilians and civilian populated areas under threat of attack in the Libyan Arab Jamahiriya'.

[155] See Schmitt, 'Targeting and international humanitarian law in Afghanistan', at page 323, where he argues with regard to military advantage that: 'The notion does not extend to winning hearts and minds, a point illustrated by agreement that destroying enemy civilian morale does not qualify as advantage vis-à-vis the definition of military objective.'

[156] See for example Blum, 'The fog of victory', at page 415.

[157] Bothe, 'The protection of the civilian population and NATO bombing on Yugoslavia', at page 535. The entire passage says: 'Do traditional considerations of military necessity and military advantage have a legitimate place in a conflict the declared purpose of which is a humanitarian one, namely, to promote the cause of human rights? The thought would deserve further consideration that in such a conflict, more severe restraints would be imposed on the choice of military targets and of the balancing test applied for the purposes of the proportionality principle than in a "normal" armed conflict.'

[158] Naturally, the use of force may be restricted by other sources, such as rules of engagement implementing the purpose of the mandate. See Chapter 4.

[159] This appears to be questioned by De Cock, 'Operation Unified Protector: targeting densely populated areas in Libya', at page 29, where he asks: 'one of the issues that arose was whether or not the objective was limited to jus ad bellum. Was it necessary to have a direct and causal link between the military objectives planned by NATO and the strategic objective of protecting the civilian population? In other words, each time the crew decided to strike a particular target did they need a direct link to the protection of the civilian population, or was this strictly the overall strategic objective and the end state?'

military operation in Libya in 2011. The task[160] was interpreted by NATO States to encompass:

> NATO conducts reconnaissance, surveillance and information gathering operations to identify those forces *which present a threat to civilians and civilian-populated areas*. Acting on this information, NATO air and naval forces can engage targets either on the ground or in the air. Targets are determined by NATO's operational Commanders and to date, targets struck include tanks armoured personnel carriers, air-defence systems, storage facilities, command and control centres and artillery around and approaching key civilian areas.[161]

A similar statement was made by the NATO Ministers of Defence, subsequent to a working lunch: 'By maintaining a high operational tempo and carrying out precision strikes against legitimate military targets, we have seriously *degraded the ability of the Qadhafi regime to attack civilians* and relieved the pressure on civilian populated areas such as Misratah. Our operations are being conducted with the outmost care to avoid civilian casualties.'[162]

Thus, the military planning resulted in typically military targets, offering typically military advantages.[163] The following statement of the US Defence Secretary also supports this assertion: 'NATO strikes are becoming more and more effective at degrading the Qadhafi regime's military capability.'[164] Despite criticism of being drawn into a military campaign for regime change in Libya by default, the military tasks of attacking military capabilities, remains illustrated.[165] Furthermore, when it came to the assessment and execution of

160 The task of protecting civilians and civilian centres was taken on by the NATO led operation 'Unified Protector' on 31 March 2011. See NATO Fact Sheet, Operation Unified Protector Protection of Civilians and Civilian-Populated Areas. See also Taylor, 'Military operations in Libya', at page 10.

161 Taylor, 'Military operations in Libya, at page 12. Emphasis added.

162 NATO Statement on Libya, 8 June 2011, NATO Official texts. Emphasis added.

163 See as well De Cock, 'Operation Unified Protector: targeting densely populated areas in Libya', at page 29.

164 Quoted at page 21 in Taylor, 'Military operations in Libya'.

165 See for example the article by Mezran, 'Libya's lessons on Syria', where he argues that: 'In Libya, the United States and its allies initially stated that their aim was limited to protecting civilians. Based on that stated mission objective "regime change" through the continuation of air raids on Muammar al-Qaddafi's assets was not a goal. However, based on how the protection of civilians was to be achieved, the United States and its NATO allies implicitly found themselves rapidly involved in a regime change campaign almost by default. Protecting civilians meant that they had to stop the advancement of the Libyan military toward the rebels' stronghold in Benghazi. This meant striking both the advancing military columns and targeting the command and control posts from where the Libyan regime sent orders to attack civilians. The necessary rush to intervene to protect civilians meant that NATO became inadvertently engaged in an intervention without a coherent vision and with

'necessary means', a senior official in the US administration gave his blessing to the discretion of the military commander regarding assessment of military advantage:

> NATO has agreed to take on the mission of protecting civilians and that mission will be executed in the – by the commanders, in the best way they judge possible . . .
>
> And we – all 28 allies, every single one, agreed that that should be the case. And if it is judged by the commanders that there's a need to bomb forces of the Libyan regime, then the forces of the Libyan regime will be bombed, and no one is going to be able or in a position to challenge that. That is a military judgement to be made by the military authorities, and we, as an alliance, agreed today to give the supreme allied commander of Europe that authority.[166]

As argued in Chapters 4 and 6 above, consistency in the application of humanitarian and military considerations does not mean that humanity will tip any consideration to the detriment of military necessity. This is the case even in armed conflicts where the said purpose is of a humanitarian character. If priority was given to humanitarian considerations (with an alleged basis in the Martens Clause), beyond the balance prescribed in each positive rule, this exercise would contravene the very essence of the Clause itself, which is to apply 'in cases not covered by the Protocol'. Apart from some arguments in favour of interpretative restrictions,[167] it thus appears to be clear that the concept of military advantage is the same, subject to the circumstances ruling at the time – and subject to the commander's margin of appreciation. The notion of the circumstances ruling at the time does not encompass the entire war as such, nor the reasons for resort to force (*jus ad bellum*).[168]

Having said this, the political reasons behind the conflict may motivate additional guidelines for the use of force, beyond those in the LOAC. It might be that, due to the ambition to reduce civilian losses to an absolute minimum, the physical area of manoeuvre is limited and therefore also the ability to seek military advantages. Such restrictions are dealt with in Chapter 15.

limited understanding of the political, public relations, and reconstruction activities that would be required in order to achieve a desirable outcome.'

166 Taylor, 'Military operations in Libya', at page 13. Footnotes omitted.

167 See Laursen, 'NATO, the war over Kosovo, and the ICTY investigation', at page 788, where he argues that: 'jus ad bellum justifications, such as humanitarian intervention, influence, or aid in the interpretation of jus in bello rules, as long as the goal and objective is a better, more comprehensive protection of individual persons'.

168 On the notion of 'circumstances ruling at the time', see Section 14.5. On the relationship between *jus ad bellum* and *jus in bello*, see Chapter 1.

14.9 MILITARY ADVANTAGE AND THE SPECIFIC ISSUE OF USE OF FORCE TO REPRESS INTERNATIONAL CRIMES

Related to the issue of distinguishing the military advantages from the aim of forcing a change in the negotiating attitude of the adversary – or from the overall aim of protecting the civilian population – is the issue of repression of serious international crimes. In a recent book chapter Kolb discusses whether serious, large scale international crimes can be repressed by the use of armed force and, therefore, asks whether (for example) means of transportation for deportation of civilians to extermination camps qualify as lawful targets. That is, despite the fact that the bombardment has a 'humanitarian purpose' and is not aimed at 'weakening the enemy forces', and hence cannot be expected to offer a military advantage.[169] Kolb discusses possible alternative bases for attacking the means of transportation (railway) out of which the following are legal bases, a 'state of necessity', United Nations Security Council (UNSC) mandate, Responsibility to Protect doctrine, State practice subsequent to AP I and a teleological expansion of the wording of AP I, and the final one is a question of accepting the violation of AP I article 52(2). Notwithstanding the question of 'accepted violation' of AP I, Kolb argues that a teleological expansion of AP I article 52(2) is arguable (because the purpose of the provision, which is to protect the civilian population, is better served this way), despite its dangers.[170] The practical importance of the issue is narrow, but significant. The specific question raised by Kolb only arises where armed forces engage in serious criminal activity, not amounting to acts of warfare such as regular attacks (then they would be targetable), against protected persons.

I recognise the importance of addressing the issue, but I fail to see the need for a teleological application of AP I in order to repress the criminal activity. First of all: criminal activity as such is a matter for law enforcement agencies and is, as a point of departure, not conduct of hostilities. That said, law enforcement agencies (for practical purposes the police) may not always be in a position (either by their will or their ability) to repress criminal activity committed by a State's armed forces. The fact that the police are not capable (or willing) to repress the crimes does not, however, mean that the law enforcement paradigm is inapplicable. Crimes can be repressed by deadly force when that is, under the circumstances, proportionate to the threat (this is law enforcement proportionality, not the proportionality rule as dealt with

169 Kolb, '"Humanitarian bombardments" in jus in bello?', at page 116, for his legal point of departure with regard to *lex lata*.

170 Ibid., at pages 123–4.

elsewhere in this book).[171] Use of force is based on the threat posed towards the third person, not the status of the object (as under the LOAC). Furthermore, international law does not prohibit armed forces from repressing crimes (this is subject to national regulation and division of powers), it simply prescribes how and when. Therefore, I see it as a matter for the law of individual self-defence and law enforcement to repress crimes with the force necessary and proportionate to the threat posed. Furthermore, if repression of the crimes is met with armed resistance, an armed conflict may in fact occur and the LOAC will apply. In this last situation, there is no need to resort to analogies or teleological interpretations in order to attack the means of transportation.

14.10 MILITARY ADVANTAGE AND THE SECURITY OF THE ATTACKING FORCES

14.10.1 *The 'Controversy'*

For various reasons, the question of whether the 'security of the attacking forces' can be seen as military advantage has become a matter of controversy. The 'controversy' of this inclusion seems to rely upon a factual presumption that: "The understandable modern attitude of military commanders that they will not expose their subordinates to unnecessary risks tends to increase the danger to civilians."[172] This statement may seem too sweeping – it may just as well be the case that *in some conflicts* commanders are reluctant to expose their subordinates to unnecessary risks, whereas in other conflicts exposure to risks may be the chosen alternative. Nevertheless, the issue of the security of the force was already subject to controversy during the drafting process of AP I. At that time, the controversy took place as disagreement over the question of whether the security of the attacking force could exempt parties to the conflict from the rule on presumption of civilian status now laid down in article 52(3).[173] The question was not solved[174] and although a presumption of civilian

[171] This is enshrined in the ECHR article 2 and the International Covenant on Civil and Political Rights, article 6.

[172] Rogers, 'Zero-casualty warfare', at page 168. See as well, among others, Boivin, 'The legal regime applicable to targeting military objectives in the context of contemporary warfare', at page 45.

[173] An account of this is given by Geiss, in 'The principle of proportionality', at page 75.

[174] The UK statement on interpretation of article 50 clearly enshrines considerations of military necessity, stating that the rule applies only in cases of 'substantial doubt' and not 'as overriding a commander's duty to protect the safety of troops under his command or to preserve his military situation, in conformity with other provisions of the Protocol'. Printed in Schindler and Toman, *The Laws of Armed Conflicts*, at page 816.

status *may* imply an increased risk on the attacking force, this presumption (without exception) certainly does not indicate a general duty to accept an increased risk to own troops.[175]

In order to address the different aspects of the issue of the security of the attacking forces, I shall start off with the linkage to military necessity.

14.10.2 *Military Necessity, Threats to the Mission and the Security of Forces*

It goes without saying that armed forces have a need to preserve own forces, otherwise the war is lost. In order to have military success you need to have forces left – both personnel and materiel. This is also why certain defensive measures easily may amount to a military necessity. Therefore, the probability of success includes a consideration of the threat to the mission. A great threat to the mission (and then to the security of own forces) reduces the probability of success. It is common sense for a military commander to avoid spilling his own forces. These considerations are often also referred to as economy of force.[176]

As a point of departure it should therefore suffice to remember the undisputable core of military necessity, which is the permission of measures necessary to weaken the enemy forces, and which in turn can be seen as a reflection of the perseverance of own forces. That it is a necessity to conduct war in such a way as not to take too great losses should therefore not be controversial – it lies at the heart of the necessities of war. Considerations of necessity determine for example how much forward in the terrain a troop can advance in order not to expose itself to attack from the enemy. Military necessity determines the eventual presence and size of forces behind enemy lines, and so forth. Then a few remarks on terminology.

14.10.3 *The Confusion of Terminology: 'Security of the Attacking Forces' vs 'Force Protection'*

The heading of this section uses the expression also used by several States with regard to military advantage: the 'security of the attacking forces'. Occasionally, the expression 'force protection' is used to discuss the (apparently) same issue.[177] 'Force protection', however, is not identical to the overall notion of the security of

175 Geiss, 'The principle of proportionality', at page 76.

176 On certain defensive operations as military necessity, see Section 14.3. For general remarks on economy of force, see above, Chapter 2. See as well the US DoD Manual, which states that 'The principle of proportionality has been viewed as a legal restatement of the military concept of economy of force', at para. 5.12.3.1.

177 See for example Geiss, 'The principle of proportionality'.

the attacking forces. Force protection measures are passive and active precautions taken, such as the wearing of bulletproof vests, helmets as well as the use of armoured vehicles and protection by fences around the camp.[178] Even if one uses the expression more widely, in order to include threats to the mission more broadly, the expression easily leads to confusion between conduct of hostilities and individual self-defence – which are two separate legal regimes and should not be lumped together in one argument. Under the legal concept of self-defence, military advantage is not an issue, while under the LOAC, the resort to violence is not limited to countering an imminent threat.[179] I therefore prefer the expression 'security of the attacking force'.

14.10.4 *Military Advantage: Disadvantage Avoided*

With regard to the 'military advantage' in the proportionality balance, a number of States have clearly stated: 'That the term "military advantage" involves a variety of considerations, including the security of attacking forces.'[180]

The military 'advantage' here appears as a 'disadvantage avoided' and despite the widespread opinion of States that military advantage includes the security of the attacking force, some scholars (including the majority of the Group of Experts in the Tallinn Manual[181]) have raised the question of whether the advantage is sufficiently 'concrete and direct' to the attack, to count in the proportionality equation.[182] I do not share the opinion that the

178 The definition of 'Force protection' in NATO AAP-6 is: 'All measures and means to minimize the vulnerability of personnel, facilities, equipment and operations to any threat and in all situations, to preserve freedom of action and the operational effectiveness of the force', at page 2-F-5. For a US definition see *US DoD Dictionary of Military and Associated Terms*: 'Preventive measures taken to mitigate hostile actions against Department of Defense personnel (to include family members), resources, facilities, and critical information', at page 94.

179 In my view, Henderson confuses the arguments when he argues that the 'security of the attacking force' points at the attacking individuals. See Henderson, *The Contemporary Law of Targeting*, at pages 199–200.

180 Reservation made by New Zealand and Australia to the AP I articles 51(5)(b) and 57(2)(a)(iii), in Roberts and Guelff, *Documents on the Laws of War*, at pages 508 and 500. The same statement is made in the Canadian Manual, at para. 415, page 4-4; and the US DoD Manual, para. 5.12.2 at pages 263–4.

181 Tallinn Manual, Commentary 15 to rule 113, at page 476. The argument in the Tallinn Manual is not equal to that of Geiss (see below). The majority of Experts argue that the consideration is suited under the duty to take feasible precautions in attack.

182 This – or a similar – comment is presented by Geiss, 'The principle of Proportionality', at pages 78–9. See also Boivin, 'The legal regime applicable to targeting military objectives in the context of contemporary warfare', at page 46, where it is argued that: 'The potential for military casualties by the attacking side in the process of the attack itself are strictly speaking not part of the equation.'

requirement of 'concrete and direct' is *particularly* suited to qualify or disqualify the security of the attacking force as military advantage in the proportionality rule. This requirement certainly applies to the security of the attacking force as it does to all other potential advantages – without excluding the considerations at the outset. An example is the attack on two ISAF fuel trucks, captured by Taliban, that took place in Kunduz area in Afghanistan in 2009. In fear of Taliban attack by the use of the captured truck, a German colonel requested air support in order to destroy the two trucks. During the attack, a number of civilians were killed. The destruction of the captured fuel trucks could reasonably be expected to offer a military advantage.[183] The tank was a military objective, and the concern that a tank may be used against own forces is not a hypothetical and speculative consideration.[184]

As with other military advantages, the advantage needs to relate to the 'attack as a whole' and not the whole war.[185] Therefore, the security of the belligerent party as such will not be a concrete and direct military advantage related to the *attack*. I do argue, however, that the question remains a concrete one and will – with significant practical importance – be subject to the consideration of 'excessiveness'. The decisive point will often be that of the *relative weight* of the security of the attacking forces, under the concrete circumstances.[186] I do not see the question of relative weight as the beginning of a sliding scale – as some commentators seem to do.[187] And, I don't accept the factual presumption that commanders will 'intuitively' consider the life of own soldiers so precious that they will outweigh a certain amount of collateral damage.[188] In short, I do not see the advantage of the security of the attacking force as something qualitatively different from other military advantages. The consideration between collateral damage on the one hand and the security of the attacking force on the other hand is just as difficult as a consideration between collateral damage on the one hand and the advantage of destroying military command and control facilities on the other hand.

183 The incident was investigated by the German prosecution and finalised in a report commented upon above, see Heintschel von Heinegg and Dreist, 'The 2009 Kunduz Air Attack', at pages 848–9.

184 In another direction, see Geiss, 'The principle of proportionality', at page 81, who argues that the advantage is speculative

185 In this direction, see also Geiss, ibid., at page 81.

186 That it is a matter of relative weight also seems to be presumed in the OTP Report where it was stated that: 'To what extent is a military commander obligated to expose his own forces to danger in order to limit civilian casualties or damage to civilian objects?' OTP Report, at para. 49. On relative weight in general, see Chapter 15.

187 Oeter, 'Comment', at page 58.

188 Ibid.

I shall illustrate my point with an example of close air support (CAS). This example must not be confused with the duty to take feasible precautions in attack under AP I article 57, which are dealt with later in this book.[189] CAS can be released on short notice by small units who find themselves under extremely high risks. Imagine a situation where two troops have engaged in combat (a so-called TIC: troops in contact, which is not pre-planned) at the outskirts (closer than 200 metres) of a village with approximately 250 civilian inhabitants. The troop of State A drives a military vehicle which is technically advanced, containing crypto-facilities with military intelligence. The troop of State B drives Land Cruisers. Both troops are armed only with individual weapons. Troop A cares for their crypto-equipment and fears the consequences of enemy capture of that equipment. They request close air support in their fight against troop B. What is the military advantage of the close air support of State A? It is the combination of destroying the enemy troop *and* preserving own personnel and mission essential materiel. This advantage has to be weighed against the expected damage done to parts of the village. Imagine now the situation without the crypto-materiel, but with the request for air support (and leave out the details of weaponeering on the plane for the sake of the argument), what is the military advantage for State A? It is the destruction of enemy forces (maximum one troop) and the reflected preservation of own forces. In both examples the military advantage encapsulates that of preservation of own troops and materiel, but in the latter case this advantage weighs significantly less.[190] Similar examples can be made with other types of materiel such as fighter planes and submarines. I therefore argue that, when it comes to the security of the attacking forces, it is particularly useful to distinguish between *relevance* and *weight*. The security of the attacking force is among the relevant considerations to assess as military advantage, but its relative weight may vary quite a lot. In fact, the relative weight can vary from exceptional necessity to relatively minor advantages. The relative weight of the military advantage is dealt with in more detail in the next chapter.

189 The distinction between proportionality and the duty to minimise collateral damage to the extent feasible is pointed out for example by Boivin, 'The legal regime applicable to targeting military objectives in the context of contemporary warfare', at page 38.

190 I do not agree with Geiss, 'The principle of proportionality', at page 81, where he argues that the destruction of a tank which drives through a village only offers a hypothetical advantage. The destruction of the tank will – as always – offer a military advantage on the attacking side, just as the destruction of other materiel which is military by nature. The advantage here is clearly not hypothetical and speculative in that it is uncertain at what time the tank will be used against own forces. This argument itself is speculatively construed.

15

The Commander's Ultimate 'Margins': Assessing Excessiveness and Feasibility

15.1 THE 'EXTREMELY DIFFICULT' DECISIONS

The notion of flexible rules in the LOAC is accounted for above, in Chapter 4, where I argue that the key to strike a proper balance in each case is to combine realistic room for subjective appraisal with objective limits to the commander's concrete assessment. The room for subjective appraisal – as well as the challenges thereto[1] – is particularly prominent in the notion of excessiveness under the proportionality rule, as well as in the conception of feasible precautions in attack.

There is an inherent tension in the proportionality rule between the wording 'concrete and direct' – interpreted to be 'indicative of missions confined to a smaller area'[2] – on the one hand and the military advantage interpreted to be an 'overall military advantage' anticipated from the 'attack as a whole', on the other hand. These requirements may lead to an 'extremely difficult decision-making process' on the shoulders of commanders, sometimes at a relatively low level of command.[3] Both 'excessiveness' and 'feasibility' are featured by being

[1] It has for example been argued in a rather pessimistic way that: 'Despite the wide acceptance of the applicability of some notion of proportionality under customary international law, the principle proves difficult to interpret in practice. The task of balancing similar values that cannot be quantified – military gains and humanitarian considerations – entails a wide margin of appreciation and is bound to yield a less than satisfactory outcome.' Boivin, 'the legal regime applicable to targeting military objectives in the context of contemporary warfare', at page 42.

[2] Rauch, 'The concept of military necessity in the context of the law of War', at page 24.

[3] Ibid.

highly discretionary and incumbent upon the commander's assessment of necessity. For this reason, these norms are devoted separate discussion in this chapter.

15.2 ASSESSING EXCESSIVENESS IN THE PROPORTIONALITY RULE

15.2.1 *The Point of Departure: an Insoluble Problem*

When is collateral damage 'excessive' to the concrete and direct military advantage anticipated? Treaty law contains no guidance to the meaning of the word 'excessive'. It is utterly clear that the weighing of these unlike quantities and values requires the judgment of a reasonable commander,[4] but beyond this point, nothing seems clear.[5]

The notion of 'excessiveness' is the core of the question of the *relative weight* of military advantage. As noted at the beginning of the previous chapter, relativity has at least two dimensions in this connection. The weight of military advantage is obviously relative to the weight of collateral damage, but it is also relative to the objective sought to achieve, which has been the topic of the foregoing chapters. It is clearly a military task to determine the weight attributed to the military advantage of destroying a particular object under the circumstances ruling at the time and in accordance with the military operational plan. It appears intuitively reasonable that a military commander can say that in this operation it is of great importance to take control over the opposing forces' C2, and therefore to destroy a communication node on top of a hillside. The obvious problem of assessment arises when the same commander is asked to compare the weight of destroying the communications node, for the loss of one civilian, two civilians or a frequently visited restaurant. How is he, or she, who is trained for military tasks, supposed to measure the value of one or ten human lives in comparison to the military advantage?

4 Dinstein, *Conduct of Hostilities*, at page 159.

5 In the OTP Report it is stated in para. 48 that: 'It is much easier to formulate the principle of proportionality in general terms than it is to apply it to a particular set of circumstances because the comparison is often between unlike quantities and values.'

To determine the meaning of the term 'excessive' is not an exact science,[6] and opinions on its content differ.[7] Furthermore, it must be clear that reasonable commanders might disagree as to whether the expected casualties would be excessive – without any of them necessarily violating the law.[8] These differences in opinion are among what the commander's margin of appreciation allows for. At the same time differences in opinion truly matter in this issue, being the real cornerstone of the proportionality consideration.

15.2.2 *Military Necessity and 'Excessive' Collateral Damage*

The principle of proportionality 'is an attempt to balance the often conflicting interests of military necessity on the one hand and humanitarian protection on the other when taking precautions in attack'.[9] The military necessity–humanity balance is at its peak in the proportionality rule, where 'The give and take of military necessity and humanity is apparent in the relative nature of the term "excessive".'[10] Accordingly, if there has been a shift[11] in this balance, away from military necessity and towards humanity, this shift is primarily influencing the consideration of 'excessiveness'. An alleged 'shift' is visible, for example, in the remarks by the Norwegian delegate, presented at the AP I Diplomatic Conference, and cited in Section 14.2. The AP I Diplomatic Conferences ended up, as previously accounted for, with a compromise on the proportionality rule, leaving out an explicit reference to 'proportionality', and instead inserting the notion of 'excessiveness'. Both terms are highly flexible. 'Excessiveness' does not indicate a diminished

[6] In the US DoD Manual, it is stated that: 'Determining whether the expected incidental harm is excessive does not necessarily lend itself to quantitative analysis because the comparison is often between unlike quantities and values', para. 5.12.3, at page 265. In the first version of the Manual (2015) it was, however, stated at page 245 that: 'The weighing or comparison between the expected incidental harm and the expected military advantage does not necessarily lend itself to empirical analyses.' The word 'empirical' is changed to 'quantitative'. The meaning does not appear to be significantly altered, although 'quantitative' has a more narrow and specific meaning than 'empirical'. See also the OTP Report where it was pointed out that among the unsolved questions to discuss under the proportionality rule were 'What is the standard of measurement in time or space?', at para. 49.

[7] See for example the remark made by Wright in 'Excessive ambiguity', at page 820, where he refers to 'expert' descriptions varying in the same conference panel from: 'shock the conscience' to 'clearly unreasonable' or 'unreasonable'.

[8] US DoD Manual, para. 5.10.2.3, at page 245. On the differences among commanders, see as well for example, Dill, 'Applying the principle of proportionality in combat operations', at page 4.

[9] UK Manual, at page 86. See also Corn et al., *The Law of Armed Conflict*, at page 124.

[10] Beer, 'Humanity considerations cannot reduce war's hazards alone', at pages 804–5.

[11] See Chapter 6.

weight devoted to military necessity at the expense of humanitarian considerations. Some argue in favour of 'closing the gap' between military necessity and humanity in the proportionality analysis and therefore argue to reformulate military necessity in order to align with humanity.[12] As of today, the argument does not appear to reflect *lex lata*.

The flexible notion of the rule has led scholars to express their concern. Kalshoven asks whether there is: 'an upper limit beyond which collateral damage that is not excessive in view of the absolutely imperative military necessity of the attack, will by it's terrible scale become unacceptable nonetheless?'[13] This question reveals Kalshoven's position on the question discussed just below, that excessiveness is a relative concept and that the proportionality rule does not necessarily forbid extensive civilian losses. I shall return to this issue in a moment, but first an argument with regard to the role of *military necessity* in this context. References to the concept of military necessity sometimes appear confusing, in relation to excessiveness.[14] It appears to be, primarily, when the advantage amounts to a necessity, that even extensive civilian losses can be justified by referring to the proportionality rule.[15] In this, I agree with Kalshoven that the proper question to ask is whether there can be an upper limit at all? I do not, however, believe that the question need to be asked rhetorically and regrettably. Despite my view that military necessity may justify (by law, not necessarily ethically) extensive civilian losses, I believe that the most proper test to limit collateral damage lies in the notion of the relation to the concrete and direct advantage of the *attack as a whole*. From this perspective, it is also possible to address seemingly endless questions of State survival and excessiveness. Such as the statement in the dissenting opinion by Judge Higgins in the Nuclear Weapons Case:

12 Beer, 'Humanity considerations cannot reduce war's hazards alone', at pages 818–20. Beer is arguing in favour of the 'constraining potential' of the 'necessity principle'. Beer is relying upon a 'professional military standard' and arguing that this standard should be a matter of law. The weakness of this argument is that the standard referred to has emerged from Counterinsurgency Operations (COIN) and is not necessarily suited for all other circumstances.

13 Kalshoven, 'Remarks'.

14 For example the remark made by Melzer in a footnote: 'The determination that incidental injury to civilians would be "excessive", implies that the harm caused by such injury does not outweigh the military necessity of achieving a concrete and direct military advantage.' See Melzer, 'Targeted killing or less harmful means?', page 106. It is not clear to me what function Melzer attributed to military necessity here, apart from that the word necessity has a causal element. My perspective on these functions is accounted for in Section 14.3.

15 I do not attribute my own distinctions between military advantage and military necessity to Kalshoven.

> It must be that, in order to meet the legal requirement that a military target may not be attacked if collateral civilian casualties would be excessive in relation to the military advantage, the 'military advantage' must indeed be one related to the very survival of a State or the avoidance of infliction (whether by nuclear or other weapons of mass destruction) of vast and severe suffering on its own population; and that no other method of eliminating this military target be available.[16]

The last part of the quoted passage appears to be a reference to necessity in its most crude form: where there is no other method available. The problem in the statement does not, however, lie here. It appears above, when Higgins relates military advantage to State survival. This notion is rejected above, and the point for repetition is: the notion of the 'attack as a whole' must be limited to exclude the 'entire war', otherwise the test of 'excessiveness' becomes endless. This view appears to be acknowledged in Israeli national case law, in the Beit Sourik Case, where the Israeli High Court said that '. . . even the needs of the army are the army's military needs and not the national security interest in the broad meaning of the term'.[17]

With these assertions presented, I shall turn to a more dogmatic account of the notion of 'excessiveness'.

15.2.3 *Relative Is Not Absolute*

The ICRC has equated 'excessive' with 'extensive', displaying the following position:

> The idea has also been put forward that even if they are very high, civilian losses and damages may be justified if the military advantage at stake is of great importance. This idea is contrary to the fundamental rules of the Protocol; in particular it conflicts with Article 48 '(Basic rule)' and with paragraphs 1 and 2 of the present Article 51. The Protocol does not provide any justification for attacks which cause extensive civilian losses and damages. *Incidental losses and damages should never be extensive.*[18]

In other words, the ICRC argues that there is an absolute limit for civilian losses, referred to as 'extensive' losses. This reading is not compatible with the wording of the treaty text, which is relative by nature, not absolute.[19] Although

[16] Legality of the Threat or Use of Nuclear Weapons, Advisory Opinion, dissenting opinion of Judge Higgins, at para. 21.

[17] Beit Sourik Case, at para. 27. The passage is also cited above, in Section 14.7.

[18] AP I Commentary, at paras. 1979–80, page 626. Emphasis added.

[19] In this regard, see also the AMW Manual, Commentary to rule 14, at page 92, pointing out that 'The concept of excessiveness is not an absolute one.' For a comparison, see as well the AP

supporting the view of the ICRC, Human Rights Watch points out that: 'Excessive damage is a relational concept, not quantifiable in terms of a fixed number of civilians dead or injured, or houses destroyed.'[20] Beyond the support of Human Rights Watch, the ICRC's view has by no means gained widespread support – at least not in legal literature, where the opposition seems to have been most direct.[21] The underlying problem is, however, worth sympathy – where is the legal limit to extensive losses? One part of a limitation lies (as indicated above) in the requirement of concrete and direct – one of the other relative aspects of military advantage. Related to the question of excessiveness vs extensiveness is the question sometimes posed: what to do when there is no *clear* excessiveness?

15.2.4 *When in Doubt ...?*

Military commanders are sometimes compelled to act, despite their doubts.[22] The ICRC argues that the interests of civilians should *prevail* in matters where the decision does not stand out as clear to the commander:

> Of course, the disproportion between losses and damages caused and the military advantages anticipated raises a delicate problem; in some situations there will be no room for doubt, while in other situations there may be reason for hesitation. In such situations *the interests of the civilian population should prevail*, as stated above.[23]

That civilian interests will prevail in matters of doubt cannot be seen simply as a prolongation of the presumption of doubt laid down in AP I article 50(1), and therefore lacks basis in treaty law. In the AMW Manual, it is explicitly stated that 'The term "excessive" is often misinterpreted. ... It applies when there is

I article 56, dealing with the special protection of works and installations containing dangerous forces, where an absolute wording in fact *is* used. See Chapter 17.

20 Human Rights Watch, Needless Deaths in the Gulf War, Chapter 1.

21 Dinstein, *Conduct of Hostilities*, at page 156. Schmitt, 'Military necessity and humanity in international humanitarian law', at page 805; De Cock, 'Operation unified protector and the protection of civilians in Libya', at page 232; Henderson, *The Contemporary Law of Targeting*, at page 224. See also the introductory handbook published by the Danish armed forces where it is argued that it must be an obvious disparity between the military advantage anticipated and the expected collateral damage: 'Princippet om proportionalitet indebærer, at der ikke må være et åbenbart misforhold mellem den forventede konkrete og direkte militære fordel, som er forbundet med et angreb, og den forventede skadevirkning på civile og civile objekter.' Güntelberg, *Introduktion til folkeret*, at page 88.

22 The US DoD Manual states that 'the principle of proportionality does not preclude commanders from taking decisive action in doubtful cases', para. 5.10.4, at page 249.

23 AP I Commentary, at paras. 1979–80, page 626. Emphasis added.

a significant imbalance ... The fact that collateral damage is extensive does not necessarily render it excessive.'[24] This view is supported in earlier literature, inspired by the treaty negotiations leading up to the AP I. Based upon the fact that the wording of the treaty is of no guidance when it comes to the meaning of the word 'excessive', Rauch argues that: 'only substantially or obvious excessive effects would result in the attack being unlawful'.[25] In a similar manner Bothe, Partsch and Solf argue that: 'Despite the impossibility of quantifying the factors of the equation, a plain and manifest breach of the rule will be recognizable.'[26] The emphasis on 'significance' or 'substantial' overweight of civilian losses is also supported in more recent literature, as by Dinstein, who argues that: 'The adjective "excessive" means that the disproportionality is not in doubt ...'[27] The reference to 'obvious excessive effects' also finds support in the wording of the Rome Statute article 8(2)(b)(iv) where the word 'clearly' is added. The reference to the Rome Statute must be done with awareness of the fact that violations of the Statute amounts to war crimes, whereas a violation of AP I article 51(5)(b) certainly does not necessarily amount to a war crime. The exact scope of 'significant' overweight is, however, not clear. Human Rights Watch argue that: 'Such damage need not be so great that it "shock the conscience" of the world. Rather, its avoidance requires a good-faith balancing of disparate probabilities – the foreseeability of collateral damage and the relative importance of a particular military target.'[28]

We are still left with abstract uncertainties, upon which the commander will have to decide. Neither do States' military manuals seem to provide further concrete guidance other than simply restating the vagueness with alternative terms.

In the Canadian Manual it is simply referred to 'a rational balance',[29] which certainly does not add clarity to the meaning of 'excessiveness'. In the Norwegian Manual it is referred to lawful proportionate collateral damage vs unlawful disproportionate collateral damage, but the threshold for excessiveness is not specified.[30] This threshold is not specified in the UK Manual either, apart from the fact that the concrete military advantage should be 'identifiable and quantifiable',[31] nor in the US DoD Manual, apart from that it

24 AMW Manual, Commentary to rule 14, at page 92.
25 Rauch, 'The concept of military necessity in the context of the law of war', at page 24.
26 Bothe, Partsch and Solf, *New Rules*, at page 352.
27 Dinstein, *Conduct of Hostilities*, at page 155.
28 Human Rights Watch, Needless Deaths in the Gulf War, Chapter 1.
29 Canadian Manual, at page 2-3.
30 Norwegian Manual, at pages 33–5.
31 UK Manual, at pages 86–7.

should be 'clearly excessive' and that the assessment should consider 'any relevant moral, legal, and military factors',[32] or in the German Manual.[33]

An alternative formulation can, however, be found by Oeter in Fleck's Handbook, where it is held that the proportionality rule implies that: 'The collateral damage which inevitably occurs on the occasion of nearly every attack is justifiable only in so far as losses to the "innocent" civilian population are *commensurate* with the military advantage which the operation sought to achieve.'[34] This formulation is of interest because when the two relata on the scale (military advantage and collateral damage) are 'commensurate' they weigh the same, and are – as questioned above – on equal footing. If 'commensurate' is to be interpreted as what is not 'excessive' and thus a requirement for lawfulness, it implies that 'excessive' means *any overweight* on the side of the scale with collateral damage. Furthermore, that the scale need to drop *significantly* below, in order to be unlawful. Such an interpretation could support the ICRC position (if it is intentional) and is clearly at odds with the view of the other commentators above. This interpretation also seems to be at odds with the wording chosen in the Rome Statute, referred to above.

The legal standard of 'excessiveness' is impossible to apply if the only guidance consists of yet other flexible formulations. The concept cries out for practical illustrations: which advantages are usually attributed 'heavy weight' in the proportionality balance?

15.2.5 *'High Value Targets' and Other Targets*

As pointed out at the beginning of this section (and in the previous chapter), the issue of 'excessiveness' invites the weighing of military advantage in at least two dimensions: towards the objectives sought to achieve and towards the expected collateral damage. The first will often determine the second. A high value target (HVT)/high pay-off target (HPT) can more easily justify collateral damage than targets of a more 'simple' value. A high value target is in NATO terms understood as 'A target of significance and value to an adversary, the destruction, damage or neutralization of which may lead to a disproportionate advantage to friendly forces.'[35]

32 US DoD Manual, para. 5.12.3 at pages 266–7.
33 German Manual, paras. 404–5, at pages 53–4.
34 Oeter, 'Methods and means of combat', para. 459, at page 196. Emphasis added.
35 NATO AAP-6.

An (historic)[36] example is the sinking of the steam ferry *Hydro* on the Norwegian lake Tinnsjøen, on 20 February 1944. Sinking the ferry was considered a necessity in order to prevent Hitler from gaining access to heavy water from the Vemork factory at Rjukan. Naturally, the military advantage anticipated from the attack was therefore high. The transport of heavy water barrels over Tinnsjøen was the weakest part of the transportation route out of Rjukan. To sink *Hydro* through a sabotage operation was therefore, under the circumstances, considered the only alternative to deny Hitler from gaining the critical ingredients to develop a nuclear bomb.

Among objects that usually are ascribed the value of being high value targets are C2 facilities and military commanders of high rank in crucial positions. Examples of the first can be seen from Operation Desert Storm in Iraq in 1991, where the USA argued in favour of the military advantage of destroying bridges in order to disrupt C2, despite the presence of civilians:

> Attack of all segments of the Iraqi communications system was essential to destruction of Iraqi military C2. C2 was crucial to Iraq's integrated air defense system; it was of equal importance for Iraqi ground forces. Iraqi C2 was highly centralized. With Saddam Hussein's fear of internal threats to his rule, he has discouraged individual initiative while emphasizing positive control. Iraqi military commanders were authorized to do only that which was directed by highest authority. Destruction of its C2 capabilities would make Iraqi combat forces unable to respond quickly to Coalition initiatives. Baghdad bridges crossing the Euphrates River contained the multiple fiber-optic links that provided Saddam Hussein with secure communications to his southern group of forces. Attack of these bridges severed those secure communication links, while restricting movement of Iraqi military forces and deployment of CW and BW warfare capabilities. Civilians using those bridges or near other targets at the time of their attack were at risk of injury incidental to the legitimate attack of those targets.[37]

Both bridges and electrical power plants may easily turn into military objectives and are dealt with as such above, in Chapter 8. The attention devoted to these objects are also caused by the fact that they, being military objectives, on numerous occasions are of considerable importance to the adversary's military action and thus may provide a substantial military advantage upon destruction. C2 systems often rely upon electrical power and are usually of vital

36 Being a historic example, neither the definition nor the proportionality rule were applicable. I still regard the example illustrative, taking the particular importance of heavy water into account.

37 Final Report to Congress, at page 699.

importance to destroy – particularly if the systems are modern. The situation is completely different when it comes to for example a troop of armoured tanks or a storm-trooper squadron. Their value, although naturally being effective, as military objects by nature, is not vital in order to get an upper hand at the opposing forces military power *system*. If seen from an operational command level of military planning, it is more likely that the choice between attacking the armoured tanks or the storm-troopers is a question of timing and lower priority – while the issue of the opposing forces' C2 can amount to a matter of necessity. There will be no other rational choices than to proceed with paralysing C2. As seen, the examples also illustrate the distinction made above, between military advantages and military necessity. While advantages can be alternative, like choosing between storm-troopers or armoured tanks at a given time and place, attacks on C2 can be unavoidable at the time, in order not to fail the mission completely.

An essential part of the C2 system is the enemy leadership. The group of scholars and professionals addressing the ICTY Trial Chamber decision in the Gotovina trial argued in fact that: 'few targets are designated as higher in value than enemy strategic leadership' and that in the case of Milan Martic, 'any reasonable commander' would attribute him 'extremely high value'.[38] The same position (on the relative weight attributed to military leaders) appear to be upheld by the USA in a 2016 law and policy report published by the White House.[39] The examples shown also lend support to the assertion that: 'The more integral the proposed target is to the military strategy, the higher the level of likely civilian casualties and damage to civilian objects that will be acceptable.'[40] Furthermore, targets with a high value to the chosen military strategy can prove difficult to distinguish from targets that can produce an advantage to the 'survival of the State'. While the ultimate advantage of a war can be the survival of the State, the survival of the State is rejected as a military advantage of the attack.

38 'Application and Proposed Amicus Curiae Brief Concerning the 15 April Trial Chamber Judgment and Requesting that the Appeals Chamber Reconsider the Findings of Unlawful Artillery Attacks during Operation Storm', at page 25, para. 26.

39 The White House, Report on the Legal and Policy Frameworks Guiding the United States' Use of Military Force, at page 19, states that: 'It is well- and long-established that under the law of armed conflict, States may target, specific, individual members of an enemy force as well as individuals directly participating in hostilities. For example, during World War II, U.S. Navy forces lawfully shot down the aircraft of Admiral Yamamoto, the commander of the Japanese navy, specifically because he was on board. His loss was a significant setback for the Japanese war effort.'

40 Gardam, *Necessity, Proportionality and the Use of Force by States*, at page 100.

15.2.6 *The Relative Positioning of the Parties*

Being linked to the circumstances ruling at the time, the relative weight of the military advantage will also relate to the positioning and relative strength of the parties to the conflict. As noted by Schmitt: 'A weaker party is likely to assess the military advantage accruing from its attack as high. This is because when one chronically suffers defeats, any success looms large.'[41] Obviously, the assessment of the relative strength of the parties to the conflict flows from each party's intelligence that is reasonably available at the time.[42]

15.2.7 *A Remark on the Other Side of the Scale: Relaxed Weight of Collateral Damage?*

In the treaty text of AP I the reference to collateral damage (i.e. loss of civilian life, injury to civilians, damage to civilian objects, or a combination thereof[43]) is done without differentiation as to whether the incidental effects hit objects or persons. In Section 13.2 I raised the question of whether the relative weight of collateral damage differs, and if so, on which premises? Having no clear answer in treaty law, the issue is subject to differing in opinions. Two distinctions may be made, out of which the true difficulties seem to lie in the second category. First, we may distinguish between objects and persons, in that civilian persons should be given greater consideration than civilian objects (without prejudice to the special protection devoted to, for example, cultural property as dealt with Chapter 17).[44] Second, the question may be posed whether 'some civilians are more equal than others' before the law, that is to say whether some *deserve* greater protection than others under the proportionality rule. It must be emphasised that the issue at stake is not whether they become lawful targets, but how heavily their loss or injury count in the balance towards the military advantage anticipated from the attack.

Some guidance on this question is found in the rules on special protection devoted to certain categories of personnel, such as medical personnel, wounded and sick, women and children and civil defence personnel.[45] The guidance here may, however, only serve as a point of departure, as the rules on special protection are broader than the general protection from attack and are,

41 Schmitt, 'Asymmetrical warfare and international humanitarian law', at page 28.
42 See Chapter 4.
43 AP I article 51(5)(b).
44 US DoD Manual, para. 5.12.1.1, at page 261.
45 Dinstein argues that 'a dozen civilians dining in a restaurant do not weigh as much as a dozen patients and doctors in an infirmary. Otherwise, what is the real meaning of the special protection accorded to the latter?', in *Conduct of Hostilities*, at page 160.

for example, also directed at the possibility to perform specific functions.[46] Furthermore, while women and children enjoy special protection in some aspects regarding their vulnerability, this does not mean that civilian women as such count more than civilian men in the proportionality calculation. For the present purposes, the special protection regarding women and children primarily covers expecting mothers and mothers with small children as well as children in general (see Chapter 17).

Other situations arise where civilians are in close proximity to a lawful target and have, apparently, accepted the risk thereof. This is the case with civilian workers in a munition factory or crew members on airfields and with civilian technical support of military infrastructure of any kind. Their presence will not immunise the military objective from attack and it appears to be a tenable legal position that those civilians working in or at a military objective by consequence will receive less protection from the proportionality rule.[47]

Finally, there is a contentious issue of the use of human shields. When shielding is clearly performed voluntarily, the act may amount to direct participation in hostilities and as such cause the loss of protection.[48] When shielding is achieved through compulsion of any sort, however, the issue is more delicate and despite the fact that the party using humans as shields bear responsibility thereof,[49] the situation nevertheless requires that the civilians are included in the proportionality assessment.[50]

The difficulties that these situations may lead to, has led the USA to state that the failure on the hand of the defender, to protect its own civilians, does not require a higher military advantage correspondingly on the other side of the scale.[51]

Situations involving involuntary human shields may be almost impossible to solve satisfactorily and will raise difficult questions with regard to what measures are considered feasible precautions in attack (see Section 15.3 below). Above all, situations where the relative weight of civilian life has to be assessed by a military commander represent perhaps the most insoluble area of assessment during conduct of hostilities. As opposed to the assessment of military advantage, which may be challenging enough, the assessment of

46 See Chapter 17.

47 In this direction, Bothe, Partsch and Solf, *New Rules*, at page 336, comparing the situation to that of sick bays on board warships. See as well Oeter, 'Methods and means of combat', para. 446, at page 176. The same position is taken in the US DoD Manual, para. 5.12.3.3, at page 268.

48 See Chapter 11. See also for example the Norwegian Manual, at page 55.

49 US DoD Manual, para. 5.12.3.4, at pages 269–70.

50 See Norwegian Manual, at page 56.

51 Final Report to Congress, at pages 699–701.

civilian life calls for value judgments outside the military sphere – judgments that military personnel possess no better or worse qualifications for than any other layperson. The fewer distinctions drawn in this regard is possibly for the best.

15.3 'FEASIBILITY'

The notion of 'feasibility' appears in three articles in the AP I. Article 41(3) places a duty to take all 'feasible precautions' in order to ensure the safety of prisoners of war who have fallen into the power of an adverse party under unusual conditions. Articles 57 and 58 prescribe the duty to take precautionary measures for those who plan or decide upon an attack and for those liable for attack. The duty to take feasible precautions against the effects of attack thus applies both ways: on the attacker and on the attacked. The headings reflect this: 'Precautions in attack' (article 57) and 'Precautions against the effects of attacks' (article 58).

In article 57, feasibility relates to two core duties incumbent upon the military commanders: that of properly identifying a military objective as a lawful target and that of avoiding or minimising collateral damage. The article states that those who plan or decide upon an attack shall:

(i) do everything feasible to verify that the objectives to be attacked are neither civilians nor civilian objects and are not subject to special protection but are military objectives within the meaning of paragraph 2 of article 52 and that it is not prohibited by the provisions of this Protocol to attack them;
(ii) take all feasible precautions in the choice of means and methods of attack with a view to avoiding, and in any event to minimizing, incidental loss of civilian life, injury to civilians and damage to civilian objects.

The word 'feasible' simply refers to something that is 'possible to do easily or conveniently'.[52] The notion of 'feasible precautions' is understood similarly, by a number of the ratifying States, to encompass 'that which is practicable or practically possible, taking into account all circumstances ruling at the time, including humanitarian and military considerations'.[53] The same

[52] Soanes and Stevenson, *Concise Oxford English Dictionary*, at page 519.

[53] Statement of Canada, printed in Roberts and Guelff, *Documents on the Laws of War*, at page 502. Similar statements were made by Algeria, at page 499; Austria, at page 500; Italy, at page 507; Belgium, at page 501; Federal Republic of Germany, at page 504; Ireland, at page 506; the Netherlands at page 508; Spain, at page 509; the United Kingdom, at page 510.

understanding is repeated in the wording in Protocol III to CCW 1(5). This understanding of the rule shows – as noted by one commentator[54] – a clear reference to the concept of military necessity in its foundational function.

Recalling that the yardstick of the commander's assessment in all situations is that of the reasonable commander, the question of feasibility with regard to precautionary measures coincides with reasonableness in many aspects. Furthermore, the core of the concept of 'feasibility' relies both upon a 'fairly broad margin of judgment' and (within this) the considerations of military necessity.[55]

The expectation of what is reasonably available at the time is closely linked to 'the circumstances ruling at the time' which is among the elements of the definition of military objectives. As seen in the passage in the Canadian Manual: 'Commanders, planners and staff officers are required to take all "feasible" steps to verify that potential targets are legitimate targets. However, such decisions will be based on the "circumstances ruling at the time".'[56]

What then, are feasible measures to verify that potential targets are legitimate targets?

15.3.1 *'Feasible to Verify'*

The rule in AP I article 57(2)(a)(i) contains two elements: feasibility and verification, where the one affects the other. The rule is of paramount practical importance in setting the standard for commanders' concrete 'firing guidance' to subordinate forces. What measures ought to be prescribed by commanders under specific circumstances in order to make sure that their attacks in fact are directed at lawful targets?

The ordinary meaning of the verb 'to verify' is to 'confirm' or 'prove'[57] that the target is what it is presumed to be. This must not, however, be confused with a specific level of certainty, which is addressed elsewhere in the AP I, as the doubt rules. The rule in article 57 addresses reasonable *measures* to make

54 See Rauch, 'The concept of military necessity in the context of the law of war', at page 23.

55 AP I Commentary to article 57, at para. 2210, page 684. See also Rauch, 'The concept of military necessity in the context of the law of war', at page 21, where he argues that: 'Military necessity is always part of the evaluation, consideration and decision making process in those cases . . .'

56 Canadian Manual, at para. 418(2), at page 4-5.

57 Oxford Dictionary at: www.oxforddictionaries.com/definition/american_english-thesaurus/verify.

the decision as certain *as possible*, not the level of doubt.[58] However, the two issues will naturally be considered together in practice. The duty to verify that an object is a military objective relates not only to the status of being military, as opposed to civilian, but also to the eventual special protection that the object may enjoy, such as being a medical facility, cultural property or works and installations containing dangerous forces.[59]

The 'feasible to verify rule' is often applied by the military as 'positive identification', so-called PID.[60] The jargon is a linguistic pleonasm and as such not ideal to describe a rule. Identification is identification, the adjective 'positive' does not add clarity, but it might give a psychological illusion of being 'even more sure', in addition to drawing upon military terms and expressions like 'positive' and 'affirmative' in order to confirm something. In a legal context, however, the phrase 'positive identification' does not add more than what is already accounted for, namely that an objective is verified as military. I will stick to the labelling of the treaty text in the following.

The very concept of 'verification' presumes some sort of recognition. You cannot verify that you have found a military objective unless you know what you are looking for. In cases concerning enemy military materiel this recognition is, at least at the outset, easy. The use of stealth functions and advanced military camouflaging equipment may obviously make the recognition more difficult. Creating such difficulties lie at the core of the method of ruses of war, which is a lawful deceptive manoeuvre – all contributing to the totality of the 'fog of war' and, eventually, calling for the commander's reasonableness. In cases where objects that are normally used for civilian purposes are being used for military purposes, these may be even harder to 'recognise', and additional information may be required. Eventually, the need for additional information in such cases aligns with the rules on presumption of civilian status for objects normally used for civilian purposes.[61] The ICRC argues that if there is only a 'slight doubt' as to whether an object is a military objective, additional information is required.[62] The reference to 'slight doubt' appears too strict,[63]

58 For a discussion of the rule of doubt, see Chapter 7. The level of certainty must be 'reasonable', not complete. With regard to precautions in attack, see also Boothby, *The Law of Targeting*, at page 121.

59 See Chapter 17.

60 For a legal context and discussion of the use of the expression, see for example Merriam, 'Affirmative target identification', at pages 84–5. See also Schmitt, 'Targeting and international humanitarian law in Afghanistan', for example at pages 316–17.

61 See Chapter 7.

62 AP I Commentary to article 57, at page 680, para. 2195.

63 In this direction, see Dinstein, *The Conduct of Hostilities*, at page 165; Boothby, *The Law of Targeting*, at pages 121–2; Henderson, *The Contemporary Law of Targeting*, at page 163.

and at odds with the acknowledgement of the inevitable uncertainties of warfare.[64] One may easily foresee cases where there is slight doubt, yet reasonable to attack and not feasible to make further verifications on the status of the object.[65] Ideally, intelligence should be collected from the 'inside' of an object, for example by the use of human sources inside a building. In many cases, security reasons preclude this option – it is not feasible. Problems thus arise in cases where, for example, an object is being used for the first time as an effective contribution to military action. In these cases, recognition is not truly possible and unavoidable uncertainties arise. This is within the frame of reasonableness. Then, when enemy behaviour at a certain stage becomes familiar, the 'map of recognizable conduct' needs updating. Such updating is a continuous process and a military commander's deeply rooted challenge. If he or she lags too far behind this continuous update, the limits of reason – and of his or her freedom to assess – are met.

The ICRC argues:

> The evaluation of the information obtained must include a serious check of its accuracy, particularly as there is nothing to prevent the enemy from setting up fake military objectives or camouflaging the true ones. In fact it is clear that no responsible military commander would wish to attack objectives which were of no military interest. In this respect humanitarian interests and military interests coincide.[66]

It is true that humanitarian and military interests coincide – until a certain point: the point where the potential danger meets the doubt in question, in other words where time gets critical. Among the different measures and circumstances that affects whether feasible precautions have been taken to identify the target are: the time and resources available, the risk to own forces, the potential military advantage of attacking the target at the time, the possible collateral damage anticipated, the weather, topography and relative positioning of forces in order to possibly keep 'eyes on target' etc.[67] Two examples may illustrate how the conception of 'feasible measures' may change according to the circumstances.

64 See Chapter 4.

65 In the OTP Report, at para. 29, it is argued that: 'The obligation to do everything feasible is high but not absolute. A military commander must set up an effective intelligence gathering system to collect and evaluate information concerning potential targets. The commander must also direct his forces to use available technical means to properly identify targets during operations.'

66 AP I Commentary to article 57, at pages 680–1, para. 2195.

67 See for example: the Norwegian Manual, at pages 29–30; US DoD Manual, at pages 138–40; Boothby, *The Law of Targeting*, at page 122; Henderson, *The Contemporary Law of Targeting*, at pages 162–5.

In the first case, there is suspicion that enemy forces have a weapons cache, hiding portable air defence (MANPADS), in a house otherwise appearing as a civilian house. The following measures make it *highly likely* that the target constitutes a military objective as suspected: a trustworthy human source on the inside of the building reporting that there are weapons being stored inside, in combination with additional information stating the same. The additional information may come from satellite images or pictures from an unmanned aerial vehicle (UAV) showing that weapons have been carried inside the house, and no corresponding images of weapons being carried out. In that case, the measures provide an ideal certainty. In another situation, there might not be a human source on the inside of the house and the only feasible information accessible is from a trustworthy source reporting a planned weapons transport. There might be available UAV pictures, indicating that weapons have been carried in, but no corresponding confirmation that the weapons have not also been carried out again. In this latter case it may be considered as *likely* that the target is actually a military objective and the pending question is whether it is feasible with additional information in order to confirm that the MANPADS are (still) in the house. The answer depends on the circumstances. Additional human sources may be feasible to acquire, but human sources are also the most uncertain sources, taking into account that information has often travelled through several mouths. If technology is available, surveillance above the house can be started and continued until, for example, the weapons are observed being carried out of the house. Finally, own forces can visit the house in order to verify themselves whether MANPADS are actually being stored in the house or not. The latter alternative provides the highest degree of certainty and *may* in some cases be considered feasible – in a case as the one described here – if the risk to own forces is considered acceptable. The latter question is at the core of the commander's margin of appreciation.[68] It might even be that he or she considers the risk of MANPADS being armed (untouched) as lower than the risk of sending own forces to search the house. The feasibility of a multitude of information gathering in the foregoing example hinges on the overall scenario: if

68 In the OTP Report, at para. 29, it is argued that: 'Both the commander and the aircrew actually engaged in operations must have some range of discretion to determine which available resources shall be used and how they shall be used. Further, a determination that inadequate efforts have been made to distinguish between military objectives and civilians or civilian objects should not necessarily focus exclusively on a specific incident. If precautionary measures have worked adequately in a very high percentage of cases then the fact they have not worked well in a small number of cases does not necessarily mean they are generally inadequate.'

MANPADS are actually considered an asset for the enemy forces, this indicates that there is no other strategic air defence accessible to deny access to the area. Furthermore, as long as there is no strategic air defence or other assets denying access to the area, it may actually be feasible to approach the house by own forces, and as such gather more reliable information.

Let us then consider a second scenario where the enemy possesses an advanced strategic air-defence system, making it impossible for own forces to get access to the area where the system assumedly is being placed. It might be that the air-defence system gives the enemy free space to target own forces within a certain radius. While access to the area is denied, the feasibility to verify that the right object and area is located is correspondingly low. Yet, the possible advantage of destroying the enemy air-defence system is potentially high. A commander may in that case accept fewer measures to verify the target as well as a higher degree of uncertainty and still be 'reasonable'. It is thus both the nature of the target as well as the commander's overall risk assessment which make up the ingredients of 'feasible measures'.[69]

15.3.2 *'Feasible . . . with a View to Avoid and Minimize'*

The rule in AP I article 57(2)(a)(ii) obliges commanders to take all feasible precautions *with a view* to avoid or minimise collateral damage. As with almost all other rules in the LOAC, this one also deals with reasonable foresight. The commander is obliged to seek to reduce collateral damage as far as possible. Whether the result actually reflects his aspirations is another issue. The rule is not the same as the proportionality rule, although the two rules are in practice intertwined. Excessiveness is a separate consideration that addresses the comparison between advantage and collateral damage. However, the way an attack is planned to be carried out will often decide whether the threshold of excessiveness is reached or not. The latter case is a matter of precautions, which is an integrated part of military planning. The rule does not prescribe that specific methods or weapons must be chosen if these will result in diminished collateral damage. Again, the notion of feasibility refers to the

69 In the same direction see for example the article by Corn, 'Targeting, command judgment, and a proposed quantum of information component', at page 441. Corn suggests a 'quantum of information framework to facilitate the effective implementation of the military objective test', which is a model drawn upon US domestic law. Beyond his point of departure, I do not subscribe to his suggested levels of information required. For example, I do not share his views that the information required in order to target objectives, that are military by nature, can be circumscribed to 'operational instinct'. See for example his illustrations made at page 495.

commander's different options under the circumstances, accepting that the same or similar military advantage is still to be pursued.[70]

Among the measures to consider as 'feasible' are those mentioned above with regard to identification of military objectives.[71] However, when considering feasible measures to minimise collateral damage during an attack, two additional precautions appear with great force: weapon selection and warnings. In total, the timing, the risk to own forces, the choice of weapons and ammunition (weaponeering) and warnings stand out as crucial elements in the consideration of feasibility with regard to avoiding collateral damage.[72]

The law is way too vague and flexible to establish a specific duty to use precision guided munitions in urban areas.[73] If resort to precision guided munitions was a practically possible option in the concrete situation, however, this fact may also be decisive for the legal consideration of feasibility.[74] In this direction, see for example the statement made in the aftermath of the first Gulf War, by Human Rights Watch: 'Given the well-publicized technologically advanced munitions available to the allied forces in this conflict, Middle East Watch believes that the most discriminating weapons should have been used in attacks against military targets in populated civilian areas.'[75]

The recurring issue of the security of the attacking force – also referred to as 'force protection' and dealt with separately above, in Chapter 14 – may in many cases form a substantial part of feasibility considerations, in addition to being a part of the military advantage of the attack itself. The examples made above, with regard to identification of military objectives, clearly illustrate how the security of the attacking force may play a decisive role. In the first case (with the house presumably being a weapons cache with MANPADS), the security of own forces allows for a different range of precautionary measures than in the latter case (of the strategic air-defence system placed in an area where access is denied). The alternative ways of neutralising the threat from the weapons cache

70 Boothby, *The Law of Targeting*, at page 124; Boivin, 'The legal regime applicable to targeting military objectives in the context of contemporary warfare', at page 38.

71 See above, Section 15.3.1.

72 The UK Manual lists the following, at page 83: the importance of the target and the urgency of the situation, intelligence about the target (what it is being used for etc.), the characteristics of the target itself, for example whether it houses dangerous forces (such as chemical weapons). What weapons are available, their range, accuracy, and radius of effect, conditions affecting the incidental loss or damage, such as the proximity of civilians or civilian objects in the vicinity of the target or other protected objects or zones, the risks to his own forces.

73 Dinstein, *The Conduct of Hostilities*, at page 170; Boothby, *The Law of Targeting*, at page 124.

74 Boivin, 'The legal regime applicable to targeting military objectives in the context of contemporary warfare', at page 40.

75 Human Rights Watch, Needless Deaths in the Gulf War, at page 124.

are numerous compared to the possibilities to deal with enemy strategic air defence. The potential risk of collateral damage may vary accordingly. In the first case, there is first and foremost the possibility simply to avoid bombing the house from the air or by indirect fires (for example artillery), by sending own forces to take control of the house and the weapons inside. Second, if the intelligence gathering possibilities are optimal, it might be possible to attack the weapons while they are being carried out of the house, and as such spare the building and its surroundings from a bigger blast. Third, if a more conventional attack is chosen because the risk to own forces is considered too high to search the house, it might still be feasible with eyes on target through the use of forward air controllers (FACs) and as such contribute to minimise collateral damage.

Following the attack on the Al-Firdus bunker in Iraq in 1991,[76] one of the pending legal questions was whether feasible precautions could have been taken in order to avoid the tragic result of civilian deaths. While Human Rights Watch questions why the intelligence on the target was not updated with images that could have revealed civilian presence, others refer to 'normal intelligence gathering methods', arguing that if these had proved reliable in the past, this was sufficient for the standard of reasonableness.[77] Under the circumstances, taking into account the premeditated concurrent use of the bunker as a shelter by the Iraqi armed forces, it is difficult to conclude otherwise than that feasible measures were taken to establish sufficient information on the target. A final question concerning precautionary measures appears however: that of issuing warnings. Accepting that it appeared reasonable at the time to rely on information that the target was a military objective, a warning could, arguably, still have been issued with respect to the surrounding civilian population.[78]

15.3.3 *Feasible Precautions Applied in Afghanistan*

A case study illustrating precautionary procedures of recent date is the International Security Assistance Force (ISAF) mission in Afghanistan from 2002/3 until 2017.[79] Although the conflict in Afghanistan is a non-international

[76] See Chapter 4 as well.

[77] Human Rights Watch, Needless Deaths in the Gulf War, at page 137. Barber, 'Scuds, shelters and retreating soldiers', at page 689.

[78] It does not make sense, however, to argue, like Human Rights Watch does in Needless Deaths in the Gulf War, page 126, that a warning should have been issued in order to evacuate civilians from the shelter – if one first acknowledges that it was reasonable to rely on the information that there was no civilian use of the building.

[79] The international presence today has the consent of the Afghan Government and as well basis in UN Security Council resolutions, mandating the NATO force ISAF to use 'all necessary means' in order to support security, stability and transition in Afghanistan. The mandate for

armed conflict, it is nevertheless illustrative with regard to conduct of hostilities.[80]

In Afghanistan, as elsewhere, the air war has been 'a dominant feature of the war'.[81] Civilian casualties have shown a disturbing trend and been a repeated and major concern for the military operations in Afghanistan, for the UN,[82] by participating States,[83] the ICRC,[84] as well as ISAF and Operation Enduring Freedom (OEF) themselves. The urge to minimise collateral damage led the (different) commander(s) of the ISAF forces (COMISAF) to issue 'civilian casualties directives' (sometimes referred to as CIVCAS directives) to his subordinate forces from 2008 and onwards, stressing among others that the 'outmost care should the taken to minimize any damage'.[85] In 2009, strict guidelines for the use of indirect fire, such as artillery, were issued:

> I cannot prescribe the appropriate use for every condition that a complex battlefield will produce, so I expect our force to internalize and operate within my intent ... The use of air-to-ground munitions and indirect fires against residential compounds is only authorized under very limited and prescribed conditions.[86]

The exact conditions for when indirect fire in residential compounds was releasable was classified information. The imposed limitations resulted, however, in situations where the risk to own forces finally made General Petraeus to state one year later that: 'Subordinate commanders are not authorized to

ISAF was established by UN Security Council Resolution 1386(2001) and was later extended a number of times, last by UN Security Council Resolution 2069(2012) (until 13 October 2013). The US led operation, Operation Enduring Freedom (OEF), does not have a mandate from the Security Council, but coordinates its activities with ISAF according to UN Security Council Resolution 2069(2012). The UN Assistance Mission in Afghanistan (UNAMA) is not dealt with here, as it has not conducted combat operations.

80 One of the most problematic legal issues with regard to the armed conflict in Afghanistan is that of the status of the different armed groups fighting against the Afghan government and its allies, see Dinstein, *Conduct of Hostilities*, page 55. This issue is beyond the scope of the present discussion.

81 Schmitt, 'Targeting and international humanitarian law in Afghanistan', at page 309.

82 See for example UN Security Council Resolutions 1674(2006), 1738(2006), 1849(2009) and 2096(2013).

83 See the Norwegian concern expressed in: www.regjeringen.no/nb/dep/ud/kampanjer/bistand_afghanistan/politikk.html?id=598732.

84 See for example the 2012 ICRC Report on Afghanistan, at page 242 ff.

85 ISAF Headquarters, Kabul: COMISAF's Tactical Directive, 30 December 2008 (ISAF Tactical Directive, 30 December 2008).

86 ISAF Headquarters, Kabul: COMISAF's Tactical Directive, 6 July 2009 (ISAF Tactical Directive, 6 July 2009).

further restrict this guidance without my approval.'[87] The development illustrates the checks and balances inherent in the notion of feasibility. The feasible precautions were in this case the result of, on the one hand, the commander's assessment of the accepted level of risk to own forces (repeatedly confused during the ISAF mission as 'self-defence') and, on the other hand, the aim of protecting civilians.[88] COMISAF's 'intent' represents, in this case, his margin of appreciation: 'My intent is to eliminate ISAF-caused civilian casualties across Afghanistan, and minimize civilian casualties throughout the area of operations by reducing their exposure to insurgent operations.'[89] Furthermore, as direction, COMISAF states that: 'every Afghan is a civilian until otherwise apparent; all compounds are civilian structures until otherwise apparent; in every location where there is evidence of human habitation, civilians are present until otherwise apparent'.[90] The quoted passage entails not only a presumption of civilian status for persons and objects, but also for civilian presence unless 'apparent'; a presumption which arguably goes beyond the requirements of the treaty text. This has become a prominent feature of the conflict in Afghanistan – that politically imposed restrictions exceed the limits of the LOAC.[91] That the ROEs and SOPs were considered as distinct from the LOAC was also illustrated by the German prosecutor's report in the Kunduz incident of 2009.[92] The ISAF practice in this regard must be viewed as context specific and not as practice formative for customary international law.[93]

87 ISAF Headquarters, Kabul: COMISAF's Tactical Directive, 1 August 2010. (ISAF Tactical Directive, 1 August 2010.) See ISAF News Release, August 2010, releasing unclassified parts of the Directive.

88 ISAF Headquarters, Kabul: COMISAF's Tactical Directive, 30 November 2011, where it is stated that: 'We must balance our pursuit of the enemy with our efforts to minimize the loss of innocent civilian life and our obligation to protect our troops . . . all planning and execution of operations account for our obligations to employ force consistent with the principles of military necessity, proportionality, distinction and humanity in accordance with LOAC.'

89 Ibid.

90 Ibid.

91 The restrictions are, however, political – and legally binding as orders – but not a part of the LOAC. See for example, Schmitt, 'Targeting and international humanitarian law in Afghanistan', at page 312.

92 The Prosecutors report is accounted for and commented upon in English by Heintschel von Heinegg and Dreist, 'The 2009 Kunduz Air Attack'; and commented upon in Chapter 14, with regard to military advantage. On the relationship to ROE, see page 850. It should also be remarked that the authors of the article regret the absence of a clarification on the relationship between Chapter VII of the UN Charter and the LOAC. Furthermore, that armed forces are 'in desperate need of clarification of the clause "with all necessary means"'. On these points, see page 865.

93 I cannot see that the mentioned practice points in the direction of being formation of a customary rule. On the contrary, the political tone of the limitations is – as illustrated above – manifest and *opinio juris* seems lacking, although practice arguably can be retrieved.

Concerning feasibility, however, the guidelines in the tactical directives illustrate what Commander ISAF continuously has assessed as feasible – taking into account the security of the attacking force, mission accomplishment and minimising collateral damage. In the case of ISAF, protection of civilians became a cornerstone of the mission itself. The CIVCAS directives came out in the wake of ultimatums given from Karzai to the USA and NATO with regard to civilian casualties.[94] The importance of reducing civilian casualties in order to succeed has been a remaining issue and is for example expressed in the ISAF press release in response to a United Nations Assistance Mission in Afghanistan (UNAMA) report[95] on the protection of civilians in 2013:

> Protecting innocent Afghan civilians is the cornerstone of ISAF's mission. It is a sacred trust and responsibility that the Coalition forces take very seriously. Our deeds and the results of our long-term civilian casualty mitigation efforts demonstrate our resolve. While we have more to do, we are committed to the work ahead and the success of the combined effort to protect the Afghan people.[96]

Precautionary measures in order to reduce collateral damage therefore simultaneously enhance mission accomplishment. Consequently, the threshold for feasibility becomes lower. When precautionary measures align with mission accomplishment, these measures are also more easily assessed as feasible.

In the same direction, see Schmitt, 'Targeting and international humanitarian law in Afghanistan', at page 328.

94 See for example Peter, 'Karzai gives ultimatum on civilian deaths'.

95 The figures according to the 'Afghanistan Mid-Year Report 2013 on Protection of Civilians in Armed Conflict', includes a 14 per cent increase in deaths and 28 per cent increase in injuries from 2012 to 2013, a total of a 23 per cent surge in civilian casualties from the year before. The report is prepared by UNAMA and is retrievable at: http://unama.unmissions.org/LinkClick.aspx?fileticket=EZoxNuqDtps%3d&tabid=12254&language=en-US; the figures are also referred to in the UN press release: www.un.org/apps/news/story.asp?NewsID=45536#.UkMtooZmiSo (accessed 25 September 2013).

96 ISAF Press Release, 31 July 2013.

PART IV

THE EXCEPTIVE FACE OF MILITARY NECESSITY

16

Destruction and Seizure of Property When Military Necessity Requires

16.1 A HISTORICAL RULE WITH NARROW BUT SIGNIFICANT VALUE

This chapter contains an account of the rule governing destruction or seizure of property during hostilities.[1] As early as in the Codification Era in the nineteenth century, permission to destroy or seize property when required by military necessity was codified in treaty law.

Despite not being a treaty, the Lieber Code is illustrative and frequently cited. Article 15 (quoted in Chapter 3) contains, among others, a sweeping permission: 'Military necessity admits of all direct destruction of life or limb of "armed" enemies … of all destruction of property, and of all withholding of sustenance or means of life from the enemy; of the appropriation of whatever an enemy's country affords necessary for the subsistence and safety of the army …' In a prohibitive language, the 1899 and 1907 Hague Regulations article 23(g) confirms a similar right by stating that it is prohibited 'To destroy or seize the enemy's property, unless such destruction be imperatively demanded by the necessities of war.'

During the same epoch, a number of examples from State practice can be found in history, such as during the Franco-Prussian War (1870–1),[2] and the South African War.[3] The sweeping practice of scorched earth tactics was

[1] The rule on destruction and seizure of property during belligerent occupation lies outside the scope of this book.

[2] See also Chapters 6 and 12, on *Kriegsraison* and the aspects of 'total war' and loss of civilian protection from attack.

[3] The war was subject to criticism throughout Europe, outside the British Isles, both during and after the war took place. Britain first regarded the Transvaal opponents as merely criminals, but eventually regarded the whole war as an international war. See for example: Neff, *War and the Law of Nations*, at page 264. Britain was a party to the Geneva Convention of 1864 as well as the (then) recently adopted Hague Convention on Land Warfare from 1899.

subject to persistent criticism from France[4] and Europe outside the British Isles,[5] respectively. In British defence it was argued, with regard to the Hague rule on destruction of property in particular, that 'Now nothing can be more imperative in war than the preservation of the communications of the army.'[6] The 'communications' in this regard was actually pointing back at the situation where guerrillas were given shelter in farms,[7] which were subsequently being burned, in order to somehow 'smoke-out' the opponent.[8] The effect, however, was dubious.[9]

Today, the 1907 Hague Regulations apply by wording during conduct of hostilities in land warfare, but the quoted rule has acquired the status of customary international law and applies throughout the different domains of warfare.[10]

In this chapter, I address seven different aspects of the rule on destruction of property. First, its scope under customary international law. Second, the apparent opposition and mutual exclusion of 'necessity' and 'wantonness'. Third, that the scope of the rule today is limited to military operations not amounting to attacks as defined by the AP I article 49. Fourth, and in connection with the foregoing point, the absence of a distinction between military objectives and civilian objects – that is to say that destruction of military objectives is always lawful a fortiori, and that the practical scope of the rule thus relates to civilian objects. Fifth, that the notion of 'property' is glaringly unaddressed in legal literature, yet seemingly a familiar concept, at least in its core essence. Sixth, that the notion of 'imperative' at the outset does not appear to add any difference to the material substance; what arguably matters are the examples, and, seventh, that an explicit assessment of military necessity is *not required* when seizure, capture or destruction is justified by other specific rules granting the right to capture for prize or as war booty.

4 Particularly harsh (and biased) criticism of Prussia was raised by the French (and thus enemy citizen) Andler, *'Frightfulness' in Theory and Practice*, see pages 37–9, where he argues refers to an unlawful use of incendiaries, looting and reprisals against the civilian population.

5 In the South African War, which was hard on the British forces in particular after the Boer's commencement of guerrilla tactics, approximately one year in, the British implemented a sweeping 'scorched earth' tactics in response. See Nasson, *The South African War*, pages 217–18. Nasson also refers to statements by the British Army, which said: 'The problem of the Boers lies not only in their armies. They are in the main a rather hostile people, who have also to be subdued in order for our present business to be brought to an end.'

6 Doyle, *The War in South Africa*, at page 89.

7 Ibid., at pages 88–9.

8 Both the actual farm-burning and the concentration camps have been argued to be a part of the scorched earth policy. See Nasson, *The South African War*, at page 222.

9 Ibid., at page 223.

10 For examples, see Section 16.8.

16.2 THE RULE IN TREATY LAW AND CUSTOMARY LAW

The prohibition in the 1899 and the 1907 Hague Regulations of destruction and seizure of enemy property unless 'imperatively demanded by the necessities of war'[11] has reappeared with slight alterations both in the First, Second and the Fourth Geneva Conventions of 1949,[12] as well as in the statutes of international war crimes tribunals.

In the London Agreement for the Nuremberg Tribunal, war crime was defined as 'wanton destruction' or 'devastation ... not justified by military necessity',[13] whereas the Statutes of the ICTY and ICC criminalises destruction of property within two contexts: as grave breaches of the Geneva Conventions and as violations of treaty or customary law in general.[14] The requirement of 'extensive' destruction and appropriation of property (in the first context) exclusively relates to the war crime of breaching the Geneva Conventions – that is 'if committed against persons or property protected by the Convention'.[15] Destruction of other public or private property is dealt with in the Hague Regulations and does not amount to grave breaches of the GCs.[16]

The two different forms of criminalisation in the ICTY and Rome Statutes do not appear to affect the general rule governing conduct of hostilities.[17] The ICRC Customary Law Study encapsulates the rule of customary law in its rule 50 as 'The destruction or seizure of the property of an adversary is prohibited, unless required by imperative military necessity.'[18] While the exact wording may differ slightly,[19] similar rules are incorporated into a vast number of States' military manuals and national legislation.[20]

11 1899 and 1907 Hague Regulations, article 23(g).
12 GC I article 50; GC II article 51; and GC IV article 147.
13 London Agreement for the International Military Tribunal, article 6(b). On the meaning of 'destruction vs. devastation', see Section 16.8.
14 ICTY Statute article 2b and Rome Statute article 8(2)(a)(iv), and ICTY Statute article 3b and Rome Statute article 8(2)(b)(xiii).
15 GC I article 50; GC II article 51; and GC IV article 147.
16 ICRC Commentary on the First Geneva Convention 2016 article 50, at para. 3006, pages 195–6.
17 The ICTY case law also seems to support that 'extensive' is a particular criminal law requirement, see for example the cases of Blaskic Case, Trial Chamber Judgment (para. 234 ff.) and Martic Case, (para. 92). On the specific formulation 'carried out unlawfully and wantonly', see further Section 16.3.
18 ICRC CIHL, rule 50.
19 The dubious added value of the requirement of 'imperative' is dealt with in Section 16.7, and Chapter 2.
20 See the enumeration done in the ICRC CIHL. Older examples include the Lieber Code articles 15 and 16, and the Brussels Declaration article 13(g).

While the 1907 Hague Regulations govern land warfare, neither the criminalisation nor the corresponding customary rule appear to be limited to the land domain. As a point of departure, the rule prohibiting destruction or seizure of enemy property, unless required by imperative military necessity, is applicable in all domains of warfare: air, sea, land, cyber and space. The fact that the San Remo Manual, the AMW Manual and the Tallinn Manual only deal with destruction or seizure of property within the context of the natural environment and cultural property (or occupation as well in the Tallinn Manual), does not alter this point of departure, as there appears to be no clear legal reason for the lack of regulation under these instruments.[21] Having stated this point of departure, the actual scope of the prohibition – and the permission to destroy or seize property when required by military necessity – will vary according to (a) permission to capture or seize property according to the rule governing war booty or prize and (b) rules granting special protection to certain categories of property.

16.3 NECESSARY AS OPPOSED TO WANTON DESTRUCTION OF PROPERTY

In the context of destruction of property, military necessity appears, at least at the first glance, as the opposite of wantonness. Lieber Code article 16 states, among others that: 'Military necessity does not admit of ... the wanton devastation of a district.' In the London Agreement article 6(b) and ICTY Statute article 3(b) the prohibition is expressed as: 'Wanton destruction ... not justified by military necessity', while the GC I article 50 and the ICTY Statute article 2(d) criminalises destruction 'not justified by military necessity and carried out unlawfully and wantonly'. In the latter version, wantonness relates to the behaviour of the person, while necessity relates to an objective fact. As such, the notion of wantonness fits with criminal law – perhaps rather than with international law of armed conflict as such. It also fits the ordinary meaning of the word as a 'cruel or violent action', or as 'deliberate and unprovoked'.[22] The ICRC Commentary to the GC I article 50 supports this understanding while addressing 'wantonly' as equivalent to 'vicious', 'unreasonably and maliciously risking harm while being utterly indifferent to the consequences'.[23] Simply put, 'carried out wantonly' relates to a subjective state

[21] See the San Remo Manual, rule 44; the AMW Manual, rule 88; and the Tallinn Manual, rule 149, at page 549. The Tallinn Manual neither refers to military necessity, nor to wantonness in the black letter rule.

[22] Soanes and Stevenson, *Concise Oxford English Dictionary*, at page 1626.

[23] See ICRC Commentary on the First Geneva Convention 2016, at para. 3016, pages 206–7, also relying upon the Blaskic Case (see above).

of mind on the hand of the perpetrator, while necessity relates to objective facts. *He* was reckless vs *it* was necessary. It is therefore theoretically possible to argue that an act reasoned by military necessity can be performed wantonly. Having said this, acts carried out wantonly will, for all practical purposes, never be considered militarily necessary. Furthermore, an act of necessity could hardly be considered an act of wantonness at the same time. A militarily necessary act is one that is required in order to achieve a military aim or objective, having a reasonable connection to this aim or objective.[24] Acts of wantonness, on the other hand, are those acts that lack such reasonable connection to the military aim. They are tortious acts carried out either maliciously or carelessly, for example speeding in open terrain, just for the rush of it, without thought for the stress and danger imposed on grazing livestock nearby. Needless to say, all acts of plunder, pillage and sheer vandalism are also wanton.[25] The common denominator for these acts is the lack of reasonable connection to military ends, and instead being motivated by private gains – whether these be greed, revenge or destructive lust.

Although not identical in all aspects, military necessity and wantonness thus appear to be mutually exclusive in practice. Consider the following example: let's say it was necessary to drive at speed with an armoured vehicle through a pine wood plantation, since enemy forces had taken control over the alternative road. The destruction caused to the plantation while driving over it was justified by military necessity. If the driving was carried out wantonly, those parts of the driving that were considered wanton would also be unnecessary. At this stage, legal analysis also becomes delicate, considering the commander's margin of appreciation. If, on the way through the pine wood forest, it was possible to avoid the plantation and drive through a felled area not yet being planted, this option should be chosen if easily available under the circumstances ruling at the time,[26] especially taking into account the time, level of threat and need of taking cover. If the reasonably available route is not chosen and the pine wood plantation is destroyed, it is hard to argue that the destruction was a result of an act required in order to reach the military aim (necessity): the advance and preservation of own forces. In any case, the duty to take constant care to spare civilian objects (and persons), according to the AP I article 57, would apply to this example.

24 See Chapter 2.

25 Pillage is criminalised as a separate crime and not dealt with further. See for example Rome Statute article 8(2)(b)(xvi).

26 See Chapter 4.

Military necessity may justify numerous acts, not limited to attacks on military objectives. Furthermore, military necessity cannot, in the context of destruction of property, be defined by reference to the definition of military objectives, as suggested by the ICTY in the Strugar Case.[27] On the other hand, a military objective satisfies the necessity test, as pointed out by the ICTY Appeals Chamber in the Prlic case.[28] The practical scope of application is the topic in the next two sections.

16.4 PRACTICAL SCOPE OF APPLICATION I: OPERATIONS NOT AMOUNTING TO ATTACKS

The rule prohibiting destruction of property not justified by military necessity (wanton destruction) applies to the entire spectrum of military operations during conduct of hostilities. This implies that military necessity, *in principle*, can be invoked against all destruction of property during conduct of hostilities. With regard to attacks, however, the AP I states that these only may be directed against military objectives (see below on military objectives vs civilian property).[29] The definition of attacks found the in the AP I expresses customary international law of armed conflict as well,[30] and states: '"Attacks" means acts of violence against the adversary, whether in offence or in defence.'[31] This definition is wide and meant to encompass not only defensive operations as well as offensive (as said in the treaty text), but 'combat action' more broadly.[32] Furthermore, 'attacks' covers acts of violence that are not exclusively directed at opposing *forces* – it clearly covers attacks directed against civilians or acts that by mistake hit civilians.[33] Although this definition is wide, it is not meant to encompass 'military movement or manoeuvre as such'.[34] 'Acts of violence' cannot reasonably be said to cover every act performed by military forces in the theatre during conduct of hostilities; some acts are more useful to categorise within the ambit of 'destruction of property'.

Military movements and manoeuvres may easily cause destruction to enemy property, and in these cases the 1907 Hague Regulations article 23(g) and the corresponding customary rule, apply.[35] As long as the movement or

27 The Strugar Case is also cited in Chapter 14.
28 ICTY, Prlic Case, at para. 411.
29 AP I article 48, see Chapter 7 above.
30 AMW Manual, article 1(e); Tallinn Manual, Commentary 2 to rule 92.
31 AP I article 49(1).
32 AP I Commentary, at para. 1880, page 603.
33 AMW Manual, Commentary to rule 1(e).
34 Bothe, Partsch and Solf, *New Rules*, at page 329.
35 See for example the examples in the US DoD Manual, at pages 263–4.

manoeuvre does not amount to an act of violence (which for example would be the case with 'show of force' manoeuvres), the right to destroy or seize enemy property has a wider scope than the right to attack military objectives.[36] Among such destruction is therefore the incidental damage resulting from movements done during, for example, transport of troops in a combat zone. This means that civilian property is protected against wanton destruction even if the act does not amount to an attack, and conversely, that it is lawful to destroy or seize the same property when required by military necessity, through acts or conduct not amounting to attacks. Examples are dealt with in Section 16.8, below.

Furthermore, the wording in the rule in the 1907 Hague Regulations is not limited to situations when an area is under the control of the destroying party. In fact, the provision is found under the heading 'hostilities' and separate rules govern situations when territory is under the control of the opposing party (occupation).[37] Despite this, both a number of States' military manuals as well as commentators deal with the rule on destruction of property *only* in the context of occupation.[38] This may appear misleading and contribute to the confusion over the relationship between the AP I rules and the Hague rule.

Finally, the rule governing destruction of property during hostilities governs, according to an ordinary understanding of the wording, operations prior to, and in the aftermath of, actual troops in contact. This means that it also covers situations when combat action is *not* going on, such as movements and positioning of forces, transportation of troops into theatre etc. In this regard the statements made by the ICTY in the Oric and Martic cases appear wrong (or perhaps exclusively focused on major demolition of civilian settlements). In

36 US DoD Manual, at page 261, where it is stated that the rule applies 'outside the context of attacks'. Dinstein, *Conduct of Hostilities*, at page 288.

37 1907 Hague Regulations, article 42. GC IV article 53 reiterates the content of article 23(g) in the Hague Regulations.

38 UK Manual, at page 299 paras. 11.75 and 11.75.1 with footnote 131, refers to situations where destruction is 'absolutely necessary'. The rule is only dealt with in the context of occupation, under the heading 'enemy property in occupied territory' and juxtaposed to the provision in the GC IV article 53. The UK Manual also explicitly states that the protection of civilian property 'on the battlefield' is dealt with elsewhere. The Norwegian Manual deals primarily with booty of war and not incidental destruction of property arising from conduct of hostilities beyond that damage that results from attacks directed against the adversary. See page 181. In the German Manual, destruction of property is not dealt with as a separate permission under the conduct of hostilities, see Chapter 4 (conduct of hostilities) vs Chapter 5 (occupation). See as well Olasolo, *Unlawful Attacks in Combat Situations*, at pages 91–2, who argues that the rule in the Hague Regulations should be limited to applying when an area is under the control of the opposing force. In the Canadian Manual, however, destruction, capture and seizure of property is dealt with as a separate legal basis, and not limited to situations of occupation.

the Oric Case the Trial Chamber argued that 'after the fighting has ceased, destruction can in principle no longer be justified by claiming "military necessity"'.[39] The statement seems to be a consequence of (wrongly) tying the prohibition on destruction of property onto everything that does not fulfil the criteria of being a military objective (see below).

All that said, destruction of property is, even though required by military necessity, subject to the duty to show 'constant care' towards the civilian population, civilians and civilian objects, as laid down in the AP I article 57(1).[40]

16.5 PRACTICAL SCOPE OF APPLICATION II: DESTRUCTION OF CIVILIAN PROPERTY

While attacks shall be limited to military objectives, the rule governing destruction of property governs, in practice, civilian property. When an object qualifies as a lawful target, it is a fortiori also necessary to destroy the same object.[41] The US DoD Manual states that: 'After all, if sufficient military necessity exists to justify attacking an object as reflected by that object meeting the definition of military objective, then imperative military necessity would also exist to justify seizing or destroying that object by measures short of attack.'[42] The assessment of military necessity under the rule governing destruction of property therefore has its independent scope of application when it comes to civilian property. Conversely, military necessity cannot be defined simply by referring to the definition of military objectives as done by the ICTY in the Strugar Case.[43]

Some argue, however, in favour of an opposite position, claiming that the simultaneous application of the Hague rule and the AP I could imply that attacks that are otherwise lawful according to the AP I could be unlawful according to the Hague rule if they are not military necessary.[44] Even though

39 See the ICTY Oric Case, Trial Chamber Judgment, at para. 588. It should also be said that the ICTY actually allows for destruction based on military necessity in a limited fashion. And in the Martic Case, para. 93: 'In principle, destruction carried out before fighting begins or after fighting has ceased cannot be justified by claiming military necessity.'

40 AP I article 57(1) applies also on the conduct of operations more broadly, and is not limited to attacks.

41 See the ICC Pre Trial Chamber decision in the Katanga and Chui Case, at paras. 312 and 313.

42 US DoD Manual, at page 263.

43 See Strugar Case, at para. 295. The Strugar Case is also dealt with in Chapter 17, with regard to cultural property.

44 Olasolo, *Unlawful Attacks in Combat Situations*, at pages 90–1, where he, in fact, he argues that military necessity may circumvent the status of legality in two ways.

the older Hague rule is based on the 'broad and undetermined notion of "necessities of war" (military necessity)',[45] the assertion that a lawful attack also can imply wanton destruction of property (which is the implication of unlawfulness according to the Hague rule), appears as nothing but construed as wrong. Ironically, the confusion appears to stem from, precisely, the undetermined notion of 'necessities of war'. It should be clear, however, that an attack on an object which is expected to produce a military advantage cannot at the same time be wanton. Although necessity and advantage are distinct legal concepts – and despite the fact that advantage is arguably 'less severe' than necessity – the presence of either one of the two precludes the finding of 'wanton acts of war'. Furthermore, the Hague rule does not permit attacks that are prohibited by the rules in the AP I.[46] If an attack is not expected to produce a military advantage, considerations of military necessity cannot trump the assessment done according to the rule in AP I article 52(2). On the other hand, if an attack is otherwise lawful, no separate assessment of imperative military necessity with regard to the incidental damage is required.[47]

16.6 THE NOTION OF 'PROPERTY'

The prohibition against destruction of property is widely formulated.[48] Both private and public property fall within the scope of the prohibition.[49] Furthermore, the notion of 'property' is linguistically wider than 'objects', that are traditionally understood in the context of the LOAC as 'visible and tangible' things.[50] 'Property', on the other hand, includes, by the ordinary meaning given to the word, 'a thing or things belonging to someone'.[51] As a point of departure, 'property' includes, but is not limited to, a piece of land, buildings and movables. 'Property' also includes 'realizable securities',[52] such

45 Olasolo, *Unlawful Attacks in Combat Situations*, at page 90.

46 US DoD Manual, at pages 262–3.

47 In this regard, see Chapter 13, as well as Section 16.8 below. With regard to the notion of collateral damage, see the ICC Pre Trial Chamber decision in the Katanga and Chui Case, at para. 313.

48 Dinstein, *Conduct of Hostilities*, at page 287.

49 Greenspan, *The Modern Law of Land Warfare*, at page 281. Dinstein, *Conduct of Hostilities*, at page 287.

50 AP I Commentary to article 52(2), at paras. 2007–8. This approach is supported by the majority in the Tallinn Manual, see Commentary 5 to rule 100, at page 437.

51 See for example Soanes and Stevenson, *Concise Oxford English Dictionary*, at page 1151. A similar understanding appears in the ICC Elements of Crimes, with regard to article 8(2(b)(xiii).

52 See 1907 Hague Regulations, article 53, at page 80. This provision only applies during occupation, but there is no reason to interpret 'property' differently for the purposes of article 23(g) and customary law.

as interest-bearing bonds,[53] which more often than not only 'exist' electronically, and not as a physical document.[54] Contrary to the view presented by the majority in the Tallinn Manual, it may be argued that 'property' includes intangible objects as well as tangible objects.[55] In fact, given the technological development in the administration of valuables, as well as other identifiable possessions that it is possible for someone to own, it appears counter-intuitive to exclude certain intangible possessions from the term 'property'. The decisive criterion should rather be focused on the ownership. The notion of ownership by an adversary also appears to have been central in the practice of the ICC, which stated in the Mbarushimana Case: 'As found by the Chamber in the Katanga case, the property in question may be moveable or immoveable, private or public, but must belong to individuals or entities aligned with, or having an allegiance to, a party to the conflict, adverse or hostile to the perpetrator.'[56]

16.7 DOES THE REQUIREMENT OF 'IMPERATIVE' ADD ANY VALUE?

According to the Hague rule,[57] destruction of property is prohibited unless '*imperatively* required by military necessity'. The adverb 'imperatively', when placed in addition to 'necessities of war', indicates by its wording that necessity as such is not enough for lawfulness – it must be *more* than necessary. The practical implication of the requirement of 'imperative' is, however, unclear.[58] This lack of clarity is partly caused by the adverbial and adjectival inconsistency throughout the GCs as compared to the Hague Regulations[59] and partly by the wording itself: imperative may also be read *into* the notion of necessity, as an integral part of it.[60] The choice of different wording in the GCs[61] and the Hague Regulations has

53 Dinstein, *The International Law of Belligerent Occupation*, at page 211.

54 I disagree with the majority of the Tallinn Manual, expressed in Commentary 6 to rule 100 at page 437, that data is not property.

55 Ibid., see also Commentary to rule 142, at pages 534–5 with regard to the notion of 'cultural property'.

56 The ICC Pre-trial Chamber I, Mbarushimana Case, at para. 171.

57 As well as the formulations of the rule in the ICRC CIHL and the Rome Statute, see Section 16.3.

58 McCoubrey, 'The nature of the modern doctrine of military necessity', at page 224; Dinstein, *Conduct of Hostilities*, at page 12.

59 See Chapter 2.

60 The *Merriam Webster Dictionary* refers to 'necessary' as an 'imperative duty'.

61 The corresponding provision in GC IV article 53, applying during occupation, uses the phrase 'absolutely necessary'.

met criticism for being somewhat random.[62] Differences in terminology aside, the provisions do not necessarily represent a different threshold.[63]

The requirement of 'imperatively' found in the 1907 Hague Regulations was left out of the London Agreement, leaving the threshold for a war crime higher than a simple violation of treaty law. The impact of this more lenient test has been subject to disagreement and leaves no guidance for the content of customary law.[64] If anything, the lack of clarity has only become more manifest after the adoption of the ICTY and the Rome Statute, which have applied both (different) tests: the ICTY applies the (linguistically) more lenient test in its article 3(b), while the Rome Statute applies the test as laid down in the 1907 Hague Regulations article 23(g) in its article 8(2)(xiii). To sum up, it should therefore suffice to say that the adverb 'imperatively' does not appear to add substance to the requirement of military necessity.

16.8 PRACTICAL SCOPE OF APPLICATION III: THE MODES OF DESTRUCTION AND SEIZURE

16.8.1 Destruction, Devastation, Damage and Seizure

It has already been pointed out in Section 16.4 above that the primary scope of application for the prohibition of destruction of property concerns operations that do not amount to attacks. In the present section, I shall address some practical aspects of the modes of destruction and seizure, including some examples from history.

The Hague Rule and customary law refer to 'destruction or seizure' as prohibited acts. The provisions criminalising destruction of property invariably refer to 'destruction or devastation' and to 'destruction or seizure'. The London Agreement article 6(b) as well as the ICTY Statute use the former phrase pointing out, however, that that the two nouns 'destruction' and 'devastation', are similar.[65] The Rome Statute, on the other hand, uses destruction and seizure.

62 See Draper, 'Military necessity and humanitarian imperatives', at page 140, who expresses that: 'the two provisions do not chime well' and 'the Convention has done little to clarify the uncertainties of the law implicit in the cases'.

63 Dinstein, *The International Law of Belligerent Occupation*, at page 196. In the ICRC Commentary of 1952, the differences in language is not commented upon, only the different area of application with regard to occupation.

64 See Schwarzenberger, *International Law*, at page 134 vs McCoubrey, 'The nature of the modern doctrine of military necessity', at page 224, where the latter argues that the practice of the International Military Tribunal does not support a loosened standard in general.

65 ICTY Strugar Case, at para. 291, commenting on the ICTY Statute article 3(b).

With regard to the different forms destruction may amount to, the ICC stated in the Mbarushimana Case that: 'In the view of the Chamber, the war crime of destruction of property may be carried out through acts such as setting fire to, pulling down, or otherwise damaging the adversaries' property.'[66]

Many acts may in practice amount to 'destruction' of property, including the less destructive act of 'damage'. Examples from State practice and case law concerning different forms of setting fire to property, such as houses, food storages, crops, dwellings and livestock, are numerous and in many cases the examples have one feature in common: destruction has been done in order to deny the enemy of its potential use of the property. The next section provides a brief overview of practice and law in this regard.

16.8.2 Deny of Enemy Use and Scorched Earth Tactics

Scorched earth tactics have been applied on countless occasions throughout history in order to deny the enemy use of that property. There are four aspects that are important to point out with regard to destruction of property in order to deny enemy use: first, that it may be considered a necessity to destroy enemy property in order to deny the enemy armed forces from using it.[67]

Second, that in many cases (probably most cases) that same property would qualify as a military objective[68] and also lawful to attack. Third, that the act of destruction would qualify as an attack and thus be governed by the AP I rules and fourth, that destruction of property in order to deny the enemy from using a certain area *may* be lawful within the limited auspices laid down by the AP I, but this access to apply the scorched earth tactics today is for most practical purposes limited to the defence of own territory against an invading force.[69] The majority of practice by States and older case law is therefore of limited illustrative value to shed light on the scope of the rule today, but some remarks may nevertheless be useful.

In most recent cases dealt with by international tribunals, destruction of housing, crops, food storages etc. have been considered criminal destruction

66 See the ICC Mbarushimana Case, at para. 171.

67 See for example the Commentary to the AMW Manual, rule 88, Commentary 4, at page 206, where it is pointed out that the scorched earth tactics must be distinguished from wanton destruction of property.

68 See Chapter 8. Objects would in this case often qualify as military objectives because of their purpose or use.

69 See AP I article 54 and the special protection of objects which are indispensable for the survival of the civilian population, in Chapter 17.

of property of the civilian population,[70] while a couple of examples of destruction actually considered militarily necessary also occur in older case law. Among these, the much cited and exceptional acquittals in the High Command Case and the Hostage Case.[71] In the High Command Case the Tribunal stated:

> directing an operation against certain villages 'used by the partisans as a base of operations', with instructions to seize the cattle, horses, and chickens and most of the food, but further directing a small amount of food be left for the population at the direction of the commander of the operations. We cannot say this order was illegal. Likewise an order of XXXIX Corps issued on 7 December 1941, regarding a forced retreat, called for the destruction of food and fodder that could not be taken along in the retreat. The destruction of these foodstuffs would tend to hamper the advancing enemy and we cannot find it was not justified under the exigency of the situation. We do not find any criminality under this phase of the case.[72]

In order to distinguish the lawful acts from the unlawful (in these cases criminal as well) ones, two aspects are worth noticing: first that the destruction of property in order to hamper enemy advance must be based on real necessity, not a hypothetical scenario and, second, that the question of necessity in fact relies upon whether it was reasonable for the commander in question to assess the facts as a situation of necessity.

First a few remarks on the first aspect, that military necessity does not mean a hypothetical scenario.[73] Both older and more recent case law appear to support this. In the High Command Case as well as in the subsequent von Manstein case it is stated respectively that destruction of property could not be used as a pre-planned measure, but only when there was no other 'reasonable

70 From the practice of the ICC, see the Harun Case and the Kushayb Case as well as the Katanga and Chui Case. From the practice of the ICTY, see the Nikolic Case, the Karadzic and Mladic Case, the Rajic Case, the Blaskic Case, the Kordic and Cerkez Case, the Nalelic and Martinovic Case, the Milosevic Case, the Hadzihasanovic Case, the Babic Case, the Strugar Case, the Brdanin Case, the Ademi and Novac Case, the Hazic Case, the Zupljanin Case, the Oric Case, the Boskoski and Tarculovski Case, the Cermak and Markac Case as well as the Gotovina Case. See https://ihl-databases.icrc.org/customary-ihl/eng/docs/v1_rul_rule50 (accessed 13 June 2019).

71 In the commentary to the Law Reports of Trials of War Criminals the exceptional character of this acquittal is, however, emphasised, see Commentary on the Law Reports of Trials of War Criminals, vol. 15, at page 176.

72 High Command Case, at page 48. See also Downey, 'The law of war and military necessity', at pages 259–60 commenting on the case.

73 In the same direction, see Draper, 'military necessity and humanitarian imperatives', at page 141, arguing that there must be concrete and urgent reasons for the destruction.

alternative course of action'.[74] Furthermore: 'Now first and obvious comment on the wording of this article is that the requirement is "necessity" and not "advantage". The second is that necessity must be an imperative one.'[75] In the present case, the destruction was not held to be one out of necessity: 'it was really the carrying out of a policy planned a considerable time before, policy which the accused had in fact been prepared to carry out on two previous occasions and now was carrying irrespective of any question of military necessity'.[76]

A similar position was taken more recently, by the Eritrea-Ethiopia Claims Commission.[77] The Commission considered military necessity with regard to destruction of property in a number of claims, but then with regard to occupied territories.[78] Also the ICTY appears to have set the same standard when it comes to actual and present necessity, referring to an example where 'preventive destruction' could be justified by military necessity in concrete cases to prevent combatants from retaking a building in order to launch attacks from it.[79] Another example where destruction did not appear to have been based on real and present necessity was the application of scorched earth tactics during the first Gulf War in 1991.[80] During their retreat from Kuwait in

74 See the comments made by McCoubrey, 'The nature of the modern doctrine of military necessity', page 225.

75 Ibid., at page 522.

76 Ibid., at page 523.

77 The Eritrea-Ethiopia Claims Commission was established in 2000 pursuant to a bilateral agreement (The Algiers Agreement) and was given the mandate to consider claims arising from violations of international humanitarian law during the armed conflict between the two states taking place from 1998 to 2000.

78 Permanent Court of Arbitration, Case, no. 2001-02, Eritrea-Ethiopia Claims Commission, Eritrea's Claims 2, 4, 6, 7, 8 and 22, at para. 88, where it is stated that: 'Ethiopia has not suggested any reason why the destruction of any of the properties in question could have been rendered "absolutely necessary" by military operations other than simply to prevent their reuse by Eritrea if and when it should regain control of Senafe Town. The Commission does not agree that denial of potential future use of properties like these, which are not directly usable for military operations as are, for example, bridges or railways, could ever be justified under Article 53.'

79 See the ICTY Trial Chamber Judgment in the Oric Case, at para. 588, cited in Section 16.4. The building used as an example by the ICTY would in my opinion qualify as a lawful target and thus be a fortiori lawful to destroy, as pointed out in Sections 16.4 and 16.5.

80 The first Gulf War (also referred to as the Persian Gulf War and Operation Desert Storm), started with the Iraqi invasion of Kuwait on 2 August 1990 and was followed by the US led attack on Iraq from 17 January 1991 to 28 February 1991. As the Iraqi invasion in Kuwait aroused immediate international condemnation and agreement on Security Council Resolutions 660 and 661, the US led Operation Desert Storm attacked Iraqi forces on 17 January, subsequent to the passing of UN Security Council resolution 678, authorising states to use 'all necessary means' in order to force Iraq out of Kuwait after 15 January.

January and February 1991, Iraqi forces set fire to approximately 600 oil wells and caused massive environmental, long-term damage.[81] The Iraqi retreat was a result of the US led military intervention and massive international condemnation. As the war between Iraq and Kuwait was clearly coming to an end the destruction does not appear to have been based on imperative military necessity in order to hamper the advance of Kuwaiti forces. Arguably, the destruction could even fall within the prohibition of AP I article 54 and as such only be permissible on own territory in defence of an invading force (see Chapter 17).

Then to the second illustrative aspect of the distinction between necessity and acts that are not militarily necessary: the reasonable commander.

16.8.3 Commander's Decision of Military Necessity

The notion of the 'reasonable commander' is introduced in Chapter 4 above. The standard of reasonableness partly had its origin in the case against Lothar Rendulic, who was charged with the crime of wanton destruction of property, while applying the 'scorched earth' tactics in a devastating manner[82] to Finnmark in the North of Norway.[83]

The decision is remarkable in (at least) two ways. First, that the magnitude of destruction was not questioned as long as the anticipation of Russian advance was reasonable and, second, that the destruction was not *in fact* necessary, but it was reasonable to believe so.[84] The second aspect touches upon the relationship between the norm and the person assessing the norm, as addressed above, in Chapter 4. As argued there, although the notion of necessity primarily is a matter of objective fact, the commander's subjective appraisal of the facts before him (or her), under the circumstances ruling at the time, sometimes almost wipes out the distinction between the norm and the person assessing the norm. The difference between (and the difficulties related to) the rule and its factual determination with regard to destruction of property was pointed out in the High Command Case as well:

81 See further Chapter 17.

82 See the account given in the Hostage Case, at page 68.

83 See the Hostage Case, at page 68, cited in Section 4.5. In particular, the Tribunal noted: 'There is evidence in the record that there was no military necessity for this destruction and devastation. An examination of the facts in retrospect can well sustain this conclusion. But we are obliged to judge the situation as it appeared to the defendant at the time.'

84 This is pointed out for example in Best, *War and Law since 1945*, at page 328 ff. and Solis, *The Law of Armed Conflict*, at page 265. See also for example the quotation from the High Command Case, taken from Dunbar, 'Military necessity in war crimes trials', at page 451.

> The devastation prohibited by the Hague Rules and the usages of war is that not warranted by military necessity. This rule is clear enough but the factual determination as to what constitutes military necessity is difficult. Defendants in this case were in many instances in retreat under arduous conditions wherein their commands were in serious danger of being cut off. Under such circumstances, a commander must necessarily make quick decisions to meet the particular situation of his command. A great deal of latitude must be accorded to him under such circumstances. What constitutes devastation beyond military necessity in these situations requires detailed proof of an operational and tactical nature.[85]

Difficulties aside, the actual determination of military necessity in such cases is an integral part of conduct of hostilities.[86] The commander's margin of appreciation in this case[87] includes 'a great deal of latitude' upon determining the content of military necessity. In the quoted passage, it is thus difficult to distinguish explicitly between the flexibility in the norm and the threshold of reasonableness on the part of the commander.

16.8.4 Diminishing Enemy Ability to Sustain Operations: the US View

A particular issue is that of property sustaining the enemy's ability to wage war through its economic outcome. According to the US view it may be militarily necessary to destroy or seize enemy property in order to diminish the enemy's ability to conduct or sustain operations, such as the destruction of narcotics production – for example the opium fields in Afghanistan and the Confederate cotton production during the American Civil War.[88] This view is consistent with the US view on the definition of military objectives – and opposed to the view widely shared as representing international treaty and customary LOAC.[89] Destruction of war sustaining capabilities will easily fall within the scope of attacks and must therefore be limited to military objectives as defined in the AP I article 52(2).[90] Consequently, the view of the scope of military objectives will taint the permission to destroy the same objects, as

85 High Command Case, at page 93. This point is also made in the U.S. Supreme Court, *Korematsu* v. *United States* case, at pages 244–5. See also Dunbar, 'Military necessity in war crimes trials', at page 451.

86 See for example Solis, *The Law of Armed Conflict*, at page 264: 'Determining what constitutes military necessity is a duty of the battlefield commander.'

87 See for example McCoubrey, 'The nature of the modern doctrine of military necessity', at page 237.

88 US DoD Manual, at page 264.

89 See Chapter 8 above.

90 AP I articles 48 and 52(2).

military objectives are a fortiori necessary to destroy, as explained above (Sections 16.4 and 16.5).

16.8.5 Incidental Damage Resulting from the Movement of Military Forces

Imperative military necessity may justify use or destruction of all sorts of private or public property that may be utilised by the enemy.[91] As referred to above, in many cases destruction of railways or lines of communication – as are mentioned in particular in the Hostage Case – are a fortiori lawful to destroy because they are military objectives. Thus, it is the incidental damage to private and public property resulting from the movement of military forces that appears most practical with regard to the scope of the Hague rule. Early examples in case law demonstrate that incidental damage is permitted by military necessity, and that this is distinct from wanton destruction of property, such as looting.[92]

Incidental damage – in this regard distinct from incidental damage resulting from an attack directed at a military objective[93] – is that damage to property 'unhappily chanced to stand in the field of those operations'.[94]

[91] See the much cited phrase in the Hostage Case. At page 66 the tribunal states: 'The destruction of property to be lawful must be imperatively demanded by the necessities of war. Destruction as an end in itself is a violation of international law. There must be some reasonable connection between the destruction of property and the overcoming of the enemy forces. It is lawful to destroy railways, lines of communication, or any other property that might be utilized by the enemy. Private homes and churches even may be destroyed if necessary for military operations. It does not admit the wanton devastation of a district or the willful infliction of suffering upon its inhabitants for the sake of suffering alone.' From the same epoch, see also Greenspan, *The Modern Law of Land Warfare*, at page 283.

[92] See for example the Zafiro Case from the British-United States Arbitral Tribunal during the 1920s, analysed by Schwarzenberger, *International Law*, at pages 132–4. In the Zafiro Case from 1925, the question was in fact whether the looters were acting on their own or on behalf of the state. Their looting was clearly not reasoned by military necessity. See *D. Earnshaw and Others (Great Britain)* v. *United States (Zafiro Case)*, VI 160 (American and British Claims Arbitration Tribunal). The case is commented by Schwarzenberger in ibid., at page 132.

[93] See Section 16.5 on the scope of the rule with regard to civilian property, and the ICC Pre Trial Chamber decision in the Katanga and Chui Case, at para. 313.

[94] See the case of *Luzon Sugar Refining Company Ltd. (Great Britain)* v. *United States* VI. The Tribunal held that damage to a pumping station was 'incidental' to the suppression of an internal revolution, and therefore: 'The foreign residents, whose property unhappily chanced to stand in the field of those operations, have no ground of complaint against the United States which had no choice but to conduct them where the enemy was to be found. No complaint is made that the troops were out of hand or did anything beyond what the operations necessarily involved.' The matter of 'no choice' is dealt with above, in Chapter 2 on the elements of necessity.

Some examples from older case law are the digging of trenches across farmers' fields,[95] or the destruction of property in order to secure the health of own troops, such as was the case in the Hardman Claims, during the occupation of Siboney in the Spanish-American War in 1898.[96] In the latter case, American forces burned down certain houses out of fear of Yellow Fever. The Tribunal held that: 'In law, an act of war is an act of defence or attack against the enemy and a necessity of war is an act which is made necessary by the defence or attack and assumes the character of *vis major*.'[97] Furthermore, 'that the destruction required for their safety was consequently a necessity of war.'[98]

Then, there are a number of present examples of incidental damage, frequently experienced by States, that may result from the movement of military forces, both on land, at sea and in the air (or from the air).

Air forces may produce different sorts of damage as a result of low overflights. In particular situations low and fast overflights may cause shattered glass as a result of the sonic boom from an aircraft travelling faster than the speed of sound.[99] In other cases low overflights may result in stress-related damage on husbandry facilities, such as reindeer herds, fox and mink farms, which again turn into economic loss.[100] While such damage is possible to avoid during peacetime military exercises, they may be a result of military necessity during armed conflict as the circumstances may point out the chosen route as the only feasible alternative in order to avoid enemy anti-access aerial denial systems.

Naval forces may for example create damage on anchored or moored private yachts or smaller boats, as a result of waves or undertow in the wake from torpedo boats driving in formation through narrow sea lanes or channels. Anchored vessels may be smashed against the shore, moorings may be disrupted and fishing nets may be drawn up. Furthermore, piers and quays may crack under the weight of the cargos of naval vessels which are discharged on

95 See the example of the German trench digging through Rumanian fields during WWII. The case is commented upon by Schwarzenberger, *International Law*, at page 134.

96 *William Hardman (Great Britain)* v. *United States*, Vol. VI, pages 25–6.

97 Ibid., at page 26.

98 Ibid.

99 A spectacular example of this (admittedly outside the context of an armed conflict) was the glass breaking incident at the Brazilian Supreme Court, caused by its armed forces, in July 2012. See for example Gayle, 'They're in SO much trouble: low-flying Brazilian air force pilots shatter every window of the country's Supreme Court'.

100 More specifically, the reindeer doe may abort her calf due to stress, fox mothers may eat their cubs and mink may escape.

them. Even submarine telegraph cables may incidentally be drawn up in the wake of maritime vessels passing at speed.[101]

Land forces may create a vast number of different sorts of damage in addition to the older examples mentioned at the beginning of this section. Due to the size and weight of military vehicles, they may create damage to roads and bridges which may have been constructed primarily for lighter means of transportation. Even more specifically, Main Battle Tanks (MTBs) driving with 'snow shoes' on regular asphalt during wintertime create massive destruction to the roads. Military vehicles driving off-road may cause extensive damage to, for example, pine wood plantations, cultivated land and strawberry fields. In addition to potentially damaging roads and bridges, military vehicles easily tear down fences, house corners and mail boxes. These damages have proved to be even more frequent as a result of snowploughing in the support of advancing military forces.[102]

A point in common for the three domains is that armed conflict may create situations of stress and urgency which preclude optional routes of movement. Furthermore, it is a fact that the combination of heavy vehicles and relatively inexperienced drivers or captains (soldiers or young officers barely having turned the age of twenty) under situations of stress, lack of rest and sleep, will be prone to mistakes. The important point, however, is that these mistakes can be reasonably expected from the average soldier or young officer in a similar situation. They are within the ambit of what is reasonable to expect when determining situations of necessity.

Destruction can also be a result of necessary movements and manoeuvre by unmanned or even autonomous vehicles in the three domains – and probably also in the cyber domain. In principle, the point of departure is the same as with manned vehicles, vessels and aircraft. Incidental damage to property in the wake of military manoeuvre is accepted. One aspect is different however: the stress of active warfare does not affect the unmanned vehicle, vessel or aircraft. Errors of navigation must therefore be judged from a different perspective. Sometimes a machine can reasonably be expected to perform less navigational errors than a human being. At present there appears to be international hesitation against employing fully autonomous *weapon* systems. Unarmed systems, however, are not burdened with the same scepticism. Autonomous systems for Intelligence, Surveillance and Reconnaissance

[101] Thanks to my colleague, Navy Commander Thomas Slensvik, for helping me with examples experienced by the Norwegian Navy.

[102] Thanks to my colleague, Lieutenant Colonel Palle Ydstebø, for helping me with examples experienced by the Norwegian Army.

(ISR) are more likely to be used on a wider scale, both on land and in the air, and not least subsea. The Norwegian system called 'Hugin' is one well proven example of such systems.[103] From the time Hugin is submerged and until it is recovered to the mother vessel, it autonomously follows a pre-programmed route. The system has advanced forward looking sonar and obstacle avoidance routines to detect deviations from the terrain information it has been programmed with. However, it may fail to react correctly to or detect obstacles, thereby creating damage to seabed ecology such as cold-water corals, or to manmade installations such as fishing nets and aquaculture installations. As long as the intelligence collection is considered necessary for the support of ongoing operations (which it presumably is) in the armed conflict, and the mistakes made are considered accidental rather than systematic programming mistakes or even malicious programming, the incidental damage is not wanton.

16.8.6 Seizure (Including Use) of Property

The Hague rule and its corresponding rule in customary law includes 'seizure' on an equal footing with 'destruction'. While a literal interpretation of 'seizure' primarily refers to taking possession over movable property, it appears that also the 'use' of enemy property appears to fall within the notion of 'destruction and seizure of property'.[104] While extensive use of enemy property often will be an issue during belligerent occupation (and hence is governed by the law of occupation), the use of enemy property is also a practical measure during the actual conduct of hostilities. Examples of the latter may include (but not be limited to), the use of ports or military barracks; buildings used for housing combatants, wounded and sick; buildings used for observation and reconnaissance posts, concealment and cover; and property used for defensive purposes.[105] A measure similar to the use of property for reconnaissance and observation is the use of property for forward air controlling (FAC) functions, for example performed by special operation forces behind enemy lines. In some instances, even the use of broadcasting facilities may be permitted, if a careful assessment of *military* reasons makes it necessary.[106]

103 See the information provided by Kongsberg Maritime at www.km.kongsberg.com/ks/web/nokbg0240.nsf/AllWeb/D5682F98CBFBC05AC1257497002976E4?OpenDocument (accessed 8 May 2017).

104 See for example US DoD Manual, at page 263.

105 See examples in ibid.

106 Such practice is for example presumed to be lawful under certain circumstances according to the NATO Rules of Engagement.

16.9 NO EXPLICIT ASSESSMENT OF NECESSITY REQUIRED FOR BOOTY OF WAR AND CAPTURE FOR PRIZE

Capture of property as booty of war or for prize is governed by specific rules. When capture or destruction is lawful according to these specific rules, the acts are also *ipso facto* militarily necessary and will not amount to acts of wantonness.

Booty of war is not codified in treaty law[107] and encapsulates, primarily, movable public property captured on the battlefield. All military materiel – with some exceptions[108] – can be captured as booty of war and also that in private possession,[109] and governmental property which is not of a military character can also be captured as war booty, although opinions differ to some extent on this latter point.[110] Outside this, destruction or seizure of enemy property is only permitted when justified by military necessity under the umbrella of the Hague rule accounted for above.

All enemy vessels (not only warships) can be captured for prize adjudication outside neutral waters,[111] and all civilian aircraft can be captured for prize adjudication on the ground or outside neutral airspace.[112] Even neutral vessels and aircraft may be captured as prize under certain conditions.[113] The air and sea warfare differs from land warfare: while the right to capture private property is only exceptional during land warfare, in: 'sea warfare enemy civilian vessels can be captured as prize with a view to interfering with the enemy's trade and lines of commercial communication. The same applies in air warfare, where a civilian aircraft is liable to capture as prize solely on account of its enemy character.'[114]

Finally, two aspects are worth highlighting: first, that the distinction between civilian persons and property on the one hand and military objectives on the other is not decisive when it comes to war booty and prize. Second, that the justifying force of military necessity primarily comes into force beyond the

[107] Downey, 'Captured enemy property', at page 488; Dinstein, *Conduct of Hostilities*, page 282.

[108] See however, below Chapter 17, on the status of military medical materiel and property.

[109] ICRC CIHL, rule 49; Norwegian Manual, at page 181; Greenspan, *The Modern Law of Land Warfare*, at page 281; US DoD Manual, at page 262.

[110] US DoD Manual, at page 262; Dinstein, *Conduct of Hostilities*, at pages 282–3; Greenspan, *The Modern Law of Land Warfare*, page 281. Opposite: ICRC CIHL, Commentary to rule 49, which does not include non-military state property. The Norwegian Manual does not mention non-military state property.

[111] San Remo Manual, rules 135–8.

[112] AMW Manual, rule 134.

[113] San Remo Manual, rule 146; AMW Manual, rule 140.

[114] AMW Manual, Commentary 3 to rule 134, at page 273.

scope of the right to war booty and prize. On this point, differing opinions appear among commentators however. Some also rely on military necessity for the purposes of booty of war and argue that '. . . any property which is useful in war or is taken or seized on the ground of military necessity for the purpose of depriving the enemy of its use or of turning it into its captor's advantage is considered captured enemy property'.[115] Others argue, on the contrary, that 'Public enemy property which may be seized as war booty is limited to movables on the battlefield, and these need not be for military operations or necessity.'[116] The practical implications of such differing views must not be exaggerated. The point of the customary rule on war booty appears simply to be that in cases covered by the rule, the seizure is presumptively necessary, whereas outside the scope of the rule, necessity must be explicitly assessed by the commander.

[115] Downey, 'Captured enemy property', at page 488.
[116] Lew, 'Manchurian booty and international law', at pages 584–92.

17

Military Necessity and Rules on Special Protection

17.1 GENERAL REMARKS

The principle of distinction protects civilians and civilian objects against direct and indiscriminate attacks. Beyond the principle of distinction, the LOAC devotes special protection to certain persons as well as objects. Persons benefiting from special protection are both civilians – for whom the special protection constitute an *extra protection* – as well as combatants – for whom the special protection constitute the *exception* from otherwise being a lawful target. Special protection from attack is devoted to women and children, enemy combatants *hors de combat*, parachutists from aircraft in distress, parlementaires, medical personnel, religious personnel, civil defence personnel, relief personnel and journalists.

When it comes to objects, special protection is devoted to cultural property, medical units, the natural environment, works and installations containing dangerous forces as well as objects indispensable to the survival of the civilian population. Special protection entails more than prohibitions on attack, it also entails specific limitations upon military methods of warfare – in particular siege war and scorched earth tactics, both of which have traditionally been justified and applied on the basis of considerations of military necessity (see Chapter 16).

Certain instances of special protection are reasoned by *particular* considerations of humanity, and do not appear to be at odds with military necessity, such as the protection of women and children (see below for details). Other instances of special protection have stronger features of a balance towards military necessity, where the latter has yielded to humanitarian (or other) concerns. Examples are the protection of civil defence personnel and military medical personnel (see below for details). Other instances of special protection again are based on a slightly different balance from the humanity–

necessity scale, and instead construed in order to enhance reciprocity and protect the good faith between belligerents, for instance the protection of parlementaires.

17.2 PROTECTION OF COMBATANTS *HORS DE COMBAT*

17.2.1 *Protection against Direct Attacks*

Combatants are lawful objects of attack as long as they are not *hors de combat.* The ICRC Commentary states that: "The safeguard of the enemy "hors de combat" on the battlefield is the logical and natural complement to the preceding provision which prohibits the refusal to give quarter."[1] The definition of enemy combatants *hors de combat* was first laid down in the 1907 Hague Regulations article 23(c) and is now considered customary law,[2] codified in the AP I article 41:

1. A person who is recognized or who, in the circumstances, should be recognized to be 'hors de combat' shall not be made the object of attack.
2. A person is 'hors de combat' if:

    (a) he is in the power of an adverse Party;
    (b) he clearly expresses an intention to surrender; or
    (c) he has been rendered unconscious or is otherwise incapacitated by wounds or sickness, and therefore is incapable of defending himself; provided that in any of these cases he abstains from any hostile act and does not attempt to escape.

As for the principle of distinction and the protection of civilians which is accounted for above, the protection of enemy combatants *hors de combat* can also arguably be said to be based on the St Petersburg Declaration. The Declaration states that for the purpose of weakening the enemy military forces 'it is sufficient to disable the greatest number of men'.[3] Hence, once combatants are *hors de combat,* further attacks are not militarily necessary.[4] The ICRC goes even further than stating the firm status as customary law and links the protection of the enemy *hors de combat* to the whole fundament of the LOAC: 'the whole secret of the law of war lies in the respect for a disarmed man'.[5]

1 In AP I Commentary, at para. 1601, page 480. On denial of quarter, see Section 17.4.
2 ICRC CIHL, rule 47; Bothe, Partsch and Solf, *New Rules,* at page 252.
3 St Petersburg Declaration, see Chapter 3; and Bothe, Partsch and Solf, *New Rules,* at page 252.
4 Bothe, Partsch and Solf, *New Rules,* at page 252.
5 AP I Commentary to article 41, at page 480, para. 1601.

When being *hors de combat* a soldier is – with regard to the protection against direct attacks – on same footing as civilians (not performing DPH).[6] The protection extends, however, only to direct attacks and not incidental damage resulting from attacks on lawful targets nearby.[7] Combatants who are *hors de combat* do not turn into civilians and the question of whether they are comprised within the notion of 'collateral damage' is contested.[8]

The protection against attack enters into force both in clear-cut cases where a person *is recognised* as *hors de combat,* and in cases where the person – according to what could have been expected from a reasonable man – *should have been* recognised as *hors de combat.*[9]

The protection lasts as long as the criteria[10] for being *hors de combat* remains; there is no room for invoking military necessity as an exception.[11] Persons *hors de combat* enjoy specific protection against reprisals.[12]

17.2.2 *The Definition of Persons* Hors de Combat

The provision refers to 'persons' and not only (lawful) combatants. By this wording it also encapsulates civilians.[13] The protection of civilians against direct attacks in this connection makes best sense when seen in relation to the DPH rule;[14] also irregular combatants and persons conducting DPH are protected against direct attack when they are *hors de combat* in accordance with the rule in AP I article 41.

Persons 'in the Power' of the Adverse Party

The protection of persons *hors de combat* is overlapping (in time and space) with the protection as POW under the GC III (and the AP I): 'the enemy "hors de combat" is protected at whatever moment he is considered to have "fallen into the power" of his adversary'.[15] It also overlaps with the categories of protected persons in GC I, II and IV who are sick, wounded, shipwrecked or civilians in the power of an adverse party (for example during belligerent

6 AP I Commentary, at para. 1602, page 482.
7 Bothe, Partsch and Solf, *New Rules*, at page 253.
8 See Section 13.2.
9 AP I Commentary, at para. 1608, page 483.
10 See Section 17.3.
11 AP I Commentary, at para. 1609, page 484.
12 See Section 12.4.
13 AP I Commentary, at para. 1606, page 483.
14 See Chapter 11.
15 AP I Commentary, at para. 1602.

occupation).[16] A further account of the standard of treatment offered persons in the power of the adverse party falls, however, outside the scope of the present book which deals solely with the conduct of hostilities.

The rule in AP I article 41(3) also governs persons 'in the power of the adverse party' entitled to POW status, and is important in that it has a twofold expression: persons who have 'fallen into the power of an adverse Party under unusual conditions of combat which prevent their evacuation as provided for in Part III . . . shall be released and all feasible precautions shall be taken to ensure their safety'. First, the rule is based on the absolute prohibition of killing persons in the power of the adverse party, even for considerations of urgent necessity (for example the necessity of hiding ones presence in hostile territory).[17] Second, the rule provides an alternative to the prompt and humane evacuation of prisoners from the combat zone according to GC III articles 19 and 20. For long range reconnaissance units and commando raids for example, article 41(3) leaves an option (to disarm and release) which is far more practical.[18]

Combatants Who Are Surrendering

There is no internationally recognised mode of 'surrendering'.[19] The protection as *hors de combat* commences from the 'clear intention' to surrender. It is not necessary that surrender is completed, but the intention must be clear.[20] Clear situations of surrender are those where, for example, the soldier raises his hands – with or without arms – or raises a white flag.[21] At sea or in the air the alternatives of raising hands or waving with flags are not practical. In the air, the intention to surrender ought to be communicated on a 'common radio channel such as a distress frequency'.[22] At sea, the traditional signal of surrender is to strike the flag.[23] Military necessity can never justify the refusal of an unconditional surrender.[24]

16 Bothe, Partsch and Solf, *New Rules*, at pages 253–4.
17 See Section 17.4 on the prohibition of denial of quarter and the comments with regard to the Peleus Trial where operational necessity was argued by the defence.
18 Bothe, Partsch and Solf, *New Rules*, at page 256. AP I Commentary, at para. 1625, page 489.
19 Norwegian Manual, at page 68.
20 AMW Manual, rule 127, at page 266. See also UK Manual, at page 57; Norwegian Manual, at pages 67–8.
21 AP I Commentary, at para. 1618, pages 486–7.
22 AMW Manual, rule 128, at page 267. See also the AP I Commentary to article 41 which refers to the method of 'waggling the wings' of the aircraft, at para. 1619, page 487.
23 AMW Manual, Commentary to rule 127(a), at page 266. See also AP I Commentary, at para. 1619, page 487.
24 AP I Commentary, at para. 1619.

Occasionally, situations may arise where capture of surrendering personnel is difficult. In these situations, communication between the surrendering personnel and the captor is crucial. Such situations may arise, for example, where a small unit (for example a squad) encounters a surrendering company, or even a battalion, or where enemy personnel on the ground offer surrender to air forces.

In the first example, the possibility for the small unit to capture the surrendering company does not only rely on the possibilities for reinforcement, but equally on the compliance among the surrendering personnel to abide by instructions given by their captors. The potential danger inherent in situations of numerous surrendering personnel underscores the importance of strict adherence to the criteria laid down in AP I article 41(2)(c), that those who surrender must 'abstain from any hostile act' and not 'attempt to escape' (on these requirements, see Section 17.3).

In the other example, of offering surrender to an airplane, situations may be roughly divided into two: first, those situations where capture is clearly not feasible,[25] such as where a military aircraft over enemy controlled territory observes enemy combatants raising their hands towards the aircraft. In these situations, no valid situation of surrender appears to arise, as there are no possibilities to comply with the additional requirements laid down in AP I article 41(2)(c). Arguably, enemy combatants offering surrender by raising their arms under such circumstances do not enjoy status as *hors de combat*. Second, there are situations which may pose challenges, but where capture may be feasible, such as where a helicopter or an aircraft encounters enemy combatants offering surrender in a territory where reinforcement by ground troops or landing is possible. In these situations, the importance of strict compliance with the requirements of laying down arms and refraining from attempts to escape as well as any hostile acts again become crucial. For example, simply raising one's arms is not enough to clearly communicate an intent to surrender from a tank. The tank and its weaponry must be placed in a passive position and then dismantled, before awaiting instructions from the captors upon where to assemble.

While it is true as said above, that military necessity can never justify a refusal to accept an unconditional surrender, it is also true that military necessity plays a part in defining the surrender as such (or the validity of it). The notion of feasibility, as introduced in the examples above, is a reference to

[25] Feasibility is introduced as a requirement in the US DoD Manual, at para. 5.9.3.3, relying, among others, upon the US experiences in the 1991 Gulf War. On the notion of surrender and the Gulf War, see further just below.

military necessity (as seen, particularly, in Chapter 14 on precautions in attack). The notion of feasibility here lies at the commander's assessment of the situation. In this regard, it should be noted that while immunity from attack is the default position of civilians, combatants are presumptively lawful targets. This basic difference also underlies the rule governing enemy combatants who are *hors de combat* due to surrender. Even though the core of the rule granting protection to those who are *hors de combat* relies in 'the respect for a disarmed man',[26] attacks on able-bodied enemy combatants are usually considered militarily necessary. Those combatants offering surrender will therefore also bear the responsibility for communicating their harmlessness clearly to their enemies. The commander's assessment of the situation becomes a key to establish communication between the surrendering personnel and the captors. He or she must assess the level of threat, adapt suitable instructions for enforcing the capture and finally how to proceed with evacuation.

Finally, surrender must not be confused with retreat,[27] which can be used for regrouping and thus necessitate an attack. One example of retreating, but not surrendering, combatants – although devoted criticism in public media – was the US attack on Iraqi forces retreating from Kuwait on Highways 80 and 8 (later labelled the 'Highways of Death') in March 1991.[28] Although the attack appeared devastating and gained criticism in public media, it was probably not a violation of the LOAC. The military necessity of attacking combatants was still present. Activities amounting to loss of protection are dealt with in Section 17.3.

The argument presented above (that those in the power of the adverse party under GC I–IV also enjoy protection as *hors de combat* according to AP I article 41(2)(a)) must not, however, be reversed. Although a person has status as *hors de combat* due to surrender, this is not the same as gaining status as a protected person according to GC III or IV. The protection (of being *hors de combat*) thus entails protection against attack, but it does not infer the rights as POWs until the person is 'into the power' of the adverse party.[29]

Combatants Who Are *Hors de Combat* Due to Wounds or Sickness

The protection of combatants in AP I article 41 who are *hors de combat* due to wounds or sickness coincides with the protection offered according to AP

26 AP I Commentary to article 41, at para. 1601, page 480.
27 AMW Manual, Commentary to rule 127(a), at page 266.
28 The incident is introduced in Sections 9.4 and 9.5.
29 Bothe, Partsch and Solf, *New Rules*, at page 254.

I article 8 and succeeds the rule in the 1907 Hague Regulations article 23(c) which prohibits the killing or wounding of an enemy who no longer has any 'means of defence'.[30] It is not the sickness or wound in itself which makes the person inviolable for attack, but the fact that he is *incapacitated* by the wounds or sickness and therefore unable to defend himself.[31] A wounded person who takes a continued part in hostilities remains a lawful target.

17.3 LOSS OF PROTECTION AGAINST ATTACKS

17.3.1 *General*

The protection of persons as *hors de combat* is: '... provided that in any of these cases he abstains from any hostile act and does not attempt to escape'.[32]

If a person resumes hostile activity or attempts to escape, the notion of military necessity resurrects and justifies direct attacks against that person. The provision points – by wording – back at all the categories of persons being *hors de combat* in accordance with article 41. The alternative of 'escape' fits, however, poorly with those who are unconscious or otherwise incapacitated by wounds or sickness.[33] The duty to abstain from hostile activity encompasses for example tactical intelligence transmission.[34] Being *hors de combat* is not compatible with an attempt to evade, and this covers as well the repeated abuse of the protected status by feigning intention to surrender. The feigning of intent to surrender may easily turn into acts of perfidy[35] if used in order to gain protection from attack only to resume combat activity afterwards.

17.3.2 *Loss of Protection by Resort to Perfidy*

Ruses of war belong to those tactics which have been practiced by belligerents since time immemorial[36] and which from a very early age have been subject to

30 1907 Hague Regulations article 23(c).

31 AP I Commentary, at para. 1620.

32 AP I article 41(2)(c).

33 Bothe, Partsch and Solf, *New Rules*, at page 255.

34 AMW Manual, rule 127(b) with commentary at pages 266–7. Transmission of tactical intelligence is considered direct participation in hostilities. On the notion of direct participation in hostilities, see Chapter 11 above.

35 AP I article 37, at page 730. See also Bothe, Partsch and Solf, *New Rules*, at page 255.

36 See Grotius above, Chapter 3, on 'stratagems'. From history the examples are numerous, from Hannibal and Alexander the Great, to the American Civil War and the attack on Pearl Harbor etc. For an account of early historic examples, see Fleck, 'Ruses of war and prohibition of perfidy', at pages 273 ff.

regulation. Ruses of war should contribute to reach the objectives of war without the loss of human lives (or less losses).[37] Alongside the use of ruses of war as a lawful measure is the prohibition of perfidious acts, which invites the confidence of the adversary in order to abuse their trust for one's own advantage.

The treaty threshold between lawful ruses of war and unlawful perfidy was established in the 1907 Hague Regulations article 23(b) and AP I article 37. Killing or wounding an adversary by resort to perfidy constitutes a war crime and the prohibition is part of customary international law.[38] Capturing an adversary under false pretences is a perfidious act only for those who are parties to the AP I.[39] A deceptive act alone is not enough to constitute a war crime, it must be conducted in order to kill or injure (or capture).[40] The two provisions are not, however, identical, neither in wording nor in scope. While the first provision simply refers to killing or wounding the adversary 'treacherously', the AP I gives examples of both lawful ruses of war and prohibited perfidy. Furthermore, the AP I provision requires that the perfidious act must rely on a breach of confidence (where the perpetrator alleges a claim of protection), while the Hague provision is broader. The broader area of application of the Hague provision is still in force.[41]

Perfidious tactics – for example to wave a white flag and show a false intention to negotiate in order to kill or wound the adversary – may prove useful for achieving military advantages, and – again if necessity were the sole yardstick to guide the conduct in war – therefore necessary. When it comes to perfidy, military necessity has yielded not only to humanitarian considerations, but also to expectations of 'honour' and perceptions of a 'fair play'.[42] As such, the distinction between lawful ruses of war and unlawful perfidy may be cultural dependent – depending upon the conception of honour and cowardice during wartime which is prevailing at the time and place.[43]

37 Ibid., at page 276.

38 AMW Manual, rule, 111, at page 244; Bothe, Partsch and Solf, *New Rules*, pages 233–4; ICRC CIHL, rule 65.

39 AMW Manual, Commentary to rule 111, at page 244; UK Manual, at page 60, stating that the acts of killing or wounding amount to war crimes; Dinstein, *Conduct of Hostilities*, at page 231. In the ICRC CIHL it is argued in the Commentary to rule 65 – which includes capture as a part of customary law – that State practice supports this position (of including capture). The references to State practice is, however, dubious. One reference is for example to the 'Swedish IHL Manual', which in reality was non-existent at the time.

40 Bothe, Partsch and Solf, *New Rules*, at page 235.

41 Dinstein, *Conduct of Hostilities*, at pages 266–9; Bothe, Parsch and Solf, *New Rules*, at page 235.

42 See AP I Commentary, at page 430, para. 1485.

43 Fleck, 'Ruses of war and prohibition of perfidy', at page 272.

Considerations of honour and 'chivalry'[44] are certainly not the overriding considerations in order to degrade the impact of military necessity; humanitarian considerations are present by an inducement to create respect for the protective regime for those who are protected as civilians or *hors de combat*.[45] If all sorts of foul play by abuse of the protective status were lawful, there would be no inducement for the belligerent parties to guarantee the protection of those who are wounded, sick or surrendering etc. In turn, this could put the whole principle of distinction at risk – a development which would not even be defensible by a reference to military necessity alone.

17.4 MILITARY NECESSITY AND DENIAL OF QUARTER

The AP I article 40 states: 'It is prohibited to order that there shall be no survivors, to threaten an adversary therewith or to conduct hostilities on this basis.' The provision succeeds the provision in 1907 Hague Regulations article 23(d).

As late as during the aftermath of WWII the question of killing helpless survivors from a shipwreck was raised in the Peleus Trial[46] where a German submarine had sunk a merchant vessel. The accused submarine commander, Heinz Eck, argued that the killing was lawful due to 'operational necessity' because his submarine should not be found by the enemy. The Court rejected his plea, arguing that the operational aim of saving the vessel and its crew could have been achieved more effectively without such acts of cruelty since the submarine could have been removed as quickly as possible from the scene. The Court did not, however, conclude on the question whether helpless survivors in a last instance could have been shot, *if* it was considered operationally necessary.[47] This question can be answered unequivocally in the negative today.

The prohibition of denial of quarter is directed at the *threat* of killing defenceless people,[48] in addition to affirm the already established sanctity of those who are *hors de combat*.[49] There is no possibility to invoke exceptional military necessity in situations such as that of the Peleus Trial – or other similar situations.[50] A comparable situation is that of a small unit which

44 Bothe, Partsch and Solf, *New Rules*, at page 233.

45 Ibid.

46 The Peleus Trial I.

47 Ibid., at pages 15–16.

48 AP I Commentary, para. 1591, at pages 474–5.

49 AP I Commentary, para. 1592, at page 475.

50 See GC II articles 12–15 with regard to shipwrecked persons who enjoy the same protection as wounded and sick and as well POW status provided that the conditions are fulfilled.

encroaches upon enemy forces in hostile territory, capturing them with no means of keeping them in their power and with the legitimate fear of having their position disclosed, who consider killing the captured enemy personnel. The law leaves no option for killing, although it might be considered necessary from a military point of view. Humanitarian concerns have in other words trumped military necessity and rendered the inviolability of human life absolute. A violation of the prohibition of denial of quarter may be tantamount to a war crime according to the Rome Statute article 8(2)(b)(xii).

17.5 PARACHUTISTS FROM AIRCRAFT IN DISTRESS

AP I article 42(1) states that 'No person parachuting from an aircraft in distress shall be made the object of attack during his descent.' This temporary protection against direct attacks is devoted to combatants who are, due to the circumstances, not able to defend themselves (as opposed to airborne troops who are lawful targets during their descent[51]), as well as civilians (the wording encompasses 'persons') descending from an aircraft in distress. The protection of parachutists in distress is related to the protection of enemy combatants *hors de combat*,[52] which is dealt with separately above, but not identical to it.[53] In fact, the provision gave birth to controversy during the Diplomatic Conference exactly because opinions differed with regard to whether one was to view parachutists as actually escaping with no reason for protection, or as combatants *hors de combat*.[54] The majority of views saw parachutists in distress as comparable to the shipwrecked persons protected by the GC II article 12 and the *hors de combat* provision in AP I article 41.[55] The difference between the treaty protection of *hors de combat* and parachutists is found in the time given parachutists to surrender upon reaching the ground; a person who has parachuted 'shall be given an opportunity to surrender before being made the object of attack, unless it is apparent that he is engaging in a hostile act'.[56] Combatants (and civilians taking a direct part in hostilities) are otherwise lawful objects of attack due to military necessity.

51 AP I article 42(3).

52 In the UK Manual, at page 58, the relationship is described as 'follows from the protection of those *hors de combat*'.

53 Dinstein, *Conduct of Hostilities*, at pages 194–5.

54 AP I Commentary, at page 494, para. 1636.

55 AP I Commentary, at page 495, para. 1637.

56 AP I article 42(2), at page 732.

17.6 MEDICAL AND RELIGIOUS PERSONNEL AND UNITS

The special protection devoted to medical personnel is provided that they are assigned by a party to the conflict 'exclusively to the medical purposes'.[57] In Additional Protocol I article 15(5) religious personnel are devoted the equal respect and protection as medical personnel. In the following, religious personnel are therefore not dealt with in further detail.

The protection of medical personnel is derived from the protection of the wounded and sick being *hors de combat* and thus not necessary to attack.[58] In this manner the protection of medical personnel is also distinct from the tasks of the veterinarians, who are not protected as medical personnel.[59] Medical personnel can consist of both civilian as well as military personnel as long as they are 'assigned to' such tasks by a party to the conflict.[60] Both those persons assigned for medical purposes as well as administrative personnel are protected.[61] Furthermore, medical personnel of aid societies and personnel of medical units or medical transports are devoted special protection,[62] as well as when belonging to a neutral or other State which is not a party to the conflict, provided that the personnel are made available to a party to the conflict.[63] In sum, the definition of medical personnel is wide, leaving out individual physicians operating outside the framework of a State or an organisation through which the State can exercise control.[64] The assignments may be permanent or temporary.[65] When the GCs distinguished between permanent and auxiliary personnel[66] the AP I expands the possibilities for being temporary assigned – or in that case, 'devoted'[67] – provided that the personnel are 'exclusively' engaged in medical tasks during their assignment.[68] The requirement of being 'exclusively engaged' in medical tasks reflects the scope of the special protection of medical personnel – and the loss of the same protection. It is the latter threshold which is of most interest for the purpose of the present book.

57 GC I article 24; AP I article 8(c).
58 AP I Commentary, at para. 347, page 124.
59 Dinstein, *Conduct of Hostilities*, at page 197.
60 AP I article 8(c)(i), at page 718.
61 Ibid.
62 AP I article 8 (c) (ii and iii); GC I articles 24 and 26.
63 AP I article 9.
64 Bothe, Partsch and Solf, *New Rules*, at pages 105–6.
65 AP I article 8(c).
66 GC I articles 24 and 25.
67 AP I Commentary, at para. 392, page 132.
68 Ibid., at para. 390. Temporary medical personnel are thus better protected than 'auxiliary personnel' in the GC I; see Bothe, Partsch and Solf, *New Rules*, at page 109.

As far as objects (and not persons) are concerned, the term 'medical units' is understood broadly, encompassing fixed or mobile, permanent or temporary, military or civilian units organised for medical purposes – including medical transportation[69] and evacuation.[70] Fixed and mobile medical units enjoy protection from attack and shall at all times be respected and protected by the parties to the conflict.[71] The protection of medical units 'shall not cease unless they are used to commit, outside their humanitarian function, acts harmful to the enemy'.[72] As opposed to the provisions governing the protection – and loss of protection – of objects there is no separate provision dealing with the discontinuance of protection of persons. However, the threshold for the loss of special protection of medical *units* is applied also for *persons*.[73]

The notion of acts harmful to the enemy is a broad concept. 'Harmful acts' encompass both the infliction of direct and indirect harm and thus transcends (as far as persons are concerned) the notion of DPH.[74] It is therefore misleading to exemplify 'harmful acts' by referring to the concept of DPH.[75] Surely, acts which constitute DPH will usually also fall within the scope of acts harmful to the enemy, but not the other way around. During the drafting process, the concept was apparently already established. According to the explanation of the ICRC the notion covered: 'Acts the purpose or effect of which is to harm the adverse Party, by facilitating or impeding military operations".'[76] The Commentary to the AP I also mentions the acts of sheltering able-bodied combatants and using the hospital as an observation post, as examples of acts harmful to the enemy, as well as 'any attempts at deliberately hindering his military operations in any way whatsoever'.[77] One limitation is, however, in-built in the provision itself: it is only when committed 'outside their humanitarian function' that acts harmful to the enemy will deprive the personnel and unit of their special protection. This implies that some acts may be considered harmful to the enemy and that they therefore would reason that the deprivation of protection was appropriate if military necessity was to prevail. Humanitarian considerations have, however, trumped that particular

69 Particular rules apply with regard to the protection of medical aircraft, coastal rescue crafts and hospital ships. These rules are not dealt with here.

70 AP I articles 8(e) and (f)–(j).

71 GC I article 19; AP I article 12.

72 GC I articles 21 and 22; and AP I article 13 (1).

73 ICRC CIHL rule 25 with commentary. Dinstein, *Conduct of Hostilities*, at page 201.

74 Dinstein, *Conduct of Hostilities*, at page 202; AP I Commentary, at para. 551, page 175. On the notion of DPH, see Chapter 11.

75 In this direction see the ICRC CIHL, in the Commentary to rule 25.

76 Quoted from AP I Commentary, para. 550, at page 175.

77 Ibid.

consideration. The ICRC Commentary provides an example where the intent to inflict harm is absent: 'a mobile medical unit accidentally breaks down while it is being moved in accordance with its humanitarian function, and thereby obstructs a crossroads of military importance'.[78] Taking into account that the concept is far-reaching, the treaty text itself exemplifies certain acts which shall not be considered as acts harmful to the enemy: 'that the personnel of the unit are equipped with light individual weapons for their own defence or for that of the wounded and sick in their charge'.[79]

The loss of protection conveys the *special* protection as medical personnel, not necessarily protection against attacks. Subsequent to loss of special protection, the personnel and units retain their original protection against attacks according to their primary status. This means that if the medical personnel are civilians, they can only lose their protection against direct attacks if they are taking a direct part in hostilities. If the medical unit is civilian, it loses its protection against attack only if it qualifies as a military objective. The situation may thus arise that a medical unit has lost its protection against attack, while the participating individual (in fact performing acts harmful to the enemy) remains protected against attacks – yet having lost his/her special protection. If the personnel are military non-combatants they are still protected against direct attacks, but as opposed to civilian medical personnel, military medical personnel will not count as collateral damage under the proportionality assessment during an attack against (for example) a medical unit having lost its protection.

With regard to objects, the special protection of medical units does not only comprise protection against attacks, but also places restrictions upon the use of military medical units in the hands of enemy forces. While enemy military materiel usually may be seized or used as war booty (Chapter 16), enemy *mobile* medical materiel enjoy absolute protection against use.[80] For fixed medical units, the point of departure is the opposite: they are subject to the laws of war, i.e. they may be used and administered in accordance with the 1907 Hague Regulations article 55, unless they are required for the care of the wounded and sick The protection may cease, however, in cases of 'urgent military necessity'.[81] If this exception is invoked, alternative

78 AP I Commentary, para. 552, at page 175.

79 AP I article 13(2)(a).

80 GC I article 33(1); ICRC Commentary on the First Geneva Convention 2016 article 33, at paras. 2329–30. The same point is also made in, for example, the Norwegian Manual, at page 181.

81 GC I article 33(2).

arrangements must be made for the wounded and sick.[82] The provision is a delicate *via media*[83] between humanitarian considerations and the necessities of war, referring to a cumbersome three-step consideration: fixed medical units may be used, according to the requirements of war, but only if they are not required for the wounded and sick, and even then an exception may be invoked. Despite this delicate formulation, there is not significant practice among States in the recent decades as to which situations may qualify as 'urgent military necessities'.[84] Finally, invocation of military necessity is exhaustively governed by the GC I and the AP I, and the 1907 Hague Regulations article 23(g) may not be applied.[85]

17.7 CIVIL DEFENCE PERSONNEL AND ORGANISATIONS

Civil defence organisations and their personnel, as defined in AP I article 61,[86] are protected and entitled to perform their tasks 'except in case of imperative military necessity'.[87]

Military necessity here serves as an exception which may be invoked in order to limit the performance of the tasks of defence personnel, not to cease the protection from direct attacks.[88] Imperative reasons of military necessity are exemplified in the Commentary as the conflict with a major operational plan,[89] or as imposing instructions of deviation on a civil defence aircraft which operates close to the lines of the adversary.[90]

The latter protection: 'shall not cease unless they are used to commit, outside their proper tasks, acts harmful to the enemy. Protection may, however, cease only after a warning has been given setting, whenever appropriate, a reasonable time-limit, and after such warning has remained unheeded.'[91] In this regard the special protection of civil defence personnel is comparable to that of medical personnel – with an *almost* identical wording to the provision in AP I article 13 on the loss of protection for medical personnel and materiel. The difference is related to the tasks of civil defence personnel and medical

82 ICRC Commentary on the First Geneva Convention 2016 article 33, at para. 2335.
83 ICRC Commentary of 1952, to GC I article 33, at pages 275–6.
84 ICRC Commentary on the First Geneva Convention 2016 article 33, at para. 2337.
85 ICRC Commentary on the First Geneva Convention 2016 to GC I article 33, at para. 2339.
86 'Personnel' is defined in AP I article 61(a), 'Organizations' are defined in article 61(b).
87 AP I article 62.
88 AP I Commentary, at para. 2441, page 739; Bothe, Partsch and Solf, *New Rules*, at page 446.
89 AP I Commentary, at para. 2445, page 740. AMW Manual, at page 211.
90 Bothe, Partsch and Solf, *New Rules*, at page 448.
91 AP I article 65.

personnel. While article 13 refers to 'humanitarian function', article 65 uses the expression 'proper tasks'.

The difference is noticeable when it comes to the application of the loss of protection for acts which are considered harmful to the enemy – and hence the necessity of directing attacks directly at personnel or objects which used to have a protected status. Medical personnel work closely with *and for* the armed forces but with an exclusively humanitarian function.[92] It is the humanitarian character of their work which deserves protection – their proximity to the armed forces and hence their utility for the armed forces are considerations which are clearly based on military necessity, and which point in the opposite direction of protection, but which have yielded under the humanity–necessity balance. When it comes to civil defence however, considerations of military necessity are not so close at hand. The 'proper tasks' of civil defence personnel is to protect the *civilian population*. The difference in tasks and utility for the armed forces, as well as the potential necessity for the adversary to attack, has a bearing on the application of the notion of 'acts harmful to the enemy'. As explained above (regarding medical personnel), the notion of 'acts harmful to the enemy' is wider than the notion of 'direct participation in hostilities', since harmful acts can be committed almost by accident. When applying the article by its word on civil defence personnel, it implies that *civilian* personnel may lose its *special* protection from attack according to a lower threshold than other civilians. The solution becomes absurd – what is then the point of special protection? There is no basis in military necessity which points in the direction of *lessened* protection for civilian defence personnel – as opposed to military medical personnel. The solution laid out in the commentaries, as well as the AMW Manual, is that civil defence personnel resume their normal civilian protection for acts which do not constitute direct participation in hostilities.[93] Although this solution appears somewhat strained in the wording of the protocol, it appears to be the correct one. States' military manuals do not seem to address this construction particularly – but at least they do not state that civil defence personnel become lawful targets upon the loss of special protection.[94]

17.8 CULTURAL PROPERTY

Cultural property, without being referred to specifically by that term, has been entitled to be spared 'as far as possible', both by the 1907 Hague Regulations

[92] AP I Commentary, at para. 2590, page 771.
[93] Bothe, Partsch and Solf, *New Rules*, at page 457; AMW Manual, pages 214–15.
[94] Norwegian Manual, at page 83; UK Manual, at page 97.

and the 1907 Hague Convention on Bombardment by Naval Forces, provided that the same property is not, at the same time, used for 'military purposes'.[95] The notion of 'as far as possible' can be read as a reference to military necessity.

The 1954 Hague Convention on Cultural Property defines the expression[96] and codifies the duty to respect property of 'great importance',[97] and establishes as well the regime of special protection for cultural property of 'very great importance'[98] in times of armed conflict. The protection is also reiterated in the AP I article 53 and covers both use and attack[99] and is reflective of customary LOAC.[100] The obligations for belligerents in order to respect cultural property can nevertheless be waived in 'cases where military necessity imperatively requires such a waiver'.[101] Furthermore, and as a response to a prior violation of the Conventions by one of the parties to the conflict, the protection may be temporarily withdrawn 'in exceptional cases of unavoidable military necessity'.[102] The same interpretative challenges arise here, as with regard to other provisions containing a reference to aggravated necessity.[103] Apart from the fact that waiving the *special* protection obviously is intended to require a more severe situation than waiving the 'normal' protection,[104] and – as explicitly required – the decision of a higher command,[105] it is difficult to be more specific on the meaning of the aggravated terms. Some clarifications to the application of the term 'imperative military necessity' may have been offered by the twofold criteria laid down in the Second Protocol to the Hague Convention, adopted in 1999, which states in article 6(a) that the object is both turned into a military objective by function *and* that there is no other 'feasible alternative available' to achieve a similar military advantage. The Second Protocol is not, however, reflective of customary LOAC in its

95 1907 Hague Regulations, article 27; 1907 Hague Convention on Bombardment by Naval Forces, article 5. Both conventions refer to edifices of religion, art, science, charity and historic monuments.

96 Ibid., article 1.

97 Ibid.

98 Ibid., article 8.

99 With regard to use see 1954 Hague Convention on Cultural Property articles 4(1)–(2) and 19(1), as well as the Second Protocol to the Hague Convention articles 6(b) and 22(1), and the AP I article 53(b). With regard to attacks, see 1954 Hague Convention articles 4(1) and (2), as well as Second Protocol on Cultural Property, article 6(a) and AP I article 53(a) (which relates to 'acts of hostility', which is broader than the notion of 'attacks').

100 ICRC CIHL rules 38 and 39.

101 1954 Hague Convention on Cultural Property, article 4; ICRC CIHL articles 38 and 39.

102 1954 Hague Convention on Cultural Property, article 11.

103 See Chapter 2.

104 Dinstein, *Conduct of Hostilities*, at page 210.

105 Article 11(2), division commander or equivalent.

entirety, and the totality of requirements laid down in article 6 can therefore not be applied in general.[106] The wording of article 6 reflects that of the AP I. The general relationship between destruction of property and the definition of military objectives according to AP I article 52(2), is accounted for in Chapter 16 above, but it was also specifically addressed by the ICTY in the Strugar Case.[107] The Strugar Case concerned, among others, attacks on the Old Town of Dubrovnik on 6 December 1991 by the Jugoslav National Army (JNA) (allegedly) against Croatian positions. The shelling of Dubrovnik lasted throughout the day in an attempt to gain control of Mount Srd, a hillside on top of Dubrovnik under Croatian control.[108] The JNA had positioned themselves (among others) at Zarkovica, outside the city of Dubrovnik, providing artillery support for the advance of own troops against Mount Srd. While JNA advancing troops (allegedly) were under fire from Croatian positions in Dubrovnik, the JNA positioned at Zarkovica answered the (alleged) fire from the Old Town of Dubrovnik with (among others) light antitank portable weapons.[109]

As pointed out by the Tribunal, this case was full of factual uncertainties.[110] This is also contributing to its illustrative usefulness. Whether the JNA was aiming at the Old Town was subject to controversy, whether the weapons used could disperse over the Old Town although aimed at its outside was subject to controversy, whether the JNA was actually answering Croatian fire was subject to controversy – and if they were, the need for the duration of the response was subject to controversy. Finally, the time lapse between the incidents – in 1991 – and the time of the trial – in 2005 – was in itself a huge source of uncertainty. Upon these uncertainties the Tribunal stated that: (i) there were no Croatian positions in the Old Town;[111] (ii) even if there were, this fact could not justify the response in intensity and duration; (iii) there were no justifiable reasons to believe that there were Croatian positions in the Old Town;[112] and (iv) even if positions outside the Old Town were aimed at, this would not cause shells to

106 For example, the obligation in article 6(d) to give advance warning has not achieved the status as customary LOAC.

107 The ICTY Statute criminalises 'seizure, destruction or wilful damage' (military necessity is not mentioned). ICTY Statute, article 3(d). It is worth pointing out that the phrase 'cultural property' not is mentioned. This is similar to the criminalisation in the Rome Statute article 8(2)(b)(ix).

108 Strugar Case, at paras. 113–17.

109 Strugar Case, at paras. 117–27.

110 Strugar Case, at paras. 5–10.

111 Strugar Case, at paras. 185 and 193.

112 Strugar Case, at para. 195.

fall over the Old Town.[113] Having arrived at these factual findings, the legal discussion became easier.

Relying upon its own previous jurisprudence and treaty law as expressed in the 1907 Hague Regulations article 27, the Hague Convention on Cultural Property article 4 and the AP I article 53, the Trial Chamber stated: 'Nevertheless, the established jurisprudence of the Tribunal confirming the "military purposes" exception which is consistent with the exceptions recognised by the Hague Regulations of 1907 and the Additional Protocols, persuades the Chamber that the protection accorded to cultural property is lost where such property is used for military purposes.'[114] The Tribunal's reasoning on this point – where protection is lost if the property is used for military purposes (the expression from the 1907 Hague Conventions cited above) – has been denoted as a 'sensitivity' by the ICTY to 'maintain the necessity-humanity balance'.[115] Whether it might appear as 'sensitivity' to this balance as far as the legal point of departure is concerned, the Tribunal's reasoning with regard to the facts did not leave equally much 'sensitivity' towards military necessity.

The Trial Chamber found that not any of the destroyed buildings were being used for military purposes, and military necessity could thus not justify the attacks.[116] The Appeals Chamber upheld this decision, arguing that: 'Hence, the Trial Chamber reasonably concluded that the direct perpetrators of the crime were aware of the protected status of the cultural property in the Old Town and that the attack on this cultural property was deliberate and not justified by any military necessity.'[117]

For the purpose of drawing up the legal limits to the commander's assessment of military necessity, the Tribunal's findings on these points are of interest. The scenario represents general challenges which any reasonable commander is likely to face: a mission to gain control over a hillside while being under attack and being required to respond to the fire in order to secure own forces. Counter-attacks by the use of artillery in urban areas pose a number of problems, yet they may easily be considered a necessity (notwithstanding that the attack may still be unlawful due to humanitarian concerns, such as in the proportionality rule). Furthermore, the deliberate misuse of objects endowed with special protection (such as cultural property in the

113 Strugar Case, at paras. 204–14.
114 Strugar Case, at para. 310.
115 Schmitt, 'Military necessity and humanity in international humanitarian law', at page 818.
116 Strugar Case, at para. 328.
117 Strugar Case, at para. 329. The position taken by the Trial Chamber was upheld by the Appeals Chamber, at paras. 279–80.

Strugar Case) by a technologically less advanced enemy is sometimes to be expected. Finally, artillery (understood in a broad sense) is an area weapon. Rocket artillery is not made to hit a single target within an urban area – and nothing next to it. When used as designed these weapons hit a target area, in many cases shaped as an elliptical area.[118] While the use of area weapons in densely populated areas poses a number of questions with regard to the prohibition of indiscriminate attacks and the duty take feasible precautions in attacks, their use will, as a point of departure, be considered necessary by a reasonable commander. In light of these observations, the Tribunals findings in the Strugar Case are noteworthy for the purposes of defining the limits of the commander's assessment of military necessity.

17.9 WORKS AND INSTALLATIONS CONTAINING DANGEROUS FORCES

Works and installations containing dangerous forces enjoy special treaty protection. AP I article 56(1) and (2) say:

1. Works or installations containing dangerous forces, namely dams, dykes and nuclear electrical generating stations, shall not be made the object of attack, even where these objects are military objectives, if such attack may cause the release of dangerous forces and consequent severe losses among the civilian population. Other military objectives located at or in the vicinity of these works or installations shall not be made the object of attack if such attack may cause the release of dangerous forces from the works or installations and consequent severe losses among the civilian population.
2. The special protection against attack provided by paragraph 1 shall cease:
   (a) for a dam or a dyke only if it is used for other than its normal function and in regular, significant and direct support of military operations and if such attack is the only feasible way to terminate such support;
   (b) for a nuclear electrical generating station only if it provides electric power in regular, significant and direct support of military operations and if such attack is the only feasible way to terminate such support;
   (c) for other military objectives located at or in the vicinity of these works or installations only if they are used in regular, significant and

118 Cross, Dullum, Jenzen-Jones and Garlasco, 'Explosive weapons in populated areas', at page 32. See as well Chapter 5.

> direct support of military operations and if such attack is the only feasible way to terminate such support.

This provision was an invention of AP I and is not reflective of customary LOAC, which requires parties to take 'particular care'.[119] The AP I provision devotes special protection to objects which would usually be considered a necessity to destroy. Flooding of dykes was for example used by the Germans during WWII in the Netherlands, in order to hamper enemy advance. Furthermore, both nuclear electrical generating stations and dams may easily qualify as military objectives when providing power to the armed forces. Attacks on works and installations containing dangerous forces must almost inevitably be expected to cause extensive collateral damage. This is what is captured by paragraph 1 of article 56: attacks which may be expected to cause 'severe' losses among the civilian population. This threshold differs in meaning from 'excessive' in the proportionality rule. The rule is therefore not just a simple restatement of the proportionality rule.[120] On the contrary, 'severe' refers to what might be an absolute threshold (by the ICRC labelled as 'important' or 'heavy'[121]) which does not necessarily imply that the losses anticipated will be excessive (on excessiveness as a relative and not absolute threshold, see Chapter 15). This deviation from the proportionality rule constitutes the source of opposition by non-contracting State parties to the AP I as well as the basis for reservations made by other States, France and the UK in particular.[122] The reason behind the US view is expressed as follows:

> The negotiating history throws little light on what level of civilian losses would be 'severe'. It is clear, however, that under this article, civilian losses are not to be balanced against the military value of the target. If severe losses would result, then the attack is forbidden, no matter how important the target. It also appears that article 56 forbids any attack that raises the

119 The ICRC CIHL rule 42 states that parties to the armed conflict must show 'particular care' if and when attacking works and installations containing dangerous forces. Dinstein, *Conduct of Hostilities*, at page 194; and Oeter, 'Methods and means of combat', at page 217, states the same with regard to the customary point of departure. See, however, below for details.

120 Dinstein, *Conduct of Hostilities*, at page 228. In an opposite direction, see Oeter, 'Methods and means of combat', at page 217.

121 AP I Commentary, para. 2154, at pages 669–70.

122 As a reservation to AP I article 56, the UK has stated that it 'cannot undertake to grant absolute protection to installations which may contribute to the opposing Party's war effort, or to the defenders of such installations, but will take all due precautions in military operations at or near the installations referred to in paragraph 1 of Article 56 in the light of the known facts, including any special marking which the installation may carry, to avoid sever[e] collateral losses among the civilian populations; direct attacks on such installations will be launched only on authorisation at a high level of command.' A similar statement is made by France.

> possibility of severe civilian losses, even though considerable care is taken to avoid them.[123]

At the core of this statement lies the lack of possibility to take the value of the target into account, which means that considerations of military necessity have yielded to humanitarian concerns in article 56 – to the opposition of certain States.

For States whose commanders are obliged to perform an assessment of 'severity', the ICRC points out that this assessment relies, here as elsewhere, upon common sense and the good faith of the commander.[124] The discretionary challenges incumbent upon the commander in the context of dangerous forces thus appear almost infinite.[125] While on the one hand the commander is required to use his or her most reasonable judgment, he or she is also expected to undertake particularly thorough factual estimates, as the notion of 'severity' in practice has to be assessed '. . . on the basis of objective elements such as the proximity of inhabited areas, the density of population, the lie of the land etc'.[126]

The protection devoted to these objects under paragraph 1 (here including the objects in their vicinity) only ceases according to an aggravated qualification of military objectives and precautions in attack as stipulated in paragraph 2. The object must provide 'regular, significant and direct support' of military operations, as opposed to merely 'effective contribution' in the provision in AP I article 52(2), which 'establishes a conspicuously higher standard than, say, 'effective contribution to military action''.[127] This threshold may pose different difficulties in application with regard to each of the three categories in AP I article 56. While the wording is undoubtedly vague and in evident need of clarification,[128] the ICRC presumes that 'these terms merely express common sense, i.e., their meaning is fairly clear to everyone'. This 'clarity' is expounded upon as follows:

> The word 'regular' relates to time. It means that accidental or sporadic use is not sufficient; there must be some continuity in the use, or at least some rhythm. The word 'significant' is less precise, but must be understood in relation to a scale of degrees of significance that may be established. The support must not be negligible nor should it be merely an incidental

123 US DoD Manual, page 271, footnote 423, citing the US view on the legal status of AP I article 56.

124 AP I Commentary, para. 2154, at pages 669–70.

125 In this same direction, see Oeter, 'Methods and means of combat', at page 220.

126 AP I Commentary, para. 2154, at pages 669–70.

127 Dinstein, *Conduct of Hostilities*, at page 228.

128 Ibid.

> circumstance, but it must be sizeable having a real and effective impact. The term 'direct' means: not in an intermediate or a roundabout way. Thus the relation between the act and its effect must be close and immediate. What is meant is support which would benefit military operations themselves and not merely intermediary objectives which themselves would be related to such operations.[129]

The latter part of the quotation, relating to the 'intermediary objectives', is subject to controversy. 'Intermediary objectives' can for example be nuclear electrical generating stations providing power to the defence industry. With regard to this distinction, Oeter states that: 'What directly supports warfare in such a case is the industry supplied with power, not the power station in itself. However, even such a primarily defence industry-related function should probably be regarded as a "regular, significant, and direct contribution".'[130] The ICRC disagrees with this view, on the ground that the expression 'military operations' does not cover factories producing armaments, ammunition and military equipment.[131]

The problem concerning terms that are supposed to be understood by the commander according to his or her 'common sense' (see Chapters 1 and 4 for general remarks in this regard) arises here as well (as with 'necessity' and 'advantage'). For example: absent exemplification, the 'common sense' approach to the term 'significant' may vary substantially. These variations may become increasingly present when (i) 'effective contribution' to military action is to be distinguished from (ii) 'regular, significant and direct support' to military operations. Taken into account (among others) that 'effective contribution' also entails a requirement of time (and therefore in this regard cannot be understood clearly distinct from 'regular'), I only see one utterly clear distinction: (ii) requires something 'more' than (i) in order to waive the special protection granted according to article 56 (1).

Furthermore, an attack on the object must be the 'only feasible way' to terminate the support. As is the case with cultural property this latter requirement entails a qualified causal requirement of military necessity.[132] Non-nuclear power stations do not fall within the scope of protection in the first place (unless they are in the vicinity of dams, dykes or nuclear electrical generating stations), and an attack upon these must be assessed by the AP

[129] AP I Commentary, para. 2162, at page 671.
[130] Oeter, 'Methods and means of combat', at page 220.
[131] AP I Commentary, para. 2165, at page 672.
[132] See Chapter 2.

I article 52(2) and, subsequently, the proportionality rule.[133] Finally, objects enjoying special protection from attacks in AP I article 56 are not protected from destruction or being rendered useless, as long as it is within the threshold of AP I article 54, in particular article 54(5) (see Section 17.11).[134]

From this, I am able to make three points: first, that the notion of 'severe' in AP I article 56(1) actually is something distinct from a proportionality assessment – it requires a particularly challenging prognostic requirement[135] which is not relative to the military advantage anticipated from the attack. In this, the commander receives some guidance, albeit challenging to perform. Second, the special protection granted in AP I article 56(1) can, although the attack may be expected to cause 'severe' losses among the civilian population, be lifted under particular circumstances which are very difficult to outline clearly, but which entail that the military objectives may nevertheless be attacked if their contribution is significant enough – more than what amounts to effective contribution to military action – and if the attack is the only feasible way to terminate the support. In the assessment made under paragraph 2, those considerations of military necessity that were excluded from paragraph 1 appear somehow to be reinserted again. Third, under customary LOAC, particular precautions are to be taken if and when works and installations containing dangerous forces are attacked and may be expected to cause 'severe' losses among the civilian population.

17.10 NATURAL ENVIRONMENT

The status and protection of the natural environment under the LOAC are subject to debate. There is no agreed definition of the natural environment. Yet, there is a presupposed common understanding of the concept.[136] It appears clear that the Pacific Ocean and the Amazon rainforest are parts of the natural environment, but it is not equally clear whether the lawn in front of my house constitutes 'natural environment'. Furthermore, the 'natural environment' may overlap with other categories under the LOAC. While the natural environment in principle is a civilian object[137] and enjoys protection

133 Oeter, 'Methods and means of combat', at page 220, appears to make the same point, although phrased as if the objects do not fulfil the criteria in para. 2 of article 56 – which they are not required to fulfil in the first place as they do not fall within the scope of para. 1.

134 AP I Commentary, at para. 2152, page 669.

135 Oeter, 'Methods and means of combat', at page 220.

136 A feature which is similar to that of the 'military advantage'.

137 ICRC CIHL, rule 43 A with commentary. See also for example, Oeter, 'Methods and means of combat', at page 213.

against destruction, direct attacks and excessive collateral damage, parts of the natural environment may qualify as a military objective by its location, purpose or use (but not by nature). In these cases, its capture, destruction or neutralisation is lawful whenever the two criteria of AP I article 52(2) are fulfilled. An example is the use of parts of the natural environment for different forms of camouflage, whereby the assessment of military necessity is in-built in the definition of military objectives.[138] In other cases than those where parts of the natural environment constitute a military objective, the natural environment may fall within the scope of the notion of 'property' and thus be destroyed when required by military necessity.[139] Numerous practical examples from history (e.g. application of scorched earth tactics and starvation as a method of warfare) fall within this latter category. In recent history it is perhaps the destruction of oil wells which has gained most attention. The release of oil and damage to oil rigs may lead to damage comparable to that dealt with in the prohibition of attacks on installations containing dangerous forces. However, the rule in AP I article 56 exhaustingly governs dams, dykes and nuclear electrical generating stations.[140] The release of oil must therefore be viewed in light of the protection of the environment and the rule permitting destruction when justified by military necessity. In all incidents, feasible precautions must be taken in order to minimise incidental damage to the environment.

The special treaty protection of the natural environment *as such* appeared for the first time in the Environmental Modification Convention (ENMOD) in 1976[141] and in the AP I the year after. AP I article 35(3) states that: 'It is prohibited to employ methods or means of warfare which are intended, or may be expected, to cause widespread, long-term and severe damage to the natural environment.' And then in article 55:

1. Care shall be taken in warfare to protect the natural environment against widespread, long-term and severe damage. This protection includes

138 For a codification of this position, see article 2(4) of the Protocol III to the CCW.

139 ICRC CIHL, rule 43 B. Some refer to Legality of the Threat or Use of Nuclear Weapons, Advisory Opinion, at para. 30, where the Court refers to necessity and proportionality. This statement does, however, seem to address the *jus ad bellum* and not the *jus in bello*. For a particular statement with regard to the notion of 'property', see Roscini, 'Targeting and contemporary aerial bombardment', at pages 437–8, who argues that it is unclear whether 'property' encompasses natural goods.

140 AP I Commentary, para. 2150, at pages 668–9.

141 Convention on the Prohibition of Military or Any other Hostile Use of Environmental Modification Techniques (ENMOD) 10 December 1976. The threshold in the ENMOD differs from the one in the AP I.

a prohibition of the use of methods or means of warfare which are intended or may be expected to cause such damage to the natural environment and thereby to prejudice the health or survival of the population.

2. Attacks against the natural environment by way of reprisals are prohibited.

The threshold for protection according to this provision is high (in this regard, higher than in the ENMOD[142]), requiring both 'widespread', 'long-term' *and* 'severe' damage. The protection afforded according to the treaty applies regardless of the advantage the operation may offer to the attacker.[143] This fact, that States are *not* allowed to take considerations of military necessity into account when the damage is great enough, seems to lie at the heart of the opposition against the customary status of the rule in AP I.

Although stated in rule 45 of the CIHL study that the AP I article 55 rule is established as customary law, this position seems questionable.[144] The USA has taken a clear position against the customary status of the rule (labelled a persistent objector in the CIHL study), stating that widespread, long-term and severe damage to the natural environment is only prohibited if 'their use is clearly excessive in relation to the concrete and direct overall military advantage anticipated'.[145] A justification for the opposition against the customary status of the rule is provided by the example of a State A that hides a chemical and biological weapons arsenal in a rainforest and has an imminent plan to launch an attack against State B. According to the AP I rule, State B would be prohibited to launch an attack against the weapons storage if the attack would be expected to cause widespread, long-term and severe damage, although the attack would not be expected to cause excessive civilian collateral damage as such.[146]

142 In the ENMOD, the threshold criteria are alternatives and not cumulative requirements. According to article 1, the hostile use of environmental modification techniques having widespread, long-lasting or severe effects as the means of destruction, damage *or* injury to any other State party. However, the ENMOD is limited in another aspect, namely that of applying only in cases where the natural environment is used as an 'instrument of war'. For this reason, the opposition against the ENMOD is not the same as towards the AP I provision. See for example, US DoD Manual, at pages 377–8.

143 Roscini, 'Targeting and contemporary aerial bombardment', at page 439.

144 Legality of the Threat or Use of Nuclear Weapons, Advisory Opinion, at para. 31; and Roscini, 'Targeting and contemporary aerial bombardment', at page 440. In an opposite direction, see the OTP Report, at para. 15.

145 US DoD Manual, at pages 378–9.

146 Ibid., the manual's footnote 219.

17.11 STARVATION AND OBJECTS INDISPENSABLE TO THE SURVIVAL OF THE CIVILIAN POPULATION

17.11.1 *A Historical Backdrop of Siege War, Starvation and Military Necessity*

AP I article 54(1) contains a general prohibition of starvation of civilians 'as a method of warfare'. The provision was an innovation with the AP I, although the GC IV already provides for aid in favour of the most vulnerable groups as well as safeguards the necessities of life for the civilian population.[147] Although being an innovation of the AP I, the rule has now gained the status as customary international law.[148] The scope of the prohibition of starvation is determined by the rest of AP I article 54,[149] but in order to grasp the potential of the provision in the context of military necessity, it is fruitful to take a brief look back at history.

Starvation has, from early times, been seen as a necessary measure in order to reach the ends of war, the weakening of the enemy forces. The Lieber Code of 1863 states in article 17 that: 'War is not carried out by arms alone. It is lawful to starve the hostile belligerent, armed or unarmed, so that it leads to the speedier subjection of the enemy.'[150] Starvation of the civilian population has been achieved through the use of siege warfare and in order to grant the effectiveness of the siege it is also stated in the Lieber Code, article 18 that: 'When a commander of a besieged place expels the noncombatants, in order to lessen the number of those who consume his stock of provisions, it is lawful, though an extreme measure, to drive them back, so as to hasten the surrender.'[151] While history has shown the brutal results on the civilian population in besieged towns, the method was nevertheless considered necessary and lawful all the way through WWII.[152]

The present prohibition on starvation as a method must be seen partly as a reaction to the magnitude of devastation resulting from the German siege of Leningrad from September 1941 to January 1944 where Hitler's plan was to raze the city to the ground in order to acquire its territory. Consequently, the prohibition on starvation as a method of warfare limits the belligerents' resort

147 AP I Commentary to article 54, at page 652, para. 2083; GC IV articles 23 and 53; Bothe, Partsch and Solf, *New Rules*, at pages 378–9.

148 AMW Manual, rule 97 (a); ICRC CIHL, rule 53; Dinstein, *Conduct of Hostilities*, at page 218. Use of starvation as a method of warfare is also criminalised as a war crime in the Rome Statute article 8(2)(b)(xxv).

149 Official Records of the Diplomatic Conference CDDH/215/Rev.1, at para. 73.

150 Lieber Code article 17.

151 Ibid.

152 High Command Case, at page 563.

to measures traditionally perceived as a military necessity. Siege war has in its traditional form (directed at the civilian population) practically been prohibited by the AP I rule in article 54[153] – although it is clear that blockade is not covered by the prohibition and is (still) subject to the law of naval warfare.[154] With regard to land (and air[155]) warfare, however, the necessities of war finally yielded to humanitarian considerations with regard to starvation. With regard to the scorched earth tactics, the picture is more uncertain. It remains therefore to discuss the actual impact on military necessity and the traditional methods of warfare from the AP I prohibition.

17.11.2 AP I Article 54: Limitations upon 'Traditional' Military Necessity

AP I article 54(2) has a wide scope in order to support the prohibition to use starvation as a method of warfare. The text of paragraph (2) says:

> It is prohibited to attack, destroy, remove or render useless objects indispensable to the survival of the civilian population, such as foodstuffs, agricultural areas for the production of foodstuffs, crops, livestock, drinking water installations and supplies and irrigation works, for the specific purpose of denying them for their sustenance value to the civilian population or to the adverse Party, whatever the motive, whether in order to starve out civilians, to cause them to move away, or for any other motive.

Alongside the prohibition of starvation as a method of warfare, this provision, which protects certain objects according to their function, also enjoys customary status.[156]

The alternatives 'attack, destroy, remove or render useless', are chosen in order to 'cover all possibilities',[157] and therefore gives objects which are indispensable for the civilian population a wider protection than simply protection from attacks. The enumeration of objects is not exhaustive and the provision can arguably also extend to electrical power supplies which provide drinking-water purification, such as those destroyed during the first Gulf War in 1991.[158]

In addition to siege warfare, which is mentioned specifically above, article 54 covers (among others) scorched earth tactics – when this is applied in such

153 Dinstein, *Conduct of Hostilities*, at page 255.
154 San Remo Manual, rules 102–3; Bothe, Partsch and Solf, *New Rules*, at page 380; ICRC CIHL Commentary to rule 53.
155 AMW Manual, article 97(a), at page 221.
156 AMW Manual, rule 97(b), in Commentary page 221; ICRC CIHL rule 54; and the Rome Statute article 8(2)(b)(xxv) where a violation of the rule is made a war crime.
157 AP I Commentary, at page 655, para. 2101.
158 See Chapter 13.

a way that it denies the civilian population of objects which are indispensable for their survival.[159] While 'imperative military necessity' has been the justification for applying the scorched earth tactics throughout history, it is not immediately clear what role military necessity is given with regard to objects indispensable for the survival of the civilian population. Initially, the scope and function of 54(2) can be read as a provision that limits which measures can be invoked by reference to the military necessity umbrella in the 1907 Hague Regulations article 23(g).

In addition to the obvious requirement of 'indispensable for the survival' of the civilian population, two conditions are set out to limit the scope of the prohibition: first that the prohibition only covers destruction of the objects 'for the specific purpose of denying them for their sustenance value', and second that military necessity provides for exceptions in the following sub-provisions (3) and (5).[160]

First a remark on the requirement of 'specific purpose', which was carefully drafted[161] in order to make it explicit that the provision extends only to acts done for the purpose of denying the objects their 'sustenance value' for the civilian population or to the adverse party.[162] The notion of 'purpose' has, however, led to confusion since 'motive' is clearly rejected in the same provision. From the drafting process it was pointed out that:

> Another confusion in paragraph 2 is caused by the interplay of purpose and motive. The only attack, destruction, etc. that is prohibited by this paragraph is that which is done for the purpose of denying the objects to the adverse Party or to the civilian population. In principle that is fairly clear, but the sentence does not read easily, because that statement is followed by the words 'whatever the motive that produced that purpose, whether to starve out civilians, to cause them to move away, or any other motive'.[163]

This confusion is easy to understand, since it quite often in practice is difficult to distinguish between the purpose of an act and the motive behind it.

159 Bothe, Partsch and Solf, *New Rules*, at page 379. On scorched-earth practice in general under the rule on destruction of property, see Chapter 16.

160 AP I Commentary, para. 2105, at page 656.

161 This requirement was not included in the ICRC's Draft Article 48, which said: 'It is forbidden to attack or destroy objects indispensable to the survival of the civilian population, namely, foodstuffs and food-producing areas, crops, livestock, drinking water supplies and irrigation works, whether it is to starve out civilians, to cause them to move away or for any other reason. These objects shall not be made the object of reprisals.' See Official Records of the Diplomatic Conference, Vol. 1, part three.

162 Bothe, Partsch and Solf, *New Rules*, page 381. The same wording is reiterated in the AMW Manual, Commentary 2 to rule 97(2).

163 In Official Records of the Diplomatic Conference CDDH/215/Rev.1, para. 75.

Particularly when it comes to the practice of scorched earth, the role of the 'purpose' of the act will often be decisive for lawfulness. The purpose of destroying a field of crops can be to hamper the enemy advance, and the act will be lawful. If the purpose of the act is to deny the civilian population the crops for food, the act will be unlawful. What role does eventual motive play here? It is possible to argue that the problem arises at the outset, by the requirement of 'purpose'. If that notion was out of the provision, the rule would have been a straightforward special protection of objects which are indispensable for survival of civilians. It would also be a specific limitation upon military necessity. With the requirement of 'purpose', however, military necessity seems to remain the decisive factor: if there is a military purpose of destroying the field of crops, the act is arguably outside the scope of the prohibition.[164] The consequence of this reading of the provision is that the prohibition remains almost without force with regard to scorched earth tactics – while it will still prohibit siege warfare in its traditional form.

The same 'confusion' with regard to the requirement of 'purpose', makes the scope of the exception in article 54(3), unclear:

> The prohibitions in paragraph 2 shall not apply to such of the objects covered by it as are used by an adverse Party:
>
> (a) as sustenance solely for the members of its armed forces; or
> (b) if not as sustenance, then in direct support of military action, provided, however, that in no event shall actions against these objects be taken which may be expected to leave the civilian population with such inadequate food or water as to cause its starvation or force its movement.

This provision is unclear in more aspects than the relationship to the 'purpose of the act': objects that are used as sustenance 'solely for the members of its armed forces' (*litera* (a)) will hardly be considered as 'indispensable for the survival of the civilian population', as required by article 54(2), and therefore fall outside the scope of the prohibition for this reason. The situation is different for so-called dual-use objects, when they are both indispensable for the survival of the civilian population and used in support of the armed forces. Such objects will fall within the prohibition of article 54(2) if the purpose of destruction is to deny the objects of their sustenance value to the adverse party – for example irrigation works. The purpose of 54(2) has not, however, been to prohibit destruction of food or supply for the armed forces. Paragraph 3(b) thus permits destruction of

[164] In AP I Commentary, footnote 13, at page 655, it is stated that: 'Bombarding an area to prevent the advance through it of an enemy is permissible, whether or not the area produces food.'

such objects according to a higher threshold than that for attacking objects which would otherwise qualify as military objectives according to article 52(2). It furthermore entails a separate threshold for destruction of objects which could otherwise have been destroyed (outside the scope of attacks as governed by article 52(2))[165] by reference to the 1907 Hague Regulations article 23(g) according to 'imperative military necessity'. In both aspects the rule in article 54(3) entails a limitation upon military necessity due to humanitarian concerns; military necessity can only be invoked in an aggravated form.

Then, in article 54(5), military necessity is given an additional exceptional role: 'In recognition of the vital requirements of any Party to the conflict in the defence of its national territory against invasion, derogation from the prohibitions contained in paragraph 2 may be made by a Party to the conflict within such territory under its own control where required by imperative military necessity.' The actual scope of this provision is also unclear. This is partly because national law governs destruction of property on a belligerent State's own territory (to the extent the destruction is not prohibited by AP II article 14),[166] and partly because the provision seems to presume the prohibition of destruction of a field in order to hamper the enemy advance (which the drafters presumed remained lawful, due to the purpose of the act). The following sentence illustrates the confusion: 'Although para. 5 of article 54 would in the future prohibit a scorched earth policy by the retreating forces of an Occupying Power as was the situation in the two cited cases, it would still permit such devastation by a defending Party in its own territory.'[167] Even further, the provision is unclear with regard to the threshold of 'imperative military necessity', which is exactly the same threshold as that found in the 1907 Hague Regulations article 23(g).[168] What should be the watermark for distinguishing the one from the other, given that the AP I article 54(5) aspires to be a higher threshold than the one provided in the Hague Regulations? The rule in article 54 certainly induces military commanders to be extra careful with regard to objects which may be indispensable for the survival of the civilian population. But with regard to enemy advance and own forces' retreat

165 On the relationship between article 52(2) and 23(g) in general, see Chapter 16.

166 This was also pointed out by delegates at the Diplomatic Conference, see Official Records of the Diplomatic Conference CDDH/215/Rev.1, para. 77.

167 Bothe, Partsch and Solf, *New Rules*, at page 379.

168 The AP I Commentary illustratively states at page 659, para. 2122, that: 'In the case of imperative military necessity a belligerent Power may in an extreme case even destroy objects indispensable to the survival of the civilian population in that part of its own territory which is under its control.'

he or she is left with little guidance for considering military necessity but that which is already found in the Hague Regulations.

17.12 OTHER RULES ON SPECIAL PROTECTION AND CONSIDERATIONS OF MILITARY NECESSITY

'Parlementaire' is used as a term to describe someone who negotiates between the belligerent commanders. The unnecessary character of attacking the 'messenger' is obvious. The inviolability of the parlementaire is thus firmly established,[169] most known by reference to a white flag, the flag of truce, signalling a will to negotiate and calling for protection in this errand. The inviolability of the parlementaire is not repeated explicitly in treaty law after 1907, but the protection is reflected in the rule on perfidy in AP I article 37(1)(a). Killing an opponent by resort to perfidy by the feigning of an intent to negotiate is considered a war crime according to the Rome Statute article 8(2)(b)(xi). Furthermore, in cases of repeated perfidy by one belligerent, it may be considered necessary for the opponent to adopt to the perfidious activity. Alongside the argument that it is unwise and unnecessary to kill the messenger, it may be necessary to direct an attack against a person feigning the status of a parlementaire. Hence, *feigned* status is not protected status.

Women are devoted special protection in article 27 in the GC IV and AP I article 76(1). The latter provision entails protection regardless of whether the woman is a civilian (and hence enjoys civilian protection) or a combatant in the power of an adverse party,[170] and states that 'Women shall be the object of special respect and shall be protected in particular against rape, forced prostitution, and any other form of indecent assault.'[171] Such acts are by treaty law considered manifestly *unnecessary* and unrelated to the success of the armed conflict. Although some bizarre argumentation could advocate the actual usefulness of such conduct – for example to create fear and perception of enemy dominance in the civilian population – the law (also customary international law[172]) establishes a clear preference to humanitarian considerations.

The same provision furthermore provides protection for pregnant women and women with 'dependant infants' against prolonged uncertainty with

169 1907 Hague Regulations, article 32. See also UK Manual, at page 259.

170 AP I Commentary, para. 3051, at page 892.

171 And AP I article 76(1).

172 See Rome Statute article 8(2)(b)(xxii), which establishes rape, sexual slavery, enforced prostitution, forced pregnancy, enforced sterilisation or any other form of sexual violence as a war crime. The same position is held in the ICTY Trial Chamber decision in the Delalic Case, at paras. 476–7.

regard to detentions and as well an *absolute* prohibition on the execution of death sentences.[173] Under circumstances where the woman is either pregnant or has responsibility for a 'dependant infant' the death penalty was – by the treaty drafters – considered *inhumane*.[174] Hence, although it might – from a State perspective – be considered *necessary* to inflict the death penalty on a female individual sentenced, for example, by having committed a serious act of sabotage, the treaty provision has decided that humanity trumps necessity in the cases where the execution would adversely affect the unborn child – or the infant.[175]

The Rome Statute extends the prohibition of sexual exploitation in a material aspect, criminalising as well enforced sterilisation and forced pregnancy, and in a personal aspect, not limiting the protection to women.[176]

The special protection devoted to children in armed conflict is – apart from the protection emanating from the protection of women with infants above – concentrated on the prohibition of indecent assault[177] and the recruitment of child soldiers below the age of fifteen.[178]

The Rome Statute article 8(2)(b)(xxvi) states that it is a war crime to conscript or enlist children under fifteen years of age – or to use them to participate actively in hostilities. Furthermore, alongside the prohibition of executing a death sentence on pregnant women and women with infants (above), it is prohibited to execute a death penalty on a person 'who had not attained the age of 18 at the time the offence was committed'.[179] As with women accounted for above, also with children below the age of eighteen, humanitarian considerations have trumped any perception of necessity with regard to executing the death penalty for serious crimes – although the crime may pose a serious threat to the security of the state.

The special protection granted children when it comes to the prohibition of recruiting child soldiers is, however, somewhat misleading when it comes to protection against direct attacks. While it is a war crime to recruit child soldiers, child soldiers – when taking a direct part in hostilities – are lawful targets.[180] The necessity of attacking those participating in hostilities (despite being forced into it and being a child) thus trumps the humane aspect of

173 Ibid. and AP I Commentary, at page 895, para. 3169.
174 AP I Commentary, at page 895, para. 3168.
175 See AP I Commentary, at page 892, para. 3148, where it is argued that the idea behind the prohibition of execution of death sentences is to protect the unborn child.
176 Rome Statute articles 8(2)(b)(xxi) and (xxii).
177 AP I article 77(1).
178 AP I article 77(2).
179 AP I article 77(5).
180 See for example Norwegian Manual, at page 63.

protecting the child. This is partly a result of the inherent difficulties of determining the age of an approaching enemy; whether a person is fifteen or nineteen can be difficult – if not impossible – to tell at a distance. The protection offered children is therefore dependent upon those recruiting – or rather not – them.[181] This legal construct – that a child with special protection also can be considered a lawful target – certainly does not solve the *moral* difficulties of approaching a child with a weapon.

Relief personnel are those persons who form part of the assistance provided in a relief action.[182] They are entitled to 'respect and protection' and their activities or movements may only be limited or restricted in cases of 'imperative military necessity'.[183] Beyond these provisions, the protection against direct attacks relies on the main rule of distinction and the definition of lawful targets (including the threshold for direct participation in hostilities), as accounted for above in Chapters 7–11.

The rule in AP I article 79 simply confirms the civilian status of journalists, although they fulfil their mission in an area of armed conflict. They enjoy no special protection beyond their protection as civilians. Conversely, they lose their protection when taking a direct part in hostilities,[184] for example through the passing of tactical intelligence information to troops on the ground. Having said this, those who are accredited as 'war correspondents' will gain the status as prisoners of war upon capture.[185]

181 See AP I article 77(2), placing a duty upon the belligerent parties to take 'all feasible measures' in order to keep the children below the age of fifteen out of participating directly in hostilities.
182 AP I article 71, relief actions are defined in article 70.
183 AP I articles 71(2) and (3).
184 Dinstein, *Conduct of Hostilities*, at page 199.
185 AP I article 79(2); and GC III article 4.

PART V

CONCLUSIONS

18

Conclusions: Limitations to the Commander's Assessment of Military Necessity

18.1 OVERVIEW: LIMITATIONS IN DIFFERENT WAYS

The legal limits to the military commander's assessment of military necessity are addressed in four different parts in this book. The commander's assessment is in some contexts left with little guidance and a wide margin of appreciation and in other contexts with almost no margin, where considerations of necessity are consumed entirely (for practical purposes) by the law.

In part I the military margin of appreciation is presented as the limits of law (Chapter 4). The margin of appreciation is both an inevitable part of military necessity and the distinction between law and arbitrariness (Chapters 2 and 4). Military necessity as such is not a limitation upon the commander's assessment, but the right to invoke necessity is limited. Military necessity is limited by humanitarian concerns and the general rule of limitation (Chapter 6).

In part II distinction is presented as a limitation upon military necessity (Chapter 7). In this part the constituent elements of lawful targets and protected objects and persons are presented and discussed. The principle of distinction includes both a permission to attack lawful targets and a prohibition to attack protected objects and persons. The permissive part is justified by military necessity and the prohibitive part entails a limitation due to humanitarian concerns (or even other State interests) (see in particular Chapter 10).

In part III the rules effectuating the principle of distinction (the prohibition of indiscriminate attacks – including the proportionality principle – and the duty to take precautions in attack) illustrate the wide margins devoted to military commanders when having to balance between necessities of war and humanitarian concerns in the most conspicuous way (Chapters 14 and 15). Except from parts of the prohibition of indiscriminate attacks (Chapter 12) these rules cry out for the commander's assessment and are a result of treaty compromises leaving limitations upon commander's assessment vague, ambiguous and wide.

In part IV military necessity is presented as a limited exception. Military necessity appears seemingly less vague than in situations discussed under part III, yet challenges still arise due to the fact that older and more recent treaty law are not harmonised (Chapter 16) as well as the fact that some specific exceptions are difficult to distinguish from general rules on protection (Chapter 17).

18.2 NECESSITY AND THE ASSESSMENT OF NECESSITY: SOMETIMES ONE AND THE SAME

On some occasions, the rule referring to military necessity and the assessment of that rule are so closely linked that the rule appears to be, as argued in Section 4.2.3, what the commander assesses it to be. This observation embodies a delicate challenge: to combine realistic room for subjective manoeuvre with objective limits to the commander's assessment of military necessity. The combination of subjective assessment with an objective threshold established in the legal norm is illustrated in the commander's assessment of military advantage, as discussed in Chapter 14 and concluded below in Sections 18.5 and 18.8. In other parts of the LOAC, the commander's assessment of military necessity is (almost) entirely consumed by legal regulations, such as the scope of the prohibition of unnecessary suffering of combatants and the definition of lawful combatancy, as discussed in Chapters 9 and 10 and concluded in Section 18.6 below. In these latter cases, pending issues regarding military necessity have emerged at the stage of treaty drafting, rather than in the application of the law.

18.3 THE BASICS OF MILITARY NECESSITY: MEANS TO ENDS AS A FEATURE OF WAR ITSELF

18.3.1 An Unaltered Challenge: 'The Object of War'

Some aspects of military necessity appear unaltered since the time of Hugo Grotius. Wantonness was for example already denoted by Gentili (Section 3.1) as the very opposite of necessity, and later repeated in the Lieber Code (Section 3.2), before being included in the modern provisions of international criminal law (Chapter 16). Those measures that lack a war aim are *un*necessary (Section 2.5). The war aim – or 'object of war' – is difficult to grasp properly, as the issue of 'means to ends' (introduced in Chapter 2) arises as a revolving ghost which refuses to resolve. As war by itself is a venture of allocating and applying certain means to achieve certain ends, the notion of *necessity* connotes to a 'for what' (Section 2.3). The notion of an 'object of war' is undefined by treaty law and easily merges with political reasons for warfare. While I present the point of departure as a broad – but limited to actual war-fighting – conception of the 'object of war', the practical answer is that the 'object of war' constitutes military advantages (Chapter 14 and Section 18.8 below).

18.3.2 *The Elements of Military Necessity: Limited Permission*

Among the eight features of military necessity as introduced in Chapter 2 is the feature of military necessity as a justification or permission for lawful acts of war. Treaty law does not enumerate those acts which are justified on the basis of military necessity (Section 2.6), but some measures (means and methods) of warfare are considered inherently militarily necessary in order to achieve the aims of warfare, such as attacks against combatants and military objects (lawful targets) (Chapter 7). Yet, the permissive nature of military necessity is limited (Chapter 6, and Section 18.7 below) and does not transcend established treaty and customary rules of the LOAC.

18.3.3 *The Elements of Military Necessity: Not a Matter of Natural Science*

The issue of 'means to ends' (as introduced in Chapters 2 and 3, see Section 18.3.1 above) does not only connote the question of 'for what', but also *how* 'necessity' connotes the desired end or aim. The answer to this second question of means to ends (Section 2.4) remains unclear, but it is clearly not a matter of natural science between cause and effect (Section 2.4). On the contrary, definitions of military necessity simply seem to emanate from the ordinary meaning of the word – in a very ordinary manner. Consistent with the approaches seen in dictionaries, States' manuals and international courts and tribunals have applied what resembles an intuitive interpretation of the word 'necessity', using explanatory words like 'indispensable', 'essential' and 'required' (Section 2.4).

This 'intuitive' distribution of meaning to the concept of military necessity (for the general point of departure in this regard, see Section 1.6) is also illustrative for (at least within reasonable limits) the application of terms and expressions which lack treaty definition. In this study this feature is seen particularly regarding the legal notion of 'military advantage' (Chapter 14), where the meaning given to the concept seems to have been presumably known, regarding the notion of 'excessiveness' under the proportionality rule – as well as with regard to the term 'proportionality' (Chapters 13 and 15). An intuitive perception of legal concepts may conceal differences in opinion that may appear (and reappear) at a later stage – such as the question whether 'necessary' also means 'urgent' and the question of whether 'necessary' implies 'proportionate to the end sought' (a 'silent' requirement of proportionality, dealt with in Chapter 13).

18.4 THE MILITARY COMMANDER'S ASSESSMENT: MARGIN OF APPRECIATION

18.4.1 As the Limits of Law

A military margin of appreciation is presented both as a feature (element) of necessity as such (Section 2.9) and as the limits of law (Chapter 4). Arbitrary use of force represents the opposite of lawful use of force. Limitless use of force, such as that prescribed in the old doctrine of *Kriegsraison* (and accounted for in Chapters 4 and 6), is arbitrary. It is in this context that a military margin of appreciation represents the limits of law. The margin appears where the law contains flexible rules which call for the military commander's discretion – the assessment. In Section 4.3 I introduced three categories of legal limits on the commander's exercise of this discretion: the limits inherent in the established interpretation of the legal rules, eventual limits shaped as guidelines for interpretation and the limits of the subjective appraisal, shaped as the standard of 'reasonableness'. Roughly speaking, this entire book can be subsumed under these three categories of limitations (not to be confused with the four aspects of limits to the commander's assessment reflected in the overall four parts of the book, see Section 18.1) – either one or two, or all three, at the same time. In Section 18.4.2. I present conclusions on the second (objective) category of limitations upon the commander's assessment of military necessity: the scope of the Martens Clause and other guidelines for interpretation. In Section 18.5 I present conclusions on both the limitations placed on the subjective appraisal of the commander's assessment, as well as the (lack of) guidelines in, or attached to, treaty provisions.

18.4.2 The Scope of the Martens Clause Is Limited and Other Guidelines Should Impose Cautious Limitations upon the Commander's Assessment

Among the 'general rules of interpretation' I discuss the Martens Clause in Section 4.4.1 and argue that this Clause can hardly be seen as a guideline for interpretation. The Clause does not appear to be of substantive influence when establishing the meaning of treaty rules. Consequently, it does not place a general limitation upon military necessity when accounted for in treaty law. I argue that the scope of the Clause is of practical importance first and foremost *in cases not covered* by treaty law, which is to say that it alludes to customary LOAC. However, even in this latter context the Clause does not appear to contain additional limitations upon military necessity. This is because customary LOAC has not proven to contain additional limitations upon military necessity (see Section 18.7).

Concrete guidelines for interpretation of flexible terms and expressions in the LOAC are scarce, if present at all. In Section 4.4.2 I argue that standardisation of the military commander's assessment of military necessity should be done with caution. Examples of concrete guidelines – or standardisation – are ROEs and SOPs issued by States' governments or force commanders, either permanent (standing) or for each operation. Neither ROEs nor SOPs amend or alter the content of the LOAC and should be seen as measures to control subordinate commanders' assessment of military necessity in given situations. As argued in Section 15.3.3, such measures could easily lead to unforeseen (and undesired) restriction of subordinate commanders' possibility to preserve their own forces. In other words, to an undesired restriction of their margin of appreciation. Furthermore, standardisation ought not to be done by international courts or tribunals in order to change a margin of appreciation to a 'margin of error'. As summed up in Section 18.5, treaty law hardly imposes general or specific guidelines for the commander's assessment of military necessity – beyond what follows from the general rules of interpretation.

18.5 ASSESSMENTS OF NECESSITY LEFT WITH LITTLE GUIDANCE

18.5.1 Reasonable Commanders Guided by 'Good Faith' and Common Sense

The third category of limitations to the commander's discretion, the yardstick of (subjective) assessment – dealt with in Section 4.5 and referred to as the 'Rendulic Rule' – entails a comparison with a reasonable commander. The reasonable commander is any military commander, vested with command authority, who must live up to the requirements of acting in good faith and making decisions based on information reasonably available at the time. These two requirements, which in practice easily overlap, entail a balance between excusable and culpable ignorance of fact, particularly illustrated by the doubt rules and the presumption of civilian status. In Section 7.9 I formulate the key issue, regarding doubt, as a question of when a commander's belief that the target is a military objective, is *reasonable*. In response to this question I argue that when available intelligence supports that it is at least *likely* that the target is a military objective, the decision of whether to attack or not is a matter within the commander's margin of appreciation – and subject to the requirements of feasible precautions in attack. In many aspects, the question of feasibility coincides with reasonableness (Section 15.3).

Some of the most challenging assessments to be performed by military commanders are those left with least guidance by the treaty text itself, where it arguably (see Sections 4.4, 4.5 and 17.9) is up to the 'common sense' and 'good faith' of the commander to assess. Among these are the proportionality assessment and the corresponding duty to take feasible precautions in attack, the assessment of cease of protection of works and installations containing dangerous forces and provisions calling for an assessment of 'aggravated' military necessity.

18.5.2 *The Proportionality Assessment: Effectuating the Principle of Distinction*

The proportionality rule is presented in this book as the effectuation of the principle of distinction and is as such a limitation upon the unfettered resort to military necessity (Section 13.2). The principle of distinction, at its core, represents a clear-cut distinction to the commander's assessment of military necessity: attacks against protected objects or persons are prohibited, notwithstanding their potential utility, such as in the case of terror attacks (Chapter 12). The details of its application, however, pose challenges for the commander's assessment. The treaty definition of military objectives has been accused of leaving too much for the commander's assessment by establishing a generic and abstract definition without accompanying exemplifying lists for the commander's guidance (Section 7.7). Without such treaty lists (although there are other lists), the military commander is both left with a wide margin of appreciation and a correspondingly high expectation of reasonableness and good faith (Chapter 4 and Section 18.5.1 above). Above all, it is the assessment of military advantage which calls for the commander's discretion. The military advantage is a common point of assessment for both military objectives and the proportionality assessment, concluded upon below, in Section 18.8.

In addition to an assessment of the military advantage, the proportionality assessment includes an ultimate balancing of necessity and humanitarian concerns through the issue of 'excessive' collateral damage.

This assessment not only reveals the difficulty of streamlining the relative weight attributed to military advantage (Chapter 15 and Section 18.8), but also the non-military task of foreseeing and quantifying the future loss of civilian life and damage to civilian property (Section 13.2). I argue, in Section 13.2, that the question of indirect, or reverberating, effects on civilian life or property is a matter of reasonable foreseeability and is not, as such, excluded from the proportionality assessment. Being a part of the proportionality assessment, the estimate of potential reverberating effects may appear to be a significant challenge for commanders in the field.

The assessment of excessiveness is unaccompanied by guidelines and not an exact science. Furthermore, reasonable commanders may disagree on the issue without the one or the other being a violation of the LOAC (Section 15.2). Necessity may (legally) justify extensive collateral damage, and I argue in this context that the limitation upon the assessment of excessiveness instead lies in the relation to the notion of the concrete and direct military advantage of the 'attack as a whole'. By saying this I mean that the focus on the limitation to the commander's assessment relates to the scope of military advantage as a relative concept, rather than on the notion of excessiveness (Section 15.2 and Section 18.8 on the military advantage).

18.5.3 *Works and Installations Containing Dangerous Forces*

Works and installations containing dangerous forces are granted special protection in treaty law (Section 17.9). In this treaty rule (which is not reflective of customary law) the flexible terms and expressions already present in the proportionality rule are aggravated. This is why the assessment is highlighted here – as an outstanding example of assessments of necessity left with little guidance, but with high expectations when it comes to reasonableness and good faith. As is the case with other rules granting special protection, it is difficult to discern the substantive difference between 'general' and 'special' protection. While the proportionality rule prohibits attacks which may be expected to cause 'excessive' collateral damage, the rule protecting works and installations containing dangerous forces prohibits attacks which may cause 'severe' losses among the civilian population. 'Severe' must be understood as distinct from 'excessive' in that the latter is relative, while the former is absolute. The rule prohibiting severe losses among the civilian population limits military necessity explicitly. Having said that, the difference between 'severe' losses and 'excessive' losses is in practice far from explicit. I argue in Section 17.9 that the discretionary choices incumbent upon the commander in these challenges appear almost infinite. Furthermore, the undoubtedly vague criteria in paragraph 2 of the rule are presumed by the ICRC to express 'common sense'. This approach is burdened with challenges. I argue in Section 17.9 (as predicted in Section 1.6) that a common sense approach may conceal differences in interpretation among military commanders and actually invite unequal application of the law.

18.5.4 *Aggravations*

Similar challenges to those related to the specific issue of works and installations containing dangerous forces arise with regard to the use of treaty aggravations of military necessity in general. Aggravations of military necessity, such as 'imperative' or 'absolute', are hardly of any guidance to the commander's assessment of necessity (Section 2.8) and even the aggravated form of military necessity does not mean 'impossibility' to do otherwise. Variations in treaty law expressions are numerous, inconsistent and appear in certain cases somewhat random (Section 16.7). There is therefore hardly any substantive difference between necessity in its 'simple' and its 'aggravated' form. While the use of aggravations may (linguistically) appear as guidelines, the result seems rather to be the opposite: inconsistent use of aggravations may in the worst case be a source of confusion and unequal application of the law, rather than streamlining the commander's assessment.

18.6 ASSESSMENTS OF MILITARY NECESSITY LEAVING LITTLE ROOM FOR THE COMMANDER'S DISCRETION

Several other assessments – than those mentioned in Sections 18.5.2–18.5.4 – leave less room for the military commander's discretion, either because the wording in the treaty text is less flexible or because it is not up to each *commander* to assess. Examples of assessments of military necessity where the treaty texts are less flexible are those defining combatants and the prohibition of indiscriminate attacks. An example of a rule which is usually not up to the commander to assess is the prohibition of superfluous injury and unnecessary suffering. Although the assessment of means and methods of warfare is inextricably linked to considerations of military necessity, this assessment is usually performed at State level (see Section 9.5).

The treaty definition of lawful combatancy is the result of a long and vexed process with deeply rooted oppositions in the views upon the necessity of clandestine warfare (Section 10.5). Finally, the issue of lawful combatancy is almost in its entirety resolved at the level of treaty formulation, leaving commanders with a small, yet significant, challenge: to assess when combatants 'cannot so distinguish themselves' in (the few) situations falling within the scope of the AP I article 44(3) (see Section 10.6).

In the prohibition of indiscriminate attacks, as expressed in AP I article 51(4) *litera* (a) and (b), and reflective of customary law (Section 12.3), necessity has already yielded to humanity at the stage of treaty formulation. The military commander's margin of appreciation is therefore of limited (for practical purposes non-existent) scope beyond the duty to take feasible precautions in attack, as implicitly required in particular in AP I article 51(4)(a) and corresponding customary law.

18.7 THE RIGHT TO INVOKE MILITARY NECESSITY IS LIMITED: NOT A LIMITATION

The right to invoke military necessity is limited – but must not be confused with a limitation, which is a separate rule (Chapter 6). The fact that it (the permission) is limited means that it cannot be invoked as an exception from prohibitive rules. Military necessity may be invoked only when specifically accounted for, and as an in-built consideration in treaty provisions. There are a number of limitations upon military necessity. In fact, almost the entire treaty schism contains limitations upon military necessity, out of which the principle of distinction (Chapter 7), the principle of proportionality (Chapters 13 and 15) and the prohibition of unnecessary suffering (Chapter 9) are the most prominent. Furthermore, military necessity is not a limitation in the sense of a 'double requirement' (Chapter 13). Conduct which is otherwise lawful does not 'also' have to be necessary. For example, attacks against lawful targets are a fortiori also militarily necessary. No additional assessment is required. There is, among others and as accounted for in Chapter 9, no duty to 'capture rather than kill' an enemy combatant.

18.8 MILITARY ADVANTAGE IS SOMETHING OTHER THAN MILITARY NECESSITY

18.8.1 Necessary for a Military Advantage

In Chapter 14, I discussed the relationship between military necessity and military advantage. I argued there that military advantage is an expression of military necessity in its foundational form, and that it, as such, must be understood distinctly from military necessity in its exceptional form. I argue that military advantage differs from military necessity in four aspects and that both advantage and necessity are the opposite of wanton acts of war (Section 14.3 and Chapter 16). Among the differences is the question of how necessity and advantage connote the notion of 'means to ends' (the other differences are language, severity, subjectivity). In fact, some rules of the LOAC explicitly connect necessity to advantage as means connect to ends. The 'end' (also referred to as the 'object of war' above in Section 18.3.1) may therefore, for practical purposes, be said to consist of military advantages, whether these advantages amount to the successful conclusion of war, complete or partial submission etc. (see Section 2.3). In many aspects it is seen that while any military necessity ultimately will entail a military advantage, not every military advantage amounts to a necessity.

Military advantage is of a relative nature and there are at least three aspects regarding the relative scope of military advantage which often are the source of confusion and differences in opinion.

18.8.2 *Subjective, but Limited by Circumstances*

The notion of military advantage relates to the person assessing the advantage: an advantage relative to whom? (Section 14.3) Albeit subjective (see in particular Chapter 4 for a general account of 'subjectivity') military advantage is limited in time and space by the adjectives 'concrete and direct' and 'definite'. The military advantage of the 'attack as a whole' may include advantages at each level of military command, from technical/tactical to strategic. Yet, a military advantage does not entail the 'entire war'.

18.8.3 *Differences in Circumstances, Not Rules*

Military advantage must be assessed relative to plans, aims and other circumstances (Section 14.5). Out of these, the different 'circumstances ruling at the time' should not be confused with a *different rule*. The rule is made to adapt to a fluid reality throughout the 'fog of war' and does not change even though the war may be characterised as 'new', 'coercive' or 'humanitarian' (Sections 14.7–14.8).

18.8.4 A *Relative Weight, Burdened with Doubt*

Finally, military advantage and collateral damage are distributed with weight relative of each other under the proportionality assessment. This distribution of relative weight, under the assessment of 'excessiveness', is not an exact science (see Chapters 4 and 15). Decisions by military commanders are by their very nature burdened with uncertainty (Chapters 4, 7 and 15), particularly concerning the question whether expected collateral damage must be assessed as excessive to the military advantage anticipated. The mere existence of doubt does not (need to) tip the scale in a humanitarian favour. Furthermore, the very notion of relativity in the proportionality rule means that the upper limit is not absolute. The general rule of limitation (see Chapter 6) must, however, be borne in mind.

18.9 THE PRACTICAL SCOPE OF CONSIDERATIONS OF MILITARY NECESSITY TODAY: A TWOFOLD APPEARANCE

The adoption of the AP I in 1977 has left little room for considerations of military necessity beyond treaty law. In practice, the commander's assessment of military necessity is bound to those following explicitly or implicitly from the treaty or corresponding customary rule (see Chapter 13). Perhaps the only room left for considerations of military necessity under customary LOAC concerns belligerent reprisals (see Chapter 12).

Arguably, military necessity has turned from being one sweeping (and scaled) principle to become at least two different concepts: a consideration and an exceptional rule. Military necessity has achieved more than one face under the law governing conduct of hostilities.

Bibliography

BOOKS, ARTICLES AND GOVERNMENTAL PUBLICATIONS

Adler, Gerald J., 'Targets in war: legal considerations', *Houston Law Review*, vol. 8 (1970): 1–46.

Agius, Maria, 'The invocation of necessity in international law', *Netherlands Law Review*, vol. 56, no. 2 (2009): 95–135.

Andenæs, Johs, 'Okkupasjonstidens likvidasjoner i et rettslig lys', *Tidsskrift for Retsvitenskap* (1948): 1–31.

Andler, Charles, *'Frightfulness' in Theory and Practice: As Compared with Franco-British Usages* (Fisher Unwin, 1916).

Arai-Takahashi, Yutaka, 'Excessive collateral civilian casualties and military necessity: awkward crossroads in international humanitarian law between state responsibility and individual criminal liability', in Christine Chinkin and Freya Baetens (eds.), *Sovereignty, Statehood and State Responsibility: Essays in Honour of James Crawford* (Cambridge University Press, 2015): 325–40.

Aras, M. H., Miloglu, O., Barutcugil, C., Kantarci, M., Ozcan, E. and Harorli A., 'Comparison of the sensitivity for detecting foreign bodies among conventional plain radiography, computed tomography and ultrasonography', *Dentomaxillofacial Radiology*, vol. 39, no. 2 (2010): 72–8.

Arnold, Roberta and Wehrenberg, Stefan, 'Article 8: mental element', in Otto Triffterer and Kai Ambos (eds.), *The Rome Statute of the International Criminal Court: A Commentary*, 3rd ed. (C. H. Beck, Hart and Nomos, 2016).

Barber, Peter, 'Scuds, shelters and retreating soldiers: the laws of aerial bombardment in the Gulf War', *Alberta Law Review*, vol. 31, no. 4 (1994): 662–91.

Bartels, Rogier, 'Dealing with the principle of proportionality in armed conflict in retrospect: the application of the principle in international criminal trials', *Israel Law Review*, vol. 46, no. 2 (2013): 271–315.

Bartels, Rogier, 'Discrepancies between international humanitarian law on the battlefield and in the courtroom: the challenges of applying international humanitarian law during international criminal trials', in M. Matthee et al. (eds.), *Armed Conflict and International Law: In Search of the Human Face* (TMC Asser Press, 2013): 339–78.

Bashi, Sari, 'Justifying restrictions on reconstructing Gaza: military necessity and humanitarian assistance', *Israel Law Review*, vol. 49, no. 2 (2016): 149–69.

Baxter, Richard, 'So-called unprivileged belligerency: spies, guerrillas, and saboteurs', *British Yearbook of International Law*, vol. 28, no. 323 (1951).

Beer, Yishai, 'Humanity considerations cannot reduce war's hazards alone: revitalizing the concept of military necessity', *European Journal of International Law*, vol. 26, no. 4 (2015): 801–28.

Best, Geoffrey, *Humanity in Warfare* (Methuen, 1983).

Best, Geoffrey, 'Restraint in war in historical and philosophical perspective', in Astrid J. M. Delissen and Gerard J. Tanja (eds.), *Humanitarian Law of Armed Conflict: Challenges Ahead: Essays in Honour of Frits Kalshoven* (Martinus Nijhoff Publishers) (1991): 3–26.

Best, Geoffrey, *War and Law since 1945* (Clarendon Press, 1994).

Biddle, Tami Davis, *Rhetoric and Reality in Air Warfare: The Evolution of British and American Ideas about Strategic Bombing, 1914–1945* (Princeton University Press, 2002).

Bill, Brian J., 'The Rendulic "Rule": military necessity, commander's knowledge, and methods of warfare', *Yearbook of International Humanitarian Law*, vol. 12 (2009): 119–55.

Blix, Hans, 'Area bombardment: rules and reasons', in Michael N. Schmitt and Wolff Heintschel von Heinegg (eds.), *The Conduct of Hostilities in International Humanitarian Law*, vol. 1 (Ashgate, 2012).

Blum, Gabriella, 'The fog of victory', *European Journal of International Law*, vol. 24, no. 1 (2013): 391–421.

Boivin, Alexandra, 'The legal regime applicable to targeting military objectives in the context of contemporary warfare', Centre for International Humanitarian Law, Research Paper Series, no. 2 (2006).

Boothby, William H., '"And for such time as": the time dimension to direct participation in hostilities', *International Law and Politics*, vol. 42 (2009–10): 741–68.

Boothby, William H., *The Law of Targeting* (Oxford University Press, 2012).

Bothe, Michael, 'The protection of the civilian population and NATO bombing on Yugoslavia: comments on a report to the Prosecutor of the ICTY', *European Journal of International Law*, vol. 12, no. 3 (2001): 531–5.

Bothe, Michael, 'War crimes', in Antonio Cassese, Paola Gaeta and John R. W. D. Jones (eds.), *The Rome Statute of the International Criminal Court: A Commentary*, vol. 1 (Oxford University Press, 2002).

Bothe, Michael, Partsch, Karl Joseph and Solf, Waldemar A., *New Rules for Victims of Armed Conflicts, Commentary on the Two 1977 Protocols Additional to the Geneva Conventions of* 1949, 2nd ed. (Martinus Nijhoff Publishers, 2013).

Boye, Thorvald, *Haandbok i Folkeret* (Grøndahl, 1918).

Bring, Ove and Körlof-Askholt, Anna, *Folkrätt i krig, kris och fredsoperationer* (Norstedts Juridik, 2010).

Byman, Daniel L., Waxman, Matthew C. and Shapiro, Jeremy, 'The future of U.S. coercive airpower', in Zalmay Khalilzad and Jeremy Shapiro (eds.), *Strategic Appraisal: United States Air and Space Power in the 21st Century* (Rand Corporation, 2002).

Cannizzaro, Enzo, 'Proportionality in the Law of Armed Conflict', in Andrew Clapham and Paolo Gaeta (eds.), *The Oxford Handbook of International Law in Armed Conflict* (Oxford University Press, 2014).

Cassese, Antonio, *International Criminal Law*, 2nd ed. (Oxford University Press, 2008).

Cassese, Antonio, 'The Martens Clause: half a loaf or simply pie in the sky', *European Journal of International Law*, vol. 11 (2000).

Carnahan, Burrus, 'Lincoln, Lieber and the laws of war: the origins and limits of the principle of necessity', *American Journal of International Law*, vol. 92, no. 2 (1998): 213–31.

Carnahan, Burrus, '"Linebacker II" and Protocol I: the convergence of law and professionalism', *American University Law Review*, vol. 31, no. 861 (1981–2).

Christoffersen, Jonas, *Fair Balance: Proportionality, Subsidiarity and Primarity in the European Convention on Human Rights* (Martinus, Nijhoff Publishers, 2009).

Clausewitz, Carl von, *On War*, edited and translated by Michael Howard and Peter Paret (Princeton University Press, 1984).

Cohen, Amichai, 'The Lebanon War and the application of the proportionality principle', International Law Forum, Research Paper No. 6–07 (2007).

Conan Doyle, Arthur, *The War in South Africa: Its* Cause *and Conduct* (London: Smith, Elder & Co., 1902).

Corn, Geoffrey S., 'Targeting, command judgment, and a proposed quantum of information component: a fourth amendment lesson in contextual reasonableness', *Brooklyn Law Review*, vol. 77 (2011–12): 437–98.

Corn, Geoffrey S., Hansen, Victor, Jenks, M. Christopher, Jackson, Richard, Jensen, Eric Talbot and Schoettler, James A., *The Law of Armed Conflict: An Operational Approach* (Aspen Publishers, Walter Kluwer, 2012).

Coupland, Robert, 'Humanity: what is it and how does it influence international law?', *International Review of the Red Cross*, vol. 83, no. 844 (2001): 969–90.

Coupland, Robin M., *The SIrUS Project: Towards a Determination of Which Weapons Cause 'Superfluous Injury or Unnecessary Suffering'* (International Committee of the Red Cross, 1997).

Crawford, James, *The International Law Commission's Articles on State Responsibility. Introduction, Text and Commentaries* (Cambridge University Press, 2002).

Crawford, J. W., 'The law of noncombatant immunity and the targeting of national electrical power systems', *The Fletcher Forum of World Affairs*, vol. 21, no. 2 (1997).

Cross, Kenneth, Dullum, Ove, Jenzen-Jones, N. R. and Garlasco, Marc, Explosive weapons in populated areas: technical considerations relevant to their use and effects, Special Report, Ares Armament Research Services (2016).

Cryer, Robert, *Prosecuting International Crimes* (Cambridge University Press, 2005).

De Cock, Chris, 'Operation Unified Protector and the protection of civilians in Libya', *Yearbook of International Humanitarian Law*, vol. 14 (2011).

De Cock, Christian, 'Operation Unified Protector: targeting densely populated areas in Libya', *Military and Strategic Affairs*, vol. 4 (2012).

De Saussure, Hamilton and Glasser, Robert, 'Air warfare Christmas 1972', in Peter D. Trooboff (ed.), *Law and Responsibility in Warfare: The Vietnam Experience* (The University of North Carolina Press, 1975).

Det Kongelige Forsvarsdepartement, Kongelig Resolusjon, 23 March 2011, Fullmakt til deltakelse med norske militære bidrag i operasjoner til gjennomføring av FNs sikkerhetsrådsresolusjon 1973 (2011).

Detter, Ingrid, *The Law of War*, 2nd ed. (Cambridge University Press, 2000).

De Vattel, Emmerich, *The Law of Nations or the Principles of Natural Law* (T. and J. W. Johnson, 1758, republished 1853).

Dill, Janina, 'Applying the principle of proportionality in combat operations', in Oxford Institute of Ethics, Law and Armed Conflict, Policy Briefing (2010), www.elac.ox.ac.uk/downloads/proportionality_policybrief_%20dec_2010.pdf (accessed 7 May 2017).

Dinstein, Yoram, 'Legitimate military objectives under the current jus in bello', in Andru E. Wall (ed.), Legal and Ethical Lessons of NATO's Kosovo Campaign, *International Law Studies*, vol. 78 (2002): 139–72.

Dinstein, Yoram, 'Unlawful combatancy', *Israel Yearbook on Human Rights*, vol. 32 (2002): 247–70.

Dinstein, Yoram, 'The interaction between customary international law and treaties', *Recueil des Cours*, vol. 322 (2006): 243 ff.

Dinstein, Yoram, 'Distinction and loss of civilian protection in international armed conflicts', in Michael D. Carsten (ed.) International Law and Military Operations, *International Law Studies*, vol. 84 (2008): 183–98.

Dinstein, Yoram, *The International Law of Belligerent Occupation* (Cambridge University Press, 2009).

Dinstein, Yoram, *War, Aggression and Self-Defence*, 5th ed. (Cambridge University Press, 2012).

Dinstein, Yoram, 'The principle of proportionality', in Kjetil Mujezinovic Larsen, Camilla Guldahl Cooper and Gro Nystuen (eds.), *Searching for a 'Principle of Humanity' in International Humanitarian Law* (Cambridge University Press, 2013).

Dinstein, Yoram, *Non-international Armed Conflicts in International Law* (Cambridge University Press, 2014).

Dinstein, Yoram, 'Military necessity', in *Max Planck Encyclopedia of Public International Law (MPEPIL)* (Oxford University Press, 2015), at para 1–7.

Dinstein, Yoram, *Conduct of Hostilities*, 3rd ed. (Cambridge University Press, 2016).

Dolzer, Rudolf, 'Commentary', in Andru E. Wall (ed.), Legal and Ethical Lessons of NATO's Kosovo Campaign, *International Law Studies*, vol. 78 (2002).

Doswald-Beck, Louise (general editor) and International Institute of Humanitarian Law, *San Remo Manual on International Law Applicable to Armed Conflicts at Sea* (Cambridge University Press 1995).

Downey, William Gerald Jr., 'Captured enemy property: booty of war and seized enemy Property', *American Journal of International Law*, vol. 44, no. 3 (1950): 488–504.

Downey, William Gerald Jr., 'The law of war and military necessity', *American Journal of International Law*, vol. 47 (1953).

Dörmann, Knut, *Elements of War Crimes under the Rome Statute of the International Criminal Court* (ICRC/Cambridge University Press, 2003).

Dörmann, Knut, 'The legal situation of "unlawful/unprivileged combatants"', *International Review of the Red Cross*, vol. 85, no. 849 (2003): 45–74.

Dörmann, Knut, 'The definition of military objectives', in Gian Luca Beruto (ed.), *The Conduct of Hostilities, Revisiting the Law of Armed Conflict, 100 Years after the 1907 Hague Conventions and 30 Years after the 1977 Additional Protocols* (San Remo, International Institute of Humanitarian Law, 2007): 78–85.

Dörmann, Knut, 'Article 8: mental element', in Otto Triffterer and Kai Ambos (eds.), *The Rome Statute of the International Criminal Court: A Commentary*, 3rd ed. (C. H. Beck, Hart and Nomos, 2016).

Draper, G. I. A. D., 'The status of combatants and the question of guerilla warfare', *British Year Book of International Law*, vol. 45 (1971):173–218.

Draper, G. I. A. D., 'Military necessity and humanitarian imperatives', *Military Law and the Law of War Review*, vol. 12 (1973).

Dunbar, N. C. H., 'Military necessity in war crimes trials', *British Yearbook of International Law*, vol. 29 (1952).

Dunlap, Charles, 'The end of innocence: rethinking noncombatancy in the post-Kosovo era', *Strategic Review* (Summer 2000): 9–17.

Engle, Eric, 'The history of the general principle of proportionality: an overview', *Dartmouth Law Journal*, vol. X (2012).

Feinstein, Andrew, 'Where is Gaddafis vast arms stockpile?', *The Guardian*, 26 October 2011, www.theguardian.com/world/2011/oct/26/gadaffis-arms-stockpile (accessed 7 May 2017).

Fenrick, William J., 'The rule of proportionality and Protocol I in conventional warfare', *Military Law Review*, vol. 98 (1982).

Fenrick, William J., 'Targeting and proportionality during the NATO bombing campaign against Yugoslavia', *European Journal of International Law*, vol. 12, no. 3 (2001): 489–502.

Ferrell, William H., 'No shirt, no shoes, no status: uniforms, distinctions and special operations in international armed conflict', *Military Law Review*, vol. 178 (2003): 93–140.

Fleck, Dieter, 'Ruses of war and prohibition of perfidy', *Military Law and the Law of War Review*, no. 13 (1974): 273 ff.

FM 27-10, US Department of the Army Field Manual, *The Law of Land Warfare* (US Field Manual) (Washington D. C. Headquarters Department of the Army, 1956, as amended 1976).

Forsvaret, *Manual i krigens folkerett* (Norwegian Manual) (Forsvarssjefen, 2013).

Gasser, Hans Peter and Dörmann, Knut, 'Protection of the civilian population', Dieter Fleck et al. (eds.), *The Handbook of International Humanitarian Law*, 3rd ed. (Oxford University Press, 2013): 231–321.

Gardam, Judith, 'Proportionality and force in international law', *American Journal of International Law*, vol. 87, no. 3 (1993): 391–413.

Gardam, Judith, *Necessity, Proportionality and the Use of Force by States* (Cambridge University Press, 2004).

Garner, Bryan A. (ed.), *Black's Law Dictionary*, 10th ed. (Thomson Reuters, 2014).

Garraway, Charles, '"Combatants" – substance or semantics?', in Michael Schmitt and Jelena Pejic (eds.), *International Law and Armed Conflict: Exploring the Faultlines. Essays in Honour of Yoram Dinstein* (Martinus Nijhoff Publishers, 2007): 317–34.

Gayle, Damien, 'They're in SO much trouble: low-flying Brazilian air force pilots shatter every window of the country's Supreme Court', *The Daily Mail*, 2 July 2012, www.dailymail.co.uk/news/article-2167773/Theyre-SO-trouble-Low-flying-Brazilian-air-force-pilots-shatter-window-countrys-Supreme-Court.html (accessed 15 May 2019).

Geiss, Robin, 'Military necessity: a fundamental "Principle" fallen into oblivion', in H. Ruiz Fabri, R. Wolfrum and J. Gogolin (eds.), *Select Proceedings of the European Society of International Law, 2008* (Hart Publishing, 2010): 554–68.

Geiss, Robin, 'The principle of proportionality: force protection as a military advantage', *Israel Law Review*, vol. 45 (2012).

Gentili, Alberico, *De Iure Belli Libri Tres* (Carnegie Endowment for International Peace, Division of International Law, 1933).

German Federal Ministry of Defence, Joint Service Regulation (ZDv) 15/2, *Law of Armed Conflict Manual* (German Manual) (2013).

Gillard, Emanuela-Chiara, 'Proportionality in the conduct of hostilities: the incidental harm side of the assessment', Research Paper International Law Programme (Chatham House, 2018).

Gjelsten, Roald, 'Marinens beredskap 1960-90; Kampklar i Nordflåtens skygge', Oslo Files on Defence and Security, no. 4 (2011).

Grant, Rebecca L., 'Michael C. Short: airman undaunted', in John A. Olsen (ed.), *Air Commanders* (Potomac, 2013).

Gray, Christine, *International Law and the Use of Force*, 3rd ed. (Oxford University Press, 2008).

Green, James A. and Waters, Christopher P. M., 'Military targeting in the context of self-defence actions', *Nordic Journal of International Law*, vol. 84 (2015) 3–28.

Green, L. C., *The Contemporary Law of Armed Conflict* (Manchester University Press, 2008).

Greenspan, Morris, *The Modern Law of Land Warfare* (University of California Press, 1959).

Greenwood, Christopher, *Essays on War In International Law* (Cameron May, 2006).

Grotius, Hugo, *The Rights of War and Peace*, edited and with an introduction by Richard Tuck, from the edition by Jean Barbeyrac 1738 (Liberty Fund, 2005).

Güntelberg, Heidi, *Introduktion til folkeret* (Forsvarsakademiet, 2014).

Hallion, Richard P., 'Charles A. Horner: Desert Storm maestro', in John A. Olsen (ed.), *Air Commanders* (Potomac, 2013).

Hampson, Francoise, 'Necessity and proportionality in the Gulf Conflict', *Proceedings of the Annual Meeting (American Society of International Law)*, vol. 86 (1–4 April 1992): 45–58.

Hampson, Francoise, Military necessity, crimes of war, www.crimesofwar.org/a-z-guide/military-necessity/ (accessed 22 April 2016).

Hancke, Heinz Marius, 'The 1923 Hague Rules of Air Warfare – a contribution to the development of international law protecting civilians from air attack', *International Review of the Red Cross*, vol. 33, no. 292 (1993): 12–45.

Hart, H. L. A. and Honoré, Tony, *Causation in the Law*, 2nd ed. (Oxford University Press, 1985).

Hart, H. L. A., *The Concept of Law*, 2nd ed. (Oxford University Press, 1994)

Hayashi, Nobuo, 'Requirements of military necessity in international humanitarian law and international criminal law', *Boston University International Law Journal*, vol. 38 (2010): 39–140.

Hayashi, Nobuo, 'Military necessity as normative indifference', *Georgetown Journal of International Law*, vol. 44, no. 2 (2013): 675–782.

Hayashi, Nobuo, 'Contextualizing military necessity', *Emory International Law Review*, vol. 27, no. 189 (2013): 189–283.

Hayashi, Nobuo, 'Basic principles', in Rain Liivoja and Tim McCormack (eds.), *Routledge Handbook of the Law of Armed Conflict* (Routledge, Taylor & Francis Group, 2016): 89–105.

Hayashi, Nobuo, *Military Necessity* (Leiden University, dissertation for PhD, Repository, 2017).

Heintschel von Heinegg, Wolff and Dreist, Peter, 'The 2009 Kunduz Air Attack: the decision of the Federal Prosecutor-General on the dismissal of criminal proceedings against members of the German armed forces', *German Yearbook of International Law*, vol. 53 (2010): 833–66.

Heintschel von Heinegg, Wolff, 'The law of armed conflict at sea', in Dieter Fleck et al. (eds.), *The Handbook of International Humanitarian Law*, 3rd ed. (Oxford University Press, 2013).

Henckaerts, Jean Marie and Doswald-Beck, Louise, *International Committee of the Red Cross Customary International Humanitarian Law (CIHL)* (Cambridge University Press, 2005, reprint 2009) Also accessible with updated commentaries at: ICRC, Customary IHL Database, https://ihl-databases.icrc.org/customary-ihl/eng/docs/v1_rul_rule50 (accessed 4 January 2017).

Henderson, Ian, *The Contemporary Law of Targeting* (Martinus Nijhoff Publishers, 2009).

Hersh, Seymour, 'Overwhelming force: what happened in the final days of the Gulf War?', *The New Yorker* (2000).

Higgins, Rosalyn, *Problems and Process: International Law and How We Use It* (Clarendon Press, 1994).

Holborn, Hajo, 'The Prusso-German School: Moltke and the rise of the general staff', in Peter Paret (ed.), *Makers of Modern Strategy: From Machiavelli to the Nuclear Age* (Clarendon Press, 1986).

Howard, Michael, *The Franco-Prussian War: The German Invasion of France, 1870–1871* (Methuen, 1981).

Howard, Michael, 'Empire, race and war in pre-1914 Britain', *History Today* (December 1981).

Howard, Michael, 'Constraints on warfare', in Michael Howard, George J. Andreopoulus and Mark R. Schulman (eds.), *The Laws of War: Constraints on Warfare in the Western World* (Yale University Press, 1994).

Huber, Max, 'Die kriegsrechtlichen Verträge und die Kriegsraison', *VIII Zeitschrift fuer Voelkerrecht* (1913).

Hume, David, *Philosophical Essays: Concerning Human Understanding* (A. Millar, 1748).

Hull, Isabel V., 'Military necessity and the laws of war in Imperial Germany', in Stathis N. Kalyvas, Ian Shapiro and Tarek Masoud (eds.), *Order Conflict and Violence* (Cambridge University Press, 2008): 352–77.

ICRC, Commentary on the First Geneva Convention: Convention (I) for the Amelioration of the Condition of the Wounded and Sick in Armed Forces in the Field, 2nd ed., 2016, https://ihl-databases.icrc.org/ihl/full/GCI-commentary (accessed 7 June 2019).

ICRC, Interpretive Guidance on the Notion of Direct Participation in Hostilities under International Humanitarian Law (Interpretive Guidance), *International Review of the Red Cross*, vol. 90, no. 872 (2008): 991–1047.

International and Operational Law Department, *Operational Law Handbook* (The Judge Advocate General's Legal Center and School, US Army, 2015).

Ipsen, Knut, 'Combatants and non-combatants', in Dieter Fleck et al. (eds.), *The Handbook of International Humanitarian Law*, 3rd ed. (Oxford University Press, 2013): 79–114.

Jachec-Neale, Agnieszka, *The Concept of Military Objectives in International Law and Targeting Practice* (Routledge, 2014).

Jaworski, Eric, 'Military necessity and civilian immunity: where is the balance', *Chinese Journal of International Law*, vol. 2, no. 1 (2003): 175–206.

Johansen, Sigrid Redse, 'The occupied and the occupier: the case of Norway', in Kjetil Larsen, Camilla Guldahl Cooper and Gro Nystuen (eds.), *Searching for a 'Principle of Humanity' in International Humanitarian Law* (Cambridge University Press, 2013).

Johansen, Sigrid Redse, 'Mission command and command responsibility', *The Royal Swedish Academy of War Sciences Journal* (2017).

Kalshoven, Frits, 'Remarks', *Proceedings of the Annual Meeting* (American Society of International Law), vol. 86 (1–4 April 1992).

Kalshoven, Frits, *Belligerent Reprisals* (Martinus Nijhoff, 2005).

Kalshoven, Frits, *Reflections on the Law of War: Collected Essays* (Martinus Nijhoff Publishers, 2007).

Kalshoven, Frits and Zegveld, Liesbeth, *Constraints on the Waging of War*, 4th ed. (ICRC/ Cambridge University Press, 2011).

Keen, Maurice, *The Laws of War in the Late Middle Ages* (Routledge and Kegan Paul, 1965).

Kelsen, Hans and Tucker, Robert W., *Principles of International Law* (Holt, Rinehart and Winston, 1966).

Kleen, Rikard, *Kodificerad Handbok i Krigets Lagar* (Norstedt & Söner, 1909).

Kleffner, Jann, 'Section IX of the ICRC Interpretive Guidance on Direct Participation in Hostilities: the end of ius in bello proportionality as we know it?', *Israel Law Review*, vol. 45 (2012): 35–52

Kolb, Robert, 'The main epochs of international humanitarian law since 1864 and their related dominant legal constructions', in Kjetil Mujezinovic Larsen, Camilla Guldahl Cooper and Gro Nystuen (eds.), *Searching for a Principle of Humanity in International Humanitarian Law* (Cambridge University Press, 2013).

Kolb, Robert, '"Humanitarian bombardments" in jus in bello?', in Hans-Joachim Heintze and Pierre Thielbörger (eds.), *From Cold War to Cyber War: The Evolution of the International Law of Peace and Armed Conflict Over the Last 25 Years* (Springer, 2016): 113–27.

Kolb, Robert and Hyde, Richard, *An Introduction to the International Law of Armed Conflicts* (Hart Publishing, 2008).

Kolb, Robert and Del Mar, Katherine, 'Treaties for armed conflict', in Andrew Clapham and Paola Gaeta (eds.), *The Oxford Handbook of International Law in Armed Conflict* (Oxford University Press, 2014): 50–91.

Koskenniemi, Martti, *From Apology to Utopia: The Structure of International Legal Argument* (Cambridge University Press, 2007).

Laursen, Andreas, 'NATO, the war over Kosovo, and the ICTY investigation', *American University International Law Review*, vol. 17, no. 4 (2002): 765–814.

Letter from the Norwegian Ministry of Defence to the Defence Staff, dated 24 March 2011.

Lew, Daniel, 'Manchurian booty and international law', *American Journal of International Law*, vol. 40 (1946): 584–92.

Lewis, David K., *Counterfactuals* (Blackwell, 1986).

Luttwak, Edward, 'Give war a chance', *Foreign Affairs*, vol. 78, no. 4 (1999).

MacIsaac, David, 'Voices from the central blue: the air power theorists', in Peter Paret (ed.), *Makers of Modern Strategy: From Machiavelli to the Nuclear Age* (Clarendon Press, 1986): 624–48.

Maguire, Peter H., *Law and War: An American Story* (Columbia University Press, 2001).

McClintock, A. D., 'The law of war: coalition attacks on Iraqi chemical and biological weapons storage and production facilities', *Emory International Law Review* (1993).

McCoubrey, Hilaire, 'The nature of the modern doctrine of military necessity', *Military Law and the Law of War Review*, vol. 30, no. 215 (1991).

McDougal, Myres S. and Feliciano, Florentino P., *Law and Minimum World Order: The Legal Regulation of International Coercion* (Yale University Press, 1961).

Melzer, Nils, 'Targeted killing or less harmful means? Israel's High Court judgment on targeted killing and the restrictive function of military necessity', *Yearbook of International Humanitarian Law* vol. 9 (2006): 87–113.

Menzies, Peter, *Counterfactual Theories of Causation* (Stanford Encyclopedia of Philosophy, 2008).

Meron, Theodor, 'Francis Lieber's code and principles of humanity', *Columbia Journal of Transnational Law*, vol. 36 (1998).

Meron, Theodor, 'The Martens Clause, principles of humanity, and dictates of public conscience', *American Journal of International Law*, vol. 94, no. 1 (2000): 78–89.

Meron, Theodor, *The Humanization of International Law* (Martinus Nijhoff Publishers, 2006).

Meron, Theodor, 'Customary humanitarian law today: from the academy to the courtroom', in Andrew Clapham and Paola Gaeta (eds.), *The Oxford Handbook of International Law in Armed Conflict* (Oxford University Press, 2014): 37–50.

Merriam, John, 'Affirmative target identification: operationalizing the principle of distinction for U.S. warfighters', *Virginia Journal of International Law*, no. 56 (2016): 83–145.

Mezran, Karim, 'Libya's lessons on Syria' foreign affairs', 4 September 2013, http://foreignpolicy.com/2013/09/04/libyas-lessons-on-syria/ (accessed 26 March 2016).

Meyrowitz, Henri, 'Reflections on the centenary of the Declaration of St. Petersburg', *International Review of the Red Cross*, no. 93 (1968): 611–25.

Meyrowitz, Henri, 'The principle of superfluous injury or unnecessary suffering, from the Declaration of St. Petersburg of 1868 to Additional Protocol I of 1977', *International Review of the Red Cross*, vol. 34, no. 299 (1994): 98–123.

Militærmanual om folkeret for danske væbnede styrker in internationale militære operationer (Danish Manual), København, Forsvarministeriet/Værnsfælles Forsvarskommando, 2015, www2.forsvaret.dk/omos/publikationer/Publications/Attachments/34/Militærmanual%20AF%20SEPT%202016.pdf (accessed 2 May 2017).

Morgan, J. H., *The German War Book: Being 'The Usages of War on Land'* (translated version) (Murray, 1915).

Nasson, Bill, *The South African War* (Bloomsbury Academic, 1999).

NATO, Glossary of Terms and Definitions, AAP-6, 2013, www.dtic.mil/doctrine/doctrine/other/aap6.pdf (accessed 29 April 2017).

Neff, Stephen, *War and the Law of Nations: A General History* (Cambridge University Press, 2005).

Nurick, Lester, 'The distinction between combatant and noncombatant in the law of war', *The American Journal of International Law*, vol. 39, no. 4 (1945): 680–97.

O'Brien, William V., 'The meaning of "military necessity" in international law', *World Polity: A Yearbook of Studies in International Law and Organization* (Spectrum Publishers, 1957).

O'Brien, William V., *The Conduct of Just and Limited War* (Praeger, 1981).

O'Connell, Mary Ellen, 'Historical development and legal basis', in Dieter Fleck et al. (eds.), *The Handbook of International Humanitarian Law, 3rd ed.* (Oxford University Press, 2013).

Oeter, Stefan, 'Comment: is the principle of distinction outdated?', in Wolff Heintschel von Heinegg and Volker Epping (eds.), *International Humanitarian Law Facing New Challenges* (Springer, 2007): 53–62.

Oeter, Stefan, 'Methods and means of combat', in Dieter Fleck et al. (eds.), *The Handbook of International Humanitarian Law, 3rd ed.* (Oxford University Press, 2013): 115–231.

Office of the Judge Advocate General, Joint Doctrine Manual, *Law of Armed Conflict at the Tactical and Operational Levels* (Canadian Manual), B-GJ-005–104/FP-021 (Office of the Judge Advocate General, Canada, 2001).

Ohlin, Jens David and May, Larry, *Necessity in International Law* (Oxford University Press, 2016).

Olasolo, Hector, *Unlawful Attacks in Combat Situations: From the ICTY's Case Law to the Rome Statute* (Martinus Nijhoff Publishers, 2008).

Olsen, John Andreas, *Strategic Air Power in Desert Storm* (Cass, 2003).

Oppenheim, Lassa and Lauterpacht, Hersch, *Disputes, War and Neutrality* (Longmans, 1952).

Otieno, Mbori, Wabuke, Emma and Otieno, Smith, 'The fission and fusion in international use of force: relating unlawful use of force and the war crime of disproportionate force not justified by military necessity', *Case Western Reserve Journal of International Law*, vol. 48, nos. 1 and 2 (2016): 303–28.

Parks, Hays W., 'Rolling thunder and the law of war', *Air University Review*, vol. 33 (1982).

Parks, Hays W., 'Air war and the law of war', *Air Force Law Review*, vol. 32 (1990).

Parks, Hays W., '"Special Forces" wear of non-standard uniforms', *Chicago Journal of International Law*, vol. 4 (2003): 493–560.

Parks, Hays W., 'Asymmetries and the identification of legitimate military objectives', in Wolff Heintschel von Heinegg and Volker Epping (eds.), *International Humanitarian Law Facing New Challenges* (Springer, 2007): 65–116.

Parks, Hays W., 'Military objectives', in Gian Luca Beruto (ed.), *The Conduct of Hostilities, Revisiting the Law of Armed Conflict, 100 Years after the 1907 Hague Conventions and 30 Years after the 1977 Additional Protocols* (San Remo, International Institute of Humanitarian Law, 2007): 72–7.

Parks, Hays W., 'Part IX of the ICRC DPH Study: no mandate no expertise, and legally incorrect', *International Law and Politics*, vol. 42 (2010): 769–830.

Parks, Hays W., 'Perspectives and the importance of history', *Yearbook of International Humanitarian Law*, vol. 14 (2011).

Pejic, Jelena, '"Unlawful/enemy combatants": interpretations and consequences', in Michael Schmitt and Jelena Pejic (eds.), *International Law and Armed Conflict: Exploring the Faultlines. Essays in Honour of Yoram Dinstein* (Martinus Nijhoff Publishers, 2007): 335–57.

Pictet, Jean S., *The Geneva Conventions of 12 August 1949: Commentary* (International Committee of the Red Cross, 1952).

Pictet, Jean S., *Development and Principles of International Humanitarian Law* (Martinus Nijhoff Publishers, 1985).

Pigaroff, Donald K. and Robinson, Darryl, 'Article 30: mental element', in Otto Triffterer and Kai Ambos (eds.), *The Rome Statute of the International Criminal Court: A Commentary*, 3rd ed. (C. H. Beck, Hart and Nomos, 2016).

Program on Humanitarian Policy and Conflict Research Harvard University (HPCR), *Commentary on the HPCR Manual on International Law Applicable to Air and Missile Warfare* (AMW Manual) (2010).

Rabus, W. G., 'A new definition of the levee en masse', *Netherlands International Law Review*, vol. 24, no. 1–2 (1977): 232–41.

Ragone, P. A., 'The applicability of military necessity in the nuclear age', *Journal of International Law and Politics*, vol. 16, no. 4 (1984).

Rauch, Elmar, 'The concept of military necessity in the context of the law of war', *Military Law and the Law of War Review*, vol. 19 (1980, English version).

Reichberg, Gregory M., Syse, Henrik and Begby, Endre, *The Ethics of War: Classic and Contemporary Readings* (Blackwell Publishing, 2006).

Reeves, Shane and Thurnher, Jeffrey, 'Are we reaching a tipping point? How contemporary challenges are affecting the military necessity-humanity balance', *Harvard National Security Journal Features* (2013): 1–12.

Roberts, Adam, 'Land warfare: from Hague to Nuremberg', in Michael Howard, George, J. Andreopoulus and Mark R. Shulman (eds.), *The Laws of War. Constraints on Warfare in the Western World* (Yale University Press, 1994): 116–39.

Roberts, Adam and Guelff, Richard, *Documents on the Laws of War*, 3rd ed. (Oxford University Press, 2000).

Robertson, Horace B., 'The principle of the military objective in the Law of Armed Conflict', *US Air Force Academy Journal of Legal Studies* (1997): 35–70.

Rogers, A. P. V., 'Zero-casualty warfare', *International Review of the Red Cross*, vol. 82, no. 837 (2000).

Rogers, A. P. V., 'Combatant status', in E. Wilmshurst and S. Breu (eds.), *Perspectives on the ICRC Study on International Humanitarian Law* (Cambridge University Press, 2007): 101–27.

Rogers, A. P. V., *Law on the Battlefield*, 3rd ed. (Manchester University Press, 2012).

Roscini, Marco, 'Targeting and contemporary aerial bombardment', *The International and Comparative Law Quarterly*, vol. 54, no. 2 (2005): 411–43.

Sandoz, Yves, Swinarski, Christophe and Zimmermann, Bruno (eds.), *Commentary on the Additional Protocols of 8 June 1977 to the Geneva Conventions of 12 August 1949 (AP I Commentary)* (Martinus Nijhoff Publishers, 1987).

Sassoli, Marco, 'Targeting: the scope and utility of the concept of "military objectives" for the protection of civilians in contemporary armed conflicts', in David Wippman and Michael Evangelista (eds.), *New Wars, New Laws? Applying Laws of War in 21st Century Conflicts* (Martinus Nijhoff Publishers, 2005).

Sassoli, Marco, 'Ius ad bellum and Ius in bello', in Michael Schmitt and Jelena Pejic (eds.), *International Law and Armed Conflict: Exploring the Faultlines. Essays in Honour of Yoram Dinstein* (Martinus Nijhoff Publishers, 2007): 241–65.

Sassoli, Marco, Bouvier, Antoine A. and Quintin, Anne, *How Does Law Protect in War* (ICRC, 2011).

Schachter, Oscar, 'Implementing limitations on the use of force: the doctrine of proportionality and necessity', *American Society of International Law (ASIL) Proceedings* (1992): 39.

Schindler, Dietrich and Toman, Jiri, *The Laws of Armed Conflicts* (Martinus Nijhoff Publishers, 2004).

Schmitt, Michael N., '"Direct participation in hostilities" and 21st century armed conflict', in Horst Fischer et al. (eds.), *Crisis Management and Humanitarian Protection: Festschrift für Dieter Fleck* (Berliner Wissenschafts-Verlag, 2004).

Schmitt, Michael N., 'Humanitarian law and direct participation in hostilities by private contractors or civilian employees', Expert Paper submitted at the Second Expert Meeting on the Notion of Direct Participation in Hostilities (International Committee of the Red Cross, 2004).

Schmitt, Michael N., 'Targeting and humanitarian law: current issues', in Richard B. Jaques (ed.), *International Law Studies* vol. 80, IX, Issues in International Law and Military Operations (2006): 151194.

Schmitt, Michael N., 'Asymmetrical warfare and international humanitarian law', *Air Force Law Review*, vol. 62 (2008): 1–42.

Schmitt, Michael N., 'Targeting and international humanitarian law in Afghanistan', *The War in Afghanistan: A Legal Analysis, International Law Studies*, vol. 85 (2009): 307–39.

Schmitt, Michael N., 'Deconstructing direct participation in hostilities: the constitutive elements', *International Law and Politics*, vol. 42 (2009/2010): 697–739.

Schmitt, Michael N., 'The Interpretive Guidance on the Notion of Direct Participation in Hostilities: a critical analysis', *Harvard National Security Journal*, vol. 1 (2010): 5–44.

Schmitt, Michael N., 'Military necessity and humanity in international humanitarian law: preserving the delicate balance', *Virginia Journal of International Law*, vol. 50 (2010).

Schmitt, Michael N. (general editor), *Tallinn Manual 2.0 on the International Law Applicable to Cyber Operations* (Tallinn Manual), 2nd ed. (Cambridge University Press, 2017).

Schwarzenberger, Georg, *International Law as Applied by International Courts and Tribunals, vol. II: The Law of Armed Conflict* (Steves and Sons Limited, 1968).

Soanes, Catherine and Stevenson, Angus (eds.), *Concise Oxford English Dictionary*, 11th ed. (Oxford University Press, 2008).
Solf, Waldemar A., 'Protection of civilians against the effects of hostilities under customary international law and under Protocol I', *American University International Law Review*, vol. 1, no. 1 (1986): 117–35.
Solis, Gary D., *The Law of Armed Conflict: International Humanitarian Law in War* (Cambridge University Press, 2010).
Spaight, J. M., *Air Power and War Rights* (Longmans, Green and Co., 1924).
Supreme Headquarters Allied Powers Europe, 'Allied Command Operations Comprehensive Operations Planning Directive (COPD V2.0)' (2013).
Taylor, Claire, 'Military operations in Libya', SN/IA/5909 (House of Commons Library, 2011).
Taylor, Frederick, *Dresden: Tuesday 13 February 1945* (Bloomsbury, 2004).
Trooboff, Peter D., *Law and Responsibility in Warfare: The Vietnam Experience* (The University of North Carolina Press, 1975).
Tuck, Richard, *The Rights of War and Peace: Political Thought and the International Order from Grotius to Kant* (Oxford University Press, 1999).
UK Ministry of Defence, *The Manual of the Law of Armed* (UK Manual) (Oxford University Press, 2005).
US Department of Defence (DOD), Joint Publication 1–02, *Dictionary of Military and Associated Terms* (US Department of Defence, 2001, amended 2009).
US Department of Defence (DoD), *Law of War Manual* (US DoD Manual) (2015, as amended 2016), Department of Defense Directive 2311.olE, DoD Law of War Program (9 May 2006).
US DoD Dictionary of Military and Associated Terms (amended May 2017), www.dtic.mil/doctrine/new_pubs/dictionary.pdf (accessed 7 June 2017).
US Law of Armed Conflict Deskbook, 5th ed., 2015, www.loc.gov/rr/frd/Military_Law/pdf/LOAC-Deskbook-2015.pdf (accessed 19 April 2017).
Van Creveld, Martin, *The Age of Air Power* (Public Affairs, 2011).
Venturini, Gabriella, 'Necessity in the law of armed conflict and in international criminal law', *Netherlands Yearbook of International Law*, vol. 41 (2010): 45–78.
Verri, Pietro, *Dictionary of International law of armed conflict* (International Committee of the Red Cross, 1992).
von Holtzendorff, Franz, *Handbuch des Völkerrechts: auf Grundlage Europäischer Staatspraxis* (Habel, 1885).
von Liszt, Franz, *Das Völkerrecht: Systematisch Dargestellt* (Haering, 1898/1906).
von Ullmann, E., 'Völkerrecht: Neuarbeitung auf der Grundlage der 1.Auflage', in *Handbuch des Offentlichen Rechts* (Mohr, 1908).
Walne, George, 'AFP 110–31: international law – the conduct of armed conflict and air operations and the Linebacker bombing campaigns of the Vietnam War' (Center for Naval Analyses, 1987).
Warden III, John A., *The Air Campaign* (Excel Press/iUniverse, 2000).
Watkin, Kenneth, 'Assessing proportionality: moral complexity and legal rules', *Yearbook of International Humanitarian Law*, vol. 8 (2005).

Watkin, Kenneth, 'Opportunity lost: organized armed groups and the ICRC "Direct Participation in Hostilities" Interpretive Guidance', *International Law and Politics*, vol. 42 (2009/2010):641–95.

Weiler, Joseph and Deshman Abby, 'Far be it from thee to slay the righteous with the wicked: an historical and historiographical sketch of the bellicose debate concerning the distinction between jus ad bellum and jus in bello', *European Journal of International Law*, vol. 24, no. 1 (2013): 25–61.

Westlake, John, *International Law: Part II: War* (University Press, 1907).

Wright, Jason D., 'Excessive ambiguity: analysing and refining the proportionality standard', *International Review of the Red Cross*, vol. 94, no. 886 (2012): 819–54.

TREATY DRAFTS, UN DOCUMENTS AND TRAVAUX PREPARATOIRES (CHRONOLOGICAL ORDER)

Hague Rules of Aerial Warfare (1923), Parliamentary Papers, Cmd 2201, Miscellaneous No 14, in Schindler, Dietrich and Toman, Jiri, eds., *The Laws of Armed Conflict*, at page 319.

Draft International Convention on the Condition and Protection of Civilians of Enemy Nationality Who Are on Territory Belonging to or Occupied by a Belligerent, Recommended by the XVth International Red Cross Conference, in Schindler, Dietrich and Toman, Jiri, eds., *The Laws of Armed Conflicts*, at page 445 (1934 Tokyo Draft on the Protection of Civilians).

ICRC Draft Rules for the Limitation of the Dangers Incurred by the Civilian Population in Time of War, 1956, in Schindler, Dietrich and Toman, Jiri, eds., *The Laws of Armed Conflict*, at page 341.

UN GA res 2444 (1968), in Schindler, Dietrich and Toman, Jiri, eds., *The Laws of Armed Conflict*, at pages 345–6.

The Distinction between Military Objectives in General and Particularly the Problems Associated with Weapons of Mass Destruction, Resolution adopted by the Institute of International Law at its session in Edinburgh, 9 September 1969, Schindler, Dietrich and Toman, Jiri, eds., *The Laws of Armed Conflict*, at pages 351–2.

Conference of Governmental Experts (1971), vol. III.

Official Records of the Diplomatic Conference on the Reaffirmation and Development of International Humanitarian Law Applicable in Armed Conflicts (Geneva 1974–1977) (Bern: Federal Political Department, 1978), vols. I–XVI.

Draft articles on Responsibility of States for Internationally Wrongful Acts, with commentaries, in *Yearbook of the International Law Commission*, 2001, vol. II, Part Two, as corrected.

UN Doc. A/CN.4/318/Add.5–7. Addendum – Eighth Report on State Responsibility by Mr Roberto Ago, Special Rapporteur.

REPORTS, INTERNET PAGES ETC. (CHRONOLOGICAL ORDER)

AIR 16/487: Despatch on War Operations, February 1942–May 1945, by Air Chief Marshal Sir A. T. Harris, AOC in C Bomber Command.

XXI International Conference of the Red Cross, 'Reaffirmation and Development of the Laws and Customs Applicable in Armed Conflict', Report submitted by the ICRC, Geneva (1969) (ICRC Istanbul Report).

Folkrätten i krig, Statens Offentliga Utredningar (SOU) 1984: 56.

US Strategic Bombing Surveys, European War/Pacific War, reprinted by Air University Press Maxwell Air Force Base, Alabama 36112–5532 (1987).

Conduct of the Persian Gulf Conflict: An Interim Report to Congress (Diane Publishing, 1991).

Human Rights Watch, Needless Deaths in the Gulf War: Civilian Casualties during the Air Campaign and Violations of the Laws of War (Human Rights Watch, 1991).

Final Report to Congress: Conduct of the Persian Gulf War, Pursuant to Title V of the Persian Gulf Conflict Supplemental Authorization and Personnel Benefits Act of 1991 (Public Law 102–25) (1992).

Final Report to the Prosecutor by the Committee Established to Review the NATO Bombing Campaign against the Federal Republic of Yugoslavia (2000) (OTP Report) at the International Criminal Tribunal for the former Yugoslavia (ICTY), www.icty.org/x/file/Press/nato061300.pdf (accessed 10 April 2017).

Second Expert Meeting on the Notion of Direct Participation in Hostilities (2004) Summary Report by Nils Melzer (International Committee of the Red Cross and the T. M. C. Asser Institute).

Third Expert Meeting on the Notion of Direct Participation in Hostilities (2005) Summary Report by Nilz Melzer (International Committee of the Red Cross and the T. M. C. Asser Institute).

Report from the Expert meeting on Targeting Military Objectives (University Centre for International Humanitarian Law, 2005).

ISAF Headquarters, Kabul: COMISAF's Tactical Directive, 30 December 2008 (ISAF Tactical Directive, 30 December 2008), www.nato.int/isaf/docu/official_texts/Tactical_Directive_090114.pdf (accessed 7 May 2017).

European Commission for Democracy through Law (Venice Commission), Report on the Democratic Control of the Armed Forces, Adopted by the Venice Commission at its 74th Plenary Session (Council of Europe: CDL-AD, 2008, 004), www.venice.coe.int/webforms/documents/default.aspx?pdffile=CDL-AD(2008)004-e (accessed 1 May 2017).

ISAF Headquarters, Kabul: COMISAF's Tactical Directive, 6 July 2009 (ISAF Tactical Directive, 6 July 2009), www.nato.int/isaf/docu/official_texts/Tactical_Directive_090706.pdf (accessed 7 May 2017).

Folkrätt i væpnad konflikt: svensk tolkning och tillempning, SOU 2010:72.

ISAF Headquarters, Kabul: COMISAF's Tactical Directive, 1 August 2010 (ISAF Tactical Directive, 1 August 2010). See ISAF News Release, August 2010, releasing unclassified parts of the Directive.

Peter, Tom A., 'Karzai gives ultimatum on civilian deaths', The Christian Science Monitor, 30 May 2011, www.csmonitor.com/World/Asia-South-Central/2011/05 30/Karzai-gives-US-ultimatum-on-civilian-deaths (accessed 15 May 2019).

NATO Fact Sheet, Operation Unified Protector Protection of Civilians and Civilian-Populated Areas, June 2011.

Operational Media Update, NATO and Libya, 2011, www.nato.int/cps/en/natohq/news_71994.htm (accessed 30 November 2014).

Operational Media Update 29 July 2011, www.nato.int/nato_static/assets/pdf/pdf_2011_07/20110730_110730-oup-update.pdf (accessed 1 December 2014).

The Guardian, Saturday 30 July 2011, www.theguardian.com/world/2011/jul/30/nato-bombs-libya-tv-transmitters (accessed 1 December 2014).

'NATO strikes Libyan TV satellite facility', 2011, www.nato.int/cps/en/natolive/news_76776.htm (accessed 1 December 2014).

ISAF Headquarters, Kabul: COMISAF's Tactical Directive, 30 November 2011, www.rs.nato.int/images/docs/20111105%20nuc%20tactical%20directive%20revision%204%20(releaseable%20version)%20r.pdf (accessed 30 March 2016).

ICC, Elements of Crimes, International Criminal Court, 2011.

Letter to the Chief of Defence regarding the use of Cyber Warfare in the armed forces (Norwegian Ministry of Defence, 3 September 2012).

2012 ICRC Report on Afghanistan, at page 242 ff., www.icrc.org/eng/assets/files/annual-report/current/icrc-annual-report-afghanistan.pdf (accessed 7 May 2017).

Human Rights Watch, 'Ukraine: unguided missiles killing civilians', 24 July 2014, www.hrw.org/news/2014/07/24/ukraine-unguided-rockets-killing-civilians (accessed 21 October 2014).

International humanitarian law and the challenges of contemporary armed conflicts, Report by the International Committee of the Red Cross (Geneva, October 2015, 32IC/15/11) (ICRC 2015 Report).

The White House (2016), Report on the Legal and Policy Frameworks Guiding the United States' Use of Military Force and Related National Security Operations, www.whitehouse.gov/sites/whitehouse.gov/files/documents/Legal_Policy_Report.pdf (accessed 13 December 2016).

North Atlantic Treaty Organization, Standard, AJP-3.3 Allied Joint Doctrine for Air and Space Operations, Edition B Version 1, NATO Standardization Office (NSO) © NATO/OTAN, April 2016.

North Atlantic Treaty Organization, Allied Joint Publication 01, NATO Standardization Office (NSO) © NATO/OTAN, February 2017.

The White House, Crafting tragedy, http://georgewbush-whitehouse.archives.gov/ogc/apparatus/crafting.html (accessed 27 May 2016).

Index